Pretrial Advocacy

ASPEN PUBLISHERS

Pretrial Advocacy
Planning, Analysis, and Strategy

Second Edition

Marilyn J. Berger
Professor of Law
Seattle University School of Law

John B. Mitchell
Professor of Law
Seattle University School of Law

Ronald H. Clark
Distinguished Practitioner in Residence
Seattle University School of Law

Monique C.M. Leahy
Principal, Wordsworth Publishing
Reston, Virginia

Wolters Kluwer
Law & Business

AUSTIN   BOSTON   CHICAGO   NEW YORK   THE NETHERLANDS

Aspen Publishers
Attn: Permissions Department
76 Ninth Avenue, 7th Floor
New York, NY 10011-5201

To contact Customer Care, e-mail customer.care@aspenpublishers.com, call 1-800-234-1660, fax 1-800-901-9075, or mail correspondence to:

Aspen Publishers
Attn: Order Department
PO Box 990
Frederick, MD 21705

Printed in the United States of America.

1 2 3 4 5 6 7 8 9 0

ISBN 978-0-7355-6366-7

Library of Congress Cataloging in Publication Data

Pretrial advocacy : planning, analysis, and strategy / Marilyn J. Berger ... [et al.]. — 2nd ed.
      p. cm.
    Rev. ed. of: Pretrial advocacy / Marilyn J. Berger, John B. Mitchell, Ronald H. Clark. c1988.
    Includes index.
    ISBN 978-0-7355-6366-7 (pbk. : alk. paper) 1. Pre-trial procedure—United States. I. Berger, Marilyn J. II. Berger, Marilyn J. Pretrial advocacy.

    KR8900.B4 2007
    347.73'72—dc22

                                                            2007003843

ABOUT WOLTERS KLUWER LAW & BUSINESS

Wolters Kluwer Law & Business is a leading provider of research information and workflow solutions in key specialty areas. The strengths of the individual brands of Aspen Publishers, CCH, Kluwer Law International and Loislaw are aligned within Wolters Kluwer Law & Business to provide comprehensive, in-depth solutions and expert-authored content for the legal, professional and education markets.

CCH was founded in 1913 and has served more than four generations of business professionals and their clients. The CCH products in the Wolters Kluwer Law & Business group are highly regarded electronic and print resources for legal, securities, antitrust and trade regulation, government contracting, banking, pension, payroll, employment and labor, and healthcare reimbursement and compliance professionals.

Aspen Publishers is a leading information provider for attorneys, business professionals and law students. Written by preeminent authorities, Aspen products offer analytical and practical information in a range of specialty practice areas from securities law and intellectual property to mergers and acquisitions and pension/benefits. Aspen's trusted legal education resources provide professors and students with high-quality, up-to-date and effective resources for successful instruction and study in all areas of the law.

Kluwer Law International supplies the global business community with comprehensive English-language international legal information. Legal practitioners, corporate counsel and business executives around the world rely on the Kluwer Law International journals, loose-leafs, books and electronic products for authoritative information in many areas of international legal practice.

Loislaw is a premier provider of digitized legal content to small law firm practitioners of various specializations. Loislaw provides attorneys with the ability to quickly and efficiently find the necessary legal information they need, when and where they need it, by facilitating access to primary law as well as state-specific law, records, forms and treatises.

Wolters Kluwer Law & Business, a unit of Wolters Kluwer, is headquartered in New York and Riverwoods, Illinois. Wolters Kluwer is a leading multinational publisher and information services company.

One might question how much nerve it requires to strap on a parachute and jump out of an airplane the first time. It is the second time, when you know what is coming, that is the test. When we chose to completely revise and update this book, plainly a project of several years, all of our family and friends knew what was coming—long periods when we would be totally distracted or when we would simply disappear for unpredictable spans of time. Nevertheless, they again took the leap with us, an act of such wondrous strength and love that to fully express our gratitude and love in mere words is well beyond our capacities.

To Albert J. and Dorian S.
Marilyn J. Berger

To Eva, David, Sarah, J.P., and Tyler—my family.
John B. Mitchell

To Nancy, Brady, Soojin, Malachi, Riley, Clancy, Kara, Colby, and Darren
Ronald H. Clark

To John, Shea, and Sean
Monique C.M. Leahy

And to Laurie Sleeper and her family, our administrative assistant, without whom the plane would never have even gotten on the runway.

Summary of Contents

Contents

Preface to Second Edition

It's been nearly 20 years since the first edition of this book appeared in print. The world around us has changed in so many ways, and predictably, the practice of law, too, has seen dramatic changes. This book reflects the evolving technical, technological, and strategic knowledge base required of a litigation advocate in the early twenty-first century, where changes such as the significant role of technology in practice, the extensive use of experts, the increasing importance of non-litigation dispute resolution, as well as significant changes in doctrine that are now standard procedure are all part of the landscape. This new edition also incorporates the pedagogical lessons we have learned from using the book in classes for the past two decades.

Technology permeates our existence and has been assimilated into every area of practice from research databases, e-discovery, e-filing, document storage, billing forms, conflicts checks, and client files to trial exhibits. Accordingly, we have created a chapter on case development (Chapter 3) in which we discuss various computer-based options for organizing your files and case documents. In addition, we have included a chapter on creating visuals (Chapter 10), which includes computer generated graphics, such as PowerPoint, and video animations. You should also note that the case file used in all the course exercises is on a CD, reflecting the trend toward a paperless environment, and an optionally available DVD has been created with a video of the scene of the crime/civil cause of action, samples of deposition taking, and sample computer graphics for settlement and court presentations.

Experts are now even more pervasive as our society becomes more technically specialized. In law, it is now a rare case in which there is not an expert involved. To practice in the early twenty-first century, you must be able to work with experts for your side and be able to competently deal with any opposing experts. We have, therefore, greatly expanded the number and variety of areas of expertise appearing in the interviewing and deposition exercises—including an exercise in which a deposition is being taken to lay the grounds for a *Daubert* motion.

Dispute resolution has emerged as a significant aspect of the modern advocate's practice. Drama, tension, and excitement aside, trials tend to be expensive, emotionally draining on clients, and can make relations between parties requiring future cooperation difficult. The recognition of this over the past 20 years—including data indicating that most civil and criminal cases settle before trial—has appropriately led to a systematic study of negotiation and the explosion of the world of Alternative Dispute Resolution. Thus, we have significantly expanded both the content and the sophistication of the negotiations chapter (Chapter 12) and the ADR chapter (Chapter 13).

Legal doctrine and *procedure* have also changed. The significant revisions of the Federal Rules of Civil Procedure since our previous edition are incorporated into the chapter on pleading (Chapter 7) and the chapter on discovery (Chapter 8). This edition also incorporates revisions in the Rules of Professional Conduct brought about by Ethics 2000.

Finally, we've been teaching with these materials for the past 20 years, and we've learned quite a bit in the process. We have refined the hypotheticals to more effectively guide student learning, we have greatly expanded the number and types of practice tips and examples, and we have made the checklists at the end of each chapter far more useful for both classroom use and eventual practice.

Notwithstanding all these changes, the fundamentals of effective litigation advocacy remain constant. Cicero would still be a great lawyer should he miraculously appear today (once he learned how to use e-mail). The essential approach and foundational knowledge from our original book have not changed: We have written this edition strictly adhering to the five pedagogical pillars upon which our original text was constructed.

1. First, we present the various skills (negotiation, interviewing, discovery, and so forth) as part of an interrelated strategic endeavor, not as a series of fragmented performances.
2. Second, we present this endeavor guided by the conception of case theory (Chapter 2).
3. Third, learning takes place through experiential hands-on exercises that consist of both planning questions and detailed attorney and witness performance instructions. In this edition, we have grouped the performance and discussion Assignments at the end of the book, with a full table of contents for easy access to them.
4. Fourth, all exercises are founded upon extensive criminal and civil case files, both of which evolve from the same incident.
5. Fifth, the exercises are filled with realistic ethical issues.

We invite your enthusiastic response to advocacy in our technologically exciting world. Please write us with your comments and suggestions at mjb@seattleu.edu.

Marilyn J. Berger, John B. Mitchell, Ron H. Clark & Monique C.M. Leahy

Monique C.M. Leahy, John B. Mitchell, Marilyn J. Berger, and Ron H. Clark

Acknowledgments

The cover of this book indicates that it is the work of four authors. Yet there were truly so many other individuals, in so many capacities, that were essential to this book. Their combined contributions are visible to us on every page. We do more than thank them; we share credit with them for this work.

Kwame Amoeteng, Seattle University School of Law graduate, 2002.

Authors of *The Appellate Prosecutor*.

Mimy Bailey, Seattle University, class of 2007.

William S. (Bill) Bailey, Attorney and Adjunct Professor of Law, Seattle University School of Law.

Mike Bitando, General Manager of The Garage billiards hall and bowling.

Nancy Clark, artist and editor.

Fred Dekay, Adjunct Professor at Seattle University School of Law.

Tyler Fox, Industrial Technology, Seattle University School of Law.

Steve Fury, Attorney.

Captain Tag Gleason, Seattle Police Department, Violent Crimes Section.

Alan Kirtley, Associate Professor of the University of Washington School of Law.

Law Students at Seattle University School of Law.

Gretchen Ludwig, Director of the Garage movie.

The Honorable Judge Terrance Lukens, Adjunct Professor of Law, Seattle University School of Law.

Dr. Norman Mar, Ph.D.

Hannalore Merritt, Seattle University School of Law, class of 2009.

Rebecca Miller, Officer, Seattle Police Department, East Precinct.

Theodore Myhre, Legal Writing Professor of Law, Seattle University School of Law.

The Honorable Judge Jack Nevin, Pierce County Superior Court and Adjunct Professor of Law, Seattle University School of Law.

Kyle C. Olive, Attorney.

Rex Prout, Assistant Chief, Enforcement & Education, Washington State Liquor Control Board.

Richard Sherwin, Professor and Director New York Law School's Visual Persuasion project.

Laurie Sleeper, Seattle University School of Law, administrative assistant.

John Jay Syverson (Jay), photographer, OnPoint Productions, Seattle.

Kirk Van Scoyoc, Actor.

Justin Walsh, Seattle University School of Law student and law clerk, class of 2008.

Matt Williams, Attorney and Adjunct Professor of Law at Seattle University School of Law.

Katherine Wimble, graphics artist.

Ric Wyant, Forensic Scientist, Firearm/Toolmark Section, Crime Laboratory Division, Washington State Patrol Firearms examiner for the Washington State Patrol Crime Laboratory.

The Honorable Mary Yu, King County Superior Court.

Stephanie Zimmerman, Director of Instructional Technology at Seattle University School of Law.

And a special thank you to Aspen Publishers: Steve Errick, Managing Director; John Devins, Developmental Editor; and Carmen Corral-Reid, Senior Manuscript Editor.

Introduction

This book is intended to provide you with the experience of being a practicing attorney engaged in pretrial activities. Through a series of criminal and civil problems as well as supportive commentary and case files, the book presents an approach to thinking about, planning, and performing detailed and realistic problems that simulate a wide range of pretrial practice situations and foster the kinds of analytic processes needed to solve these problems.

A discussion of our theory and approach to lawyering in an adversary system is reserved for Chapter 1; the object of this introduction is to provide you with a basic understanding of how the book is structured and its intended use.

A. STRUCTURE

This book is divided into 13 chapters followed by Chapter 14, which is an overview of the experiential learning envisioned for this course and the assignments for the class. Each chapter covers a separate pretrial subject area—for example, witness interviews, discovery, and negotiation. The substance of each chapter elaborates a theoretical approach to the particular pretrial skill that is the subject of that chapter, provides demonstrations of that approach as applied to hypothetical situations, and offers a series of practical and strategic pointers in the subject area. The examples that we provide in the text are intended to be just that, examples. They are not meant to be exhaustive, but are merely intended to illustrate the point in question. Where possible, the text also includes references to sources that may be of help to you.

In each chapter, the text concludes with checklists that you may consult when you plan to employ the pretrial skills that are the subject of that chapter.

Each performance assignment simulates a different adversarial practice situation—plaintiff's interview with a neutral witness, defendant's interview with an expert witness, defendant making a motion to compel discovery, plaintiff responding to a motion to compel discovery. Most of the problems are based on a single, but complex, fact pattern that manifests itself in two fictitious cases—a criminal case, *State v. Hard,* and a civil case, *Summers v. Hard.*

The role or perspective you assume may shift from one problem assignment to another. Thus in the civil case, your entire approach to a particular problem may vary depending on whether you are a defendant's privately retained attorney or an attorney representing a defendant's insurance company. Your instructor will clarify each of these roles—and your connection to them—as they appear. Each problem contains a preparation section that refers to the background reading you must do in order to work through the problem. Usually, this reading will include the text from one or more chapters and materials from the case file on the CD included with this book. There are also references to rules of evidence, civil procedure, and criminal procedure.

Case Files: The criminal and civil case files for *State v. Hard* and *Summers v. Hard* on the CD provide the factual and legal details for the problems. The files include diagrams, documents, expert reports, jury instructions, pleadings, research memoranda, statutes, and witness statements. The research memoranda are a special feature. The memoranda are composed of fictional cases from our fictional jurisdiction, the State of Major. The memos provide all the research you need to deal with the multitude of legal issues in the problems. Of course, your instructor may prefer that you instead research and use appropriate real cases from your jurisdiction.

Actors' Guide: The simulated pretrial skills performances generally involve role-play. Someone in the class must play the client who is being counseled or the expert economist who is interviewed or the custodian of records whose deposition is being taken. In order to make these simulations as realistic as possible, your instructor has been provided with a witness guide that contains for distribution all the information each actor requires to make his or her performance realistic—memorable background materials detailing the particular witness's personal history, information about the witness's knowledge of the case, and instructions for how the witness is to behave and respond during the particular assignment.

Additionally, the witness guide contains confidential instructions that at times will be given to the students who are playing the attorneys, for example, during negotiation exercises.

B. METHODOLOGY

The book offers a choice of one or more of five learning methodologies from which your instructor will choose:

Reading: The text provides a wealth of information about each skills performance ranging from theory to practice, including illustrations of any given approach so you can understand how the ideas are applied in practice. All of this information will assist you in working through the corresponding problems. The occasional references to other authors' work in the field give you the opportunity for further reading that can broaden your appreciation and understanding of the area.

Discussing: As just described, many of the assignments provide opportunities for you to discuss substantive issues and pretrial strategies.

Performing: The assignments provide the opportunity to learn through simulated performances (interviewing, counseling, arguing motions). The experience of role-playing a witness, or just observing the role-play of fellow law students, will also give valuable insights into the factors that constitute competent attorney performance.

Writing: Assignments also offer a variety of writing opportunities, from planning memos and discovery motions to pleadings and declarations for Constitution-based pretrial motions. As such, many of these involve developing the type of legal analysis you have perfected in law school, translating that analysis into an adversary perspective, and then communicating your position by persuasive writing to the appropriate audience.

Critiquing: Following your performances, you will gain a great deal from the critique of your work by your instructor and perhaps from fellow class members as well. Furthermore, even as a nonperforming class member, learning by example how to critique and what to critique will greatly enhance your ability to evaluate, and thereby improve, your own subsequent planning and performances.

C. ICONS AND BOXES

Throughout the chapters, boxes appear containing information and covering topics that include checklists, substantive law, facts of a hypothetical, illustrations, and practical tips. The topical material within each box is designated by the following:

Checklists

Facts of a Hypothetical

Illustration of a Point

Ethical Rules, Statutes, or Procedural Rules

D. FINAL THOUGHTS

Learn well. In a blink, you will have graduated from law school, passed the Bar, and will be practicing law. Your clients will totally rely on you. They will entrust their families, businesses, freedom, and even their very lives to your care and competence. Learn well . . . and have fun.

Pretrial Advocacy

1 Entering the Advocate's World

1 Entering the Advocate's World

"Resolve to be honest at all events: and if in your judgment you cannot be an honest lawyer, resolve to be honest without being a lawyer. Choose some other occupation."

Abraham Lincoln (1809–1865)

"Well, I got a . . . traffic ticket. I went to court, I got the cop on the stand, and I argued with him until he admitted he was wrong. And the judge, this Judge Malloy. All the while he's laughing and smiling. And then afterwards, he asks me to go to lunch with him. Then he says to me, 'you know what? You'd be a good litigator.' I didn't know what the hell he was talking about, I don't know what a litigator is. I never thought of becoming a lawyer. But this Judge Malloy, who's from Brooklyn, too? He did it, so all of a sudden, it seemed possible. So I went to law school."

Vinny Gambini, *My Cousin Vinny*

I. PRETRIAL ADVOCACY

Effective pretrial advocacy is critical because over 90 percent of all civil and criminal cases are disposed of without trial. Pretrial advocacy and preparation are the keys to either a favorable case disposition if the case is resolved without a trial or to success in trial.

This book and accompanying CD and companion DVD will provide you with the experience of being a practicing attorney engaged in pretrial activities including forging a relationship with the client, case development and analysis, formulating the case theory and theme, interviewing witnesses, pleading, formal discovery, taking and defending depositions, creating trial visuals, pretrial motions' advocacy, counseling, engaging in alternative dispute resolution, and negotiating.

This overview explains an approach to pretrial and trial. Also, this chapter provides you with summary descriptions of how both civil and criminal cases generally progress. Finally, you will learn how the materials will give you the experience of engaging in pretrial practice.

II.   THE ADVOCATE'S WORLD

Pretrial and trial advocacy is intended to exist and function in a world where the attorney must deal with the following factors:

- Human relationships,
- Money and time constraints,
- Ethical responsibilities, and
- An institutional process that moves in time.

A.   Human Relationships

As an attorney you will be dealing constantly with people, and no approach to practice can be effective unless you appreciate the full significance of this. Your clients may be shy, arrogant, or over-trusting; witnesses may be friendly, hostile, or just unwilling to get involved; opposing attorneys or co-counsel can be pleasant, rude, or even intimidating; judges and court personnel are kind and helpful or cold and indifferent; and jurors will run the spectrum. Whatever the mix of characters and temperaments, you must be able to deal with them all: working closely with some, obtaining the cooperation of others, gaining the respect of one, finding a way to relate to the next.

B.   Resource Constraints

Your clients will almost never have a blank check to give you for work on a case. They simply cannot afford the fantasy case where you take every conceivable deposition, research every imaginable legal point as if you were preparing a brief for the Supreme Court, or fly witnesses in from Europe. You may not be given resources to hire private investigators to conduct an investigation, so you and your law clerk may have to do the sleuthing. Similarly, you may not be given resources to hire an expensive expert, so a low-fee local expert or a volunteer interested in the issue may have to be located. Moreover, even if the client has the money to spend, the case simply may not be worth the outlay. Running up $15,000 in costs and fees in a $5,000 dispute would quickly bring your sense of judgment into question.

Furthermore, time is itself a resource, unrelated to its price per hour. You only have so much time to devote to a given case. No matter how many hours of your time a client can pay for, you will have other cases and clients. And you will have a life to live, too. You thus have to continually prioritize the allocation of your time among tasks within a single case, among your various cases and clients, and among your personal needs.

Accordingly, when you look at sections of the text, such as those covering witness interviews and discovery, keep in mind the context of the realities of the economic and time constraints you are almost certain to face.

C.   Ethical Relationships

One way to get a sense of the nature and scope of your ethical responsibilities is to comprehend some of the reasons why you have these responsibilities.

Dependence

You will usually represent a client who neither fully comprehends nor can dispassionately deal with the legal process. As such, your client is often totally dependent on you for help with his or her problem and likely is entrusting future fortunes, family, or even the client's life to you. This *dependence* in itself demands from the attorney an ethical awareness.

Power

In representing this person, however, you must also remain cognizant that you function in a world in which the very words you utter can have an effect upon, and eventually even transform, the reality of the wider society. For example, you may stand in a courtroom and convince a panel of judges that a criminal statute is unconstitutional and that the application of their ruling should be retroactive. Outside of that courtroom, the decision will result in overturning the convictions of hundreds of incarcerated persons. This is a world in which you tap an enormous reservoir of power. It is not your own power, and no intellectual superiority or special moral goodness on your part accounts for your access to it. It is simply that you know the words, the forms, the incantations that can bring the powerful engine of the legal institution into action. This power also demands your ethical awareness.

Influence

Moreover, in this world of power you can actively influence both the legal and factual nature of the case and thereby the results. Law students are weaned on appellate opinions where the facts are frozen within the borders of a two-dimensional page. In these appellate opinions, if "the blue car ran the red light," then the blue car ran the red light. While facts are facts, the sources of facts can be fluid, not frozen. By this we mean witness testimony or document evidence is only as solid as the reliability of the witness or authenticity of the document. No traffic accident will take place in the courtroom. No blue cars will appear; no red lights will be seen. All there will be is the evidence that you as the lawyer will bring into court or into settlement discussions. The evidence about blue cars and red traffic lights may be information from interviews with a witness who initially has "the impression" that "a blue-greenish vehicle entered the intersection just around the time the light changed from yellow." This evidence will then be filtered through evidence rules governing admissibility and may be challenged by cross-examination pointing out "but, sir, the sun was in your eyes." Finally, this "blue-greenish" car will be the subject of your and your opponent's arguments in which you both try to persuade either your adversary in settlement discussions or a jury. At every stage, therefore, the influence of one or another lawyer contributes to shaping the final nature and impact of the evidence in the case.

Similarly, legal issues, so neatly frozen in appellate opinion, are often the final result of some lawyer's choice among various alternatives of how he or she would raise, frame, characterize, focus, and develop a record in support of the client's legal position. This *influence* demands ethical awareness as well.

Client, Justice System, and Society

What ethical responsibilities then derive from your position relative to the client, the legal institution, and society? First, you are responsible for putting effort, skill, and loyalty into achieving the interest of your client. In so doing, you must recognize that winning a short-term acrimonious battle will not always serve the client's true interests when the client must maintain an ongoing, cooperative relationship with the other party. Nevertheless, your actions are still guided by the need to represent your client's interests.

The reasons why the attorney's actions are determined by the client's interests are not only embedded in the theoretical underpinnings of the adversary system, but are found in the day-to-day reality, touched on earlier, that your clients usually place themselves totally in your protection. Given this trust, the least you owe the client is loyalty and competence.

The client poses one focus for your ethical concern and responsibility. In recognition of the world of power that you move in and that you can actively influence, however, you must display integrity toward the court, your opponent, and the wider society. Much of this area of responsibility is expressed in Rules of Professional Conduct, which provide the legitimate parameters of ethical conduct. Violation of ethical rules, such as those dealing with conflicts of interest and possession of confidences from former clients whose interests are adverse to current clients, may result in a court ordering your removal from a case (including an order that you return all fees) or even a malpractice action against you.

Your Reputation

Even without the formal Rules of Professional Conduct, there are powerful informal sanctions reserved for an attorney who lacks integrity. Reputations spread fast, and opponents quickly learn whom they can trust and, therefore, cooperate with, and those to whom they will not give an inch. Judges are also aware of reputations. Because most judicial decisions are entrusted to the court's sound discretion (whichever way the court rules will be upheld on appeal), a lawyer whom the court trusts to be thoroughly familiar with the law, to accurately state the facts, and to candidly present his or her positions will consistently be given the benefit of the court's discretion over an attorney with a lesser reputation. Thus, coming full circle, you cannot effectively carry out your responsibility to your client unless your reputation for integrity is positive.

Just as important, and perhaps least subject to clear articulation, you have the responsibility to exercise your skills as a thoughtful, principled human being.

D.   A System Moving in Time

The following two sections provide you with a rough sense of the flow of events within a civil and criminal case from inception through trial. Here we are not attempting to provide you with a precise time line or to detail typical time requirements dictated by court rules (say, the time allotted between the filing of a complaint and the date of a deposition). Compared to the complex, interrelated, and often fluid nature of the various aspects of the actual process, these summaries of the processes may appear mechanical and even a bit misleading. But it is our intention to provide you with a relative reference point in time and space. As such, it will be helpful to review this section from time to time throughout the course in order to reorient yourself within the pretrial process.

III. PROGRESSION OF A CIVIL CASE

A.   Initial Stage

A civil case usually begins by a referral or some other communication in which the potential client contacts an attorney. There may be a pending matter that needs attention, such as a response to a lawsuit, or the client may wish to commence a lawsuit of his or her own. Depending on the amount of time available to investigate the client's problem, the amount of information provided at the initial interview, or other circumstances, the attorney may decide to take the potential case.

Or in some instances the attorney may want to begin an informal investigation of the facts (interviewing witnesses, reading and obtaining documents from the client, other individuals, or public records, and so on) or may hire an investigator to undertake this informal fact-gathering. The attorney also does preliminary legal research to determine the potential legal theories. This is required by ethical considerations, such as in Federal Rule of Civil Procedure II or the equivalent in state court rules.

After the informal investigation, the attorney will decide to proceed with the case or refer the case out. If the attorney proceeds and if the case is one that needs to be litigated, the attorney may decide to contact the opposing party or that party's attorney if the party is represented and make inquiries about the facts as the opposition sees them, potential settlement, or even make a demand for settlement.

B.   Pleading

Generally, initial settlement attempts often are not successful. Therefore, the attorney drafts, serves, and files pleadings: a complaint or petition for the plaintiff; an answer for a defending party. In the case of a defending party, the attorney may decide to file preliminary pretrial motions attacking the plaintiff's pleadings, such as motions to dismiss for improper venue, improper subject matter jurisdiction, motion for judgment on the pleadings, and so on. Likewise, on receipt of responsive pleadings from a defending party, the plaintiff might consider filing motions attacking the responsive pleading.

C.   Discovery

Depending on the jurisdiction, the court might require a pretrial or discovery case conference in which the schedule of the case is discussed, including discovery sequence, motions, and a tentative trial date. In federal courts, the rules require that the attorneys meet and confer to work out a discovery plan and how they will proceed with initial disclosures and then formal discovery. This plan is then submitted to the court for approval. The court might limit and direct the discovery that the parties can do and its sequence, and even discuss settlement or other alternatives including mediation or other alternative dispute resolution.

The attorneys then begin formal discovery. They might send interrogatories, request production of documents or admissions, take depositions, and so on. Most of the discovery is self-executing, that is, arranged by the attorneys, unless there is a problem. In that situation, the attorneys may resort to court to file motions, such as a motion to compel the production of certain documents.

D. Motions and Negotiation

More motions may be filed and argued, such as a motion for summary judgment. Another pretrial/settlement conference may be held. Some courts use this opportunity to strongly encourage settlement of the case. Other courts generally use the pretrial conference as an opportunity to get the case ready for trial. In federal court, the judge might schedule a number of conferences. The judge might review the issues still in contention, discuss witnesses who will testify and exhibits that will be used, rule on motions *in limine* (which deal primarily with evidentiary matters), and consider proposed jury instructions.

Throughout the pretrial process the attorneys might discuss settlement, but this is especially so when the issues have been refined and the case is in a trial posture. Here, the attorneys begin in earnest to negotiate. They are influenced by their respective assessments of the risks of going to trial or by the possible economic (attorney and expert witness fees) and non-economic (stress on client, publicity) costs of pursuing such a course or by pressure from a trial judge who makes it clear that he or she believes that reasonable attorneys would settle the case and not take up time on the judge's trial calendar.

E. Counseling

As an attorney you will find that counseling your client, witnesses, and other attorneys involved in a case is a process that occurs throughout the pretrial and trial process. Your client might want to file a lawsuit immediately and you will have to explain the advantages and disadvantages of litigating—including the time and costs involved, the possibility of settlement, or the potential for a damages recovery—and the time period within which a lawsuit must be filed. Or, your client might want you to include bloody photographs to demonstrate her child's injuries and you will have to counsel her about the possible risks: even should you get by evidentiary objections at trial, the appellate court may reverse the judgment because it decides that the unfair prejudice created by the photographs substantially outweighed their probative value or opposing counsel may turn this evidence on you, arguing that you are trying to inflame the jury's sympathy and emotions to distract from serious weaknesses in the liability portion of the case. In discussing this with your client, moreover, you will also have to consider the proper allocation of decision-making responsibility between you and your client as well as the need to maintain your client's trust and confidence. Also, there may be other considerations that have an impact on the case that may require you to counsel the client, such as when the client has an alcohol problem or has no funds or needs immediate protection from violence.

F.   Trial Sequence

Assuming that settlement negotiation was unsuccessful, the pretrial conference disposed of the motions *in limine,* and both attorneys submitted their proposed jury instructions, the case will be tried. The trial sequence could begin with a waiver of a jury trial. Then the trial would be a bench trial in which the judge serves as the trier of fact. In the absence of a jury waiver, the trial begins with jury selection *(voir dire);* opening statements (the defense can reserve its opening statement until the beginning of the defense case); the plaintiff's case-in-chief composed of direct examinations of witnesses each followed by the defense cross-examining plaintiff's witness; the defense case, again a series of direct and cross examinations. Both plaintiff and defense can orally make motions for judgment as a matter of law (directed verdict) after the opponent's opening statements, after an opponent's case-in-chief, or at the close of either side's case.

Assuming that the motion for judgment as a matter of law (directed verdict) is not granted, the court then informs the attorneys of the court's jury instructions that will be read to the jury; the attorneys can, out of the presence of the jury, take exception to the court's determination of instructions and argue their points. Jurisdictions differ in their order of closing argument—some courts instruct the jury and then allow closing argument, other jurisdictions allow closing argument and then instruct the jury. The plaintiff begins closing argument, then the defense argument is heard. Again, jurisdictions differ over whether plaintiff's lawyer will be permitted to make a rebuttal argument. The jury retires to deliberate—the exhibits, and in some jurisdictions, the jury instructions are given to the jury to take to the jury room. Finally there is a verdict regarding damages or hung jury and post-trial motions (motions for setting aside the verdict or altering the verdict, motions asking for a new trial or appealing, motions for additur, remittitur, bond for appeal). After trial and post-trial motions, the losing party may appeal.

IV.   PROGRESSION OF A CRIMINAL CASE

A.   Initial Stage

Ordinarily, for the defendant, a criminal case begins with an arrest. The arrest may be made on the scene by an observing police officer or following an investigation that may be brief or lengthy or after the convening of a secret grand jury. The prosecution's investigation will generally be carried out by the police under direction of an investigating officer, though the prosecutor may assign post-complaint investigation to a prosecutor office's investigator. The arrest may precede formal filing of charges or take place at the defendant's voluntary surrender to authorities after charges have been filed.

Generally, it is also near the time of arrest that the defense attorney comes into the case (although sometimes an attorney arranges the initial surrender of a suspect). The first meeting with the client may be in jail, where counsel attempts to arrange bail or it may take place in counsel's office as the potential client shops around for an attorney to retain. In or out of jail, however, the client is often indigent and defense counsel is a public defender or some other form of appointed counsel.

In many cases the prosecution will first learn of the case after the police have arrested the defendant and the case is submitted to the prosecution for a charging decision. In other cases, the case will be submitted to the prosecutor for filing before arresting the defendant. The police and prosecutor may consult in the investigation, pre-arrest, and pre-charge stages.

B. Charging

Generally, the prosecutor decides whether to file charges and what to charge. If a decision to charge is made (perhaps after the prosecutor's request for further investigation by the police has been met), a charging pleading document will be filed with the court. Generally, for misdemeanors, the prosecutor will file a complaint in the lower trial court, usually called a district or municipal court, upon which the defendant will face trial. Also, law enforcement may file a citation (traffic citation, shoplifting) in a lower court.

For felonies, the procedure for bringing the charge will vary among state and federal jurisdictions. In some jurisdictions, the prosecutor will file a charging pleading called an *information* in the upper trial court, generally called the superior court, upon which the defendant will face trial for the felony. In still others, the charge will be stated in a complaint filed in the lower court, which then becomes the focus of a *preliminary hearing* where the prosecutor presents evidence to establish probable cause to believe the case should be bound over for trial in superior court. If, after the conclusion of the preliminary hearing, the judge (or magistrate, as the judicial figure at a preliminary hearing is sometimes called) finds probable cause to exist for the charge, the defendant is bound over for trial to the superior court where an information containing the charges found supportable at the preliminary hearing is filed.

In other jurisdictions, the prosecutor will bring the case before a grand jury, which, if it finds the charges well founded, will return an *indictment*. Many jurisdictions have available more than one of these charging procedures.

C. Arraignment and Bail

After charges have been filed, the defendant will be brought into court for the procedure known as an *arraignment*. Technically, it is here that charges are read, a copy of the charging pleading served on the defendant, and defendant's plea, almost always not guilty, entered on the record. But many other things may occur, including the setting of bail. Defendant, if not yet represented, may be given a short continuance to obtain counsel prior to entering a plea. A motion to reduce bail may have been scheduled to be heard at this time and will be argued. The court may set a date for all pretrial motions to be filed and/or heard.

D. Discovery

After arraignment, both the prosecution and defense will be engaged in informal discovery (e.g., witness interviews, disclosing witness statements). Around this time, formal discovery motions will be filed by the defense, and by the prosecution when constitutionally permitted. The discovery permitted by the court will then be turned over and evaluated by the attorneys.

E. Motions and Negotiation

Pretrial motions (suppression, change of venue, and so on) will be filed and set for hearing. The opposing counsel may file a response, and the motions will subsequently be heard and ruled on by the court, often after a full evidentiary hearing with witnesses.

Negotiation may take place all through the process although defense counsel should first have conducted sufficient investigation and formal discovery to have a good grasp of the defendant's position. If a disposition is reached, a formal plea hearing will be set to put the plea on the record and to ensure that the defendant understands the rights the defendant is waiving and the consequences of the conviction. After the guilty plea is entered, the court will usually set a date for sentencing and may order a study and pre-sentence report by the probation department to assist in that task. Actual sentencing will follow.

F. Counseling

Counseling the defendant-client begins with the first interview ("When we get you out on bail, it would be good if you enroll in that voc-tech program to show the court you're serious about getting your life in order . . .") and continues through trial ("You can put your neighbor on as a character witness, but let me tell you the problem . . .") and beyond ("If we get bail on appeal, you'll be out, but if the appeal is denied a year later you'll probably have to serve the six months' sentence. On the other hand, if you begin serving your time now . . .").

The prosecutor also will be involved in counseling. Although the prosecutor represents the people of the jurisdiction and not the individual victim (including surviving family members) the prosecutor will often counsel the victim. For example, the prosecutor will counsel a sex assault victim about a wide variety of matters including what to expect at trial, testifying, and how to cope with the stress of trial. The prosecutor will notify the victim of potential case dispositions (e.g., dismissal of charges, plea agreement), consult with the victim, and seek victim input. Counseling may be done directly by the prosecutor, by a member of a victim assistance unit, or by both.

G. Trial Sequence

If no plea agreement or other disposition is reached, trial follows. The sequence of events at trial is fairly universal: motions before the court regarding significant evidentiary issues (*in limine* motions); jury selection *(voir dire);* opening statements by the prosecutor, then defense attorney (defense may reserve until the commencement of its case); the prosecution case-in-chief (direct examination by the prosecutor and cross-examination of witnesses by the defense); the defense case, which will consist of direct examination of defense witnesses and cross-examination by the prosecution (of course, the defense may put on a pure reasonable doubt defense—not put on any evidence and rest after the prosecution's case-in-chief); prosecution rebuttal, defense surrebuttal if any, submission of instructions to the judge and arguments over instructions; reading of instructions to the jury (in some jurisdictions, instructions are given after closing argument); closing arguments, (prosecution begins, defense follows, prosecution gets rebuttal in jurisdictions that allow the prosecutor to make a rebuttal argument); verdict (or hung jury); post-trial motions (motion for new trial, bail on appeal, and so on). Sentencing will follow a guilty verdict.

2 Formulating the Case Theory

2 *Formulating the Case Theory*

"The theory of the case is a product of the advocate. It is the basic concept around which everything revolves."

James McElhaney, *McElhaney's Trial Notebook* (2005)

"Whatever the commentators may say, a trial is not really a struggle between opposing lawyers but between opposing stories."

Johnnie L. Cochran, Jr., *Journey to Justice* (1996)

I. CASE THEORY

The case theory provides a structure that will serve as the organizing principle for all of your pretrial and trial endeavors. It will guide every activity from interviewing, pleadings, discovery, and pretrial motions to jury selection, witness examinations, and opening statement and closing argument. It is the core concept that runs throughout your work as an advocate.

This chapter examines how to develop a case theory in both criminal and civil cases. You will learn how to develop a case theory as plaintiff's counsel. And you will learn about the varied case theories available to defendants and how, as defense counsel, you can fashion a defense case theory.

II. DEVELOPING THE CASE THEORY

A. Case Theory Components

The case theory has two interdependent components: the *legal theory* and the *factual theory*. For clarity, the legal and factual theories are discussed separately, but the two concepts are interrelated, linked together through law, information, and the client's objectives.

CASE THEORY

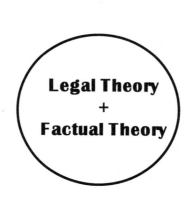

The legal theory is a legal framework developed by a lawyer from interpretation, analysis, and expansion of legal rules and standards (found in cases, statutes, and regulations). It is a framework from which the lawyer posits that, if the facts exist as alleged and under applicable legal burdens, the client is legally entitled to the relief sought. Thus, even though based on the law, one cannot say that the legal theory is the law. It is one attorney's interpretation of law. In practice, some legal theories will be beyond dispute (negligence in an automobile accident) while others may encounter quite vigorous opposition (strict liability of handgun manufacturers to those injured by the intentional use of those weapons).

The factual theory is the party's story justifying relief under the legal theory and is based on all the evidence, and logical inferences from the evidence in the case. In criminal cases the defense may put on a pure reasonable doubt defense—not put on any evidence and rest after the prosecution's case-in-chief. There the defense story will really be a commentary on the deficiencies in the prosecution's story.

B.   Legal Theory

The specific development of the legal theory will vary according to whether you are the attorney for the plaintiff or for the defendant. The principal difference between civil and criminal legal theories is the legal source of the theory. Civil legal theories of both plaintiff and defendant may be founded on common law cases, statutory enactments, administrative regulations, and so on. For most prosecutors in a criminal case, however, there are no common law crimes, only statute-based crimes, limiting the legal theories to those found in the statutes. Criminal defendants, on the other hand, may base a legal theory on a creative interpretation of a range of legal sources as does his or her civil counterpart.

The advocate must also consider the possibility of multiple or back-up theories, which we discuss later in this chapter.

C. Relationship Between the Legal and Factual Theory Components

When selecting and developing a case theory, recognize that the legal and factual theories are interrelated. They are linked together by the client's objectives, the law, and the available information. Tentative case theories start to develop when you possess even minimal information. These hypotheses, à la Sherlock Holmes, arise at an early stage (perhaps even before talking to the client or other witnesses) and are subsequently sifted through as you learn more of your client's objectives, acquire more information, and understand more of the law's applicability to the client's case. Early theorizing is possible because, in each situation, there are generally finite legal theories available, and under each legal theory there is a somewhat foreseeable spectrum of facts that will strengthen or weaken the supporting factual theory.

Client's Objectives

Perceiving the client's *objectives* (be acquitted of the crime, obtain damages, avoid damages, get an injunction), you then research the law to find authority for a legal theory that can achieve these objectives. Imagine you are representing a client accused of burglary. An acquittal is your client's initial objective and therefore the initial focus of your case strategy. Research reveals that the legal theories available to achieve this objective include a mental defense, lack of intent, and misidentification. Therefore, the objective of acquittal can be reached in many ways using more than one legal theory.

Evidence

Your legal theory, in turn, leads you to seek *evidence* from which you can develop a factual theory to support the legal theory. In a burglary case, you as defense counsel would look for information that the defendant has a history of mental problems or was intoxicated at the time of the offense or thought he was entering his own home or that eyewitnesses were biased, or had perceptual problems, and so on.

The information you obtain will then limit the available legal theories. If the defendant in the burglary was caught by police in the home, a reasonable doubt based on misidentification will not be a viable legal theory. Limiting the available legal theories may then alter the client's objectives, bringing you back full circle. If no viable legal theories remain after analysis of the available evidence in the burglary case, the client's objectives may have to be changed from acquittal to a satisfactory plea bargain.

III. PLAINTIFF'S CASE THEORY

A. Legal Theory

Civil Plaintiff

For the civil plaintiff, the legal theory corresponds to the claim for relief (damages for negligence, slander, or breach of contract or the right to possession of land through adverse possession, for example). The civil plaintiff's legal theory asserts that the plaintiff can, under the burden of proof, establish every element of the civil claim. Thus, to propose a legal theory of negligence is to assert that counsel can prove, by a preponderance of the evidence, that (1) the defendant had a duty of care to the plaintiff, (2) the defendant committed an act that breached that duty, and (3) as a proximate result of that breach, (4) the plaintiff suffered compensable harm.

The Prosecutor

For the prosecutor, the representative of the people and the plaintiff, the legal theory will correspond to the statutory definition, including any interpretation by the courts, of the particular crime involved (e.g., burglary, second-degree theft, arson, conspiracy to import a controlled substance). The prosecutor's legal theory asserts that the prosecution can establish within the required burden of persuasion every element of a statutory offense. Accordingly, to propose the legal theory of burglary is to allege that the government can prove, beyond a reasonable doubt, that (1) the defendant (2) entered a dwelling (3) that belonged to another (4) at nighttime (5) with the intent to commit a crime.

B. Selecting the Legal Theory

The potential legal theories for a particular circumstance (an automobile accident, a failed business, a violent death) may be numerous. How then does counsel for plaintiff choose a legal theory? This requires a two-part process.

Identifying Potential Legal Theories

In the *first* part of this process, after considering case law, periodicals, discussions with fellow attorneys, and so on, counsel for the plaintiff will attempt to conceive all of the potential legal theories. These will be based on accepted statements of existing law and plausible arguments for expansion and modification of that law, that the available information suggests. When initially developing a legal theory, the lawyer also considers potential information that reasonably may be found during subsequent fact-gathering. This first part of the process of developing and selecting plaintiff's legal theory is illustrated with the *Injured Motorcyclist* case.

Story

STEP 1—IDENTIFYING POTENTIAL LEGAL THEORIES

The *Injured Motorcyclist* Case

Imagine you represent the plaintiff Jay Solomon, a motorcycle driver who was hit by a car while stopped at a red light.

Through your own knowledge and research, you immediately think of several possible legal theories for the plaintiff:

- Intentional tort,
- Negligent operation of the car,
- Negligent maintenance of the car (worn brakes),
- Negligent repair of the car by some third party, and
- Defective manufacture of the car.

Which of these potential theories, however, should you choose as your initial legal theory?

Assessing Strengths and Weaknesses

In the second part of this process where the preferable legal theory is chosen, counsel for the plaintiff answers the question of which theory is preferred by assessing the strengths and weaknesses of each potential legal theory. In this second step, plaintiff's counsel simultaneously considers the legal theory:

1. In the abstract,
2. In relation to other potential theories, and
3. In conjunction with the available and potential evidence in the case.

Think again about the *Injured Motorcyclist* case with these considerations in mind.

STEP 2—ASSESSING STRENGTHS AND WEAKNESSES

The *Injured Motorcyclist* Case

1.   Assessing the Legal Theory in the Abstract

Look at the potential legal theories (intentional tort, negligent operation) in the abstract. Are any so novel as to invite a likely defense attack on their legal propriety? It does not seem so in this case.

2.   Assessing the Legal Theory in Relation to Other Potential Theories

Look at the practical advantages and disadvantages of each of these potential legal theories in comparison with each available theory. A theory of defective manufacture may require far more expensive and complex expert testimony than a theory of negligent repair. A theory of intentional tort will require establishing a much greater level of culpability on the part of the defendant than is required for a theory of negligent maintenance. A theory of negligent operation may only require obtaining the evidence of a single neutral eyewitness, or even the evidence of your own client, while a theory of defective manufacture may require gaining court-ordered access to thousands of pages of corporate documents. On the other hand, if the defendant-driver is uninsured and indigent, the manufacturer may be the only source for damages.

3.   Assessing the Legal Theory in Conjunction with the Available and Potential Evidence in the Case

At the same time, assess the legal theory in conjunction with available and potential evidence. Assume that through interviewing, investigation, and discovery you obtain information indicating that the brakes are fine and that the car is mechanically perfect. This evidence would eliminate defective manufacture, negligent repair, and negligent maintenance as viable legal theories. Also assume that several witnesses claim to have seen the defendant-driver talking on a cell phone and drinking a latte at the time he hit your client. That information would greatly weaken any theory of intentional tort, but would support negligence as a good tentative legal theory.

C. Factual Theory

The factual theory is more than an accumulation of relevant information. It is constructed from the mass of evidence you have (and that you reasonably believe you might subsequently obtain) to support your legal theory. While the case theory is made up of two components—the legal and factual theories—the factual theory can be conceptualized as also having two subparts. The factual theory must be (1) *factually sufficient* to support the legal theory, and (2) *factually persuasive.* It can be viewed as follows:

CASE THEORY

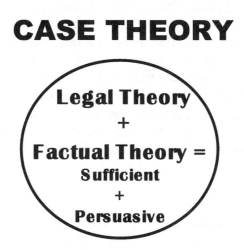

Legal Theory
+
Factual Theory =
Sufficient
+
Persuasive

Factually Sufficient

As plaintiff's counsel, your factual theory must be factually sufficient to support your legal theory. Generally, you must assert sufficient facts to legally fulfill every element of the law on which you base the plaintiff's claim. To illustrate how the factual theory is developed, assume that you are a prosecutor assigned to what has been called the *ATM Murder* case.

The *ATM Murder* Case

Story On April 11th of last year, Robert and Claire O'Toole were on their way to meet their friends for dinner and a movie. It was about 8:00 p.m. when Robert pulled his car into a parking space across the street from a branch of his bank and ran across the street to an outside ATM. He was getting some cash for the evening. His wife watched as he

continues ▶

drew out the cash and was placing it in his wallet. The man who had been standing behind him, seemingly waiting for his turn, tried to grab the wallet from Robert's hand. Robert resisted. The man stabbed Robert in the stomach and ran off down the street. Claire ran to her husband. She called 911 on her cell phone. The police and EMTs arrived within minutes, but Robert died on the way to the hospital.

Police apprehended Donald Wilcox two blocks away because he matched the description given by Claire O'Toole. In Wilcox's pocket were five $20 bills, one $5 bill and four $1 bills. The bank records show that Robert O'Toole had withdrawn $100 in five $20 bills. Later at a lineup, Claire identified Wilcox as the man who stabbed her husband. A photograph taken by the camera at the ATM shows part of the face of the man standing behind Robert, and that portion of the face looks like Wilcox's face. However, the photograph does not provide enough of the facial features to clearly establish by itself that Wilcox was the man.

Assume that you spoke with the investigating detective, witnesses, and studied the relevant photographs, bank records, and the 9-11 call record.

You examine the facts to determine whether they are sufficient to prove that Wilcox committed murder in the first degree. The murder statute states that a person commits first degree murder if the person "commits or attempts to commit the crime of robbery in either the first or second degree . . . and in the course of or in furtherance of such crime or in immediate flight therefrom, he or she, or another participant, causes the death of a person other than one of the participants." Your statutes define robbery in the first degree as a robbery with a deadly weapon and further defines robbery as follows:

> A person commits robbery when he or she unlawfully takes personal property from the person of another . . . by the use or threatened use of immediate force, violence, or fear of injury to that person . . . Such force or fear must be used to obtain or retain possession of the property, or to prevent or overcome resistance to the taking; in either of which cases the degree of force is immaterial.

Are the facts sufficient to prove Wilcox committed murder in the first degree? The robbery can easily be proven through Claire's testimony. The man used deadly force—the knife—to take Robert's wallet after he put the money from the ATM into it. The crime is then elevated to felony murder in the first degree because the element of "causing the death of a person" during the robbery can likewise be proven through Claire's testimony. Another critical element is the identification of the murderer, and Claire will testify that Wilcox is the person who stabbed her husband, and her testimony is corroborated by the ATM photograph.

Assuming that you can prove these facts, if the defense moves to dismiss your case after you rest, the judge will deny the motion, ruling that you have established a prima facie case and that it should be up to the jury to decide whether it has been proven beyond a reasonable doubt. The *factual sufficiency* component of your case theory is satisfied.

Persuasive

So, you as the prosecutor have a story with a plot, and it is factually sufficient to support your legal theory of felony murder in the first degree: Mr. Wilcox came up behind Mr. O'Toole who had just taken money from an ATM. Wilcox stabbed O'Toole when O'Toole resisted the taking of his money. And Mr. O'Toole died from the stab wound.

However, it is not enough to just prove a factually sufficient case. You want to persuade the jury to render the verdict that the defendant is guilty beyond a reasonable doubt. To create a persuasive story requires attention to at least these six key essentials:

- Human values,
- Human needs,
- Human story,
- Believable and understandable story,
- Quantity of evidence, and
- Quality of evidence.

Human Values

To be persuasive, the factual story should be about human values that the jurors share and care about. These are values that are common in the community, such as: honesty, fair treatment, safety, family, and so on. Having a factual story that radiates human values is critical in swaying a jury.

The history of Dr. Jack Kevorkian's trials provides a striking illustration of the importance of human values to a jury. Dr. Kevorkian was prosecuted repeatedly for assisting in suicides. Prosecutors presented evidence that was factually sufficient to support the murder charges, Prosecutors successfully got past a motion to dismiss for insufficient evidence, but factual sufficiency was not enough. Three times Dr. Kevorkian was acquitted and on another occasion the court granted a mistrial when the jury deadlocked. What the defendant had was a story about human suffering and mercy, and that story, with human values at its core, was compelling. It was not until Dr. Kevorkian went on national television helping a man commit suicide and goading prosecutors to charge him that he was eventually convicted.

Human Needs

One of the values that we all care about is the fulfillment of human needs. We all want food, sleep, love, freedom, belonging, safety, and other human needs. While this value could have been discussed in the prior section, it is discussed separately to stress its importance to the factual theory. The plaintiff is usually telling a story of deprivation of human needs, such as safety, financial security, or love. In this regard, Abraham Maslow's theory regarding human needs is helpful. Professor Maslow, who was the chair of the psychology department at Brandeis, created Maslow's pyramid of human needs. He theorized that each person has these needs. Jurors can relate to the deprivation of these human needs. Therefore, counsel should focus on these fundamental needs when crafting the story.

MASLOW'S PYRAMID

Being Needs

Self-actualization

Esteem Needs

Belonging Needs

Safety Needs

Physiological Needs

Deficit Needs

HUMAN VALUES AND NEEDS

The *ATM Murder* Case

In the *ATM Murder* case, the prosecutor might emphasize the value of safety in jury argument:

"Ladies and gentlemen, this case is about a commodity that each of us holds dear—our personal safety—the freedom to go to an ATM and take out cash without the fear of being robbed."

A Human Story

Counsel's story has a plot, but that plot is only a skeleton. Meat must be put on the bones. The story must be brought alive or the jury just won't care. To accomplish this, counsel will want to tell a story about a real human being, someone that the jury can care about. To this end, the plaintiff will want to elicit from witnesses at trial as much human background information as the law allows.

A HUMAN STORY

The *ATM Murder* Case

In the *ATM Murder* case, the prosecutor during pretrial investigation would want to find out as much background information as possible about Claire and Robert O'Toole and during the prosecution's case-in-chief elicit admissible testimony about them as people. This could include their ages, how long they had been married, information about their children, and how they were employed. The goal is to paint a picture of these two principal players as living, breathing human beings, not one-dimensional stick figures.

Believable and Understandable Story

Trial work is storytelling. Whether plaintiff or defense counsel, the attorney crafts the trial evidence and/or lack of evidence into a story to tell the jurors. To be a convincing story for the jury it should be one about values that matter to the jurors as well as a story about real people with whom the jurors can empathize. Like any story, the trial story must have a plot. More than that, it must be a believable plot. A believable plot for the jury is one that the jurors believe comports with both common experience and common sense. It has been often said: "In trial the better story wins." We would modify that axiom slightly to: "The better story well told wins." And failing to tell a believable story might leave an opening for jurors to frame the story instead of you . . . and it might not be favorable to your case.

These propositions have been borne out by studies of jury decision-making in criminal cases. Sociologists Lance Bennett and Martha Feldman in *Reconstructing Reality in the Courtroom* (1981) determined that jurors assembled evidence produced in fragments throughout the trial into a story and then in deliberations evaluated the story to determine whether it made sense. Researchers Nancy Pennington and Reid Hastie in their article *A Cognitive Theory in Juror Decision Making: The Story Model,* 13 Cardozo L. Rev.

519, 520 (1991) report that when making decisions jurors use stories to sort the information presented at trial and compare their personal stories with those offered at trial.

The problem is that life doesn't always make sense. At least life doesn't always make sense so that the jurors will conclude that the story presented at trial comports with their experiences or beliefs in human behavior and the way life works. Belief: A rape victim will attempt to escape when given a chance. But there are instances when a rape victim does not try to escape when she has the opportunity. Belief: An abused child will report what happened. But there are cases where children abused by an authority figures (stepfather, priest, teacher) did not report the abuse. Belief: Corporate executives know what is going on in their business. But a CEO of a multimillion dollar corporation may not know that his chief financial officer was cooking the books. Belief: A domestic violence victim would call the police, leave the batterer, or at least tell someone about the beatings. But it has happened that a domestic partner shot her partner whom she claims abused her for years and yet she never called the police or left the abuser.

In the *ATM Murder* case, you as the prosecutor, have a story that may not make sense to the jurors: the defendant Donald Wilcox was arrested two blocks away from where the robbery-stabbing took place. If Wilcox committed the crime, jurors might conclude it makes no sense that he would remain nearby. Even though this doesn't make sense, you don't want the jury to leap to the conclusion he didn't commit the murder. This is when your story is critical to the success of the case.

It is when the potential conflict between reality and juror preconceptions exists, that getting the full story before the jury is so important. By full story, we mean the story that accounts for or explains human behavior and events that may not otherwise make sense to the jurors. This may involve having the rape victim explain that fear of injury prevented her from trying to escape. Or calling an expert to explain Child Abuse Syndrome and that it is not uncommon for a child not to complain. Or to support the abused defendant's self defense claim in the murder case, defense counsel could call an expert in Battered Woman Syndrome to explain the cycle of violence. In the *ATM Murder* case, eliciting testimony that Wilcox lived in the neighborhood could be sufficient.

Another critical point is that the jury must understand the story's plot. Trials may be complex in three ways. First, many stories involve numerous events and/or players. Second, in many cases the subject matter involved in telling the story is in part comprised of technical information, for example, scientific methodologies. Third, in many cases the story involves both of the first two complexities. To make a complex story digestible by the jurors, counsel can use experts to translate and explain technical information. Visuals, such as summary charts, PowerPoint presentations, or other sorts of charts, are valuable tools to make complex information accessible to the jurors.

Quantity of Evidence

Even if your story is supported by enough evidence on each element of your legal theory to get past a motion for judgment as a matter of law (a directed verdict) or dismissal at the close of the plaintiff's case, that does not mean that enough evidence has been presented to convince a jury. The judge will review the evidence in the light most favorable to the plaintiff when considering a motion for judgment as a matter of law or dismissal. On the other hand, the jury will have a higher burden of proof when weighing the evidence—a preponderance of the evidence in a civil case and beyond a reasonable doubt in a criminal case.

QUANTITY OF EVIDENCE

The *ATM Murder* Case

If all the prosecution offered was Claire O'Toole's testimony that she identifies the defendant Donald Wilcox as the person who took her husband's wallet and stabbed him, the trial judge would still deny a defense motion to dismiss on the basis of insufficient evidence of identification. The judge would rule that viewing Mrs. O'Toole's testimony in a light most favorable to the prosecution, made a prima facie case on the identification issue. The judge would most likely state that the jury would weigh her testimony and decide whether the prosecution proved that Wilcox was a murderer beyond a reasonable doubt.

To persuade the jury, the prosecutor would argue that based upon Claire O'Toole's testimony alone defendant Wilcox is beyond a reasonable doubt the person who robbed and murdered Robert O'Toole. Then, the prosecutor could argue the quantity of evidence that corroborates Claire O'Toole's testimony on identification. That evidence includes Wilcox appearance, which matched the initial description given by Claire O'Toole; the ATM photograph showing what looks like a portion of Wilcox's face; Wilcox's possession of five $20 bills, the exact amount and number of bills that Robert O'Toole had withdrawn; and the defendant's presence within a short distance from where O'Toole was robbed and stabbed.

Quality of Evidence

No matter how much evidence you have to support your story, it will do you little good if that evidence or the story itself is not believable, that is, if it suffers quality problems. Thus, establishing the believability of your witness and the witness's testimony is essential.

To be believable, the story must appear coherent and comport with the fact finder's common sense and everyday experience with human nature. In short, it must make sense. If the prosecution's story does not make sense, the jury is likely to translate that lack into reasonable doubt. If a civil plaintiff's story does not make sense, the jury is likely to give credence to the defense's story.

In the *ATM Murder* case, we focus more narrowly on the eyewitness testimony, rather than the overarching trial story of the plaintiff or defendant. Evidence offered by this pivotal witness must make sense to the jurors so that the jury doesn't find a weakness leading to a reasonable doubt.

QUALITY OF EVIDENCE

The *ATM Murder* Case

In the *ATM Murder* case, Claire O'Toole is the prosecution's key witness. Without her, insufficient evidence exists on the element of the defendant's identification as the murderer. The quality of Claire as a witness and of her testimony is essential to a conviction. To persuade the jury, she must appear to be a credible, unbiased witness. The prosecutor will want to elicit testimony that would make her identification of Wilcox believable, such as that there was adequate lighting, no obstructions between her car and where the robber stood, she had a clear view of the robber's face and sufficient time to get a good look at the robber, and so on.

IV. DEFENSE CASE THEORY

A. Types of Theories

The potential theories available to a civil or criminal defendant are far more varied than those available to the plaintiff. Plaintiff's case theory, both the legal theory and the factual theory, is an attack on the defendant. The plaintiff, through his or her case theory, is accusing the defendant of breaching a contract, negligence, murder, violating a lease, manufacturing hazardous products, and so on. The defendant can respond to this attack in three ways:

- The defendant can focus on weaknesses in the plaintiff's case theory, thereby attempting to blunt the attack.
- The defendant can launch a separate counterattack.
- The defendant can decide that negotiation is the most viable alternative.

1. Attacking Weaknesses in the Plaintiff's Case Theory

Defense legal theories that strike at weaknesses in the plaintiff's case theory will focus their attack in one or more of four directions:

- Attack the *legality* of the plaintiff's case theory. (There is no such legal theory.)
- Attack the factual sufficiency of the plaintiff's case theory. (Such a legal theory exists, but the party's factual allegations are insufficient as a matter of law to raise the legal theory.)
- Attack the *persuasive sufficiency* of the plaintiff's case. (Though such a legal theory exists and sufficient facts have been presented to get by summary judgment motions and motions for a directed verdict, the fact finder should not be persuaded given the applicable burden of persuasion.)
- Attack *procedural aspects* of the plaintiff's case theory. (The party is barred because of some procedural rule, such as a statute of limitations or lack of personal jurisdiction.)

2. Counterattack or Affirmative Defense

In addition, there are defense legal theories that do not specifically attack the plaintiff's legal or factual theories, but rather are independent defense claims. These are termed *affirmative defenses,* which state that even if the plaintiff's legal theory cannot be attacked, the defendant should not be liable, or defendant's liability at least should be mitigated, due to some affirmative grounds such as fraud, self-defense, or accord and satisfaction.

Defense legal theories based on attacks on persuasive sufficiency and on affirmative defenses provide the principal focus for defense litigation strategies in these materials. Yet, attacks based on legality, factual sufficiency, and procedural concerns (e.g., motion to dismiss, motion for summary judgment) also constitute legal theories, although you might not initially think of them as such. This may be because these theories are generally directed to the court, which, rather than the jury, will make any factual findings required under the theories. Nevertheless, one must consider and understand these theories in order to be a competent advocate.

3. Negotiation and Settlement

The defendant can decide that negotiation is the most viable alternative. However, even if the case strategy centers on obtaining some form of settlement, an attorney nevertheless wants to develop the best possible case theory in order to provide leverage in that eventual negotiation. We will therefore discuss developing a case theory under the first two methods of attack here and leave the discussion of negotiation to Chapter 12.

B.   Legal Insufficiency

A defense legal theory that attacks the legality of plaintiff's case theory focuses on the validity of plaintiff's claim under existing law. This type of attack takes the position that, as a matter of law, plaintiff's legal theory should not be recognized as one for which the court will provide a remedy. In this type of attack, plaintiff has raised all the elements of his or her claim, but it is arguable that the claim itself should not be recognized. For example, plaintiff's claim, which attempts to hold a gun manufacturer liable for the intentional use of a handgun by a third party, will be subject to a defense argument that no such claim exists at law. Or a criminal statute may be subject to a defense contention that the criminal statute is unconstitutional on its face, and so forth.

These types of defense legal theories are developed by analyzing plaintiff's legal theory within the context of relevant substantive law. This analysis, of course, is not a neutral inquiry, but takes place from an ends-means perspective. Defense counsel begins with the position that a claim for relief is not stated because current law (statutes, regulations, cases) does not recognize the claim as presented by plaintiff. Counsel then scrutinizes plaintiff's claim and the existing law in an attempt to develop a plausible argument to sustain that position. Of course, there may not be a plausible argument for this position, and defense counsel then will have to focus on other lines of attack.

To illustrate this and other theories, assume you represent defendant Professor Abraham Wilson in a libel action that has come to be known as the *University Defamation* case.

The *University Defamation* Case

Story

The plaintiff, student Dorian E. Leonard, alleges that Professor Wilson, now the defendant, wrote on a desktop computer in the professor's private office, in 30 point font: "Reminder - tell Dean that D.E.L. is selling drugs to students." Leonard further alleges that several fellow students saw the notation when they surreptitiously entered the professor's office to play a prank on him. Plaintiff's attorney has pleaded that as a result of this defamation, which plaintiff has alleged is false, Leonard suffered significant general damages.

In raising the defamation-in-libel legal theory, the plaintiff asserts that he or she can prove, by a preponderance of the evidence: (1) defendant intentionally or negligently published matter defamatory to some third person; (2) the matter was understood as defamatory of plaintiff; (3) causation; (4) damages.

The line between a problem of legality and one of factual sufficiency is often an inexact one. For example, you review the *University Defamation* case. Libel requires only general damages for a claim, but slander generally requires an allegation of special damages. While libel is generally considered to pertain to written matter and slander to oral assertions, one can make a plausible argument under relevant case law that the real difference between the two is the relative permanence or transitory nature of the defamatory remark. Under this analysis you could argue on behalf of defendant Wilson that because the message on the computer screen is transitory (just a reminder note to himself), slander, not libel, is involved. That being so, plaintiff, who has only alleged general damages, thereby failed to allege all elements of slander and has arguably failed to state a claim for relief. As such, plaintiff's theory could be attacked on legality grounds. At a later time, however, the problem will quickly become one of factual sufficiency: Plaintiff will also need sufficient information from which he can allege special damages.

C. Factual Insufficiency

Legal theories based on attacking the factual sufficiency of plaintiff's case theory center on the lack of a sufficient quantum of evidence to submit the case to a jury—that is, plaintiff has failed to make a prima facie case. A factual sufficiency attack takes the position that even if such a legal theory exists, plaintiff's allegations are insufficient as a matter of law to permit a reasonable fact finder to find one or more elements of the claim. For example, there is no evidence in a breach of contract suit of any consideration. Or the only evidence in a robbery case, due to a successful motion suppressing the victim's identification of the defendant, is that the defendant was seen within a block of the victim's home.

These defense theories are developed by assessing plaintiff's factual theory in the context of plaintiff's legal theory.

FACTUAL SUFFICIENCY

The *University Defamation* Case

Plaintiff Leonard's story in the defamation case provides the opportunity for an attack on factual sufficiency. The defamatory matter was revealed to students who surreptitiously entered the professor's office. One element of the legal theory of defamation requires that the matter be published to some third person either intentionally or negligently. Under these circumstances, you, as defense counsel, could consider a possible legal theory of factual insufficiency and move for a summary judgment on the grounds that no reasonable fact finder could determine that the publication was your client's fault under the facts presented, i.e., the students were not supposed to be in Wilson's office, they entered the office without permission, and Wilson did not intentionally or negligently make the remark to these students.

Now that we have discussed legal and factual insufficiency, these categories need further comment. While we have categorized factual insufficiency as "factual" for purposes of organization, one could also reasonably have classified it under "legality" inasmuch as it refers to factual insufficiency as a matter of law. Like most such attempts at categorization, alternative schemes are plausible. In fact, defense legal theories could also have been divided according to the decision-maker assessing the defense legal theory: (1) those decided by the court (procedural attacks such as venue and lack of personal jurisdiction; failure to state a claim; legally insufficient information to allow claim to be considered by the trier of fact); (2) those decided by the fact finder after the court has determined that there is a prima facie case (affirmative defenses; procedural attacks such as the statute of limitations); and (3) those decided by the fact finder without an initial determination by the court (defense based on persuading the fact finder that plaintiff has not carried its burden as to one or more elements of its legal theory). The categorization employed in these materials, however, was chosen because it facilitates discussing the development of the various defense legal theories.

D. Persuasive Insufficiency

An attack on the persuasive sufficiency of plaintiff's case theory focuses on plaintiff's inability to convince a jury of the plaintiff's position. This type of attack takes the position that even if plaintiff's allegations are sufficient to be submitted to the jury, the jury should find that the plaintiff has failed to carry its burden of persuasion as to one or more elements of the civil claim or statutory crime (e.g., expert testimony regarding the cause of the plaintiff's disability precludes a finding of proximate causation between the car accident and physical injuries or credibility problems with an eyewitness to an assault raise reasonable doubts).

The defense attack recognizes the elements of the plaintiff's case that could make it persuasive and seeks to blunt them. The attack may entail showing the implausibility of the plaintiff's story or the absence of sufficient quality or quantity of evidence to support the story.

Blunting the Persuasive Elements

Defense counsel can use two thrusts:

1. **Exclude as much of the plaintiff's supporting evidence as possible.** Defense counsel can make pretrial motions in limine to exclude evidence that plaintiff's counsel could utilize in an effort to get the fact finder to empathize or sympathize with the plaintiff. For example, defense counsel could move to exclude gruesome photographs of the plaintiff's injuries under Federal Rule of Evidence 403 because the unfair prejudice of the photographs outweighs any probative value they might have.

2. **Develop a competing human story with human values.** Defense counsel can blunt the persuasive elements of the plaintiff's case by presenting a human story that competes with and nullifies the plaintiff's persuasive story. For example, in a criminal case the defense counsel can seek to humanize the defendant and stress the important value of loss of freedom through incarceration of an innocent person. Some cases come with ready-made competing human values. For example, the plaintiff files a complaint for negligence alleging that he was riding in a car driven by his friend, the defendant. Plaintiff alleges that the defendant drove negligently and collided with a telephone pole, injuring the plaintiff and at the same time killing the defendant's son. The impact of plaintiff's injury will certainly be blunted by the fact that the defendant's son was killed in the same accident. In the University Defamation case, the defense could tell the human story of Professor Wilson doing his job and trying to curb drug trafficking at the university.

Deficiencies in Quantity, Quality, and Plausibility: Defense Counsel Telling a Parallel Story

The jurors will use a story to filter and sort information, and jurors' decision-making will compare the stories presented with what they understand to be common experience and common sense. The jurors will construct their own story. They will reject stories that don't make sense to them. Jurors, understanding that they are to determine whether the plaintiff has met the burden of persuasion and that they are to determine the credibility of witnesses, will be receptive to arguments regarding the quantity and quality of the plaintiff's proof. Therefore, defense counsel will analyze the plaintiff's story to detect flaws in it.

One approach to detecting deficiencies in quality, quantity, and plausibility of the plaintiff's case is to imagine the perfect plaintiff's case on the available evidence. Once that perfect case is constructed, defense counsel compares and contrasts it with the actual facts of the case. With this analysis, the deficiencies in the plaintiff's case are revealed, and the defense can build a story and argument from the lack of evidence.

For example, assume you are defense counsel in the *ATM Murder* case.

IMPLAUSIBLE STORY

The *ATM Murder* Case

The perfect prosecution case on identity would be one where Mrs. O'Toole stood three feet from Wilcox and got a clear look at his face under a street light. The ATM camera would have gotten a full-face picture of Wilcox. O'Toole's wallet would have been found on Wilcox or at least it would have been found discarded. He would have been arrested across town where he hid after fleeing the scene.

You, as defense counsel, can compare these with the facts of the prosecution's case and argue that the prosecution has not offered a sufficient quantity of evidence to prove Wilcox guilty beyond a reasonable doubt:

"It makes no sense. If Donald had murdered Mr. Wilcox, he wouldn't have remained a mere two blocks away. He would have gotten as far away as possible. If Donald had taken Mr. Wilcox's wallet, the police would have found it on him or if it had been thrown away the police would have recovered it with Donald's fingerprints on it. There are many reasonable doubts in this case. It's a tragedy that Mr. Wilcox was murdered. Don't make this a double tragedy by convicting what the lack of evidence has shown to be an innocent man."

E. Procedural Insufficiency

Defense legal theories that attack procedural aspects of plaintiff's case theory encompass such procedural considerations as the failure to obtain personal or subject matter jurisdiction, lack of venue, or the expiration of a statute of limitations.

These legal theories are developed by comparing a list of available procedural bars (derived from the interpretation of cases, statutes, court rules, and so on, as well as any unique, creative analysis that adds to the list in a particular case) with all information relevant to these procedural postures that exists in the case. Subsequent information, whose significance is appreciated because you have the list of procedural bars and their corresponding elements in mind, may, moreover, add possible procedural grounds as the case progresses.

PROCEDURAL ASPECTS

The *University Defamation* Case

In the defamation case, suppose D.E.L. filed the defamation action in federal court alleging that subject matter jurisdiction is based upon diversity of citizenship. D.E.L. asserts he is a citizen of Maine and that your client is a citizen of Texas. After looking at the college records, defendant learns that D.E.L. signed an affidavit to obtain reduced in-state tuition in which he asserted that he considered himself a citizen of Texas. Defendant could procedurally attack plaintiff's choice of the federal forum for lack of subject matter jurisdiction.

F. Affirmative Defense

Defense legal theories do not have to be restricted specifically to attacking plaintiff's legal or factual theory. The defense may raise an independent claim that, if successful, will preclude or mitigate plaintiff's right to relief under its case theory. When asserting this claim, known as an "affirmative defense," defense counsel is taking the position that even if plaintiff has established all the elements of its theory, defendant has a legal defense based on case law or statute (e.g., fraud in the inducement, latches, insanity). Some affirmative defenses attack the propriety of plaintiff's behavior, accusing the plaintiff, say, of delay or fraud, much as plaintiff's legal theory attacks the defendant. Other affirmative defenses merely assert that the defendant has done no wrong, claiming privilege, perhaps, or insanity. In criminal law, some authorities reserve the use of the term "affirmative defense" to those defenses that carry a burden of proof, but the term when used here does not carry that implication.

As independent claims for relief, seeking to deny or mitigate plaintiff's claim, affirmative defenses are comprised of elements, just as plaintiff's legal theories are. For example, in setting forth an affirmative defense of self-defense in using deadly force, a defendant is asserting that under the applicable burden of proof, which in some jurisdictions is on the defense and in others on the prosecution, (1) defendant reasonably feared he or she was threatened with death or great bodily injury, (2) the threat was imminent, and (3) the amount of force used in defense was necessary.

It should not be surprising, therefore, that the process for selecting an affirmative defense is analogous to the process of selecting the plaintiff's legal theory. Likewise, plaintiff's attacks on a defense case theory founded on an affirmative defense will parallel the types of attacks a defendant generally can make against a plaintiff's legal theory. For instance, the prosecution can argue against a self-defense claim on the theory that the defendant has failed to establish the element of reasonable force.

In developing an affirmative defense, you must determine the affirmative defenses theoretically possible in the case. This requires examining plaintiff's legal theory. Every legal theory carries with it a number of accepted affirmative defenses found in cases, statutes, or court rules, as well as the possibility of new affirmative defenses that evolve out of a creative analysis of case trends. These new or creative affirmative defenses are also likely to arise through inductive thinking: information in a case can provide a brainstorm for a new affirmative defense theory. You will then seek supporting and analogous authority to uphold the theory.

Consider the evidence that is, and reasonably may be, available in the case. Try to match this evidence, and the inferences from the evidence, with the required elements of each potential affirmative defense. When appropriate, also consider each affirmative defense in the abstract and in conjunction with other affirmative defenses.

AFFIRMATIVE DEFENSES

The *University Defamation* Case

In the *University Defamation* case, your research revealed a number of potential affirmative defenses to defamation: truth, absolute privilege, consent, and so on. Knowing that not all of these defenses

> are likely to be appropriate to your case, you next reviewed the known evidence in your case. From this review, you realized that the alleged defamation occurred as part of an attempt to warn the dean about drug sales to students. Matching this information to the list of potential affirmative defenses, you would conclude that the conditional "public protection" privilege could offer an affirmative defense and, therefore, a possible legal theory for the defense in the case.

V.   MULTIPLE LEGAL THEORIES

There are three situations in which a party might offer more than one legal theory in a case.

A.   Evidence Gathering

First, counsel may pursue several tentative legal theories during the evidence-gathering phase, which usually, but not always, takes place at a relatively early stage. As facts are uncovered, these multiple tentative theories generally are eliminated or abandoned because of lack of evidence to support them, inconsistency, or strategic concerns. Counsel will usually try to reduce the number of legal theories as quickly as is feasible, since the evidence-gathering process itself is far more efficient if guided by a single legal theory.

B.   Strategic Sequence

Second, multiple legal theories may be used in strategic sequence. A defendant in a breach of contract case may begin by alleging a procedural bar, then, failing in that, move to dismiss for failure to state a claim for relief, and finally end up arguing the case on the basis that the plaintiff's witnesses regarding the element of consideration are too biased to be believed. This use of multiple theories illustrates the concept of the back-up theory. This concept reflects the necessity that an attorney constantly plan for every conceivable contingency and alternative throughout representation of the client.

C.   Alternatives

Third, a party may present the fact finder or the adversary in negotiations with alternative legal theories. The plaintiff in a contract dispute may allege both a breach of contract and fraud. A prosecutor may charge the same defendant with theft and burglary. At some point, however, the factual theories—the stories—underlying the alternative legal theories may become so divergent, or even inconsistent, that a choice must be made prior to negotiation or trial.

CONSEQUENCES OF ASSERTING ALTERNATIVE THEORIES

The *ATM Murder* Case

Imagine now that you represent Donald Wilcox in the *ATM Murder* case. You have two alternative legal theories: (1) reasonable doubt of misidentification and (2) insanity. Only a partial picture of the robber was taken by the ATM camera and Mrs. O'Toole was near, but not directly next to, the robber. Mr. Wilcox has a long history of mental illness, and your expert is ready to testify that he was insane at the time he stabbed Mr. O'Toole, believing that Mr. O'Toole had just stolen money from the bank.

Now, analytically, these two theories are not inconsistent - "There is a doubt my client is the man who was identified taking Mr. O'Toole's wallet and stabbing him. But even if he is that man, he was insane at the time." Fine. But what do you as defense counsel do when Ms. O'Toole testifies? Cross-examine to show that she could not clearly see the robber or otherwise try to impeach her identification? Then, what do you do, call your psychiatrist to testify that Mr. Wilcox was suffering from a delusion when he stabbed the victim? If counsel tries to mix and advance both theories, the jury will receive mixed messages. At best, they will be confused; at worst, they will perceive that counsel is desperately groping for anything in order to win, without any regard to what really happened.

VI. CASE THEORY AS A GUIDE TO ALL PRETRIAL ACTIVITIES

The case theory serves as a guide for all of your pretrial activities, such as:

- **Client Interviews**—You interview your client to obtain information to develop, support, modify, or discard plausible case theories.
- **Informal and formal discovery**—Informal investigation such as witness interviews and formal requests for discovery is aimed at obtain-

ing information to sift through plausible case theories and to focus on information that will support your existing theories or undercut your opponent's.

- **Pleading**—Affirmative civil pleadings incorporate plaintiff's legal and factual theories; responsive pleadings embody variations of defense legal theories. Criminal pleadings basically incorporate the prosecutor's legal theory.

- **Motions**—Pretrial motions, which are structured by a motion theory analogous to a case theory, are commonly used to obtain information helpful to your case theory or to keep out evidence helpful to your opponent.

- **Negotiation**—In negotiation, strengths and weaknesses of the respective case theories will be a central factor as you and the opposing party weigh the risk of litigation, attack weaknesses during bargaining, and so forth.

- **Counseling**—Counseling will often involve providing advice bearing on the execution of the case theory either directly (should the client testify in a criminal case?) or indirectly (should you recommend substance-abuse counseling when your client's alcohol problem is getting in the way of his or her ability to cooperate or even the ability to appear in court?).

VII. ETHICAL CONSIDERATIONS

All of the advice we have given in this chapter about putting together a persuasive story is premised on this proposition: "Facts do not change." Facts are facts. However, some witnesses are malleable. It is not only proper, we believe it is critical that you detect facts that will make your case persuasive. On the other hand, it is unethical to coach a witness into a false or misleading story that may be more persuasive. ABA Rule of Professional Conduct 3.4 states: "A lawyer shall not:. . . (b) falsify evidence, counsel or assist a witness to testify falsely, or offer an inducement to a witness that is prohibited by law."

For example, in the *ATM Murder* case, the prosecution's case would be more persuasive on the issue of identification if Mrs. O'Toole got a good, long look at the face of the man who stabbed her husband. In interviewing her, the prosecutor should ask her about the lighting, her distance from the robber when she saw him and so on. However, the prosecutor should not coach or lead her into a story that is not true.

✓ A CASE THEORY CHECKLIST

Formulating a Case Theory

1. Guide to Pretrial Activities

The case theory is a guide to pretrial.

- ❑ *Client Interviews*—Obtain information to develop, support, modify, or discard plausible case theories.
- ❑ *Informal and formal discovery*—Obtain information that will support your existing theories or undercut your opponent's.
- ❑ *Pleading*—Incorporate the plaintiff's legal and factual theories; responsive pleadings embody variations of defense legal theories.
- ❑ *Pretrial Motions*—Use to obtain information helpful to your case theory or to keep out evidence helpful to your opponent.
- ❑ *Negotiation*—The strength of respective case theories are central factors in weighing the risk of litigation and attacking the other side's case in bargaining.

2. Ethical Considerations

Witnesses should not be coached into giving false or misleading evidence nor evidence be misused or destroyed that would support the case theory.

Developing Plaintiff's Case Theory

Legal Theory

- ❑ *Civil plaintiff:* Assert that each element of the claim and damages can be proven by a preponderance of the evidence.
- ❑ *Prosecution legal theory:* Allege that every element of the crime can be proven beyond a reasonable doubt.
- ❑ Apply a two-step process in selecting a legal theory:
    1. Research to identify all possible legal theories that may apply to the case.
    2. Assess the strengths and weaknesses of each potential legal theory considering the legal theory:
        - ✓ In the abstract;
        - ✓ In relation to other potential theories;
        - ✓ In conjunction with the available and potential evidence in the case.

Factual Theory

❑ Appreciate that a good factual theory is both *factually sufficient,* i.e., it is sufficient to support the plaintiff's legal theory and *factually persuasive,* i.e., it will convince the fact finder (jury or in a bench trial, the judge) to render the verdict that the plaintiff is seeking.

Factual Sufficiency

❑ Identify all the elements of the civil complaint or criminal charge.
❑ Present sufficient evidence on each element to establish a prima facie case.

Persuasive Story

❑ Keep in mind that your story must convince regular people who reflect a fairly broad spectrum of American society. Make sure your story contains the six essential elements to tell a persuasive story:
  ✓ The factual story is one about *human values* (family, freedom, fairness) that the jurors believe in.
  ✓ The story is about the deprivation of *human needs* (safety, love).
  ✓ The story is about *human beings* who are brought to life by the evidence and who the jurors can care about.
  ✓ The story is *believable* and *understandable* in that it is clear, comports with stories that the jurors are familiar with, and it makes sense.
  ✓ A sufficient *quantity* of evidence supports the story so that the elements are proven in accordance with the burden of proof.
  ✓ The *quality* of evidence, i.e., credible witnesses and credible testimony, supports the story.

Defense Case Theory

Three Types of Defense Case Theories

❑ Attack the weaknesses in the plaintiff's case theory:
  ✓ Attack its *legality;*
  ✓ Attack its *factual* sufficiency;
  ✓ Attack its *persuasive* sufficiency;
  ✓ Attack its *procedural* sufficiency.
❑ Raise an affirmative defense, or
❑ Negotiate.

Legal Sufficiency of Plaintiff's Case Theory

❑ Show that the plaintiff's legal theory is not valid under existing law (e.g., it's unconstitutional).

❑ Note that a fine line exists between legal and factual insufficiency.

Factual Sufficiency of Plaintiff's Case Theory

❑ Assert that the plaintiff has not proven one or more elements with sufficient evidence to establish a prima facie case so the case should not be submitted to the jury.

❑ Assert that the plaintiff has not proven one or more elements of the complaint by a preponderance of the evidence in a civil case or beyond a reasonable doubt in a criminal case.

Persuasive Sufficiency of Plaintiff's Case

❑ Blunt the plaintiff's attempt to tell a human story about human values by:

  ✓ Moving to exclude as much as possible of the plaintiff's evidence from which that story could be told, and

  ✓ Tell a competing human story with human values.

❑ Attack deficiencies in quality, quantity, and plausibility of the plaintiff's case by using the perfect plaintiff's case approach.

Procedural Insufficiency

Attack the procedural aspects of the plaintiff's case theory (e.g., the statute of limitations has passed, improper venue)

Affirmative Defense

Raise an independent claim, an affirmative defense, that will either mitigate or preclude a plaintiff's verdict.

Case Theory Standards for Plaintiff and Defendant

Multiple Legal Theories

Three situations when a party may want to offer more than one legal theory:

❑ During the early *evidence-gathering* stage before focus has narrowed to a limited number of legal theories.

❑ When the theories are used in *strategic sequence,* for example, move to dismiss for insufficient evidence, and failing that argue that the plaintiff has not met the burden of proof.

❑ When *alternate* theories exist, for example prosecutor charges murder in the first degree but argues the lesser included crime of murder in the second degree.

3 *Developing and Managing the Case*

3 *Developing and Managing the Case*

"Detection is, or ought to be, an exact science, and should be treated in the same cold unemotional manner. You have attempted to tinge it with romanticism, which produces the same effect as if you worked a love-story into the fifth proposition of Euclid."

Sherlock Holmes to Dr. Watson, *The Sign of Four*
by Arthur Conan Doyle (1859–1930)

"In the criminal justice system, the people are represented by two separate yet equally important groups: the police, who investigate crime; and the district attorneys, who prosecute the offenders. These are their stories."

Law and Order, television series originally
aired in 1990 on NBC

I. DEVELOPING AND MANAGING THE CASE

The development of the case starts the moment you get involved in the case and goes on until it is submitted to the jury. Case development involves a variety of processes designed to enhance your case including fact investigation, legal research, application of strategies for organizing the information and so on. Case development is never more intensely pursued than during the pretrial phase. Upcoming chapters are devoted to investigating and developing the case with client and witness interviews, written discovery, depositions, creation of trial visuals, and motions. This chapter provides an overview of those activities and highlights their interrelationships. Further, you will learn about these other areas important to case development: legal research, the selection and utilization of experts during the investigation, the search for and preservation of physical evidence, and ethical considerations during the investigation.

This chapter also covers how to manage your case information so it is filed in an orderly manner and is understandable and retrievable. You will be introduced to an organizational tool we call a "fact-development diagram." This diagram provides an approach to investigating and organizing the investigation and the information you uncover. Finally, the chapter offers techniques and systems for organizing and managing the case, with an emphasis on electronic case management software.

II.   PLANNING CASE DEVELOPMENT

A.   Case Theory as a Guide

All case development activities are aimed at a single goal: finding information that bears upon your tentative case theory (the components of which are the legal and factual theories) and a related appreciation of the opposing side's case theory. In this investigation you are hunting for information both favorable and unfavorable because you want to understand the case's strengths and weaknesses.

Particularly at the outset of case development, you must be open to finding factual evidence that will modify, or even change, your factual theory to such an extent that the legal theory must change. Indeed, early in the case, your search for the facts will aid you in selecting among competing legal theories or in deciding to abandon a legal theory.

To illustrate the importance of an investigation of the facts and the gathering of evidence to support your legal theory, assume that you are considering representing the plaintiff, 23-year-old Litonya Barefoot, in the *Bicycle-crosswalk* case. You need to develop a case theory.

The *Bicycle-Crosswalk* Case

Story

Ms. Barefoot has told you that she was commuting by bicycle to Major University on October 11th, where she is a graduate student in psychology. As is her habit, she crosses the arterial of 12th Avenue in a westbound direction, which immediately adjoins the campus. There are two westbound crosswalks at the intersection of 12th and Marion where the collision occurred. There is a flashing yellow light up above to catch the attention of motorists. There isn't a stop sign for northbound nor for southbound traffic on 12th. Ms. Barefoot was hit while in the crosswalk, sustaining injury to her right shoulder and left hip.

After meeting with Ms. Barefoot, you requested a copy of the police report of this incident.

Your initial legal theory is that the motorist, Tyler Sullivan, was negligent in that he failed to see the bicyclist in the marked crosswalk and did not yield the right-of-way to her. As a necessary prerequisite to developing your legal theory, you must first research the applicable law for the right-of-way in crosswalks. You find the following statute in the motor vehicle code:

CROSSWALKS

(1) The operator of an approaching vehicle shall stop and remained stopped to allow a pedestrian or bicycle to cross the roadway within an unmarked or marked crosswalk when the pedestrian or bicycle is upon or within one lane of a half of the roadway upon which the vehicle is traveling or onto which it is turning.

(2) No pedestrian or bicycle shall suddenly leave a curb or other place of safety and walk, run, or otherwise move into the path of a vehicle which is so close that it is impossible for the driver to stop.

After reviewing the pertinent statute governing the right-of-way, you then want to construct the factual theory to support your legal theory. You begin by reviewing the police report. You learn that Sullivan received a citation and the matter is currently pending. You also found out that because of an increased focus on pedestrian and bicycle safety in the jurisdiction, this case was investigated thoroughly by the police. It includes the investigating officer's report, which includes a narrative, witness statements, a photograph taken by a bystander immediately after the collision (shown below), visibility photographs, and a live action study on videotape.

The investigating officer, Kim Jarvis, reached the conclusion that Tyler Sullivan should have been able to see the bicyclist, yielding the right-of-way and avoiding the collision. You decide to take Ms. Barefoot's case.

You want to argue the following factual theory: that the bicyclist was in the crosswalk, that the oncoming car failed to yield the right-of-way, that your client left the curb and entered the crosswalk at a time when it was safe to do so, when it was possible for an oncoming driver to stop. You can only make this factual argument because the evidence according to your preliminary reading of the police report supports this as a tentative factual theory. However, you still need to investigate further to gather all the facts. If additional evidence exists contradicting these factual assertions of liability by Tyler Sullivan, the motorist, your legal and factual theory might be weak or without support, and the case may lack merit.

As you learn about both the formal and informal methods of developing the case in the upcoming chapters, you will see that your best compass is the case theory. It will always point you to the facts and law that shed light on the case.

B.   Legal Theory—Researching the Law

For plaintiff's counsel, the question might be: "Which comes first—the facts or the law?" The answer is: "The facts." The client provides the factual story and seeks counsel's legal advice. Counsel begins with at least some initial research to determine what legal theories may be viable. On the other hand, defense counsel's starting point is the law as asserted by the plaintiff; research into the law, and then investigation of the facts flows from there. As the case is developed factually, more expansive and in-depth research is conducted.

It is beyond the scope of this book—or any single book—to explore all the potential substantive laws that might be the basis for law suits, defenses, or all procedures. It is up to you, as the advocate, to determine the law applicable to your client's situation.

Research Areas

Your pretrial research will cover a broad range of subjects, such as:

PRETRIAL RESEARCH AREAS

- **Forum**—Where (federal or state court and venue within the jurisdiction),
- **Timing**—When to file (the statute of limitations),

- **Procedure**—How to plead and serve process (joinder of parties, claims, capacity to sue, service of process),
- **Substantive law** governing the legal theory component of your case theory—What action or defense (negligence, comparative negligence, products liability, contracts, murder, conspiracy, and so forth), and
- **Evidentiary matters**—Admissibility of evidence (suppression of unlawfully seized evidence under the Fourth Amendment, authenticity of a document).

Research Resources

You may well begin and end your research online using Westlaw or Lexis. The computerized research will get you into applicable case law, statutes, and court rules. The following are illustrative pretrial Internet links that also are useful:

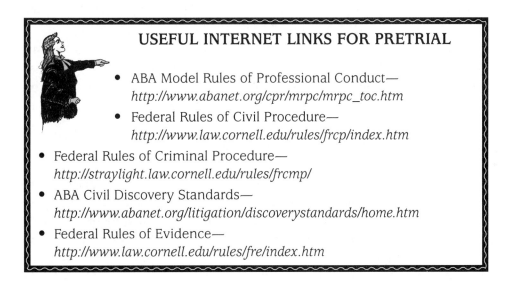

USEFUL INTERNET LINKS FOR PRETRIAL

- ABA Model Rules of Professional Conduct—
  http://www.abanet.org/cpr/mrpc/mrpc_toc.htm
- Federal Rules of Civil Procedure—
  http://www.law.cornell.edu/rules/frcp/index.htm
- Federal Rules of Criminal Procedure—
  http://straylight.law.cornell.edu/rules/frcmp/
- ABA Civil Discovery Standards—
  http://www.abanet.org/litigation/discoverystandards/home.htm
- Federal Rules of Evidence—
  http://www.law.cornell.edu/rules/fre/index.htm

Your research may delve into hornbooks (a nice start to research because they provide overviews of the subject matter), law reviews, American Law Reports (ALR), statutes, court rules, and other practice materials.

C. Organizing the Fact Investigation

We suggest a fact-development diagram that will help you organize and conduct your factual investigation. If you represent the plaintiff, the chart begins with column 1, listing the elements of your legal theory (e.g., negligence). Column 2 lists the principal factual assertions to support the elements of the legal theory. Column 3 lists the evidence that supports or detracts from your assertions. Columns 4 and 5 are the sources of the evidence (e.g., witnesses, documents) and the investigative method (e.g., witness interviews) that could be used to uncover the evidence. Column 6 contains the evidentiary concerns you have about the admissibility of that evidence.

For defense counsel, the first column contains the elements of the plaintiff's legal theory that the defense can attack and/or the affirmative defense (comparative fault (contributory negligence)) and the elements of the defense. If the first column contains the elements of the plaintiff's claim, the second column would contain factual assertions that could be used to attack the elements. Otherwise, the subject matter for each column remains the same as the plaintiff's fact investigation diagram.

When you fill in this fact-investigation diagram, you will have an organizational tool that structures the investigation and provides you with an overview of the case. This diagram will direct you to what factual information you need to acquire, *where* you will locate the source that contains the information, and the range of available *investigative methods* to use. To learn how to complete the diagram and use it to organize and plan case development, see the model on the bicycle-crosswalk case, Section III B (page 63).

By filling in the diagram, you will graphically see what evidence you have and what you are missing. When you have determined what you are missing, you can brainstorm to determine what the possible sources are for the evidence. And, you can prepare a "to do" investigation checklist.

D. Avoiding Tunnel Vision

The two goals of case development are (1) to identify all potential legal theories that are applicable to the incident as you know it and (2) to find all of the facts relating to that incident. At the outset of case development, your legal research and fact investigation should be far-reaching and broad enough to consider all possibilities. You are engaged in the process of shaping factual theories that might support the potential legal theories you are sifting through. In this hunt for supporting facts, you must remain open-minded. You may find evidence that modifies, or even changes, your factual theory. Your factual theory may be changed to such an extent that alteration of your legal theory becomes necessary. In other words, you should be ready to question and revise your understanding of the incident based upon newly uncovered evidence. It is essential that you not develop tunnel vision that will prevent you from perceiving or looking for new evidence or new legal theories. Also, early in the case, this search for evidence will aid you in selecting among competing legal theories.

When you have settled upon a legal theory, you can prepare a fact-development diagram and plan a thorough investigation. While you never want

FACT DEVELOPMENT DIAGRAM

1. Elements	2. Factual Allegations	3. Evidence	4. Sources of Information	5. Investigation Method	6. Evidentiary Concerns
Plaintiff's legal theory (divide into elements) Or **Defendant's legal theory** (divide into elements of plaintiffs legal theory that are subject to attack; also list separately each element of any affirmative or other defenses)	**Factual or opinion assertions** supporting each element	**Evidence** that could support or attack the factual assertions underlying each element	**Sources** of information	**Case Development method** • Interviews • Expert consultant • Documents	**Evidentiary concerns** • Evidentiary foundations that are required

to develop tunnel vision, you will narrow your focus as the case develops. If you represent the plaintiff, you will devote your investigation to uncovering evidence to support the elements of your legal theory and uncover evidence that detracts from your legal theory. If you represent the defendant, you will concentrate on how you will attack the elements of the plaintiff's legal theory and/or search for evidence that supports your affirmative defense. The search is not just for facts that are legally sufficient to support the legal theory. The search is also for the second part of the factual theory—facts that will persuade the jury.

As part of your initial investigation you will want to collect and preserve evidence that may be used in preparation of your case, whether for settlement or trial.

Once you know the basic facts and applicable law in the bicyclist-crosswalk case, it is important to personally go to the scene and observe traffic conditions, motorist and pedestrian behavior patterns, and sight lines. For example, do pedestrians typically have to "challenge" motorists at this location (get their attention by moving into the crosswalk, attempting to make eye contact)? Do pedestrians typically look both ways? How busy is this intersection? How congested is traffic at the time of the event in issue? Do cars generally drive slower or faster than the posted speed? Drive your own car on the same route as the motorist did that day. How visible are pedestrians as you approach the intersection? Are there any obstructions that prevent the driver or bicyclist from being clearly seen? Stand on the corner in the position of the bicyclist. How far away can oncoming cars clearly be seen? How long does it take a pedestrian or bicyclist to cross this street? How long does it take a motorist to stop, once a pedestrian is seen? How adequate are the traffic controls and signs at this location?

It is important to turn your instincts loose to process everything that is happening in the scene around you, becoming an expert on it. Once you have had adequate time to process the scene, take photographs to illustrate the patterns, behaviors, and physical facts that your senses and instincts have given you, paying particular attention to how such photographs will both support and detract from your legal theory. Don't just look for what favors your client's position. Part of avoiding tunnel vision is anticipating what facts and theories will be available to your opponent. Better to know these from the very beginning, if possible, developing effective responses to them as you build your case.

Focus Groups—A Valuable Way To Test Assumptions

Tunnel vision can result with even the most careful analysis and investigation. It is human nature to look for facts that are consistent with an opinion and reject or ignore those that are inconsistent. While the lawyer develops a working hypothesis that seems sound, lay people or even your adversary might not believe the "story."

For this reason, lawyers have increasingly used a marketing research tool—the focus group. You assemble a group of people obtained through a newspaper advertisement and present basic facts about your case to them. For example, in the Bicyclist-crosswalk case, you might show them photos of the intersection, the police report, and witness statements and summarize the factual contentions of both sides and the applicable law. Each member of the group would then answer a questionnaire about which side would prevail and why, the credibility of each side's theories and contentions, and whether they would need additional information about the case before making a decision. Once the individual questionnaires are completed, you then have the focus group discuss the case together, videotaping the discussion. Well in advance of trial, the focus group will identify your hot button issues and whether your legal theory or theories are on the right track. It will also tell you what the demographics of your ideal decision makers might be. In fact, some lawyers do focus groups on significantly important cases before agreeing to represent the client, learning if there are significant unseen problems that would make representation unwise.

E. Economic Factors

When you set out to develop the case, you will want to prepare an estimate of how much your legal research and the fact investigation will cost. Your client will want to know not only how much it will cost but how you arrived at the dollar figure. The answers depend on how far you go with the case. If you negotiate a settlement shortly after a complaint is filed, the cost will be low when compared with the expense of full pretrial and trial.

Even if you are a prosecutor, publicly funded defense attorney, or an attorney working on a contingent fee basis who will not log billable hours for your case development work, you still have to keep in mind the resources you may require. In criminal prosecution and defense, you must balance the significance of the case (e.g., death penalty versus first-time shoplift) against available public resources in even conceptualizing the scope and manner of your legal and factual investigation. For a civil attorney taking a case on a contingent fee, you could go broke if you fail to realistically estimate how much a case will cost you.

You should estimate the number of hours you will spend on each of these activities:

- Legal research,
- Investigation of the facts,

- Pleadings,
- Discovery,
- Pretrial hearings,
- Settlement discussions,
- Trial preparation, and
- Trial.

In addition to determining the cost of your services by multiplying the number of billable hours times your hourly rate, you should calculate the case costs including, among other things:

- Court clerk filing fees,
- Investigator's fee,
- Expert witness fee, and
- Court reporter fees for depositions.

F. Informal and Formal Fact Investigation

Civil Case Development

Civil case development methods can be categorized as follows: (1) informal case development and (2) initial disclosure and formal discovery. They can be subdivided as follows:

CHECKLIST

Civil Case Development Methods

Informal Fact Investigation

- Client interview
- Witness interviews
- Scene visit
- Expert witness consultation
- Scientific testing by expert
- Development of demonstrative evidence
- Demand for access to public records under law (e.g., Freedom of Information Act)
- Request for disclosure to counsel

Discovery: Initial Disclosure and Formal Discovery
Federal Rules of Civil Procedure

Required Initial Disclosure – Rule 26(a)

Interrogatories – Rule 33

Requests for Production – Rule 34

Medical/Mental Examinations – Rule 35

Subpoena Duces Tecum – Rule 45

Depositions – Rules 27 – 32

Requests for Admissions – Rule 36

For any given case, you will probably use both formal and informal fact investigation. Why would you use informal methods? Informal fact investigation has a number of advantages.

- First, it's **inexpensive** (a phone call, walking over to someone's office). In contrast, a formal discovery device such as a deposition is expensive. Even interrogatories can run up the bill for the client when the attorney is being paid by the hour for their preparation and evaluation.

- Second, it's **simple.** No formal devices or procedural hoops are involved as are in something like drafting and serving a subpoena duces tecum or request for production of documents. Again, informal fact gathering can be a walk through the site of an accident or a meeting over a cup of coffee at a café.

- Third, it's **unbounded in time, scope, or location** by any formal legal rules. Formal discovery generally may not take place prior to the filing of the complaint; while interrogatories, depositions, and such may only be served or scheduled within timelines explicitly set by the Federal Rules of Civil Procedure and its state counterparts. Informal investigation can be done at any time you choose, before or after a formal action is filed. Also, formal discovery rules have limits—whether a particular device is limited to parties (e.g., requests for admissions are limited to parties), limits as to the geographic radius under which some device can be used (e.g., subpoena to appear at deposition), and such. Informal discovery has no such constraints as to either target or location.

- Fourth, informal fact investigation can be **done without announcing** that you are seeking information as part of a lawsuit. A witness may be far more candid if they don't understand that their statements may be eventually used to support the filing of a legal claim or the claim itself. Of course, you must be aware of the ethical rules circumscribing dealing with represented witnesses, potential parties, and non-parties discussed in Chapter 6 on Witness Interviewing, page 135.

- Fifth, it can be **quicker and easier** than a formal discovery method such as deposition. Thus, you could go through all the trouble of drafting a subpoena duces tecum for the witness to bring a document to the deposition. Or you could just call opposing counsel and ask for the document.

- Sixth, the **case may not require much in the way of formal discovery** because the evidence is readily available without having to seek it from the opposing party. For instance, informal fact investigation is especially suitable for gathering evidence from neutral or cooperative witnesses.

For example, in the *Bicyclist-crosswalk* case, your informal fact investigation activities could include:

INFORMAL FACT INVESTIGATION

The *Bicycle-Crosswalk* Case

- Your client interview with Litonya Barefoot to determine what happened.
- Interviews of eyewitnesses listed on the police report.
- Visits to the scene of the collision, observing traffic patterns, times, and distances. This can also include a drive through with your own car, using the same path as the northbound striking vehicle.
- You might also want to consult with an accident reconstruction expert, who will assist with time and distance calculations, as well as with determining the visibility of Tyler Sullivan, the potential defendant driver, at various points prior to the collision. If Tyler Sullivan is represented by counsel, you will not be able to speak with him, either personally or through your investigator. However, you can take sworn declarations from the eyewitnesses. You will want to do this if they have additional details to offer that are not included in the police report.

If there was diversity jurisdiction allowing you to file the *Bicycle-crosswalk* case in federal court, obtaining information from the defendant's attorney will require Rule-controlled discovery, which encompasses initial disclosure as set out in Fed. R. Civ. P. 26(a) (note that some state courts have also adopted this part of the federal rules). Both state and federal courts provide for formal discovery devices, such as in Fed. R. Civ. P. 27-36. For instance, requests for production and interrogatories can be used to obtain witness statements or expert witness reports. You could depose the defendant to establish what he saw before the collision and what he was doing just prior to the collision. Chapters 8 and 9 on written discovery and depositions, discuss initial disclosure and which of the various formal discovery devises is best suited to obtain the desired information.

Criminal Case Development

The choice between formal and informal discovery methods is not, in the main, a concern in criminal case development once charges have been filed. Generally, informal fact investigation methods are used. Chapter 8 on discovery (pages 231, 270-72) discusses how formal discovery is handled in the criminal justice system.

Investigations in the pre-charging phase are also generally informal in nature. Law enforcement officers interview witnesses, collect evidence, and so on. A grand jury or inquiry judge can be utilized by the prosecutor to gather evidence, including summoning a witness before the grand jury and compelling the witness to testify under oath. As such, the grand jury could be considered to be a formal discovery device. Likewise, a warrant to search and seize evidence could be viewed as another formal means of gathering evidence.

III. INFORMAL CASE DEVELOPMENT

A. The Investigator

In criminal cases, law enforcement (the local police department, Federal Bureau of Investigation, sheriff's office) gathers the evidence. The prosecutor may serve as an advisor or in some instances lead the investigation. Some prosecutors' offices have their own in-house investigators. Hired or in-house investigators perform investigations for defendants in criminal cases.

For civil cases, no set pattern exists. The investigation could be assigned to a hired or in-house investigator or a paralegal (think Erin Brockovich in the movie) or an attorney. In later chapters, you will learn about investigation conducted through both client and witness interviews. The client, with your guidance, may also act as the investigator, keeping notes and collecting records and physical evidence.

B.   The Expert: Consultant and Witness

The Fact-Development Diagram

An expert consultant can be crucial in case development by providing or directing you to fact and opinion evidence, in assisting with the formulation of the case theory, and in the analysis of the other side's case theory. But, how do you know whether an expert can assist in a particular case? As with other aspects of case development planning, the fact-investigation diagram is a good starting point.

In this regard, let's apply the diagram to the *Bicycle-crosswalk* case (page 64). One tentative legal theory that you are pursuing is negligence by the motorist, Tyler Sullivan. In the first column of the diagram, you list the elements of that claim for relief. As an illustration, we will focus upon the element of duty as set out in the motor vehicle code: "The defendant operator of the approaching vehicle shall stop and remain stopped to allow a bicyclist to cross the roadway within a marked crosswalk when the bicycle is upon or within one lane of a half of the roadway upon which the vehicle is traveling. The bicyclist entered the crosswalk at a time it was safe to do so." The factual assertion is that "Plaintiff Litonya Barefoot, the bicyclist, was in the crosswalk and that the oncoming car failed to yield the right-of-way, that the plaintiff left the curb and entered the crosswalk at a time when it was safe to do so, when it was possible for an oncoming driver to stop. The defendant motorist should have seen the bicyclist in sufficient time to stop and avoid the collision."

To support this assertion we have Ms. Barefoot's story that she was in a marked crosswalk with a flashing yellow light overhead at a time it was safe to cross, and that she looked both ways before entering the crosswalk and proceeded slowly. Suddenly she saw defendant Sullivan's Honda Civic coming at her at a high rate of speed. There was no way to avoid being hit by defendant's car at that point. All this is reflected in the first two columns of the following fact-development diagram.

Using your common sense and the information you've acquired to date, you realize that other allegations bearing upon the element of duty might be possibilities. For instance, there was a van exiting a nearby parking lot that partially obscured the vision of the northbound traffic on 12th. It may be possible for plaintiff to argue that the defendant driver was either speeding at the time of the collision or was inattentive to traffic just prior to the collision. Ms. Barefoot, however, is not qualified as an expert to express an opinion, for example, on whether the parked van had indeed obscured the defendant motorist's visibility of the bicyclist or whether the defendant was speeding at the time. You would probably conclude that an expert, conducting motion and impact tests, may be able to render an opinion that the

motorist was speeding, and/or a van had obstructed the defendant's view of the crosswalk, and/or that the bicyclist should have realized that if she was in the crosswalk she would not be visible to a motorist in time for the motorist to stop (remember, you want to know the bad as well as the good). At this juncture in the case development, you might benefit from an expert with whom you can consult. (See the Fact Investigation Diagram, page 64.)

A consulting expert may be hired just for preparation of litigation and therefore information generated by the expert and the expert's opinion are likely to be privileged as work product. An expert retained to testify at trial must be disclosed during discovery and this expert's information is not privileged. It may be that a consulting expert may later become a designated expert for trial. A consulting expert may provide information on issues such as:

- What *fields of expertise apply?*
- What are the *issues* (if any) to which an expert could even speak?
- *Who* are the experts qualified to provide testimony in these fields?
- What *evidence* and *sources* of evidence should you seek through your informal investigation and the formal discovery process?
- What *evidentiary concerns* exist (e.g., Is the expert qualified? Is there a scientific basis for the opinion?)?
- What are the strengths and weaknesses in the *defense case theory,* including potential defense expert testimony?

FACT INVESTIGATION DIAGRAM IN THE *BICYCLE-CROSSWALK* CASE

1. Elements	2. Allegations	3. Evidence	4. Sources of Information	5. Investigation Method	6. Evidentiary Concerns
1. Duty	Marked crosswalk	Photos of scene	Police report	Client interview	Admissibility of witness opinions • Lay opinions • Expert
The motorist failed to yield the right of way to the bicyclist in the crosswalk, as required by the statute; did not stop to allow bicyclist to cross roadway in a marked crosswalk	Flashing yellow light Bicyclist proceeded slowly Bicyclist looked both ways Bicyclist was visible Def. was speeding Def. not paying attention (on cell phone)	Measurements Witness statements supporting plaintiff Possible allegation that client entered crosswalk when unsafe	Possible expert consultation	Witness interviews Possible expert consultation Accident reconstruction technology	

The Elimination Process: Should You Retain an Expert?

You have now determined that you could use an expert and have focused on the field of expertise required: accident reconstruction. An accident reconstructionist can recreate the scene prior to and at the time of the collision to provide time and distance estimates that will allow you to state when the motorist should have seen the bicyclist, when he should have applied his brakes, and whether that would have allowed him to avoid the collision. The accident reconstruction expert can also provide an opinion as to speed and whether the view of the crosswalk was obstructed creating an unsafe condition. All that, however, does not mean that you will in fact hire an expert. The next stage is a process of elimination. Matters coming into play at this stage include, among others, economic factors, the lack of any available scientific technique, an absence of evidence, and the existence of a better approach.

Economic Factors

Expert/consultant witnesses can be expensive, and the cost may be prohibitive. While the prosecutor in a homicide case may be able to obtain the services of publicly funded crime laboratory experts, and criminal defense attorneys may be able to obtain court-appointed experts for their indigent clients, private counsel, such as plaintiff's counsel in a products liability case, generally does not have this advantage. Private counsel must consider expense funds at every stage, beginning with case development, when an expert may provide valuable advice and technical information right through expert investigation (e.g., scientific testing) and, ultimately, trial testimony.

You need to consider whether you can justify the expense of employing an expert's services. You may decide not to use an expert because in your judgment (perhaps after consultation with an expert or after self-education on the technical aspects) you conclude that an expert will not support your legal theory or is not likely to produce the results you want or that considering what an expert would add to your total case presentation, it's just not worth the expense. On the other hand, if you would choose to have an expert if you could, but expense in relationship to the valuation of the case is problematic, you might consider more creative options. For example, in the Bicyclist-crosswalk case, consider using the investigating police officer as your expert because she supports your legal theory.

Even when the case merits an expert because of conflicting testimony and expenses are not an issue, as plaintiff's counsel you still might decide initially only to employ an accident reconstructionist as a consultant during early case development, reserving further decisions about the use of experts until you have a better understanding of your case.

Scientific Techniques Unavailable

Another factor that can help determine if you will use an expert in a case investigation is whether there exists some scientific technique that is capable of producing useful information for your case. For instance, your consulting expert could advise you that the type of testing that you thought would be useful is not an option because the scientific technique has not been perfected. In other words, the technique is not commonly accepted as reliable in the scientific community and may not be used at trial. You will need to determine what scientific test is applicable in your jurisdiction—whether the Frye or Daubert test—and comply with the requirements. See Chapter 9.

Absence of Evidence

The absence of any evidence to be tested would block pursuing expert investigation and testimony. While it might seem inconceivable that critical evidence might be unavailable for testing, it could turn out that the intersection has been significantly altered since the collision, for example.

A Better Approach

You may decide that using other evidence such as lay testimony, exhibits, or even argument in lieu of expert testimony is tactically a better approach. For example, you could conclude that the accident reconstructionist's testimony would be weak and that you would be better off presenting what happened through Ms. Barefoot's testimony and that of the investigating officer Kim Jarvis, arguing to your adversary in settlement discussions or to a jury that it is common sense to draw a conclusion that an experienced bicyclist such as Litonya Barefoot would not have entered the crosswalk unless it was safe to do so. On the other hand, if there are too many conflicting statements of eye witnesses this argument may not be convincing.

A Model for Selecting an Expert

Assuming that after this process of elimination you still want an expert consultant, you have arrived at the point when you will need to choose a specific expert. Initially, you should be aware that an expert may be selected for you without your direct involvement. In the *Bicyclist-crosswalk* case, the investigating officer, Kim Jarvis, may have decided that the defendant Sullivan was speeding and issued a citation for speeding. In this instance, it is likely that you will be calling the investigating officer as your expert witness. Similar circumstances occur with medical experts—so that the plaintiff's attorney might call the treating doctor as the medical expert in the case.

In the usual situation, however, you will have to select the expert your-self. We propose a model decision-making process for the selection of a specific expert that involves an analysis of the person in the light of four considerations.

1. Conclusions Compatible with Your Case Theory

Analysis of whether or not to choose a particular person as an expert begins at the beginning—your case theory. Underpinning your decision to select the person as your expert is the premise that the expert will provide testimony helpful in proving your case theory or in attacking your opponent's case the-ory. Therefore, a primary consideration is whether the person would make investigative findings and provide helpful testimony.

That does not mean that you seek out an expert who will mechanically say what you want them to say. Quite the contrary. In the first place, in every aspect of your planning and preparation, you want to know about pos-sible problems with proving your case theory. The domain of expertise is no exception. For example, as plaintiff's counsel in our bicyclist-crosswalk case, you want a knowledgeable expert who will candidly tell you whether the motorist had sufficient time and distance to avoid the collision. Rather than bulling ahead towards an inevitably disastrous trial, you now can consider options such as developing a new case theory that can withstand expert scrutiny or seeking quick settlement or advising the client to stop pursuing the lawsuit to avoid putting good money after bad.

In the second place, one of the worst mistakes an attorney can make with an expert is to try to push the expert into an opinion beyond what his or her expertise can support. This is both professionally uncomfortable for the expert and will most likely result in transforming helpful into harmful evi-dence. Imagine that an accident reconstructionist expert tells you that "while I cannot say absolutely that the speed of the motorist caused the collision, I can say unequivocally that the speed is in no way inconsistent with having resulted in the collision." Of course you'd like the expert to say, "absolutely caused," but that's not what her expertise can support. So take what she is giving you, run with it, and look to amass enough non-expert evidence cor-roborating your causation theory such that, in combination with the expert's opinion of consistency, you will get past any summary judgment motion and be well on your way to settlement or to a jury. On the other hand, if you try to force the expert away from "consistent" to "caused," the expert likely will appear uncomfortable and unsure, will probably get hammered by oppos-ing counsel in a deposition and at trial, and you will have not only lost the helpful evidence the expert had to offer, you will now have harmed your entire case by showing the fact finder that you are willing to present weak, noncredible evidence.

Let's think about this desire for an expert who can support your case theory in the criminal context. Assume that you are the prosecutor assigned to a homicide case and that it is your job to oversee case development. Assume for the moment you want to establish that the suspect, the boyfriend, committed the crime. Let's look at the *Bite-mark* case.

The *Bite-Mark* Case

Story   A jogger in Laurelhurst park spotted Tamica Roy's dead body in a wooded area next to the jogging path. During the autopsy, the medical examiner observed what appeared to be a bite mark on the victim's left shoulder. Ms. Roy's boyfriend was Brandon Robinson. The night before Ms. Roy's body was discovered, a neighbor overheard a loud quarrel in the apartment that Ms. Roy shared with Mr. Robinson.

The Prosecutor

A forensic odontologist could examine Ms. Robinson's body, photograph the marks, and take impressions. The odontologist could then compare photographs and impressions of the suspect's teeth with the photographs and impressions of the marks and finally reach conclusions regarding whether Mr. Robinson's teeth made the bite marks.

In deciding whether to use a particular odontologist, you might want a person who is likely to investigate and come to the conclusion that Mr. Robinson's teeth made the bite marks. Realistically, you recognize the possibility that scientific investigation may lead to findings that are either inconclusive or exclude the suspect as the person who left the marks. In the latter situation, the scientific investigation would produce exculpatory evidence that either would justly lead to the exoneration of innocent Mr. Robinson or, if the prosecution believed under the circumstances that there still existed sufficient evidence of guilt, would have to be disclosed to the defense.

If your only obligation were to prove the case, if you had no obligation to seek justice, you would think only about finding a bite-mark expert who could credibly tell you what you wanted to hear, tempered by the previous discussion of the dangers of trying to force the expert to say more than his or her expertise can support. A more cynical viewpoint is that an expert is a commodity to be shopped for. This viewpoint certainly may be offensive to all those who would hope that scientific testing and expert opinion would be objective and not subject to outside influences such as who hired the expert. Realistically, however, some experts may be influenced. Further, science is not cut-and-dry. Reasonable people can differ, situations can be ambiguous, and, especially in "soft" sciences such as those studying human behavior, an expert who routinely works with attorneys, and who adopts an ends-means perspective, can plausibly support a position that is 180 degrees from that of an opponent's expert.

Now stand back from what we've been doing. While the prosecutor may want to find the expert who will make favorable findings, again, blind attachment to such an approach has intrinsic perils. Paramount is the danger that this expert is merely a hired gun who will distort any factual situation to reach the result desired by the party who employed him or her. This carries two problems. A talented forensic faker can demean the justice system as well as the legal profession, no matter what the verdict might be. On a more practical level, the distortion may be exposed at trial. In fact, any evidence during the trial that the expert's work has been influenced by an excessive fee arrangement, bias toward a party, or personal inclination may greatly diminish the expert's testimony and possibly damage the entire case.

Above all, as the prosecutor, you have an ethical obligation that overrides any tendency you might have to select a biased expert. Your duty is to do justice, not just to convict. Mindful of this principle, you should decide to choose the expert based on the person's expertise in the field, as well as the person's investigative and forensic skills. More about skills of the expert can be found in the next section.

Defense Counsel

Now consider the decision-making processes of defense counsel in the same criminal case. Your responsibility as defense counsel is to ensure that Mr. Robinson, who is constitutionally guaranteed competent representation, receives the best defense ethically possible. That does not involve responsibility to seek potentially damaging information. Therefore, you as defense counsel would want to choose the expert who would render a favorable finding. For example, in the *Bite-mark* case, you would want an expert who would be likely to find that the marks on the body were either not bite marks or if they were bite marks, that the marks either excluded Mr. Robinson or were inconclusive. You could consider the prior performance and other factors (the expert has customarily testified for the defense) in deciding whether to employ the person. However, you as Mr. Robinson's attorney, like the prosecutor, would be concerned about hiring a person who might be vulnerable to being exposed as having a bias or interest or who cannot be trusted to proceed forthrightly and honestly.

2. Skills of the Expert

One approach to choosing an expert is to evaluate the characteristics of possible experts against a profile of the ideal expert witness. While you may not find the perfect expert witness, the profile will allow you to weigh the strengths and weaknesses of potential experts. Think about the characteristics of the ideal expert witness. Commonly, an expert will perform two functions: one as investigator and another as witness. The person's abilities in these areas should be major considerations.

The Expert as Investigator

An ideal expert would be a highly competent investigator and recognizable as an expert in the field. Preferably, the investigation would personally involve the expert during evidence-gathering. The expert would carefully examine all evidence, perform appropriate scientific tests, and prepare or suggest for preparation demonstrative evidence that would be helpful in illustrating the expert's testimony (e.g., photographs, models). Implicitly, this means that the expert should be someone with whom you can work well.

The Expert as Witness

- **Qualified Under Evidence Rules**

Now consider the profile of the ideal expert witness from the perspective of the expert's role as a witness. First, there are issues of admissibility to be determined by the court. Thus, the expert must be able to *qualify* under the appropriate state or federal evidence rule, such as Federal Rule Evid. 702, that the expert can impart helpful specialized or technical knowledge to the jury based upon his or her "knowledge, skill, training, or experience." In assessing expertise, be certain to match the specific expertise with the "scope" of the testimony you desire. In other words, an expert cardiologist testifying about a heart attack precipitated by a painful beating may be successfully objected to if she attempts to go too deeply into orthopedic injuries. Part of qualifications might also include the very legitimacy of the proposed expertise, (e.g., polygraphy) or the particular methodology used by the expert (e.g., whether an epidemiologist used proper data and studios). In some states, the court will decide this latter question based on the so-called *Frye* standard (whether the area of expertise or particular methodology is "generally accepted in the scientific community"); while in other states and all federal courts, the judge will apply the *Daubert* standard ("reliable methodology"), discussed in Chapter 9 Depositions, pages 328 to 330.

- **Qualified in the Eyes of the Jury**

Even assuming the expert's testimony is admissible under evidence rules, an attorney must consider how persuasive the expert will be in convincing the trier of fact to accept her opinion. An expert's qualifications, just discussed as a legal requirement, are obviously also a significant part of the expert's persuasiveness, especially if they are particularly impressive or better than the qualifications of an expert called by the opposing party.

- **Impartiality and Objectivity**

The ideal expert would also be a person the jury would perceive as impartial and objective. Information about the expert that you might consider in deciding whether the person probably will project these qualities, includes whether the witness has testified more often for one side in a lawsuit than the other, whether the person has a financial interest in the case, whether the expert usually finds the same facts or comes to the same conclusions, whether an employment bias exists (the expert testifies in favor of the party who has hired her), whether personal or professional bias is a factor (the expert adheres to a particular theory over which there is a dispute).

- **Communications Skills**

Assess what the potential charisma rating is. Jurors care very little for the resume-type qualifications that tend to impress lawyers. Your adversary will also recognize any deficiencies in your expert's "charisma" and that will affect settlement or in criminal cases, plea bargaining. The expert with the best resume does not necessarily win a case. While jurors certainly expect an expert witness to be knowledgeable, the expert's attitude and communications skills are far more important in determining credibility. A know-it-all expert with a superior, condescending attitude who speaks in pedantic jargon-laden phrases may be quickly rejected. The same result for a prickly, defensive expert who is combative and hostile on cross-examination. Think of your favorite teacher in school. What made you like and respect that teacher so much? The same principle applies to expert witnesses in court. Jurors like experts who are helpful and accessible, making eye contact and engaging them. It also helps if the expert has warmth, enthusiasm for the subject, and a sense of humor. Like your favorite teacher in school, the best experts also know how to illustrate scientific or technical principles by appealing to the visual sense. For example, in the *Bicyclist-crosswalk* case, you should be on the lookout for an accident reconstruction expert who has taught courses to law enforcement officers and who has access to the variety of government-funded studies on bicycle-motorist collisions at crosswalks.

3. Practical Problems

Three frequently encountered practical problems facing an attorney trying to choose an expert are how to locate a suitable expert, how to compensate the expert, and how many experts to employ.

Locating Experts

A reliable way to find a suitable expert who most closely matches the perfect expert witness profile is to consult with lawyers, experts, and others whose judgment you trust and who have firsthand knowledge of the expert's ability. The Internet and legal databases provide an excellent way to locate experts in every field. The lawyer grapevine is one of the most commonly used and most effective way of locating good experts. For example, in the *Bicyclist-crosswalk* case, you could look for other reported verdicts and settlements in similar cases in your jurisdiction. These will list not only the type of case and the name of the lawyer, but also the experts used. If you call the lawyer, you will get an in-depth report of how well the particular expert worked. Many lawyer organizations also have a computer listserve where members share information. You could send out an email asking for suggestions on experts (remembering, of course, not to divulge any sensitive information about your case, in that this is not confidential). In addition, you may resort to directories of forensic evidence experts, such as *The Forensic Science Directory* (National Forensic Center). Also, jury verdict sheets, bar association materials, and news reports may contain information about experts.

Compensation

You also need to be concerned about compensation of the expert witness. Forensic experts tend to be relatively expensive, as many people in that field do not wish to get involved in the stresses and inconveniences of testifying. Accordingly, experts who do agree to consult in cases typically expect to receive a premium for the significant time and trouble involved in doing forensic work. As previously mentioned, government attorneys may be provided with no-cost services from a publicly funded state or local crime laboratory or be able to call upon the services of the Federal Bureau of Investigation Crime Laboratory for assistance. Beyond that, a prosecutor or an indigent defendant may be able to request a court-appointed expert and have the court order payment from either a state or local budget.

In civil cases, economics plays a key role in hiring an expert, since rarely will courts appoint experts. Generally, expert witness fees in civil cases are high and are often cost prohibitive to many, noncorporate clients. Expert fees may contain provision for travel, hotels, and other accommodation.

Therefore, carefully weigh the costs and benefits of an expert to your case. Determining the fee, the hourly rate, and cost reimbursements may be difficult and may require consultation with other attorneys or other sources.

If an expert made observations and reached conclusions (say, as a treating physician) before becoming a court-appointed expert, local law may provide that the person may be subpoenaed and required to testify for only the usual fee paid to a lay witness. While compelling testimony without an expert fee might be economical, you may well be faced with a recalcitrant witness.

Number of Experts

Finally, you must decide on the number of expert witnesses to employ. First, while you may want to call several experts to speak on a single issue so that each, in effect, corroborates the other and the jury does not get the sense that only one person's opinion is being heard, there are some possible problems with this tactic that you should consider. The risk is that multiple expert witnesses in the same field might render contradictory or somewhat inconsistent findings or opinions or rely on different bases for their opinions and therefore undermine each other's credibility. Second, while experts testifying about different issues are generally not going to contradict each other, there still remain concerns. A case inundated with expert witnesses, techniques, and jargon may become confusing. A frequent complaint from jurors is undue repetition—lawyers tend to go over and over the same material. Jurors in our media-centric age are sophisticated consumers of information—they get the point very quickly. Attention spans are very short and there is a preference for economy and simplicity. Saturation bombing of redundant information through a parade of experts quickly causes resentment—jurors feel that it insults their intelligence. The lawyer that does that quickly loses favor. Also, to the extent your case appears to center on expert testimony, you may lose the genuine underlying emotions and equities in your case, replacing them with a series of academic questions answered by experts, and may precipitate a battle of experts in which the jurors will flip a coin between your experts and your opponent's. Third, the expense of hiring multiple experts may also be a determinative factor.

C. Handling Demonstrative, Physical, and Documentary Evidence

Because of the vital importance of visuals to persuasive advocacy, Chapter 10 is devoted to the creation of visuals. Also, in that chapter, we stress the importance of a scene visit and how it should be carried out.

Fact investigation also entails the location, inspection, and preservation of physical and documentary evidence. In a criminal case, law enforcement has set procedures for evidence collection, labeling and preserving it in an evidence room until trial. For example, in the *Bite-mark* case, the pathologist or a detective would have photographed the bite marks on Ms. Roy's body and filed them and the negatives in a safe place. The impressions of Mr. Robinson's teeth would have been packaged, given an evidence label and number, and stored in the evidence room of the police department. The chain of custody for the evidence would be carefully maintained.

The same principles apply to civil case evidence collection and preservation. Remember that in the *Bicyclist-crosswalk* case, we suggested that the intersection of the crash with the passage of time might conceivably be altered. What should the lawyer do to prepare for this possibility? As soon as the attorney learned about the case, he or she should have visited the scene of the crash, directed that it be photographed and videotaped, and have made a timely decision about hiring an expert, such as an accident reconstructionist.

The attorney also needed to establish a system of labeling and storing the evidence from the intersection and the related expert reports so that witnesses will later be able to effectively use this evidence to testify about the scene as it was when the crash occurred. None of this would be difficult to do in the *Bicyclist-crosswalk* case, though such organization, storing, and preservation would be significantly more difficult with fungible physical evidence, which needs to be placed in a container, sealed, labeled, and stored in a place protected from outside tampering. Special consideration must be given to the preservation of organic material such as perishable products or human or animal components. In any case, proper preservation of vital evidence is critical to success at trial.

IV. MANAGING THE CASE

As your case develops, it may seem at times like you face an oncoming avalanche of information—thousands of pages, a mass of e-mails and other electronically stored information, deposition transcripts and videos, correspondence, and much more. You will need to organize and manage this burgeoning information. Your management system should file the information in an orderly fashion so you can easily search and retrieve what you want when you want it. That system should facilitate a privilege review and production of discovery. And, when you go to trial, the management system should enable you to locate, retrieve, and effectively display the information you want to the fact finder. This section is devoted to management systems that will help you accomplish these goals.

A. Electronic Case Management

Software is available to manage the information onslaught that can be part of your pretrial litigation. This software is designed to do the following tasks, among others:

- Receive and store the information in a database,
- Sort the information by categories, such as chronology, people, events, and issues,
- Search the database to locate and retrieve desired information,
- Facilitate case analysis by sorting and other analytical functions,
- Annotate documents and images in the database,
- Redact objectionable portions of a transcript,
- Manage transcripts, and
- Conduct a privilege review and produce discovery.

Computer software that is intended for the creation and/or display of visuals is covered in Chapter 10, which discusses visuals.

CASE MANAGEMENT AND TRIAL PRESENTATION SOFTWARE

The following lists some case management and trial-presentation software:

- **Concordance** from Dataflight Software, Inc.—case management software that accommodates large cases—*www.dataflight.com*
- **CaseMap** from Casesoft—case management and analysis software—*www.casesoft.com*
- **Summation** from CT Summation—case management and trial presentation software—*www.summation.com*
- **Visionary** from Visionary Legal Technologies—case management and trial presentation—*www.visionarylegaltechnologies.com*
- **PowerPoint** from Microsoft—trial presentation software—*http:office.microsoft.com*
- **TrialDirector** from InData, Co—trial presentation software—*www.indatacorp.com*
- **Sanction** from Verdict Systems—trial presentation software—*www.verdictsystems.com*
- **Trial Pro** from IDEA, Inc.—trial presentation software—*www.trialpro.com*

What follows are an overview and sampling of what the electronic management software does and offers. This will enable you to understand how the software operates and more importantly what this software can do for you in pretrial litigation and trial. However, to truly have a grasp what this technology offers you need to experience it. Most of the software mentioned above offer trial periods so you can test the product, and some offer webinars, which are seminars online that can walk you through the use of the software. The following are some ways in which the electronic software operates.

Database

First, the lawyer, paralegal, and/or outside litigation support service (e.g., Litigation Abstract, Inc. or Visionary Legal Technology) creates the electronic management system's database. Documents and images (e.g., a photographic exhibit) are scanned into the system. Electronic documents such as transcripts of depositions, e-mails, pleadings, and other electronic information are coded, numbered and loaded into the system. Initially, this information may be entered into a database such as Microsoft's Access and later imported into the case management software. Widely used case management software include Concordance, Summation, and CaseMap.

Search and Retrieval

A feature common to management software is the ability to search for, locate, and retrieve what is needed from a mass of information. Using words, topics or phrases the software rapidly locates the information sought. For example, if you are planning to depose a witness, you can search for the witness's name in all the database information including prior testimony, inner-office memoranda, e-mails, correspondence, and so on.

Case Analysis

Electronic case management software provides a case organization and analysis tool somewhat like the fact-development diagram discussed earlier in this chapter at p. 53. However, the electronic tool is more efficient and flexible.

CaseMap is an example of what computer technology can do for case organization and analysis. CaseMap provides a spreadsheet that interlinks the essentials of a case: facts; objects (i.e., people, places); issues; questions (i.e., things the lawyer is searching for) and legal research. As the case is developed, new information, e.g., a new witness, is added to the spreadsheet. The program also has a thinking tool that permits the user to evaluate the information (e.g., positive rating for a witness). The software interlinks the spreadsheet's information so that with a double click all information relating to a particular person can be called up. CaseMap can also be used to export information to TimeMap, a software program that will create a timeline of events.

During case preparation, information can be annotated and flagged so key information can be later located and retrieved. For example, Summation has a feature that allows the user to highlight, like a yellow highlighter, "Hot-facts," which can be later called up from the database. Another example of how the software can aid in analysis is Summation's transcript digest feature by which the lawyer highlights portions of the deposition transcript, types in marginalia, and transfers the highlighted and annotated transcript excerpts to a digest for retrieval.

Hosting the Database

Electronic case management allows the database to be accessed over the Internet. Therefore, for instance, multiple law firms working on a products liability case could share information online. Or an expert could review case information online.

Discovery

Using electronic management software, such as Concordance, the lawyer can do a privilege review and redact where necessary, and produce discovery. Also, the software can imprint production numbers, like the Bates Stamp (the old-fashioned Bates stamp used to hand-stamp numbers on all desired documents, while the Bate Stamp Program has since electronically replaced the original Bates Stamp or Bates Numbering Machine), and thereby tracks documents for production in discovery. The electronic management tools are compatible with the concept of utilizing electronic technology to facilitate discovery as discussed in Chapter 8 on discovery.

Pretrial, Trial, and Settlement Presentations

For trial, alternative dispute resolution, or settlement conferences, the images and documents stored in the electronic management software may need to be transferred to trial presentation software—TrialDirector, Sanction, Visionary, TrialPro, and PowerPoint. This presentation software is used to display the images, such as photographs, documents, portions of a deposition transcript to the other side, for negotiation purposes, for instance, or to the fact finder. Chapter 10 is devoted to visuals and the utilization of presentation software.

B. Everything in Its Place

Preparation is the key to favorable pretrial litigation and to success in trial. And you can't be prepared if you are not organized. You will eventually settle on an organizational system that works best for you. It may be primarily electronic in nature or it may be paper-based, utilizing trial notebooks, accordion files, file drawers, or some combination of these systems. Whatever system you adopt, in order to be effective it must be orderly and enable you to store information easily and retrieve it quickly. The following are essentials for your organizational system.

Journal

Your organizational system should include a chronological case journal of significant things that you do regarding the case. For example: "5/23/XX – Received telephone call from plaintiff's counsel, Alfred Campbell, and scheduled a meeting on 6/28/XX at his office." However it is stored, electronically or on paper, it should be recorded with the case file not just in a daily planner. The journal can come in handy in recalling dates and sometimes helping you prove an event took place. For example, the judge might inquire into whether you conferred with opposing counsel before bringing a motion.

To-Do List

So that you do not neglect to do an essential task, have a to-do list for your case. As you complete the tasks, you can check them off. It is also important that you give due dates to the items on your list. For example: "Set deposition of "Myrna Torrie by 5/19/XX."

Your to-do list generally will include two types of deadlines: self-imposed deadlines and those imposed by others, for example, judge's deadline for submission of a trial brief. When faced with an imposed drop-dead due date (judge-imposed deadlines are normally firm), you should schedule a due date far enough in advance of the final date so that if unforeseen events occur as they will (e.g., your computer with no back-up crashes), you can still make the deadline. Law school provides a nice opportunity to put this approach into practice by creating your own deadline in advance of the one set by the professor.

With experience, you will create a stock to-do list with deadlines assigned for accomplishing each task. Ask other experienced lawyers in your jurisdiction if they have such to-do lists that are calendared by due date and whether you can adapt it to your use. This stock to-do list can be added to and should be augmented for each new case.

Thinking File

You're commuting to work and *flash!* you get an insight for your closing argument. Brilliant. In the middle of the night the idea comes to you for that case theme that you had been searching for. Again, brilliant. A week later or a day later, and you are struggling to remember those brilliant thoughts. Brilliant but forgotten because they weren't written down.

At the outset of any case, open electronic or paper files for your thoughts. Then record your brainstorms as they come to you. The notes will prove invaluable later as you plan a particular pretrial or trial activity. Normally, at the outset of any case, as with any new endeavor, the mind will offer a wealth of thoughts and those fresh ideas are some of the best. In particular, you should create thinking files on these topics:

- Themes and theories,
- Settlement,
- Demonstrative evidence,
- Jury selection,
- Opening statement,
- Cross-examination, and
- Closing argument.

Trial System

Whatever method you decide upon for taking information to court either pretrial for settlement or for trial (trial notebook, accordion files, electronic, other methods, or some combination) you will most likely settle on a system that for the most part is organized by pretrial or trial activity. A standard set of trial notebooks includes these tabbed subdivisions:

- Journal,
- To-do List,
- Thinking,
- Settlement,
- Pleadings,
- Motions,
- Jury selection,
- Opening statement,
- Witnesses—tabbed by witness and including direct examination outline or questions, prior statements including depositions,
- Cross-examination—prior statements, questions, and also tabbed by witness,

- Jury instructions, and
- Closing argument.

V. ETHICAL CONSIDERATIONS IN CASE DEVELOPMENT AND MANAGEMENT

A. Supervising the Investigation

Ethical considerations for different case development methods are discussed in the chapter on each subject. For instance, the ethical requirements for conducting witness interviews are covered in Chapter 6 on Witness Interviewing. But, what are your ethical responsibilities if you are not the person conducting the interview? What are your responsibilities if your paralegal is going to conduct the witness interview?

ABA Model Rule of Professional Conduct 5.3 sets out the ethical responsibilities of a partner or managerial equivalent in a law firm or an individual lawyer directly supervising a nonlawyer employee for the conduct of that employee. Rule 5.3 (a) provides that the *manager* is to "make reasonable efforts to ensure that the firm has in effect measures giving reasonable assurance that the person's conduct is compatible with the professional obligations of the lawyer; . . ." Under Rule 5.3 (b), the *direct supervising lawyer* is to "make reasonable efforts to ensure that the person's conduct is compatible with the professional obligations of the lawyer; . . ."

Rule 5.3 (c) states that the lawyer is responsible for the nonlawyer's conduct that would be a violation of the rules of professional conduct if engaged in by a lawyer if:

> (1) the lawyer orders or, with the knowledge of the specific conduct, ratifies the conduct involved; or
>
> (2) the lawyer is a partner or has comparable managerial authority in the law firm in which the person is employed, or has direct supervisory authority over the person, and knows of the conduct at a time when its consequences can be avoided or mitigated but fails to take reasonable remedial action.

B. The Expert

As you recall from our discussion of selecting an expert in the *Bite-mark* case, while counsel might want to find an expert who would provide testimony supporting the case theory, this desire for favorable results is hazardous. The expert's bias may be apparent to the jury or the expert may be unreliable and produce faulty results. However, when does a lawyer cross the line by employing an expert to provide favorable results and violate the rules of professional responsibility?

Clearly the line is crossed if the expert testifies falsely and the lawyer knows that the testimony is false. ABA Rule of Profession Conduct 3.3 (a)(3) provides that a lawyer shall not "offer evidence that the lawyer knows to be false. If . . . a witness called by the lawyer, has offered material evidence and the lawyer comes to know of its falsity, the lawyer shall take reasonable remedial measures, including, if necessary, disclosure to the tribunal. A lawyer may refuse to offer evidence, other than the testimony of a defendant in a criminal matter, that the lawyer reasonably believes is false."

C.   Preservation and Spoliation

In developing and managing the case, the lawyer has an obligation to insure the preservation of evidence and to prevent spoliation. This is particularly important concerning electronic information that is vulnerable to destruction. The obligations are discussed in Chapter 8 on discovery at page 247.

✓ THE CASE DEVELOPMENT CHECKLIST

The following are standards of performance for effective case development:

Case Theory Guide to Case Development

- ❑ Explore tentative legal theories that fit your early understanding of the facts of the case.
- ❑ Use the tentative legal theories as guides to search for evidence supporting those legal theories.
- ❑ Be open to looking for factual information about the incident or incidents involved and to the possibility that the new information may change both your legal and factual theories.

Researching Legal Theories

- ❑ As plaintiff's counsel, begin by identifying viable legal theories based on an understanding of the facts provided by the client.
- ❑ As defense counsel, research the legal theories and facts alleged by the plaintiff, and research possible defenses.

❑ Research the following, among other areas of the law:
- ✓ The forum—state or federal,
- ✓ Timing—when to file,
- ✓ Procedure—how to plead and serve process,
- ✓ Substantive law, and
- ✓ Evidentiary matters.

✓ Take advantage of research resources, particularly those on the Internet.

Organizing the Fact Investigation

❑ Create a fact-investigation diagram that will organize and identify what needs to be proved or disproved and what evidence is possessed or needs to be located.

❑ Use the fact-investigation diagram to create a "to-do" investigation checklist.

Avoiding Tunnel Vision

❑ Appreciate the two goals of case development: (1) identify all potential legal theories that are applicable to the incident and (2) find the facts relating to that incident.

❑ To achieve these goals, guard against developing tunnel vision, which blinds the researcher and investigator from seeing or seeking new legal theories, revised factual theories, or new evidence.

Economic Factors

❑ Establish a guesstimate of the different components of case development cost.

❑ Estimate the hours the lawyer will devote to each activity (e.g., discovery).

❑ Estimate the costs for litigation (e.g., court reporter fees for depositions).

Informal or Formal Case Development

❑ Understand **informal** case development tools available:
- ✓ Client interview,
- ✓ Using an investigator,
- ✓ Witness interview,
- ✓ Scene visit,

✓ Expert witness consultation,

✓ Scientific testing by expert,

✓ Preserve evidence,

✓ Development of demonstrative evidence,

✓ Demand for access to public records (Freedom of Information Act), and

✓ Request for disclosure to counsel.

❑ Understand the **formal** case development tools available:

✓ Required Initial Disclosures—Rule 26(a)

✓ Interrogatories—Rule 33

✓ Requests for Production—Rule 34

✓ Medical / Mental Examinations—Rule 35

✓ Subpoena Duces Tecum—Rule 45

✓ Depositions—Rules 27—32

✓ Requests for Admissions—Rule 36

The Expert Consultant

❑ Use the fact-investigation diagram to decide whether having an expert as a consultant would help in case development.

❑ Analyze the need for an expert versus the reasons not to employ an expert consultant:

✓ Cost,

✓ The scientific techniques are unavailable,

✓ The evidence that needs to be tested is unavailable, and

✓ A better approach exists without an expert.

❑ Assess whom to select as the expert:

✓ Will the expert provide favorable conclusions,

✓ Is the person skilled as an expert, an investigator and a witness, and

✓ Practically, consider the use of the expert (e.g. cost).

❑ Locate potential trial exhibits as evidence.

❑ Label, package, and preserve the evidence so it complies with evidence admissibility rules.

❑ Ensure that a chain of custody can be proven for fungible evidence.

❑ Develop exhibits for motions, settlement, and trial.

Ethical Considerations in Case Development

❑ Ensure that nonlawyer employees involved in case development comply with the Rules of Professional Conduct.

❑ Do not use false expert witness testimony.

4 Forging the Attorney-Client Relationship

4 *Forging the Attorney-Client Relationship*

"Deceive not thy physician, confessor or lawyer."

Spanish Proverb

"Concepts of justice must have hands and feet . . . to carry out justice in every case in the shortest possible time and the lowest possible cost. This is the challenge to every lawyer and judge in America."

Warren E. Burger (1907-1995)

I. THE ATTORNEY-CLIENT RELATIONSHIP

In this chapter, you will learn about the nature of the attorney-client relationship, how to plan for your initial contact with the prospective client, techniques for forging and maintaining a positive relationship, your ethical responsibilities, and how to organize and conduct your practice once you have agreed to represent the new client. Aspects of the interview that are applicable to both a client and non-client witness (i.e., gathering substantive information about the case) are covered in Chapter 6 on witness interviewing.

The special relationship between an attorney and a client is composed of three concurrent relationships: legal, economic, and cooperative. Each attorney-client relationship can be understood in this way.

A. Legal Relationship

The attorney-client relationship is a *legal* relationship. The formation of this legal relationship is less a matter of tactical choice than a product of the substantive law of the controlling jurisdiction. Nevertheless, it will affect your overall relationship with a client in a number of respects. This legal relationship commits you to a particular set of duties (e.g., confidentiality, loyalty), subjects you to professional discipline for breaching those duties, opens you to civil liability (e.g., a malpractice action for missing a statute of limitations), locks you into a relationship from which you may need court approval to withdraw, often adds a constitutional dimension to your activities (e.g., in a criminal case where the attorney's duties and obligations are circumscribed by the Sixth Amendment or in a civil case by the Fifth Amendment), and provides a basis on which to build a cooperative relationship (e.g., through competence and diligence), while at the same time your professionally required duties of confidentiality, loyalty, and zeal help instill client trust.

B.   Economic Relationship

The attorney-client relationship is an *economic* relationship. At its most basic, this generally involves obtaining a fee for your representation. Developing an equitable economic relationship is particularly important. A perception by the client at any point that the fee arrangement is unfair will have a negative impact on the cooperative relationship. Without fair fees from enough of your cases, you in turn will not have the economic resources to competently carry out representation. For attorneys appointed to represent indigent clients, economics can play a more subtle role in the relationship between the attorney and client. Raised in a market economy where the byword is you get what you pay for, some indigent clients may initially distrust their attorney's abilities. Or, aware that the attorney is being paid by the government, some indigent clients may initially think that the attorney is part of the system and, therefore, not have trust in the attorney's loyalty to their cause.

C.   Cooperative Relationship

The attorney-client relationship is a *cooperative* relationship, one where the client's trust in the attorney's abilities and motives is given in return for the attorney's commitment to give loyalty to the client (expressed as zeal for the client's interests or respect for the client's confidence), and to employ competence and diligence in the client's cause. The importance of developing this relationship is obvious—without it you will find it difficult to get the information from the client that is needed to develop your case theory, and you will lack the client cooperation that is required to put the theory into practice. When a good working relationship is missing, the client listens dutifully to your advice and then does what he or she pleases—destroys business records against your advice, goes to the home of the estranged spouse in violation of a restraining order, and so on. In contrast to the economic relationship, which is usually established around the time of the first interview, the cooperative relationship is constantly evolving. Nevertheless, the initial interview may well set the tone for the future growth of this cooperative relationship.

II. PLANNING FOR THE INITIAL INTERVIEW

The initial face-to-face meeting with the prospective client, more than most other contacts, will often determine the course of your attorney-client relationship. When properly conducted, the initial contact will form the basis for the decision by the client whether to retain you as counsel and for your decision whether to accept or decline the representation. It will establish mutual attitudes of trust and confidence and present a picture of you and your firm to the prospective client.

A. Setting the Objectives for the Interview

The initial client contact is too important to be approached haphazardly, relying solely on intuition or your powers of perception to come through for you. You need a plan with a definite objective.

Whatever the precise form of your plan, it will be developed in the context of three basic objectives. These same three objectives will repeat themselves in subsequent interviews and contacts with your client throughout the case.

- First, you will seek *information* from the prospective client that will help you formulate a case theory. Because the approach to gathering this type of information is identical for witnesses and clients, this objective is explored in Chapter 6 on interviewing witnesses.
- Second, you will *advise the client about what to expect.* For instance, you will advise the client about what the next steps are in settlement discussions or in answering a complaint filed against the client.
- Third, you will strive to *develop the legal, economic, and cooperative relationships.*

Your specific objectives may be narrower than those suggested here. In a criminal case where the client is in custody, the only objectives of the initial interview might be to meet the client, get information for a motion to reduce bail, and to then set up the next interview.

Nevertheless, the objectives you set will drive the initial interview with each new client.

B.   Preparing for the Interview

Your initial contact with a potential client is very important as it sets the tone for a functioning, cooperative attorney-client relationship. In an effort to achieve an effective attorney-client relationship you should take three steps: (1) learn about the prospective client's situation; (2) do preliminary research of the potential applicable law, and (3) anticipate interpersonal matters and problems.

Learn About the Prospective Client's Situation

In an effort to develop a cooperative relationship with the client, where the client has confidence in your abilities, you should be prepared and conversant in the client's situation from the start. To be conversant with and carry out your plan you need to know something about the legal and factual aspects of the prospective client's case. To do so you must first gather all reasonably available information about the potential client's situation.

In this chapter, we show you how to apply the concepts and techniques of forging the attorney-client relationship. The hypothetical *Bagshaw* case, to which you are about to be introduced, serves as an illustrative case not only in this chapter but throughout the rest of the book.

The *Coach Bagshaw* Case

Story   Suppose that you just received a phone call from Mansfield University former women's basketball coach Marilyn Bagshaw. Coach Bagshaw has been referred to you by a colleague, who, like you, is also a Mansfield University alum. You spoke briefly with Coach Bagshaw on the phone and scheduled an appointment to meet with her in your office tomorrow morning at 9:30 a.m. Often you will find out something about the potential client's situation from the telephone conversation during which the initial appointment is arranged, and in this case you learned that Coach Bagshaw wants to discuss her termination by the university and that she is quite upset.

Bagshaw's termination has been front-page news in your small town's newspaper, the *Intelligencer*, ever since the University fired her three days ago. You have been following the story as it unfolds in the media. According to those accounts, the Collegiate Sports Commission (CSA) had been investigating Bagshaw for gambling on intercollegiate women's baseball and soccer games. Bagshaw told the investigators and the Mansfield University athletic director that she had not gambled. But, when the investigation revealed that Bagshaw had gambled sizeable sums at a charity event, the athletic director summarily fired her.

To become more informed about Bagshaw's situation, you use the Internet to check the archives of the *Intelligencer.* Your research refreshes your memory about other conflicts between Bagshaw, and the athletic director and the University's administration. You learn that following last year's winning season, rumors were rampant that Bagshaw was being courted by other universities for a coaching position. When reporters questioned the coach asking whether she was interviewing with other teams about coaching positions, she denied it. By happenstance a reporter caught Bagshaw visiting with the president of Entman University. Bagshaw later admitted that she had discussed a coaching position at Entman U., but she declined the job offer. She publicly apologized to the athletic director for misleading him about whether she was entertaining other offers.

Obviously, the situation of few potential clients will be so public as to have news accounts that you can use to prepare for the initial interview. But, you have other sources that you can check so you will have all reasonable information about the potential client's situation. Your office staff can be an excellent resource if you plan accordingly. By giving your paralegal/legal assistant instructions on how to interact with new prospective clients, you can gain information that will help you prepare for the initial interview. The paralegal who is your client intake representative and makes the appointment with a prospective client might also gather information about the client's emotional state or personality traits.

INSTRUCTIONS TO YOUR PARALEGAL/LEGAL ASSISTANT

Instruct your paralegal to ask the potential client for:

- Full name and correct spelling
- Contact information, including name, address, phone number, contact person
- A convenient time to meet during timeframes that you have set aside in your calendar to meet with new clients
- The nature of the client's concern: "If you don't mind, could you tell me what you wish to consult with the attorney about?"

continues ▶

> Instruct your paralegal to observe the client's demeanor and report his or her impressions to you.
>
> As an alternative, you can have a form for each prospective client to fill out before your meeting. See the office "Information Report" checklist in Part VI, Effective Case Management for the New Client.

Obtaining information by using these types of sources has advantages and disadvantages that you should consider. For example, using a client form for information-gathering may not be appropriate for every situation. Consider your personal style, the type of client you generally represent (unschooled or elderly people may have difficulty with written forms), and the types of cases you usually handle (tax, family, corporate). Nevertheless, even with minimal information, you can get a sense of the general legal areas involved in a prospective client's case and begin to familiarize yourself with the applicable body of law pertaining to those areas. At some point in your career, especially if you specialize, you will be able to perceive a wide range of potential legal issues and theories with only bare-bones information.

Preliminary Research of Applicable Law

Your early consideration of potentially applicable bodies of law will give you a sense of the spectrum of legal theories reasonably available and, therefore, the basis for a fact-gathering plan. Based on your telephone conversation with Coach Bagshaw, you know that she thinks that she was unfairly terminated and that the university breached its contract with her. Bagshaw had three years left to go on her five-year contract. You decide to do a cursory review of unlawful termination law. Of course, the best solution for the client may not be one that leads to litigation. In Bagshaw's case, a quick settlement and/or rehiring (the university is two months away from basketball season and without a head coach) may be far more beneficial than unlawful termination litigation pursued under a brilliant case theory. You also decide that you need to explore the regulatory powers of the Collegiate Sports Commission.

An awareness of the spectrum of available legal theories cues you in to the potential information from the client that could be relevant to these legal theories, allowing you to appreciate the significance of this information if it emerges or seek it if it doesn't. For example, if you think the Collegiate Sports Commission may have pressured the athletic director to fire Coach Bagshaw and your initial research reveals that such action may provide grounds for a cause of action for contract interference against the CSA, any information about the CSA's investigation and communication with the University will be of particular interest to you. Keep in mind that at this stage your research is preliminary—just to get you started on developing the case and relationship with a potential client.

Anticipate Interpersonal Matters and Problems

You also want to be able to deal with difficult interpersonal matters that may arise with the client in a way that effectively resolves the matter, instills confidence in your ability to deal with difficult situations, and demonstrates concern with the client's welfare as an individual. This is most likely to happen if you have already anticipated the situation by paying careful attention to the tenor of early contacts with the client or have listened for hints in conversations with relatives and acquaintances. Exposure to some information, such as information tending to tarnish the credibility of your client or witnesses, will alert you to the need for a plan to handle these matters.

For example, media reports about Bagshaw assert that she has been deceitful. According to the newspaper stories, she admitted to having misled the public and the athletic director concerning meeting with other universities about coaching jobs, and she allegedly lied about gambling. Also, you have come across articles about alleged recruiting violations. You are alerted to the possibility that Bagshaw may not be completely candid with you. With this information gleaned from your background preparation, you should devise a tentative plan with your potential client to deal with such interpersonal matters. You may decide to concentrate on being very straightforward with Bagshaw and to stress the need for her to be completely truthful with you on all matters.

III. CONDUCTING THE INTERVIEW

During the first interview, you will be gathering information, imparting information to the client—primarily about what the client may expect, and developing the three relationships (legal, economic and cooperative) with the client, and deciding whether to take the case.

A. Information Gathering

This chapter concentrates on areas exclusive to the client during the initial phases of the attorney-client relationship. As mentioned earlier, Chapter 6 on witness interviewing covers areas that are applicable not only to the client witness but to any non-client witness, particularly when the interview is on the substance of the case. To conduct effective client interviews requires the application of the principles discussed in both chapters. For instance, while this chapter examines only the initial client contact aspects of the Bagshaw interview, Chapter 6 revisits the initial interview with Coach Bagshaw and applies considerations for additional client interviews, such as how to gather facts to develop the case theory.

The following diagrams illustrate the content of this chapter and Chapter 6 that provide guidance for interviewing the client and other witnesses.

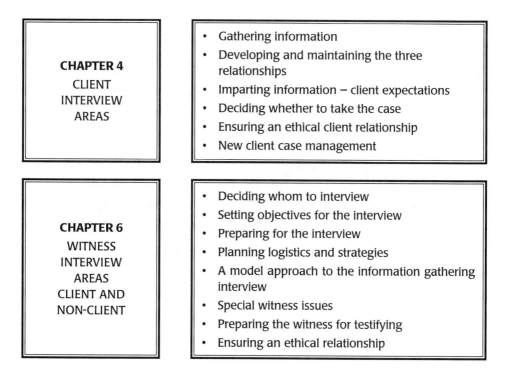

CHAPTER 4
CLIENT INTERVIEW AREAS

- Gathering information
- Developing and maintaining the three relationships
- Imparting information – client expectations
- Deciding whether to take the case
- Ensuring an ethical client relationship
- New client case management

CHAPTER 6
WITNESS INTERVIEW AREAS
CLIENT AND NON-CLIENT

- Deciding whom to interview
- Setting objectives for the interview
- Preparing for the interview
- Planning logistics and strategies
- A model approach to the information gathering interview
- Special witness issues
- Preparing the witness for testifying
- Ensuring an ethical relationship

The initial interviews with the client will generally take place when your analysis of the case is in its early stages. Later, you will gain far more sophistication as your knowledge of the client and case increases. At this point, however, there might not even be a case to consider. The client may want your advice on how to avoid being sued or on whether to file a complaint, the client may need you to write a letter or make a telephone call, or the client may just want to drop the whole matter by the day of the interview. So, although your case theory may always be in some process of development and refinement throughout the case, it is likely that your initial case theory or potential theories will not even begin to crystallize until after you've begun talking to the client.

B. Developing and Maintaining the Three Relationships: Legal, Economic, and Cooperative

The three relationships the attorney has with a client serve as focal points for the initial interview.

Building the Legal Relationship

To forge a strong relationship with the client, counsel should educate the client on the attorney-client privilege. For example, during your initial interview with Coach Bagshaw, you explain that the relationship of client and attorney is a professional one, involving the highest personal trust and confidence. It is the attorney's legal obligation to maintain confidentiality in the attorney-client relationship. The privilege protects disclosures that a client makes to the attorney in confidence, for the purpose of securing legal advice or assistance. You tell her that it is important that she understands that confidences disclosed to the attorney cannot and will not be disclosed to others, and that without the client's consent private information will stay private. In addition, you advise Bradshaw that the obligation of an attorney to preserve the confidences and secrets of a client continues even after termination of the attorney's employment. Finally, you advise Bradshaw not to discuss the case with others because statements a client makes possibly could be used against the client later, and could breach attorney-client confidentiality.

SIGNED AUTHORIZATIONS

At the time of the client interview, you also will want to obtain signed authorizations to obtain, among other things:

- employment records from present and past employers including job applications and W-2 forms;
- doctor, hospital, and other medical records;
- police reports;
- other governmental documents such as birth, marriage, divorce, passport, tax, and license records and certifications;
- school records;
- union records;

continues ▶

> - awards;
> - pre and post-injury photographs,
> - bills and bank statements, and/or
> - power of attorney.
>
> Medical authorizations, powers of attorney, and other authorizations often are needed for effective representation.

A signed power of attorney from the client may be needed when handling specific issues of the case. At the end of this chapter on page 107 is a Model General Authorization, which should be presented to and signed by the client. It provides for the release to counsel of relevant documents.

Establishing the Economic Relationship

Setting the Fee

At the end of the client interview, after you have decided to accept the case, you need to discuss the employment agreement. How will you communicate the fee arrangement to the client? While some new lawyers are uncomfortable discussing the financial terms with the client, it is an economic reality that an attorney must collect fees from clients in order to pay the bills of a law office. The client is merely being asked to pay for services rendered. Therefore, it is an important aspect of not only setting the fee but also of collecting it that the subject be talked about in a straightforward and business-like manner. The explanation should cover the precise terms of the fee, the basis for the fee, and what is expected of the client concerning payment.

In both criminal (except those involving an indigent client) and civil matters, the attorney may require a retainer at the time that the attorney accepts the case. The retainer must be placed in a separate trust account. Then, the attorney will bill at an hourly rate against the account and deduct ordinary costs, with the client receiving an accounting of these expenditures.

Costs

You must make clear to the client the difference between "fees" and "costs", i.e., that the attorney is paid a fee for the work performed and that costs must be reimbursed by the client no matter what the result of the case. The usual costs include long distance phone charges, photocopying, and exhibit preparation. Extraordinary costs, such as travel for an expert witness, may be incurred. Counsel should seek prior approval by the client of all extraordinary costs.

Written Fee Agreement

A written fee agreement formalizes the attorney-client relationship and contains the fee provision. ABA Model Rules of Professional Conduct Rule 1.5(b) states a preference that the fee agreement be in writing. Counsel usually uses a standardized agreement and has the client review and sign the agreement. It is important that a written employment agreement be executed, because an oral agreement may result in confusion or misunderstanding later. Further, such disputes are subject to close scrutiny under a state's Rules of Professional Conduct.

The employment agreement states the work to be performed, the division of attorney-client authority (counsel makes procedural and tactical decisions; the client makes all substantive decisions), and how the fee will be calculated (either hourly, a fixed or contingent fee, or another agreed-upon method of payment) and what costs may be incurred and how the costs will be paid, particularly any extraordinary expenses. The agreement may specify a retainer amount to be paid before representation commences and how fees and costs are billed against the retainer. It may state the attorney's hourly rate and rates for paralegal and staff assistance. In all cases the fee must be reasonable. The agreement also may provide for the duration of the representation, for example, until settlement, through trial, up to but not including appeal, until a final judgment. Clients like clear fee information. Put all fee policies in writing and generally have the client sign a fee agreement. Communicate details clearly to the client and check that the client fully understands all aspects of the employment agreement. Get the business aspects of lawyering settled and out of the way so you can focus yourself totally on representation. At the end of this chapter at page 107 is a Model Employment and Contingency Fee Agreement, which can be tailored to a specific client and the needs of that representation.

Whatever billing format you use, keep exact records, documenting all your activities on your client's behalf, even if the activity took only a few minutes (".1 hours: discussed resetting Furman deposition with opposing counsel"). Clients are happier if they can see what they are paying for. Reasonableness is an important factor in billing practices. For instance, billing by the quarter hour for a phone call that took two minutes (e.g., confirming the client will be at a 9:00 A.M. hearing the next day) is irksome and detracts from the confidence the client has in the attorney.

Ethical Requirements

ABA Model Rule of Professional Conduct Rule 1.5 provides ethical guidelines for fee arrangements. Rule 1.5 prohibits the setting of an unreasonable fee. As far as the practicality of setting a fee, ask fellow attorneys for a range of appropriate fees. In a civil case, your fee will generally be set at an hourly rate (unless contingent). It will reflect your level of experience, expertise, area of practice, and overhead.

In a criminal case involving an indigent client, defense counsel may be either a public defender working for a public defender agency or counsel appointed to represent the client. If the defendant can afford to retain an attorney, usually the attorney will set an hourly rate. Factors determining the level of remuneration include labor expended, the attorney's experience, and the difficulty of the issues involved and at times, the potential severity of consequences involved, that is, the magnitude of the responsibility you are accepting (e.g., defense of a death penalty case). Rather than set an hourly rate, some attorneys will set a flat fee for the case based upon its nature (e.g., charging a set fee for a driving under the influence of intoxicants case). Or, the attorney may set flat fees tied to different stages of the proceedings (for example, $3000 through the motions and $5000 more if it goes to trial). Model Rule 1.5(d) (2) prohibits contingent fees in criminal cases.

The Cooperative Relationship

Rapport Building

In order to establish an enduring, positive relationship with the client, you will first need to develop a rapport. Rapport building requires people skills tailored to the client. You have several choices for how to build a rapport.

- You can begin the interview with *small talk* about your experiences in common with the client.
- You can *empathize* with the client's situation.
- You can *sell* the potential client on your abilities.

RAPPORT BUILDING

The *Coach Bagshaw* Case

At your first meeting with Coach Bagshaw, your conversation could begin with:

- Small Talk: "Coach, as a Mansfield alum, I so admire how you turned the Lions into a winning team over the last couple years."
- Empathy: "Coach, this publicity along with the university administration's conduct these past couple days must be taking a toll. How are your spouse and teenagers taking it?"

Usually, it will be best to enter the interview with several rapport-building options in mind, and make your choice depending on the actual situation. This may even involve using several options over a single session. Ultimately, you are striving to develop a relationship in which the client will be candid with you, will be comfortable with you and your decisions, and will believe that you are trustworthy.

In order to gain the trust of the potential client, you may need to market your abilities. You could do this by providing a sketch of your professional background as part of your introduction to the client. This could also be provided to the client prior to the initial interview in the form of a brochure. You could also draw the client's attention to your past experience in the area of practice that the situation calls for. For example, you could tell Coach Bagshaw about your trial work and successful negotiations of contract disputes with the university.

Potential Clients with Special Considerations

Special consideration should be given to the needs and concerns of special needs clients: incompetent, minor, physically or mentally challenged, and other extraordinary clients. A guardian may be appointed to represent the interests of these clients. Special arrangements may need to be made for access to offices and the courthouse and for maximum understanding by the client of all aspects of the case. Going the extra distance to assist these clients enhances the cooperative relationship.

Some interpersonal problems may arise which make the development of a cooperative relationship difficult, if not impossible. Suppose you are a public defender who works for RAP (Representation for Accused Persons, a public defender agency). You have been assigned to represent Chris Richardson, who is charged with a hate-crime assault. When you greet Mr. Richardson for the first time in jail, he acts surprised that you are the same person he has talked to on the telephone. At the meeting, he expresses some reluctance to work with you. You suspect that this is because you are black. Later, he tells your supervisor that he would like someone he can "relate to better." Will you confront the client with his suspected racial prejudice against you? Ignore the attitude of the client and do the best job possible? Or will you try to convince him not only of your expertise but also that minority representation when charged with this crime is likely to give him a strategic advantage in a jury trial? Should the supervisor ignore the client's request? Or should the supervisor try to convince him of your abilities? Should another lawyer in the office represent Richardson? Or should RAP tell the client that unless he is represented by you, that the office will no longer represent him?

Women, at times, can face analogous problems with a client due to gender. Or one might encounter religious or ethnic prejudice in a client. Be prepared in the event such an unfortunate situation should occur and plan your response, leaving flexibility for actual circumstances. Determine whether an interpersonal problem can be overcome or if a cooperative relationship and representation is not possible.

C.   Imparting Information—Client Expectations

Parts of the initial interview are used to give information to the client. This information usually consists of what the client can expect from the attorney, what the attorney expects in turn from the client, and what the client can expect from the process the client is about to face. For instance, you have anticipated the need to discuss with Coach Bagshaw the necessity that she be scrupulously truthful with you; recounting the truism that a person should always be truthful with his or her priest, doctor, and lawyer. Often, you will need to alleviate the client's concerns. For instance, you may want to explain to Bagshaw what to expect during the litigation if and when filing a complaint is considered.

The discussion about what to expect may range from clarifying the fee arrangement, articulating the client's duties regarding keeping appointments, and detailing how the client will have to assist with interrogatories, to explaining what to expect at an arraignment, what an answer to a complaint is, the nature of the attorney's duty of confidentiality, who the client should not talk to, the lawyer's role at a deposition noticed by the adversary, and so on. By clarifying these various expectations, you can accomplish a number of objectives: The attorney-client relationship is enhanced when the expectations of both parties are clear from the start, the client can play a more effective, contributing role in the overall strategy when he or she understands the nature of the process, and the client is likely to feel less stress if expectations are clear and the process less mysterious.

Counsel should carefully examine and explain to the client any difficulty of establishing liability before accepting the representation. Liability often is clear to the client but may be difficult to establish by counsel, particularly if there are multiple defendants in the case. In addition, the attorney must consider the potential for recovery of damages. Even a clear case of liability may result in little or no damages. Never promise your client an award or a settlement.

IV. DECIDING WHETHER TO ENTER INTO THE RELATIONSHIP

To take the case, or not take the case? That is the question. A variety of factors may dictate that you should decline to represent the perspective client. Information developed at the client interview may make this case or client incompatible with representation by you. The nature of the case may be outside your field of practice. You may have current time constraints. Personality problems may preclude effective representation of the client. A conflict of interest may exist between this perspective client and representation of a current client.

A potential client walks into your office. She has fallen down what she believes was an unsafe staircase in a department store. Her side was sore for a week, but she feels fine now and, according to her doctor, will suffer no lasting damage from the fall. She incurred $1500 in out-of-pocket medical expenses, her employer's insurance plan having covered the remainder. Should you take this case? First, you know slip-and-fall cases are generally difficult to win. Juries tend to believe people trip because they weren't watching what they were doing. So you will have to put much effort into preparation if you are going to come up with a convincing claim. Second, there will be real expenses in pursuing the case. You will probably have to take depositions, and you will need an expert to testify about the structural unsoundness of the staircase. Based on verdicts in these types of cases in your jurisdiction, the most you believe a jury would award is a few thousand dollars, and you would bill $300 an hour or a 40 percent contingency fee after the client pays costs out of her share. This case is simply not worth the time and expense to you or the client, unless you find something about it that would make you want to take it pro bono or you can get the department store to enter into some method of alternative dispute resolution (e.g., mediation or arbitration) that could quickly resolve the case. On the other hand, you might advise her how to negotiate with the insurance adjuster for the department store.

After the initial client interview, counsel will want to reassess and sift through all of the information obtained from the prospective client to determine if the case should be accepted and to determine how to handle the case. In deciding whether to accept the case, the lawyer will want to consider numerous factors, such as what strategies are appropriate and what legal theories are applicable to the matter. Also, counsel must consider what information or facts are potentially harmful to the client and what the client said that was not credible or that counsel will want to corroborate. Counsel should compile a list of other information to obtain, either from the client or through investigation, such as the identification of witnesses and relevant documents. For example, in the Bagshaw case you will want to review her contract with the university. Consideration of whether the client would be a good witness and would cooperate with counsel is important.

If counsel decides not to accept the representation, it is important to confirm a rejection in writing. Include information about the reasons why you declined to accept the employment, any applicable limitations period or deadlines, advise him or her to contact other counsel immediately to pursue the matter, and thank him or her for consulting with you. This letter may be needed in the future to refute that an attorney-client relationship was formed.

V.   ENSURING AN ETHICAL RELATIONSHIP

The only way to make sure that you maintain an ethical relationship with your client is through adherence to your jurisdiction's rules of professional responsibility.

Solicitation

One consideration the professional rules of conduct have an impact on is the solicitation of clients. Counsel must become familiar with the solicitation prohibitions in their jurisdiction and strive to avoid improper prospective client contact. An attorney who personally solicits employment may be disbarred, suspended, or reprimanded. An attorney may contact an accident victim for legitimate investigative purposes and is not barred from representing the victim if requested to do so. However, an arrangement with a doctor whereby, for consideration, the doctor recommends an attorney to injured persons, may well result in disciplinary action.

Frivolous Actions

What if after interviewing Bagshaw about the facts, she insists that you file a complaint against the Collegiate Sports Commission for interfering with her university contract? If you believe that insufficient facts exist at this juncture to file the complaint, pleading it would be a frivolous action, barred by the ABA Model Rules of Professional Conduct Rule 3.1 and Fed. R. Civ. P. 11. You must try to dissuade Bagshaw, and, if that fails, withdraw. In a criminal case, you must explain the realistic risks and consequences of pushing a frivolous defense to trial to the client, but after that, under Model Rule 3.1 you "may nevertheless so defend the proceeding as to require that every element of the case be established."

Competency

Some new clients seek representation on matters that counsel is not familiar with or competent in. Or, counsel may have a conflict of interest. In these situations, it may be ethically best not to accept the representation but to refer the case to another attorney.

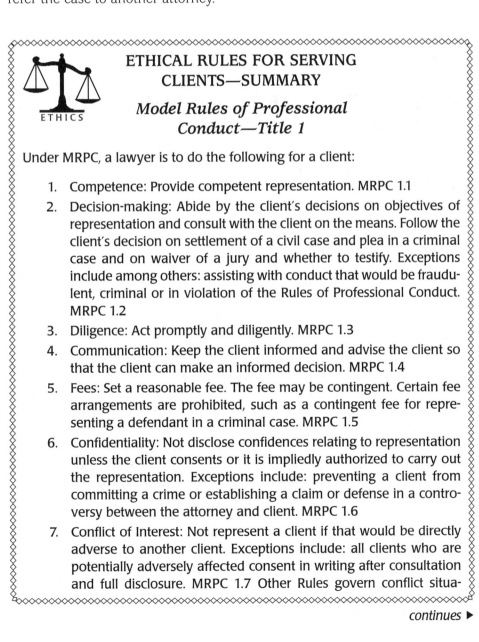

ETHICAL RULES FOR SERVING CLIENTS—SUMMARY

Model Rules of Professional Conduct—Title 1

Under MRPC, a lawyer is to do the following for a client:

1. Competence: Provide competent representation. MRPC 1.1
2. Decision-making: Abide by the client's decisions on objectives of representation and consult with the client on the means. Follow the client's decision on settlement of a civil case and plea in a criminal case and on waiver of a jury and whether to testify. Exceptions include among others: assisting with conduct that would be fraudulent, criminal or in violation of the Rules of Professional Conduct. MRPC 1.2
3. Diligence: Act promptly and diligently. MRPC 1.3
4. Communication: Keep the client informed and advise the client so that the client can make an informed decision. MRPC 1.4
5. Fees: Set a reasonable fee. The fee may be contingent. Certain fee arrangements are prohibited, such as a contingent fee for representing a defendant in a criminal case. MRPC 1.5
6. Confidentiality: Not disclose confidences relating to representation unless the client consents or it is impliedly authorized to carry out the representation. Exceptions include: preventing a client from committing a crime or establishing a claim or defense in a controversy between the attorney and client. MRPC 1.6
7. Conflict of Interest: Not represent a client if that would be directly adverse to another client. Exceptions include: all clients who are potentially adversely affected consent in writing after consultation and full disclosure. MRPC 1.7 Other Rules govern conflict situa-

continues ▶

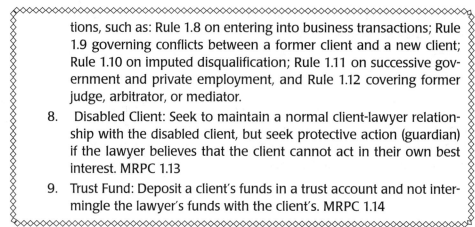

> tions, such as: Rule 1.8 on entering into business transactions; Rule 1.9 governing conflicts between a former client and a new client; Rule 1.10 on imputed disqualification; Rule 1.11 on successive government and private employment, and Rule 1.12 covering former judge, arbitrator, or mediator.
>
> 8. Disabled Client: Seek to maintain a normal client-lawyer relationship with the disabled client, but seek protective action (guardian) if the lawyer believes that the client cannot act in their own best interest. MRPC 1.13
>
> 9. Trust Fund: Deposit a client's funds in a trust account and not intermingle the lawyer's funds with the client's. MRPC 1.14

VI. EFFECTIVE CASE MANAGEMENT FOR THE NEW CLIENT

Two significant and practical considerations when beginning a new relationship with a client are (1) setting up the client's file for your office and (2) depositing any client money in your client trust account.

The Client's File

You should supervise or personally set up and organize the client's file immediately after accepting the employment. You do this because you will receive documents and correspondence and possibly handle investigative and medical reports and other record requests and must know where these are located to access them quickly.

The most important reason to organize the client file is to determine any limitations or deadline periods and highlight these in the file. In addition, these periods must be entered in the office tickler system that should notify counsel that a deadline is coming up. Counsel may want to keep a docket system for the client such as a desk or pocket day-minder and record important dates. It is important to use more than one system and to have a backup system to prevent overlooking a critical deadline or limitations period.

The client file can be organized with sections for:

- Information Report for the Initial Client Contact – See page 110 at the end of this chapter
- Correspondence
- Investigation
- Legal Research

- Discovery
- Witnesses
- Expert Consultant and Witness
- Settlement Negotiations
- Pleadings, Motions, Court-Related Documents
- Trial
- Evidence
- Damages
- Billing

The complexity of the case will dictate how the file is organized and whether supplemental files are needed. Supplemental files may be needed for bulky documents or evidence, deposition transcripts, extensive medical reports, or a complex trial notebook.

As a practicing lawyer, you will have to maintain an organized and efficient management system for your cases, and this will require that you pay close attention to details. The contents of the file should be kept in chronological order, and loose papers should not be tolerated as they are easily lost. The attorney-client Employment Agreement is often attached to the inside cover of the main file along with the initial client interview information. Maintaining the file cannot be stressed enough as it is critical to effective representation. Proper case management requires counsel to periodically review the file and determine the status of each ongoing aspect. For example, during the discovery process counsel should review the status of outstanding discovery to determine if answers are made and received timely, and if not, that discovery is completed or requested or a motion to compel filed. If a retainer was obtained it should be deposited in the attorney or firm's trust fund. The client's information and fee agreement particulars should be added into the billing and accounting system.

✓ CLIENT INTERVIEW CHECKLIST

The following are standards of performance for conducting an effective initial client interview (excluding the witness-interviewing aspects, which are covered in the Chapter 6):

Overall Interview Performance

☐ Do adequate background preparation for the interview
☐ Have a set of objectives in mind

❑ Conduct a structured and well-organized interview

❑ Behave in a confident and professional manner

❑ Anticipate and have a suitable approach for dealing with problems that could arise during the interview

Information Gathering

❑ Gather adequate background information from the client (e.g., contact information, education, marital status, employer).

❑ Consult the section in Chapter 6 covering information gathering applicable to both client and non-client witnesses.

Attorney's and Client's Expectations

❑ Explain what the client can expect from you, the attorney

❑ Discuss what you expect from the client (e.g., keeping appointments)

❑ Explain the upcoming process (e.g., answering the complaint)

❑ Discuss what to expect from the justice system

❑ Explain other matters unique to the client's case

Legal Relationship

❑ Discuss the confidential nature of the attorney-client relationship

❑ Seek authorization to obtain pertinent information (e.g., medical records, asking for power of attorney), including obtaining signed authorization forms

Economic Relationship

❑ Convince the client that you are worthy of being retained

❑ Set a reasonable attorney's fee

❑ Discuss the fee with the client

❑ Set a reasonable retainer. Place any client monies received in the attorney's trust account

❑ Make clear the terms of payment

❑ Explain the difference between the fee and costs

❑ Have the client sign an employment agreement

Cooperative Relationship

❑ Develop a rapport with the client

❑ Recognize and grapple with interpersonal problems (e.g., prejudiced client)

Ethical Relationship

❑ Recognize and handle ethical matters (e.g., conflicts of interest, client's attempt to get the attorney to coach him)

MODEL GENERAL AUTHORIZATION TO RELEASE DOCUMENTS TO ATTORNEY

Date: _____

To: _____

The undersigned authorizes you to furnish and disclose any and all information in your possession, including police, medical, and other reports or records, that may in any way relate to a matter involving the undersigned, regarding the accident or incident on or about _____ [date], or regarding the determination of damages resulting from this accident or incident to _____ [attorney/law firm].

A photocopy of this General Authorization is considered as valid as the original.

_____ [Client]

_____
Printed Name

MODEL EMPLOYMENT AND CONTINGENCY FEE AGREEMENT

I _____, the undersigned client (hereinafter referred to as "I," "me," or the "Client") do hereby retain and employ _____ and the law firm of _____ (hereinafter referred to as "Attorney"), as my Attorney to represent me in connection with the following matter:_____.

Under this Employment and Contingency Fee Agreement (hereinafter referred to as "Agreement") Client authorizes Attorney on my behalf to undertake negotiations or institute legal proceedings or file any lawsuit necessary. I further authorize Attorney to retain and employ, at my expense, the services of any experts as well as the services of other outside contractors, as Attorney deems necessary or expedient in representing my interests. I also understand that Attorney may associate with counsel outside of the firm to assist in the handling of this matter and I authorize Attorney to retain and employ other attorneys with my prior knowledge and consent. The combined fee of Attorney and all other attorneys is limited as stated in Section A below.

A. ATTORNEY FEES. As compensation for legal services, Client agrees to pay Attorney as follows:

continues ▶

Contingency Fee: Attorney receives the following percentage of the amount recovered before the deduction of costs and expenses, as stated in Section C below.

_____% if settled without a lawsuit
_____% in the event a lawsuit is filed
_____% in the event a trial commences
_____% in the event an appeal is filed by any party

It is understood and agreed that this employment is upon a contingency fee basis and, if no recovery is made, Client will not be indebted to Attorney for any sum whatsoever as Attorney Fees. If Attorney associates with outside counsel to assist in the handling of this matter, I understand all Attorneys are only entitled to one fee that is divided between them, pursuant to their agreement. In the event of recovery, costs are to be paid out of my share of the recovery.

B. POWER OF ATTORNEY. Attorney cannot, without first obtaining the informed consent of Client, enter into any binding agreement to settle or compromise Client's claims. Subject to that limitation, Client empowers Attorney to sue, to receive any and all payments, to endorse any and all checks, to sign any and all documents, of whatever nature, to obtain medical records and other personal information, and to do everything generally necessary for the prosecution of Client's legal matters as if Client were present. Client agrees that this Power of Attorney is continuous until expressly revoked in writing.

C. ADVANCES AND EXPENSES (hereinafter referred to as "costs"). Out of Client's recovery, in addition to paying Attorney's Fees, I agree to pay all costs in connection with Attorney's handling of the claim or lawsuit that is the subject of this Agreement out of any settlement and/or judgment. I agree costs will be billed to my account as they are incurred. A copy of my account will be provided to me on request. I hereby agree to reimburse Attorney out of the first settlement and any other settlements, if necessary, for costs. Costs may include, but are not limited to, the following: an open file fee of $125, long distance telephone charges (billed at actual cost), photocopying (25 cents per page), postage, facsimile costs ($2.50 per page), delivery charges, medical records/bills, charts, models, photographs, blow-ups, and other demonstrative aids and evidence, deposition costs and fees, expert fees, subpoena costs, court costs, sheriff's and service fees, travel expenses (including, but not limited to, air fare, lodging, mileage (based on the rate set by the Internal Revenue Service), automobile rental charges, and meals), investigation fees, and payments made, owed, and/or guaranteed, for treatment rendered to Client. In addition, clerical staff overtime will be charged at 1.5 times the base hourly rate paid to the staff who work that overtime. The base hourly rates for clerical staff range from $_____ per hour to $_____ per hour. These costs only pertain to overtime that might be required in the handling of Client's specific claims.

If Client decides to terminate Attorney's employment, Client agrees to pay all costs, as set forth in this Section C, out of any settlement and/or judgment ultimately obtained. If I decide not to pursue this matter, I agree to pay all costs, as set forth in this Section C, regardless of whether there is any recovery in this matter.

If an advance deposit for costs is being held by Attorney Client agrees to promptly reimburse Attorney for any amount in excess of what is being held in advance.

Advance required _____ Yes _____ No

Client agrees to advance $\$\_\_\_\_\_$ for costs, which amount will be deposited in Attorney's trust account and will be applied to costs and expenses as they accrue. Should this advance be exhausted, I agree to replenish the advance promptly on Attorney's request. If I fail to replenish the advance within ten (10) days of Attorney's request. Attorney has, in addition to other rights, the right to withdraw as my Attorney.

D. LINE OF CREDIT. In the event Attorneys find it necessary to obtain a line of credit specifically to fund the costs of Client's case, the interest paid by Attorney on this line of credit and principal is an expense to be reimbursed with all other costs and advances out of my share of the proceeds of any judgment or settlement.

E. INTEREST AND ATTORNEY'S FEE FOR ENFORCEMENT. If any Attorney's fees or costs and expenses are not paid within ten (10) days of Attorney's mailing of a statement to Client, I further agree to pay interest thereafter on any balance due at the rate of _____ percent (__) per annum. I further agree to pay the reasonable attorney's fee of any attorney employed by Attorney to seek enforcement of this Agreement.

F. PRIVILEGE. Client agrees and understands that this Agreement is intended to and does hereby assign, transfer, set over, and deliver to Attorney as fee for representation of Client in this matter an interest in the claim or lawsuit that is the subject matter of this Agreement, any proceeds or recovery under the terms and conditions stated in this Agreement, in accordance with the provisions of _____ Revised Statutes, and that Attorney has the privilege afforded by _____ Revised Statutes.

G. NO GUARANTEE. Client acknowledges that Attorney has made no promise or guarantee regarding the outcome of Client's legal matter. In fact, Attorney has advised me that litigation in general is risky, can take a long time, can be very costly and can be very frustrating. I further acknowledge that my Attorney has the right to cancel this Agreement and withdraw from this matter if, in Attorney's professional opinion, the matter does not have merit, I do not have a reasonably good possibility of recovery, I refuse to follow the recommendations of Attorney, I fail to abide by the terms of this Agreement, and/or if Attorney's continued representation would result in a violation of the Rules of Professional Conduct.

Attorney is not a tax attorney and makes no representations regarding the tax implications of any settlement or judgment recovered. Tax implications, if any, of any settlement or judgment should be made in conjunction with Client's accountant and/or a tax attorney.

H. COOPERATION. Client agrees to cooperate with Attorney and to be available for conferences, depositions or other negotiations, including court appearances. Client agrees to review all materials sent to Client by Attorney promptly on receipt. In the event of inquiries, complaints, or misunderstandings that Client may have, Client agrees to promptly bring those matters to the attention of Attorney. Client must keep Attorney informed of Client's contact information including current residence and business addresses, as well as residence and business telephone numbers.

I. SETTLEMENT, COMPROMISE, RELEASE or DISCONTINUANCE. It is further agreed that Attorney, or those associated with Attorney, or Client may not, without the consent of the other, settle, compromise, release, discontinue or otherwise dispose of the claim or lawsuit that is the subject of this Agreement.

J. STATUTORY ATTORNEY'S FEES. In the event of recovery under the provisions of a statute or under any other law that specifies the attorney's fees to be paid, Attorney fees must be paid in accordance with the maximum allowed by law.

continues ▶

K. ALTERNATIVE DISPUTE RESOLUTION. In the event of any dispute or disagreement concerning this Agreement, Attorney and Client agree to submit to arbitration by the _____ State Bar Association Lawyer Fee Dispute Resolution Program.

L. ADDITIONAL TERMS. Attorney and Client agree to the following additional terms: _____.

M. APPLICABLE LAW. This Agreement is governed by the law of the state of _____.

N. TERMINATION OF REPRESENTATION. Client understands that I have the right to terminate the representation on written notice to that effect. I understand that I will be responsible for any fees and costs incurred prior to the discharge or termination. It is also understood that Attorney has a right to terminate representation on written notice to that effect. I understand that should Attorney terminate this representation, I will be responsible for any fees and costs incurred prior to the discharge or termination.

O. ENTIRE AGREEMENT. Client has read this Agreement in its entirety and I agree to and understand the terms and conditions stated in the Agreement. I acknowledge that there are no other terms or oral agreements existing between Attorney and Client. This Agreement may not be amended or modified in any way without the prior written consent of Attorney and Client.

This Agreement is executed by me, the undersigned Client, on this _____ day of _____, 20__.

CLIENT:

Print Name: _____

Signature: _____

This Agreement is hereby accepted on this _____ day of _____, 20__.

ATTORNEY _____

By: _____

Print Name: _____

Memoranda Report for the Initial Client Contact

The following Memoranda is a model form that either you or an office staff person completes during the initial client contact or at the client interview.

1. Date:
2. Attorney Handling:
3. Referred by:
4. Client
    Name:
    Address:

Phone:

Social Security No.:

Date of Birth:

5. Personal Information

Marital status:

Children (names, ages, and contact information):

Other dependents (relationship and contact information):

Education:

Employer:

Employer address and phone:

Prior event/injury that were similar or lawsuits involved in within the last ten years:

Other attorneys consulted with on this matter:

6. Event Information

Date of event:

Time:

Day of week:

Location:

Type of event (accident, injury, arrest, breach of contract occurrence, money owed, etc.)

Weather conditions:

Persons causing the event/injury:

Persons witnessing the event/injury:

Description of what happened:

Description of any medical treatment:

Description of any property, such as an automobile, involved:

Accident or medical reports or other documentation of event/injury:

Report of event/injury made to police, doctor, insurer, or others:

Date and time reports made:

Insurance:

Name and contact information of insurers:

Name and contact information of agent:

Date report made to insurer:

Content of report to insurer:

Insurance benefits statements:

5 *Counseling the Client*

5 *Counseling the Client*

"A lawyer's advice is his stock and trade."

Abraham Lincoln (1809 - 1865)

"One cool judgment is worth a thousand hasty counsels. The thing to do is to supply light and not heat."

Woodrow Wilson (1856 - 1924)

I. COUNSELING

Counseling is a major part of a lawyer's work, because an attorney is so often called on to advise a client, crime victim, witness, or co-counsel in the resolution of a range of problems. This chapter explores how to identify the problem that calls for counseling, set counseling objectives, decide whether to counsel, and determine the extent to which you should counsel. In addition, you will learn counseling techniques and approaches. While our discussion focuses on client counseling, the counseling approaches and techniques ordinarily work just as well for counseling witnesses, co-counsel, paralegals, friends, and family.

Generally, you will be counseling your client on matters directly relating to those for which you were retained. Counseling might involve decisions whether to litigate, testify before a grand jury, obtain a physical examination, present a particular defense, settle the dispute, and so on. When representing clients in matters not involving litigation, counseling may concern tax strategy or business, estate, or trust planning. However, counseling also may involve matters that are not as clearly related to the matters in which you represent the client (a drug problem, personal dispute with a friend). In this chapter, we present an approach to counseling that governs both those situations directly arising from your representation as well as those situations that are only tangentially related to the representation of your client.

II. PLANNING COUNSELING

A. Identifying the Problem

Preparation

Generally, preparation for identifying the counseling needs of a client and the type of counseling technique to use will be much like the preparation for client interviewing. Recall that you should obtain, preferably even in advance of your initial meeting with your client, factual, legal, and personal information about the client. The more you know about and have an appreciation for the client's personality, legal case, and even some of the client's personal affairs, the more readily you will be able to identify the problem.

If you are aware of a matter that potentially may require counseling, even if it is not directly related to the legal matter for which you have been retained, you might ask your client to prepare a written account of the situation (assuming that the matter does not arise unexpectedly and require immediate attention), bring appropriate documents to the counseling meeting, and so forth.

When representing a client, you may be consulted about many different issues, some of which present the need for professional or specialized help. Therefore, it is helpful to maintain a comprehensive list of potential referrals, such as community social services—mental health professionals, hospitals, health treatment centers, accountants, applicable governmental agencies, juvenile facilities, and so on.

Information Gathering

To illustrate how to gather information and identify a problem that requires counseling, assume that you are about to meet a potential client, Malorie Leinart, in a matter referred to as the *Battered Spouse* case. Malorie's husband is Vince Leinart.

INFORMATION GATHERING

The *Battered Spouse* Case

When you meet Malorie at the door of your office and shake her hand, you detect a strong odor of alcohol on Malorie's breath. You ask Malorie, "What can I do for you?" Malorie states, "I want to leave my husband."

You need to obtain information that will help you identify the counseling problem. You might immediately think of two potential problems to explore. Your first inclination is to suggest legal advice, such as filing a petition for dissolution. But you should resist the tendency of the lawyer in you to put your client's problems into a legal box. At this stage, you need to decide if you know enough about the facts. Your second inclination might be to explore the extent and nature of Malorie's drinking problem. But does she in fact have a drinking problem?

Rather than guessing where to begin, you should gather additional information. Because interviewing and counseling are often a simultaneous process, let's concentrate on information-gathering for this counseling matter. Suppose that you ask, "Can you tell me more about your situation?" Malorie responds:

> "Vince, my husband, beat me and the kids last night. He's done this for the past eight years we've been married. I am scared he is going to kill one of us."

Now, because you have gathered information rather than jumping right to the legal or obvious problems, you can tentatively identify some potential issues: dissolution, marital counseling, possible assault and battery, child abuse, and possibly help for Malorie's drinking.

Keep in mind that Malorie could request advice on a wide range of subjects—some related to the matter you are retained to handle, some remote, some seemingly purely personal. Also, unlike the potential counseling matter, some problems for counseling do not easily identify themselves. A client may not come in and readily explain her situation as Malorie did: "I am a battered woman; help me." Rather, the person may not recognize the full scope of potential problems involved ("My husband and I don't get along. He comes home after drinking a lot "). Or she may not be willing to acknowledge the problem ("I understand; I'm real frustrating to be around. . . That bruise? I bumped into a cabinet door").

B.   Setting Counseling Objectives

After identifying the problem, you will need to set the objectives for your counseling. Generally, in counseling there are three interrelated objectives.

Objective 1: Maintaining a Good Attorney-Client Relationship

When you contemplate counseling your client, it is prudent to keep in mind that you want to always maintain a good working relationship with the client.

All the good advice in the world will fall on deaf ears if you have lost the client's trust and good will. For example, if you confront Malorie about her drinking and counsel her to get help for her drinking problem, she may become defensive or offended. So, always remember that your objective is to maintain a good relationship and the techniques you use to approach the problem may be as important as the advice you give.

Objectives 2 and 3: Achieving the Client's Long-Term Case Strategy and Achieving the Client's Short-Term Counseling Objectives

Generally, in counseling there are two additional interrelated objectives:

- Your client's *long-term case strategy*—the ultimate result that your client desires regarding the matter that you are retained to handle and
- Your client's *short-term counseling objectives*—resolution of particular matters about which your client is requesting counseling.

These interrelated objectives are significant aspects of your legal representation of the client. They are important to achieve, and they require the use of all of your legal and people skills. If you feel you do not have certain skills, such as an ability to interact with your client regarding counseling, it is imperative you seek assistance to improve this skill, perhaps through a Continuing Legal Education program or other support. Improving this skill will make you a better attorney in the long run.

COUNSELING OBJECTIVES

The *Battered Spouse* Case

In the *Battered-spouse* illustration, you will need to identify your client's short-term counseling objectives, particularly since they may focus your activity in directions that differ somewhat from your case strategy.

Long-term Case Strategy

Obtaining a dissolution is a long-term case strategy that involves bringing a full-blown law suit.

Short-term Counseling Objectives

Short-term counseling objectives that are directly related to your long-term case strategy for Malorie and the children may focus on protecting Malorie and her children from further physical harm by Vince. As such, you may need to counsel her about the advisability of locating temporary emergency shelter; securing short-term financial support should she leave home; arranging private therapeutic counseling and some marital counseling; and seeking police protection and a restraining order from the court. Note that you must determine whether in your jurisdiction you have an ethical and/or legal duty, transcending the duty to maintain client confidences, to report crimes of child abuse and spousal battery to the proper authorities regardless of the client's wishes. Some of these objectives can be accomplished by filing for a dissolution, others by your counseling advice and referral to appropriate community services.

C. Deciding Whether to Counsel

Deciding whether to counsel depends primarily upon whether the subject of the counseling is related to the matter for which you have been retained. If it is directly related to the matter of representation, the decision generally is that counseling is within the sphere of the employment. You do not need to counsel your client on matters outside that scope.

TO COUNSEL OR NOT

Concerning the Matter of Representation

The *Battered Spouse* Case

Counseling Malorie concerning her dissolution or child custody litigation is part of your legal representation. If Malorie seeks your advice as to the child custody hearing, you must decide how to counsel her based on the case strategy goal of obtaining custody of the children for Malorie. However, there is more to Malorie's situation that requires consideration and, more importantly, has an impact on the case strategy. Whether and how you choose to address that is a critical decision.

Concerning Malorie's drinking, you might be tempted to respond, "Malorie, I am here and available to advise you about your dissolution and child custody; everything else is your problem." Your response might be appropriate because the drinking problem is a personal matter.

However, her drinking may have an impact on the case strategy. In your opinion, counseling may be needed so that her drinking does not negatively affect the case. To determine whether counseling is proper, you must analyze the effect that the short-term counseling objectives might have upon your case strategy. Consider asking yourself. "How is my client's dissolution and child custody affected by the short-term counseling

continues ▶

matter—Malorie's drinking?" Malorie's long-term case strategy might be affected by evidence of her drinking—that is, such issues as her inability to provide adequate care for the children because of hangovers, poor witness credibility if the case goes to trial, and so on. Therefore, you might decide to counsel your client.

Other Matters

On the other hand, if the counseling matter does not remotely affect your client's case strategy, you might be inclined to not counsel.

We in no way suggest that being a lawyer means that you have a license to ignore human needs and remain insensitive to human conditions. Your role as an attorney is often critical in a client's life, and as such, you should consider the many interrelated facets of the representation. But you need to be aware of the inherent risks in your involvement.

You need to consider the impact of counseling on sensitive issues and whether this might strain or confuse your attorney-client relationship. You need to consider whether counseling interferes with the case strategy. You need to recognize and be prepared to respond appropriately to circumstances that range from times when your client just needs someone to talk to, to times when the client might be on the edge of suicide (in this case professional help should be sought immediately), to times when the client is in need of solely legal representation.

After considering the case and the inherent risks associated with counseling, you must determine what is best for the client during your representation of the matter.

D. The Extent of Counseling

You have decided to counsel your client. Now you must examine the extent of your involvement. The extent of your counseling involves a choice that falls somewhere along a spectrum ranging from the most intensive type of involvement (e.g., you provide the therapy), to the least intensive type of involvement (e.g., you make a referral to someone else or an agency). No specific rules exist that we can tell you to apply that will magically help decide the scope of your involvement. But we can suggest a number of factors to consider:

- Your comfort zone,
- Your competency level in the area of counseling,

- The effect on your long-term case strategy,
- The availability of other counselors (among family and friends, or community agencies),
- The nature of the problem, and
- Your relationship with your client.

COMFORT ZONE AND COMPETENCY

In the Comfort Zone—But Outside the Zone of Competency

The *Battered Spouse* Case

Suppose you are the type of person who enjoys helping people with their problems. Caution: beware of acting outside the zone of your competency. Like most attorneys, you probably lack the educational skills and training to engage in therapeutic counseling. Therefore, generally, unless you are specifically trained to be a therapist, as a lawyer you cannot and should not attempt to give Malorie therapeutic advice about her drinking problem. That is beyond your competence and expertise. You should limit your counseling to those things you are trained to do as an attorney.

Outside the Comfort Zone

Now suppose that you are the type of person who feels uncomfortable counseling on any matter that does not present a legal issue directly related to the legal case. You might believe that Malorie's drinking is none of your business. Does that mean you can say no to counseling Malorie? As previously discussed, many seemingly peripheral matters may prove to affect your client's legal case. Your personal comfort zone is, therefore, not a reason to avoid counseling, but it will influence the scope of that counseling.

Suppose that you want to limit the extent of your counseling role regarding Malorie's drinking: You wish only to advise Malorie to seek professional help for her drinking problem. Even this limited role has scope decisions. You will need to determine the extent of your role in referral. Will you suggest an appropriate person or agency? Will you set up the appointment? Accompany Malorie to the appointment or send someone from your office? Follow up to see if Malorie kept the appointment? The extent of your involvement even in this limited counseling role depends on many of the same factors discussed in determining the spectrum of counseling advice.

E. Counseling Advice

There are usually many solutions available to resolve a problem, each of which might have attendant risks and benefits (deciding whether to settle the case, present a defense, pose for newspaper photographs). Our approach entails evaluating the alternative solutions in the context of considering the solution's effect on the case strategy and the client's objectives.

The Process

The process for coming up with options and advice for the client once you have identified the problem is as follows:

- The first step is to *identify the various solutions* to the client's problem.
- Second, each potential solution is *evaluated* within the set of counseling objectives: (1) maintaining the good attorney-client relationship, (2) meeting the client's short-term objectives, and (3) either advancing or at least not impeding the long-term case strategy.
- Third, utilizing the partnership approach (described in the next section), the options and your advice are *presented to the client* for decision making.

As an illustration, let us turn to a more problematic situation in the *Battered Spouse* case. The counseling matter is tangentially related to your long-term case strategy but will the advice you give harm or hinder your case strategy?

ADVICE

The *Battered Spouse* Case

Imagine that Malorie wants a dissolution and custody of the children. You have commenced litigation by filing a complaint. Malorie owns a house in which she and the children presently reside. There is no dispute as to Malorie's separate and distinct ownership. Malorie asks your advice: "I want to sell the house. It just has too many bad memories. What do you think?"

Step 1—Identifying the Solutions

Here Malorie has not only identified the problem—"bad memories" but also she has proposed a solution—sell the house.

Step 2—Evaluate the Solutions

Although the two matters (bad memories and the long-term case strategy) are not directly related to one another, potentially decisions as to one could affect the other. Your case strategy as to the child custody case is to obtain the best result you can for your client: custody of the children and adequate child support. If you advise your client to sell the house for the sake of her emotional well-being, however, that decision may be harmful to your legal position on custody since the house is a positive factor for child custody. It provides a place for the children to live and allows the children to remain in the same school and maintain friendships. Sale of the house may be disruptive to the children. If you advise Malorie to keep the house, on the other hand, she may face a sadness and depression that will affect the quality of her life and her children's lives.

You need to consider how counseling advice about the house sale can be reconciled with your case strategy as to the child custody case. In this example, your client's needs in the custody case and in the house sale appear to be divergent (need for stability in the children's life versus moving and finding personal peace that will result in disrupting the continuity in the children's lives). In dealing with this apparent dilemma, you could apply a process we suggest for reconciling what appear to be divergent positions. In Malorie's case, by examining the underlying interests that motivate each of the two seemingly divergent matters of house sale and child custody (a home for the children and the stability afforded by a house in the same general neighborhood area; your client's need to start a new life unburdened by constant reminders of the painful past), you might be able to develop alternatives that could further both your client's short-term objectives and your case strategy. You could advise her to sell the house and use the house sale money to purchase another house in the same general neighborhood. Now that you have evaluated the options, it's time to take the third step—to discuss the solutions that you have evaluated with Malorie so she can consider the ramifications of selling or not selling the house and reach a decision.

The Client's Questionable Decision

Suppose that after you have discussed all the various options and considerations with Malorie, she decides that the house must be sold. The money from the house sale might be totally inadequate to purchase alternative housing in the same neighborhood, and rental housing may not be available.

The decision on the short-term matter seems harmful to your case strategy in the child custody case. If that occurs, and your client insists on pursuing the short-term objective, your only alternative might be to counsel your client to accept the consequences and then to put forth your best effort to minimize the damage to your representational strategy ("The source of stability that Malorie gives her children is not some home in some neighborhood. It is her loving and strength that provides their stable environment, and as the psychologist's affidavit states, to remain in that house would have been so painful for Malorie as to jeopardize her ability to provide that loving strength"). Or, at some point, you may even consider changing your long-term case strategy. If the client's decision puts you in the position where you would be committing unethical or illegal conduct, you must withdraw from representing the client.

III. COUNSELING TECHNIQUES

A. Authoritarian and Partnership Approaches

Counseling techniques will depend on your basic approach to counseling. Two common approaches are the authoritarian and the partnership approaches. A lawyer could draw upon one or the other depending on the circumstances while utilizing one of the approaches as the predominant style of counseling.

Authoritarian

Some attorneys insist on, and their clients acquiesce in, attorney-controlled decision making: "I will tell you how this case is going to be run; how you are going to act in court; . . . " Such choices are a matter of style or sometimes of necessity because of the personality or abilities of the client. For example, some clients would be petrified by the entire process if their attorneys did not assume the role of absolute authority figure. However, this approach can result in a disgruntled client, who desired a more collaborative role and felt left out of the process. This is a troublesome approach, one that a client will either embrace or abhor.

Also, you should be aware that this type of approach might present ethical problems, as discussed in the next section on the partnership approach, because the attorney may make important case decisions. Even if you follow this authoritarianism you should explain the decision to your client, although it might not be a full, meaningful consultation with the client.

Partnership

Counseling can be approached as a partnership between the attorney and the client. A counseling partnership implies that the attorney is competent to give the advice the client seeks; that the attorney acts as an adviser, not decision maker; that the client is receptive to receiving advice, and that the client is able to make appropriate decisions on his or her own behalf.

The partnership approach is also compatible with the approach espoused by the ABA Model Rules of Professional Conduct. Rule 1.2 (a) states:

> . . . a lawyer shall abide by a client's decisions concerning the objectives of representation and . . . shall consult with the client as to the means by which they are to be pursued. A lawyer may take such action on behalf of the client as is impliedly authorized to carry out the representation. A lawyer shall abide by a client's decision whether to settle a matter. In a criminal case, the lawyer shall abide by the client's decision, after consultation with the lawyer, as to a plea to be entered, whether to waive a jury and whether the client will testify.

Further, Rule 1.4 requires the lawyer to consult with the client and keep the client informed. According to that Rule, the attorney is to keep the client reasonably informed about the status of the case, consult with the client about how to accomplish the client's goals, and promptly inform the client of any decision or circumstance where the client's informed consent is necessary, and so on. The Comments to Rule 1.4 embrace the Rules partnership approach as follows:

- "(1) Reasonable communication between the lawyer and the client is necessary for the client effectively to participate in the representation. . .
- "(5) The client should have sufficient information to participate intelligently in decision making concerning the objectives of the representation and the means by which they are to be pursued, to the extent the client is willing and able to do so."

We advise you to employ the partnership approach if it seems a plausible one given the particular client. Our partiality stems from our desire to work in a collaborative mode with clients because we believe that, for most, they will be a better informed, more effective advocate in such a relationship, and we find this approach is in total harmony with the Rules of Professional Conduct. Naturally, because under this approach the client is the decision maker and partner, the client may decide that he or she does not want to be heavily involved in the case and may authorize you to act without detailed communication.

To illustrate the approaches, imagine that you represent Harvey in an eviction action.

AUTHORITARIAN versus PARTNERSHIP

The *Eviction* Case

Harvey is a shy, disheveled young man. He has begun to telephone you once or twice a week to discuss his eviction case and just chat. You have invited Harvey to your office to counsel and prepare him for his deposition. Let's begin planning techniques for counseling Harvey.

When you counsel Harvey, you want to prepare him for his deposition. You are particularly concerned that Harvey make a good impression at the deposition; a good impression will surely aid your case strategy of eventual settlement. Therefore, you want to advise him on how to dress, how to answer questions, and generally on how to present himself.

Authoritarian Approach

If you use this approach with Harvey, you might advise Harvey outright: "This is how I would like you to dress for your deposition . . ."

Partnership Approach

Let's consider performance techniques that encourage a counseling partnership. For example, consider your professional demeanor—do you encourage client discussion? As in interviewing, you can promote client discussion by posing open-ended questions; by listening to your client (reflective and active listening); and by choosing language that generally establishes and maintains rapport and empathy with your client. Deposition preparation of Harvey that employs a partnership style might sound like this:

> "Now, let me explain the setting of the deposition. It will take place in plaintiff's counsel's office. Of course, all the attorneys will be dressed just like they are in court—in business suits. You want to create a good impression. Let's talk about what would be appropriate dress for you as the deponent. What would you like to wear to create a good business-like impression?"

B.   Written or Verbal Advice

Will your advice be written or verbal? Will it be effective to send Harvey a letter advising him about his deposition preparation—how to respond to questions, his choice of appropriate dress, the role of a deposition, and so on? Or will you consider sending him a DVD where he can see what you are talking about? Generally, written advice provides a structure for documenting and organizing relevant information for your client. In a letter, whether it is an opinion letter or one specifically describing the deposition, a basic structure can generally be used. You can identify the issue or problem, provide the information that you considered and relied on (legal and nonlegal), evaluate the information, and present your opinion as to potential options and the consequences. A letter explaining the deposition process that also includes specific instructions can therefore achieve many of your counseling ends.

But written advice can have disadvantages. It might be given too much weight by a client merely because it is written and seems more official. A letter may also appear too business-like and impersonal and thus be a some-what alienating device. Or the letter might contain flaws because you did not have all the information. For example, even though an opinion letter may contain a disclaimer as to its inaccuracies or explanations as to its incompleteness, it may nevertheless be read as authoritative.

As you can imagine, verbal advice also has advantages and disadvantages. Although it can be more informal, it can be disorganized, it is more time-consuming, and the client can more easily forget what you have said or may attend to your remarks in a very selective way.

IV. FOLLOW-UP ON COUNSELING

You should plan what will happen if you give particular counseling advice. That plan should contain follow-up to see if the advice was followed, whether the problem was rectified, and case re-evaluation.

FOLLOW-UP

The *Eviction* Case

In the *Eviction* case, suppose that Harvey fails to follow your advice and disagrees about how he should present himself at the deposition. Then you must reevaluate your case in light of Harvey's refusal to follow your advice, considering the impact of that refusal on your case strategy. It probably will make a favorable settlement unlikely.

V. ETHICAL CONSIDERATIONS

You need to consider ethical dilemmas that can occur and how these concerns might affect the content of your counseling. Many of the ethical considerations discussed in Chapter 4 on forging the client relationship are applicable to counseling the client. More specifically, the following are ethical considerations that should be considered when counseling:

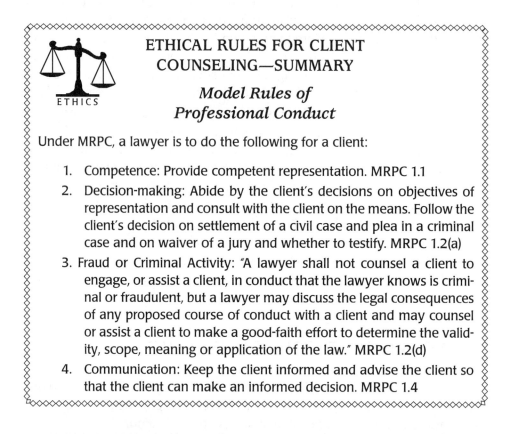

ETHICAL RULES FOR CLIENT COUNSELING—SUMMARY

Model Rules of Professional Conduct

Under MRPC, a lawyer is to do the following for a client:

1. Competence: Provide competent representation. MRPC 1.1
2. Decision-making: Abide by the client's decisions on objectives of representation and consult with the client on the means. Follow the client's decision on settlement of a civil case and plea in a criminal case and on waiver of a jury and whether to testify. MRPC 1.2(a)
3. Fraud or Criminal Activity: "A lawyer shall not counsel a client to engage, or assist a client, in conduct that the lawyer knows is criminal or fraudulent, but a lawyer may discuss the legal consequences of any proposed course of conduct with a client and may counsel or assist a client to make a good-faith effort to determine the validity, scope, meaning or application of the law." MRPC 1.2(d)
4. Communication: Keep the client informed and advise the client so that the client can make an informed decision. MRPC 1.4

✔ COUNSELING CHECKLIST

The following are standards of performance for effective counseling:

Identifying the Problem

❑ Prepare for identifying the needs of the client by learning as much as possible about the client's case, personality, and personal situation.

❑ Maintain a comprehensive list of referral resources, e.g., social service agencies, treatment centers, and so on.

❑ Keep an open mind and gather as much information as possible.

Setting the Counseling Objectives

❑ Keep in mind maintaining a good relationship with the client.

❑ Have a long-term case strategy.
❑ Set short-term objectives for counseling.

Decide Whether to Counsel

❑ Generally counsel if short-term objectives for counseling either advance or at least are not inconsistent with the long-term case strategy.
❑ Give serious consideration to not counseling if the matter is outside the scope of the representation or the scope of competency.

Extent of Counseling

Determine the extent of counseling within a range, from no counseling to intensive personal counseling to referral to some other person or agency based upon these factors:

❑ The lawyer's comfort zone,
❑ The lawyer's competency,
❑ The effect on the case strategy,
❑ The availability of other counselors,
❑ The nature of the problem, and
❑ The relationship with your client.

Counseling Advice

❑ Identify the potential solutions to the problem.
❑ Evaluate the potential solutions by assessing whether they further the client's short and long-term objectives and the objective of maintaining a good relationship with the client.

Counseling Techniques

❑ Recognize the authoritarian and partnership approaches and styles and the advantages and disadvantages of each approach.
❑ Consider whether the advice is better communicated verbally, in writing, or both.

Follow-up on Counseling

❑ Follow-up on counseling to determine whether the problem has been addressed and solved.
❑ Based upon the follow-up findings, reevaluate to determine what steps, if any, need to be taken.

Ethical Considerations

❑ Keep the client informed and advise the client so that the client can make informed decisions.

❑ Abide by the client's decisions on the objectives of the representation and consult with the client on the means to reach those objectives.

❑ Follow the client's decision on settlement of a civil case and plea in a criminal case and on waiver of a jury and whether to testify.

❑ Do not knowingly counsel or assist a client in criminal or fraudulent conduct.

6 *Witness Interviewing*

6 *Witness Interviewing*

I. THE WITNESS INTERVIEW

This chapter covers identifying and locating witnesses, deciding whom you should interview, planning the logistics involved (when and where to do the interview and whether you should be accompanied or do it alone), setting objectives for the interview, encouraging the witness to communicate with you, gathering information pertinent to the case, and preparing the witness for trial. The witness to be interviewed could be friendly, neutral, or adverse. The interview approach offered here is the same for all witnesses (except for those client-specific areas discussed in Chapter 4), so the witness could be your client, a prospective client, or a person who saw or heard something or somehow is involved in the case.

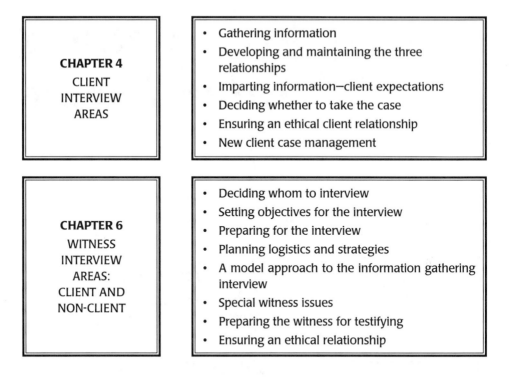

CHAPTER 4 CLIENT INTERVIEW AREAS	• Gathering information • Developing and maintaining the three relationships • Imparting information—client expectations • Deciding whether to take the case • Ensuring an ethical client relationship • New client case management
CHAPTER 6 WITNESS INTERVIEW AREAS: CLIENT AND NON-CLIENT	• Deciding whom to interview • Setting objectives for the interview • Preparing for the interview • Planning logistics and strategies • A model approach to the information gathering interview • Special witness issues • Preparing the witness for testifying • Ensuring an ethical relationship

II. WHOM TO INTERVIEW

Identifying and Locating Witnesses and Other Evidence

Your client and friendly witnesses can be the best sources for identifying and locating other witnesses. During your client and witness interviews, you can inquire about other persons who were present at the event in question and their whereabouts. You will also want to ask the witnesses about physical and documentary evidence and where these are located. Formal discovery (e.g., interrogatories) will enable you to uncover other potential witnesses. If the witness was present at the scene of the event when it took place, if possible you would want to interview that witness at the scene to better understand what took place and where it happened at the site.

Deciding Whom to Interview

Whom do you want to interview? The answer is that you want to interview everyone who sheds light on your case theory or your opponent's case theory. However, for many reasons, particularly time and money constraints, this may not be possible. You should never rely upon a statement by a witness in your pretrial preparation or call a witness to the stand at trial unless you have personally interviewed that witness. The stakes are too high and not meeting with the witness before beginning direct examination can result in surprising and potentially devastating testimony. While this is our advice to you based on our experience, some lawyers will interview only expert witnesses and essential fact witnesses before trial. And sometimes there are reasons for not interviewing a witness or witnesses.

What are the reasons you may not want to interview a witness? The witness may be too far away geographically to visit without great expense; the witness may already have given a statement to some agency or to the police that tells you all you need to know; you may know that the witness will refuse to speak with you; you may not be able to reach him or her on the phone, and the impeachment value of this refusal at trial is not worth the time and expense of tracking the witness down at home or the workplace, you may not want to give the witness a sense of how you will approach him or her at an upcoming deposition or trial, and you are concerned that the interview could provide the witness with some information that he or she could use to prepare for you. Of course, in an interview you could also get a sense of the witness and pin him or her down on helpful points for the subsequent examination under oath. But you might already have planned to take his or her deposition anyway and feel there is little advantage to doing a prior interview.

If you decide you do want to interview the witness and the witness is represented, under ABA Model Rule of Professional Conduct 4.2, you cannot do so ethically without first obtaining his or her attorney's permission. If the witness is unrepresented and reasonably facing potential liability in the matter you are investigating, you must make the interests you are representing clear. ABA Model Rule 4.3.

III. PLANNING FOR THE INTERVIEW

A. Setting Objectives

Your witness interview will be designed either:

- to gather information about the case
- to prepare the witness for settlement discussions, a deposition, or trial, or
- a combination of these objectives

Later in this chapter we will discuss techniques that you can use to prepare a witness for settlement discussions, a deposition, or trial. But, for now, let's examine the first objective—gathering information, because understanding its importance will guide you in planning the information you want to obtain in their interview.

The information gathered in your witness interviews provides one of the most important sources for understanding your, and your opponent's, case theory, handling your factual assertions, dealing with any negative information that arises, observing the witness's credibility, and providing a basis for settlement negotiation. The primary reason for obtaining information from the witness is to know both the good and the bad in advance so you can deal with it. The information helps evolve, support, or modify your case theory and probe the strengths and weaknesses of your opponent's theory.

Even though the case theory provides a main focus for the witness interview and the information obtained from it, the case theory should not constitute a constraint on the breadth of your information gathering. The information you obtain should provide a basis for understanding the facts of your case and determining which facts you will assert as determinative in the case. A good attorney can and must deal with virtually every potential negative that arises, but it's far better if these negatives do not come packaged as last-second surprises. Hearing them from a witness well in advance allows for adequate investigation and preparation. The witness interview gives you the first chance to observe the witness's demeanor and whether what is said is credible. Also, the information you learn may assist with negotiations or settlement of the case.

B. Preparing for the Interview

Familiarizing Yourself with the Case

With these objectives in mind, you can begin background preparation for your interviews by reviewing your case theory and all the factual and legal information you have obtained and then factoring in any information you can find about the particular witness. If you are dealing with an expert witness, you will also want to obtain a copy of the expert's vitae, read technical articles and texts to familiarize yourself with the general vocabulary in the area of expertise, review works written by the expert, and even prepare yourself by talking to other experts. Also, there are some subscription services that maintain a vast database containing the various trial and deposition testimony of thousands of forensic experts. A discussion of the process of selecting an expert appears in Chapter 3.

You will want to gather together all available documentary and physical evidence that you want to discuss with the witness. This could include photographs, diagrams, contracts, and anything else that sheds light on the case. Determine what in a specific document is important for the witness to confirm, refute, or elaborate on.

Prepare the Potential Legal Theories—The Value of Jury Instructions

You should familiarize yourself with applicable patterned jury instructions. Keep in mind that jury instructions are not persuasive legal authority in arguments to the judges. Pattern instructions ordinarily have been drafted by committee and even if they have an appellate court's stamp of approval and have been published as guides for trial lawyers to use in drafting proposed instructions, they are not the jurisdiction's law. Rather, trial and appellate courts rely on statutes, appellate decisions, court rules, and other legal authority in making decisions. Pattern jury instructions, however, do constitute the law for jurors, and they can help you in creating legal theories.

As an example of how pattern jury instructions can be utilized to construct legal theories, imagine you are representing a plaintiff in a wrongful death case. You know that damages are one element of your legal theory, and that part of your witness interviewing should be directed at finding information regarding this element. However, if you look at the instruction the jury is likely to receive for wrongful death damages, you will see that damages contain sub-elements. One factor in the instruction for a jury in assessing the measure of damages for wrongful death is that they should consider "[w]hat the decedent could reasonably have been expected to contribute to his [survivor, children, dependent mother and father] in the way of support, love, care, guidance, training, instruction and protection." You will find jury instructions, such as the one governing wrongful death damages, can provide a precise focus for your interview, and will alert you to seek information that directly corresponds to the very categories (or sub-elements) of damages that the jury will consider in its deliberations.

JURY INSTRUCTIONS

The *Wrongful Death* Case

Suppose you want to interview a neighbor who knows the survivors and knew the decedent. Using the pattern jury instruction on damages, you might explore the various sub-elements within the instruction when interviewing the neighbor and plan to ask:

- "Can you tell me about Donald's relationship with his children?"
- "Was he actively involved with them in sports?"
- "Did he have any hobbies?"
- "So, he taught Kathy how to play the piano. How often were they involved in this activity together?"

C. Planning Logistics and Strategies

When to Interview

"The sooner the better" is the answer to the question of "when should you interview a witness?" There are advantages to talking to witnesses early in a case—not the least of which is to satisfy the legal requirement of Federal Rule of Civil Procedure 11: "Representations to the Court require an attorney or unrepresented party is certifying that to the best of the person's knowledge, information, and belief, formed after a reasonable inquiry under the circumstances," that the claims are nonfrivolous and have evidentiary support before a complaint is filed. There are also tactical advantages to interviewing the witness before the battle lines have been clearly drawn. The witness may not yet appreciate the full significance of his or her information or have even thought through his or her involvement. Accordingly, the witness may be less selective in the information he or she provides and how he or she characterizes it. Also, details will be fresher in his or her mind and the witness will not be as likely to have begun the process of "filling in." People like their stories to be complete and coherent. Thus, over time, details that do not neatly fit together or gaps in a story will gradually be filled in by the mind, without conscious realization, as the tale is retold. On the other hand, without a real sense of what the case may be about, you may have difficulty in the interview knowing what information to pursue as it emerges, where to focus your questions, and so on. This could be a real problem if you are likely to get only one crack at interviewing a particular witness.

Although you may have only a single opportunity to interview your opponent's witnesses, it is common and good practice to meet with your own witnesses two or more times. At the early interviews, you will concentrate on gathering information about the case. Later, you will meet with your witness to prepare the witness to testify at a deposition and/or at trial.

Where to Conduct the Interview

Where you interview the witness is a matter of judgment, of choosing between the alternatives: the home, their office, your office, a coffee shop, or the scene of the crime or incident. The objective for the interview—gathering information—will dictate your choice for the interview's location.

Your Office

Getting the witness to come to *your office* has a number of advantages. You don't have to take time traveling out of the office and you have access to a variety of helpful resources—secretaries and devices for taking statements, extensive case files and legal materials, duplicating equipment, your own telephone, and so on. If the meeting is to be held in your office, you may want to plan the desired mood. Are you comfortable, with the witness and you facing each other in padded armchairs? Are you exuding authority, with you sitting behind a large desk and the witness positioned at a distance?

Witness's Home

A witness will likely be confident and at ease at *home*. When you interview a witness in his or her home, you gain insight into the person's background. The witness will generally lack the sense of hurry and self-consciousness that often accompanies meetings at the workplace, where the time clock ticks and fellow workers pass by and stare. The witness's comfort and ease can assist you in building a rapport and thereby gaining information. However, if you just appear at someone's home without prior invitation, you risk resentment and perhaps refusal to allow the interview because of your unannounced intrusion into the witness's sanctum. On the other hand, if you call ahead, the witness may also refuse, or initially agree but then back out when the witness has "had time to think about it" or to talk to the opposing party (with whom his or her sympathies align) and not be home at the time of the appointment. An alternative place might be to suggest a neutral public place, such as a coffee shop. But be mindful of noise and being overheard.

Witness's Office

On some occasions, you will decide to interview the witness at the *witness's office* because the visit will reveal useable information to you. Normally you will interview or depose your opponent's expert witness in your office. However, on the occasions that you go to your opponent's expert's office it may be seen as a show of courtesy, a recognition of the expert's tight time schedule. This may make the expert more receptive to your questioning. As you look across the expert's bookshelves, you may spot books that you can use on cross-examination under the learned treatise hearsay exception (asking the witness on cross, "It is reliable authority, isn't it? Isn't it a book you have on your own bookshelf, doctor?").

The Scene

Interviewing a witness at the *scene* where the event took place (e.g., the crime scene or the scene of the automobile collision) will give you a much better understanding of what took place. The witness can point out where events occurred. To get even a clearer picture of what happened, the witness may be able to demonstrate the incident. For example, a robbery victim could show the prosecutor how far the defendant was from her when he demanded her purse. Finally, when you see the scene, you will get ideas about how you can use visuals (e.g. diagram, photographs) to display the scene in settlement discussions or a brochure or to the jury.

Whether or Not to Be Accompanied

When you are interviewing a friendly witness or your client, generally you will not need to be accompanied. This is not to say that you can't have another person, such as an investigator, present and taking notes.

However, if there is the slightest possibility that the witness may be adverse to you or there is any reasonable possibility they could change or recharacterize what they tell you when it comes time for them to testify, always have another person present as a prover witness. As a lawyer at trial, you are prohibited (except under extremely narrow circumstances) from testifying as a witness. Generally, ethical rules forbid an attorney from testifying in the same case the attorney is trying. ABA Model Rule 3.7. If that witness that you interviewed by yourself changes his or her story at trial, you will not be able to impeach the witness with the prior inconsistent interview statement. However, if you had a witness—a prover—present, you can confront the witness with the statement and call your prover in rebuttal if the witness denies making the statement.

Preserving the Interview Information

You have choices to make about how you wish to preserve the information. You can take notes, tape or video the interview, or have the witness write out a witness statement or sign a transcribed statement.

At least three considerations go into deciding whether to record the interview: likely disclosure, the need for diplomacy, and the need to have the witness adopt the statement.

Disclosure

First, before you take a witness's statement, be aware that eventually it is likely to be seen by the opposing party. The witness statement may be used as evidence at trial under certain circumstances. For example, even if the work-product privilege is held to apply to witness statements unaccompanied by any of your analysis (which is a legal position that is not certain to prevail), the privilege may be overcome if the opponent can show special need. Likewise, if the witness reviews the statement for a deposition or trial, then the statement may be admissible pursuant to evidentiary rules concerning using documents to refresh a witness's recollection at trial or deposition.

Diplomacy

Second, if you do decide that you want to pin down the witness with a recorded statement, you might have to use some diplomacy in getting the witness to cooperate ("I want to accurately record your statement. This is for your protection as well as mine. No one will be able to say that you said anything but what is recorded here").

Adoption of the Statement

Third, to be useful for impeachment, the witness must adopt the statement. Make the witness read it over carefully before he or she signs it. Have the witness write in any corrections if you have had the statement typed. The point is that you do not want the witness to be able to claim later while testifying that the statement is incorrect as to some crucial point. In fact, some attorneys deliberately put minor typos and mistakes in the statement that the witness then finds and corrects by hand. This is to raise the inference that the witness reviewed the statement carefully in order to undercut any subsequent claim that she "never really read it." We view this as a questionable practice that does not reflect the level of candor and integrity that counsel should exhibit.

IV. MODEL APPROACH TO THE INFORMATION GATHERING INTERVIEW

You need a structure for your interview to gather information.

- It should have a guiding objective.
- It should involve rapport building.
- It should have a beginning, middle, and an end.

The following is an approach that you can use and at its core is the "funnel structure" for identifying and gathering information from the witness.

A. Case Theory as a Guide

Your witness interview is aimed at gathering information:

- information that supports, undercuts, or alters your legal or factual theories (and will, therefore, also influence your overall representational strategy as well as the content of your pleadings, your future fact-gathering, and your strategy if you eventually go to trial);
- information that bears on the credibility of the witness (which will also affect your case theory); and
- information that is relevant to a negotiated settlement.

The hypothetical *Coach Bagshaw* case is used here to illustrate how the model interviewing approach works. As you will recall from Chapter 3, to prepare for the information gathering part of the Bagshaw interview, you will recall that you have attempted to familiarize yourself with the case. After your initial phone conversation with Coach Bagshaw, you went online to search the archives of the local newspaper. You refreshed your memory about her prior conflicts with Mansfield University's administration, the gambling investigations, her termination three days ago, and other facts. You will need to review the case details contained on pages 90-91.

You prepared the potential legal theories on which to base your case by doing a quick review of recent wrongful termination appellate decisions. And, you reviewed the state's pattern jury instructions on wrongful termination to determine the elements that may need to prove. You have not had time to research the regulatory powers of the Collegiate Sports Commission (CSC).

B.   Developing a Rapport

You want to establish a rapport with the witness so the witness will cooperate during the interview, allow you to conduct subsequent interviews, if necessary, and not fight when examined by you at a deposition, evidentiary hearing, or trial. With Coach Bagshaw, you have engaged in small talk and expressed empathy for her situation.

C.   Gathering Basic Information

At some point, you want to collect critical information about the witness's background and about how to contact the witness. When and how this is done depends primarily on who the witness is. With a client or prospective client, such as Coach Bagshaw, you or your office staff may collect this at the outset using the Information Report contained in Chapter 4 at pages 91-92; it contains the critical information about the prospective client or client and how to contact the person. With a friendly witness, you also might seek this information at the outset of the interview. On the other hand, with a neutral or adverse witness, you might seek this information after you have determined whether the witness is of value to you and after you have established a relationship where you are confident that the person will give you accurate information. Because witnesses relocate, you want the contact information to include home, work, and cell phone numbers; work and home addresses, and contact information for friends and relatives. Also, you want to determine when the witness may be unavailable so you know about potential conflicts with deposition, settlement negotiations, and trial dates.

Background information (e.g., age, education, employment, family situation, life experiences, and so on) is important not only in helping you gauge how good a witness will be when testifying but also in constructing your persuasive factual story and in determining relationships between the parties and witnesses. With an expert witness, the person's training and experience in the field is needed to qualify the expert at trial. With a lay witness, the personal history will help you develop the human story that is essential to persuading the fact finder. You want to know the bad and the good. You want to assure the witness that it is important that all the harmful information be revealed to you because only then can you seek to protect the witness. Often, the other side is aware of the harmful information. If you are unaware of damaging information, you cannot protect the witness by, for example, making a motion in limine to exclude the witness's prior conviction that does not meet the requirements of Evidence Rule 609.

You also will want to know the relationships between the parties and this witness. Does this witness have a bias in favor or against one of the parties? Does the witness have an interest in the outcome of the action?

D. Funnel Structure of the Interview

Attorneys approach and organize a witness interview in a variety of ways. The widely used four-step "funnel" organization (so termed because its information-gathering focus starts broadly, then begins to narrow) is useful in achieving the basic objectives of this skills performance. If the "funnel" approach is perceived as a general, flexible guide and not a rigid, mathematical formula, it may be your best method for obtaining the information you need. After all, not every attorney and client will impart information and develop a relationship in exactly the same manner and sequence. An interview conforming to the funnel model is based on the four steps graphically illustrated as follows:

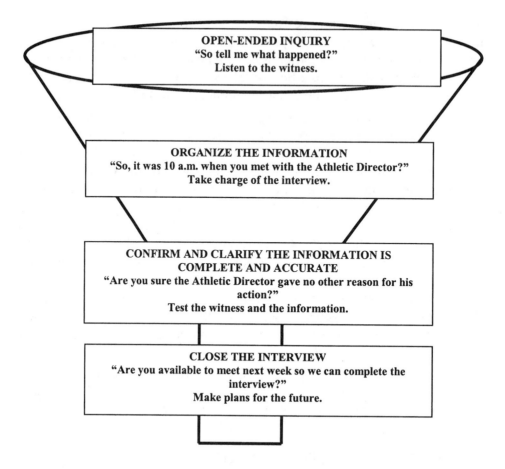

Step 1. Open-ended Inquiry

After introducing yourself and putting the witness at ease by gathering background information about the witness, you begin to develop a rapport with the witness and to gain information by using nonleading questions (e.g., "So, tell me, what happened?"). This sort of inquiry allows the witness to vent emotions, builds rapport by indicating the attorney's interest in the witness's story, avoids coaching the witness, and most of all, permits you to hear what the witness really wants to say. Using an open-ended inquiry also allows you to determine what information the witness has personal knowledge of, not just what he or she heard from others. This will be critical at all stages of the case because a foundation of personal knowledge must always be established and hearsay testimony will be dismissed as speculative and excluded at trial unless it is offered for non-hearsay purposes or falls under an exception to the hearsay rule, in which cases the witness's personal knowledge that the statement was made will suffice.

After chatting with Coach Bagshaw about her successes at your alma mater and expressing concern for both her and her family, you ask her to tell you what happened. She begins by talking about a meeting that occurred five days ago. She and the athletic director, Owen O'Connor, met with two Collegiate Sports Commission investigators. Bagshaw was prepared to discuss rumored recruiting violations, but the investigators asked her about whether she had gambled on college sports within the last five years. Bagshaw tells you that she was "caught off guard" and denied gambling both to the investigators and then again in a private discussion with the athletic director right after the meeting.

At this juncture in the interview, you are tempted to interrupt Bagshaw. You have several questions, such as: "Had you gambled?" and "Why didn't you just admit it if you had gambled?" You might want to have Bagshaw back up and explain the allegations of recruiting violations. But, resist the temptation to interrupt. This is the time when you want to listen closely to how the witness wants to tell the story in as broad a manner as possible. You are at the mouth of the funnel. The time for narrowing the funnel will come later. For now, just listen and jot down your questions. Use reflective listening as the witness relates what happened because that shows the witness that you are paying attention (e.g., "If I understand correctly, you were surprised when the investigators inquired about gambling."), and helps insure that you are accurately perceiving what the witness intends to communicate.

Bagshaw goes on to tell you that she had gambled on college basketball with her friends at a charity event. On the day after meeting with the CSC investigators, she remembered a memorandum from Mansfield University's compliance officer that the form of gambling she had engaged in was permissible. She contacted the compliance officer and obtained a copy of the memorandum. Coach Bagshaw next consulted with her business adviser, Donna Fent, about what action to take. Then, she called the CSC investigator, and admitted to the investigator that she had gambled but not in violation of CSC or University regulations. She and Fent went to the athletic director and explained the situation. At that meeting Athletic Director O'Connor offered Bagshaw the options of resigning or being fired. O'Connor acceded to Bagshaw's request to meet with the university president first.

Next, Bagshaw tells you that on that night after she contacted the CSC and the athletic director she was summoned to the home of the Mansfield University's president. She met with the president and athletic director, and they reviewed what happened over the past two days. The following morning, she was called into the athletic director's office, and O'Connor informed her that she was being terminated.

Step 2. Organize the Information

After listening closely to the witness's story, you go back over the information and begin to take control of the interview as you gradually shift away from the open-ended phase of the interview. ("Let me get this straight. Three days ago, you were called into the athletic director's office and were summarily fired.") This puts information in a form that an attorney can use and begins a transition in the interview from rather free-flowing storytelling to a point where you start to take charge and begin to organize the information. Again, in summarizing the witness's information in order to form this chronological structure, you are also impressing on the witness that you are paying attention.

For an expert witness, you will need to gain a firm understanding of the field of expertise involved and the applicable scientific theories and techniques. Use the Internet, books, and law research services to grasp the basics, including terminology, before going to the interview. This will save time and jump start your learning curve. You will ask the expert to define terms and to explain clearly, using analogies when appropriate, and to clarify methodologies and technology.

In your interview with Bagshaw, you decide to widen the mouth of the funnel and get a firm understanding of the timeline of significant events. You ask her when she first noticed any conflicts between herself and the university administration. She recounts the incident in which she interviewed with Entman University when she was publicly denying any interest in another coaching position. She relates that the Athletic Director O'Connor was upset when he learned about the Entman University interview. However, she says everything had been settled amicably with O'Connor.

Step 3. Confirm and Clarify the Information Is Complete and Accurate

Probing Questions

You begin focusing your questions on specific points you perceive as important. Of course, you may be doing some of this throughout the interview. At this point you confirm and clarify specific information, questioning the witness about further areas and details that seem appropriate. For example, with an eye-witness in a criminal case, you would use this phase of the interview to test the witness's ability to perceive and to determine whether the witness really could have seen what the witness says he or she saw. So you'd ask whether the witness needed glasses to see objects at a distance even though the witness was not wearing glasses on the day of the event. It is at this step that you begin sifting through tentative case theories.

This third step can be illustrated in the *Coach Bagshaw* case. Your information-gathering questions explore in detail whether you have a case theory. In other words, you probe for facts sufficient to support your tentative legal theory of wrongful termination.

CONFIRM AND CLARIFY, COMPLETE AND ACCURATE

The *Coach Bagshaw* Case

During the third step, you want to clarify and verify the witness's information. For instance, your interview of Bagshaw zeros in on whether the university had any legitimate grounds for firing her. You ask:

- "Did the athletic director, the university president or anyone else connected with the university warn you that you were in jeopardy of losing your job prior to the meeting with the athletic director three days ago?"
- "Were you ever told that you were in peril of losing your job because of alleged recruiting violations?"
- "What exactly were the allegations of recruiting violations?"
- "Did the university sanction or warn you in any way as a result of the allegations of recruiting violations?"

Labeling for Clarity

If you have a number of relatively similar events that the witness has told you about and that you and the witness must accurately coordinate (such as a series of telephone calls or meetings), or if you and the witness must review a sequence of events over time, you need to develop a way to designate each of these events so you know the one to which the witness's information applies and the witness is clear what is being sought ("Let's call the time period in which you had seen the blueprint, but before you received any money, the 'first period' when we discuss this." . . . "Now, we're talking about the second phone call, the one where he asked you to put the proposal into writing").

Complete and Accurate

Obtaining complete and accurate information is, of course, a critical issue. Another issue of significant ethical concern and debate is whether, before obtaining your witness's story, you should reveal all the legal and factual information you already know about the case. Note the complexity of this issue. You do not want to, and legally and ethically cannot, assist the witness in developing false testimony. You do, however, want the witness to give you the full and accurate information necessary for carrying out effective representation. If before obtaining the witness's story, you show the witness relevant documents or the statement of some witness (favorable or unfavorable) or tell the witness about the other side's case or about the applicable law, you run a risk. The witness may consciously tailor his or her story to fit the facts or the law or, perhaps, may have the story subtly changed by suggestion, sometimes to the witness's detriment. If you do not give this information to the witness prior to obtaining the witness's story, you also run a risk.

Daily life is filled with a mass of data, only a minute fraction of which is relevant to a particular lawsuit. Without the focus offered by first showing the witness some witness statements, the witness may not be able to recollect significant details or provide full and accurate information. When a client goes to a tax lawyer who asks, "do you have any other business expenses?" it would not be surprising if the witness responded, "what other categories of things can constitute a business expense?" It is not that the witness is trying to cheat; the witness simply does not know what information among all the work-related data in his or her mind is legally significant.

Which risk then are you going to take? Will you risk fabricated testimony to get a complete story? On the other hand, must you presume that, given any opportunity, your witness will cheat and lie (especially in the criminal area where the client is constitutionally presumed innocent)? Is there a genuine risk that, without some initial direction, the client may give inaccurate information and then become committed to this inaccuracy to his or her detriment? These again are complex issues on which there is wide disparity of opinion.

Some believe that in the criminal arena the entire system is directed at giving the benefit of the doubt to the defendant, thereby willingly risking the acquittal of guilty people to ensure that the innocent are not convicted. These practitioners reason the decision as to which of the above risks to take has already been resolved by the central philosophy of the criminal justice system itself. Others strongly disagree, positing that the ethical issues involved cannot be resolved by reference to the existence of constitutional procedural concepts such as reasonable doubt. Whatever your view, if you have a client who your instincts tell you might be trying to use your expertise to create a false story, you can try to diplomatically obviate the problem. To do this you might state: "I really need to hear your story first, and then I can figure out what law may be involved. . . . I wouldn't speculate about the law here until I know what's going on." If this strategy is not successful and you continue to feel wary of your client's story, you can refuse the representation

(ABA Model Rules 1.2(d)(e) and 1.16) or withdraw if you have already been retained (ABA Model Rule 1.16).

Step 4. The Closing

You've arrived at the end of the interview and now must make plans with the client for the next steps that will be taken ("We need to meet again. Are you free Wednesday morning at . . ."). Here, as the attorney, you set the course for the next stage—arrive at a date for the next appointment, instruct the client to drop by certain documents, confirm a court date, and so on. However, if you are uncertain whether you will be representing the client, you might want to confirm the next steps you will take to arrive at a decision.

After meeting with Coach Bagshaw, you have decided to take her case. You conclude the interview by having her sign an employment agreement and scheduling a follow-up meeting.

THE FUNNEL

The *Motorcyclist Injury* Case

One final illustration of the interview approach, this time in the motorcyclist personal injury case. After completing Step 1 of the funnel (rapport building, gathering contact information, and listening to the eye-witness's story, another motorist who saw the accident) and Step 2 (organizing the information and getting a chronological account), the interviewer should use the methods of Step 3 to verify and clarify the facts and the methods of Step 4 to close the interview.

Step 3—Verifying and Clarifying Facts

- "Could you diagram the scene for me?"
- "Where exactly was your car when the accident happened?"
- "What was the weather like at the time of the accident?"
- "Did you observe the injuries? Could you describe them for me?"
- "What was the nature of the property damage that you saw?"
- "Were there other witnesses there?"
- "Had you consumed any alcohol that night?"
- "Were there any obstructions to your view?"

Step 4—Closing

- "Can we reduce what you just said to writing so we have a fresh written account of what happened?"

E.   Unfriendly Witness Interview

This funnel approach to witness interviewing is usually effective for friendly witnesses (yours and many neutral ones) and even sometimes for adverse witnesses. However, often the approach will need to be modified for unfriendly witnesses. While the rest of the funnel model remains useful, the following modifications may need to be made.

Develop a Rapport if Possible: Use Commanding Statements and Probing Questions

While small talk and expressing empathy might work for some reluctant witnesses, for other unfriendly witnesses you may need more compelling arguments. You can articulate your duty—"All I'm trying to do is to find out what really happened from a neutral witness like you." Or, "I really would like to save both of us time and money by just talking to you now. Then, we may be able to avoid having to depose you."

Focus on Important Information

When you ask an unfriendly witness to tell you "what happened?", you're likely to be met either by silence or a more promising: "What do you want to know?" When dealing with a recalcitrant witness, you can skip to Step 3 in the funnel structure. Begin by focusing your questions on important areas. Ask questions to clarify and verify information.

Lock in Witness Information

Try to lock an unfriendly witness into useful information—such as a concession that bolsters your case theory or undercuts the other side's theory, an improbable story, or impeachment evidence (e.g., the witness was a friend of the opposing party).

V.   SPECIAL WITNESS ISSUES

Individual characteristics of the witness call for individualized approaches. As with the unfriendly witness, the approach taken with many witnesses should be altered from a standard approach.

Children and the Elderly

Children and elderly persons serve as good illustrations of witnesses for whom you might need to adjust your approach. A young child, say six years of age, may be impressionable and easily led to please the interviewer, anxious and afraid to speak, lacking in communication skills, borderline competent, or presenting a combination of these difficulties. Techniques to adopt when interviewing a young child witness include establishing a rapport with the child by meeting in a familiar setting and talking about nonthreatening topics, such as the child's dog, not leading a susceptible child, questioning the child about things the child knows to determine whether the child knows the difference between the truth and a lie (e.g., a question to a five-year old: "If I said that you were ten years old would I be lying or telling the truth?"), and keeping the interview brief.

An elderly person, as with a young child, may present competency problems. During the interview, questioning can explore the elderly person's cognitive abilities. Hearing and other infirmities that come with age may need to be addressed. For instance, if the witness is hard of hearing, the lawyer will want to know the extent of the impairment and whether an elevated voice level would help the witness. At a deposition or at trial, the lawyer will want to condition the persons present at the deposition and the prospective jurors during voir dire to expect that the witness has a hearing impairment that requires the lawyer to speak loudly. Equally important, the lawyer will want to know if the hearing impairment affected the witness's ability to perceive (asking, "Could you hear the defendant say, "I shot him" if you were standing 50 feet away?" may be critical). Also, the lawyer may determine whether the elderly witness will need assistance getting to the courthouse and if so how to provide transportation.

Gender

Gender-related problems provide yet another illustration. Suppose an attorney is a woman and the witness states, "I would feel much better if I spoke to a man about these matters. This conversation shouldn't be for a woman to hear. It is too obscene." Will you, as a female attorney, agree with the witness and get a man to do the interview? Or will you try to convince the witness that you have sufficient professional expertise and life experience to hear the matter? If so, will you tell the witness about similar cases you worked on? Will you insist that the witness explain his position and argue with him about your capabilities? Will you be jeopardizing the case if you insist on interviewing this witness? What reaction do you expect from the witness? Hostility? Understanding? A change in his opinion? If he proves hostile, will you tell him that he is "offensive"? If you have an emotional outburst, will you be able to obtain the information you need? Will other members of your firm subsequently be impeded from obtaining this information if you have an outburst? Will you tell anyone else about the witness's attitude? Will that depend on such factors as the witness's age, background, or importance to the case?

Men can also face gender-related problems in an interview. A woman who is a sexual assault victim may feel uncomfortable or even be completely unwilling to discuss her situation with a male attorney. Or a female witness, such as a chief financial officer, may talk down to a male attorney. If so, does the attorney insist the witness stop being condescending and "get off it?" Can the male attorney obtain the information he needs after this outburst? Be sensitive to gender concerns and be prepared to handle them.

VI. PREPARING THE WITNESS TO TESTIFY

The trial date is approaching. It is time to prepare your witness for trial. Your central goal is to prepare the person to be an effective communicator, projecting confidence and testifying clearly and credibly. The following compiles information that you should go over with your witness before putting the witness on the stand, including providing information to the witness about the courtroom and courthouse behavior, preparing the witness on the substance of the testimony, and helping the witness with how to testify. As will be discussed in Chapter 9 on taking a deposition, similar witness preparation is essential to prepare a witness to testify at a deposition if your purpose at the deposition is to preserve the deponent's testimony for trial (see page 308).

A. Preparing the Witness for the Courtroom

The courtroom can be an intimidating setting for a witness, even an experienced expert witness. The more that you familiarize the witness with what to expect in the courthouse and courtroom, the more likely the person will be less nervous and appear comfortable, confident, and credible. You will want to explain the layout of the courtroom and who will be in the courtroom when the witness testifies. Consider a pretrial trip to the courtroom with the witness so that the person will feel more at ease. For example, a young child should visit the courtroom in advance because the child may freeze up and not be able to answer questions in a foreign setting.

You can explain how to get to the courthouse and to the courtroom and that the witness should not discuss the case in or around the courthouse hallways or in the elevator because prospective jurors may be nearby. The witness should avoid any contact with other witnesses and potential jurors and be mindful that the witnesses have been excluded from the courtroom until summoned into it.

B. Preparing the Witness on the Substance

The Witness's Role and Preparation on the Substance

The Witness's Role

The witness should be informed about where their testimony fits in the case. This will give your witness an understanding of his or her role and where you and opposing counsel may be headed with the questions. Discuss the necessity of the witness telling the truth. Explain that you need to know about any damaging information because only if you know about it can you protect the witness. For instance, you could use a motion in limine to get the court to exclude from the trial the witness's prior act of misconduct that has no bearing on the case. Don't forget to ask if your witness has any concerns and answer those concerns.

Prior Witness Statements

Have your witness review each and every one of the witness's prior statements line by line, explaining that at trial a witness may be examined on prior statements at trial. Tell the witness that if any part of the prior statement is inaccurate, the witness should tell you and explain to you why it is inaccurate or why this statement differs from another statement. The witness should be advised that the prior statement is not binding; the witness is only bound by a responsibility to tell the whole truth.

The Witness's Story

Go through the witness's story, particularly probing the information critical to the case theories and the witness's credibility, checking for inaccuracies, inconsistencies, and previously unrevealed information. Pay attention to the witness's estimates of time, distance, and other measurements. Some witnesses are particularly bad at estimating. For instance, a witness may tell you that an event could not have taken more than a minute, when it actually took nearly five minutes. To get an accurate estimate of the time it took have the witness look at his or her watch, think back to the event and say "start" and "stop" when the witness has had the same period of time pass by, and see how long it took according to the witness's watch.

Direct Examination

The Walk Through

Part of pretrial is preparing a witness to testify at trial (this preparation is equally applicable to preparing one of your witnesses to be deposed). In preparation for direct examination (or a deposition you are taking of one of your witnesses), you will have listened to the witness discuss what happened and had the witness review prior statements, and you will hone in on critical areas going over the facts with the witness. After this, you prepare your direct examination questions. Then, walk through the direct examination with the witness so the witness knows what you will ask and the order of your questions. The witness will gain confidence, and you will know how the witness will respond to your questions.

The Exhibits and Courtroom Demonstrations

Make sure that your witness has seen every piece of physical evidence that you will have the witness discuss on direct examination and potentially on cross-examination. Nothing is more awkward than showing a witness a diagram at trial that the witness has never seen before, asking the witness whether they can identify it, and receiving a negative reply. Before engaging in a courtroom demonstration, practice it with the witness beforehand. Walk through the sequence of events of the demonstration and what it will show. Otherwise, you may become a footnote in courtroom history ("If it doesn't fit, you must acquit.").

Cross-Examination

To prepare the witness for cross-examination, you need to step into opposing counsel's shoes and think of the questions that your opponent will ask on cross-examination. Then, practice the cross-examination with the witness. During your practice cross, you can use the techniques that opposing counsel may use on the witness, such as trying to get the witness rattled or angry or say inconsistent things. In the next section, we discuss how to prepare your witness to testify credibly and accurately.

C. Preparing the Witness on how to Testify

While you are prohibited by ethical rules, such as ABA Model Rule of Professional Conduct 3.4 (b) ("A lawyer shall not. . . counsel or assist a witness to testify falsely") from coaching a witness as to what to say, you may advise your witness on how to testify. In essence, you want to prepare your novice witness to be a good communicator—confident, clear, and credible. You should cover at least the following four points.

Appearance

First, appearance does matter, and the witness should dress appropriately for the courtroom. You could explain that the lawyers will be dressed in business attire. If appropriate, a witness may dress in uniform. And, appearance is more than just clothing. You should discuss sitting up straight, distracting habits (gum chewers), personal hygiene (clean, well-kept hair), and looking directly at the jury when testifying on direct.

Courtroom Rules

Second, explain courtroom rules and that witnesses should abide by them. For instance, you can discuss objections and that the witness should stop talking when an objection is made. Tell the witness what "sustained" and "overruled" mean. Explain that a trial's purpose is to find the truth and that the witness should candidly admit mistakes and inconsistencies. Explain that it is alright to admit it if the witness does not know or can't remember something and that if the witness cannot recall, then the witness may refresh his or her memory, and that you will help the witness to do so.

Communication on Direct Examination

Third, you can discuss how to behave on direct examination, explaining that this is the witness's opportunity to communicate with the fact finder. For example, for a jury trial, you can tell the witness that you will ask most of your questions from the far end of the jury box. This will cue the witness to look down the jury box toward you, to speak clearly and loudly enough so the juror furthest away can hear, and to look directly at the jurors and tell them what happened. The witness is talking to the jurors; they are the people who will decide what happened, and no one else in the room matters as much as they do in a jury trial. This is a good opportunity to explain to the witness that jurors are just members of the community whose job it is to decide what happened in the case. They are looking to the witness to explain that to them. They have no axe to grind with the witness, and they can be trusted to listen fairly to the witness's testimony. This may put the witness at ease.

Communication on Cross-Examination

Fourth, you can explain how to behave on cross-examination. Cover the difference between direct and cross. On cross-examination the witness is not telling the fact finder what happened as much as responding to opposing counsel's questions. Consequently, the witness usually should look at opposing counsel, not the jury, listen carefully to each question and answer it directly and briefly. The witness should not volunteer information. The witness should behave in a courteous manner and never become provoked. You can explain that quarrelling with a lawyer gains little. Tell the witness that if he or she does become angry, after the witness finishes testifying and leaves the courtroom, the lawyer remains and can argue at the end of the case that the witness's angry demeanor showed that the witness had an interest in the case. You can also alleviate some of the witness's trepidation about cross-examination by explaining that as long as the witness tells the truth, the witness has nothing to fear because the jury will know that it is the truth. Also, you may review some of the tricks of cross-examination. For instance, on cross, counsel may ask whether the witness discussed the case with anyone, and the way the question is asked may suggest some impropriety in discussing testimony prior to trial. You can then explain that it is perfectly proper to discuss testimony with you, the attorney, pretrial. Then, make the point that the witness should not try to figure out where counsel is going with the question, just listen to the question and answer it directly.

VII. ENSURING AN ETHICAL RELATIONSHIP

The Rules of Professional Conduct are designed to promote fair and forthright dealings with witnesses, to further justice by protecting witnesses from a lawyer's improper conduct, and to maintain the integrity of lawyers. For instance, under the Model Rule of Professional Conduct 4.1(a), you cannot make false or misleading statements of material fact to a witness. Thus, you could not claim to a witness in a highway collision case that your accident reconstruction expert determined that the collision occurred in a way that you know it did not.

However, what about feigning emotions, offering sympathy to the witness even if you have none, or conjuring up homey stories of "Daddy's garage and old tow truck" when, in fact, your father was a doctor in New York who only went into a gas station when the taxicab in which he was riding pulled in to refuel? A technical reading of the rule may lead to the conclusion that the rule has not been breached because no misrepresentation has been made as to a material fact. However, a strict reading of the rule might well find that this analysis is questionable, it may not be within acceptable parameters and may actually be a violation of the rule, subjecting counsel to discipline. You are advised against making statements of this kind. By misleading a witness in this manner you not only may lessen your personal sense of self-worth, but risk your professional reputation and credibility as others learn of your tactics (and sooner or later they usually do learn of them). In those tough circumstances when your personal moral sense seriously conflicts with your ability to get information helpful to your client, you may have to seriously contemplate withdrawal from the case. This same expansive approach should be applied to other ethical rules applicable to witness transactions, including the major rules which are summarized below.

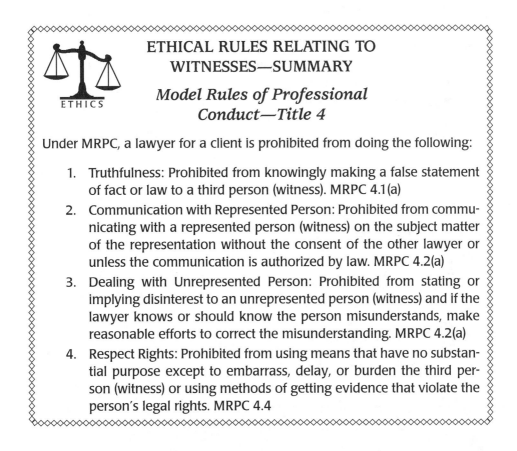

ETHICAL RULES RELATING TO WITNESSES—SUMMARY

Model Rules of Professional Conduct—Title 4

ETHICS

Under MRPC, a lawyer for a client is prohibited from doing the following:

1. Truthfulness: Prohibited from knowingly making a false statement of fact or law to a third person (witness). MRPC 4.1(a)

2. Communication with Represented Person: Prohibited from communicating with a represented person (witness) on the subject matter of the representation without the consent of the other lawyer or unless the communication is authorized by law. MRPC 4.2(a)

3. Dealing with Unrepresented Person: Prohibited from stating or implying disinterest to an unrepresented person (witness) and if the lawyer knows or should know the person misunderstands, make reasonable efforts to correct the misunderstanding. MRPC 4.2(a)

4. Respect Rights: Prohibited from using means that have no substantial purpose except to embarrass, delay, or burden the third person (witness) or using methods of getting evidence that violate the person's legal rights. MRPC 4.4

✓ THE WITNESS INTERVIEW CHECKLIST

The following are standards of performance for conducting an effective witness interview (excluding the client-only aspects, which are covered in the previous chapter):

Overall Interview Performance

❑ Determine which witnesses to interview, when, and where to interview.

❑ Do adequate background preparation for the interview.

❑ Set objectives.

❑ Conduct a structured and well-organized interview.

❑ Behave in a confident and professional manner.

❑ Anticipate and have a suitable approach for dealing with problems that could arise.

Case Theory as a Guide

❑ Have potential case theories in mind.

❑ Prepare potential legal theories (review the jury instructions).

Preserve the Interview

❑ When interviewing an adverse witness, be accompanied by a prover witness.

❑ Preserve the witness's interview (take notes, tape record, or get a written witness statement).

Rapport Building

❑ Develop rapport with the witness.

❑ Handle problems posed by problematic, adverse, and/or hostile witnesses.

Background Information

❑ Collect contact information.

❑ Gather background information pertinent to the witness's credibility.

❑ For an expert witness, explore training, experience, and education needed to qualify the witness as an expert.

Funnel Approach

Step 1—Begin with an open-ended inquiry (e.g., "Tell me what happened?) and do not interrupt the witness's storytelling.

❑ Listen carefully to the witness's account.

❑ Use reflective listening to show the witness that the witness is being heard.

Step 2—Begin to take over the interview, putting the witness's account into an organized and/or chronological order.

❑ Question in a logical storytelling fashion.

Step 3—Narrow the focus by concentrating on important, specific points.

❑ Obtain complete information on critical issues.

Step 4—Verify the accuracy of the information.

Unfriendly Witness

❑ Attempt to build a rapport with techniques suitable to an unfriendly witness.

❑ Modify the funnel approach to the information-gathering interview by going to step 3, focus on important information.

❑ Seek to lock the witness into useful information (e.g., concessions supporting the case theory, an improbable story, or impeachment evidence).

Special Witness Issues

❑ Determine if there are special concerns, such as the age of the witness, the witness's gender, or the presence of a physical or mental impairment.

❑ Determine how to handle the special issues and if any accommodations are needed.

Preparing the Witness to Testify

❑ Familiarize the witness with the courthouse, the courtroom, and court personnel.

❑ Inform the witness of court prohibitions, such as having no contact with jurors.

❑ Explain the importance of telling the truth.

❑ Tell the witness where the witness fits in the big picture of the trial.

❑ Have the witness review and correct inaccuracies in all prior witness statements.

❑ Explain the importance of appearance (dress, body language, eye contact).

❑ Cover court procedures (e.g., objections).

Preparing the Witness for Direct Examination

❑ Have the witness examine all potential exhibits.

❑ For an expert witness, review predicate questions to qualify the witness, have the witness define terms and discuss ways to simplify the explanation of the expert's findings and opinions.

❑ Practice direct examination.

❑ Discuss jury communication (look at the jurors, speak clearly, tell the truth).

Preparing the Witness for Cross-Examination

❑ Practice likely cross-examination questions with the witness.

❑ Discuss how to answer opposing counsel's questions (listen, answer directly, and don't volunteer).

❑ Review cross-examination tricks with the witness.

❑ Explain the importance of maintaining composure (be courteous with opposing counsel and don't lose temper).

Conduct the Interview in an Ethical and Professional Manner

❑ Know the professional rules of conduct, ask proper questions, and act as an attorney should.

Concluding the Interview

❑ Satisfactorily terminate the interview (e.g., with a client, signing an employment agreement or with a witness, scheduling another interview).

❑ Confirm all contact information so that you can reach the witness in the future.

7 *Strategic Pleading*

7 *Strategic Pleading*

"*Lawsuits are war. It's simple as that. And they begin the same way: with a declaration of war—the complaint. . . . When you're a small firm and they're a big one it's easy to be intimidated. Don't be—that's what they want. . . . I don't run away from bullies.*"

John Travolta in the movie *A Civil Action* (1998)

"*In general, I think the analogy of litigation to war is overdone. While there are similarities (including the critical importance of planning, discipline, and logistics), you can't get hurt in litigation unless your charts fall on you. Nevertheless, before the Microsoft case was done I knew what Travolta was talking about.*"

David Boies, *Courting Justice: From New York Yankees vs. Major League Baseball to Bush v. Gore, 1997-2000* (Miramar Books, 2004)

I. PLEADINGS

Pleadings, like other parts of the pretrial process, use a goal-oriented approach—specifically, ends-means thinking. Using ends-means thinking to plead means that any pleading you draft will be guided by a case strategy, that is, those overall objectives that you want to accomplish for your client. This chapter explores how to develop those objectives and draft pleadings to accomplish them. It discusses an approach to drafting that is case-theory directed and satisfies technical, procedural, and ethical requirements.

To begin, let's review the basic terminology of pleadings and the types of pleadings that will be discussed throughout this chapter.

A. CIVIL PLEADINGS

For civil cases, there are two types of pleadings: affirmative and responsive pleadings.

Affirmative Pleading

An *affirmative pleading* describes a legal claim for which the substantive law provides a remedy. Affirmative pleadings include a complaint (also referred to as a petition, bill, or writ), a counterclaim, a cross-claim, and a third-party complaint.

Responsive Pleading

A *responsive pleading* is a defendant's response to plaintiff's allegations. Responsive pleadings include answers and replies filed by a defending party. In many jurisdictions, a defendant can file an answer (also referred to as a response or reply) and/or a motion (such as a motion to set aside the complaint or motion to strike). Under the Federal Rules a defending party can respond by an answer and a motion simultaneously or by an answer or motion solely. This chapter discusses answers. For a full discussion of motions, see Chapter 11.

A defendant must answer plaintiff's complaint in compliance with the rules of procedure of the jurisdiction where the complaint has been filed. Generally, the answer admits or denies the complaint's allegations, states affirmative defenses, and/or requests relief. Federal Rule of Civil Procedure 8(b) provides that a defending party shall "state in short and plain terms the party's defenses to each claim asserted and shall admit or deny the averments upon which the adverse party relies. If a party is without knowledge or information sufficient to form a belief as to the truth of an averment, the party shall so state and this has the effect of a denial."

Admit or Deny

First, a defendant must admit or deny each of the plaintiff's allegations in the complaint.

Affirmative Defense

Second, defendant, in addition to responding to plaintiff's allegations, must assert its affirmative defenses in the answer or risk waiving those defenses. An *affirmative defense* does not deny the truth of the plaintiff's contentions but instead asserts that, even if plaintiff's contentions are true, other facts prevent the plaintiff from obtaining relief from the defendant. For example, the defendant could assert that the statute of limitations has passed and the suit is barred. The Federal Rules of Civil Procedure and many jurisdictions require the pleading of certain affirmative defenses in the answer, and if an affirmative defense is not plead, it is waived.

Request for Relief

A request for relief includes asking for dismissal, damages, an injunction, declaratory relief, restitution, or specific performance. There are two types of relief—equitable and legal. Certain claims and remedies historically are considered to be equitable, others legal. If you request a remedy that historically is classified as equitable (e.g., injunctions, specific performance, restitution), your selection of a remedy may determine whether you have a jury as the fact finder. For instance, a purely equitable request for relief, such as a request for injunctive relief, may preclude your client's right to a jury trial.

Format for Civil Pleading

Both affirmative and responsive pleadings consist of four parts:

- The caption (providing information about the court, the parties, the case number, the jurisdiction, and the type of pleading),
- The *body* (a description of the event, including claims, defenses, and the parties involved),
- The *remedy* (or request for relief), and
- The *signature*.

We will refer to these four parts again when discussing how to organize information for your pleading.

Code versus Notice Pleading

In the civil arena there are, theoretically, two styles of pleading, *code pleading* and *notice pleading*. Typical code pleading rules require that the complaint contain a statement of facts that constitutes a cause of action. Notice pleading requires a "short and plain statement of the claim showing that the pleader is entitled to relief" (Fed. R. Civ. P. 8(a)).

Some commentators find practical differences between notice and code pleading: They suggest that code pleading requires strict adherence to pleading the elements of the substantive law and that notice pleading merely requires setting forth facts. Other commentators argue that only philosophical differences exist, and any practical distinctions that might result are insignificant when drafting is concerned. They base their position on the fact that both code and notice pleading require legal and factual sufficiency. They argue that, even in notice pleading, facts must have legal relevance in describing how the event occurred, who was involved, why the client is entitled to relief, and what relief is sought. In this text, we take the position that a pleading must be legally and factually sufficient (i.e., be able to withstand defense legal theories attacking legality and factual sufficiency). We have not made distinctions in drafting because of code or notice pleading rules.

Specific Allegations

You also need to be aware of procedural rules that require specific factual allegations. For example, the Federal Civil Procedure Rules require specific allegations if fraud, mistake, or special damages are pleaded. Procedural rules in other jurisdictions might not require or might even prohibit certain allegations from being pleaded (e.g., specific monetary amounts for general damages).

B.   Criminal Pleadings

In the criminal arena, the only pleading is the charging document, which relates the criminal offenses the defendant is facing. Generally, the charging document is referred to by three names, although terminology may vary somewhat among jurisdictions. When filed at the inception of a case in the lower trial court by the prosecutor, it is called a *complaint;* when filed by the prosecutor in the superior court or when embodying the probable cause determination of a court after a preliminary hearing, an *information;* when incorporating the findings of a grand jury, an *indictment.*

These charging documents can be significant to advocates in a number of ways. First, defense counsel, depending on the jurisdiction, may be able to file a demurrer to the charging pleading on the grounds that the statutory offense pleaded is unconstitutional, the pleading does not charge a crime, the pleading reveals some defense on its face (e.g., statute of limitations), or the pleading does not give sufficient information for the accused to prepare a defense. This last ground may be used as a means for discovery when accompanied by a request for a bill of particulars.

Second, due process considerations of fair notice will limit the variance permitted between this pleading and subsequent proof at trial. It is hard to imagine that a court would let a prosecutor who has charged a June burglary prove at trial that the burglary really happened in December. Whether the court would allow amendment of the pleadings to conform with the proof for a one or two-day variance, on the other hand, would vary with the specific circumstances of the case.

Third, the charging pleading in a prior case may have a bearing on a claim that the defendant is facing double jeopardy in a current case.

II. PLANNING THE CIVIL PLEADING

A. Setting the Objectives for Pleading

Ultimately, your pleadings should be designed to accomplish your overall case objective (e.g., an early settlement, a large amount of money). In addition to reflecting a case strategy, the pleading also serves specific functions within the legal system. Therefore, your pleading will need to reflect and accomplish interrelated goals. We refer to these interrelated goals as pleading objectives:

- Formally invoking the court's jurisdiction by asserting a claim you allege is within its jurisdictional competence,
- Giving notice of claims or defenses to your adversary, the trier of fact, and the public,
- Narrowing the issues in controversy,
- Framing the issues for discovery, and
- Persuading and educating your adversary with the aim of resolving the dispute (judgment on the pleadings, summary judgment, settlement, or, as a defending party, dismissal).

Your case theory will also provide a framework for determining the actual content of your pleading. Later in this chapter, we explore how your case theory guides your choice of claims, parties, and relief within the pleading.

Discovery and Pleading

Discovery and pleading are inextricably tied together. Discovery allows you to obtain the broadest amount of information that will support your case, refute your adversary's case, and develop other potential issues. Federal Rule of Civil Procedure 26(a) on initial disclosures includes identifying information of individuals with discoverable information "that the disclosing party may use to support its claims or defenses. . . ." Because pleading is based on specific legal theories, the inclusion of claims, parties, and relief within the pleading helps to crystallize the issues. Yet, to ensure full discovery, pleading should be inclusive of all potential case theories supported by law and fact. For example, in an automobile rear-end collision, if you do not plead a claim that the car was defective, you could potentially be precluded from discovery of relevant facts that might support a products liability claim because your pleading did not cover that issue.

Negotiation and Pleading

Pleading and negotiation are also interrelated. For instance, if you plead and then negotiate, you need to consider how the pleading content will affect negotiation. Is your pleading a persuasive tool? Then perhaps your pleading, because it is persuasive, will entice your adversary into negotiation. Is your pleading vituperative or hostile? This may hinder your negotiation efforts.

Overall Case Strategy and Pleading

This chapter presents our approach for drafting affirmative and responsive pleadings. We emphasize that the drafting of a pleading is an endeavor that must be carried out in the context of your case strategy and with an appreciation of its impact on other pretrial tasks—case theory determination, factual investigation, the scope of discovery, and negotiation. We believe that pleading is a tool that allows the advocate to accomplish a case strategy. To illustrate our approach, this chapter includes two examples of pleadings, both based on the Federal Rules of Civil Procedure (see pages 206-210). We are mindful that there are differing pleading styles, philosophies, and requirements (such as code and notice pleading) that can affect drafting. Nevertheless, we believe that by presenting these examples we can best demonstrate a framework that you can adapt for your drafting style and jurisdictional requirements.

B. Preparing to Draft Pleadings—Civil Case Theory Development

Before filing a pleading in a civil case you have an ethical duty and procedural requirement under Federal Rule of Civil Procedure 11 to make a reasonable investigation and inquiry of law and fact under the circumstances. See Part VI discussing counsel's ethical considerations in detail (pages 217-219). This section discusses the preparation and planning you need to undertake before you are ready to draft a pleading. This lengthy preparatory process is in fact your first step in actually drafting a pleading. Also, this section covers the procedural rules applicable to drafting pleadings.

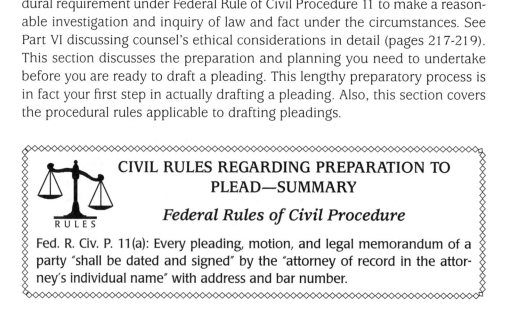

CIVIL RULES REGARDING PREPARATION TO PLEAD—SUMMARY

Federal Rules of Civil Procedure

Fed. R. Civ. P. 11(a): Every pleading, motion, and legal memorandum of a party "shall be dated and signed" by the "attorney of record in the attorney's individual name" with address and bar number.

MEANING OF THE SIGNATURE:

"The signature of . . . an attorney constitutes a certificate by . . . the attorney that the . . . attorney has:"

- read the pleading, motion, or legal memorandum,
- to the best of the attorney's knowledge, information, and belief, formed after reasonable inquiry, it is well grounded in fact and is warranted by existing law or a good faith argument for the extension or reversal of existing law, and
- that the document is not interposed for any improper purpose (e.g., to harass).

CONSEQUENCES IF UNSIGNED OR SIGNED:

- NOT SIGNED: Stricken unless signed promptly when brought to the attention of the attorney
- SIGNED IN VIOLATION OF THE RULE: This can result in an appropriate sanction that may include paying the other party's reasonably incurred expenses.

You may recall from our discussion of the development of a case theory that only events, things, or occurrences that are legally significant (cognizable by substantive law) result in a remedy. Similarly, in pleading, only occurrences that are legally and factually sufficient can form the basis of your pleading. Thus, the substance of your pleading also must be based on a legal theory.

Legal Sufficiency

Your pleading must be legally and factually sufficient or else your complaint may be dismissed upon motion by your opponent. Legal sufficiency means that your claim states a basis for relief and thereby withstands an attack on legality. Factual sufficiency is discussed below.

There are two types of legal theories that affect the legal sufficiency of a pleading, "tried-and-true" and "cutting-edge" theories.

"Tried-and-True" Legal Theories

Tried-and-true legal theories are well-grounded in legal precedent, custom, and statutes. Generally, a pleading based on tried-and-true legal theories will be legally sufficient. Thus, when planning your pleading, you will review case law, statutes, and jury instructions and adopt tried-and-true claims or defenses, parties, and relief for inclusion in your pleading.

Cutting-Edge Legal Theories

Cutting-edge legal theories are just that, the cutting edge of established law. These legal theories can be problematic. If you plead based on a cutting-edge legal theory, you may subject your pleading to attack by a motion to dismiss for failure to state a claim, judgment on the pleading, or summary judgment. Yet, there may be circumstances in which, because of your case strategy, you want to plead a cutting-edge legal theory because this theory potentially expands the scope of a lawsuit by adding new claims, parties, or remedies. You are, in effect, creating new law.

As an example, over the years the new legal theory of tortious breach of contract emerged, which allows recovery of punitive damages, a remedy not available in contract. Likewise, strict liability for dangerous products has been extended to the manufacturer, thus expanding the parties who could be joined in a lawsuit. As in developing your case theory, to plead a cutting-edge theory (whether it relates to claims, parties, or relief), you should search for clues in case law footnotes, dicta, or dissenting opinions or in law review articles, legal periodicals, or specialized legal journals. Search other areas of law for applications that could be applicable to your facts. For example, the application of tort concepts to a business contract situation resulted in the tortious interference with contract claim.

Cutting-edge legal theories can also be developed by your own factual theorizing. Some facts that you possess may not suggest any of the accepted legal theories. Instead, these novel facts may suggest a new legal theory to fit them. More than likely, however, you will try to plead novel facts within an established claim rather than through the proposal of a novel one: Your pleading will be less likely to be subject to attack for tried-and-true claims and relief than for cutting-edge claims and relief.

Factual Sufficiency

In addition to legal sufficiency, your pleading must resist attacks on factual sufficiency. Factual sufficiency under Federal Rule of Civil Procedure 8(a) requires "a short and plain statement of the claim showing the pleader is entitled to relief." Factual sufficiency means that your complaint pleads the necessary facts to satisfy the elements of your legal theory. Therefore, your pleading must describe factually, and not in the abstract, the event that gave rise to your client's injury, the person who caused it, and the remedy you seek—that is, the claim, the party, and the relief. But pleading your factual theory must be done in a legally significant manner. The elements of your legal theory will provide the structure for pleading your story of what occurred. Essentially, this story is your factual theory.

To determine which facts to plead, whether for a tried-and-true or cutting-edge legal theory, you might examine cases for guidance. You may find, however, that some facts that are essential for an element of a claim or defense are missing (e.g., the exact date of the incident, specific location of the event). If you reasonably believe in good faith that these missing facts may be obtainable, you can file the claim (or defense) alleging the facts upon "information and belief."

C. Organizing the Information—Mapping the Potential Pleading

To illustrate how our approach to drafting pleadings works, we use a plaintiff's complaint in the hypothetical *Alby* case. The same approach and thought processes, however, are applicable to drafting an answer, with the exception that defendant's answer must respond to allegations in plaintiff's complaint. To see how our approach is applied to a responsive pleading, see the answer at pages 209-210. Now to apply the approach:

The *Alby* Case

Story

Imagine that you represent the plaintiff-driver, Albert J. Alby, in a hypothetical automobile accident case. Albert Alby lives, works, votes, and registers his car in California and has a summer home in Oregon. He owns and operates a bakery in California. Clark Brady lives in Texas and is a registered nurse. On June 15, 20XX (last year) Alby and Brady were driving on Interstate Highway 5 in the State of Major. Brady crashed into the rear of Alby's red sports car. The week before the crash, Alby made an appointment to have his gas pedal adjusted. At the scene, Alby told the police that his car abruptly slowed down. Both Alby and Brady suffered personal injuries and property damage. Alby was hospitalized and incurred hospital and medical bills of $15,000; two weeks of lost profits to his business, $5,000; property damage of $10,000, and general personal injuries set at $50,000.

Brady was not injured, but had $8,000 property damage. Brady was given a breathalyzer test at the scene and registered a .25 blood-alcohol level. The state highway police issued a citation to Brady for violation of State of Major motor vehicle code section 14.0, which provides "it is unlawful to operate a motor vehicle while intoxicated. . . . Presumption of intoxication is .08."

Your research disclosed that the Major State Supreme Court in *Susanah v. David*, 182 Maj. 3d 118, 236, firmly establishes common law negligence and negligence per se, allowing only compensatory damages. In addition, footnote 2 states in part:

> A level of intoxication which exceeds the presumptive .08 intoxication level is outrageous. People driving while so intoxicated should be punished.

A recent law review article by Professor Waldman, "Excessive Intoxication—The Case for a New Tort," 3 Maj. L. Rev. 1, argues a new legal tort theory based on excessive intoxication while driving—"reckless endangerment."

As Alby's attorney you wish to consider how your case strategy can be implemented by your pleading. A major aspect of our planning approach to pretrial advocacy involves organizing information and mapping a potential pleading. Organization is of particular importance in pleading. You will be gathering, or already have gathered, a vast amount of legal and factual information, and pleading requires that this information be presented in a highly structured manner. We have found it helpful to organize information by following the actual structure of a pleading: the caption, the body, the remedy or request for relief, and the signature. By organizing in this fashion, you simultaneously map out the potential pleading.

We include four charts that will help you organize the type of information you potentially might use for drafting affirmative and responsive pleadings based on the Federal Rules of Civil Procedure. The charts are broadly designed, allowing you to include all kinds of information that potentially might be of benefit in preparing your case strategy. As with all our suggestions, feel free to adopt or modify these charts to reflect your organizational needs.

- **Chart 1** is a plaintiff's chart containing the basic information: jurisdiction, parties, and potential forum (state or federal court).
- **Chart 2,** also a plaintiff's chart, contains plaintiff's case theory information: legal theories (i.e., negligence and negligence per se and the elements of each), the facts to prove each element, and finally the remedy.
- **Chart 3** is a defendant's chart, organizing the defendant's answer to each of plaintiff's allegations in plaintiff's complaint.
- **Chart 4** is another defendant's chart organizing and mapping affirmative defenses, counter claims, and third party claims.

In order to observe how these charts organize information, we will be referring to the *Alby* case. Later in this chapter, these facts will be used again in our illustrations and in our pleading examples to demonstrate our approach to drafting a pleading (see pages 206-210). Let's assume the attorneys for Alby, the plaintiff, and Brady, the defendant, have obtained the following information:

CHART 1: Plaintiff's Complaint Chart— Caption, Parties, Jurisdiction

Chart 1 organizes information for drafting the caption and the first paragraph of the body of a complaint. This opening paragraph describes the parties and subject matter jurisdiction according to Federal Rule of Civil Procedure 10. The chart may also be of help to a defendant in raising a procedural attack on the pleading.

CHART 1: Plaintiff's Complaint Chart—Caption, Parties, Jurisdiction		
Jurisdictional Requirements	**Parties**	
1. Subject matter jurisdiction (elements)	Plaintiff (Alby)	Defendant (Brady)
a. Diversity of citizenship (28 U.S.C. §1332(a)		
(1) individuals from different states	California	Texas
(2) $75,000 in dispute	$50,000 personal injuries,	$8,000 property damage
	$5,000 lost profits,	
	$15,000 medical expenses,	
	$10,000 property damage	
b. Federal question	None	None
2. Venue (elements for diversity jurisdiction, 28 U.S.C. §1391)		
a. Place where the cause of action arose	Accident in State of Major	Accident in State of Major
b. Corporation's residence	Not applicable	Not applicable
c. Individual's residence	Resides in California, summer home in Oregon	Resides in Texas
3. Appropriate court and preferences for venue		
a. State court	States of Major, California, and Oregon	State of Texas
b. Federal court	United States District Courts in Major, California, and Oregon	United States District Court in Texas

The legal elements for party description and subject matter jurisdiction provide the structure for the factual allegations. Chart 1 also includes a framework for listing information relevant to personal jurisdiction and venue, even though the Federal Rules of Civil Procedure do not require a plaintiff to affirmatively plead jurisdiction and venue. Including these legal elements in the chart will help Alby's attorney to draft the pleading properly.

Note that venue for a corporation is based on a corporation's residence, which is defined by 28 U.S.C. §1391(c) as the location where the corporation has its principal place of business, the places where it is licensed to do or does business, and its places of incorporation. Venue for an individual for diversity jurisdiction is based on an individual's place of residence. Venue is appropriate either where all plaintiffs reside or all defendants reside. Selecting an appropriate state or federal court takes into consideration personal jurisdiction, venue, and subject matter jurisdiction criteria. Strategy decisions as to which court to select reflect such issues as geographical convenience of client and attorney, choice of law to be applied, and selection of the decision maker.

CHART 2: Plaintiff's Complaint Chart— Claim, Party, and Relief

Chart 2 organizes information for a plaintiff to draft the remainder of the body (including the claim, the party, and the injury) and the relief portion of an affirmative pleading. This chart can also help the defendant in determining whether there are legal and factual deficiencies in plaintiff's pleading. Chart 2 also provides a framework for including a factual theory, legal theory, and documents. By including this framework, the chart can be used either to formulate this information for the pleading or response or to plan a case strategy.

CHART 3: Defendant's Answer Chart— Responding to Plaintiff's Allegations

Chart 3 is based on a response to the sample complaint at page 206. This chart can help organize an answer to a plaintiff's allegations. The structure of the chart is based on the four ways one can respond to plaintiff's allegations: (1) admit, (2) partially admit and partially deny (partially admit and partially deny means that, in the paragraph you are responding to, some of the facts are true and some may not be true or even known. For example, suppose plaintiff pleads in Paragraph 5 that Defendant Brady, the owner of a blue sedan, was proceeding south. A potential response by Defendant Brady might be: Defendant admits part of Paragraph 5, i.e., he is the owner of a

CHART 2: Plaintiff's Complaint Chart—Claim, Party, and Relief

Legal Theory	Factual Theory	Legal Claim	Legal Elements of Claim	Facts to Plead	Documents	Parties	Remedy
Negligence	Intoxication (Brady)	Common law negligence	Duty owed	Event occurred on 6/15/XX		Plaintiff: Alby (owner, driver). Defendant: Brady (owner, driver).	
	Failure to keep a careful lookout			Alby driving car on public highway	Alby's car registration		
				Brady driving car on public Highway	Brady's car registration		
			Breach of duty	Brady: .25 blood-alcohol level while driving	Police report, breathalyzer test, state police citation		
			Proximate cause of injury	Brady crashed into Alby	Three witness statements under oath		
			Injury and relief	$10,000 property damage, pain and suffering	Bills for car repair and car rental		General damages $10,000 pain and suffering
				$15,000 doctor and hospital expenses, $5,000 lost profits	Doctor and hospital bills, bakery financial books and records		Special damages, $20,000

continues ▲

CHART 2: Plaintiff's Complaint Chart—Claim, Party, and Relief *(Continued)*

Legal Theory	Factual Theory	Legal Claim	Legal Elements of Claim	Facts to Plead	Documents	Parties	Remedy
Negligence Per Se	Brady was presumptively intoxicated (above a .08 blood-alcohol level) and was driving while intoxicated, which is in violation of State of Major motor vehicle code §14.0	Negligence Per Se	Duty	State of Major vehicle statute protects Alby, a driver, from Brady, who was Driving while intoxicated on a public highway on 6/15/XX	Statute, police citation	Plaintiff: Alby (injured driver). Defendant: Brady (owner, driver).	
				Brady had a .25 blood-alcohol level (tested by the police shortly after the crash). A blood-alcohol level of .08 is presumption of intoxication.			
		Breach of duty					
		Proximate injury		Brady crashed into Alby	Three witness statements under oath		
		Injury and relief		$10,000 property damages, pain and suffering	Bills for car repair and car rental		General damages, $10,000, pain and suffering
				$55,000 doctor and medical bills	Doctor and hospital bills		Special damages, $20,000
				$5,000 lost profits	Bakery financial books and records		

CHART 3: Defendant's Answer Chart—Responding to Plaintiff's Allegations				
Plaintiff's Allegations (corresponding to the numbered paragraphs in plaintiffs complaint)	Admit	Partially Admit/ Partially Deny	Denial	Denial Because of Lack of Information Sufficient to Form a Belief
1. Subject matter jurisdiction is based on diversity jurisdiction.				1. (Don't know if Brady is truly a citizen of TX)
2. Plaintiff Alby is a citizen of CA.				2. (Same as allegation 1)
3. Defendant Brady is a citizen of TX.	3			
4. The matter in controversy exceeds $75,000.			4	
5. On 6/15/XX Alby and Brady driving south on Highway 5 in Jamner, Major.	5			
6. Defendant Brady negligently crashed into Alby.			6. (Brady was not negligent; Plaintiff might have a defective gas pedal)	
7. Brady proximate cause of injuries to Alby. Property and personal damages, loss of income.			7. (Don't know all the facts)	
8. Alby incurred medical and hospital expenses, loss of profits, loss of wages.			(Same as allegation 7)	
17. Special damages, $20,000			17	
18. General damages according to proof at trial			18	
19. Punitive damages, $500,000			19	
20. Costs, interests, and other relief			20	

blue sedan, but he denies the rest of the paragraph, i.e., he was proceeding east, not south), (3) deny, (4) deny with a reason (upon information and belief). When a responding party lacks knowledge of the actual facts, the defending party can assert lack of information and can deny the allegation

Chart 3 can help a responding party list each of plaintiff's allegations or compare plaintiff's allegations with the facts that defendant knows to exist or in good faith believes to exist. Defendant's response to each plaintiff allegation can then be recorded under the appropriate category. A plaintiff can use the chart to determine the facts and issues in controversy and refute defendant's responses.

In Chart 3, the plaintiffs' allegations correspond to the *Alby v. Brady* complaint, paragraphs 1 through 8 (including the last claim for relief) and paragraphs 17 through 20 (pertaining to general relief requested for negligence). The numbers in the remaining four columns also correspond to the paragraphs in plaintiffs' complaint.

CHART 4: Defendant's Answer Chart—Affirmative Defense, Counterclaim, Third-Party Complaint

Chart 4 is similar to Chart 2 in that it organizes information according to the legal elements within an affirmative defense, counterclaim, cross-claim, or third-party complaint. Some commentators maintain that affirmative defenses do not have to factually plead legal elements. But because affirmative defenses are subject to motions as to their legal and factual sufficiency, the better view is to plead defenses according to the requirements of the legal elements.

This chart provides a framework for including legal and factual theories and documents. Using Chart 4 for organizing an affirmative defense can help organize information that is relevant to a counterclaim against plaintiff or to cross-claims against other defendants. Additionally, it can help you focus on whether a third-party complaint is necessary in the event a defendant was not joined as a party by plaintiff. A plaintiff, in turn, can use this chart to determine the legal and factual sufficiency of a defendant's response claims.

As you will note, this chart illustrates one theory for comparative fault (contributory negligence). There may be additional factual theories that Brady could assert for contributory negligence, such as negligent repair of the gas pedal by the car repair shop; defectively manufactured gas pedal; or defect occurring because of negligence in shipping of the car. If these other factual theories were to be included in the chart, they would require the same application of the listed legal elements with the relevant facts, documents, parties, and so on to be filled in the appropriate places.

CHART 4: Defendant's Answer Chart—Affirmative Defense, Counterclaim, Third-Party Complaint

Legal Theory	Possible Factual Theories	Legal Elements of the Defense	Facts	Documents	Parties Named in the Lawsuit		People Not in the Lawsuit but Potentially to be Joined as Defendants	Remedy	Potential Pleading to be Filed	Miscellaneous Things to Do
					Plaintiff	Defendant				
Contributory Negligence (also referred to as comparative fault or comparative negligence)	Duty to keep car in good repair if it is driven on a public highway	Duty	Alby and Brady were driving their cars on a public highway on 6/15/XX in the State of Major		Alby	Brady				Investigation as to road construction and other obstacles on highway proves negative.
		Breach of duty	Alby's car abruptly slowed down on the highway. Alby may have had a faulty gas pedal that needed repair. OR	Police report	Alby				Counterclaim in Brady's answer	Obtain repair documents for Alby's car. Investigation: contact private investigator, other attorneys specializing in products liability.
			Alby's car abruptly slowed down on the highway. Alby had an appointment to have his gas pedal repaired one week prior to the crash.	Police report, Alby's statement to the police at the scene	Alby					Obtain repair records from automobile repair shop.

continues ▲

CHART 4: Defendant's Answer Chart—Affirmative Defense, Counterclaim, Third-Party Complaint (Continued)

Legal Theory	Possible Factual Theories	Legal Elements of the Defense	Facts	Documents	Parties Named in the Lawsuit		People Not in the Lawsuit but Potentially to be Joined as Defendants	Remedy	Potential Pleading to be Filed	Miscellaneous Things to Do
					Plaintiff	Defendant				
			Alby either did not get the repair done or did not see to it that it was done properly and continued to drive with a faulty gas pedal.							Think about third-party complaint by Brady against repair shop.
		Proximate cause of injury	Alby's abrupt slowing down on the highway because his gas pedal may not have been working properly caused Brady to unavoidably crash into Alby.	Car repair bills	Alby					
		Injury	$8,000 property damage to Brady's car.		Alby			$8,000 and according to proof at trial	Counterclaim and/or motion dismissing plaintiff's complaint. Think about third-party complaint.	

III. DRAFTING THE CIVIL PLEADING

A. Case Theory and Strategy as Guides

Now let's begin the drafting process, using the *Alby* civil case as an illustration. First, you must develop your case theory and strategy. As Alby's attorney you believe liability against Brady is strong and damages are easily provable. Your beliefs are based on documentary proof of Brady's intoxication and proof of damage. You have multiple case strategies: to settle the case at the earliest possible time, obtain maximum compensation for your client, and prepare yourself for litigation if the case does not settle. Your pleading should reflect these strategies by making a persuasive case on liability and damages, and by drafting it in such a way that it is sufficient to give notice, narrow the issues in controversy, and frame issues for discovery. Be mindful that, although you have multiple case strategies and pleading objectives, some might be more important than others.

In the *Alby* case, your primary objective is to make your pleading persuasive and give sufficient notice of Alby's claims. How can your pleading accomplish these particular case strategies? Accomplishing your objectives requires selecting:

- The subject matter *jurisdiction* and *venue,*
- The legal *claim or defense,*
- The *parties,* and
- The *relief* that is consistent with your client's objectives.

Now we turn to those decisions.

B. Pleading Subject Matter Jurisdiction and Venue

Considerations in Selecting a Forum

Consider the selection of a forum. Will you choose federal or state court? Which geographical location within the forum? Answers to these questions begin by determining whether you can establish that the desired court has subject matter jurisdiction and that the court is the proper place, that is, the proper venue for the action. Customarily, jurisdiction and venue are pled right after the caption in the complaint.

Provided you can plead and prove that the court has jurisdiction and is the proper venue, your strategic decision also may be based at least on which forum offers the most favorable

- Quality of the judges,
- Composition of the juries,
- Procedural or evidentiary rules,
- Time delays in hearing the case,
- Availability of appellate review,
- Cost of review,
- Familiarity with court procedures, and
- Litigation cost difference.

Subject Matter Jurisdiction

Subject matter jurisdiction is determined by which court has authority over the action. Subject matter jurisdiction is a creature of constitutional and statutory law. Therefore, careful review of the requirements to establish original or limited jurisdiction is necessary for proper pleading (see the discussion of state and federal court jurisdiction following). Failure to establish subject matter jurisdiction can result in dismissal of the complaint.

State Court

Ordinarily, a *state court* by statute is a court of *general jurisdiction,* meaning that it has subject matter jurisdiction over any proper legal action from torts to contract disputes. You need only state in your pleading: "The state of Major has jurisdiction over this action."

Federal Court

However, a *federal court* is empowered by Article III of the United States Constitution and federal statutes to decide only certain cases—a court of *limited jurisdiction.* For example, a federal court has subject matter jurisdiction over controversies presenting a federal question and those involving citizens of different states and involving over $75,000 exclusive of interest and costs—diversity jurisdiction. Consequently, you will need to both plead and be able to establish that the federal court has subject matter jurisdiction. For example, you could plead for diversity jurisdiction: "Plaintiff is domiciled in Washington state and is a citizen of Washington state. Defendant is a corporation incorporated under the laws of the State of New York having its principal place of business in a state other than the state of Washington. The matter in controversy exceeds exclusive of interests and costs, the sum specified in 28 U.S.C.A. §1332. Subject matter jurisdiction is founded on diversity of citizenship under U.S.C.A. §1332."

Venue

Venue, the place where the action will be heard is determined by statute or court rule. State statute or court rule may provide for venue to be in the place where the defendant resides, where the plaintiff resides, where the action arose, and so on. Federal venue is governed by 28 U.S.C.A. §1391 (and in some instances by specific statutes.) For instance, for a diversity case, venue governed by 1391(a) generally providing for either "1) where any defendant resides, if all defendants reside in the same state, a judicial district in which a substantial part of the events or omissions giving rise to the claim occurred, or a substantial part of the property that is the subject of the action is situated, or 3) . . . where any defendant is subject to personal jurisdiction at the time the action is commenced, if there is no district in which the action may otherwise be brought."

C.   Claims and Defenses

The following legal, procedural, and strategic factors will guide you in deciding what claim or defense to plead:

* Your *legal theories,*
* Whether you have the *burden to plead,*
* *Procedural rules regarding joinder* of claims and defenses, and
* Your overall *case strategies.*

Legal Theories as Guides

What claim or defense will you plead? Your answer depends on the legal theory you select to support the claim or defense. Also, Fed. R. Civ. P. 8(e)(2) provides:

* that the claim or defense may be *alleged alternatively or hypothetically,*
* that a party may allege *as many separate claims or defenses as the party has,* and
* that the claims or defenses *may be inconsistent.*

However, obviously, all statements in a claim or defense are subject to the obligations of Rule 11 requiring an attorney signature reflecting the reading of all court documents, the making of a reasonable inquiry regarding both law and facts, and not interposing a document for an improper purpose.

Consider which claims Alby should plead. As preparation for drafting your pleading, you focused your efforts on selecting a legal theory, which will be the basis for the claims or defenses, parties, and relief you will plead.

You engaged in this process when you researched tried-and-true and cutting-edge law and examined the facts in your client's case.

You developed three plausible legal theories. Two legal theories are based on tried-and-true negligence law in the State of Major: common law negligence based on Brady's intoxication, and negligence per se (breach of State of Major statute for intoxication). The third legal theory is based on a plausible interpretation of the State of Major Supreme Court case, *Susanah v. David*, which in a footnote stated, "[e]xcessive intoxication might recklessly endanger others." A law review article by an eminent professor also suggests that driving while excessively intoxicated might potentially be considered a "new tort."

Tried-and-True Negligence Claims

What claims are suggested by these three legal theories? Two claims, common law negligence and negligence per se, are suggested by the tried-and-true legal theories. There are facts to support both tried-and-true claims as indicated by the police report—Brady's intoxication while driving and breach of a State of Major statute by being intoxicated while driving.

Some commentators believe that you need not plead separate and distinct claims that are derived from identical substantive law but raise different factual or legal theories of negligence. Others disagree. But if you plead only one claim for negligence, you must be careful that the statement of the claim is sufficiently broad to include all legal and factual theories of recovery.

Cutting-Edge Reckless Endangerment Claim

The third legal theory is at the cutting edge of the law because it is potentially expanding negligence law by suggesting a new tort claim, reckless endangerment, based on a new legal theory. A claim such as reckless endangerment is essentially just a more expansive use of facts and relief for a negligence claim (outrageous conduct instead of negligent conduct, punitive damages instead of only compensatory damages).

Therefore, the same elements used in the established negligence claim could constitute the reckless endangerment claim. The facts in Alby's case fit a reckless endangerment interpretation. Brady's .25 blood alcohol level is well beyond the blood-alcohol level for negligence. But suppose instead of .25, Brady's blood-alcohol level was .12. If most negligence claims of driving while intoxicated are based on a blood alcohol level between .09 and .15 in a jurisdiction basing a violation on a .08 level, Alby's facts would be weak for attempting to assert a cutting-edge claim for reckless endangerment.

WHAT CLAIMS TO PLEAD

The *Alby* Case

The legal and factual components of your case theories guide you in determining what claim to plead.

Legal Theories

- Tried-and-true—firmly established legal theories:
  - ◇ Common law negligence
  - ◇ Negligence per se
- Cutting-edge—Reckless endangerment

Factual Theory—Common Law Negligence

Imagine as Alby's attorney that you assert a claim for common law negligence. The facts you allege will be structured by the elements of the legal theory—duty, breach, cause, injury.

Duty:	1.	On June 15, 20XX, Alby and Brady were driving on a public highway in the State of Major.
Breach of Duty:	2.	Brady negligently drove his car into Alby,
Cause:	3.	Causing Alby to suffer injuries that hospitalized him.
Injury:	4.	Alby had medical expenses totaling $5,000 and personal injuries of $50,000.

Burden of Pleading

The burden of pleading is generally determined by procedural rule, although sometimes it is determined by statute, case law, or established custom. Who has the burden to plead certain aspects of the case is important because a failure to meet the burden may have adverse consequences for your client. The burden of pleading is particularly important in determining the content of your pleading—that is, in determining whether something must be plead as a claim or defense.

For example, in most jurisdictions, procedural rules establish that a plaintiff in an affirmative pleading has the burden of pleading a defendant's negligence but is not required to plead the absence of his or her own negligence.

Thus, a plaintiff does not have to plead, "I was wearing a seat belt at the time of the crash." Instead, the procedural rule establishes that a plaintiff's negligence is an affirmative defense that the defendant has the burden of pleading, and if this is not plead this defense may be waived—in this case, that the plaintiff failed to wear a seat belt resulting in injury. Yet some jurisdictions have the opposite procedural rule and place the burden on the plaintiff to plead the absence of negligence by plaintiff. Therefore, it is very important that you become aware of how the particular rules in your jurisdiction allocate the burdens of pleading.

Joinder of Claims or Defenses

You need to consider how procedural rules can affect which claims or defenses you can join in your pleading and which ones you must plead in order to avoid waiving those claims or defenses. Some procedural rules allow and even encourage that all claims and defenses be joined in one lawsuit. For example, a plaintiff can plead unrelated claims of negligence and contract against a defendant.

Procedural rules established by case law, such as res judicata, collateral estoppel, and statutes of limitation might require you to join claims because you may be precluded from raising the claim or defense in a subsequent law suit. Therefore, you might have to plead, in the same lawsuit, two claims or defenses that you may not have wanted to join (a medical malpractice claim against the treating doctor and a claim for common law negligence against the driver of the automobile). Or you might join two affirmative defenses (accord and satisfaction and fraud).

You also need to be aware of other procedural rules that can limit defenses that may be joined. For example, a defending party can plead only affirmative defenses related to the claim or transaction alleged by the plaintiff.

Case Strategies as Guides

Now stand back and consider: Do these claims or defenses help achieve your case strategies? Because a motivating force in determining which claims to plead will be your case strategy, you must decide what you want to achieve and how this pleading can help advance toward that goal. Let's suppose, for illustration, that your case strategy is to try to settle the case for the greatest amount possible. In order to achieve this strategy, the pleading should be legally sufficient and factually sufficient and convince your adversary to settle for the maximum amount of compensation for Alby.

Both claims based on negligence will be sufficient and persuasive, if sufficient facts are pleaded, because they are established by present law. But your objective of maximizing damages might not be achieved by pleading only the two negligence claims. Relief under a negligence theory is limited to compensatory damages and would not maximize compensation for Alby since damages for negligence under State of Major case law do not include punitive or treble damages.

Maximizing damages might be better achieved by pleading the reckless endangerment claim, which suggests the potential for punitive or treble damages. But there are two serious drawbacks to a reckless endangerment claim. First, since a reckless endangerment claim is at the cutting edge of the law, it is not established, thereby subjecting it to an attack because of legal insufficiency. Second, a claim for reckless endangerment might not be as persuasive to your opponent because it is a novel claim.

As Alby's attorney you will have to decide which claims will best achieve your case strategy. Does that mean you plead only those claims that are strongest, such as the tried-and-true claims? Or do you include your cutting-edge claim even though it is legally problematic? There are two philosophies. The view that suggests you only plead your strongest, nonproblematic claims is based on practical considerations of avoiding costly and time-consuming attacks on your pleading. The other view is that you plead all plausible claims, including claims that are inconsistent, as long as they have a reasonable basis in law and fact. This position views pleading as a potential negotiation tool. Thus, the third claim might provide leverage in negotiating. Any problems with the third claim can eventually be resolved by dismissing the cutting-edge claim, but why do that now? Adopting this view, you tentatively plan to plead all three claims and to eventually sort out the claims or defenses that are the most likely to be proved at trial.

D. Proper Parties

Important strategy questions for all parties are at issue here. Is the plaintiff a proper party? Is the defendant? Should defendant file a cross-claim against a codefendant? If plaintiff has not joined a defendant, should you, as the responding party, file a third-party complaint? For clarity of analysis, we have posed discrete questions for determining claims, parties, and relief. But in actuality the approach to party determination is part of a concurrent analysis similar to that for determining claims or defenses. Here too you will consider:

- Your *legal theories,*
- *Procedural rules regarding joinder*—this time joinder of parties, and
- Your overall *case strategies.*

Legal Theories as Guides

Similar to determining which claims or defenses to plead, the decision as to what parties to include is determined by the legal theory that supports the claim or defense you are relying on. In order to name a party, either as a plaintiff or a defendant, the party must have a causal connection to the event as defined by the legal theory. For example, suppose a bystander witnesses a bloody accident and suffers emotional distress by witnessing the impact. The bystander wants to file an action for emotional distress against the defendant-driver. Is the bystander a proper party plaintiff? If the law is that no duty is owed to unrelated bystanders who suffer emotional distress as a result of witnessing a bloody accident, the bystander is not a proper party because the bystander is not causally connected to the event under the present law of negligence.

THE PARTIES TO PLEAD

Legal Theory as the Guide

The *Alby* Case

Analyze whether there are sufficient facts to connect the potential party to the legal claim. In the *Alby* case, Brady is a proper party because:

- He is causally connected to the accident under negligence law.
- He owed a duty to Alby to exercise reasonable care.
- He breached that duty by crashing into Alby's car and allegedly was the proximate cause of the accident.
- Factually, Brady is connected to the event since he is the owner and driver of the automobile that crashed into Alby.

Rules Governing Joinder of Parties

You should review procedural rules, case law, and statutes on party joinder because they can affect your case strategy by defining whom you can and *must* name as a party and how you technically describe a party. For instance, you may want to selectively name a party in order to pursue a particular strategy. Suppose your strategy in a products liability case is to assert a claim against the manufacturer only. Nevertheless, a procedural rule for joinder of parties may require that you must join the retailer as a party because the rules define the retailer as an essential party.

On the other hand, you may want to join a party but different procedural rules or substantive law governing personal jurisdiction, subject matter jurisdiction, venue, or service of process may prohibit you. For instance, you may decide not to join a potential defendant because the person lives in a foreign country and service would be difficult.

Rules of civil procedure govern who may be joined as parties. Federal Rule of Civil Procedure 20 provides for permissive joinder not only of plaintiffs but also of defendants. The Rule permits that plaintiffs may be joined if they have a claim and that defendants may be joined in one action if there is asserted against them "either jointly, severally, or in the alternative in respect of or arising out of the same transaction, occurrence, or series of transactions or occurrences and if any question of law or fact common to all these persons will arise in the action." State court rules usually also favor permissive joinder.

Case Strategy as a Guide

Finally, consider your overall case strategy. Analyze how joining a party would help or hurt your case.

- Will it burden your *financial and time resources?*
- Will it *complicate or confuse the issues?*
- Will it adversely affect your *negotiation or trial strategy?*

You are deciding whom to name in the *Alby* case. By naming only Brady as a defendant your case is a simple negligence rear-end collision case. But suppose Brady's intoxication was caused by drinking too much at his company's annual employee picnic. Should we name Brady's employer as a defendant? What effect does that have on your case strategy? If you name the employer, you may cause the two defendants to turn on each other to your advantage in reaching a settlement or at trial. The additional defendant complicates the issues by adding another theory of liability. By adding the employer you increase the probability of collecting a greater damage award.

However, by adding the employer you increase the likelihood that it will cost more to litigate the case. You may well spend much more time on the case because the employer will be able to devote more legal resources to the case compared to what would happen if you named only Brady as a defendant. Plaintiff's costs will increase by adding the employer because the number of witnesses, depositions, subpoenaed documents, among other things, will also increase. If you join the employer as a defendant, Brady may file a cross-claim against the employer. If you do not join the employer, your pleading is subject to attack for failure to join an essential party. A responding party can file a motion under Federal Rule of Civil Procedure 12(h)(2) to dismiss for failure to join a party. Also, Brady may file a third-party complaint thus relieving you of the time and expense of joining this defendant.

E.   Pleading a Claim for Relief

Suppose the *Alby* case strategy is to try to settle the case and obtain the most compensation. What relief will you plead?

Legal Theory as a Guide

When determining the relief to plead, you will apply an analysis similar to the one you used to determine the claims and parties to plead. Alby's relief will be based on the same legal theory that is the basis for the claim. If Alby requests punitive damages or treble damages as a remedy for negligence, then Alby's request for relief in all probability will be challenged as legally insufficient (subjecting the remedy section of your pleading to a motion to dismiss) because State of Major does not permit punitive damages for negligence. But if Alby pleads the cutting-edge claim, reckless endangerment, there is a potential for punitive relief suggested by dicta in *Susanah v. David* and the Waldman tort article.

Do the facts support punitive relief? The facts in Alby's case certainly suggest outrageous conduct, an intoxication level of .25 that is well beyond the presumptive level of .08 for intoxication. Alby's attorney could argue that punitive damages are appropriate to punish the wrongdoer and compensate the plaintiff for conduct that is far more egregious than negligence.

Case Strategy as a Guide

Does the request for punitive relief accomplish your case strategy? Pleading treble or punitive damages would be on the cutting edge. Although the pleading would appear to accomplish your objective for pleading the maximum recovery, the claim and relief probably would be subject to a motion to dismiss for legal insufficiency. Consider: If the relief can be attacked for legal insufficiency, does the requested relief achieve your case strategy? If an objective of the pleading is to plausibly raise the stakes for negotiation, then, in all likelihood, your case strategy might be well implemented. Defendant Brady now knows that if he moves to attack the legality of the reckless endangerment claim in court and loses—and, with the language in *Susanah v. David* and the general sentiment about drunk drivers, he could—the cost of settling the case at that point will increase.

THE RELIEF TO PLEAD

Legal Theory and Case Strategy as Guides

The *Alby* Case

In determining the relief to seek, your legal theory and case strategy act as guides.

LEGAL THEORY: Reckless endangerment provides for punitive damages, negligence does not. So, you seriously consider reckless endangerment because you can plead the relief of punitive damages.

CASE STRATEGY: Because punitive damages may be awarded if there is a claim for reckless endangerment, the defendant may be more amenable to early settlement, which is your overall case strategy.

Damages and Other Forms of Relief

At the end of the complaint, the complaining party states a demand for relief—what is wanted from the opposing party. As was shown in the *Alby* case, the relief demanded is determined by existing law and the legal theory; pleading negligence may result in compensatory damages but by pleading reckless endangerment the plaintiff in *Alby* could recover punitive damages.

Potential damages and other relief that may be sought are as follows:

- **Punitive damages**—Punitive damages are a monetary award designed to punish the party and to be a deterrent to others who might otherwise engage in the same conduct. The demand for relief: "for punitive damages in the amount to be proven at trial."

- **Injunctive Equitable Relief**—This is a request to the court to take action, such as order the defendant to not go within 500 feet of the plaintiff. Demand for relief: "that the court enter an injunction against the defendant prohibiting the defendant from entering onto the property located at . . ."

- **Damages**—The request is to order the opposing party to pay for the damage from the injury that party caused; this could include an award for pain and suffering. *Special damages* are those damages that are special to that plaintiff, such as medical expenses, loss of wages and profits, and so on. Fed. R. Civ. P. 9(d) requires that special damages be specifically pled. Demand for relief: "that the defendant pay damages for pain and suffering in the amount to be determined at trial."

- **Costs and Attorneys' Fees**—Demand for relief: "that the defendant pay costs and attorneys' fees." Attorneys' fees generally are awarded only when a statute authorizes an award of attorneys' fees or the contract at issue specifically provides for attorneys' fees. Usually, each party bears that party's own costs. However, the circumstances may warrant an award of costs to one of the parties.
- **Prejudgment Interest**—The request is that the other party pay prejudgment interest on liquidated damages. Demand for relief: "that the defendant pay prejudgment interest on liquidated damages."
- **Other Relief**—At the end of the list of demands, this request asks for any other relief justice requires, and this is designed to allow for further request that might otherwise be missed. Demand for relief: "that the court or jury grant other relief as justice requires."

When there is more than one defendant, the demand for relief should request that the defendants be held jointly and severally responsible for the damages.

F.   The Amount of Information to Plead

Examine how much information you should include in pleading a claim for common law negligence. There are two types of pleading methods. We have nicknamed them "bare-bones" and "fully-dressed."

Bare-Bones Pleading

Bare-bones pleading means that you include just enough information to give notice of your claims. The pleading needs to have enough facts at the outset to satisfy Rule 11. Many attorneys plead by the bare-bones method; preference for bare-bones pleading is partially due to the belief that the function of pleading is to give notice of claims and that formal discovery is the process for providing additional facts.

Fully-Dressed Pleading—Storytelling

The fully-dressed pleading method allows you to tell your story as to what occurred legally and factually. The fully-dressed method of pleading might describe legal and factual theories, document in detail the relief requested, anticipate your opponent's position and affirmatively justify your own (even though the burden of pleading may not require such justification), discard weak theories, and so on. The rationale for pleading this way is that the pleading should persuade, obtain publicity for your case, and educate the public, the court, and your adversary. Depending on the amount of information you include, this type of pleading might be highly controversial because it does not merely give notice or state the facts constituting the claim for relief, but uses pleading as an advocacy tool. It also gives your opponent a much more complete road map to your case than under notice pleading.

Pleading in the fully-dressed method might mean that your pleading will not conform to procedural rules. Your opponent might even file a motion to strike evidentiary facts. For example, procedural rules only require sufficient information to state a valid claim for relief. That means that you do not have to plead evidentiary facts or witnesses. Yet you may, by using the fully-dressed method, include evidentiary facts if your objective is to persuade your adversary.

AMOUNT OF INFORMATION TO PLEAD

The *Alby* Case

Fully-dressed Pleading

Suppose you plead Alby's negligence claim by using the fully-dressed method of pleading:

> "Three eyewitnesses—a minister and two teachers—saw defendant Brady act erratically and drive negligently through the intersection when the light was red. Brady, who had a .25 blood alcohol level, was intoxicated. Because of his intoxication, he negligently lost control of his car, crashing into plaintiff. Brady was the proximate cause of the injuries to Alby."

Bare-bones Pleading

The bare-bones method might be as follows:

> "Defendant Brady negligently and carelessly crashed his automobile into plaintiff Alby's automobile."

You could also attach exhibits such as a breathalyzer report or a police report.

The Strategic Considerations

Which method of pleading should you use?

Legal and Factual Sufficiency

First, consider how much information you need to include for legal and factual sufficiency. Recall that the type and amount of information is determined by the legal theory that is the basis for your claim or defense. Both pleading illustrations include sufficient information according to the legal elements of a negligence theory. Generally, pleading according to the elements of the legal theory you are relying on will be legally and factually sufficient for both code and notice pleading requirements. If you want to merely give notice and do not want to plead according to a legal theory, you will need to consult references in your particular jurisdiction in order to determine whether you can plead fewer facts than your legal theory suggests.

Case Strategy and Pleading Objectives

Second, consider the effect of bare-bones and fully-dressed pleading methods on your case strategy and pleading objectives. In the illustrations the case strategy was to try to settle the case for the highest amount possible. By pleading persuasively, you may promote settlement with your adversary or resolution of the dispute by summary judgment. Fully-dressed pleading will likely be more convincing than a mere bare-bones statement of negligence because it contains specific evidence that supports your factual theory. But fully-dressed pleading might also be detrimental to achieving your objectives. By explicitly including evidentiary facts, you might limit the development of other potential case theories. For instance, if you plead a factual theory of "intoxication," you might later be precluded from obtaining discovery or presentation of witnesses at trial based on a factual theory of "inattentiveness" for Alby's common law negligence claim. Of course, you can amend your pleading throughout pretrial and even at trial. Nevertheless, there may be occasions when you might be precluded because of statutes of limitations, procedural rules, or unfairness to your adversary. Therefore, a fully-dressed pleading method should also be broad enough to encompass as many potential legal and factual theories as possible.

Now examine bare-bones pleading. Does that help you to achieve your objectives? "Defendant Brady negligently and carelessly crashed his automobile into plaintiff Alby's automobile" has as its primary objective giving notice of plaintiff's claims. This pleading, although not persuasive, is factually sufficient. If the philosophy of your pleading is that it is merely a stepping stone to discovery, then bare-bones pleading is a more flexible strategy for carrying out that objective.

Local Custom

Finally, consider local custom. What is acceptable in your jurisdiction? If bare-bones pleading is the customary method of pleading and you plead using the fully-dressed method, you should be prepared for the ramifications of your break with tradition. Although ignoring local custom should not result in a motion for insufficiency, you might be perceived as failing to plead properly. And, although your pleading theoretically is persuasive, your pleading might be viewed by others as weak because it is presented in an unfamiliar manner. When the local custom is to use a bare-bones pleading, stick with this and present to opposing counsel a negotiation brochure as the persuasive device.

G. Anticipating Attacks on the Pleading

While drafting your pleading, you should anticipate the reaction to your pleading from your adversary, the court, and others. For instance, is your pleading vulnerable to a motion to dismiss, judgment on the pleading, summary judgment, failure or misjoinder of parties?

To illustrate, let's consider your pleading in Alby's case. Suppose your first claim is based on the legal theory of common law negligence. First, consider whether the pleading is subject to an attack for factual insufficiency. If you fail to include facts describing one of the legal elements, such as Alby's injury, your claim is factually insufficient. If you plead the cutting-edge claim, reckless endangerment, which requires reckless or outrageous conduct, and you fail to describe that Brady's conduct was reckless or outrageous, your pleading might be factually insufficient. Or if your pleading is so bare bones that it is deficient in giving notice of your claim—"Brady negligently crashed into Alby, breaching State of Major statutes"—such pleading might be factually deficient.

Second, consider whether your pleading will be attacked for legal insufficiency. If you plead the cutting-edge reckless endangerment claim, your pleading will probably be attacked as legally insufficient. Or if you request treble or punitive damages, you can also expect an attack on the type of relief you request because that relief is not established by law. Also, if yours is a code-pleading jurisdiction and you fail to present facts establishing all of the elements of a claim, your pleading may be attacked for legal insufficiency.

Any of these potential problems should cause you to redraft your pleading to avoid costly and time-consuming motion preparation and practice.

Thus, at the very least, draft your claim—for example, reckless endangerment—to have the strongest possible record if it is attacked and you need to defend it.

H.   Satisfying Procedural and Technical Requirements

You want to avoid an attack on your pleading based on procedural or technical insufficiency. Although technical insufficiency normally will not result in dismissal of your pleading, it is nevertheless a costly and time-consuming process to amend a pleading because of technical insufficiency. Generally, you can avoid an attack on these grounds by carefully following the local and procedural rules governing the submission of pleadings, from how they usually look—the format required by the court—to what paper to use.

Pleading Sources

Throughout this text, we have stressed the need for consulting everything from reference texts to other attorneys and court personnel. This is a special necessity in drafting pleadings because there are requirements unique to particular jurisdictions that are often a matter of custom. A word of caution is in order about particular pleading sources such as form books. Form books contain both approved court forms and forms that are generally used by attorneys in a particular jurisdiction. The Federal Rules of Civil Procedure, for example, contain an appendix of forms with stock language for complaints.

Generally, sources such as form books, and even some experienced and highly competent attorneys, might approach pleading in a technical and highly stylized manner. You might be advised, "This is the customary way to plead," when another approach would more effectively achieve your overall objectives. Or, you might even be given poorly drafted examples. Just as we continue to caution you in using our approach, we also want to add a caveat about other references. Use these resources as a source of ideas, but always use your own judgment when pleading.

Technical Format

All pleadings must conform to particular formats. Generally, procedural rules specify such requirements as paper size, paragraph divisions, topical headings, and so on. You will need to be familiar with the particular format that is appropriate or required by the court you are in.

Does your pleading have to be on a specific paper? Generally, most courts require what is referred to as pleading paper, with numbers from top to bottom along the left-hand margin. Does the caption have to appear in a certain format? Do you need topical headings? Are there specific paragraph structure rules? Do the factual allegations need to be numbered? The answer to the last question is yes—most jurisdictions require that each factual allegation be separately stated and numbered. The numbering system will vary with jurisdictions, although it will always be the rule that your numbering system must be logical. As such, use consecutive numbers that are not duplicative.

By following prescribed requirements you can avoid an attack for technical insufficiency because of incorrect format. General and local court rules, sample pleadings in form books, and experienced attorneys and court personnel (clerks, bailiffs) can help you use the proper format. You may also want to look at the examples in the appendix to this chapter.

In addition to avoiding problems, you can use the format to make your pleading more persuasive and understandable. You might use topical headings to help educate your reader and to focus issues. If you plead three claims for relief, by using a topical heading identifying each claim, your pleading will be more understandable for the adversary, court, and client. For example, one of your topical headings might read, "First Claim for Relief: Common law Negligence."

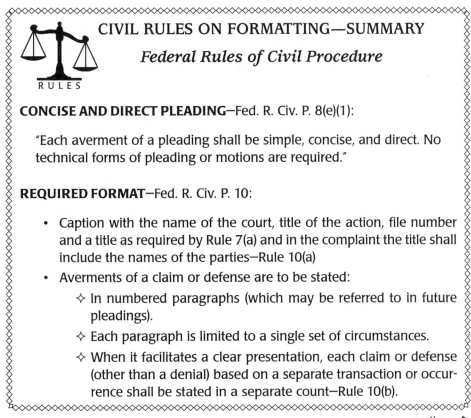

CIVIL RULES ON FORMATTING—SUMMARY
Federal Rules of Civil Procedure

CONCISE AND DIRECT PLEADING—Fed. R. Civ. P. 8(e)(1):

"Each averment of a pleading shall be simple, concise, and direct. No technical forms of pleading or motions are required."

REQUIRED FORMAT—Fed. R. Civ. P. 10:

- Caption with the name of the court, title of the action, file number and a title as required by Rule 7(a) and in the complaint the title shall include the names of the parties—Rule 10(a)
- Averments of a claim or defense are to be stated:
  - ◇ In numbered paragraphs (which may be referred to in future pleadings).
  - ◇ Each paragraph is limited to a single set of circumstances.
  - ◇ When it facilitates a clear presentation, each claim or defense (other than a denial) based on a separate transaction or occurrence shall be stated in a separate count—Rule 10(b).

continues ▶

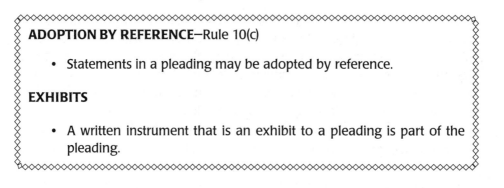

ADOPTION BY REFERENCE—Rule 10(c)

- Statements in a pleading may be adopted by reference.

EXHIBITS

- A written instrument that is an exhibit to a pleading is part of the pleading.

I.   Writing an Effective Pleading

A simple and clear writing style will transform your pleading from adequate to being a piece of work that distinguishes you as a formidable advocate who can accomplish a client's objectives. For instance, legalistic words and phrases often make a pleading difficult to understand and get in the way of the advocate's story.

Many pleadings contain meaningless, ritualistic legal jargon. Clarity is particularly important as a communication tool if the pleading is given to your client, or if it is read to the jury, as required by court rules, or disseminated to a public audience. Use plain English instead of legal jargon to make your pleading understandable and persuasive. Your pleadings should include legal jargon only when it communicates a specific legal concept. For instance, it is easier to use the legal jargon "upon information and belief" than to explain in your pleadings: "I believe in good faith that I will discover or be able to prove that . . ." When in doubt always assume that your pleading will be more understandable and persuasive if you use plain English.

Using vocabulary that is too descriptive, emotional, or flamboyant can subject your pleading to attack. Your vocabulary should specifically achieve your case strategy and your pleading objectives. If you have to amend your pleading or defend a motion because your language does not appropriately persuade, you need to consider whether your vocabulary choices are consistent with your case strategy as these consequences are time-consuming and costly for you and your client. Also, as discussed later, slanderous language is usually not conducive to building an atmosphere for rational negotiations.

Think about using your pleading to tell your client's story, including those facts that are essential to the flow of the story. By constructing your pleading according to a story, it might be more readable and ultimately more persuasive.

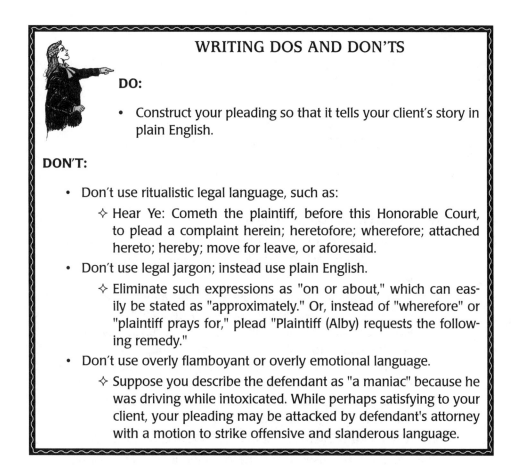

WRITING DOS AND DON'TS

DO:

- Construct your pleading so that it tells your client's story in plain English.

DON'T:

- Don't use ritualistic legal language, such as:
  ◇ Hear Ye: Cometh the plaintiff, before this Honorable Court, to plead a complaint herein; heretofore; wherefore; attached hereto; hereby; move for leave, or aforesaid.
- Don't use legal jargon; instead use plain English.
  ◇ Eliminate such expressions as "on or about," which can easily be stated as "approximately." Or, instead of "wherefore" or "plaintiff prays for," plead "Plaintiff (Alby) requests the following remedy."
- Don't use overly flamboyant or overly emotional language.
  ◇ Suppose you describe the defendant as "a maniac" because he was driving while intoxicated. While perhaps satisfying to your client, your pleading may be attacked by defendant's attorney with a motion to strike offensive and slanderous language.

J.   Focusing on the Answer

A Motion, an Answer, or Both

Let's concentrate on the responsive pleading a little more. While primarily the answer to a complaint is discussed here, the response to a counterclaim, cross-claim, or third party claim is generally governed by the same law, procedures, and strategies as the answer. The first strategic question is: Should a defendant answer or file a motion? For instance, according to the Federal Rules, a defendant can include in an answer all the matters that could be the subject of a motion, such as improper venue, process, joinder of parties, and so forth. When should either be filed? Are there time limits that create waivers? (Failure to file a motion alleging defective service of process before answering can result in waiver of the process issue. But other issues can be raised at any time either by motion or answer—e.g., lack of subject matter jurisdiction, misjoinder of parties.)

Motion

Chapter 11 is devoted to motions' practice, because it is an alternative to an answer, but motions are also explored here.

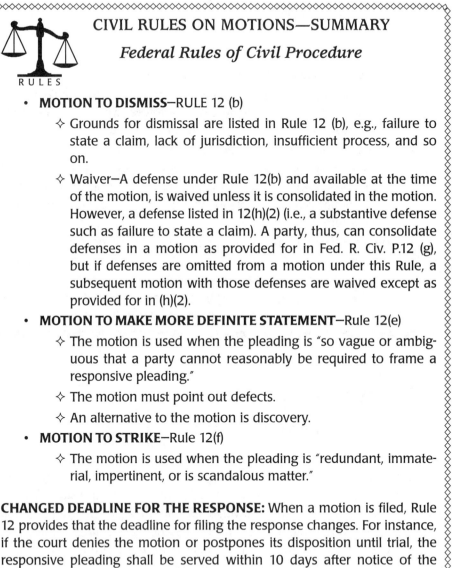

CIVIL RULES ON MOTIONS—SUMMARY

Federal Rules of Civil Procedure

RULES

- **MOTION TO DISMISS—RULE 12 (b)**
  - ◇ Grounds for dismissal are listed in Rule 12 (b), e.g., failure to state a claim, lack of jurisdiction, insufficient process, and so on.
  - ◇ Waiver—A defense under Rule 12(b) and available at the time of the motion, is waived unless it is consolidated in the motion. However, a defense listed in 12(h)(2) (i.e., a substantive defense such as failure to state a claim). A party, thus, can consolidate defenses in a motion as provided for in Fed. R. Civ. P.12 (g), but if defenses are omitted from a motion under this Rule, a subsequent motion with those defenses are waived except as provided for in (h)(2).
- **MOTION TO MAKE MORE DEFINITE STATEMENT—Rule 12(e)**
  - ◇ The motion is used when the pleading is "so vague or ambiguous that a party cannot reasonably be required to frame a responsive pleading."
  - ◇ The motion must point out defects.
  - ◇ An alternative to the motion is discovery.
- **MOTION TO STRIKE—Rule 12(f)**
  - ◇ The motion is used when the pleading is "redundant, immaterial, impertinent, or is scandalous matter."

CHANGED DEADLINE FOR THE RESPONSE: When a motion is filed, Rule 12 provides that the deadline for filing the response changes. For instance, if the court denies the motion or postpones its disposition until trial, the responsive pleading shall be served within 10 days after notice of the court's action.

In deciding whether to make a motion rather than answer the complaint, the key question is whether the motion will have any substantial, positive effect in the long run. While the defendant might make a motion to dismiss because the complaint fails to state a claim upon which relief can be granted, the consequence of your motion may merely be that the plaintiff is given the opportunity to amend the complaint. Similarly, a defense motion to make more definite may result in an amendment, and the defendant could just as well have gotten the information through a discovery request.

Framing the Answer

Federal Rules of Civil Procedure 8(b) and (c) establish specific rules regarding how the response should be framed.

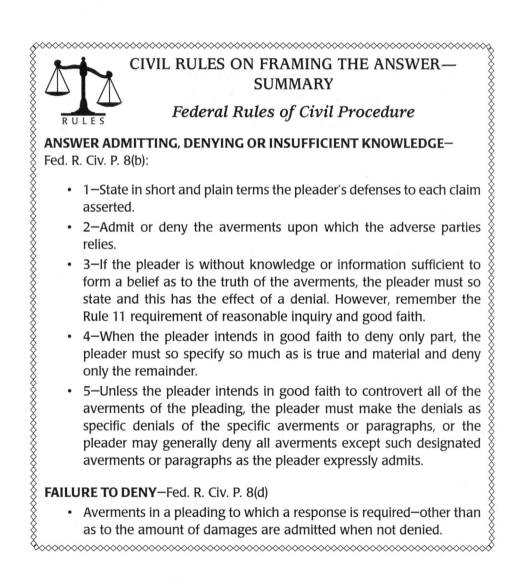

CIVIL RULES ON FRAMING THE ANSWER— SUMMARY

Federal Rules of Civil Procedure

RULES

ANSWER ADMITTING, DENYING OR INSUFFICIENT KNOWLEDGE— Fed. R. Civ. P. 8(b):

- 1—State in short and plain terms the pleader's defenses to each claim asserted.
- 2—Admit or deny the averments upon which the adverse parties relies.
- 3—If the pleader is without knowledge or information sufficient to form a belief as to the truth of the averments, the pleader must so state and this has the effect of a denial. However, remember the Rule 11 requirement of reasonable inquiry and good faith.
- 4—When the pleader intends in good faith to deny only part, the pleader must so specify so much as is true and material and deny only the remainder.
- 5—Unless the pleader intends in good faith to controvert all of the averments of the pleading, the pleader must make the denials as specific denials of the specific averments or paragraphs, or the pleader may generally deny all averments except such designated averments or paragraphs as the pleader expressly admits.

FAILURE TO DENY—Fed. R. Civ. P. 8(d)

- Averments in a pleading to which a response is required—other than as to the amount of damages are admitted when not denied.

Under the Federal Rules of Civil Procedure and common state practice, the answers to the paragraphs of allegations in the complaint may be phrased as follows:

- *ADMIT:* "Defendant (this defendant) admits the allegations of paragraph 3 of Plaintiff's complaint."
- *DENY:* "Defendant denies the allegations of paragraph 3 of Plaintiff's complaint."
- *INSUFFICIENT INFORMATION:* "Defendant does not have sufficient information to form a belief as to the truth of the allegations of paragraph 3 of plaintiff's complaint, therefore denies."
- *COMBINATION OF THE ABOVE*

Affirmative Defenses, Counterclaims, Cross-claims and Third-Party Claims

Besides admitting or denying the plaintiff's claims, the defense may either raise an affirmative defense or plead a counterclaim or cross-claim.

Affirmative Defense

A defendant can plead an affirmative defense to the complaint, such as the statute of limitations, and in doing so usually assumes the burden of proving the defense at trial. Federal Rule of Civil Procedure 8(c) contains a list of affirmative defenses including contributory negligence, accord and satisfaction, estoppel, assumption of risk, and "any other matter constituting an avoidance or affirmative defense." Rule 8(c) also provides that if a defense is mislabeled as a counterclaim or cross-claim, the court will treat it as though it had the proper designation.

Counterclaim

A counterclaim is a claim brought by the defendant against the plaintiff. A counterclaim is the equivalent of a complaint and is pled in that fashion. Federal Rule of Civil Procedure 13(a) provides for compulsory counterclaims. Compulsory counterclaims must be plead if the claim exists at the time of the lawsuit and arises out of the same transaction or occurrence. If the compulsory counterclaim is not pled, then it is waived (the exceptions to this are when the court permits it to be filed or if the counterclaim matures later). The purpose of this Rule is to allow the court to take care of all claims at the same time.

A defendant at its discretion may file a counterclaim under Fed. R. Civ. P. 13(b). The difference from a compulsory counterclaim is that the claimed fault arises out of a different transaction than the one alleged by the plaintiff.

Cross-claim

A cross-claim is brought by a defendant against a co-defendant or if there are co-plaintiffs by one plaintiff against another plaintiff. It may be brought at the discretion of a defendant. It is also like a complaint and is plead like a complaint. Under Fed. R. Civ. P. 13(g), a cross-claim may be brought if the claim arises "out of the transaction or occurrence that is the subject matter either of the original action or of a counterclaim therein or relating to any property that is the subject matter of the original action. Such cross-claim may include a claim that the party against whom it is asserted is or may be liable to the cross-claimant for all or part of a claim asserted in the action against the cross-claimant."

Third-Party Claim

A defendant or a plaintiff defending against a counterclaim may implead a non-party claiming that that third-party defendant should indemnify the party who has brought the action because of the third party's fault. Fed. R. Civ. P. 14 governs third-party claims.

K.   Other Strategic Issues

Deciding When to File

Will you file a complaint before or after negotiation? Are there prerequisites before you can file? Do you have to file a claim with an agency? Exhaust administrative remedies? Examples: Before filing a complaint against a government body, it might be necessary to file an administrative claim within a certain period of time or you might be precluded by a statute of limitations from court action; employment discrimination cases filed in federal court require exhaustion of administrative remedies with the Equal Employment Opportunity Commission prior to pleading in federal court. Carefully think about when it is best to file your pleading, taking into consideration these factors and any specific considerations of your client's claim.

Deciding What Additional Pleading You Will Do

Drafting pleadings is an evolving process, one that continues throughout your case. You will be thinking about drafting and redrafting (amending) pleadings every step of the way, from your initial client interview through your research of the law and your informal investigation of the facts, through the development of your case theory and your counseling sessions where you advise the client whether to pursue litigation or other alternatives, through formal discovery, and finally even during trial. As your view of the case evolves, and as you learn new information, you might want to think about amending your pleading to add to or change claims, parties, or relief. But at all times you need to keep in mind your case strategy, pleading objectives, and the technical procedural rules (e.g., statutes of limitations) that can control when and how you plead.

L.   Filing, Service and Electronic Means

Filing and Serving a Pleading

Who will serve process? Do you need to serve by a marshal? Registered process agent? When should you serve the pleading? (Note that service of process in some jurisdictions begins the action, while failure to serve process means that the statute of limitations is not tolled.) Who does it have to be served upon? Are there requirements for proof of service such as affidavits? Declarations? If you join a government body as a defendant, are there any special requirements to fulfill?

These questions are answered by the rules of civil procedure in your jurisdiction. The Federal Rules of Civil Procedure 3-5, after which several states have patterned their filing and service of process rules, set forth the procedures for filing pleadings and service. Under Fed. R. Civ. P. 3, a civil action is commenced when a complaint is filed with the court. In sum, Rules 4(a) and (b) provide that when a complaint is filed, the court clerk issues a summons directing that the defendant must appear and defend and notifying the defendant that failure to do so will result in a default judgment against the defendant for the relief sought in the complaint. Rule 4(c) states that the plaintiff is responsible for the service of the summons and complaint on the defendant within the time limit (usually 120 days under Rule 4(m)). Rule 4 also provides rules for waiver of service and service on diverse persons (e.g., infants, incompetents, persons in foreign countries), entities (e.g., corporations, the United States and its agencies), and so on. Rule 5 authorizes service on an attorney for a represented party and the means of serving pleadings and other papers—handing it to the person, mailing to last known address, and so on.

E-Filing and Service

Electronic filing and service is well underway in federal and some state courts. Fed. R. Civ. P. 5(e), in essence, states that the federal court by local rule can permit electronic filing with the court. A 2006 amendment to this rule authorizes the federal court by local rule to mandate e-filing but "only if reasonable exceptions are allowed." The proviso is designed to prevent undue hardship on a party. Also, a copy can be served by electronic means if the party served consents to this means of service in writing.

Electronic filing and service are both convenient (enabling Word documents to be converted to PDF files and sent from or received at locations no matter how remote) and cost effective (eliminating the filing and storage of mounds of paper). An example of the e-filing system can be found at the U.S. District Court for Western Washington, which has had mandatory e-filing since April 2004. Through local written procedures that court has described and standardized the e-filing process so that it works efficiently for the court and the litigants. Those written procedures can be reviewed on line at *http://www.wawd.uscourts.gov/wawd/welcome.nsf/main/page*. Some examples of the issues that have been resolved and explained by these written procedures are:

- The format acceptable to the court, e.g., PDF files and scanned images,
- Voluminous paper, e.g., when the document contains more than 100 pages, the judge is to be provided with a paper copy,
- Court reporter transcripts are filed electronically,
- Digitized signatures are acceptable and a process for challenging the signature's authenticity is created,
- A proposed order is electronically submitted as an attachment to a motion,
- Court orders are electronically filed,
- The party who is filing electronically provides the docket entry title when the filing becomes part of the electronic case file,
- Sealed documents are maintained in electronic format but accessible only by authorized persons, and
- Civil and criminal dockets and documents can be remotely accessed over the Internet.

If your jurisdiction has not yet adopted e-filing procedures along these lines, it will in the not too distant future. To effectively and efficiently represent your clients, both you and your legal assistant and/or paralegal staff will need to be knowledgeable about e-filing procedures.

IV. LEARNING BY EXAMPLE: CIVIL PLEADINGS

The following illustrative pleadings and marginalia commentary are designed to provide you with the nuts and bolts for drafting pleadings.

We have enhanced the examples to provide an experience similar to having a veteran litigator sitting beside you and explaining each part of the pleading. This technique is intended to allow you to become proficient in drafting pleadings right from the beginning of your law career.

These examples reflect our interpretation of federal rules and general custom and our concept of case strategy. Some lawyers might differ with our drafting content and style. Some of their disagreement might stem from different procedural rules, drafting customs, or philosophies about the function of pleadings. Instead of dwelling on these differences, we suggest that you look at the annotations describing some of the choices that we made in formulating these drafts; you might later consider these choices when drafting your own pleadings. Keep in mind that the pleading examples are not designed to meet the requirements of a particular district; they are intended to be a guide to help you think about many of the technical and strategic issues that might confront you when drafting a pleading. We urge you to supplement the Alby and Brady complaint and answer by examining applicable procedural rules, substantive law, and other lawyers' pleadings used in your jurisdiction. Then you should form and adapt your own pleading style to the particular strategy that you want your pleadings to accomplish.

COMPLAINT—*ALBY v. BRADY*

UNITED STATES DISTRICT COURT
MIDDLE DISTRICT OF MAJOR

ALBERT J. ALBY,
    Plaintiff,

    v.

CLARK BRADY,
    Defendant

Civil Action, File Number 1743

Plaintiff's Complaint for Negligence; Negligence Per Se; Reckless Endangerment

---

Subject Matter Jurisdiction and Parties

1. Subject matter jurisdiction is founded on diversity of citizenship, 28 U.S.C. §1332.

CAPTION:
The captions in Alby's complaint and Brady's answer follow the format in Federal Rule of Civil Procedure 10. The caption includes the name of the court, the title of the action, the names of the parties, the court file number, and the specific name of the pleading.

JURISDICTION:
Paragraphs 1-4 illustrate how you determine which facts to plead for subject matter jurisdiction. Subject matter jurisdiction is based on diversity jurisdiction, codified in 28 U.S.C. §1332 and interpreted by case law. The first element of the diversity statute is complete

2. Plaintiff Albert J. Alby, an individual, is a citizen of California.

3. Defendant Clark Brady, an individual, is a citizen of Texas.

4. The matter in controversy exceeds, exclusive of interest and costs, the sum of seventy-five thousand dollars ($75,000).

Claim I: Common Law Negligence

5. On June 15, 20XX, Plaintiff Alby and Defendant Brady were driving south on Interstate 5 in Jamner, Major.

6. Defendant Brady negligently crashed his automobile into Plaintiff Alby's automobile.

7. As a result of the collision, Plaintiff suffered damage to his property and person. He suffered physical and mental pain. His injuries prevented him from maintaining his business.

8. Plaintiff incurred medical and hospital expenses in the sum of $15,000, $5,000 loss of profits, and loss of wages.

Claim II: Negligence Per Se

9. Plaintiff adopts by reference paragraphs 1-8.

10. Defendant has a duty under State of Major statutes to refrain from drinking intoxicating beverages while driving and to drive his automobile while sober.

11. Upon information and belief, Defendant, while driving, was drinking intoxicating beverages and was intoxicated while driving.

12. Defendant's conduct, which violates State of Major statutes, was a proximate cause of Plaintiff's injuries.

diverse citizenship of both adverse parties. A second element of diversity jurisdiction, according to the statute, is that more than $75,000 exclusive of interest and costs be in dispute.

PARTIES:
Two requirements—legal capacity and causal connection—guide the factual description of parties in a pleading. While, under Fed. R. Civ. P. 9(a), it is "not necessary to aver the capacity of a party to sue or be sued," it is good practice to do so. You must also plead the party's causal connection—that is, that the party is legally responsible according to substantive law. Paragraphs 5, 6, and 7 in Alby's common law negligence claim illustrate causal connection to the event by stating that Brady breached his duty and caused Alby's injury.

FORMAT:
Alby's complaint generally follows the format requirements specified in the Federal Rules of Civil Procedure, including Rule 10(b) requiring the division of each factual allegation into separate paragraphs. The Rules require that you identify claims and defenses, but do not require you to specify a claim or defense by labeling it with your legal theory.

CLAIMS:
Tried-and-True and Cutting Edge—In Alby's complaint, Claims I, II, and III illustrate both tried-and-true and cutting-edge claims. Claims I and II are tried-and-true negligence claims established by the substantive law of the State of Major. Claim III, reckless endangerment, is a cutting-edge claim, plausibly an expansion of negligence and suggesting a new tort.
Bare-Bones—Paragraphs 5 through 8 illustrate bare-bones pleading. Just enough information is included to give Brady notice of the claim and relief requested.

continues ▶

Claim III: Reckless Endangerment

13. Plaintiff adopts by reference paragraphs 1-12.

14. Defendant Brady, without regard for the safety and welfare of the public, including other drivers, intentionally and with malice recklessly consumed alcohol until he was so intoxicated that he had a blood-alcohol level of .25 and then operated his automobile. (Presumption of intoxication under a State of Major Statute is .08.)

15. Defendant Brady was cited by the State of Major Highway Patrol for driving while intoxicated. A copy of the State of Major Highway Patrol breathalyzer report for Defendant Brady is attached as Exhibit A.

16. Defendant's conduct outrageously and recklessly endangered Plaintiff's safety.

Plaintiff requests relief as follows:

17. Special damages for medical, repairs, and loss of wages in the sum of $20,000.

18. General damages, including pain and suffering, according to proof at trial.

19. Punitive damages in the sum of $500,000.

20. Costs, interest, and any other relief the Court or Jury finds appropriate.

Date: January 7, 20XX+1

By

Rob Coyne - Bar No. MA 4200
Penny Sent - Bar No. MA 6800
1800 International Bank Building
Second Street
Ruston, Major

(206) 383-0000
Attorneys for Plaintiff

PLAINTIFF ALBY REQUESTS A JURY

CUTTING-EDGE:
Claim III illustrates pleading based on the cutting edge of the law. Paragraphs 14, 15, and 16 factually describe Brady's intoxication as not just a negligent act, but an intentional, malicious, outrageous, and reckless act. Note that the decision to factually describe Brady's intoxication in this manner is based on the dicta in *Susanah v. David.*

ATTACHING EXHIBITS:
Generally, documents are not attached to pleadings, except in those few instances where legal precedent, rule, or custom mandate attaching documents. In this instance, Alby's attorney might believe that attaching documents such as the police report or breathalyzer report will be a strategic help in accomplishing an advocacy objective.

DAMAGES:
Paragraph 18 illustrates when to include or exclude specific information in your pleading. Alby did not plead a specific amount of general damages in paragraph 18. This illustrates the view that a specific damage amount should not be included if it is based on guesswork and not fact. Indeed, some jurisdictions by statute or rule prohibit pleading specific figures for monetary damage.

SIGNATURE:
Every pleading must be signed by the attorney of record, Fed. R. Civ. P. 11. The signature represents that the pleading was read, drafted after reasonable inquiry, is well grounded in fact, and warranted by existing law or a good-faith interpretation of existing law.

JURY DEMAND:
Federal Rule 38(b) allows either party to request a jury trial in its pleading.

ANSWER

UNITED STATES DISTRICT COURT
MIDDLE DISTRICT OF MAJOR

ALBERT J. ALBY,   )
    Plaintiff,   )
)   Civil Action, File Number 1743
    v.   )
)   A.J. Brady's Answer,
CLARK BRADY,   )   Counterclaim,
    Defendant   )   and Cross-Claim
_____)

Defendant Brady answers Plaintiff Alby's complaint:

1. Admits paragraphs 3 and 5.

2. Denies paragraphs 6, 11, 12, 14, 16, 20.

3. Admits paragraph 15, that he was cited by the State of Major Highway Patrol, except denies knowledge or information sufficient to form a belief as to the truth of the citation and Exhibit A.

4. Is without knowledge or information sufficient to form a belief as to the truth of the allegations in paragraphs 1, 2, 4, 7, 8-10, and 13, and therefore denies those paragraphs.

FIRST AFFIRMATIVE DEFENSE:
Failure to State a Claim

5. Plaintiff's complaint fails to state a claim against Defendant Brady upon which relief can be granted

SECOND AFFIRMATIVE DEFENSE:
Contributory Fault

6. Plaintiff Alby has a duty to keep his automobile in good repair.

7. Plaintiff Alby negligently failed to keep his automobile in good repair.

8. As a result of Plaintiff Alby's negligence, Alby's automobile abruptly began to slow down, Defendant Brady unavoidably crashed into Plaintiff's automobile.

RESPONDING TO ALLEGATIONS:
Paragraphs 1 through 4 illustrate the following ways defendant Brady can answer Plaintiff Alby's allegations: admit, partially admit and partially deny, deny, deny with a reason, including lack of sufficient information.

AFFIRMATIVE DEFENSE:
Paragraph 5, Brady's first affirmative defense, illustrates the choice that the Federal Rules provide a defending party as to when to raise defenses. A defending party can simultaneously raise certain matters by responding in an answer or by motion. In paragraph 5, Brady is attacking the legal sufficiency of plaintiffs' third claim, reckless endangerment, by pleading an affirmative defense in his answer. Brady could instead have filed a motion. The choice is based on strategy.

AMOUNT OF INFORMATION:
Paragraphs 6 - 8 illustrate our interpretation of how to plead an affirmative defense. This approach is based on our interpretation of Federal Rule of Civil Procedure 8(b): A defending party should "state in short and plain terms his defenses to each claim asserted." Our interpretation of the rule is that a defendant's defense, just like a plaintiff's claim, should be legally and factually sufficient.

continues ▶

COUNTERCLAIM: Negligence

9. Defendant adopts by reference paragraphs 6-8 of Defendant Brady's Second Affirmative Defense.

10. Plaintiff Alby was responsible for causing his own injuries and is responsible for causing Defendant Brady to suffer property damage, totaling $8,000.

CROSS-CLAIM Against Defendant Manufacturer

11. Defendant Brady adopts by reference paragraphs 6-10 of Defendant's Second Affirmative Defense.

12. Upon information and belief, defendant manufacturer was negligent in manufacturing, installing, and/or shipping an automobile to Plaintiff Alby with a defective gas pedal.

13. Upon information and belief defendant manufacturer's negligence was a proximate cause of Plaintiff's and Defendant's injuries.

Defendant requests relief as follows:

14. Dismissal of Plaintiff Alby's complaint;

15. General damages against Plaintiff Alby and defendant Manufacturer according to proof at trial;

16. Costs, interest on any judgment, and any other relief the Court or Jury finds appropriate.

Date: February 1, 20XX+1   GETT AND GRABB

By

_____

Norman Gett
43 The Major State Bank Building
Jamner, Major
Telephone: (206) 383-1212
Bar No. MA. 12,800

Attorneys for Defendant Brady

COUNTERCLAIM:
Paragraphs 9 and 10 illustrate the difference between an affirmative defense and a counterclaim. Brady asserts a counterclaim, negligence, based on the same facts that support Brady's second affirmative defense. Brady's claim for $8,000 property damage against plaintiff cannot be asserted in his affirmative defense of contributory negligence. Affirmative relief cannot be granted in an affirmative defense. Brady had a choice of pleading his counterclaim in his answer or beginning a lawsuit for his damages.

CROSS-CLAIM AND THIRD PARTY CLAIM:
Paragraphs 11 through 13 illustrate how to plead a cross-claim. But note that although paragraphs 11-13 plead a cross-claim, they are technically incorrect because plaintiff Alby did not join the manufacturer as a defendant. A cross-claim is a defendant's claim against another defendant or a plaintiff's claim against a co-plaintiff. We have included this as a cross-claim to illustrate, if plaintiff had joined the manufacturer as a defendant, how the defendant would present his claim. If Defendant Brady wants to file a claim against the manufacturer, Brady would have to proceed under Rule 14—Third party practice and implead a third party.

RELIEF:
Since Brady is pleading a counterclaim and cross-claim, he could, if victorious, obtain affirmative relief of $8,000 damages. The same would have been true had he filed a third-party complaint under Rule 14.

V. PLANNING AND DRAFTING CRIMINAL PLEADINGS

Whether your future will embrace pretrial work as a prosecutor or as a criminal defense lawyer, it is important to understand how a prosecutor approaches the filing of criminal charges. As a defense lawyer, this knowledge will not only facilitate your negotiation with a prosecutor because you will understand what drives a prosecutor's charging and disposition decisions and why charge reductions or case dismissal may be the right thing to do but also this knowledge will enable you to find the defects in charging documents.

The standard criminal pleading, either a complaint, information, or indictment (definitions on page 166), which is filed with the court by the prosecution, is a procedural mechanism used to bring the defendant to answer criminal charges. The charging document is rather straightforward, tracking the applicable criminal statute or ordinance embodying the prosecutor's legal theory. Major decision making in the charging endeavor focuses on whether or not charges should be filed, and, if so what crime(s) should be filed, rather than on the way in which the charge is presented in the pleadings. In most respects, the prosecutor's approach to filing criminal charges can mirror that of the plaintiff in filing a civil complaint.

Naturally, because the defendant in a criminal case is presumed innocent until proven guilty, and possesses a Fifth Amendment right not to incriminate himself or herself, no counterparts to the civil answer, counterclaim, or cross-claim or third-party claim exist in a criminal case.

A. Setting the Objectives for Pleading

The overarching goal of a public prosecutor to seek justice was determined by the United States Supreme Court in *Berger v. United States,* 295 U.S. 78, 88, 55 S. Ct. 629, 633, 79 L. Ed. 1314 (1935). In *Berger,* the Supreme Court stated:

> The United States Attorney is the representative not of an ordinary party to a controversy, but of a sovereignty whose obligation to govern impartially is as compelling as its obligation to govern at all; and whose interest, therefore, in a criminal prosecution is not that it shall win a case but that justice shall be done. As such, he is in a peculiar and very definite sense the servant of the law, the twofold aim of which is that guilt shall not escape nor innocence suffer. He may prosecute with earnestness and vigor—indeed, he should do so. But, while he may strike hard blows, he is not at liberty to strike foul ones. It is as much his duty to refrain from improper methods calculated to produce a wrongful conviction as it is to use every legitimate means to bring about a just one.

Although *Berger* concerned a United States Attorney, state appellate courts have applied the doing-justice goal to state and local prosecutors. This doing-justice objective should guide prosecutors in their filing decisions. The Comment to ABA Model Rule of Professional Conduct 3.8, dealing with the special responsibilities of a prosecutor, provides:

> A prosecutor has the responsibility of a minister of justice and not simply that of an advocate. This responsibility carries with it specific obligations to see that the defendant is accorded procedural justice and that guilt is decided upon the basis of sufficient evidence.

Within the doing-justice parameters, the prosecutor can also be guided by other case strategies. Instead of representing a client, the prosecutor is the people's representative and should serve the public's goals. For example, like all government agencies, a prosecutor's office does not have unlimited staff; priorities must be set. Therefore, a prosecutor must select for prosecution those cases that warrant the expenditure of public time and effort. Interrelated prosecutorial charging goals include:

- To inform the defendant of the charges,
- To file charges when sufficient evidence exists to support those charges,
- To make the most economical use of limited prosecutorial resources, and
- To persuade the defendant to enter a guilty plea.

The law vests a prosecutor with wide discretion in making a charging decision. It is by strategically exercising that discretion that the prosecutor may accomplish these goals.

B.   Preparing to Draft Charging Document— Case Theory Development

As you experienced the approach to pleading a civil case in the Alby civil case, here you will also experience filing in the Portage Bay News criminal case. Imagine that you are a prosecutor and that the police have presented you with a report concerning what happened at Portage Bay News.

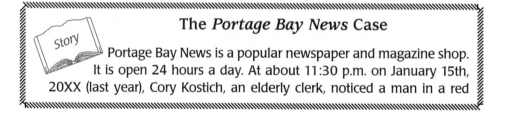

The *Portage Bay News* Case

Portage Bay News is a popular newspaper and magazine shop. It is open 24 hours a day. At about 11:30 p.m. on January 15th, 20XX (last year), Cory Kostich, an elderly clerk, noticed a man in a red

> vest, who had been browsing at the magazine rack, approach the counter.
> No one else was in the store. The man, who had his baseball hat pulled
> down, laid the magazine he was carrying on the counter, put his hand into
> his coat pocket and demanded cash from the register. The clerk handed
> over the money, and the man fled on foot. A partial print on the magazine
> matched the fingerprint of the twenty-three-year-old defendant, Jeff Lukens,
> who has a lengthy juvenile criminal history for shoplifting and a robbery.
> The clerk identified the defendant's picture in a photomontage as that of
> the robber.

Legal Sufficiency

As the prosecutor, your first charging decision in the *Portage Bay News* case
is to determine what, if any, crime has been committed. Then, second, any
charges you file must be legally sufficient, that is the defendant must be given
notice of the crime committed; the elements of the crime should be alleged,
providing the defendant with due process. In the Portage Bay News case, you
have consulted your state's statutes and determined that robbery charges
potentially could be filed against Lukens. The pertinent statutes state:

Revised Code 9A.76.010—Robbery:

> A person commits robbery when he unlawfully takes personal prop-
> erty from the person of another or in his presence against his will
> by the use or threatened use of immediate force, violence, or fear
> of injury to that person or his property or the person or property
> of anyone. Such force or fear must be used to obtain or retain pos-
> session of the property, or to prevent or overcome resistance to the
> taking; in either of which cases the degree of force is immaterial.
> Such taking constitutes robbery whenever it appears that, although
> the taking was fully completed without the knowledge of the per-
> son from whom taken, such knowledge was prevented by the use
> of force or fear.

Revised Code 9A.76.020—Robbery in the First Degree:

> A person is guilty of robbery in the first degree if in the commis-
> sion of a robbery or of immediate flight therefrom, he or she: (1) Is
> armed with a deadly weapon; or (2) Displays what appears to be a
> firearm or other deadly weapon.

> Robbery in the first degree is a class A felony.

RC 9A.76.020—Robbery in the Second Degree:

> A person is guilty of robbery in the second degree if he commits
> robbery.

> Robbery in the second degree is a class B felony.

While both robbery in the first and second degree might be viable charges, will you file anything and if so which crime will you plead?

Factual Sufficiency

Your decision as to whether you will file charges and what crime you will charge depends primarily upon the sufficiency of the evidence. If you do decide to file, the charging document must be factually sufficient in that it sets out specific facts about the particular crime committed. It is not sufficient to just allege the elements. Specifics to be alleged include the approximate date of the crime, the victim's identity, and the name of the defendant. However, unlike civil pleadings, criminal charges are normally stated in bare-bones, not a fully-dressed fashion.

C. The Charges to File, if Any

In reaching a filing decision, the prosecutor should answer at least three fundamental questions:

- First, what evidentiary standard should be satisfied before criminal charges are filed?
- Second, even if the evidentiary standard is met, do any non-evidentiary reasons exist that would justify declining to prosecute?
- Third, assuming that the evidentiary standard is met and no non-evidentiary reasons exist to decline, what type of charges and how many charges should be filed?

Evidentiary Standards

Do sufficient facts exist to support robbery charges against Lukens? What standard of evidentiary sufficiency should be applied? What degree of robbery should be charged—robbery in the first or second degree? A prosecutor can exercise discretion in determining whether to file charges and what charges to file, and the prosecutor will use some evidentiary and non-evidentiary standards that must be met before charges may be filed. Although some prosecutors have adopted written standards (e.g., requiring probability of conviction before charges would be filed), others have not.

Probable Cause

The ABA Model Rule of Professional Conduct 3.8 sets an ethical and minimal evidentiary standard for filing criminal charges, as follows:

The prosecutor in a criminal case shall:

(a) refrain from prosecuting a charge that the prosecutor knows is not supported by probable cause.

In the *Portage Bay News* case, sufficient facts exist to satisfy this probable cause standard. According to the victim, there are reasonable grounds to believe that a crime has been committed and that Lukens committed it.

Probability of Conviction

A prosecutor may adopt a higher evidentiary filing standard than probable cause. The prosecutor could require that there be a probability of conviction. This standard is at the other end of the spectrum from the probable-cause standard. While probable cause is a low hurdle, the probability-of-conviction standard is a high one and would result in charges being filed only when the prosecutor is confident that the defendant will be convicted. Utilizing this standard, the prosecutor may well decide not to charge Lukens. Only one witness, the clerk, identified Lukens as being the robber and his face was partially covered by the baseball hat. Further, it is plausible that Lukens had been at the Portage Bay News on a different occasion and handled the magazine, leaving his fingerprint.

Would-a-Jury-Be-Justified Standard

Yet a third standard could be adopted by the prosecutor. Under it, charges would be filed if available evidence is sufficient to take the case to the jury for decision, that is, if a reasonable jury would be justified in convicting the defendant based on the available evidence. This is higher than a probable-cause standard but lower than a reasonable-doubt standard. Applying this would-a-jury-be-justified standard, the prosecutor probably would file charges against Lukens because a reasonable jury, if it found the clerk's testimony credible, would be justified in convicting Lukens.

This evidentiary standard could also be applied to decide what degree of robbery—robbery in the first or second degree—should be plead. The additional element required for robbery in the first degree is whether the robber was (1) armed with a deadly weapon or (2) displayed what appeared to be a firearm or other deadly weapon. Although the robber did not display a weapon, it might be argued based on the fact that he placed his hand in his pocket and demanded money from the clerk that he must have been concealing a deadly weapon in his pocket. Under the applicable would-a-jury-be-justified evidentiary standard, a prosecutor might consider filing a robbery in the first degree charge. Or the prosecutor could decide that because the weapon was not seen by the clerk, the lesser crime of second degree robbery is a more appropriate charge.

Hybrid Approach

A fourth approach to charging reveals how prosecutorial charging practices can serve strategic objectives. A prosecutor could apply the would-a-jury-be-justified standard to crimes of violence and the probability-of-conviction standard to other crimes. Through these standards, the prosecutor's discretion dedicates greater emphasis and staff time to crimes of violence.

Non-Evidentiary Reasons to Decline Charges .

Even if sufficient evidence supports the charges, that does not mean that they automatically should be filed. Not every case that is technically fileable should be filed. The filing decision is more than a strictly legal and evidentiary one. There are several non-evidentiary grounds for declining to file charges. A nonexclusive list of reasons not to charge includes when the violation of law is only technical or insubstantial and no public interest or deterrent purpose would be served by prosecution, when a minor case may be declined because the cost of prosecution is highly disproportionate to the importance of prosecuting the offense, or when the offender is given immunity in order to obtain testimony or information reasonably leading to the conviction of more culpable individuals.

Number and Nature of Charges

Finally, the prosecutor must decide how many charges to file and what charges to file. A prosecutor should not overcharge a case in order to generate a guilty plea. The National District Attorneys Association (NDAA) has adopted national standards for prosecutors, and NDAA's Standard 43.4 states: "Inappropriate Leveraging—The prosecutor should not attempt to utilize the charging decision only as a leverage device in obtaining guilty pleas to lesser charges." NDAA Standard 9.2 provides: "The prosecutor has the responsibility to see that the charge selected describes the offense or offenses committed and provides for an adequate sentence for the offense or offenses." In essence, the tenet is that a prosecutor should not automatically file all charges, rather the prosecutor should file charges that label the gravamen of the defendant's conduct. This principle can be applied not only to the nature (e.g., degree) of the charge but also the number of charges (counts) filed.

Consider the number of crimes (counts) to be charged. Assume that Lukens had not just robbed Portage Bay New but that the robbery was only one in a spree of ten robberies The prosecutor could file all ten counts and plea bargain down to guilty pleas to five counts of robbery. Or, the prosecutor could decide that three counts accurately label the defendant's conduct and conservatively file three counts in contemplation of guilty pleas to the three counts (and decline to file the remaining five counts when the defendant pleads guilty to three counts). This approach also saves time and resources.

SAMPLE CRIMINAL PLEADING

Portage Bay News Case

SUPERIOR COURT OF MAJOR FOR JAMNER COUNTY

THE STATE OF MAJOR,	)	
	)	
Plaintiff,	)	No. 20-1-00657-7
v.	)	
	)	INFORMATION
	)	
JEFFREY A. LUKENS,	)	
	)	
Defendant.	)	
	)	

I, Anita Grant, Prosecuting Attorney for Jamner County in the name and by the authority of the State of Major, do accuse JEFFREY A. LUKENS of the crime of **Robbery in the Second Degree,** committed as follows:

That the defendant JEFFREY A. LUKENS in Jamner County, Major on or about January 15, 20XX, did unlawfully and with intent to commit theft take personal property of another, to-wit: U.S. currency, from the person and in the presence of Cory Kostich, against his will, by the use or threatened use of immediate force, violence and fear of injury to such person or his property and the person or property of another;

Contrary to RC 9A.56.210 and 9A.56.190, and against the peace and dignity of the State of Major.

VI. ETHICAL CONSIDERATIONS

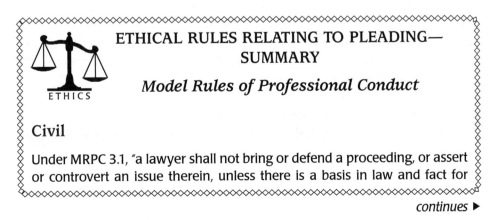

ETHICAL RULES RELATING TO PLEADING— SUMMARY

Model Rules of Professional Conduct

Civil

Under MRPC 3.1, "a lawyer shall not bring or defend a proceeding, or assert or controvert an issue therein, unless there is a basis in law and fact for

continues ▶

doing so that is not frivolous, which includes a good-faith argument for an extension, modification or reversal of existing law."

Criminal

DEFENSE COUNSEL: Under MRPC 3.1, "a lawyer for the defendant in a criminal proceeding, or the respondent in a proceeding that could result in incarceration, may nevertheless so defend the proceeding as to require that every element of the case be established."

PROSECUTOR: Under MRPC 3.8, "the prosecutor in a criminal case shall: (a) refrain from prosecuting a charge that the prosecutor knows is not supported by probable cause; . . ."

A. Civil

Federal Rule of Civil Procedure 11 provides a specific ethical duty that requires you as the attorney preparing a pleading to certify by signing it that you have read the pleading and made a reasonable inquiry that it is well-grounded in fact, warranted by existing law, and not filed for the purpose of harassment. Although Rule 11 includes specific ethical requirements, it only provides broad parameters that caution against egregious ethical breaches (filing frivolous lawsuits or dilatory motions, or filing in spite of a total failure to investigate). Determining specific ethical boundaries remains a matter of judgment since Rule 11, professional codes of conduct, and substantive law prohibit dishonest conduct or conduct prejudicial to the administration of justice. Many ethical problems, however, do not involve clear acts of dishonesty.

In our hypothetical *Alby* case, you will have to consider such ethical issues as how extensive an investigation you should do before pleading Alby's complaint. As a responding party, can you deny an allegation or must you investigate? How much of a reasonable inquiry must you engage in when responding to a plaintiff's allegations? For instance, do you have a duty to investigate the citizenship of Alby and Brady or can you allege citizenship of the parties upon information and belief? Do you need proof that the gas pedal was defective before alleging it was? Can you include *inconsistent* facts: Brady caused the accident because of his intoxicated state and Alby's gas pedal was defective, causing the accident? Can you assert a cutting-edge claim for reckless endangerment based on the Waldman law review article?

Ethical questions such as these remain issues of reasonableness and good faith according to circumstances at the time of pleading—reasonable factual investigation, reasonable interpretation of present law, reasonable basis for filing the pleading. As with these or other ethical issues, rules, although specific in nature, are difficult to apply. Rather, striving to represent your client in an ethical, but vigorous, manner will result in your maintenance of ethical judgment in pleading and a good reputation within the legal profession.

B. Criminal

To illustrate the ethical responsibilities of a prosecutor in pleading, assume that in the *Portage Bay News* case defense counsel for Jeffrey Lukens approaches you, the prosecutor, on Monday morning—the day of trial—and offers to plead her client guilty if you will amend the charge from first to second degree robbery. The judge is just about to enter the courtroom and start the trial by asking, "Are the parties ready in *State v. Lukens*?" Assume that Lukens has a lengthy criminal history of violent crimes. What you know, but defense counsel does not know, is that the victim Cory Kostich, who was quite elderly, passed away over the weekend. Do you accept the defense's offer of a guilty plea and move on to sentencing?

While you as the prosecutor are charged with the responsibility of protecting the community you represent from crime, you are also charged with protecting the defendant's rights as well. ABA Model Rule of Professional Conduct 3.8 requires that you "refrain from prosecuting a charge that the prosecutor knows is not supported by probable cause." At this moment before the judge enters the courtroom, do you still have probable cause to support any charge against the defendant? Kostich was the single eyewitness to the robbery, the defendant made no incriminating statements, and no forensic evidence establishes that he committed the crime (the fingerprint could have been left on the magazine on another date).

If no other evidence existed, you would be compelled to dismiss charges under Model Rule 3.8. But let's set aside the rules for a moment. What if you decide to accept the defense's offer, the defendant pleads guilty, and later defense counsel discovers that Kostich was dead at the time of the guilty plea? What will happen to your reputation and your effectiveness as a prosecutor in future exchanges with the defense bar and the bench?

But is all lost for the prosecution? As he was taking his last breath, Kostich said, "the stress from what that guy did—the guy I picked out in the photo display—has killed me. Damn him." During the investigation, Kostich picked out Luken's photo from a display as the robber. The detective who showed Kostich the photographic montage is available to testify to the identification. You may decide that this prior identification, incorporated into Kostich's Dying Declaration, coupled with the defendant's fingerprint on the magazine is sufficient probable cause to justify the negotiated guilty plea. Your decision to prosecute or not reflects on your ethical judgment and ultimately on your reputation in the profession.

✓ DRAFTING PLEADINGS CHECKLIST

The following are standards of performance for drafting pleadings. You can use them in drafting your affirmative and responsive pleadings.

Preparation to Draft Pleadings—Fed. R. Civ. P. 11

❑ Make reasonable inquiry to determine that the pleading is grounded in fact—

   ✓ Make reasonable inquiry and determine that the claim or defense is supported by existing law or "by a nonfrivolous argument for the extension, modification, or reversal of existing law or the establishment of new law."

❑ Do not use the pleading for an improper purpose.

Case Objectives and Case Theories as Guides for Pleading

❑ Have a case strategy (e.g., persuade your adversary to settle, narrow the controversy).

❑ Map out the pleading in a logical and organized manner—

   ✓ Make alternative allegations and avoid inconsistent claims or defenses unless either claim or defense is a likely possibility suggested by the facts.

Drafting the Pleading

❑ Draft the caption in accordance with applicable rules.

❑ Set out a claim or defense as the rules require.

❑ Adopt by reference parts of pleadings or a motion when helpful in drafting.

❑ Add a written instrument to the pleading as an exhibit when appropriate.

❑ Select the best legal theory, claim, or defense to plead.

❑ State old shoe legal claims in the pleading.

❑ State cutting-edge legal claims when appropriate.

❑ Select the correct person or entity as a party to the suit.

❑ State facts in either a fully-dressed or bare-bones manner compatible with case objectives.

❑ Decide upon the correct relief to request.

Effective Writing

❑ Satisfy other procedural and technical requirements (e.g., joinder of claims or defenses, formatting—

    ✓ Use a simple and clear writing style that is free from legal jargon and that tells the story well.

❑ Use the proper format (paper size, caption, paragraph structure, numbering of allegations, signature, address, phone number, etc.).

Other Strategic Issues

❑ Select the appropriate forum for the action.

❑ Choose a strategically good time to file the pleading.

❑ File the pleading correctly and serve the appropriate party.

Responding to Pleadings

❑ Choose the appropriate response, e.g., an answer or a motion to dismiss.

❑ Admit allegations or deny when appropriate or use a combination of admitting and denying parts of an allegation, and when you do not have sufficient facts to admit or deny state you are without knowledge or information sufficient to form a belief as to the truth of the allegations.

❑ Include affirmative defenses, cross-claims, and/or counterclaims when supported by a case theory.

❑ Consider filing a third party complaint when appropriate.

8 *Creating a Coordinated Discovery Plan*

8 *Creating a Coordinated Discovery Plan*

"Eureka! eureka!" (I have found it!).

Archimedes

"Discovery works reasonably well when you have two relatively equally matched opponents (either two large parties, each of which can afford the costs of extensive discovery, or two small ones, neither of which has many resources, and for whom discovery is therefore limited to the essentials); it works much less well where one party has the power and resources to overwhelm the other."

David Boies, Courting Justice: From New York Yankees vs. Major League Baseball to Bush vs. Gore, 1997–2000
(Miramar Books, 2004)

"If there is a hell to which disputatious, uncivil, vituperative lawyers go, let it be one in which the damned are eternally locked in discovery disputes with other lawyers of equally repugnant attributes."

Attributed to Judge Wayne E. Alley,
Krueger v. Pelican Prod. Corp.,
No. CIV-87-2385-A (W.D.Okla. Feb. 24, 1989)

I.   DISCOVERY

In this chapter, we cover discovery in both civil and criminal cases. We discuss civil discovery under Federal Rules of Civil Procedure in federal district courts since most state court jurisdictions have adopted these Rules or a version of them. Because civil pretrial practice entails an extensive discovery process with a wide array of discovery tools, civil discovery dominates most of this discussion. You will learn not only about the civil and criminal discovery processes and devices but also how to formulate and execute a coordinated discovery plan. A well thought out plan will meet your discovery objectives and case strategies. Lastly, this chapter explains how to draft discovery devices: everything from civil interrogatories to a criminal motion for discovery. Depositions are touched on here, but see Chapter 9 for a full treatment of depositions.

A.   Civil Discovery

Procedural and Substantive Rules

Legal rules, standards, and doctrine circumscribe formal civil discovery. They dictate both the procedural requirements for obtaining discovery and the scope and limits of discovery itself. Accordingly, when planning for discovery, review appropriate rules such as the Federal Rules of Civil Procedure (Fed. R. Civ. P.), which were amended in 2006 to explicitly cover electronically stored information, Federal Rules of Criminal Procedure (Fed. R. Crim. P.), local court rules, state statutes, and American Bar Association Civil Discovery Standards. While the ABA Standards do not purport to be statements of discovery law, they are useful guidelines for the parties, counsel, and the court, and they have been cited in appellate decisions. Also, you should review applicable cases, as well as determine the custom and usage of particular courts and judges (gleaned from personal observation and discussions with other attorneys and court personnel).

With this background information, you will be able to intelligently contemplate a variety of procedural matters, such as appropriate devices for discovery, discovery conferences, time requirements, and omnibus hearings, required forms for discovery requests, protective orders, and procedures for compelling responses to your discovery requests when your opponent fails to comply. This information will also help you determine what you may request and what may be requested of you. Your research will reveal the permissible scope and standards for discovery, case doctrine that deals with the appropriateness or inappropriateness of requesting certain items or types of items of information, and the grounds upon which an objection to a request for discovery can be made.

What is Discoverable?

Civil discovery is guided by rules, such as the Federal Rules of Civil Procedure, which are then interpreted by case law and local rules. Many state jurisdictions have adopted all or part of the Federal Rules of Civil Procedure for discovery.

Matters Discoverable

Fed. R. Civ. P. 26(b)(1)

R U L E

Any matter is discoverable if it is:

- **Not privileged,** and
- **Relevant** to the subject matter of the action in a **broad sense,** i.e., it appears *"reasonably calculated to lead to the discovery of admissible evidence."*

Discoverable information includes: "the existence, description, nature, custody, condition, and location of any books, documents, or other tangible things and the knowledge of any discoverable matter."

Initial Disclosure and Formal Discovery

There are two types of discovery governed by the Federal Rules of Civil Procedure: initial disclosure and formal discovery.

Required Initial Disclosures (Also Referred to as Informal Disclosure)

Depending on the court rules of the jurisdiction, the parties will be obligated to exchange certain categories of discovery without making a formal discovery demand. Fed. R. Civ. P. 26(a) for instance, compels initial discovery. The initial disclosures must be made in writing, signed, and served. Generally, these initial disclosures are part of a federally mandated scheduling conference, though certain types of actions are exempt from initial disclosure 26(a)(1)(E).

Under the Fed. R. Civ. P. 26(f), the parties are to confer and discuss claims, defenses, and possible settlement and come up with a discovery plan. Initial disclosure, according to Fed. R. Civ. P. 26(a), is to be made not later than 14 days after the scheduling conference unless the parties stipulate or the court orders otherwise. Next, the parties submit a written report to the court, and the court enters a scheduling order with time limits for, among other things, completion of informal disclosure and for discovery. Many state court rules are patterned after the federal scheme while others do not require a conference unless the parties request it.

REQUIRED INITIAL DISCLOSURE
Fed. R. Civ. P. 26(a)

RULE

- **Witnesses** "likely to have discoverable information" supporting claims or defenses and contact information (unless impeachment evidence)
- **Copy of or description by category and location of documents, electronically stored information and tangible things** supporting claims or defenses that are in the party's possession, custody or control (in practice parties usually submit a list of types of documents and so on)
- **Insurance agreement** for an insurance company that may be liable to satisfy the judgment in full or in part
- **Expert witness** who may be called at trial and a written report from that expert, and
- **A computation of any category of damages** and discoverable evidentiary material upon which the compilation is based

If a party determines that "in some material respect the information disclosed is incomplete or inaccurate," the party must **supplement** the discovery.

Formal Discovery

Discovery is characterized as "formal" information-gathering. This is so for two reasons. First, discovery is associated with a range of formal discovery devices (depositions, interrogatories) that contrast with the less structured tools of initial disclosure, and information-gathering (witness interviews, informal inspection of the accident scene). Second, the roots of discovery's very existence and legitimacy are formal. Discovery is legislatively or judicially sanctioned access to information that is in the control of your opponent or some third party. Significantly, this access is backed up by potential enforcement—a court order.

However, you should be aware that most formal civil discovery is self-executing. In practice, this formal-informal distinction is also far from clear in the criminal area. You may need a court order to interview a witness (e.g., a police informant) or to inspect the premises of a private business. On the other hand, opposing counsel may turn over documents without a formal request as a cooperative gesture.

In the scheduling conference, FRCP 26(f) provides the setting or plan for formal discovery that covers using discovery devices. Each of these civil devices has a particular use depending on the information that you want. We will review the general types of civil discovery devices and discuss how they can be used. These are the discovery tools available to you under the pertinent Federal Rules of Civil Procedure:

- Interrogatories—Rule 33
- Request for Production—Rule 34
- Physical/Mental Examinations—Rule 35
- Subpoena Duces Tecum—Rule 45
- Depositions—Rules 27–32
- Requests for Admissions—Rule 36

Interrogatories

Interrogatories are written questions that must be responded to under oath. Under Federal Rule of Civil Procedure 33(a) a party can serve *"written interrogatories; not exceeding 25 in number including all discrete subparts,"* unless leave to serve additional interrogatories is granted under FRCP 26(b)(2). They can be sent only by a party to the lawsuit to another party in the lawsuit. They are most useful for obtaining and locating information (names and addresses of witnesses, documents that may exist) or determining the basis for a party's legal and factual position. One type of interrogatory, known as a *contention interrogatory,* allows you to inquire into the legal and factual basis of a party's allegations or defenses in a pleading. For example: "What is the basis for your claim of comparative fault?" "What is the basis for your statement, `He was intoxicated,' in paragraph 5 of your answer?" Applicable rules will specify the number of interrogatories you can ask the party, such as 20 without leave of the court.

Request for Production

This discovery device, under FRCP 34, is much like an interrogatory. It is a written request that can be sent only by a party to a party to the case and allows counsel to inspect, view, and (where feasible) copy writings, documents, photographs, and other physical items, including property. A party may ask an unlimited number of document requests.

Physical and Mental Examinations

This discovery device can only be used in civil cases by a party against a party when the physical or mental condition of a party is at issue. With a strong showing to the court, witnesses may be subjected to physical or mental examinations in criminal cases.

Subpoena Duces Tecum

In the discovery context, a subpoena duces tecum is a document commanding that a nonparty to the lawsuit attend a deposition and "produce and permit inspection and copying of designated books, documents or tangible things in the possession, custody or control of that person, or to permit inspection of premises at a time and place therein specified;" Fed. R. Civ. P. 45. A sample subpoena duces tecum appears at the end of this chapter at page 286.

Depositions

Depositions are the most widely used discovery device because they can be addressed to anyone. They are usually oral examinations of witnesses under oath and are much like a "mini-trial" because you can ask questions, follow up on questions, and observe the demeanor of the witness. There are also written depositions that function much like interrogatories. Depositions are discussed in detail in Chapter 9.

Requests for Admission

Requests for admissions can be addressed only by a party to a party. They are written, must be answered under oath, and allow the requesting party to gain favorable admissions from the respondent to material relevant facts that are in dispute (for instance, the identification and admissibility of documents). Requests for admissions can be traps for the unwary. If a party does not answer a request to admit within the 30-day time period, the party is deemed to have admitted the request.

Protective Order

A motion may be made for an order protecting the party or a person from discovery resulting in annoyance, embarrassment, oppression, or undue burden or expense. Fed. R. Civ. P. 26(c). A federal court and some state courts will entertain a motion for a protective order only if the parties have previously conferred about the objection to discovery. The court can order that terms be imposed, order that discovery be barred or limit discovery to only certain areas.

B. Criminal Discovery

Criminal discovery, which is generally a product of judicial opinions, although guided by statutory or court rules in most jurisdictions, is somewhat different. It evolved slowly. Concerned with defendant perjury should the prosecution's case be known in advance, courts slowly progressed from denying all discovery to eventually requiring a stringent "good cause" showing for production of even the few items of discovery that courts would then permit defendants to obtain (e.g., the defendant's own statement to police). As criminal discovery broadened, courts in effect found good cause to apply discovery as a matter of law to a wider and wider variety of items. Thus, current criminal discovery characteristically encompasses a set, although often limited, catalog of items that might be available to the parties. Thus, under some statutes, court rules, and/or common-law doctrine, the prosecution may be required to provide the defense with witness names and statements, criminal conviction of the prosecution's witnesses, forensic evidence, items obtained in a search, and so on. Further, prosecutors have a constitutional duty to provide the defense with material exculpatory evidence bearing on guilt or punishment regardless of whether the defense has specifically requested such evidence.

In many jurisdictions, criminal discovery is the realm of the defense. With the exception of some notice of alibi and insanity statutes, the Fifth Amendment has traditionally stood as a bar to the prosecutor to obtaining a wide range of information from the defense. However, some statutes provide the prosecution with some carefully delineated discovery from the defense that goes beyond notice of alibi or insanity. Invariably such statutes will be underlain by legal rationales that the particular discovery does not violate the Fifth Amendment. Defendants may be required to give blood, writing samples, DNA samples, appear in a line-up and wear particular clothing or say particular words because the Fifth Amendment is limited to testimonial evidence, and all this evidence is nontestimonial in nature. Likewise, defendants may be required to produce incriminating writings on the theory that the core of the Fifth Amendment rests upon the concern of the government coercing testimony, and in this instance, the government did not coerce the defendant to write the document. Because the act of turning over the document could somehow incriminate the defendant, the prosecution may obtain the document but may not use the fact that the defendant provided the document in their case. On the other hand, while the prosecution in a criminal case is generally severely limited in court-ordered discovery by the Fifth Amendment, the government can do a great deal analogous to discovery through its powers of search and seizure, arrest, police interrogation, and grand jury investigation.

II.   PLANNING CIVIL DISCOVERY

A.   Setting Discovery Objectives

The list of objectives for formal discovery is dominated by the search for information:

- *to obtain information,* both good and bad, that is relevant to developing your case theory and motions, that can provide you with a basis for realistically assessing your overall position for possible settlement,
- *to create information* (e.g., obtaining a court order to conduct a scientific test), and
- *to influence your adversary* to change his or her position (e.g., an agreement to negotiate or settle or to change the grounds for settlement) by seeking relevant, but sensitive, information that the opponent does not want to release (e.g., internal management e-mails), and by making it clear to the adversary that you are serious about the case and mean to work diligently in your client's behalf. This aim may be central to a case strategy that seeks eventual dismissal of a civil suit or criminal charges or, at least, a favorable disposition.

This last objective should be clearly distinguished from using discovery as a means of grinding a less affluent opponent into submission, unreasonably delaying cases, artificially raising the costs to the opponent of noncapitulation, and so forth. These practices are, to say the least, of questionable ethical propriety. Unfortunately, however, these practices are common and an advocate must be prepared to anticipate and deal with such tactics.

B.   Discovery and Case Strategy

Every part of this discovery process ultimately is directed toward achieving the objectives of the case strategy. Accordingly, if your final objectives can best be achieved by settlement, and you are engaged in productive and cooperative negotiation sessions to that end, serving 300 document requests on opposing counsel may serve the case theory's hunger for information, but might severely harm your case strategy by escalating the litigation aspect of the case.

Summary Judgment

If summary judgment is the aim of your case strategy, discovery will be directed toward obtaining sufficient facts upon which to bring that motion.

Litigation

If litigation is to be the ultimate goal of that strategy, the information generated through discovery will be sought for a variety of uses. This information can provide support, demand modification, or even require abandonment of your case theory. Or it might suggest new case theories. It might reveal the opposing party's case theories, including the basis, strengths, and weaknesses of such theories. It might lead to more investigation, further interviews with your client, and further discovery.

Settlement

If settlement is the goal of the case strategy, discovery plays a complex role. It may support litigation, which in turn becomes a goad to negotiation. It may reveal strengths in your case theory or weaknesses in the opposition's that will affect the top and bottom of the opponent's bargaining range, as discussed in Chapter 12. It may reveal information directly applicable to your negotiation (e.g., that the opposing party has cash-flow problems, so a settlement offer that requires little cash flow may be enticing). The very pressure and projected cost from legitimate discovery may encourage settlement and influence the amount of settlement.

C. Developing a Discovery Plan—Case Theory as a Guide

A Focused Discovery Plan

Preparation of a discovery plan is tied to your general philosophy of discovery and the specific case you are involved in. There are competent lawyers who see discovery as a means to get everything imaginable. While we encourage a broad view of discovery—after all, you do not want to miss the piece of information that will suggest a new case theory or the disastrous piece of information that suggests the futility of not settling—we believe discovery should be focused. In our view, the realities of the client's financial resources and the average attorney's time resources do not suggest a philosophy of discovery that results in counsel requesting endless discovery and then being inundated by mounds of useless data. Furthermore, the courts are impatient with unfocused, shot-gun discovery requests that bog down the courts with endless hearings on the scope of discovery, vagueness, overbroadness, burdensomeness, and so forth. Note that the focus in federal courts is to institutionalize a discovery conference and plan. Fed. R. Civ. P. 26(f).

This may be less likely to happen in the average criminal than a civil case. In a criminal case, commonly only a single, isolated event is involved; the information sought by the defense is generally that which was specifically gathered by the police in investigating that event. The criminal defendant's defense can also be based on a lack of evidence in the prosecution's case, a lack that may be revealed by knowing all that the prosecution has. On the other hand, in civil actions a variety of discovery methods are available and the case may involve more than one event, resulting in the potential for random and excessive discovery.

A Coordinated Discovery Plan

Discovery should be a coordinated enterprise directed toward achieving your case strategy and developing your case theory, rather than a fragmented series of sorties pursued without overall goals and with neither a sense of how they relate to one another nor how they will be accomplished. Your discovery plan is a comprehensive overview of all the information you will seek and whom you will seek it from, and it is the basis of your legal rationale for each request. This rationale generally will emerge naturally from your analysis of what you want. The plan will also include the specific discovery devices you will use in seeking each piece of information and some consideration of likely objections you can anticipate from opposing counsel to your individual requests, as well as a sense of your possible responses to these objections. Finally, all this will be placed in the context of a timeline, ordering the use of each discovery device (interrogatories, requests for admissions, depositions) in the sequence you feel desirable. The timeline will also reflect the schedule for these devices, determined both by the court and statutory rules and by the pace you feel is desirable and feasible in light of the interests of the case and your other commitments. Many jurisdictions require a discovery plan. In federal court discovery planning is specifically structured by the rules in terms of such things as allocated time; for example, a maximum of seven hours for a deposition without leave of the court.

The following chart may be helpful in working out your plan:

DISCOVERY PLAN CHART

Claim/ Defense	Element	Facts to prove claim/ defense	Information/ Source	Discovery device	Sequence	Problems/ Evidence concerns	Date for scheduling

This chart includes: (1) A statement of your claim or defense, (2) each element of the claim or defense that embodies your legal theory (or the elements you will attack for lack of factual or persuasive sufficiency), (3) the assertions of your factual theory supporting each element, (4) the information you will request pertaining to each assertion and the source of the information (e.g., a witness, documents under the control of a custodian of records), (5) the discovery device you will employ to get this information, (6) the sequence of this device relative to other devices you will use, (7) problems/evidence concerns you may face in making your request, which include developing rationales for each request, and anticipating objections or requests for protective orders, and (8) specific dates for employing each device (when you will file interrogatories, set a deposition, and so on).

Case Theory and Discovery

Part of your preparation is mental. Specifically, you must conceptualize the role of the case theory in relation to discovery. The formal discovery process and the concept of case theory are intimately related.

Obtaining Information

First, formal discovery is a significant method for obtaining information to support or modify your tentative case theory or to adopt new case theories and to learn about your opponent's theories. The case theory will thus provide a guide in determining the information you will seek through your discovery requests, just as it did in determining the information you sought in the interviewing process.

Objections to Discovery Requests

Second, a case theory is generally central to objections to discovery requests (e.g., overbroad requests, privileged information). If the refusing party's objections are successful, the requesting party is denied information. The less information you have, however, the fewer potential "stories" and accompanying legal theories you can rely on, and the weaker those stories will tend to be. Therefore, by limiting available information, objections to discovery either tend to strengthen the refusing party's legal theories by focusing on a lack of factual/persuasive sufficiency in the requesting party's story, or keep information from the requesting party that could be used to attack the factual/persuasive sufficiency of the refusing party's story.

Legal Standards for Discovery

Third, the case theory bears a relationship to the legal standards circumscribing discovery. In a practical sense, the case theory guides not only what you will request, but also what you are legally entitled to request and the actual form your request must take. This third relationship between case theory and discovery requires further elaboration.

Where does case theory fit into the legal discovery structure? In both the civil and criminal areas, the discovery process is limited in scope by a legal structure that envisions that information will be provided only if it is "reasonably calculated to lead to discovery of admissible evidence" (civil) or there is "good cause" (criminal) that the information could bear on your case (including attacks on your adversary's case). "Reasonably calculated" and "good cause," however, are both members of the "relevance" family (in fact, Rule 26(b) specifically uses the term "relevant"), and relevance is always a function of case theory. The defendant's knowledge at the time defendant shot the victim that the victim had committed prior violent acts will be relevant to a self-defense theory as it bears on the reasonableness of defendant's fear, but will not be relevant to a misidentification theory. Thus, whether or not an item bears on your case will be determined by how you and your adversary articulate your case theories. However, you should not and do not have to bind yourself to one specific case theory in discovery. After all, one objective of discovery is to assist you in sifting through plausible alternative theories. Rather, you have the option to say, "this information could lead to information that would be admissible in support of a defense of . . ."

Your case theory, therefore, not only guides you in determining what to ask for, but provides the frame of reference for legally justifying your request under the applicable legal structure. You focus on information for discovery because it has some potential relevance to your case theories. This same type of "relevance" is implied in the legal standards for discovery. Thus, in practice, the same process from which you determined the information that you would seek in discovery will also provide the basic legal rationale for justifying the request because of the above-described relationship between the doctrinal standards and case theory. In addition to general standards for discovery found in statutory schemes and cases, special items of information may be discussed in opinions and legislative histories in such a manner as to provide guidance for your request for these items of information (e.g., the showing the defense must make in order to obtain a police officer's personnel file in a case charging resisting arrest).

RELEVANCY

The *Slip-and-Fall* Case

You represent the defendant in a negligence suit in which you are defending against a slip-and-fall claim. Plaintiff claims to have fallen because of a wet spot on the floor of the defendant's store. You believe you can successfully defeat plaintiff's claim if you can show that plaintiff's injuries (or at least their magnitude) were not caused by the fall or that plaintiff is fabricating the whole incident. You have determined that you want information concerning any of plaintiff's prior injuries and prior similar lawsuits. Prior injuries bear on a possible attack of the elements of "causation" and "damages" in plaintiff's legal theory. Prior similar suits could provide the basis for a credibility attack on plaintiff's factual theory. How can you justify obtaining this information about prior injuries and lawsuits under applicable legal standards? Look to your case theory. Your discovery request, if attacked as not meeting the legal standards for discovery, can be defended as follows:

> "This information about plaintiff's prior injuries that we've request-
> ed is reasonably calculated to lead to information that would show
> that plaintiff's injuries are not a result of the fall or that, if injured, the
> resulting damage is only slightly incremental to preexisting injuries.
> The information about prior similar suits could lead to information
> showing this is all part of an ongoing fraud scheme."

D. Five-Step Strategy for Coordinated Discovery

A suggested discovery strategy that is intended to generate a coordinated discovery plan that will accomplish its intended purposes follows. This discovery strategy has five organizational and analytical steps as follows:

A FIVE-STEP DISCOVERY STRATEGY

1. Using the case theories (i.e., legal and factual theories) as guides, determine what information you want.
2. Identify likely persons and entities that could provide that information.
3. Identify the types of information to seek.
4. Select the discovery tool suitable to the task.
5. Determine the timing and sequencing of discovery.

Step One—Using the Case Theories as Guides, Determine What Information You Want

The first step requires common sense and imagination (akin to the brainstorming you used to develop tentative case theories). This step involves a "chicken-egg" process in which you simultaneously consider both what you want and what the party from whom you might seek discovery is likely to have. You start with what you want for your case theory or what you need to undercut your opponent's theory and then look for likely sources for this information.

Categories of Information to Seek

In our experience there is generally a finite number of categories of information that could be available in discovery as follows:

CATEGORIES OF INFORMATION TO SEEK IN DISCOVERY

- Identities, addresses, and telephone numbers of witnesses
- Information possessed by particular witnesses (obtained in discovery through such devices as depositions, interrogatories, or requests for admissions; this category of information is also available informally through witness interviews)
- Pieces of paper and recorded and electronic information (e-mails, documents, records, memos, charts, policy statements, witness statements, specifications, cassette tapes, videotapes, computer programs)
- Physical and demonstrative evidence (broken camshafts, photographs, diagrams), and
- Opportunities to create information (e.g., a court order to permit your expert to examine the plaintiff)

Of course, you'd like to ask the opposition and third parties to hand over everything; that request, however, may be found a bit overbroad and vague. So how do you determine the specific information among these categories that you should request in your particular case? For that task, we have provided you with a model approach.

Case Theory Narrows the Focus

Your case theory will focus on those areas in which you will need to obtain information.

Legal Theory

Begin with your legal theory (or theories, since you will often be seeking discovery in part to choose among alternative legal theories), and those theories you suspect the opposing counsel is entertaining. While the plaintiff will be concerned with establishing every element of his or her legal theory that is the legal basis for the claim for relief, the defendant will be concerned with attacking each element. If the defendant raises an affirmative defense, the positions will be reversed. Each element of these legal theories will thus provide a separate area to focus on for discovery.

Factual Theory

Then look at the respective factual theories. You need information to support, or must become aware of information that weakens, the existing assertions in your factual theory (especially the central assertions), or you need to find information that will allow you to add assertions to fill gaps in your story. As always, you want to know the bad as well as the good. When you are aware of negative information, you may be able to deal with it within the context of your theory or by modifying or changing your theory or by seeking an acceptable settlement. Without such an awareness, disaster awaits. You also need information to undercut your opponent's story. Every assertion in your and your opponent's factual theories thus provides a potential area for discovery.

Step Two—Identify Likely Persons and Entities That Could Provide That Information

In step two, you start with likely sources (certain witnesses, types of records a person or entity is likely to keep), and assess what information these sources could contain that bears on the respective case theories. Each process, of course, yields ideas that trigger a companion process as your mind moves back and forth between the two.

This second step requires thoroughness combined with imagination. You will have already used your case theories to provide your areas of focus, and used the interrelated processes to determine the information you want within the areas. In this second step, you conceive of all the sources that could contain this information, although you might have already identified one or more sources in the first step.

While contemplating the likely sources, think about whom you will serve and with what discovery request. Will you use interrogatories to try to determine who is in possession of the information you are seeking? How will you get jurisdiction over nonparties? How will you determine the custodians of documents?

As already discussed, interrogatories and depositions can be used to discover the identities and locations of nonparty witnesses in a civil case. Nonparties can then be subpoenaed into a deposition. Once served with a subpoena duces tecum, they can also be required to produce documents and records with them.

Now we are ready to apply the first two steps in the methodology to a hypothetical automobile-repair fraud case.

The *University Auto Shop* Case

Story

You are the attorney for plaintiff in a civil fraud case. The core of your legal theory is that the defendant automobile garage, University Auto Shop, intended to defraud your client. This legal theory is based on a "story," the central assertion of which is that defendant, who was to fix all four of plaintiff's brakes, fixed only plaintiff's front brakes, while charging for repairing both front and rear brakes. Defendant acknowledges that it fixed only plaintiff's front brakes, while charging for both front and back. Defendant's "story," however, is that this was the result of a mistake when two work orders were inadvertently switched on a very busy day. This assertion of an inadvertent mistake supports a legal theory attacking the element of intent to defraud in your legal theory.

You are beginning to plan formal discovery and want to determine what information to seek. You will then determine which discovery devices to employ, the sequence of the devices, and so forth. How will you reason through this task? Begin applying the approach.

You have a tentative case theory: Civil fraud based on the repair shop having intentionally charged plaintiff for repairing both front and rear brakes while knowing that it had repaired only the front brakes. Also, after studying defendant's responsive pleading, you believe that the defendant will rely on the defense of mistake due to an "inadvertent mix-up" in repair work orders.

In this hypothetical *University Auto Shop* case, the areas indicated by analysis of your legal theory—intent to defraud—and the defendant's factual theory—mistake (due to an inadvertent switching of work orders) are fairly congruent. You want to focus on the question of mistake. But what specific information will you seek? Begin the process.

The Information You Want

The first step is to determine whether you want to bolster your case theory or undercut the defense case theory. You want information from which you can argue that the overbilling was not a mistake, but was indeed intentional (or at least you want to learn that such information does not exist or that there is contrary information). Also, you want information that could undercut this defense of mistake.

In the *University Auto Shop* case, you as plaintiff's counsel could seek to discovery your client's work order and the work order of the other person whose order defendant claims to have mistakenly switched with that of your client. Assume that the defense produces the other customer's work order. This removes your ability to argue for example, "How interesting that defendant cannot locate this other order and does not even know whose car it was. Of course the reason that it cannot be found is that it never existed. One more fraud in a seemingly endless series of deceptions." On the positive side, it provides you with a potentially powerful witness, the other customer, whom you can now interview or subpoena to a deposition.

The Sources of the Information

Then you take the second step and ask: Who might possess information bolstering our case theory or undercutting the other side's? Use your imagination. You are unlikely to have anyone tell you, "Yes, that repair job was a fraud all right." But information that the defendant's story is unlikely under current procedures ("They might have switched work orders, but then he would have been billed under the wrong order, too, and only been charged for the front brakes"), or that employees are telling materially contradictory stories in this matter (or obviously "pat" stories) would help you in arguing that the jury should infer that this incident did not occur because of a mistake.

Who or what could be the source of the information we want in the fraud case? Clearly, various employees. Thus, you need to know how to locate all potential employee witnesses (through interrogatories asking for names, addresses, and telephone numbers of all employees working at the time) so you can seek this information in a deposition. (You could employ the information-gathering methods for witness interviews described in Chapter 6.) Similarly, evidence indicating that defendant has done this same thing in the past (modus operandi) might help. Business records of the defendant (whose existence and location you have determined through interrogatories) or of some state licensing agency may contain the names of prior customers who have made complaints. However, note that only because of this brainstorming, guided by your case theory, did you even think of seeking customer names. Simultaneously, you may also be pursuing informal fact-gathering (e.g., talking to people at the Better Business Bureau). Information gained from this informal process, moreover, can be used to provide legal cause for subsequent formal discovery. You also want to find any information that supports defendant's assertion of "mistake" so you can deal with it. The same documents and witnesses already discussed will also aid in this enterprise.

Step Three—Identify the Types of Information to Seek

Now think about the types of information these persons or entities could provide, and which among these types of information could have a bearing on the focus areas for your discovery that you derived from analyzing your and your opponent's case theories. What sources of information could defendant possess? The defendant probably has written documents such as a work order, written procedures for each job, policy manuals, and such, all of which could be obtained in a request for production of documents. What types of information could these sources contain? Work orders will show what was to have been done on a particular job. Procedures and policy manuals could provide how work orders are to be handled, jobs completed and billed, and so forth. Which among these types of information could concern the area of "mistakenly" failing to repair the brakes? If your client's work order clearly indicates that it was his car (make, color, and license) upon which all four brakes were to be repaired, then a mistake may seem less likely. On the other hand, the work order may be so vague as to make a mistake believable. It may even describe plaintiff's car incorrectly. Written procedures and policy manuals may caution on the necessity of not mixing up work orders or may describe a system under which such a mix-up would be improbable. Again, however, the manuals may support your opponent. It is just as important to learn what evidence supports your opponent.

SIGNIFICANCE OF THE INFORMATION

The *University Auto Shop* Case

Generally, a helpful technique for fully appreciating the significance of the types of information you are seeking in discovery for your case theory is to *imagine how you or opposing counsel could use the information in closing argument*. After all, the closing argument is the final embodiment of your case theory:

"Ladies and Gentlemen of the jury, as you can see, no one could have looked at that work order and thought anything but that all

> four brakes were to be repaired. The defense concedes this point, as it must. Instead, defendant now claims that the orders were inadvertently switched. But, if you examine Policy Manual #6 and Procedures Section 15, you can see that it was virtually impossible for this to happen."

Step Four—Select the Discovery Tool Suitable to the Task

If you need to pound in a nail, you wouldn't reach for a screwdriver. Likewise, you want to select the right discovery tool for the job. When will you use depositions, interrogatories, requests for production, requests for admissions, requests for inspection, and requests for physical examination? What are the general advantages and disadvantages of each device? The advantages and disadvantages in this specific case? You want to consider the following factors in making your decision of whether to use a specific discovery device:

- Whether it is the best tool for the job,
- Whether your use of the device furthers your case strategy (see page 232 on the interrelationship between discovery and your case strategy), and
- How much it will cost to employ the discovery tool.

Interrogatories

As you will recall, interrogatories are written questions that must be responded to under oath. They can be sent only by parties to the lawsuit to other parties to the lawsuit. Interrogatories are most useful for obtaining and locating information (names and addresses of witnesses, types of documents that may exist) or determining the basis for a party's legal and factual position. The advantage of using interrogatories is that they are inexpensive, basically limited to the cost of preparing, copying, and mailing them.

Law offices usually have computerized interrogatory banks. As your law practice progresses, you may be aided by reference to your own interrogatory bank, which contains previously drafted interrogatories used in similar cases. However, you should use interrogatory banks cautiously and adapt the stock interrogatories to your case and circumstances. Over-reliance on a bank of interrogatory questions risks that you will not carefully think through your case well enough. A better place to start in formulating interrogatories is with the case theories. For example, as defense counsel, you can begin your analysis and drafting by carefully reviewing the other party's case theory as expressed in the complaint and go through each allegation. Many jurisdictions by local rule or judge-made rule, have limited the number of interrogatories and also assess sanctions for the clear use of irrelevant and cumulative bank-like interrogatories.

Requests for Production

Requests for production can only be served by a party on a party to the case. This discovery device is a written request to inspect, view, and (where feasible) copy writings, documents, photographs, and other physical items, including property.

The request must be specific in what it requests. A general request for "everything that you have concerning the automobile crash" is not specific enough. "All repair bills from June 20XX through the present for your 20XX - 2 Volkswagen Beetle, license number CRAZY" is a specific request. The items that you request must be in the possession or control of the party to whom you send the request. This can include the party's agents—for example, attorneys or investigators. The request is inexpensive to prepare, but like an interrogatory, must be tailored to the specific dispute.

Physical and Medical Examinations

This discovery tool, like the first two can only be used in civil cases by parties against parties when the physical or mental condition of a party is at issue. Generally, to use the device in a civil case, you need a court order, although attorneys may agree among themselves to allow an examination.

This device gives an adversary the opportunity to have an examination (physical or mental) of the other party that, in most cases, will be the allegedly injured plaintiff. This allows the adversary to confirm or refute the medical condition of the injured party.

Deposition

Depositions are more expensive than the written discovery devices. Depositions may be taken by a party from either a party or a nonparty. An oral examination of a witness under oath incurs, among other expenses, court reporter fees and costs of transcription. On the other hand, depositions are much more useful. They allow you to develop and follow up on areas of inquiry, assess the credibility of witnesses, and preserve testimony. At trial, they present an excellent device for impeachment, serving as prior inconsistent statements if the witness's trial testimony is at variance with that in the deposition. The next chapter discusses depositions in detail.

Request for Admissions

Requests for admissions are made by a party only against a party. They are written, must be answered under oath, and allow the requesting party to gain admissions that may be used during the trial of the case.

A request for admission is an inexpensive device that a party can use, for example, to find out if any particular documents will be contested and why. As with interrogatories, some courts limit the number of requests for admission. However, courts are more lenient in allowing requests for admissions, and, in some case, you may be subjected to hundreds of requests for admissions, unless the court has restricted the number.

DISCOVERY TOOLS—WHAT ARE THEY GOOD FOR?

INTERROGATORIES: *Party on party*	Gain fundamental information, e.g., names of witnesses. Not good for getting versions of the facts or details
REQUEST TO PRODUCE: *Party on party*	Get other side to produce documents and tangible items.
REQUESTS FOR ADMISSIONS: *Party on party*	Compel admissions or denials—if admitted it is conclusively proved, e.g., authentication of a document.
DEPOSITIONS: *Party on party or nonparty*	Evaluate the witness, gain concessions, preserve testimony and lock the witness in.

Step Five—Determine the Timing and Sequencing of Discovery

Strategically, you want to consider when you will use your discovery devices. As with the substance of what you seek, you should consider obtaining information in a sequence that will help you in terms of your objectives—locating more information, settlement, preservation of information, and so on. For example, it is helpful at the beginning of discovery to use interrogatories to identify whether information exists and where it is. In that way, you can decide whom you want to depose, whether certain documents exist, and, if so, where you might find them.

Additionally, you may want to inspect and copy documents before taking the deposition of a witness whom you want to question about a particular document or about information that you learned from a document. But you may not be able to wait—you might have to consider such things as the health of the potential witness. (Should I depose the 90-year-old man? Do I want to preserve his testimony?) You may even want to schedule depositions before you file a lawsuit (by court order to obtain information so you can file a lawsuit or to preserve information that may otherwise be lost before you can file suit and commence discovery). Or you may want to wait until shortly before trial to have the injured plaintiff examined since it is possible that the plaintiff's medical condition may have improved substantially. On the other hand, perhaps an early examination will help you settle the case before the plaintiff begins deteriorating. You may decide—again, strategically—to send requests for admission late in your discovery because there is a greater chance that your adversary will be able to answer them. These are just a few of the instances of the use and timing of the discovery devices. Each scheduling decision is a strategic one.

A typical order of discovery is as follows:

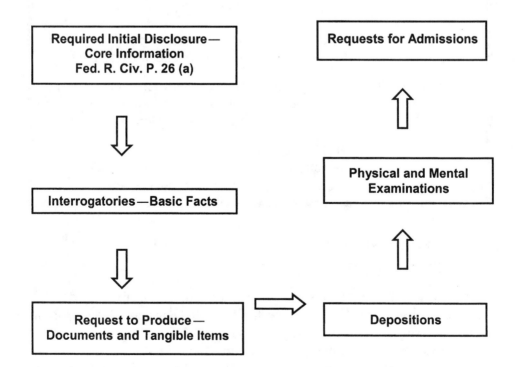

E. Preservation and Spoliation

American Bar Association Civil Discovery Standard 10 states:

> When a lawyer who has been retained to handle a matter learns that litigation is probable or has been commenced, the lawyer should inform the client of its duty to preserve potentially relevant documents in the client's custody or control and of the possible consequences of failing to do so. The duty to produce may be, but is not necessarily, coextensive with the duty to preserve. Because the Standards do not have the force of law, this Standard does not attempt to create, codify or circumscribe any preservation duty. Any such duty is created by governing state or federal law. This Standard is, instead, an admonition to counsel that it is counsel's responsibility to advise the client as to whatever duty exists, to avoid spoliation issues.

The duty to preserve is particularly important and problematic when the documents to be preserved are electronic information. Preservation of electronic information is an important concern because it has been estimated that 70 percent of all documents are never printed on paper. They exist in e-mails, instant messages, computer hard drives, and so on. Preservation is problematic because they exist in so many forms, are voluminous, can be deleted with the push of a button, and they are, once deleted, difficult to retrieve, if they can be retrieved at all. In addition, many companies have policies under which documents, especially electronic documents, are destroyed on a regular basis. Preservation obligations may require a company to halt its regular recycling of backup tapes, for example.

Nevertheless, a lawyer has the duty to advise a client on how to meet the obligation to preserve electronic information. ABA Standard 29(a) enumerates the electronic information that may be subject to a duty to preserve. When faced with the need to provide advice on this subject, you will need to research the controlling law regarding when the duty to preserve is activated, what must be preserved, and who must be told to preserve the information. In general though, the duty to preserve normally begins when litigation is reasonably anticipated, and counsel then should notify those in possession of the information (employees of a corporation who are likely to have the information) to put a "litigation hold" on the information so it is safely stored and not destroyed, that is, "spoliation." As the lawyer you must make sure you understand how the company's electronic information is being preserved and how backup tapes are being handled.

F.   The Lawyer's Signature—Certification

Accompanying every discovery request, response, or objection is the lawyer's signature block. By signing, the lawyer certifies under Fed. R. Civ. P. 26(g), or under similar state rule:

- That to the best of the lawyer's knowledge, information, and belief formed after reasonable inquiry (whether the lawyer has made a reasonable inquiry is usually determined by an objective rather than a subjective standard);
- The requests, responses, and objections are consistent with the rules and existing law or a good-faith argument for extension of the law; and
- That they were not interposed for improper purposes, such as delay or harassment, not unreasonable or unduly burdensome or expensive, given the needs of the case, discovery already had, the amount in controversy, and the importance of the issues at stake in the litigation.

Fed. R. Civ. P. 26(g) is designed to reduce delay and harassment tactics and attendant costs by imposing an affirmative duty to carry out discovery in the spirit and letter of the discovery rules. Rule 26(g)(3) provides that the court may impose sanctions for unjustified violations of the certification. Under this Rule, the court may impose "an appropriate sanction, which may include an order to pay the amount of the reasonable expenses incurred because of the violation, including a reasonable attorney's fee."

G.   E-Discovery

State or federal, large or small, no matter what kind of pretrial litigation you engage in, you will need to know about the discovery of electronically stored information. The mass of today's evidence is preserved electronically, not on paper. Practically every case involves at least e-mail evidence.

E-Discovery Rule Amendments and ABA Civil Discovery Standards on Electronic Discovery

Federal Rules of Civil Procedure were amended effective December 1, 2006 to cover electronic discovery, referred to here and elsewhere as "e-discovery." These Rules control in federal court, and they, taken together with the ABA Civil Discovery Standards on electronic discovery provide guidelines for electronic discovery in state cases as well. This section summarizes and highlights the Federal Rule E-Discovery Amendments and the ABA Standards, on electronic discovery (Section VIII, Standards 29 to 32), and explains electronic discovery.

"Electronically Stored Information"

The Federal Rule amendments apply to "electronically stored information." In Fed R. Civ. P. 26(a)(1)(B), the term "data compilation" is deleted, and the phrase "electronically stored information" substituted. The Rules do not provide a definition for this new term. This all-encompassing phrase is designed to embrace future developments. The ABA Standards provide guidance. ABA Standard 29(a) lists both electronic information that may be subject to discovery and the duty to preserve. Counsel can check the lists of data (e-mails, voice mails, animations, spreadsheets, etc.) and platforms (databases, networks, servers, etc.) to determine what to seek in discovery and what to preserve.

Federal E-Discovery Procedures

Under Fed. R. Civ. P. 26(f), as soon as practicable after a complaint has been filed but not later than 21 days before a scheduling order or conference, the parties are to conference on the preservation of electronically stored information and other e-discovery issues and concoct a discovery plan. A report on the plan, using federal form 35, is to be submitted to the court within 14 days after the meeting. Talk with the company's IT department to make sure you understand the company's system. The effect of the E-Discovery Rules is that lawyers have to understand the technology early in the case. A meeting with the company's IT department early in the case is now just as important as meeting as soon as possible with key witnesses.

ABA Standard on Civil Discovery 31 presupposes that a discovery conference should be held early in the case when *electronic discovery* is involved. Among other things, that Standard covers the various issues relating to electronic discovery (the subject matter of the discovery, identification of persons affiliated with the responding party who are knowledgeable of the system, the technology and software necessary to access the data, whether the potential data exists in searchable form, how the costs will be allocated, and so on). Also, the Standard suggests the parties consider a stipulation to court orders including initial production of subsets of material for review to determine whether further production is beneficial and the appointment of an independent technology consultant. This consultant serves as a special master in reviewing privileged electronic data without the privilege holder waiving the privilege by allowing a third party to review the information.

E-Discovery Rights and Responsibilities

Requesting Party

ABA Standards 29(b)(i) and (ii) recommend to the requesting party that the requests for electronic information should:

- State clearly whether *electronic information is sought,* but in the absence of such a statement, requests for "documents" should be construed as asking for electronic information;
- Specify *how it is to be produced*—a hard copy, an electronic form or, if appropriate, both;
- Specify the *format* (e.g., "its original format" or "native files"). Also, getting the information in its original format, for example, Word 6.0, PDF, or another format is preferable because if it is converted, it may be received in an unreadable form. Amended Fed. R. Civ. P. 34(b)(2)(ii) states that if the request for production does not state the form of production, the producing party is to provide the information as "ordinarily maintained" or "reasonably useable.") ;
- Ask for *metadata* (i.e., "ancillary electronic information that relates to responsive electronic data, such as information that would indicate whether and when the responsive electronic data was created, edited. . .");
- Ask for *software* needed to "retrieve, read or interpret electronic data"; and
- Inquire about where and how the data is stored.

Responding Party

The responding party need only provide the information in electronic form, not also in hard copy, if the information in both is identical or the differences are immaterial. Standard 29 (b)(iii).

Privileged or Trial-Preparation Material

Due to the volume of electronically stored information, the risk of turning over privileged information is increased. Amended Fed. R. Civ. P. 26(b)(5) addresses this risk by providing that if a party inadvertently provides privileged or trial-preparation information, the party may request its return and the receiving party is to comply with the request or sequester the information until the claim is resolved.

If the information technology (IT) person, who normally is not employed by the producing party, extracts electronic information for production, arguably the producing party has waived the privilege by revealing the information to a person outside the privilege. ABA Standard 32 proposes the entry of a stipulated court order to alleviate concern about waiver. The order could authorize one of these three methods: (1) the IT person would be a court-appointed special master or court officer; (2) a "quick peek" approach—with an order that production does not constitute a waiver, the producing party, without reviewing the data, turns it over to the requesting party who then identifies what documents it is interested in and the producing party would then conduct a privilege review of that; and (3) the parties agree to a third-party consultant who is not appointed as a special master or court officer. In line with the Standard, amended Fed. R. Civ. P. 16(b) provides that the federal court's scheduling order may "include any agreements the parties reach for asserting claims of privilege or as protection as trial-preparation material after production."

Undue Burden or Cost

The expense of producing electronically stored information can be significant. Also, the e-discovery may be difficult to retrieve. Amended Fed. R. Civ. P. 26(b)(2)(B) provides that a party is not required to produce e-discovery from "sources that the party identifies as not reasonably accessible because of undue burden or cost." The Rule goes on to provide:

> . . . On motion to provide discovery or for protective order, the party from whom discovery is sought must show that the information is not reasonably accessible because of burden or cost. If that showing is made, the court may nonetheless order discovery from such sources if the requesting party shows good cause considering the limitations of Rule 26(b)(2)(C).

Rule 26(b)(2)(C) lists seven considerations (e.g., specificity of the discovery request, accessibility of the information from other sources, resources of the parties, and so on) for the court focusing on the need for discovery and the expense.

Sanctions for Loss

Federal Rule of Civil Procedure 37(f) is designed to protect a party from sanctions if the party inadvertently and innocently loses electronically stored information due to "routine, good faith operation of an electronic information system" and there are no "exceptional circumstances." For example, if information is lost because the system is programmed to automatically and routinely cause deletion or overwriting without the operator's knowledge, the court, under Rule 37(f) may decide not to impose sanctions for the loss.

Some commentary, however, emphasizes that despite the safe harbor provision, companies still may have an obligation to stop automatic deletion processes such as recycling backup tapes. While this Rule has been described as providing a "safe harbor" sheltering the party against sanctions, the party moving for sanctions may claim that the loss was not due to a good-faith operation of system or that exceptional circumstances exist.

Technology to Facilitate Discovery

ABA Standard 30 envisions the use of technology to aid in the discovery process:

- By having the court order or the parties stipulate to providing electronic discovery even if the information was not originally stored in an electronic form, and
- Written discovery should be provided in an electronic version unless the parties stipulate that no electronic version is required.

III. DRAFTING CIVIL DISCOVERY REQUESTS

A. Drafting Interrogatories

Your interrogatories and requests for production are the basic written devices enabling you to obtain predicate information for depositions (telling which person to depose, which documents the person possesses) and for focusing your subsequent use of written requests.

Drafting techniques for interrogatories are guided by a variety of principles, four of which you should focus on in particular:

- Carefully compose a detailed *preamble* to your requests,
- Employ a combination of *broad and narrow questions* (a limitation on the number of interrogatories will dictate that they be broad),
- Pose questions that are *unambiguous,* and
- Ensure that the information you receive will be *clearly identified* (and identifiable).

1. Preamble and Definitions

You will have to create a "preamble" to open your written requests. This provides your personal, customized rules of the game that the opposing party must follow in answering. The preamble, which can be several pages in length, can include the particular party (spouse, corporation, partnership) to which the request is directed, the time for answering, definitions ("When using the term 'writing,' plaintiff means 'any transcription including film, video, tape recording'"), mechanics ("Answer within the space provided. If you need more space . . ."), and instructions concerning the information that is expected to be provided ("When a witness's name is provided, also include last known address and telephone number. If you cannot provide full information in response to a particular question, explain why you can't provide the information and when you plan to come in possession of the information"). Ideas for your preamble can come from form books, other attorneys' discovery papers, and your own previous preambles. But the precise preamble must be tailored to the individual needs of the particular case.

A Sample Preamble for Interrogatories and Requests for Production

Preamble for Interrogatories and Requests for Production

THE SUPERIOR COURT, THE STATE OF MAJOR
JAMNER COUNTY

JEFFERY GRAND	)	
	)	
Plaintiff,	)	No. 20 – 12154813
	)	
v.	)	PLAINTIFF'S INTERROGATORIES
	)	AND REQUESTS FOR PRODUCTION
KARA FONTES	)	TO DEFENDANT KARA FONTES
and JOHN DOE	)	
FONTES, and	)	
JASMINNA CO.	)	
a Sole	)	
Proprietorship,	)	
	)	
Defendants	)	
_____	)	

TO: Kara Fontes, Defendant

AND TO: Malachi Richardson, Defendant's Attorney

In accordance with CR 33 and CR 34, you are required to answer in writing the following Interrogatories and Requests for Production, separately and fully under oath, within thirty (30) days of their service upon you. THESE INTERROGATORIES AND REQUESTS FOR PRODUCTION ARE TO BE TREATED AS CONTINUING PURSUANT TO CR 26(e). If the information is not available within the time limits of the Civil Rules, you must answer each Interrogatory and Request for Production as fully as

continues ▶

possible within the time limit and furnish additional information when it become available. If additional space is required for answers, you may attach an additional answer sheet appropriately referenced. If additional information is discovered between the time of making these answers and the time of trial, these Interrogatories and Requests for Production are directed to that information. If this information is not furnished, the undersigned will move at the time of trial to exclude from evidence any information requested and not furnished.

DEFINITIONS:

A. The term "person" means, inclusively, an individual, partnership, corporation, or other entity or organization.

B. Where reference is made to any date or any figure, the reference is intended to connote your best approximation.

C. "Document" or "documents" includes all items within the scope of Rule of Civil Procedure 42 and, without limiting its generality, includes contracts, agreements, correspondence, letters, telegrams, reports, records, schedules, diaries, calendars, appointment books, invoices, purchase orders, books, pamphlets, accounting record and worksheets, time slips charts, diagrams, notes, estimates, summaries, appraisals, inventories, and memoranda, including intercorporate, intracorporate, interoffice, and intraoffice memoranda, and memoranda regarding conferences, conversations, or telephone conversations, any and all tapes, recorded, written, printed or typed matters of any kind or description, unless otherwise specified, and all electronically stored information including but not limited to computer or PDA inputs or outputs and backup systems.

D. When correspondence between one or more persons is requested, the request includes, without limiting its generality, any document or documents given, sent, or shown by one person to one or more other persons, however transmitted or delivered, whether or not retained by the recipient or recipients at the time of transmittal or delivery.

E. When used in relation to a person, the term "identify" means provide the name, last known address, and last known telephone number. When used in relation to a document, the term "identify" means to provide a description of the document along with its author, recipient, subject matter, and date. When used in relation to conduct, the term "identify" means to provide a description of the conduct, the actor, and the recipient, if any, of the conduct.

F. The term "Subject Contract" refers to the contract between Jeffery Grand and Jasminna Corporation to build a dock and boat moorage at 1215 E. Allison, signed on or about November 14, 20XX.

2.   Combine Broad and Narrow Questions

Use a combination of broad and narrow questions. Though guided by your and your opponent's tentative case theories, discovery must have a broad sweep. After all, your theories are only tentative at this relatively early stage of the process and you do not want to so narrow the focus of your discovery that you fail to obtain information that would indicate the possibility of other more applicable case theories. Also, you do not want information bearing on the case theories you currently have in mind to fall through the cracks because it is not specifically addressed by any particular inquiry. Broadly phrased questions fulfill the function of providing an expansive scope to your discovery. These broad questions can be placed at the beginning of a series of individual specific questions (or subparts) as lead-in questions, or at the end of a series of questions as catch-alls. Samples of lead-in and catch-all questions follow:

Sample Lead-in Interrogatories

Interrogatory 15

In paragraph xiii of your complaint, you ask for special damages. Detail all the special damages you are claiming and why you are entitled to each.

[Broad Lead-in Question]

    a. What is the amount of each special damage claim?

[Narrowly Focused Specific Questions]

    b. State the method you used to compute the amounts.

    c. Have you received any medical treatment in conjunction with any of those damage claims?

    d. If so, please provide the identity of the treating physician(s).

Sample Catch-all Interrogatories

Interrogatory 16

State all facts that support your affirmative defenses.   **[Broad Catch-all Question]**

Use of specific questions, like the ones appearing in subparts a through d in the Sample Lead-in interrogatories, allows you to focus on precise information for your case theory analysis. These specific questions also force specific information from the responding party. They are unlike the broad questions that at times can generate vague, and, accordingly, not very helpful responses. Be careful when using subparts because some rules count each subpart as a separate interrogatory. Obviously subparts may count toward your interrogatory limit.

An interesting variation on the use of narrow, directed questions involves a strategy that combines the use of contention interrogatories with requests for admissions. As you recall, contention interrogatories focus on specific factual allegations in the opposing party's pleadings and seek the basis for the allegation.

Sample Contention Interrogatories

Interrogatory 24

In paragraph 'xi' of your complaint you state "and plaintiff suffered extreme emotional distress."

    a. State all the facts upon which you base this claim.
    b. Identify all witnesses who you contend support any or all of these facts.
    c. Identify each document, including the person or persons who are in possession of and/or have control of each such document and its location, which you contend supports this claim.

---

3. Unambiguous Questions

Be certain that your questions have a clear, specific meaning—that is, be sure that they are unambiguous. Note that even narrow questions can be ambiguous.

Interrogatory 9

Identify all property, real and personal, that was given to you as a gift by plaintiff between April and July 20XX.

    a. Name all vehicles you received, providing identification numbers.

The request for "all vehicles" is certainly narrow when compared with "all property," but it is ambiguous. What constitutes a "vehicle"? Car, bicycle, horse, skateboard? Only motorized transportation? Are airplanes and boats included? Such ambiguity carries two problems. For those whose discovery philosophy is to find every excuse possible not to give information, this type of question plays right into their strategy. ("Defendant cannot answer plaintiff's Interrogatory 9, that question being too vague and ambiguous to permit a response.") For those whose discovery philosophy is to provide all information to which the other party is reasonably entitled, this question does not give sufficient guidance for providing the information.

4. Require Identification of Persons and Documents

Finally, make certain that any information about persons or documents you do receive in response to your requests is sufficiently identified so you will be able to later locate it. Note the information that is requested concerning witnesses (addresses, phone numbers) and documents (location, custodian) back in the contention Interrogatory 24, subparts b and c.

INTERROGATORIES

Fed. R. Civ. P. 33

R U L E

Device:	Written questions that must be answered in writing and under oath
Service:	By a party on a party
Good for:	Basic information, such as the identification of witnesses, documents, experts and their opinions, the sequence of events, damages information, insurance coverage, and positions on issues
Not for:	Subjective versions of facts or details
Drafting:	Have an effective preamble. Combine broad and narrow questions. Ask unambiguous questions. Require identification of persons and documents. Cover electronically stored information
How many:	Under the Fed. R. Civ. P.—25 interrogatories
Use at Trial:	Can be used as an admission of party opponent and for impeachment

---

B. Drafting Responses to Interrogatories

The Ambiguous Interrogatory

Begin your response to interrogatories by reading the instructions provided in the preamble. If anything is unclear, do not guess at the meaning. You always should have a clear idea of what the other party is seeking before answering. Assuming that you are not sure what is being requested, however, what will you do? For attorneys whose dubious philosophy of discovery is to withhold as much as possible (one technique of which is to deny information if any word in the request is ambiguous), this will provide the opportunity to return the request a month or so later indicating that, due to the particular lack of clarity, they could not provide any response. Note that it is unethical to "fail to make reasonably diligent efforts to comply with a legally proper discovery request," ABA Model Rule of Professional Responsibility 3.4(d). Additionally, Fed. R. Civ. P. 33(b)(1) requires that an interrogatory be answered "fully," indicating the intent that responses should further the goal of complete disclosure of relevant and nonprivileged information.

Attorneys whose ethical and professional philosophy of discovery is that each side should provide all requested information to which a party is reasonably entitled, will call or write opposing counsel indicating their desire to respond, and will request any clarification that is required to accomplish this end. This decision has a sufficient practical basis that we do not need to further emphasize the ethical dimension. A partial answer and an objection (see example below) is another approach to the situations where (1) while the request seems to be for everything relating to a subject, you think you know what the other side is getting at, and you want to answer while still preserving an overbreadth objection, or (2) the request asks for facts, some of which are covered by the attorney-client privilege.

Also consistent with this position that a party should respond is Fed. R. Civ. P. 26(g) and similar state rules requiring the lawyer's certification of discovery responses signifying that the lawyer has complied with the intent of the discovery rules. Consequently, you should attempt to assess the reasonable meanings of discovery requests and then try to provide complete, unambiguous responses (by giving an answer, referring to a document also available to the other party, or attaching a copy of the document). For example, a response to an ambiguous interrogatory where you nonetheless believe you know what the opposing party is seeking could be phrased: "Defendant objects to Interrogatory 31 as vague and overbroad. However, interpreting Interrogatory 31 to mean '____,' defendant answers as follows. . . ." Likewise, a request for facts, some of which are privileged and some of which are not, could be answered: "As to the request in Interrogatory 12 for the topics discussed at the meeting of 02/19/XX, Defendant objects on grounds of attorney-client privilege. As to topics discussed at 02/26/XX meeting, Defendant answers as follows. . . ."

Privileged Information

Of course, you should be certain that in providing answers you are not giving away privileged information or opening the door for a possible claim that you have waived a privilege. Before you file your response, therefore, comb through its text with a checklist of possible privileges in mind (attorney-client, work product, physician-patient). If you do feel that some request delves into privileged terrain, you can raise an objection to that request as your answer. Before you raise this claim, however, be certain that it is well founded. If such a refusal to provide information is brought before the court by your opponent on a motion to compel and you lose, even if you are clearly in good faith, courts will often assess the opponent's costs (attorney's fees, travel) to your client. Also, if the court does not regard your objection as well conceived, you may lose credibility on subsequent legal positions you take in discovery.

Sample Responses to Interrogatories

Responses to Interrogatories

Objection

ANSWER:

"Defendant objects because the requested information falls under the attorney-client privilege. Major Evidence Rule 25"

Objection/Partial Answer

ANSWER:

"Defendant objects as overbroad and unduly burdensome. Subject to and without waiving its objections, Defendant states . . ."

Provide the Answer

ANSWER

"Defendant employed Alfred Matthews and Michael Hogen during the time period stated in interrogatory # 5.

Business Record

ANSWER:

"Defendant's business record answers this interrogatory—the Articles of Incorporation for Jasminna Corporation provide the answer. At a mutually convenient time and date, plaintiff may examine and copy the Articles at the offices of Jasminna Corporation. Rule 33(c)."

Investigation Continues

ANSWER:

"At this juncture, your request is premature and the investigation continues."

E-Discovery and Business Records

As shown in the foregoing example, one response is to produce business records in answering an interrogatory. This response is explicitly authorized by Federal Rule of Civil Procedure 33(d), as follows:

> Where the answer to an interrogatory may be derived or ascertained from the business records, *including electronically stored information,* of the party upon whom the interrogatory has been served or from an examination, audit or inspection of such business records, including a compilation, abstract or summary thereof, and the burden of deriving or ascertaining the answer is substantially the same for the party serving the interrogatory as for the party served, it is a sufficient answer to such interrogatory to specify the records from which the answer may be derived or ascertained and to afford the party serving the interrogatory reasonable opportunity to examine, audit or inspect such records and to make copies, compilations, abstracts, or summaries. A specification shall be in sufficient detail to permit the interrogating party to locate and identify, as readily as can the party served, the records from which the answer may be derived.

The e-discovery amendment to this Rule adds the italicized phrase for clarification of the meaning of "business records" to include electronically stored information.

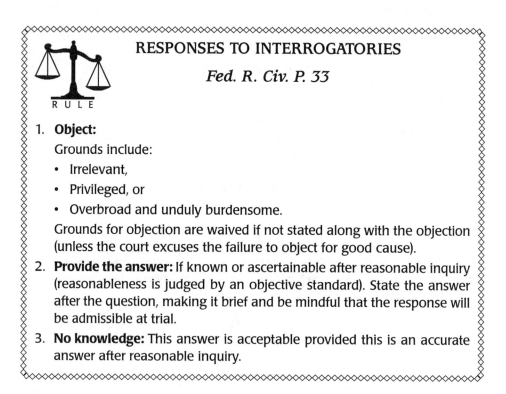

RESPONSES TO INTERROGATORIES

Fed. R. Civ. P. 33

RULE

1. **Object:**
   Grounds include:
   - Irrelevant,
   - Privileged, or
   - Overbroad and unduly burdensome.

   Grounds for objection are waived if not stated along with the objection (unless the court excuses the failure to object for good cause).

2. **Provide the answer:** If known or ascertainable after reasonable inquiry (reasonableness is judged by an objective standard). State the answer after the question, making it brief and be mindful that the response will be admissible at trial.

3. **No knowledge:** This answer is acceptable provided this is an accurate answer after reasonable inquiry.

4. **Business records:** Answer that the business records provide the information sought and this includes electronically stored information. Fed. R. Civ. P. 33(c).

5. **Investigation continues:** State this in the answer if the legal or factual matter is still in the development stage.

Updating discovery: Responses to interrogatories must be "seasonably" updated. Fed. R. Civ. P. 26(e).

Deadline: Interrogatories must be answered within 30 days after service.

C. Drafting Requests for Production

Either you have used your interrogatories to identify the existence and location of documents or things reachable under a request for production or you have decided to couple your interrogatories with a request for production. The next step is to draft the request for production. It should be comprehensive in seeking what is authorized.

Federal Rule of Civil Procedure 34(a), amended in 2006 to explicitly mention electronically stored information, authorizes requests to produce and allow the party making the request:

- "to inspect, copy, test, or sample any designated *documents or electronic discovery* (including writings, drawings, graphs, charts, photographs, sound recordings, images, and any other data or data compilations stored in any medium—from which information can be obtained, translated, if necessary, by respondent into reasonably usable form)," or

- "to inspect, copy, test, or sample any designated tangible things" that are discoverable, or

- "to permit *entry upon designated land or other property* in the possession or control of the party upon whom the request is served for the purpose of measuring, surveying, photographing, testing or sampling the property or any designated object or operation thereon" which is discoverable.

Preface

Your requests for production, just like your interrogatories, should begin with a preface defining terms and providing instructions to the respondent.

Particularity

Under Fed. R. Civ. Proc. 34(b) the item to be produced must be described "with reasonable particularity." Thus, you want to draft your requests with as much specificity as possible. For instance, this can be accomplished by describing the item in relationship to a specific timeframe (e.g., "all sales receipts for May 23, 20XX") or in reference to the other party's pleadings (e.g., "all documents that relate to paragraph 6 of Plaintiff's complaint"). A mind frame helpful to crafting requests that describe with "particularity" is to assume that the respondent will be uncooperative or even recalcitrant. By envisioning all the ways the respondent might avoid disclosure, you can refine your requests to rule out those evasions.

Interlink Requests for Production with Interrogatories

Requests for production can be interlinked with interrogatories. The interrogatories seek to identify items that requests for production can get the respondent to produce. Often, other requests for production are submitted in addition to interrogatories.

Protect Against Destruction

To shield against the destruction of evidence, it is good practice to notify the other side as soon as possible of your request, even before filing the complaint. This communication can trigger the other side's duty to preserve evidence.

Sample Interrogatories Linked with a Request for Production

Interrogatories Linked with a Request for Production

Interrogatory 7: Identify and describe the work performed by each subcontractor, person, or entity that worked on the dock and boat moorage under the Subject Contract.

ANSWER:

Interrogatory 8: Identify the following:

a. The amount that you and/or Jasminna Corporation paid each subcontractor, person or entity for work under the Subject Contract,
b. The reason for payment,
c. The date that amount was paid.

ANSWER:

Request for Production 1: Pursuant to Civil Rule 34, Request for Production is hereby made to provide a copy of payment records made by Jasminna Corporation to any subcontractors who worked on the dock and/or boat moorage covered by the Subject Contract.

REQUESTS FOR PRODUCTION
Fed. R. Civ. P. 34

RULE

Device: Written requests for documents, tangible objects and access to property

Service: By a party on a party

Good for: Obtaining documents, e-mails, and tangible objects and entry onto property

Drafting: Describe with "particularity." Cover all possible records including those electronically stored. Ask for destroyed documents and electronically stored information and the circumstances of destruction

Use in Trial: Evidence, such as documents, can be introduced at trial.

E. Drafting Responses to Requests for Production

Under Fed. R. Civ. P. 34(b), a party served with requests for production must "serve a written response within 30 days after the service of the request." Besides this, what are the respondent's obligations?

Duty to Preserve

As was mentioned earlier in Section II E., page 247, both the attorney and the client have a *duty to preserve evidence*. This includes the preservation of electronically stored information, such as e-mails, as well as paper documents. When the lawyer is put on notice that a lawsuit against the client is reasonably foreseeable, the lawyer should inform the client of the duty to preserve documents in his or her possession, control or custody that are relevant to the action.

Form or Forms of Production

"Unless the parties otherwise agree, or the court otherwise orders," Fed. R. Civ. P. 34(b)(i) requires the party to produce the documents "*as they are kept in the usual course of the business* or shall arrange and label them to correspond with the categories in the request."

The e-discovery amendments to Fed. R. Civ. P. 34(b) add that unless the court orders or the parties agree otherwise:

> (ii) if a request (for production) does not specify the form or forms for producing electronically stored information, a responding party must produce the information in a form or forms that are reasonably usable, and

> (iii) a party need not produce the same electronically stored information in more than one form.

Formulating the Response

Once requests for production are served, the first chore is to determine what of the requested items is in the client's possession, custody, and control. After that has been accomplished, the potentially discoverable items must be screened to eliminate from production any that are confidential or privileged and thus not discoverable. The written response to the requests may include objections to the requests, and under Fed. R. Civ. P.. 34(b) the reasons for the objection must be stated. If only part of the request is objected to, the other requested items must be produced. Finally, for those items that are to be produced, the attorney for the respondent can make arrangements with the requesting lawyer for the method of discovery: providing a copy of the items, permitting inspection and allowing copying of particular items, entry onto land for testing, and so on.

The responses are drafted to each request stating:

- an objection along with reasons for the objection,
- that the item does not exist, or
- that the inspection and related activity will be permitted.

Sample Responses to Requests for Production

Responses to Requests for Production
Objection
ANSWER:
"Objection—This item is not in responding party's possession, custody and control. Rule 33"

Not in Existence

ANSWER:

"The requested document does not exist."

Complying with the Request

ANSWER:

"The requested documents will be produced for examination and copying at the time and place suggested by the plaintiff and as indicated in the pretrial scheduling order."

RESPONSES TO REQUESTS FOR PRODUCTION

Fed. R. Civ. P. 34(b)

R U L E

Preservation: Inform the client to preserve relevant information.

Locate: Determine whether the client has the requested item in the client's possession, custody, or control.

Screen: Examine the information to determine whether it is discoverable.

Responses:
1) Objection on grounds of:
   - Irrelevant,
   - Privileged, or
   - Unduly burdensome or annoying
2) Requested item not in existence, or
3) State that the request will be met.

Record Keeping: Because claims of failure to make discovery can be alleged, keep accurate records of what was given to whom and when, utilizing a "Bates" stamp number. The "Bates" number is named after the Bates stamp machine. A Bates number is distinct number given to each discovery document. Example: May 23 XX 123456

Deadline: Requests for Production must be answered within 30 days after service.

F.   Drafting Requests for Admissions

Requests for admissions are not so much designed to discover what the other side knows but rather to help with a summary judgment motion and are intended to streamline the trial by gaining admissions that can be read to the jury or by the judge in a bench trial. Under Fed. R. Civ. P. 36(b), "any matter admitted under this rule is conclusively established unless the court on motion permits withdrawal or amendment of the admission." In other words, the admitted matter cannot be contradicted by evidence produced at trial. Admissions that may be obtained include: "the truth of any matter" that is a discoverable fact or of the application of law to fact or the genuineness of any document.

When drafting requests for admission, you want to begin with a preface, like the preface for interrogatories or request for production that defines terms and gives directions to the respondent. It is crucial to keep in mind the use of admissions in trial. Therefore, be cognizant that:

- *Wordsmithing* is important because the admission will be read to the jury. How will it sound in that setting?
- The admission should *facilitate the proving of your case.* For instance, tedious evidentiary predicates, authentication of documents, proof of an agency relationship are candidates for requests for admissions.
- You do *not want to seek admissions to evidence that the jury will likely find compelling* for your case, such as evidence of the client's pain and suffering. If you request and get the admission to persuasive evidence you will be precluded from offering other evidence on the subject because the admission is conclusive evidence on the subject.

Sample Requests for Admissions

THE SUPERIOR COURT, THE STATE OF MAJOR
JAMNER COUNTY

JEFFERY GRAND	)	
	)	
Plaintiff,	)	No. 20 – 12154813
	)	
v.	)	PLAINTIFF'S FIRST
	)	REQUESTS FOR ADMISSION
KARA FONTES	)	TO DEFENDANT KARA FONTES
and JOHN DOE	)	
FONTES, and	)	
JASMINNA, CO.	)	
a Sole	)	
Proprietorship,	)	
	)	
Defendants	)	

TO: Kara Fontes, Defendant

AND TO: Malachi Richardson, her attorney

The Plaintiff requests the Defendant Kara Fontes to admit or deny the truth of the following facts pursuant to Rule of Civil Procedure 36.

DEFINITIONS:

   A. The term "person" means, inclusively, an individual, partnership, corporation, or other entity or organization.
   B. Where reference is made to any date or any figure, such reference is intended to connote your best approximation.
   C. The term "Subject Contract" refers to the contract between Jeffery Grand and Jasminna Corporation to build a dock and boat moorage at 1215 E. Albomb, signed on or about November 14, 20XX.
. . .

   Request for Admission 1: Admit or deny that Kara Fontes signed the Subject Contract.

ANSWER:

   Request for Admission 2: Admit or deny that when Kara Fontes signed the Subject Contract she was the President of Jasminna Corporation.

continues ▶

ANSWER:

Request for Admission 3: Admit or deny that Jasminna Corporation is a sole proprietorship.

ANSWER:

Request for Admission 4: Admit or deny that Jasminna Corporation breached the Subject Contract by not finishing the construction of the dock and boat moorage by the date of completion established in the Subject Contract.

DATED: _____, 20XX

STANS STARBOCKS AND TULLY

_____

Riley Stans, Bar No. MA 12601
1999 Broadway N.
Ruston, Major 98105
206-993-1222
Attorney for Plaintiff Jeffery Grand

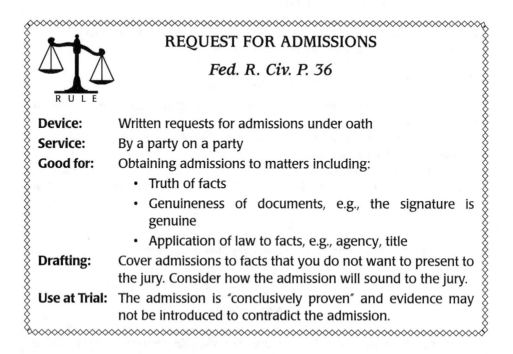

REQUEST FOR ADMISSIONS
Fed. R. Civ. P. 36

Device:	Written requests for admissions under oath
Service:	By a party on a party
Good for:	Obtaining admissions to matters including:

- Truth of facts
- Genuineness of documents, e.g., the signature is genuine
- Application of law to facts, e.g., agency, title

Drafting:	Cover admissions to facts that you do not want to present to the jury. Consider how the admission will sound to the jury.
Use at Trial:	The admission is "conclusively proven" and evidence may not be introduced to contradict the admission.

G. Drafting Responses to Requests for Admissions

If a request for admission is not answered in writing and signed by the party or party's attorney within the time limit set by court rule—Fed. R. Civ. P. 36 sets it at 30 days or another period of time set by the parties or court—it is deemed admitted. A matter admitted under Fed. R. Civ. P. 36(b) is conclusively established unless the court permits amendment or withdrawal.

Four responses exist under Fed. R. Civ. P. 36(a):

- First, an *objection* can be made, and it must be supported by the reasons for the objection. Grounds for objections include: that the matter is non-discoverable, i.e., privileged or irrelevant, or it is unduly burdensome or annoying.
- Second, the party may *admit*.
- Third, the party may *deny all or part of the request*. However, if in good faith a party must qualify the answer or deny only part, the party is to specify what part is true and then qualify or deny the rest. If a party denies and the other party proves the fact at trial, then the other party is entitled under Rule 37(b) to expenses incurred proving the fact, including the attorney's fee.
- Fourth, if in good faith the answering party can *neither admit nor deny,* the answer must state why the party cannot either admit or deny. An answering party may not give lack of information or knowledge as a reason for failure to admit or deny unless the party has made reasonable inquiry and the information known or readily obtainable by the party is insufficient to enable the party to admit or deny.

Sample Responses to Requests for Admissions

Responses to Requests for Admissions

Denial

ANSWER:

"Denied."

Qualified Answer

ANSWER:

"Defendant can neither admit nor deny because the matter in dispute is whether Jasminna Corporation "finished the work," which responding party contends it did, and the request assumes noncompliance by Jasminna Corporation."

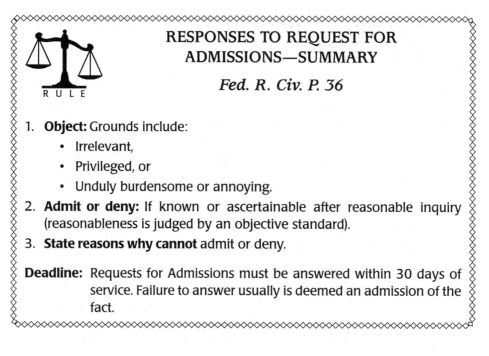

RESPONSES TO REQUEST FOR
ADMISSIONS—SUMMARY

Fed. R. Civ. P. 36

1. **Object:** Grounds include:
   - Irrelevant,
   - Privileged, or
   - Unduly burdensome or annoying.
2. **Admit or deny:** If known or ascertainable after reasonable inquiry (reasonableness is judged by an objective standard).
3. **State reasons why cannot** admit or deny.

Deadline: Requests for Admissions must be answered within 30 days of service. Failure to answer usually is deemed an admission of the fact.

IV. CRIMINAL DISCOVERY

A. Discovery Rules, Statutes, and Devices

As you will remember, there are restrictions on what the prosecution may discover in a criminal case; the defendant's constitutional protections being the primary limitation that the prosecutor cannot obtain access to what would otherwise be discoverable. There is, however, a bit of a range among jurisdictions as to what information the defendant can be compelled to provide to the state. For that reason, the discussion here is primarily devoted to defense discovery practices in criminal cases.

Court Rules and Statutes

Criminal discovery is generally regulated by statutes and court rules (such as the Federal Rules of Criminal Procedure), case law or accepted custom, and usage of a particular court. The type of discoverable information varies from jurisdiction to jurisdiction. Generally, under applicable court rules and statutes, the defense can discover such items as police reports, physical evidence, the defendant's statements, and forensic tests. A good cause showing, however, is still required for anything not provided for in the court rules.

Federal Rule of Criminal Procedure 16 on "Discovery and Inspection" provides that the following, among other information, must be provided to the defense on request:

- Generally, the defendant's statements before and after arrest in response to an interrogation by law enforcement,
- Defendant's prior criminal record,
- Documents and objects that will help the defense prepare and that will be offered by the government in its case-in-chief,
- Reports of examinations and tests,
- A written summary of testimony for any expert that the government expects to call, and so on.

Fed. R. Crim. P. 16 also contains counterpart provisions governing what the defendant must provide to the government including specific documents and objects, reports of examinations and tests, and summaries of expert witness testimony. This defense discovery is conditioned upon the government's compliance with Rule 16.

Open-File Policy or Defense Motion

In some jurisdictions, the prosecutor's office has an open-file policy, providing the defense with all but privileged portions of the case information in the prosecutor's files. Although a great deal of informal discovery of information by the prosecution takes place, and in some jurisdictions court rules or statutes require the prosecution to turn over various categories of information to the defense, in many instances, criminal discovery will be accomplished by a formal, written motion to the court. The sample defense discovery motion at the end of this chapter (page 282) provides a spectrum of items that a defendant may reasonably try to obtain, although the defendant cannot expect that this try, even though reasonable, will invariably be successful in a jurisdiction where defendants must obtain discovery through formal legal motions to the court.

Other Tools for Discovery

Preliminary Hearing

The defense has other avenues to explore in an effort to obtain full discovery. If the jurisdiction has a preliminary hearing system, that is, a lower court takes testimony and receives evidence and then determines whether probable cause exists to bind the case over for trial in a higher trial court, then the defense can utilize the preliminary hearing as a discovery device. By cross-examining the prosecution's witnesses, the defense can gather extensive information, including an assessment of the credibility of the government's witnesses.

Deposition

In Florida, depositions are taken in criminal cases. However, in other states depositions in criminal cases are generally limited to the rare instance when the witness is likely to be unavailable for trial (e.g., terminal illness, a move to Europe), though a few jurisdictions permit deposing material witnesses who refuse to cooperate in an interview (which gives some clout to the defense when a witness does not want to cooperate in informal discovery).

Bill of Particulars

In those jurisdictions in which it is recognized, a bill of particulars is a device that technically is a response to the prosecution's charging pleading (e.g., the information or complaint) and that asks for clarification of the pleading in terms of dates, means of committing the offense, and other facts that directly underlie the elements of the charge ("Your Honor, the information alleges only that my client possessed 'a controlled substance.' By this bill of particulars we seek to learn what specific substance my client is alleged to have possessed. Without that information, he does not know the true nature of the charges he is facing, and accordingly can neither enter a plea nor begin to prepare an effective defense").

B. *Brady* Material

Brady v. Maryland, 373 U.S. 83 (1963), held that the Due Process Clause imposes on the prosecution the obligation of providing full discovery to the defense of any exculpatory evidence—material evidence favorable to the defendant either as to guilt or punishment. An extensive body of case law has developed both interpreting the *Brady* obligation (the meaning of "material") and expanding it (the prosecutor must provide exculpatory information in law enforcement's possession under *Kyles v. Whitley*, 514 U.S. 419, 437 (1995)). Unlike other situations where the court rule or statute formulates a two-way street discovery approach, the defense has no obligation to provide inculpatory information to the prosecution.

V.   MOTION TO COMPEL DISCOVERY AND REQUEST SANCTIONS

A.   Determining When to Make a Motion to Compel Discovery

In both criminal and civil cases, it is common practice that the party seeking discovery initially files a request for discovery with the opposing party, resorting to the court with a motion for discovery (criminal) or motion to compel discovery (civil) if some or all of the requested information is not forthcoming. In the criminal area, the request and the motion are often filed at the same time, with the areas the parties can agree on being settled prior to the hearing on the motion. As already noted, however, there are jurisdictions where the prosecution voluntarily "opens its files" to the defendant, obviating these formal processes in most cases. In the civil area, attempts to resolve informally discovery disputes must be made before a party is permitted to resort to the courts and file a motion to compel. See the section below discussing the resolution of civil discovery disputes.

Considerations

Whether to bring a motion to compel will be determined by at least two considerations beyond the plausibility of your position—the importance of the information that is being withheld and the general behavior of the opposing party in discovery. If the opponent has been unreasonable throughout discovery you may seek to compel the discovery of even relatively minor information (although you are likely to include it in a single motion to compel with more significant information that has also been withheld) in order to expose that unreasonableness. You want this behavior to be seen by the court in the hope that the court will get involved and assist you in the future in obtaining reasonable access to information in your opponent's possession. Also, by bringing the motion, you show your opponent that you are willing to go to the trouble of filing a motion and to argue in court in order to obtain that to which you are entitled. This may give the opponent second thoughts before refusing any particular requests for discovery in the future.

Resolving Disputes over Civil Discovery

Attempt to Resolve Informally

It is a widely accepted that before moving to compel discovery the parties should seek to resolve the dispute. Federal Rule of Civil Procedure 37(a)(2) requires it, stating, "The motion must include a certification that the movant has in good faith conferred or attempted to confer with the party not making the disclosure in an effort to secure the disclosure without court action." ABA Standard on Civil Discovery 2(b)(i) states that the court should not entertain a discovery motion if the parties have not sought to resolve or narrow the issues informally. Standard 2(b)(ii) recognizes that some issues are not suitable for informal resolution, such as attorney-client privilege and work product issues, adequacy of the discovery responses, or production or the scope of discovery.

Deposition Disputes

When the parties and/or a nonparty witness cannot resolve a dispute arising at a deposition, ABA Standard on Civil Discovery 2(a)(i) indicates that a telephone conference should be conducted with the court, and if that does not solve the problem, other methods involving minimal time and expense, such as a discovery dispute conference should be employed. Parties should keep in mind that courts do not like discovery disputes and consider them generally to be a waste of judicial resources. You should make every effort to resolve disputes before burdening the court.

Other Discovery Disputes

Standard 2(a)(ii) indicates that when other disputes cannot be informally resolved, the aggrieved party can notify the court by phone (with other parties given the opportunity to be on the line) or a short letter outlining the nature of the dispute and attaching necessary documentation (to which the opposing party or affected witness or subpoena recipient may respond by similar short letter). The court is then to promptly resolve the matter, informing the parties by phone or letter-ruling.

B.   Sanctions

Fed. R. Civ. P. 37, and similar state rules, delineate the sanctions that the court may impose upon a party for failure to comply with discovery requirements. Sanctions vary depending upon the nature and severity of the violation. For example, if a motion to compel discovery is granted, under Fed. R. Civ. P. 37(a)(4), the court, after giving an opportunity to be heard, may impose upon the deponent or party causing the motion reasonable expenses in bringing the motion, including attorney's fees. If a party fails without substantial justification to make disclosure or amend a response to a discovery request as required by provisions of Federal Rule 26 and the failure cannot be characterized as harmless, the party is barred from using the evidence at trial and the court may impose additional sanctions. Fed. R. Civ. P. 37(c)(1).

C.   Drafting a Motion to Compel Discovery

What will your motion contain? What form will it take? Under court rules and statutes, must you first meet with your opponent in an attempt to resolve your discovery dispute before bringing this motion? If so, must the results of this meeting appear in a written affidavit or declaration in support of your motion? What else will you put in your affidavit or declaration? Will you seek the costs involved in bringing your motion from the opposing party?

To give you a general sense of the form of a motion, a model subpoena duces tecum criminal discovery motion is on page 286; motion for a protective order appears in Chapter 11 at page 420. Though not a motion to compel, the format of this motion will prove instructive for you. Similarly, a criminal pretrial discovery motion, also in Chapter 11 on pages 420-23 can give you a feeling for the appropriate form and structure.

THE SUPERIOR COURT, THE STATE OF MAJOR
JAMNER COUNTY

JOHN SMALL	)	
	)	
Plaintiff,	)	No. 20 – 639077
	)	
v.	)	MOTION TO COMPEL DISCOVERY
	)	
DIANA PENN,	)	
	)	
Defendant	)	
_____	)	

Defendant, by Roderick Leonard, defendant's attorney, respectfully states:

The above-entitled action is by plaintiff to recover damages for personal injuries;

In the course of diagnosis and treatment of the claimed injuries, hospital, medical and other records and reports concerning the injuries and their treatment were made;

Plaintiff has refused to allow defendant to inspect and copy the records and reports although duly requested.

Defendant requests that this court pursuant to section 34.16 of the State of Major Statutes to order plaintiff, on such terms as are just, to give consent and the right to inspect and copy the records and reports.

Dated: January 27, 20XX+1

Roderick Leonard
1008 Roosevelt Way
Ruston, Major 98102
206-555-1212
Attorney at Law
Bar No. 6344

You can find information specifically pertaining to a motion to compel discovery in court rules, from local attorneys and court clerks. In many jurisdictions, a motion to compel in a civil case may be accompanied by a request for costs (i.e., your attorney fees attendant to bringing the motion) and sanctions (a fine). In civil cases, costs may be awarded even if the opposing party acted in good faith in refusing discovery. Sanctions require a finding of bad faith or, at least, unreasonableness. Outside of the discovery arena, sanctions are rarely imposed unless there is a history established in the case that reveals a pattern of dilatory behavior on the part of your opponent. Courts simply do not like to call either party "bad." On the other hand, courts are far less tolerant of the extensive delays occasioned by the parties' behavior in discovery and see this as a major problem in the system. Abuse of the discovery process may well result in sanctions being imposed.

VI. ETHICAL CONSIDERATIONS

Ethically, an attorney is obligated to expedite litigation and not make frivolous discovery requests, ABA Model Rules 3.2 and 3.4(d). Grinding down the other side by submitting hundreds of generic questions from your document request bank would seem to run afoul of these ethical guidelines. However, if a jurisdiction does not limit the number of interrogatories permitted (many jurisdictions do have a numerical limit, and some even count subparts as individual questions) and your questions are tailored to the particular case, there will be little practical chance of someone attacking your efforts on ethical grounds, no matter how voluminous your request. You can even allege that, by providing thorough interrogatories, you are attempting to avoid the expense of depositions. However, although it is unlikely you will be subject to formal sanctions for unethical behavior, what have you done to the overall mood of the case? You have probably turned it into a war of paper, with the other side responding in kind and your client paying the bills for the endless skirmishes and battles that will ensue.

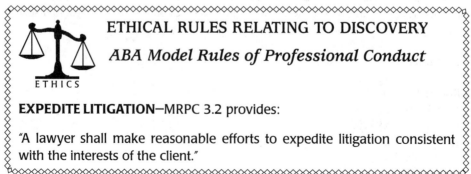

ETHICAL RULES RELATING TO DISCOVERY

ABA Model Rules of Professional Conduct

ETHICS

EXPEDITE LITIGATION—MRPC 3.2 provides:

"A lawyer shall make reasonable efforts to expedite litigation consistent with the interests of the client."

FAIRNESS TO OPPOSING PARTY AND COUNSEL—MRPC 3.4 (d) provides:

"A lawyer shall not: . . .

- in pretrial procedure, make a frivolous discovery request or
- fail to make a reasonably diligent effort to comply with a legally proper discovery request by an opposing party; . . ."

SPECIAL RESPONSIBILITY OF THE PROSECUTOR—MRPC 3.8(d) states:

"The prosecutor in a criminal case shall:

make timely disclosure to the defense of all *evidence or information known to the prosecutor that tends to negate the guilt of the accused or mitigates the offense,* and, in connection with sentencing, disclose to the defense and to the tribunal all unprivileged mitigating information known to the prosecutor, except when the prosecutor is relieved of this responsibility by a protective order of the tribunal . . ."

VII. EFFECTIVE CASE MANAGEMENT

Will you make a list of all discovery voluntarily provided by the opposing party? Will you file this list with the court? Will you detail on the record the justification for a request that has been objected to at a deposition? Will you file detailed declarations in support of *subpoenas duces tecum?* Will you articulate your case theory in a motion to compel? In what detail?

All of these questions reflect the importance of effectively managing all information relevant to the discovery process. The point is that you need to maintain accurate records so that if you need to make a discovery request to the court, you can: (1) detail what you are requesting, (2) articulate all the reasonable steps you took to obtain the discovery from your opponent before you were forced to resort to a formal motion, and (3) explain clearly why, under applicable legal standards, you are entitled to the information.

Once you obtain discovery, thoughtful management of the information likewise becomes important. Will you index the discovery by witness, elements of the offense, or cause of action to which it pertains? Will you keep it in files? Trial binders?

What you will do depends largely on personal preference and the extent of information involved. In a small criminal case, you may keep all of your information in a single file folder. In a complex antitrust suit, you may have a warehouse full of documents that are cross-indexed on a computer. In any event, you do need some system that permits both quick retrieval of information and fast correlation of the information to those aspects of your case theory or negotiations to which the information is relevant.

✓ CIVIL DISCOVERY CHECKLIST

Overall Discovery Performance

❑ Have discovery objectives compatible with case strategy (e.g., settlement, summary judgment, trial).

❑ Discovery requests focus on gathering information relevant to case theories—yours and your opponent's.

Five-Step Strategy for Coordinated Discovery Requests

❑ Step 1—Use case theories as guides to determine what information to seek.

  ✓ Identify potential information in existence.

  ✓ Use case theories to identify the information to seek.

❑ Step 2—Identify likely sources (persons and entities) that could provide that information.

❑ Step 3—Identify the types of information to seek.

❑ Step 4—Select the discovery tool suitable for the task of gathering the information based on:

  ✓ It being the best device for the task,

  ✓ Cost, and

  ✓ Compatibility of the discovery device with the case strategy.

❑ Step 5—Determine effective timing and sequencing of discovery.

Preservation and Prevention of Spoliation

❑ When the duty to preserve information begins, inform the client of the duty to preserve likely relevant documents in the client's possession and control and of the consequences of a failure to preserve.

❑ Store the documents safely to prevent spoliation.

The Lawyer's Signature—Certification

❑ Sign the discovery request, response or objection, certifying compliance with the rules requiring the following:

    ✓ That a reasonable inquiry has been made prior to signing,

    ✓ That to the best of the lawyer's knowledge, information and belief, the request, response or objection is consistent with existing law or a good-faith argument for extension of the law, and

    ✓ That it was not interposed for improper purposes.

Electronic Discovery

❑ Make sure that the discovery requests and responses include electronic information.

❑ To prevent any waiver of the attorney-client privilege through the involvement of an information technology person, enter a stipulated court order.

Drafting Interrogatories

❑ Served by a party on a party.

❑ Not objectionable (irrelevant, privilege, or unduly burdensome or annoying).

❑ Used to best advantage in obtaining basic information, such as identification of witnesses, documents, experts and their opinions, sequence of events, damages information, insurance coverage, positions on issues.

❑ Compose a detailed specific preamble to your case and to your requests.

❑ Employ a combination of broad and narrow questions.

❑ Pose questions that are unambiguous.

❑ Ensure that the information received will be clearly identified (and identifiable).

Responding to Interrogatories

❑ Review the preamble carefully to determine what is requested.

❑ Object to irrelevant, privileged, or unduly burdensome or annoying requests for information.

❏ Provide an answer if known or ascertainable after reasonable inquiry (reasonableness judged by an objective standard). State the answer after the question, making it brief and be mindful that the response will be admissible at trial.

❏ Respond that your client has "no knowledge" provided this is an accurate answer after reasonable inquiry.

❏ Respond that business records provide the information sought. Fed. R. Civ. P. 33(c).

❏ Respond that "investigation continues" if the legal or factual matter is still in the development stage.

❏ "Seasonably" update responses to interrogatories. Fed. R. Civ. P. 26(e).

Drafting Requests for Production

❏ Served by a party on a party

❏ Not objectionable requests (irrelevant, privileged, or unduly burdensome or annoying)

❏ Used to best advantage in obtaining documents, emails, and tangible objects and entry onto property

❏ Compose a detailed preamble to the requests for production.

❏ Describe the items sought with particularity.

❏ Seek electronically stored and destroyed documents and data.

❏ Interlink interrogatories and requests for production.

❏ Protect against destruction by the opposing party.

Responding to Requests for Production

❏ Inform the client that it must preserve relevant information.

❏ Determine whether the client has the requested item in the client's possession, custody, or control.

❏ Examine the information to determine whether it is discoverable.

❏ Object to irrelevant, privileged, or unduly burdensome or annoying requests for production.

❏ Respond that the requested item is not in existence.

❏ State that the request will be met.

❏ Keep accurate records of what was given to whom and when, utilizing a "Bates" stamp (number); keep records of which documents came from which witness's files.

Requests for Admissions

- ❑ Served by a party on a party
- ❑ Not objectionable requests (irrelevant, privileged, or unduly burdensome or annoying)
- ❑ Used to best advantage in obtaining admissions to matters that will streamline the trial including:
    - ✓ Truth of facts,
    - ✓ Genuineness of documents, e.g., the signature is genuine, and
    - ✓ Application of law to facts, e.g., agency, title
- ❑ Not used for matters that the requester wants to submit to the jury.
- ❑ Consider effect at trial and word the request with persuasiveness and with the fact finder in mind.

Responding to Requests for Admissions

- ❑ Object to irrelevant, privileged, or unduly burdensome or harassing requests for admissions.
- ❑ Respond by admitting or denying the request if known or ascertainable after reasonable inquiry (reasonableness judged by an objective standard).
- ❑ Respond by stating that the request can neither be admitted to nor denied and state specific reasons for the response.

Motion to Compel Discovery

- ❑ The motion is justified by the importance of the discovery material.
- ❑ The motion is justified by the conduct of the opposing party in denying access to the information.

Ethical Considerations

- ❑ Discovery requests or responses are consistent with counsel's duty to expedite litigation.
- ❑ Discovery requests are not frivolous.
- ❑ A reasonably diligent effort was made to comply with proper discovery.

Case Management

- ❑ Keep detailed records of discovery given and received.

Sample Criminal Discovery Motion

Criminal Discovery Motion

This is a representative sample taken from an actual criminal discovery motion. It is not, however, intended to be a perfect model. There are many different formats an attorney could use to present a discovery motion.

SUPERIOR COURT, THE STATE OF MAJOR
JAMNER COUNTY

STATE OF MAJOR, Plaintiff, vs. ALAN HENRY KRUB a/k/a MART FIRS, Defendant. _____	No. CR 76-0106 ESE Motion for Discovery and Inspection (with Memorandum of Authorities)

TO THE HONORABLE EDWARD S. ELLIS, Judge of the Superior Court of Major, in Jamner County:

The defendant, by counsel, requests this Court pursuant to case law and the Due Process Clauses of the Fifth and Fourteenth Amendments to the Constitution of the State of Major to order the District Attorney to produce and permit the defendant to inspect, copy, or photograph each of the following that are now known to be or are in the possession of the government or any of its agents or which through due diligence would become known from the investigating officer, or witnesses or persons having knowledge of this case:

1. All tangible objects obtained during the investigation of this case, including:
    a. All tangible objects obtained from defendant's person or effects.
    b. Tangible objects obtained from the person, effects or vehicle driven by defendant, or any home, apartment, or motel room rented by defendant.
2. All books, paper, documents, or tangible objects the government plans to offer in evidence in this case.
3. Books, paper, documents, or tangible objects upon which the government relied in returning the indictment against the defendant, or which the government plans to offer in evidence in this case.
4. All property in the possession of the government or its agents or seized by the government or its agents belonging to or alleged by the government to belong to defendant.
5. All fingerprint impressions, blood samples, clothing, hair, fiber, or other materials obtained by whatever means or process from the scene of the offense and whether such fingerprint impressions, blood samples, clothing, hair, fiber or other materials were those of defendant, or were those of some other person or persons known or unknown.
6. All comparisons of blood, fingerprints, clothing, hair, fiber, or other materials made in connection with this case, particularly including:

    a. Original photographs of any latent fingerprints obtained in the investigation of this case, together with the time, place, and manner in which the latent fingerprint was developed and photographed.

    b. Copies of all enlarged photographs or other reproductions of the latent fingerprint used for purposes of comparison, including both marked and unmarked copies of any enlargement or reproduction from which unique identification was accomplished.

    c. Complete report of the identification procedure employed, including notation of all points of identification that were isolated and used for comparison.

    d. Copies of all original and/or enlarged photographs of inked fingerprints used for comparison with latent fingerprint pictures.

7. The written report of any chemical analysis of the alleged plant material seized, prepared by the government or any of its agents or anyone at its direction, together with descriptions, test results, test dates, and determinations as to the nature or weight of the substance.

8. All results or reports of physical or mental examinations (e.g., handwriting, fingerprints, drug analyses).

9. All statements, confessions, or admissions made by defendant, whether written or oral, subsequently reduced to writing, or summarized in officers' reports, or copies thereof, within the possession, custody, or control of the government, the existence of which is known or, by the exercise of due diligence may become known to the attorneys for the government. This request includes statements made to witnesses other than police officers at any time prior to or subsequent to defendant's arrest, including the precise words attributed to defendant that caused government agents to conclude the defendant was "associated" with other co-defendants.

10. All documents, instruments, forms, or statements of any kind signed or purported to have been signed by the defendant.

11. All statements of co-conspirators, whether written or oral, subsequently reduced to writing, or summarized in officers' reports, or copies within the possession, custody, or control of the government, the existence of which is known or by the exercise of due diligence may become known to the attorneys for the government.

12. All names and addresses of persons who have knowledge pertaining to this case, or who have been interviewed by the government or their agents in connection with this case.

13. All FBI and local arrest and conviction records of all persons in Paragraph 12 the government plans to call as witnesses.

14. Written statements of all persons in Paragraph 12 whom the government does not plan to call as witnesses.

15. The transcript of testimony of all persons who testified before the Grand Jury in this case.

16. The name, identity, and whereabouts of any informer who gave information leading to the arrest of defendant, and whether the informant was paid by the government for the information.

17. All materials now known to the government, or that may become known, or which through due diligence may be learned from the investigating officers or the witnesses or persons having knowledge of this case, which is exculpatory in nature

continues ▶

or favorable material or which might serve to mitigate punishment, and including any evidence impeaching or contradicting testimony of government witnesses or instructions to government witnesses not to speak with or discuss the facts of the case with defense counsel.

18. Any information pertaining to misconduct or bad acts attributable to the informant or any government witness.

19. Information pertaining to consideration or promises of consideration given to any witnesses.

20. Information pertaining to the number of times that any witness who is not an agent of the State of Major has testified for the government before a tribunal, or any other body.

21. Information pertaining to any current or potential prosecution of any witness to be called by the government.

22. All information pertaining to personnel files on any witness to be called by the government, including whether or not such files exist, where they are, and how they are identified.

23. Provide the same records and information set out in items 18 to 22 with respect to each non-witness declarant whose statements are to be offered in evidence.

24. State whether the government obtained any information or evidence relating to this case by means of electronic listening devices, wire taps, or any form of electronic surveillance. State the circumstances under which such surveillance or eavesdropping was conducted. Provide a copy of any written transcript prepared from the eavesdropping, and an opportunity to listen to and copy electronically all recordings.

25. State whether the government obtained any information or evidence relating to this case, or the defendant, by means of searches or seizures. For each search and seizure:

    a. List the names of the law enforcement agencies and officers participating in the search or seizure, or contributing information leading to the search and seizure.

    b. List the places searched or seized, the dates, and the items or information obtained.

    c. Provide the name of any informant used to establish probable cause who might reasonably provide information bearing on the guilt or innocence, or sentencing.

    d. List the names of any law enforcement agencies or officers to whom the results of any search or seizure were forwarded, disclosed, or made available.

26. Provide defense counsel with a statement describing in detail the methods and procedures used to identify the defendant and/or co-participants as the perpetrators of the offenses alleged in the indictment, including:

    a. The names and addresses of all persons to whom photographs were exhibited for the purpose of identification, and when and where these displays took place.

    b. Copies of all photographs exhibited for the purpose of identification in connection with this case.

    c. The names and addresses of those persons who identified the defendant and/or any known co-participant from these photographs as a perpetrator of this offense, and those who were unable to identify these persons.

MEMORANDUM OF POINTS AND AUTHORITIES IN SUPPORT OF MOTION FOR DISCOVERY AND INSPECTION

"In our adversary system for determining guilt or innocence, it is rarely justifiable for the prosecution to have exclusive access to the storehouse of relevant facts. . . . [I]t is especially important that the defense, the judge and the jury should have the assurance that the doors that may lead to truth have been unlocked." *State v. Darby*, 205 Maj. 2d 274, 281 (1963).

"Courts of this state have consistently exercised their discretionary powers to provide defense-discovery in criminal cases broadly, consistently ordering discovery of the tangible evidence and information in possession of the government and police which could 'reasonably be used in, or lead to the development of, a defense at trial,' *State v. Karme*, 100 Maj. App. 3d 420, 422 (1975)." *Kincade v. Superior Court*, 169 Maj. App. 3d 333, 337 (1979).

Under *State v. Darby*, *supra*, and *Kincade v. Superior Court*, *supra*, all the requested information is properly discoverable.

Respectfully submitted,

_____

Harry C. Swings,
Bar No. 10164
Attorney for defendant
1201 Market Street
Jamner, Major 98455
Telephone: (206) 999-8999

Sample Subpoena Duces Tecum

Subpoena Duces Tecum

THE SUPERIOR COURT, THE STATE OF MAJOR
JAMNER COUNTY

JEFFERY GRAND	)	
	)	
Plaintiff,	)	No. 20 – 12154813
	)	
v.	)	SUBPOENA DUCES TECUM
	)	
KARA FONTES	)	
and JOHN DOE	)	
FONTES, and	)	
JASMINNA CO.	)	
a Sole	)	
Proprietorship,	)	
	)	
Defendants	)	
_____	)	

The State of Major to: Michael Cheung
                           Cheung Construction Inc.
                           1211 E. Ellysian St.
                           Lynnwood, Major 98102

Greetings:

YOU ARE COMMANDED to appear at the law offices of Stans Starbocks and Tully, 1920 State Street, Lynnwood, Major 98108 on May 19, 20XX + 1 at 9:00 a.m. and to testify under oath as a witness at this deposition at the request of Plaintiff Jeffery Grand in the above cause, and remain in attendance until discharged.

You are also commanded to bring the following to the deposition:

All documents and electronic information in your possession and control pertaining to Jasminna Corporation, Kara Fontes and/or John Doe Fontes, including but not limited to documents and electronic information of any kind concerning the building of a dock and boat moorage at 1215 E. Albomb, Lynnwood, Major 98111.

DATED: _____, 20XX+1

                           STANS STARBOCKS AND TULLY

                           _____
                           Riley Stans, Bar No. 12601
                           1999 Broadway N.
                           Ruston, Major 98105
                           206-993-1222
                           Attorney for Jeffery Grand

9 *Taking and Defending Depositions*

9 *Taking and Defending Depositions*

"Is there an echo in here? Your objection's been recorded. She typed it into her little machine over there. It's on the record. So now I'll proceed with my deposition of my witness."

Ron Motley—Portrayed in the movie by
Bruce McGill, *The Insider* (1999)

I. DEPOSITIONS

In one sense taking a deposition is just utilizing another discovery device, serving the overall objectives of gaining and creating information pertinent to the case theories and influencing your opponent. However, this discovery device deserves special consideration for several reasons. First, it can often produce more detailed information than the other discovery tools. You can produce a full transcript of direct and cross-examination, and it can be video-taped for the jury to see. Second, it involves in-person exchanges, unlike written discovery, and that interaction can produce less studied and controlled responses. Those responses may be helpful or harmful to your case theory. Third and most importantly, the taking of the deposition can be crafted with skill to effectively serve your trial objectives.

This chapter explores how to depose a witness, how to prepare a witness for a deposition, and how to represent the deponent when defending the deposition. You will learn how you can use your objectives and case theories to determine the content of the deposition, to frame your questions, and even to guide your manner as you conduct during the deposition.

A. Procedural and Substantive Rules

As with other discovery devices, planning to depose or defend a deposition begins with a review of legal rules, standards, and doctrine that govern depositions. Accordingly, when planning for a deposition, review appropriate rules such as the Federal Rules of Civil Procedure, Federal Rules of Criminal Procedure, local court rules, and state statutes.

In this section we discuss the procedural requirements, such as who can be deposed and when a deposition can be taken. This is not to be confused with what should be done—who should be deposed, who shouldn't be deposed, what should or shouldn't be inquired into during the deposition, and so on. Later, we discuss strategy and what should be done. For now, let's concentrate on the rules.

Who Can Be Deposed

State rules generally and Fed. R. Civ. P. 30(a)(1) provide that a party may depose both a party and a nonparty to the action.

Experts

Experts are treated separately according to Federal Rule of Civil Procedure 26(b)(4). Commonly, only those experts who will be testifying at trial are subject to discovery. If an expert will not be testifying at trial, for example an expert acting as a consultant only, the expert may not be subject to discovery unless exigent circumstances exist. Experts, those who are informally consulted, generally are never subject to discovery.

Corporations

Corporations, partnerships, associations, and government agencies are creatures of legal fiction. So, how do you obtain deposition testimony from the entity? Fed. R. Civ. P 30(b)(6) and counterpart state rules authorize a party to compel the entity to select an agent to testify on its behalf on pre-selected subjects. Under the rule, the party serves the entity with a subpoena that spells out with particularity the matters on which testimony is requested and the duty of the entity to designate a representative. The entity may then choose one or more persons in the organization to testify. The organization has a duty to prepare the witness to testify fully. Under Rule 30(b)(6) testimony taken under this rule may be "used by a party for any purpose." The testimony of the representative should be admissible as an admission by a party under Fed. R. Evid. 801(d)(2).

When a Deposition Can Be Taken

State rules usually permit the defendant to take a deposition after service of the complaint and summons, and the plaintiff may do so 30 days after service. On the other hand, Fed. R. Civ. P. 26(d) requires the parties to confer before taking a deposition unless they stipulate in writing or obtain a court order for an earlier deposition. Fed. R. Civ. P. 27(a) authorizes the taking of a deposition prior to the commencement of a lawsuit upon a showing that the federal court would have jurisdiction and that the action could not yet be commenced.

How Many Depositions and Duration

Federal Rule 30(a)(2)(A) provides that only ten depositions may be scheduled and that only under a stipulation by the parties or with the court's permission may a party conduct more than ten depositions or depose someone already deposed. While your state court rules may or may not limit the number of depositions, and even if no limit exists, you may be able to obtain a protective order to limit the number of depositions.

Fed. R. Civ. P. 30(d) provides that the duration of a deposition is limited to one day or seven hours, unless extended by stipulation of the parties or court order. Your state rules may not limit the length of the deposition, and its duration will be determined by reasonableness. The deposition notice may state the start time and that it will last until completed.

Service, Subpoena, and Notice

To obtain the attendance of a *nonparty witness* at a deposition, Fed. R. Civ. P. 30(a)(1) and 45 and their state rule counterparts require that the witness be subpoenaed. When the subpoena commanding an appearance is served, it is to be accompanied by transportation costs and fees for one day's attendance.

To obtain the attendance of a *party,* Rule 30(b)(1) indicates that a notice to the party should be sent. The same rule requires that the party desiring to take the deposition must give reasonable notice to all parties of the "time and place for taking the deposition and the name and address of each person to be examined, if known, and, if the name is not known, a general description sufficient to identify the person or the particular class or group to which the person belongs."

Production of Materials—Subpoena Duces Tecum

Court rules authorize the party taking the deposition to compel the deponent to bring documents and other materials to the deposition. State rules and Fed. R. Civ. P. 30(b)(5) provide that to compel a *party* to comply the party seeking the deposition must attach a request for production to the deposition notice. For a *nonparty* deponent, the proper way to compel production is with a subpoena duces tecum commanding that the deponent bring the material to the deposition. Fed. R. Civ. P. 45(b)(2). For a sample of a subpoena duces tecum see page 286 at the end of Chapter 8 on discovery.

Where and When

State court rules generally and Fed. R. Civ. P. 30(b)(1) allow the party taking the deposition to choose where and when it will be taken.

Persons Present

Persons who have a right to be present at a deposition are:

- The deponent,
- The parties—Fed. R. Civ. P. 30(b)(1) provides for notice to parties,
- Attorneys for the deponent and the parties, and
- An officer authorized by the court or stipulation of the parties to administer the oath—normally the court reporter.

Fed. R. Civ. P. 26(c)(5) permits the court to enter a protective order specifying that no one other than persons authorized by the order may be present at the deposition.

Recording the Deposition

Under Fed. R. Civ. P. 30(b)(2) and (3) and similar state rules, the party setting the deposition selects the method of recording the deposition (e.g., sound, sound and visual, stenographic) and bears the cost of the recording, and any other party may select an additional method of recording the deposition.

Your state may have explicit provisions regarding video depositions and may have adopted all or part of the Uniform Audio-Visual Deposition Act.

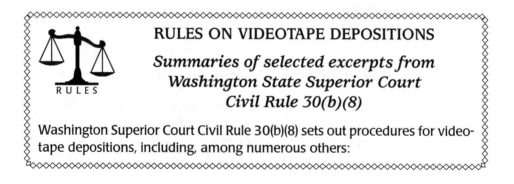

RULES ON VIDEOTAPE DEPOSITIONS

Summaries of selected excerpts from Washington State Superior Court Civil Rule 30(b)(8)

Washington Superior Court Civil Rule 30(b)(8) sets out procedures for videotape depositions, including, among numerous others:

- A stenographic record shall also be made of the deposition;
- A suitable place for videotaping—adequate lighting and reasonably quiet;
- Identification and contact information relating to the camera operator;
- If more than one tape is used, a statement of start and stop time for the tape;
- Notice of intent to offer portions of the videotape into evidence with time for objections and court rulings and editing of the tape to only admissible portions, and
- Storage of the original tape and an operator's certificate that it is a correct and complete record of the deponent's testimony.

B.   Objections

Form and Procedure

Form of the Objection

An objection at a deposition is to be "stated concisely and in a non-argumentative and non-suggestive manner." Fed. R. Civ. P. 30(d)(1). By "non-suggestive" the rule means that the objecting lawyer is not to suggest an answer to the witness with the objection.

Procedure

Normally, once an objection is made at the deposition, the officer (court reporter) makes note of the objection on the record and then the deposition proceeds with testimony, subject to the objection. Fed. R. Civ. P. 30(c). However, the attorney for the deponent may instruct the deponent not to answer when necessary to preserve a privilege, to enforce a limitation directed by the court, or to present a motion under Rule 30(d)(4), which provides that a deposition should not be conducted in "bad faith or in such manner as unreasonably to annoy, embarrass, or oppress. . .". Fed. R. Civ. P. 30(d)(1).

Grounds for Objections

Federal Rules of Civil Procedure and similar state rules exist regarding the following objections:

Disqualification of the Officer—Waived If Not Made

Fed. R. Civ. P. 32(d)(2) requires that the objection to the qualifications of the officer before whom the deposition is to be taken must be made at the beginning of the deposition or as soon as the disqualification becomes known or the objection is waived.

Form and Conduct—Waived If Not Made

Under Fed. R. Civ. P. 32(d)(3)(B), objections to the form of questions or answers, manner of taking the deposition, or conduct of the parties or errors in the oath or affirmation are waived by failure to object if the error could have been cured if an objection had promptly been made at the deposition.

Competency, Relevancy, and Materiality—Not Waived If Not Made

Irrelevant information is not discoverable. However, relevancy for discovery purposes is information "relevant to any claim or defense of any party" and relevancy is broadly defined—it "need not be admissible at the trial if the discovery appears reasonably calculated to lead to the discovery of admissible evidence." This means that information that on its face may seem irrelevant is discoverable during a deposition if it may lead to the discovery of other evidence that would be admissible. Fed. R. Civ. P. 26(b)(1). Objections on the basis of competency, relevancy, and materiality can still be made at trial; they are not waived for failure to be made before or during the deposition unless the ground for the objection could have been removed if presented at the time of the deposition. Fed. R. Civ. P. 32(d)(3)(A).

Admissibility of Evidence—Not Waived if Not Made

Fed. R. Civ. P. 32(b) provides that objections to admissibility of evidence in a deposition or part of a deposition may be made at trial "for any reason which would require the exclusion of the evidence if the witness were then present and testifying."

Privilege

Privileged information is not discoverable. Fed. R. Civ. P. 26(b)(1). This includes confidential information protected by the attorney-client privilege and the work product of opposing counsel, doctor-patient privilege, and so on.

Argumentative and Suggestive Objection

As stated above, Fed. R. Civ. P. 30(d)(1) requires that an objection be concise, nonargumentative and nonsuggestive.

Frustrating a Fair Examination

Fed. R. Civ. P. 30(d)(3) provides that no person is to impede, delay, or otherwise engage in conduct that frustrates a fair examination of the deponent. If this rule is violated the court may sanction the violator, including reasonable costs and attorney's fees.

Acting in Bad Faith, Annoying, Embarrassing, or Oppressing

Fed. R. Civ. P. 30(d)(4) prohibits a deposition examination from being conducted in bad faith or in a manner that unreasonably annoys, embarrasses, or oppresses a party or deponent. In this situation, the party or deponent may make a motion to the court coupled with a showing that this rule was violated. The court, upon finding that the rule was violated may order the officer conducting the examination to terminate the deposition or limit the scope and manner of the taking of the deposition.

C. Deponent's Review

Fed. R. Civ. P. 30(e) and similar state court rules provide the deponent an opportunity to review, correct, and sign the deposition transcript. Under the Federal Rule, a request to review and sign must be made before the completion of the deposition, and the deponent has 30 days after being notified by the officer that it is available for review. The deponent may make changes in both "form and substance" on an errata sheet. Both the original transcript and the errata sheet can be used at trial. This wide latitude in what can be changed is designed to create an accurate transcript.

II. WHO TO DEPOSE

Deciding Who to Depose

Who do you want to depose? The answer at the outset is similar to the answer given in the chapter on witness interviewing to the question: "Who do you want to interview?" That answer is: "You want to depose everyone who sheds light on your case theory or that of your opponent." Now, remove from that group your client, parties on your side of the lawsuit, and your witnesses. The remaining likely persons whom you want to depose are:

- Opposing parties,
- Nonparty key lay and expert witnesses who are aligned with the opposing parties, and
- Your witnesses who need to have their testimony preserved.

Other Considerations

The main considerations in favor of taking a deposition are whether it would serve your deposition objectives, for example, lock a witness into a story. These deposition objectives are discussed in the next section. Beyond those objectives, you will want to consider the following and other reasons why not to depose a witness:

- *Cost*—depositions are expensive,
- *Revealing and preparing the witness*—by deposing a witness, you may rehearse and educate the witness before trial (e.g., during the deposition the questioner covers the expert witness's failure to review certain documents and thereby alerts the witness to a deficiency in the basis for the expert's opinion and allows the witness to prepare for such questioning at trial), and
- *Perpetuating testimony harmful to the opposing party*—if a witness on the other side becomes unavailable, the deposition will be available and admissible at trial.

III. PLANNING TO TAKE A DEPOSITION

A. Setting the Deposition Objectives

Deposition Objectives

These five objectives commonly drive the substance and the form of taking a deposition:

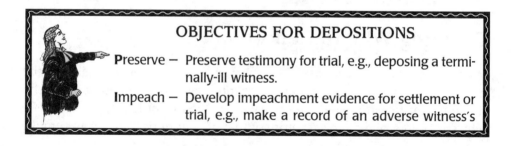

OBJECTIVES FOR DEPOSITIONS

Preserve — Preserve testimony for trial, e.g., deposing a terminally-ill witness.

Impeach — Develop impeachment evidence for settlement or trial, e.g., make a record of an adverse witness's version of events so that if the witness's testimony varies at trial the deposition may be used as a prior inconsistent statement.

Lock in — Use the deposition to lock a witness into concessions that support your case theory and that can be offered as admissions by the party opponent at trial.

Evaluate — Determine during the deposition how the witness will come across to the fact finder, e.g., determine whether the witness is credible.

Educate — Demonstrate to opposing counsel problems with the case that might increase the desire to settle.

Discover — Explore what the witness might know that would bolster your case theory or undermine the other side's so this information, or valuable information that it leads to, can be used at trial.

Admissibility and Uses at Trial

In setting objectives, Federal Rules of Civil Procedure and the Federal Rules of Evidence or state counterpart rules govern whether the deposition testimony will be admissible in trial. The following rules come into play as the grounds for the admissibility of the deposition transcript in trial:

- **Preserved Testimony—Unavailable Witness:** Fed. R. Civ. P. 32(a)(3) provides that the deposition testimony of an unavailable witness (the witness is dead or more than 100 miles away, or there are age, illness, imprisonment concerns) is admissible in lieu of the witness's live testimony. To present the testimony at trial, a stand-in for the deponent can be called to the stand to read the deponent's portions of the transcript. Or a video can be shown to the fact finder.

- **Prior Inconsistent Statement:** When the witness's testimony at trial is inconsistent with that given during the deposition, the prior inconsistent statement is non-hearsay and can be used to impeach the witness. Fed. R. Evid. 801(d)(1) provides in part: "A statement is not hearsay if—The declarant testifies at the trial or hearing and is subject to cross-examination concerning the statement, and the statement is (A) inconsistent with the declarant's testimony, and was given under oath subject to the penalty of perjury . . . in a deposition."

- **Prior Consistent Statement:** A prior consistent statement in a deposition or elsewhere is admissible non-hearsay when offered to rebut allegations of a witness's recent fabrication or improper motive or influence. Fed. R. Evid. 801(d)(1).

- **Admission of a Party Opponent:** Fed. R. Civ. P. 32(a)(2) provides:

> The deposition of a party or of anyone who at the time of taking the deposition was an officer, director, or managing agent, or a person designated under Rule 30(b)(6) or 31(a) to testify on behalf of a public or private corporation, partnership or association or governmental agency which is a party may be used by an adverse party for any purpose.

Under Fed. R. Evid. 801(d)(2), an admission of a party opponent is non-hearsay.

- **Refreshing the Witness's Memory:** A deposition of the witness or of another witness (or for that matter another document) may be used at trial to refresh the declarant's recollection of events under Fed. R. Evid. 612. This evidentiary rule allows the examiner to show a forgetful witness the transcript to refresh the witness's memory. The transcript is inadmissible.

- **Past Recollection Recorded:** If the witness still cannot recall (after an effort has been made to refresh the witness's recollection) the examiner may then rely on Fed. R. Evid. 803(5)—past recollection recorded. This Rule provides that the deposition testimony is admissible as an exception to the hearsay rule if the examiner can establish that the witness "once had knowledge but now has insufficient recollection to enable the witness to testify fully and accurately, shown to have been made or adopted by the witness when the matter was fresh in the witness' memory and to reflect that knowledge correctly. If admitted, the memorandum or record may be read into evidence but may not itself be received as an exhibit unless offered by an adverse party." This means that the witness must be prepared to testify that at some prior point in time when their recollection was fresh, he or she reviewed the deposition transcript and found it to be accurate.

Multiple Trial Objectives

A deposition may serve multiple objectives. For instance, a deposition that begins as an exploratory, discovery deposition might uncover information supporting the questioner's case theory and thus shift to an examination designed to lock the witness into concessions favorable to that case theory.

Negotiation and Settlement Objectives

Also, an attorney may have another purpose in mind for the deposition, such as exposing weaknesses in the other side's case so the opposing party will become more receptive to negotiation. Further, because depositions are time-consuming and expensive, an attorney may depose witnesses in an effort to grind down the other side, though the authors believe that this use of disproportionate resources is of dubious propriety. Also, the deposition offers an opportunity to ask questions of the opposing party, and the lawyer taking the deposition may directly ask the party deponent what it would take to settle.

A deposition transcript may also be used to convince the client to settle. The lawyer who is having difficulty convincing the client of the strength of the other side's case can show the client the harmful deposition testimony.

Summary Judgment or Other Motions Objective

Deposition transcripts may be used to support a summary judgment motion. Fed. R. Civ. P. 56(c). The concession-based examination approach described later in this chapter at pages 312-24 is useful to obtain precise and clear testimony needed to sustain a summary judgment motion.

B. Five-Step Approach for a Coordinated Discovery Plan

Depositions are just one of your discovery tools. Who you depose and the content of your examinations should fit into your overarching discovery plan. Chapter 8 explained the creation of a coordinated discovery plan through a five-step approach that was explored at length on pages 237 through 246.

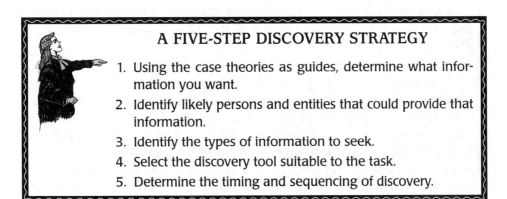

A FIVE-STEP DISCOVERY STRATEGY

1. Using the case theories as guides, determine what information you want.
2. Identify likely persons and entities that could provide that information.
3. Identify the types of information to seek.
4. Select the discovery tool suitable to the task.
5. Determine the timing and sequencing of discovery.

As a review of that discovery strategy, let's apply it to the *Coach Bagshaw* case that is described in earlier chapters.

The *Coach Bagshaw* Case

Story
You represent Marilyn Bagshaw in a wrongful termination suit against Mansfield University and the Collegiate Sports Commission (CSC). Bagshaw was the Mansfield University's women's basketball coach until the athletic director, Owen O'Connor, fired her with three years left on her five-year coaching contract.

The Collegiate Sports Commission had been investigating Bagshaw. Bagshaw thought that the meeting with the CSC investigator was to discuss minor recruiting violations, and she was caught off guard when the questions turned to gambling violations. Bagshaw told the investigator and the Mansfield University athletic director, who was present at the interview, that she had not gambled. In fact, she had gambled sizeable sums at a charity event. Later that day, Coach Bagshaw remembered a memorandum from Mansfield University's compliance officer that stated that the form of gambling she had engaged in was permissible. She immediately contacted the compliance officer and obtained a copy of the memorandum. Coach Bagshaw next consulted with her business adviser, Donna Fent about what action to take. Then Bagshaw called the CSC investigator and admitted to the investigator that she had gambled but not in violation of CSC or university regulations. She and Fent went to the athletic director's office and explained the situation to O'Connor. At that meeting, Athletic Director O'Connor offered Bagshaw the option of resigning or being fired. O'Connor acceded to Bagshaw's request to meet with the university president that evening.

That evening Coach Bagshaw was summoned to the home of Mansfield University's president. She met with the president and athletic director, and they reviewed what happened over the past two days. The following morning, Bagshaw was called into the athletic director's office, and O'Connor informed her that she was being terminated.

This was the second time Coach Bagshaw has been publicly accused of misleading the university administration. Following last year's winning season, rumors were rampant that Bagshaw was being courted by other universities for a coaching position. When reporters questioned the coach asking whether she was interviewing with other teams about coaching positions, she denied it. By happenstance, a reporter caught Bagshaw visiting with the president of Entman University. Bagshaw later admitted that she had discussed a coaching position at Entman U., but she declined the job offer. She publicly apologized to the athletic director for misleading him about whether she was entertaining other offers.

Step 1. Using the Case Theories as Guides, Determine What Information You Want

What do you want that will help your case theory or undermine your opponent's? First of all, you want evidence that will prove every element of your legal theory of wrongful termination. You want all the information that you can get to help you argue that the university did not fulfill its contract with Coach Bagshaw. Also, you know that the university's defense is that your client breached her contract by being dishonest with the university's administration, and you want to gather any information indicating that the university and/or the Collegiate Sports Commission had ulterior motives or lacked a basis for terminating Bagshaw. Also, you want to learn all that you can about any evidence that would prove harmful to your case theory or helpful to the university and the Collegiate Sports Commission.

Step 2. Identify Likely Persons and Entities That Could Provide That Information

At this juncture, you brainstorm to identify who or what entities could provide this information. Some of the sources include Athletic Director Owen O'Connor, Mansfield University President Gary Lum, CSC investigator Darren Sidbury, and CSC Commissioner Margo Willingham, as well as Dr. Tyrone Stanback, the defense expert on damages. These are many of the principal players, some neutral and several adverse witnesses, who can provide information both helpful and harmful to your case theory. Also, you want to depose the university's compliance officer Marcus Locke, whom you want to testify at trial but who will be in China caring for his ailing mother at the time of trial.

Step 3. Identify the Types of Information to Seek And Step 4. Select the Discovery Tool Suitable to the Task

While here we concentrate on the deposition discovery tool (Step 4), you take depositions as part of a coordinated discovery plan, utilizing them in conjunction with the other discovery devices. Your interrogatories to the university and the CSC have delved into who possessed information about the circumstances of Bagshaw's termination and whether any documents or electronic information existed. Your request for production sought those documents and electronic information (e.g., e-mails exchanged within the CSC that pertained to the Bagshaw investigation). Information gained with these discovery tools will become exhibits for the depositions.

Step 5. Determine the Timing and Sequencing of Discovery

You decided to begin with interrogatories and follow with requests for production. Now, you will depose parties and nonparty witnesses. You could just as well have decided that a good strategy would be to depose the key adverse witnesses soon after filing the complaint, thinking that at that stage the witness would be less prepared and more likely to provide accurate information about recent events. Later as the trial approaches, you will serve your requests for admissions.

Another question for your consideration: What will be the order in which you depose the witnesses? One approach is to begin with witnesses who are neither parties nor clearly adverse witnesses, such as employees of the CSC, to gather information that can be used when you do depose adverse witnesses, such as the athletic director and the university president.

C.   Preparation for Taking the Deposition

Preparation for taking a deposition is of critical importance; you cannot approach the deposition process aimlessly and wait until the time of the deposition to decide how you will proceed. Your purposes will dictate some of the nuts and bolts—when you will take the deposition (early or later in the litigation), the manner and thoroughness of your preparation, and your selected demeanor.

Now let's concentrate on how you prepare to take a deposition with an emphasis on the deposition of an adverse lay client or a nonparty witness. We begin with preparation techniques that are applicable to all witnesses; later at pages 324-29 we discuss special additional approaches to deposing an expert witness.

Know Your Case

Preparation includes total familiarity with all the information in your case file that pertains to the issues and the deponent (e.g., witness statements, documents).

Notice and Documents

Because you will be taking the deposition, you need to notify all parties within the timeframe specified by the rules. You need to decide whether to subpoena the deponent or send a notice. This depends whether the deponent is a party (notice) or a nonparty witness (subpoena). Although the rules require formal notice, you may be able to contact cooperative opposing counsel and schedule the deposition and then send counsel a confirming letter.

If you will need documents or particular exhibits when examining the deponent, you should obtain those before the deposition so you have time to study them. Consider obtaining the materials you think you might need by sending a subpoena duces tecum if the materials are held by a nonparty or a request to produce if the materials are in the possession of a party. Chapter 8 discusses these discovery tools in detail.

Recording the Deposition

You must make arrangements with a reliable court reporting service—confirm by letter as to the time, date, place, and travel directions; set the approximate length for the deposition; and anticipate specific needs such as a date for the transcribed transcript, fees, and so forth. If you have decided to video the deposition, you need to familiarize yourself with the court rules regarding video depositions (pages 292-93). While you or your staff could videotape the session, hiring a videographer will better ensure the quality of the tape.

Location and Setting for the Deposition

You will need to set the place for the deposition.

Location

Although the rules usually provide that the party taking the deposition may select the site, some accepted conventions exist. Nonparty witnesses are deposed where they reside or within a hundred mile radius. A defendant is deposed where the defendant resides or works. A plaintiff is deposed where the defendant works or resides or where the suit was filed.

Setting

The rules usually provide that the deposition may be taken in any setting (home, place of work), but it usually is conducted in a lawyer's conference room. If you are taking the deposition at your firm's office, you will need to reserve and arrange the seating in the conference room. Traditionally, the lawyer taking the deposition sits across from the deponent and the attorney defending the deposition sits next to the deponent. You will also need to make arrangements for enough chairs, staging if it is a videotape deposition, availability of the necessary documents and exhibits, water or coffee, and other essentials.

Stipulations

In preparation for the deposition, you will want to think about stipulations you will enter into or refuse to agree to, such as the waiver of signatures or a specific time period for review of the deposition, as well as formalities you want to observe, such as having an oath given to a deponent or filing the deposition with the court.

Therefore, be aware of the attorney who might try to sandbag you by beginning the deposition with, "Usual stipulations, counsel?" Find out what they might be. For example, one stipulation you should avoid is the waiver of the deponent's reading and signing of the deposition once it is transcribed, because you might need to rely on using the deposition in circumstances when the signature is important to show that the deponent has verified the accuracy of the deposition. A deponent has the right to read and correct a deposition, and you want this done before trial, not while you are cross-examining; avoid the possibility of the deponent/witness declaring, "No. That's not what I said. . . . No. I've never read this deposition before." You are better off meeting the "Usual stipulations?" with "We will do this deposition in accordance with the rules (state or federal civil rules)."

Objections and Directions Not to Answer

Before the deposition, try to anticipate objections. On pages 293 to 295, you will find the usual rules regarding objections that may be made at a deposition, and it is good practice to review and know those objections that can legitimately be made and those that do not apply to a deposition. If opposing counsel does object, unless the objection concerns privilege, an alleged attempt to annoy, harass, or embarrass the witness or a claim that the question goes beyond a court order, you should proceed and tell the deponent to respond to your question. The testimony is taken subject to the objection.

If it is an objection as to form and you intend to use the transcript at trial, you will want to cure any serious defect in your question by rephrasing it because to not do so could result in the exclusion of the evidence. However, don't be intimidated by opposing counsel and resulting interruptions with objections as to form. If you are conducting a discovery deposition and therefore not concerned about admissibility of the deposition testimony, you can instruct the witness to answer the question. Or, if you want to keep control of the deposition and create a deposition with admissible testimony, you can instruct the deponent to answer your question and then later rephrase it and get an answer to the rephrased question.

What if deponent's counsel directs the deponent not to answer and you believe that the instruction and grounds for the objection are wrong? If it is a significant matter that you are inquiring about, you could inform the deponent of the consequences of not responding (a hearing, additional expenditures of time and money, and so on) and ask if the deponent would like to consult with counsel about answering. After all, it is the deponent who is being asked the question.

Exhibits

Make sure well before the deposition that you have legible, facsimile copies (unmarked) of any exhibit that you intend to offer so that you can provide them to the deponent and opposing counsel while you are questioning. This will save time at the deposition. You can retain the original and offer a copy after counsel on the other side has compared the copy with the original. You will give the court reporter the exhibit for inclusion with the transcript.

When using an exhibit, you will mark it as an exhibit and refer to it specifically so the transcript is clear and understandable. Exhibits can be marked in different ways. One approach is to mark them in the order that they are used by that party for *all* that party's depositions . . . Plaintiff's Deposition Exhibit No. 1, 2, 3. Exhibits could also be numbered for each deposition beginning with the number 1.

IV. MODEL APPROACH TO TAKING A DEPOSITION

Certain aspects of every deposition are almost identical, such as swearing the witness and having opening remarks for the witness. Here we will suggest a model approach to those aspects that you can use no matter who the witness is or what the purpose of the examination is.

A. Opening Remarks

Opening remarks at the deposition are of prime importance. Be sure that you have the witness take an oath and that you deliver a complete preamble introducing essential participants and specifying the rules of the deposition. If the deposition transcript is used at trial for impeachment purposes, the preamble lecture can be used to show that the witness understood the meaning of the oath, purpose of the deposition, and so on. While no exact formula for opening remarks exists, the following transcript of questions by you, Coach Marilyn Bagshaw's attorney, to Marcus Locke, the compliance officer of Mansfield University (whom you are deposing in order to preserve his testimony for trial) illustrates a model that you can use.

OPENING REMARKS

The *Coach Bagshaw* Case

Your questions and statements to compliance officer Marcus Locke at a deposition to preserve his testimony:

To the court reporter: Please swear the witness.

To Mr. Locke:

- **Introduction and Identification:** How do you do, Mr. Locke, my name is _____. I am an attorney and I represent Marilyn Bagshaw in the case of *Bagshaw v. Mansfield University*. Ms. Bagshaw brought this suit.

- **Prior Depositions:** Have you ever been deposed before?

- **Procedures:** Mr. Locke, because you have not been deposed before, I'd like to go over some of procedures of a deposition before we start, is that alright with you? Could you verbally answer the question; the court reporter may not catch your nodding? Thank you.

- **Under Oath:** You have taken an oath administered by the court reporter. Even though we are not in a courtroom today, you understand that that oath has the same effect as one administered in court. Do you understand that?

- **The Transcript:** During this deposition, the court reporter will be recording what you say. Later the reporter will prepare a transcript of what was said here and that transcript may be used in trial. Do you understand that?

- **Unclear Questions:** If at any time during this deposition, I ask you a question that is unclear to you, please let me know and I will clarify the question for you. Can you do that? Are we agreed that if you don't call this to my attention that I can assume that you understood my question?

- **Objections:** Your lawyer may object to a question that I ask you. You should still answer my question unless, of course, your lawyer instructs you not to answer. Do you understand that?

B. Closing Remarks

Closing remarks are equally important as opening remarks. Consider effective wrap-up questions and instructions. Your last questions are designed to prevent the witness from testifying at trial to new facts and effectively claiming that he or she would have given the same answer during the deposition if only you had asked a question on the subject.

CLOSING REMARKS

The *Coach Bagshaw* Case

Your final questions and statements to compliance officer Marcus Locke at a deposition to preserve his testimony:

To Mr. Locke:

- **Complete Transcript:** Is there anything else you would like to add to any of your responses? Is there anything else that you remember about what happened relating to Coach Bagshaw? Relating to this case?
- **Chance to Correct:** Do you want to correct anything you stated here today?
- **Reading and Signing:** Counsel, would you like to tell Mr. Locke about his right to review and correct the transcript or shall I do it? Mr. Locke, the rules provide that you have a right to review the transcript and correct it, provided you do so within 30 days after it has been prepared. We'll give you notice of when it has been prepared. Do you understand that? Do you want to exercise that right?

V. DEPOSITION STRATEGIES DRIVEN BY THE DEPOSITION'S OBJECTIVES AND THE TYPE OF DEPONENT

Your approach to deposing a witness depends on your deposition objectives and the type of witness. Those objectives, as we have discussed, are usually trial-driven: preserving testimony, discovery of evidence, locking down a witness's story, evaluating the credibility of the witness to determine how the witness will come across in front of a jury, and so on. Obviously, the approach to a deposition to preserve testimony of your friendly witness is markedly different from the approach taken to deposing an adverse witness in order to impeach that witness at trial. For a particular type of witness you may have multiple objectives and you may vary your approach during the deposition. For instance, if you begin to depose a witness with a discovery objective in mind and soon learn that the witness is adverse, you may change your approach to techniques designed to impeach the witness.

A. Absent Witness—Preservation Examination

Rule Regarding Preservation

As mentioned earlier, Fed. R. Civ. P. 32(a)(3) and similar state rules authorize the court to allow a witness's deposition to be used for any purpose at trial if the court finds the witness is unavailable to testify for a number of reasons, such as death, illness, being over 100 miles from the place of trial when that absence is not caused by the party offering the deposition. So, when you anticipate that one of the witnesses you would call to testify at trial may be unavailable for trial, you need to consider conducting a deposition for the purpose of preserving that testimony and presenting it at trial.

Creating Evidence for Trial

Approach taking a deposition to preserve testimony by thinking of it as a two-dimensional. First, the deposition should be an effective direct examination, that is, one that is clear and advances your case theory. Second, you want to create a record of the testimony that will be as close as possible to having the witness actually present at trial. The deposition may also serve the function of providing evidence for motions and settlement but the essence of a preservation transcript is to have it available in lieu of a witness at trial.

Preparing the Witness

If the witness is a friendly or neutral one, your preparation of the witness for the deposition is a process very similar to that of preparing a witness for trial. In Chapter 6 at pages 152 through 156 we provide an approach to preparing a witness that you can adapt to preparing the deponent for the deposition.

Effective Examination

All of the trial techniques employed in a good direct examination are applicable to a deposition to preserve the testimony of your witness. You want to come to the deposition with an outline of the areas to cover during your examination of the witness. You may go beyond just using an outline and write out the questions that you intend to ask. With a friendly or neutral witness, you should do what you would to prepare the witness for trial: conduct detailed witness interviews, discuss how to testify, and conduct a dry run of the examination in preparation for the deposition.

Usually, you will begin with the witness's background, personalizing the witness as much as possible, and put on the record the reasons for the witness's unavailability. Your goal is to get the witness to tell the witness's story.

As much as possible, ask open-ended questions that will allow the witness to narrate. Use your questions to let the witness clarify and explain. If the person is an expert, ask questions to qualify the witness as an expert. When the testimony concerns events, chronological storytelling works well. If the witness is discussing a particular subject matter, for example, the business's financial records, the direct may move from topic to topic with transitional phrases, "Now, let's discuss the records of June 14 . . .". The examination should paint word pictures for the fact finders. Have the deponent work with demonstrative and real evidence exhibits to keep the testimony understandable and interesting. Conclude the direct on a high note if at all possible.

But what if the witness is an adverse witness? Then, your approach is like a direct examination of an adverse witness. Usually, it is a concession-based examination designed to elicit information favorable to your case theory or unfavorable to the opposing party's case theory. Rather than asking open-ended questions, the questions are mostly leading.

Objections

Avoid objectionable questions and answers. If you get an objection as to form, for instance, "leading," or "compound question," and the objection has merit, rephrase the question to cure it so that the testimony will be admissible at trial.

Video

What better way to preserve the deposition than in a video? Reading a cold deposition transcript is to watching a video deposition what reading a critic's review is to seeing the play. Or reading a wine menu is to drinking a glass of pinot noir. With a video, the fact finders can evaluate the witness's demeanor, facial expressions, and see the place where the deposition was taken and how it was conducted. To take full advantage of a video deposition requires staging—placement of the camera and people in the room so that all the action and testimony is captured on video—and preparation of the people involved, particularly the deponent.

PRESERVING TESTIMONY

The *Coach Bagshaw* Case

Excerpts of your questions to compliance officer Marcus Locke at a deposition to preserve his testimony using the subject matter, as opposed to the chronological, approach:

continues ▶

To Mr. Locke:

- **Identification:** For the record, could you state your name, spelling your last name? Where do you reside?
- **Unavailability:** Mr. Locke, directing your attention to the trial date of December 7th of this year, will you be available for trial then? Why not?
- **Background:** Mr. Locke, are you married? Any children? What are their ages? What is your current occupation? How long have you been employed as the compliance officer for Mansfield University? In your capacity as compliance officer, what are your duties? Could you describe your employment history before you became the compliance officer? Please describe your educational background.
- **Gambling:** As Mansfield University's compliance officer, did you ever issue a memorandum discussing gambling by members of the athletic department? When was that? Kindly describe the process that you went through before preparing the memorandum on gambling. (To the court reporter: please mark this as Plaintiff's Exhibit 1) I am handing you what has been marked as Plaintiff's Exhibit number 1, could you identify that document? What is it? Is this your signature on Plaintiff's Exhibit 1, entitled "Memorandum Re: Gambling on College Sports?" Please read Plaintiff's Exhibit 1. You just read the date on the memorandum; was it distributed on that day or another date? The memorandum is addressed to all members of the Mansfield University Athletic Department; that includes Coach Marilyn Bagshaw, correct?
- **Opposing Counsel:** Objection: leading. Your reaction to this objection is to direct the witness to answer and then you rephrase: To whom was the memorandum, Plaintiff's Exhibit 1, sent?

B. Discovery Deposition—Going Fishing

While a deposition is referred to as a discovery device, as you have learned, it may be intended to discover little if anything for the party deposing the witness. As you have seen, a deposition to preserve testimony is not designed to discover information. Later, we discuss depositions of an adverse witness; those depositions likewise may not be designed to uncover information, rather they may be intended to gain concessions and to lock in the witness. However, this section discusses the *discovery deposition*, which is aimed at discovering what information the witness can provide. It is akin to fishing; you are exploring what the witness knows in hopes of catching information that you don't have. What are you fishing for? Naturally, you are seeking facts, opinions, and other information; sources that are reasonably calculated to support your case theory or undermine your adversary's. However, you do not want to just limit the information you uncover to what supports your case theory: You want to uncover the harmful information as well. But, like an expert fisherman, you want to cast your line where your knowledge and expertise tells you it makes sense. Part of what opposing counsel will be doing at the deposition is judging your skill level. You want them to see that you know what you are doing, not fishing around without purpose.

Effective Examination

What are the examination techniques for an effective discovery deposition? They are the same as those applied in any good witness interview. Chapter 6 (pages 143-49) on witness interviewing offers an approach that you can use for a discovery deposition. It is the four-step funnel approach.

Step 1. Establish an Open-ended Inquiry—Begin by seeking to establish rapport with the deponent. Before the deposition begins, try to make a personal connection with the witness with some small talk and a good-natured demeanor. You can start the deposition with nonthreatening questions about the witness's job and background. Your initial questions about the case should be open-ended. Pay close attention to the witness, and ask follow-up questions, but avoid unduly interrupting the flow of what the witness has to say.

Step 2. Organizing the Information and Putting it in Chronological Order—Next, take more control over the deposition by going back over what the witness has said, organizing it, and putting it into chronological order. For each activity or subject, start at the beginning and walk systematically through the witness's testimony asking about time, place, who else was present or knew about it, the details, and how the witness knows. Don't be concerned about hearsay or other evidentiary rules (except of course for privilege). Don't neglect to ask the open-ended "how" and "why" questions. Summarize the testimony to make sure it is clearly stated in the record and can be used later at trial.

Inquire about the documentary and real evidence that you have received through discovery or had the witness bring to the deposition pursuant to a subpoena duces tecum. Examine the witness about other exhibits. Ask the witness about other physical evidence that may exist and about what might have been destroyed. Consider having the witness draw a diagram (having it marked as an exhibit) or walk through a demonstration (describing what took place for the record if the deposition is not being videoed).

Step 3. Verifying Facts and Getting Clear and Accurate Information—During this phase of the deposition, ask probing questions to test and confirm what the witness has testified to.

Step 4. The Closing—The closing step for a witness interview involves planning for the future, that is, scheduling the next meeting. The closing step in a deposition insures that the witness has provided all that the witness can: "Do you recall anything else about the meeting—anything at all?"

Objections

How will you meet objections during a discovery deposition? Because your objective is to gather information, not create an admissible transcript for trial, you can be inclined to direct the witness to answer the question if you get an objection as to form, rather than rephrasing the question. If it develops that you will want to use the testimony at trial, then consider reasking the question so as to cure any irregularity as to form. You obviously will avoid questions designed to elicit either privileged information, or information irrelevant within the standards for discovery.

C. Concession-Based Examination— Adverse Witness

Now, we come to what can be the most challenging deposition to take—that of the adverse witness. The deponent could be either an expert or lay witness; the techniques and approaches are much the same. Usually, for this type of deposition you will have two objectives in mind and those objectives will determine the techniques. First, your objective may be to learn what the adverse witness knows, and you will use the discovery deposition approach and techniques that were discussed in the previous section. Your second goal is to gain concessions from the witness—concessions that are favorable to your case theory or unfavorable to the other side's case theory. This is a concession-based examination, and the approach and techniques of that examination are radically different from those used in the exploratory discovery deposition.

As general principles, if a deposition to preserve testimony should resemble a good direct examination, a concession-based deposition of an adverse witness should resemble a good concession-based cross-examination. A concession-based deposition examination is composed of three components, which we examine in this section:

- *Content*—How to determine the content of the deposition,
- *Construction*—Once the content has been decided upon, how to construct the examination so that it is compelling, and
- *Character*—How the examiner conducts him or herself during the deposition.

Content

Content Flows from the Purpose of the Examination

The content of any adverse witness deposition should flow from the purpose of the examination. The seminal book on cross-examination, *The Art of Cross-Examination* by Francis Wellman, states that more cross-examinations are suicidal than are homicidal in nature. Wellman explains that cross-examinations often yield disastrous results because cross-examiners do not understand the primary purpose of cross. The primary purpose of cross-examination is to catch the truth. As with cross-examinations, the primary purpose of a deposition of an adverse witness should be to catch the truth—concessions that either help your case theory or undermine your adversary's. Impeachment of the witness and the witness's testimony remains a potential objective, but it is a secondary one.

Case Theory Concessions

Planning the content of the adverse witness's deposition begins with your and the other side's case theories. Begin with a firm understanding of your factual theory—the persuasive story. Consider not only the strengths of your evidence but also the values that your factual theory communicates to the fact finder (for the plaintiff in the *Bagshaw* case, an important value is to honor a contract) and the human story underlying the factual theory (the effect of the firing on both Coach Bagshaw and her family). The examination should be designed to get concessions compatible with that case theory. Also, the attorney planning the examination must have a grasp of the other side's factual theory components. For instance, in the Bagshaw case, plaintiff's counsel would recognize that the defendant university will rely on the value of honesty (Coach Bagshaw lied not only to the investigators but more importantly to the university administration, and probably the athletic director who was trying to maintain the integrity of the athletic department). The examiner will seek concessions to facts that undermine that factual theory.

Brainstorming the Content

Once you have a firm grasp of the case theories in the case, you can brainstorm to identify the content of your deposition examination. To accomplish this you will need to make two lists.

- **First List—Concessions:** On the first list, write down concessions that the adverse witness must make that will either support your case theory or undercut the other side's case theory. Note that the key word in the last sentence is must. The witness must concede the point because you can prove it directly or by inference. If the witness does not make the concession, the witness's testimony can be impeached as mistaken, false, or misguided. You begin by seeking to lock the witness into helpful information, and if you don't get it, you lock the witness into impeaching information. For example, you could ask the athletic director in the Bagshaw case whether the university had a binding five-year contract with Coach Bagshaw. The existence of the contract is an essential element of your case theory. The athletic director must concede that fact because you not only have a copy of the contract with his name on it but also witnesses who can testify to the correctness of your assertion during the examination. Should the athletic director deny the existence of the contract, he can be effectively impeached.

- **Second List—Impeachment:** You will also brainstorm to determine how you could impeach the adverse witness. During this session, one by one go down a list of areas of impeachment and write on the list the ones that apply to the witness. The following is a list of areas of impeachment that you can review during this brainstorming process:

✔ IMPEACHMENT CHECKLIST

1. Improbability
2. Prior Inconsistent Statement
3. Prior Convictions
4. Lack of Personal Knowledge
5. Mental and Sensory Deficiencies
6. Bias and Interest
7. Prior Bad Acts Probative on Untruthfulness
8. Contradiction
9. Character Witness—"Have you heard . . . ?"

> Note that an expert can be impeached by:
>
> a. All of the Above
> b. Qualifications Issues
> c. Basis for Opinion Issues (e.g., time spent; source of information relied upon; assumptions about data utilized)
> d. Learned Treatises

Brainstorming the Content—The Bagshaw Case *Illustration*

Now, let's apply this methodology to the *Coach Bagshaw* case. You, as Bagshaw's attorney, are planning the deposition of adverse witness, Athletic Director Owen O'Connor. Your case theories are that the university had a valid five-year contract with your client and wrongfully terminated her when she had three years left to go on her contract. You also claim that the College Sports Commission interfered with your client's contract by pressuring the university to fire her. You know that the university's case theory is that it had grounds for terminating Bagshaw—gambling and giving false and misleading information. Your position is that the type of gambling engaged in was not prohibited by the university or the CSC and that Bagshaw's prevarications were not only understandable under the circumstances (she was surprised by the CSC investigators whom she thought were going to ask her about minor recruiting violations), were cured by her truthful statements later in the same day and were never considered grounds for termination until the athletic director learned that gambling was not a sufficient basis by itself for terminating Bagshaw.

As you plan to take O'Connor's deposition, you reflect on the meeting that your client had with O'Connor on the day before she was fired. Both your client and her business advisor Donna Fent are prepared to testify to what took place. They will testify at trial that later in the same day that Bagshaw had been interviewed by the CSC, she called the CSC investigator to correct the record and told the investigator that she had participated in the charitable event that involved gambling and that the compliance officer for Mansfield University had previously issued a memorandum stating in essence that that form of gambling was not prohibited. Bagshaw and Fent then went to meet with O'Connor in his office. Before Bagshaw mentioned her contact with the CSC investigator, O'Connor told Bagshaw that her gambling had embarrassed the university because the CSC had already contacted the media to disclose what it had uncovered about Bagshaw's gambling. O'Connor offered Bagshaw an opportunity to resign and showed her a draft of a letter terminating her for violating CSC regulations on gambling.

At this juncture, Bagshaw told O'Connor about correcting the record with the CSC and that she had come to O'Connor to do the same. Bagshaw showed O'Connor the compliance officer's memorandum indicating that the gambling in question did not violate either CSC or university regulations. O'Connor responded that the memorandum was wrong. He said, "What do you want to do, get both me and Marcus (the compliance officer) fired?" To which Coach Bagshaw said, "No. I want you to help me fight this thing with the CSC." O'Connor told Bagshaw that it would be better for her to resign or he would add another violation to the termination letter—giving dishonest and misleading information.

With the case theories in mind, you brainstorm for concessions that O'Connor must make because you can prove them. If O'Connor does not make the concession, then O'Connor can be impeached by your proof. Another by-product of concession-based deposition examinations is that they lock the witness into a version of events, and thus create a prior statement that can be used to impeach O'Connor if he varies at trial from what he testified to during the deposition. The following are some areas that you might identify and list during your brainstorming session.

BAGSHAW CONCESSIONS

A Contract Existed and Bagshaw Was Terminated

- The university had a five-year contract with Bagshaw.
- The athletic director terminated Bagshaw when there were three years still existing on the contract.

Damages

- Bagshaw had a winning season the year before she was fired.
- O'Connor gave Bagshaw raises that made her one of the highest paid college baseball coaches.

Surprised by the College Sports Commission

- For over 20 years, O'Connor had always been told before a meeting with CSC investigators what the subject matter of the investigation was.
- Before the meeting with O'Connor and Bagshaw, he thought that the investigation concerned minor recruiting violations.
- O'Connor was caught off guard when the CSC investigators began questioning Coach Bagshaw about gambling.

Gambling Was Not Grounds for Termination

- The university's compliance officer issued a memorandum stating that this form of gambling was not prohibited.
- The memorandum was addressed to the athletic director.
- Only after Bagshaw brought up the memorandum did O'Connor mention dishonesty as a ground for termination.

Dishonesty and Giving Misleading Information Were Not Grounds for Termination

- Bagshaw corrected the record the same day.
- O'Connor never mentioned to Bagshaw that dishonesty and giving misleading information would be added as a violation to the termination letter until after Bagshaw brought up the compliance officer's memorandum which nullified gambling as the first grounds O'Connor relied on for firing Bagshaw.

Note that for each fact concession, evidence exists to prove the fact sought from O'Connor. For instance, if he denies seeing the gambling memorandum, the compliance officer's secretary can be called to testify that he hand delivered it to O'Connor for review before it was ever published. Also, the memorandum is addressed to the athletic director among others.

Now, turn to brainstorming whether there are any areas in which Athletic Director O'Connor is vulnerable to impeachment. Looking down the list of nine areas of impeachment, one—bias or interest of the witness—seems to apply. The integrity of O'Connor and the athletic department and he, as its head, had been attacked. Prior to firing Bagshaw, the media was questioning whether the athletic director was going to take action against Coach Bagshaw who once again had engaged in deception. O'Connor had also received pressure from the CSC to do something about Bagshaw. O'Connor had an interest is self-preservation. Now, he has an interest in justifying his decision to fire Bagshaw.

Construction

Now that you have determined the content of your deposition examination, you can begin the next preparation task: constructing an examination that is clear and compelling. While there are some times that an attorney taking a deposition will want to jump around, for example to catch a lying deponent, usually the examination should be designed to flow in a logical and understandable manner.

How can you accomplish this? We suggest that you think about this type of examination as you would a good cross-examination. During cross-examination, your questions are predominantly leading in form and you know what the answer will be (or, on that rare occasion, don't care what the answer is). During this type of examination, you are not exploring for information. Rather, you are using the witness to make statements that you are confident the witness will make. Simply put: This is the examiner's opportunity to testify.

Concession-Based Examination Format

An effective approach is to lay the examination out on pieces of paper using the following concession-based examination format:

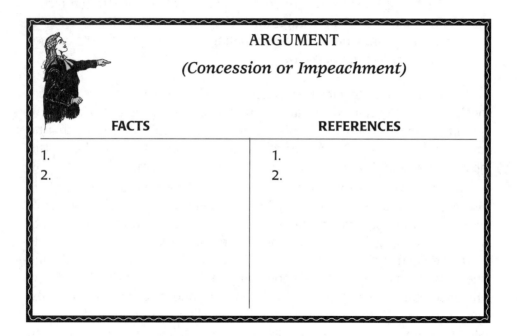

ARGUMENT	
(Concession or Impeachment)	
FACTS	**REFERENCES**
1.	1.
2.	2.

At the top of the page, put the argument that you will make at the end of the case, for example, the "Witness Lacks Credibility" because he is biased. This heading is very important because it will keep you on your subject during the examination, curbing any tendency you might have to wander. Number each page relating to that subject. When you start a new topic, start with page one. On the left side, write short statements of fact. These statements of fact are the fact concessions that you have settled on after brainstorming and then organizing the resulting information. Writing short statements has the advantage of reinforcing for you the idea that you are not on an exploratory deposition examination. Rather, you are stating facts that the witness must concede or be impeached. Second, it forces you to use the proper form of the question for an adverse witness—leading. And, it is unnecessary that you frame questions because you need only add words like "isn't that correct?" to the end of the statement or raise your voice to make the statement into a question.

Besides the advantages already mentioned, this approach is effective for two other reasons. First, the short one-fact-per question approach creates a persuasive examination on the facts because it avoids conclusion and rather leads the audience (judge or jury) to come to the conclusion on its own. Having reached the conclusion on its own, it is more likely the audience will have a proprietary interest in it and be more persuaded by it. Second, it is effective because it compels ends-means thinking. The statements (questions) are all designed with the argument—your case theory and the discrediting of the other side's case theory—in mind.

The right column is available to write references to the file (e.g., prior witness statement or e-mail) in case the witness does not provide the desired answer and you need to promptly access your proof. Also, the right column can be used to take note of any answers by the deponent that you find remarkable.

Using the Concession-Based Examination Format— The Bagshaw Case Illustration

The following are questions for Athletic Director O'Connor.

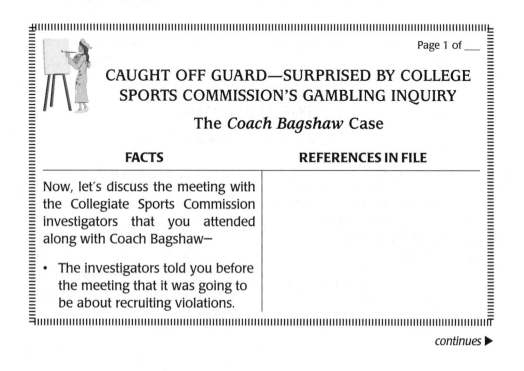

continues ▶

- The CSC investigator asked Coach Bagshaw about gambling on college sports.
- Before the meeting, the CSC never mentioned a probe about gambling to you.
- In your 20 years working in athletic departments, the CSC always stated the reason for the investigation before the meeting.
- To your knowledge no mention of gambling had been made to Coach Bagshaw before the meeting.
- You were caught off-guard by questioning about gambling.
- You were upset that you had not been given notice.
- You told this to the investigators.
- Coach Bagshaw also appeared surprised by the questioning about gambling.
- She appeared upset, too.

DISHONESTY—NOT GROUNDS FOR TERMINATION

The *Coach Bagshaw* Case

FACTS	REFERENCES IN FILE
I'd like to direct your attention to mid-afternoon on the same day that you and Coach Bagshaw met with CSC investigators.	
• Mid-afternoon Coach Bagshaw came to your office.	

- She was accompanied by Donna Fent, the Coach's business advisor.
- Coach Bagshaw informed you that she had been at a charity event and gambled on college basketball.
- She told you that she didn't think that it was prohibited gambling.
- She handed you a memorandum from the university's compliance officer, Marcus Locke.
- (Have him identify and authenticate Pl's Exhibit 16—the memorandum.)
- The memorandum, Pl. Exh. 16, is addressed to you.
- The last paragraph of the memorandum indicates that the type of gambling that Bagshaw engaged in was not prohibited.
- You told Coach Bagshaw that the memorandum was wrong.
- You said, "What do you want to do, get both me and Marcus (the compliance officer) fired?"
- Then Coach Bagshaw said, "No. I want you to help me fight this thing with the CSC."
- It was not until Bagshaw showed you the memorandum that you mentioned terminating her for providing false information.
- Up until she showed you the memorandum, you had only mentioned the gambling as grounds for her termination.

Memorandum Exhibit

Control

Professor Irving Younger, now deceased, was and still is nationally recognized for his Ten Commandments of Cross-Examination. He taught a generation of lawyers to adhere to them when conducting cross-examinations. These Ten Commandments are still taught to fledgling trial lawyers. Six are particularly applicable for taking a deposition, while others (crossed-out) may be used for some occasions:

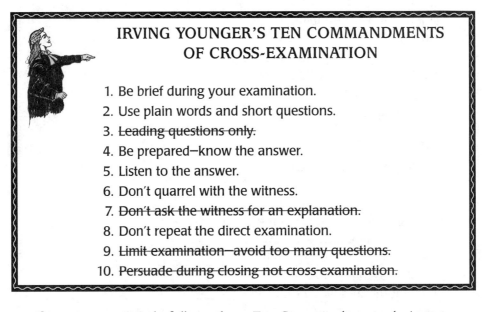

IRVING YOUNGER'S TEN COMMANDMENTS OF CROSS-EXAMINATION

1. Be brief during your examination.
2. Use plain words and short questions.
3. ~~Leading questions only.~~
4. Be prepared—know the answer.
5. Listen to the answer.
6. Don't quarrel with the witness.
7. ~~Don't ask the witness for an explanation.~~
8. Don't repeat the direct examination.
9. ~~Limit examination—avoid too many questions.~~
10. ~~Persuade during closing not cross-examination.~~

If an attorney strictly follows these Ten Commandments during a cross or any other adverse witness deposition or trial examination, the attorney will maintain control of even a witness who is intent upon evading or deflecting the question. For example, how can a witness finagle when the question posed is short, leading, non-argumentative? In conducting the concession-based deposition examination, it is best to follow Professor Younger's Ten Commandments. This is not to say that we agree that these should be *commandments* either for a concession-based deposition examination or for a cross-examination. When the witness is lying and the examiner can prove the lie, the interrogatory (nonleading) question will give the prevaricator plenty of latitude to spin the deception, which the examiner can later reveal as a falsehood. Or the examiner may ask a question to which the examiner does not know the answer because the examiner does not care what answer the witness gives. While we take issue with these being commandments, we do recommend them as *guidelines* that should be followed unless good reason exists for straying from them.

Inevitably, you, as a lawyer, will encounter the rambling, evasive witness who will backhand your question with a quick answer and then launch into a monologue, usually serving opposing party's case theory. Expert witnesses are particularly adept at this. You will encounter this problem during both depositions and in trial. How do you control the evasive witness? We suggest that the techniques that we are about to explain are effective. While these techniques can be effective at trial as well as for a deposition, we caution you that some of the techniques are confrontational, and, thus, they may offend jurors if not done properly. Jurors usually have a protective attitude towards a witness, and they don't want the witness mistreated by the lawyer. The examiner must be mindful at all times not to get tough with a witness unless the jury is ahead of the examiner and thinks that the witness should be reigned in.

The following techniques are listed in increasing confrontational tone to meet escalating levels of evasiveness by the witness.

CONTROL TECHNIQUES FOR THE EVASIVE, RAMBLING WITNESS

The *Coach Bagshaw* Case

You are deposing Dr. Tyrone Stanback, the defense expert on damages, whom you know from trial transcripts that you have read can be an evasive witness. Your questions and statements to Dr. Stanback at a deposition:

To Dr. Stanback:

Securing an Agreement: Doctor, I'm going to try to make my questions simple—most all of them will be able to be answered "yes" or "no." When I'm though, the university's lawyer will be able to ask you questions so that you can elaborate or explain your answers to my questions. Can we agree that you will answer my questions with a "yes" or "no" if that is what the question calls for?

Repeat the Question:

Q.: Doctor, did you speak with Coach Bagshaw before you reached your opinion in this case?

A.: Ramble, ramble, ramble . . .

Q.: Did you speak with Coach Bagshaw before you reached your opinion in this case?

Q.: Can you repeat the question that I asked you doctor?

Q.: Are you ready to answer the question now doctor?

Q.: Doctor, is there something preventing you from answering the question?

One final technique that you can use to control the run-away witness is to resort to the physical. Raise your hand, palm facing the witness in the universally recognized signal to stop. It usually works.

Another common method that witnesses use to evade answering the question is to quibble about the meaning or definition of words that you are using. To meet this means of evading, you can compel the witness to define the terms and go on from there.

CONTROL TECHNIQUES FOR THE EVASIVE, QUIBBLING WITNESS

The *Coach Bagshaw* Case

To Director O'Connor:

Q.: When was the subject of gambling raised with Coach Bagshaw that evening?

A.: What precisely do you mean when you say "gambling?"

Make the witness define and answer.

Q.: Tell me how you would define "gambling," then use your definition to answer my question.

A.: Well, I can't do that because I don't know if you mean "gambling" in the sense of "X," "Y" or "Z."

Q.: Why don't you answer the question for X, then assuming Y and finally assuming Z.

D. Opposing Party's Expert Witness

Now we want to shift gears and discuss taking an opposing party's expert witness deposition. This is a difficult task, but one you can master by following certain rules, all of which require your utmost concentration on planning and preparation. Primarily, you will be concerned about obtaining admissions to help your case theory and information to prepare for cross-examination to blunt your opponent's case theory.

Usually expert witnesses are deposed late in the discovery process. Under Fed. R. Civ. P. 26(b)(4)(A), an expert is to be deposed only after the expert produces the expert's report, which is required by 26(a)(2)B). Unless the parties stipulate or the court requires otherwise, the report is due not later than 90 days before the trial date or trial readiness date. Even without this requirement, a preferred approach is to depose lay witnesses first so the expert will have the optimum facts available for consideration.

While the previously described approaches—preservation, discovery, and concession-based—apply equally to expert witnesses (although you always want to determine if the expert plans any further studies, experiments, and such after the deposition), there are some other considerations and techniques that are explored in this section.

Expert Witness Fees

Fed. R. Civ. P. 26(b)(4)(C) provides that the party taking the deposition shall compensate the expert with a reasonable fee for time spent on the deposition. Because the expert already has a financial relationship with the party that has employed the expert, it is not uncommon for the parties to stipulate that they pay the fees and expenses of their own experts with leave to go to the court for a protective order for an abuse of the deposition process.

Preparation to Take the Expert's Deposition

Compiling Information

In preparation for taking the opposing party's expert witness's deposition, you want to gather and read all the information you can about the expert and what the expert relied upon in reaching conclusions in the case. A nonexclusive list of information to collect and read is as follows and also provided on initial disclosure under FRCP 26(a)(2):

- The *expert's report* (in a federal case, you should have the report required by Fed. R. Civ. P. 26(a)(2)(B). If it is a state case and the state does not have a rule like the federal rule, you can use interrogatories to gather similar information.).
- Prior *transcripts* of the expert's testimony (this will provide you not only with an understanding of how the expert may testify but also the cross-examination of the expert may provide you with some helpful areas to explore. Also, the prior testimony just may prove to be inconsistent with the expert's testimony during your deposition. Fed. R. Civ. P. 26(a)(2)(B) requires that the expert's report contain a list of trials and depositions that the expert has testified during the preceding four years).
- The expert's *publications* pertinent to your case (Fed. R. Civ. P. 26(a)(2)(B) requires that the expert's report contain a "list of all publications authored by the witness within the preceding ten years".
- The expert's current *curriculum vitae* (it is possible for a curriculum vitae to contain incorrect information).

- The *Internet* (the Internet may provide useful information about the expert, such as a web page advertising the expert's services for hire).
- *The expert's file, tests, and other reports—anything the expert relied on* in your case.

Consulting Your Expert

While you want to gain at least a fundamental understanding of the deponent's field of expertise, you will probably never master it. Nevertheless, you need to become a mini-expert in the field. That is why the best way to prepare to take the deposition is to consult with your own expert. Your expert can identify flaws in the other expert's report, tests, and other areas that should be covered during the deposition. Your expert can review the expert's curriculum vitae for overstatements, gaps, and deficiencies in expert qualifications. Your expert can examine the expert's list of publications and direct you to those that should be read because they are relevant to the case. Your expert can point you to the information that should be checked and who should be contacted to determine the validity of the information. For example, your expert can point you to the right source to determine whether the expert is licensed or a member of an organization. Your expert can help you formulate questions for the deposition.

Consult with Other Attorneys

Colleagues in your firm or other lawyers who have encountered the expert can be valuable resources concerning the expert.

The Expert's Methodology

The discovery and concession-based approaches to taking a deposition (described at pages 310-311 and 312-313) are also applicable to taking an expert's deposition. During the discovery phase, you inquire about facts that would help your case theory or hurt the other side's, including determining every opinion the expert has arrived at and the theory and facts underlying each such opinion. For the concession-based examination, you begin by brainstorming concessions that the expert must make because you can prove the fact. You then review the list of impeachment areas and decide which apply to the expert. However, three areas of impeachment exist for an expert that do not for a lay witness: (1) the expert's qualifications, (2) learned treatises, and (3) the basis for the expert's opinion. While the value and use of the first two are self-evident, the third deserves further explanation, which is provided in the next section, because it is so crucial to a successful deposition examination.

Particular Areas to Probe with Experts

In many of the ways we have already discussed, pages 310 to 323, taking an adversary expert's deposition is similar to that of an adverse lay witness. There are however, areas unique to an expert you may want to be prepared to probe.

Let's image you are representing Coach Bagshaw, and are preparing to take the deposition of the defense damage expert in the Bagshaw case, economist Dr. Campbell. The following are areas of vulnerability that you could explore.

VULNERABILITY OF AN EXPERT

The *Coach Bagshaw* Case

- **Neutrality**—Experts want to appear as neutral scientists, not as partisans conducting a business. Of course, keep in mind that this is not very useful if your own expert is in the same situation.

To Dr. Campbell:

Q.: You charge for your services? Tell me about how you charge.

Q.: What percentage of your professional income comes from consulting and testifying? (If it is too high a percentage, then this is the expert's business.)

Q.: Do you advertise? (Advertising looks less like a neutral scientist.)

Q.: Do you offer seminars? To whom?

Q.: Do you charge for the seminars? Are some people (e.g., insurance companies) given reduced rates for fee seminars? (Looks like drumming up business.)

- **Dynamics of the Opinion**—Adverse experts are good sources for providing information to weaken their own opinions.

To Dr. Campbell:

Q.: The mathematical formula you used to calculate Coach Bagshaw's economic loss from being fired—where did you get that formula?

Q.: Is it recognized in literature and/or studies in your field? Which?

Q.: Are there any other formulas you could have used? Why didn't you use that formula?

---

continues ▶

Q.: Would anyone competent in your field have used the other formula in these circumstances? Are there any criticisms that someone in you field could make about using the formula you did in a case such as this? What are they?

Q.: If you had used a different formula, would your conclusion change? Specifically how?

Q.: Will your formula always accurately determine lost income in a case such as this? Are there specific circumstances under which it would not give an accurate result? What are those?

Q.: The number you plugged into the formula for the "discount rate"— what is a discount rate? Why did you chose the one you did?

Q.: Could anyone in your field have chosen a different number? On what basis?

Q.: Would that have affected the total lost income? How?

• **Information from a Biased Source**—This is not an attack on the expert of the expert's expertise; it is a route to attack the opinion.

To Dr. Campbell:

Q.: In your calculations you took into consideration other possible coaching positions being available for Coach Bagshaw. In doing this, did you consider that censure by the CSA would lower her market rate?

Q.: And the reason that you assumed in your calculations that there would not be such a negative impact was because your employers, the defendants, assured you that the coaching profession did not function that way?

• **Factual Assumptions**—Again, this is not an attack on the expert or the expert's expertise; but if the factual information proves to be incorrect, it can be devastating to the opinion.

To Dr. Campbell:

Q.: How did you calculate the value of Coach Bagshaw's pension? (You are prepared to show through other factual evidence that Dr. Campbell only was aware of an earlier pension plan, which had subsequently been superceded to triple its value.)

The Basis—Daubert and Its Progeny

For federal courts and states that followed the federal lead, the importance of an effective expert witnesses's deposition increased with *Daubert v. Merrill*

Dow Pharmaceuticals, Inc., 509 U.S. 579 (1993) and *Kumho Tire Co. v. Carmichael*, 526 U.S. 137 (1999). Prior to *Daubert*, the *Frye* test only required that the proponent of the expert testimony establish that the scientific methodology was accepted in the scientific community before it was admissible at trial. *Daubert*, in setting aside the *Frye* test as the sole criteria for admissibility, placed the burden on the proponent of the scientific expert testimony to establish the reliability of methodology utilizing several criteria of reliability. The judicially relevant criteria according to *Daubert* include:

- Whether the theory or technique can be, and has been, tested,
- Whether the theory or technique has been subjected to peer review and publication,
- The known or potential rate of error and the existence and maintenance of standards controlling the technique's operation, and
- The level of acceptance in the scientific community.

Kumho Tire made it clear that the *Daubert* approach applies to all expert testimony, not just the scientific expert testimony ruled on in *Daubert*. With the additional burden on the proponent of the expert's testimony comes the opportunity for opposing counsel to test the vulnerability of expert's methodology using the criteria during a deposition. While *Daubert* sets a standard for admissibility of expert testimony in federal and some state courts, the nonexclusive list of factors provided also offers useful avenues to explore when assessing the weight of an expert's opinion.

Examination Concerning the Methodology

Your discovery examination should be designed to reveal any shortcomings in the expert's methodology, and thus corresponding weaknesses in the opposing party's case theory. The deposition structure can be patterned to follow and examine criteria listed in *Daubert*. For example:

EXPERT DEPOSITION EXAMINATION

Criteria: Whether the theory or technique has been subjected to peer review and publication

- Doctor, has the scientific theory that you relied upon in this case been discussed in any publication?
- What was the name of the publication and when was it published?

---

continues ▶

> - Did that publication involve a peer review?
> - What were the qualifications of the persons who did the peer review?
> - Any other publication?

This pattern of questioning can be developed for each of the *Daubert* criteria. The information derived from the exploratory examination should reveal areas of vulnerability in the basis for the expert's opinion and provide information that you can research for accuracy after the deposition. That research may well provide valuable information that can be utilized during your cross-examination of the expert at trial, or even lead to preclusion of the expert's testimony if your jurisdiction follows *Daubert*.

E.   Overcoming Problems with Defending Counsel

Taking a deposition can be an ordeal. Both defending counsel and the witness (remember the evasive witness discussed earlier in this chapter) may present you with problems. While we cannot anticipate all the individual problems that you will encounter, in this section we offer you a few common ones that you may have with the defending attorney along with suggested ways to handle them. These illustrations will enable you to use your common sense and solve these problems as they arise.

Incessant Objections

Obstreperous defending counsel may interpose too many objections in order to disrupt the examination or to rattle the examiner or for some other reason. When you encounter this or some of the other problems presented by defending counsel, it is a good practice to keep your attention on the witness and your examination. You can meet the objection by telling the witness to now answer the question and by ignoring defending counsel. Arguing with defending counsel over the grounds for the objection serves no purpose and will further interrupt the flow of your examination. You also can nip this excessive objection tactic in the bud by confronting counsel and instructing the attorney that groundless and excessive objections can result in sanctions.

Improper Coaching

Speaking Objections: Defending counsel can use a variety of methods to coach the deponent. The speaking objection is one tactic. Fed. R. Civ. P.

30(d)(1) forbids counsel from making objections that are argumentative or suggestive in nature. When this conduct by defending counsel exceeds the bounds of reasonableness, you should take the steps necessary to curb counsel's behavior.

TECHNIQUES FOR MEETING THE SPEAKING OBJECTION DURING THE DEPOSITION

The *Coach Bagshaw* Case

As Marilyn Bagshaw's lawyer, you are deposing Athletic Director Owen O'Connor, and O'Connor's lawyer, John Volker, persists in making speaking objections that coach the deponent:

To Mr. O'Connor:

> Q.: Mr. O'Connor, when did the compliance officer Marcus Locke's memorandum concerning gambling, plaintiff's exhibit 16, first arrive in your office?
>
> Mr. Volker: Objection. The witness has no first hand knowledge as to when it arrived; his secretary receives a mound of correspondence each day.
>
> A: I have no idea when my secretary received the memorandum. You'd have to ask her.
>
> Q.: Showing you plaintiff's exhibit 16, paragraph five on the last page. That paragraph states plainly that the type of gambling that Coach Bagshaw engaged in was not prohibited, correct?
>
> Mr. Volker: Objection. The document speaks for itself, and that paragraph is somewhat ambiguous.

To Mr. Volker:

Mr. Volker, you are making speaking objections that are designed to coach the witness. I'm handing you the court rules and directing your attention to Rule 30(d)(1) that prohibits suggestive objections. If you persist, I will have to terminate this deposition and make a motion for discovery sanctions.

Physical Signals to the Witness: Another coaching technique involves physical signals, such as shaking the head. To combat this behavior, begin by making a record ("For the record, counsel signaled the witness by shaking his head after I asked the question"). One method of curtailing coaching is to video the deposition so that defending counsel's behavior is visually recorded.

Taking a Break: What if deponent's counsel or the deponent asks for a break during the testimony? This request may be so they can consult or for a bodily reason. American Bar Association Standard on Discovery 18 provides that "(a)n attorney for a deponent should not initiate a private conference with the deponent during the taking of the deposition except to determine whether a privilege should be asserted or to enforce a court-ordered limitation on the scope of discovery. Subject to the provisions of subparagraph (a)(ii) (the deponent's attorney shouldn't request a recess while a question is pending except regarding privilege and whether the question goes beyond a court order) and (b) below (privilege), a deponent and the attorney may confer during any recess in a deposition."

If a question is pending, it is common practice to instruct the witness to answer that question. However, no rule exists supporting this practice, just as no rule allows the examiner to prohibit the deponent from taking the break. If the other side is taking too many breaks or using the breaks as an opportunity to engage in wood shedding, the attorney taking the deposition can make the record in the transcript that the witness has changed testimony from that given before the break, and in the case of continued abuse, seek a protective order from the court.

Offending Behavior

Again it's impossible to describe all that you may encounter from defending counsel. Counsel's behavior may be offensive in many ways. Counsel may try to insult you or the deponent, complain about the length of the deposition, and so on. As general principles, remain calm, make a record by describing the behavior in the transcript, consider videoing the deposition, and in an extreme case complain to the court.

F.   The Visual Deposition

Early in this chapter you learned that court rules permit the videotaping of depositions and that the Uniform Audio-Visual Deposition Act has specific provisions for how the videoing is to be conducted. Now we turn to the strategy involved in not just the videoing of depositions, but beyond that to the use of visuals to create a persuasive deposition for trial.

The Nature of the Video Deposition

Today's court reporting services no longer just provide transcripts of the deposition. They can provide videographers who will video the deposition. Then the service can synchronize the transcript with the video. The end product is a video that shows both the deposition and at the same time runs the transcript on the screen for the fact finder to read. Also, the videotape can show three components on the screen at the same time: the deposition, the transcript, and the exhibit being discussed.

The Strategic Value of a Video Deposition

A video deposition can prove effective in at least three common situations. First, a video of a perpetuation deposition may be compelling. For example, as a plaintiff's attorney you could show the fact finder the deposition of your terminally ill patient. Second, a video of an adverse witness's responses may be effective in impeaching that witness at trial if the witness varies from the answers given during the deposition. Third, a video deposition may serve as a deterrent to an attorney for the deponent who might otherwise be inclined to use physical coaching of the witness, or it may reveal the misconduct of counsel who fails to be deterred.

The Visual Deposition

Beyond the common usages of the video deposition is the incorporation of visuals into a deposition in order to advance the case theory or undercut the other side's case theory. This is a challenging endeavor and requires creativity. The deposition visual originates in much the same way that we describe how trial visuals are created in Chapter 10. Here, however, you will be thinking on two levels. First, what visual will advance your case theory and second, how can that visual be displayed in the deposition video that will be shown to the fact finder at trial.

THE VISUAL DEPOSITION

The *Hotel Z* Case

The Situation: You represent William Bailey who suffered multiple fractures to his leg when he fell in front of the Big Z Hotel. The steps that he fell on had chunks of concrete missing, probably due to hotel guests using rolling suitcases on the stairs. Through discovery, you have obtained hotel records showing that the hotel had deferred maintenance on the stairs due to cash flow problems and correspondence showing that the hotel had received communications from corporate to correct the problem. You want to create a video deposition of the manager that will highlight the hotel's negligence.

The Visual: Coupling Fed. R. Civ. P. 34(a), providing that a party may inspect premises with the right of the party setting the deposition to select the loca-

---

continues ▶

tion of the deposition, you move the court to have the manager deposed in front of the eroded front steps of the Big Z Hotel. When the fact finder sees the manager trying to downplay the deterioration of the steps during the deposition, the steps are visible in the background, thus undermining the hotel's case theory and advancing yours.

Securing an Agreement: Doctor, I'm going to try to make my questions simple—most all of them will be able to be answered "yes" or "no." When I'm though, the University's lawyer will be able to ask you questions so that you can elaborate or explain your answers to my questions. Can we agree that you will answer my questions with a "yes" or "no" if that is what the question calls for?

VI. DEFENDING THE DEPOSITION

A. The Defending Counsel's Role

Defending counsel has several responsibilities in representing the deponent. First, counsel should prepare the client or nonclient witness for the deposition. Second, during the deposition counsel should protect the deponent from abuse, preserve privileges, object to improper questions (form of the question) and procedures (the officer lacks the requisite qualifications), and clarify and protect the record. Counsel has responsibilities to perform in a professional manner, such as avoiding suggestive and argumentative objections.

B. Preparing for a Deposition

Preparing the Deponent

How do you prepare your client, or a witness who is friendly to your case, for a deposition by the opposing party? Preparing a deponent has two parts— preparing a deponent for the mechanics of a deposition and preparing the deponent for the substantive content of the deposition. In this section, we concentrate on both mechanical aspects and content, and provide you with a list of practical tips.

The first tip is to remember the consequences of your legal relationship with the deponent as you prepare the deponent. When the deponent is your client, your communications are privileged and you should object if the questioning during the deposition calls for privileged information. However, even otherwise privileged documents may have to be turned over to opposing counsel if the deponent used them to refresh his or her recollection in preparing for the deposition. Fed. Rule Evid. 612. On the other hand, what you discuss with a nonclient witness is not privilege protected and the examiner may question the deponent about your preparation discussions.

Case Theories and the Deponent's Role

Being deposed can be an unsettling experience. The fear of the unknown is a major contributor to the deponent's discomfort. The more the deponent knows about not only the case and his or her role in it but also the mechanics of the deposition the more likely the deponent will be a clear and confident communicator during the deposition. So, take time to explain both your legal and factual theories and what the deponent's role is in relationship to those theories. Also, explain what the opposing party's case theory is. With this knowledge, the deponent will have a better understanding of the meaning of the questions posed during the deposition.

For example, if you were preparing Donna Fent, Coach Bagshaw's business advisor, for a deposition to be taken by the lawyer for Mansfield University, you could explain that your legal theory is breach of contract by the university, that the university's legal theory is that it had grounds to fire Bagshaw (she participated in gambling on college sports in violation of CSC regulations and provided false information to both CSC investigators and the university administration). Concerning Fent's role, you could explain that she supports Coach Bagshaw's version of the meeting with athletic director O'Connor when O'Connor discussed firing Bagshaw.

Familiarizing the Deponent with the Deposition

Besides instructing the deponent about the case theories and the deponent's role in the case, the next most important thing is to familiarize the deponent with the deposition process. You should inquire whether the person has been deposed before. Assuming the person is not very familiar with the deposition process, you can begin by explaining what a deposition is. Many attorneys do this by sending a letter that outlines all the information the deponent needs to know about his or her deposition. The letter might also include documents, diagrams, prior statements, or depositions that you want the deponent to be familiar with. The checklist in this section contains the topics that you will want to cover in a letter and/or your conversation with the deponent.

Then again, many attorneys provide a short (10-15 minute) DVD or videotape, which shows how a deposition looks. DepPrep by Casesoft located at *www.casesoft.com* contains a computer slideshow that was developed by Iowa attorney David A. Hirsch along with Casesoft. To prepare for a deposition, the witness can view the DepPrep slideshow that provides tips on how to testify during a deposition. By visiting Casesoft's website, you can view the DepPrep slideshow and learn more about what a deponent should be told before the deposition.

Even with a prepared letter, video, and a slideshow tutorial, you will still want to meet with the deponent. You will want to discuss again most of the nuts-and-bolts topics because the more the deponent hears about the mechanics, which can be presented in a number of different ways, the more familiar, and hopefully less intimidating, the deposition process will appear. In your discussion you will want to provide a *general description of a deposition:*

GENERAL DESCRIPTION OF A DEPOSITION

- Information about why the other side is taking the deposition and the ways a deposition can be used (admissions, impeachment, substantive evidence)
- Length of the deposition
- The identity and function of the attorney who will be asking questions
- The anticipated manner of opposing counsel (brusque? nice?)
- Travel to the deposition location (specific directions, map)
- Anything, such as notes or a file, that the deponent brings to the deposition may be sought by the attorney taking the deposition (so tell the deponent it is wise to not bring anything to the deposition)
- Appropriate dress (suggested or mandated by you)
- The persons who will be present (parties, attorneys, court reporter) and their role
- The oath and its importance
- How the deposition testimony will be recorded
- That everything the deponent does and says is fair game, i.e., the other side may use what is said during breaks, on the elevator, and so on
- Opening remarks of counsel (what they consist of and why they are made)
- Objections to questions (how and when they are made, deponent's role when they are made)
- The right that the deponent has to review, correct, and sign the deposition
- And finally your role at the deposition. Usually you will sit next to the deponent and generally your role will be passive. But there are some

---

instances when you may find it essential to examine your client or friendly witness at the deposition. You might want to clarify misleading information lest the deponent's deposition be used at trial or for a particular purpose such as summary judgment; as such you will want to be certain that the deposition is correct and contains the information you need for your motion

You will want to give the deponent *specific advice about how to testify* during the deposition. Related discussions include witness preparation at pages 334-36. The following are essential points to cover during your discussion of how to testify:

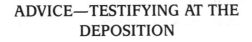

ADVICE—TESTIFYING AT THE DEPOSITION

- Tell the truth (not only tell the deponent to tell the truth because it is the most important principle in testifying but also because the lawyer taking the deposition may ask what you told the witness in preparation)
- Listen carefully to the question and make sure you understand it (ask for it to be repeated or clarified if necessary) and pause and think before answering
- Do not speculate—if the deponent does do not know the answer or cannot remember—answering that you do not know or remember is fine provided it's true (it is not improper to ask for speculation during a deposition but the deponent should not render an opinion without a basis)
- Do not argue with nor be lulled into friendship with the attorney because it can be harmful to the case
- Don't volunteer—answer the question directly and briefly
- Forcefully testify on important points (knowing the case theories and themes helps the deponent understand why certain questions are important)
- Do not reveal privileged communications (which will be explained and identified by counsel for the deponent-client)
- If the deponent makes a mistake during the testimony, tell them during a break so you can make sure that it can be corrected
- Explain objections and that when an objection is made stop talking, listen for instructions as to what to do next (usually to answer the question)
- Explain instructions to not answer the question (privilege, going beyond a protective order with the question, annoying, embarrassing, and so on)

Preparation for the content of the deposition testimony should in most cases include:

CONTENT OF THE DEPOSITION

- Discussing the anticipated subject matter of deponent's testimony in great detail
- Rehearsing the deposition with the deponent (you can do this with another attorney or a paralegal assistant playing the role of opposing counsel)
- Religiously and painstakingly reviewing prior statements, explanations for any potential inconsistencies in the deposition testimony, or any documents, and
- Reviewing any other possible exhibits, such as diagrams, photographs, maps, and the like

Preparing to Object and to Direct the Deponent Not to Answer

You will have to be prepared to make objections to opposing counsel's questions or the deponent's answers. In order to prepare, review a list of objections that are available to be made during a deposition. You will recall the list of objections at the beginning of this chapter at pages 293-95.

Again, in most jurisdictions, you will need to object to errors or irregularities in the form of the question or answers. Unless a timely objection is made at the deposition, objections to the irregular form of the question will be deemed waived. That means you must object to questions that might be ambiguous, unintelligible, compound, too general, calling for a narrative answer, asked and answered, misquoting a witness, leading, argumentative, assuming fact not in evidence, or calling for speculation. However, you do not need to object to evidentiary problems in the substantive content of the question or in testimony such as hearsay or inadmissible parole evidence. Those types of objections are preserved for trial and can be raised in that forum without first making a record at the deposition. Also, avoid making objections on grounds of irrelevancy during a deposition because relevancy in the discovery setting is broadly defined.

There are two types of questions to which you should both object and instruct the witness not to answer:

- First, Fed. R. Civ. P. 30(d)(4) prohibits a deposition examination from being conducted in bad faith or in a manner that unreasonably *annoys, embarrasses, or oppresses a party or deponent.*

- Second, questions asking for information that is *protected by some privilege* are improper (the most common examples we have encountered in litigation involve such privileges as attorney-client, work product, Fifth Amendment self-incrimination, and trade secrets). Fed. R. Civ. P. 26(b)(1).

The reasons for this should be clear to you. If you provide possibly privileged information, you not only provide the information, but likely waive the privilege as well. And under no circumstances should you permit your deponent to be abused by opposing counsel.

C. Preparing the Expert Deponent

This section discusses some of the issues you must consider in preparing your expert for a deposition to be taken by opposing counsel. The nuts-and-bolts aspects of lay depositions as discussed at pages 334-36 also apply to expert witness depositions. You must next focus on the actual preparation of your expert witness for his or her deposition. You should explain, just as you did with lay deponents, the deposition process as a whole (if the expert has never been deposed) and review the substantive content for the deposition.

Scheduling

A practical issue to consider when dealing with an expert is scheduling. You should inform opposing counsel of the scheduling needs of your expert and communicate the date for the deposition to your expert. The more each counsel cooperates on technical points, the easier the process is on everyone.

Assembling the Expert's File

Prior to the deposition, have your expert assemble the full file on the case—that is, all the information the expert relied on in rendering an opinion. You should work with your expert to ensure that the file is complete and so you can maintain in good faith that only those items that you will claim are privileged have been removed. The necessity for this preparation becomes clear as you proceed to prepare your expert for the content of the deposition—the anticipated subject matter of the questions.

Topics for Examination

Topics that will be the subject of the deposition will generally include all those areas that are ripe for cross-examination. Generally, these areas include:

TOPICS FOR EXAMINATION
OF AN EXPERT

- The possibility of bias (compensation, time spent on case, prior history of consultations and for whom); qualifications (to testify, particular expertise)
- Reliability of the scientific methodology as discussed earlier in this chapter in relationship to taking the expert's deposition
- The basis for the expert's opinions (procedures or tests, instruments used, acceptability by others)
- Learned treatises
- Underlying factual data and investigation used in rendering the opinion (time spent, data given to the expert, data developed through testing and investigation by the expert, data relied on that is acceptable in the field), and
- The expert's opinion (consistency with treatises, the factual data, other opinions by your expert)

You should review all of these areas with your expert. In particular, your expert should understand and be familiar with the assignment and the limits of the opinions that you requested. You should have your expert review prior opinions, data, and cases testified about in order to ensure consistency in the expert's factual basis and opinion. Some caveats are in particular order. Caution your expert about being too talkative, going to extremes in his or her opinion, speculating, or wandering far from his or her expertise.

VII. SEEKING JUDICIAL INTERVENTION

Only when all else fails should you seek judicial intervention to cure problems that arise in taking or defending a deposition. Before you do, make sure that it is significant matter, that you have made a record in the transcript of the conduct about which you are complaining, that you attempted to resolve the matter with opposing counsel, and that you are confident that the court will rule in your favor. Fed. R. Civ. P. 30 (d)(3) authorizes the court to sanction by imposing costs and attorney's fees on any person who impedes, delays or frustrates the "fair examination of the deponent." If a deposition is "being conducted in bad faith or in such manner as unreasonably to annoy, embarrass, or oppress the deponent or party" the federal court upon a party's motion may enter a protective order limiting or terminating the deposition.

For example, recall the series of speaking objections made by the athletic director's attorney, John Volker, during your deposition. If it persisted to the point of being obstructionist, you could terminate the deposition and set a motion for discovery sanctions. Your memorandum in support of your motion would recite the portions of the transcript during which attorney coached the deponent under the guise of objecting and rely not only on Rule 30(d)(1) that prohibits suggestive objections but also Rule of Professional Responsibility 3.4, which requires that counsel make a "reasonably diligent effort to comply with legally proper discovery request(s) by an opposing party." You could request attorney fees and costs for the deposition so far, for the motion for sanctions, and for the supplemental deposition that would be necessary because the first one was terminated.

VIII. ETHICAL CONSIDERATIONS

The ethical rules governing discovery (i.e., expedite litigation consistent with the interests of the client, not make frivolous discovery request, and not fail to make reasonably diligent effort to comply with a proper discovery request, as discussed in Chapter 8 on pages 270-72 and 276-77) are of course applicable to discovery by depositions. American Bar Association Model Rule of Professional Responsibility 3.2 states, "A lawyer shall make reasonable efforts to expedite litigation consistent with the interests of the client." Therefore, it is unethical to employ delay tactics during a deposition. For instance, it would be improper for defending counsel to use excessive objections and frequent recesses as tactics to eat up deposition time so that the deposition cannot be completed within the designated one-day time limit set by the court rule.

As you have seen, it is the duty of the defending counsel to ensure that the deposition does not invade any privilege. The attorney taking the deposition has a concomitant obligation under ABA Model Rule of Professional Responsibility 4.4 to respect the rights of third parties in obtaining evidence, and, as the Comment to Rule mentions, that includes "unwarranted intrusions into privileged relationships, such as the client-lawyer relationship."

✓ TAKING THE DEPOSITION CHECKLIST

The following are standards of performance for successfully taking a deposition:

Overall Performance in Taking the Deposition

❑ Determine who to depose, normally opposing parties, key nonparty lay and expert witnesses, and potentially unavailable witnesses.

❑ Have a set of objectives in mind.

❑ Take a structured and well-organized deposition.

❑ Behave in a confident and professional manner.

❑ Anticipate and prepare a suitable strategy for dealing with problems that could arise during the deposition (e.g., obstreperous defending counsel).

Five-Step Strategy for a Coordinated Discovery Plan

Step 1—Use case theories as guides to determine what information to seek.

❑ Identify potential information in existence.

❑ Use case theories to identify the information to seek.

Step 2—Identify likely persons and entities as sources who could provide that information.

Step 3—Identify the type of information to seek.

Step 4—Select the deposition suitable for the task of gathering the information.

❑ Is a deposition the best device for the task?

❑ Cost

❑ Compatibility of the discovery device with the case strategy

Step 5—Determine an effective timing and sequencing of depositions in the overall discovery plan.

Preparation for the Deposition

❑ Have a thorough working knowledge of the facts and law of the case.

❑ Subpoena nonparty witnesses and provide notice to party witnesses with reasonable lead time and provide notice of the deposition to all parties (schedule depositions by cooperative agreement with opposing counsel where possible).

❑ Obtain all documents and other exhibits needed for the deposition (i.e., subpoena duces tecum to nonparty witness, request to produce to a party).

❑ Arrange for recording of the deposition by a court reporter and/or videographer.

❑ Select the site for the deposition (e.g., reserve the conference room) and prepare the place (seating arrangements, exhibits present, beverages, and so on).

❑ Consider what stipulations, if any, that should be agreed to.

❑ Anticipate objections and revise the planned questions so they are not objectionable.

❑ Line up the exhibits and have copies and a numbering system for the exhibits that will be offered during the deposition.

Deposition Objectives

❑ Decide upon the objective or objectives (preserve testimony, discover information, or gain concessions or lock in a witness, evaluate the deponent) for the deposition.

❑ Understand how the deposition transcript may be used at trial (in lieu of the absent witness, prior inconsistent statement, prior consistent statement, admission by party opponent, refresh a witness's recollection, past recollection recorded), as a settlement tool, or in support of a motion for summary judgment.

Opening and Closing Remarks

❑ Have opening remarks for the deponent (designed so that if the transcript is offered at trial it will show the witness understood the situation) covering: who the lawyer is taking the deposition and whom the lawyer represents, whether the witness had ever been deposed before, the meaning of the oath, that the witness needs to answer audibly so the court reporter can report what was said that the transcript may be offered at trial, objections and the need to respond in spite of the objection unless the deponent's lawyer directs that the question not be answered.

❑ Closing remarks should cover: inquiries as to whether the testimony is complete, whether the deponent would like to add or correct anything, and advise about both reviewing and signing the transcript.

Deposition to Preserve Testimony

❑ Use this type of deposition for a witness who is unlikely to be available for trial.

❑ Prepare the deponent for a preservation deposition in much the same way a witness is prepared for trial—see pages 152-56 in the chapter on witness interviewing and add an explanation of how a deposition is conducted.

❑ Avoid objectionable questions and meet objections as to form by rephrasing if need be.

❑ Consider videotaping the testimony so the jury can view the deponent's demeanor.

Discovery Deposition

❑ This type of deposition is exploratory in nature and is intended to uncover information helpful to the case theory of the attorney taking the deposition or harmful to the opposing party's case theory.

❑ Use the funnel approach that is used in interviewing witnesses, as follows:

Step 1. Establish an open-ended inquiry, developing a rapport (asking interrogatory questions, i.e., who, what, when, where?).

Step 2. Organize the information; use chronological order.

Step 3. Verify facts and obtain and accurate information.

Step 4. Close the deposition by asking the deponent if there is anything else that should be disclosed.

❑ Because the examination is exploring for information, not creating an admissible transcript, there is less concern about whether questions are objectionable and need to be rephrased.

Concession-Based Deposition

❑ This sort of deposition examination is used to gain concessions either supporting the case theory of the lawyer taking the deposition or undercutting the other party's case theory. This approach can be coupled together with a discovery deposition approach and used during the examination of an adverse witness.

❑ Brainstorm to identify the content of this examination by asking what must this witness admit because the lawyer taking the deposition can prove it.

❑ Brainstorm to identify areas of impeachment.

❑ Construct a structured examination using the concession-based examination format.

❑ Control the witness by adhering to most of the Ten Commandments of Cross-Examination unless there is a good reason to deviate from the commandments.

Deposing the Opposing Party's Expert

❑ Compile available information about the expert: the expert's report, prior transcripts, publications, curriculum vitae, the expert's file, and Internet information.

❑ Consult with an expert about the opposing party's expert.

❑ Consult with colleagues and other attorneys.

❑ Design an examination to cover the same content as that used for lay witnesses and add the following areas of vulnerability:

✓ Deficiencies in the expert's qualifications,

✓ Learned treatises, and

✓ Flaws in the expert's methodology with an examination into Daubert criteria.

Problems with Defending Counsel

❑ Anticipate problems with opposing counsel and plan how to meet them.

Seeking Judicial Intervention

❑ Seek judicial intervention when it is a significant matter, attempts to resolve the matter with opposing counsel failed, and when it is probable that the request to the court will be granted.

✓ DEFENDING THE DEPOSITION CHECKLIST

Prepare the Deponent to Testify

❑ Explain the case theories and the role of the deponent in the case.

❑ Familiarize the deponent with how a deposition is conducted.

❑ Provide the deponent with advice on how to testify, not what to say.

❑ Discuss the subject matter of the testimony in great detail.

❑ Review all prior statements made by the witness.

❑ Rehearse the deposition.

❑ Review all potential exhibits.

Prepare to Object

❑ Review a list of available deposition objections (pages 293-96).

❑ Prepare to object to questioning that either invades a privilege or abuses the witness.

Preparing the Expert

❑ Work with opposing counsel to accommodate the expert's schedule.

❑ Have the expert assemble a case file.

❑ Review with the expert the areas that are likely to be covered during the examination.

10 *Creating Visuals*

10 *Creating Visuals*

"Not everybody trusts paintings but people believe photographs."

Ansel Adams, photographer (1902–1984)

"School kids today are doing sophisticated things with personal computers that are no bigger than text books but that outperform the largest computers of a generation ago."

Bill Gates (1955–   ) in *The Road Ahead*
(Penguin Books, 1996)

I.   VISUALS

A monumental change has taken place in trial advocacy. Today's lawyers persuade jurors with a chart showing a timeline created by computer software, with images projected on a large screen by a document camera, with a computer generated reconstruction of a crime or computer slideshow aiding in the telling of the advocate's story. Innovative and compelling trial visuals are the product of advancements in *software* (programs designed to visually display information), *hardware* (the document camera and computer) and the *creativity* of trial lawyers and businesses that design visuals.

Creating effective visuals is as much a part of your pretrial advocacy as conducting an investigation. The visuals will help organize, frame, and provide imagery for the refinement of your case theory. You cannot fully understand what you are preparing unless you appreciate how you will actually use these visuals. Therefore, we discuss some examples of using visuals at various points in trial, not to improve your use of demonstrative evidence in front of a jury, but to guide you in the initial creation of those visuals.

This chapter discusses why visuals are so critical to pretrial and trial persuasion. You will learn how to plan for and prepare the visuals and about the necessity of laying the evidentiary predicate for these exhibits. This discussion explains and shows types of visuals that may be employed in a case from settlement negotiation to trial opening statement through closing argument. Finally, you will learn when you should, and even more importantly, when you shouldn't, use trial visuals.

Visuals play an important role in many aspects of advocacy. Visuals employed during pretrial, as in a deposition, for instance, can have a persuasive effect when the deposition is introduced at trial. While most of the principles and techniques covered in this chapter are applicable to deposition visuals, additional information on effectively using visuals during a deposition is provided in Taking and Defending Depositions, Chapter 9. Another beneficial use of visuals, such as computer slideshows, is in pretrial presentations, such as those used during mediation, settlement conferences, or in preparing a witness for a deposition.

A. Why Use Visuals?

Seven reasons why lawyers use visuals:

1. **Perception and Retention**—Studies show that we retain less than 15 percent of what we hear, but we remember over 90 percent of what we both see and hear. Consequently, witness testimony accompanied by visuals is much likelier to be remembered than without them.

2. **How Jurors Learn**—Today's jurors, attorneys, and even judges, receive news and entertainment over the Internet and television in short bursts with pictures. Technology permeates our lives. Most jurors own computers or access one at work. They are receptive to and accustomed to computer information. It is how they learn.

3. **The Technology Exists**—Why employ visuals? Answer: Because you can. Technology allows lawyers to create and display visuals faster and in ways that might only have been dreamed of 20 years ago. In this chapter you will see some of what is possible to produce with today's technology.

4. **Repetition and Highlighting**—A trial lawyer is able to repeat and highlight information with visuals. For example, the lawyer elicits testimony from the witness about an event. Then, the lawyer introduces into evidence a diagram of the place where the event took place and goes back over the event having the witness use the diagram to show where certain acts occurred.

5. **Time Saver**—For a lawyer who tries a particular type of case over and over, a software program such as PowerPoint can conserve time. Rather than remaking the visual for each trial, the lawyer can develop a visual in PowerPoint, (e.g., a chart with the elements of negligence

on it) and then copy it over into a new presentation for the next trial. This is a time saver and works well (provided the lawyer remembers to change the names and dates on the chart for the new case).

6. **Create Evidence**—Need evidence? You can create demonstrative evidence. The only boundaries for a trial lawyer when it comes to demonstrative evidence are the rules of evidence and the lawyer's imagination. It is this creative process that makes pretrial and trial work challenging and rewarding.

7. **Successful Advocacy**—Trial visuals dynamically present the story and the argument. They enable the lawyer to emphasize the important aspects of the case theory. An example is the 2002 high-profile Connecticut trial of Michael Skakel, nephew of Ethel Kennedy, who was accused of murdering 15-year-old Martha Moxley in 1975 with a golf club. The state's attorney in closing argument played a portion of the defendant's tape-recorded interview while displaying slides of the trial exhibit photographs of the victim along with text from the interview on a screen. The appellate decision stated, ". . . By juxtaposing the photographs of the victim with the defendant's statements, the state's attorney sought to convey to the jury in graphic form what the state believed was the real reason for the defendant's panic, that is, that he had killed the victim. . ." *State of Connecticut v. Michael Skakel*, 276 Conn. 633, 888 A.2d 985 (Conn. 2006); cert. denied, 127 S. Ct. 578 (U.S. Conn.).

B. High-, Medium-, Low-, No-Tech

Choosing Media

Visuals come in a wide variety, ranging from a high-tech courtroom demonstration, to high-tech computer generated animation of an airplane crash to low-tech hardcopy photographs or "no-tech" markers on a white board. We do not suggest that a high-tech presentation is necessarily more effective than a low-tech or no-tech presentation. Parading an injured child's photograph, cradled in your hands, before the jurors so that you stand close to them and pause long enough so each juror can get a good look can leave an even more lasting impression than projecting the child's picture on a large screen or television monitor. The important point is that the lawyer should select the visual medium that will be most compelling.

Restraint should be exercised so that the high-tech approach is not overused. A presentation overloaded with technology may interfere with jury communication, rather than facilitate it. For example, even if sound effects can be added to a digitized slideshow, that may be an inappropriate addition that detracts from the information portrayed in the show.

The Options

Computer software enables you to select from a variety of methods for displaying visuals. For example, with PowerPoint you can develop an array of information on slides—charts, photographs, diagrams, and much more. Once the slideshow has been put together, you can project those slides onto a screen or television monitor as part of the show. In many courtrooms today, each juror has a personal monitor in front of them upon which visuals can be shown. A slide can also be printed onto letter-size paper. This piece of paper can be either introduced into evidence or used for illustrative purposes. With a document camera, the image on the paper can be projected onto a screen so all of the jurors can see it at the same time. Or the piece of paper can be enlarged to poster size with a poster-maker or by a professional copy service. The enlargement can be backed with Styrofoam board and put on an easel or just taped to a page on a flipchart.

The Software and Hardware

Software

This chapter introduces you to software and hardware. There are several software programs for creating visuals. We will suggest and show you some ways in which that software can be used. However, we will not attempt to go into depth on how to operate the software or hardware. For example, while we discuss PowerPoint software and show you some of the things it can produce, we do not go into detail on how to design slides. How-to manuals and other resources are readily available, and the companies that design these software products commonly offer free trial periods during which you can download the software from the Internet and try it out for a time, usually 30 days, without having to purchase it. At the end of this chapter, in the Pretrial Litigation Library, page 369 we suggest software products for you to explore.

PowerPoint is versatile software for creating and displaying computer slideshows. It enables the creator to customize the animation of slides so that, for example, the text will zoom in from center screen. PowerPoint also has the advantage of being provided in the Microsoft Office bundle. Power-Point slideshows work well during controlled linear presentations—opening statement, closing argument, and a direct examination of an expert witness explaining the expert's field. With an index of the slide numbers, PowerPoint can also be used to call up a slide out of order by typing the slide number and hitting "enter."

Two other popular trial software programs are Trial Director by inData and Sanction II by Verdict Systems. These programs have an advantage over

PowerPoint in that they permit the lawyer to retrieve an image, such as an individual document, by Bates number and at any time enlarge and highlight pertinent portions of it. See Chapter 3, page 77 for a description of the Bate's Stamp.

Hardware

Document Camera: DORE and ELMO and others manufacture document cameras, also referred to as "digital visual presenters." These cameras have several features in common. First the document camera (shown below) enables a trial lawyer to project an enlarged image of an exhibit on a large screen or a television monitor. The lawyer places the exhibit on the flatbed of the document camera and then zooms in or out to provide a close up or wider view of the object. This is ideal for anything from a photograph to an object the size of a penny. It replaces the need to publish an exhibit to the jury where they pass it hand to hand until each juror has examined the exhibit. Also, a transparency, such as an X-ray, may be placed on the bed of the document camera and the light source switched from above to below the transparency so that the image will be projected.

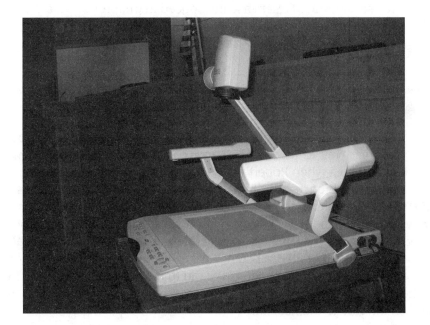

Computer: The computer is surely the most essential piece of hardware for today's lawyer. A computer is the source of slideshows, such as those produced by Sanction and PowerPoint software. The computer can either be connected to an LCD projector so it can project images onto a screen or connected to a television monitor so the image will be shown on that monitor. The lawyer can use a hand-held remote to advance or reverse the order of the slides.

Poster Maker: A poster maker can be utilized to enlarge visuals such as a photograph or a slide created using a computer. The poster-size paper can then be adhered to Styrofoam to create the traditional and reliable trial visual—the board-backed enlargement.

II.　PLANNING VISUALS

A.　Case Theory as the Guide

As with all aspects of pretrial and trial work, your case theory should serve as a guide in designing visuals. For example, to explain your *legal* theory to the jury, you can create an elements' chart as shown on page 366. Visuals can assist you to tell a persuasive *factual* story. Photographs of the persons and places involved in the action can tell a human story and bring the events to life in a settlement conference or the courtroom.

Let's revisit the *ATM Murder* case introduced in Chapter 2, Case Theory to demonstrate how the case theory is a guide and how visuals can be planned and displayed.

The *ATM Murder* Case

Story

On April 11th of last year, Robert and Claire O'Toole were on their way to meet their friends for dinner and a movie. It was about 8:00 p.m. when Robert pulled his car into a parking space across the street from a branch of his bank and ran across the street to an outside ATM. He was getting some cash for the evening. His wife watched as he drew out the cash and was placing it in his wallet. The man who had been standing behind him, seemingly waiting for his turn, tried to grab the wallet from Robert's hand. Robert resisted. The man stabbed Robert in the stomach, and ran off down the street. Claire ran to her husband. She called 911 on her cell phone. The police and EMTs arrived within minutes. But Robert died on the way to the hospital.

Police apprehended Donald Wilcox two blocks away because he matched the description given by Claire O'Toole. In Wilcox's pocket were five $20 bills, one $5 bill and four $1 bills. The bank records show that Robert O'Toole had withdrawn $100 in five $20 bills. Later at a lineup, Claire identified Wilcox as the man who stabbed her husband. A photograph

> taken by the ATM shows part of the face of the man standing behind Robert, and that portion of the face looks like Wilcox's face. However, the photograph does not provide enough of the facial features to clearly establish by itself that Wilcox was the man who robbed and killed Robert O'Toole.

B.   Scene Visit

Go to the scene of an event in order to completely understand the event. The scene is also a good place to get ideas for what visuals you want to create. Schedule the visit at the earliest opportunity.

Assume that you are the prosecutor assigned to the *ATM Murder* case. As soon as you can, you go to the place where Robert O'Toole was robbed and stabbed. Among other things, you want to learn about factors pertinent to Claire O'Toole's identification of Donald Wilcox as the man who killed her husband. Ideally you would go there at the same time of day and year so that you could see for yourself what the lighting was like. You would see where the O'Toole car was parked and how far that was from the ATM machine. If possible you would also visit the scene with a person who is familiar with what took place where and when. It would be best to go to the site with Ms. O'Toole who could guide you and orient you to the scene.

Police detectives most likely would have already generated some visuals. They would have taken photographs of the scene and probably measured distances so that a to-scale crime scene diagram could be drawn. They may have even made a video of the scene. As you think about the exhibits you intend to present at trial, you also should consider who will lay the foundation for admissibility of these exhibits and who will testify with the aid of the these exhibits. Both Ms. O'Toole and the detectives who were at the scene should be able to lay the foundation for the admissibility of these exhibits. (See Part C discussing laying an evidentiary foundation for admissibility of trial exhibits.)

If you were a sole practitioner investigating a civil case, such as an action for personal injury damages after a car accident, you would endeavor to do the same sort of things to create a visual presentation of the accident scene. You or your investigator would take photographs, measure, inspect the scene, make a video. See Chapter 3, the Bicycle-Cross-Walk Case and the photographs of the scene. All the time, you would be thinking about the witnesses who would identify and authenticate the exhibits.

While you are at the scene, you will also be contemplating whether or not to ask the judge for a jury scene visit. If the motion is granted, the jurors will be transported there and permitted to walk and inspect the scene. A jury visit could be helpful or harmful to the case theory. For example, where a defendant claims self-defense, asserting that he was frightened when the victim approached him in an alley, a trip to the secluded, dark alley crowded with drug addicts may give the jurors the sense of apprehension that the defendant felt as he was approached by the victim in that alley and lead to the conclusion the defendant did act in self-defense and should be found not guilty.

C.   Evidentiary Foundation

Planning to use visuals at trial requires that you prepare to lay the evidentiary foundation for the admissibility of the evidence. You will research the evidentiary rules and the relevant appellate decisions in your jurisdiction. The foundation for admissibility may be relatively simple, such as asking Claire O'Toole on direct examination whether the photograph of the ATM and bank is a "fair and accurate representation" of how they looked to her on the night of April 11th. On the other hand, the foundation questions for the ATM's surveillance photograph are more complicated. No person witnessed what the camera saw. The predicate involves witness testimony establishing that the camera was in working order, identifying the photograph as the one taken by the ATM camera on the night of the 11th, and that the photograph is of Robert O'Toole's face and part of the face of the man behind him.

Pretrial planning of the evidentiary foundation also requires that you anticipate attacks upon that foundation. The attack may come in the form of an objection or a motion in limine to exclude the evidence. For example, in the *ATM Murder* case, you as the prosecutor could anticipate that defense counsel will move in limine to exclude autopsy photographs of Robert O'Toole. The defense will claim that the photographs should be excluded under Evidence Rule 403 because their unfair prejudicial effect substantially outweighs any probative value they may have. To meet this motion, you need to explain why each photograph is probative (it would aid the medical examiner, explain the manner and means of Robert O'Toole's death, and so forth). To lessen the prejudicial effect and alleviate the court's concern, you could offer only a couple of the photographs.

D.   Preparing the Visual

The actual creation of the visual may be done by you, by your law firm staff or by a business that you employ to design the visuals. The software programs described earlier are user friendly, and you can create basic, yet effective, visuals on your own. When it comes to more complex visuals, computer animated video, you may need to hire not only a computer programmer but also scientists to do the physics upon which the visual is based. On the

Internet, you can locate companies that create demonstrative evidence. Two such companies are:

- Sanction – *www.verdictsystems.com* and
- Ronin Consulting – *www.roninconsulting.net*

Even if the preparation of the visual is done by someone else, you must maintain oversight and control the final product because it is your case.

When you plan to use technology in the courtroom, have a backup plan in case the technology fails. If you plan to do a computer slideshow, it is a good idea to print out your slides so you can place them on the document camera if the courtroom has one, or in the absence of a document camera, parade the slides in front of the jury one by one.

E.   Preparing to Use the Visual

Pretrial preparation of visuals entails not just creating them, you must also prepare to display them in the assigned courtroom or at a settlement conference. We discuss courtrooms but are equally mindful of settlement conferences. Many modern courtrooms and offices are equipped with all of the latest technology: a document camera; television monitors for the jurors, counsel, and the judge (enabling the judge to regulate what the jurors will see and when); a conveniently placed large screen onto which a computer slideshow, a video, and so on may be shown, and even the remnant of the traditional courtroom—the flipchart on an easel.

However, you may be assigned to a courtroom that was designed at the turn of the century—the 20th century. All that the courtroom may provide for displaying visuals may be that old reliable—flipchart on an easel. In this case, assuming that you wish to and can afford to use a document camera or a computer generated slideshow, you must scout the courtroom to determine, among other things, where to place a screen or television monitor, where to place the projector and/or document camera, where to plug in your equipment, whether extension cords are needed, and so on.

III. EXAMPLES OF VISUALS

In this section, we offer you a sampling of trial visuals. These examples are equally applicable for settlement negotiations and in any part of the advocacy process in which you want to persuade. By offering these visuals we hope that they not only show what is possible but also stimulate your imagination so that you create the visuals your case needs. As the discussion progresses, you also should come to understand when you should and when you shouldn't use trial visuals.

A. Storytelling—Opening Statement

Opening statement provides the lawyer with the best opportunity to tell the party's full and compelling story. As discussed in the Case Theory, Chapter 2, for the story to be persuasive it should be a human story involving values shared by the jurors. The opening statement should bring reality into the courtroom so the people discussed come alive and the events make sense. There is no better way to do that than with pictures.

The general proposition is: If you can tell it to the jury, you can show it. In other words, during opening statement because you are *telling* the jury what you expect to prove, you also can *show* the jury what you intend to prove. You can show the scene diagram that you intend to offer during trial. What if opposing counsel objects? [If you are in a jurisdiction in which the judge is actively involved in preparing the pretrial order, this is an issue you would want to discuss at the pretrial conference.] Then you can respond by making an offer of proof to the judge in which you lay the foundation for the exhibit. A preferred method, when you plan to show a computer slideshow that contains slides of the scene diagram, photographs of the scene, and so on during the opening, is to print the slides and preview them to both the court and opposing counsel in advance of your opening. If opposing counsel objects to any slides, you can meet the objection at the preview and, if need be, delete certain slides. By previewing the slides to counsel and the judge, you are more likely to avoid objections and interruptions during your opening.

Continue to assume that you are the prosecutor in the *ATM Murder* case and that you employ a computer slideshow to tell the story. You begin by introducing the jurors to Robert O'Toole by projecting the following photograph of him on a big screen. As the jurors look at his photograph you tell them about Robert: his name, age, occupation You tell them that on the

evening—around 8:00 PM on April 11th of last year Robert and his wife Claire were going out for dinner and a movie with their friends.

Then, you explain that Robert decided that he needed to stop and get some cash. He parked his car and ran across the street to an ATM at a branch of his bank. Here, you move to the next slides in the slideshow showing the scene. You point to the photograph to show the jury that Robert parked the car next to Jenny's restaurant and across the street from the bank.

Next, you show the bank and ATM as viewed by Ms. O'Toole from where she sat waiting for her husband. You direct the jurors' attention to the light just to the left of the ATM.

So that the jury is oriented to the scene—where the ATM was in relationship to the car, on the next slide you point out the bank to the right and the place where the O'Tooles parked, by the restaurant on the left.

At this juncture you describe how defendant Donald Wilcox grabbed for Robert's wallet, how a struggle followed, and how the defendant stabbed Robert in the stomach. With the following aerial photograph using an animated arrow you show where the defendant was arrested and its close proximity to the ATM where Mr. O'Toole was stabbed.

The remainder of the slide presentation can be seen by looking at it on the DVD that accompanies this book and is summarized below. The rest of the opening statement and slides are summarized as follows:

- **Slide—Diagram of a Human Body:** You show the jurors a diagram of a human body marked to show where Robert was stabbed. You explain that the medical examiner will testify to performing an autopsy on Robert O'Toole and determining that he died as a result of the stab wound.
- **Slide—Elements Chart:** This chart lists the elements charged in the Information alleging that the defendant Wilcox committed felony murder in the first degree. You explain to the jury that the evidence will prove the crime beyond a reasonable doubt.

Note that the same visuals could be shown during the opening statement (or at a settlement conference) without using a computer slideshow. The slides could have been printed out on letter-sized paper and placed on a document camera that would project them on a screen. Or they could be enlarged, backed, and displayed on an easel.

B. Complexities

The principal ways that trials can be complex and hard for the jury to follow are when one or both of the following exist:

- Technical information is involved and/or
- The case involves a large quantity of information (numerous actors, events, or both actors and events).

When faced with these types of complexities, the trial lawyer should think of using visuals in order to simplify and clarify the information.

Technical Information

Technical information can be daunting for many jurors. Using a visual may impart the information in a much more comprehensible way. For example, the CD that comes with this book has a PowerPoint presentation that expert witness Steve Lambert, with the South Carolina Law Enforcement Division, shows when he explains to the jury what DNA is, how it is analyzed, and what it can establish in a criminal case.

To understand how technical information can be made clear with visuals, you can visit New York Law School's Visual Persuasion Project website at *http://www.nyls.edu/pages/2734.asp*. This project and the attendant website are the creation of Professor Richard K. Sherwin. Once you reach the website, click on "Visual Litigation and Litigation Services" and then enter "Kinds of Visuals." Here you can browse through computer generated animations of a faulty filter system in a swimming pool, a collision of tractor trailer with a pedestrian in a cross walk, an umbilical cord wrapped around a baby's neck and its effect on the baby's breathing and heart rate, and many more.

When your case involves medical testimony, you will want to introduce a demonstrative exhibit that assists the physician in explaining the doctor's testimony to the jurors. For example, in the murder case, the pathologist could use a medical illustration of abdominal anatomy to show the jury where Mr. O'Toole was stabbed in the stomach. Medivisuals—*www.medvisuals.com*—is an example of a company that provides trial medical illustrations of all the different parts of the human body

A Large Quantity of Information

Federal Rule of Evidence 1006—Summary Chart

Summary charts are especially effective in clarifying and making understandable a mountain of information. The first type of summary chart is the kind covered by Federal Rule of Evidence 1006. Under that Rule, the contents of voluminous writings, recordings, or photographs that cannot be conveniently examined by the jurors may be presented by a chart, summary, or calculation. For example, mounds of medical records can be summarized and enlarged on a chart for the jurors to see.

Federal Rule of Evidence 611(a)—Summary Chart

Federal Rule of Evidence 611 states:

> (a) Control by court.
>
> The court shall exercise reasonable control over the mode and order of interrogating witnesses and presenting evidence so as to (1) make the interrogation and presentation effective for the ascertainment of the truth, (2) avoid needless consumption of time, and (3) protect witnesses from harassment or undue embarrassment.

This Rule makes no mention of summary charts. However, a body of case law, e.g., *United States v. Janati*, 374 F.3d 263 (4th Cir. (Va.) 2004) has developed under Rule 611(a). The rule provides that summary charts, "pedagogical" devises offered to help in the presentation and comprehension of the evidence, may be shown to the jury. The chart can contain, among other things, witness conclusions. Generally though, the chart is not admitted into evidence.

Timeline

When the case involves several events for the jury to grasp, a timeline visual is an excellent aid to highlight the important events and put them in chronological order.

Casesoft, found on the Internet at *http://www.casesoft.com/timemap/index. shtml,* produces Timemap software that can be used to create timelines. You enter the event date and time, and the software lays out a proportionate timeline and a box above the date into which you can enter the facts. Timemap also interacts with Casemap, which can be used to pull together a full case chronology. Then you can import the significant events from Casemap into Timemap to produce the timeline.

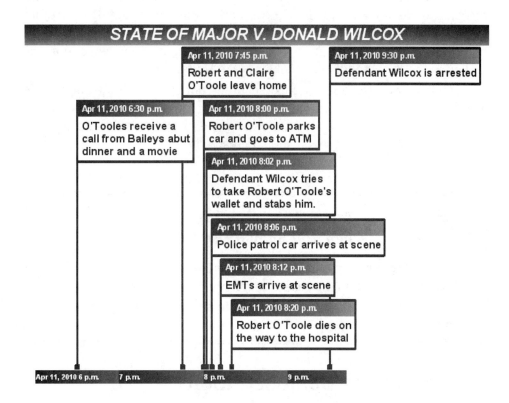

C. Improbability of the Opposing Party's Story

Sometimes the best way to debunk the other side's story is to show that it just does not make sense. For example, in *State v. Randy Roth*, recounted in Ann Rule's book *A Rose for Her Grave,* the defendant contended that his wife died when their raft capsized because a motor boat wake tipped it over. Roth claimed that when the raft turned over his wife went under water and drowned. To disprove the defendant's story, the prosecution videotaped a reenactment of two persons in the water on the raft and ran motorboats of various sizes by the raft. It did not overturn. On the DVD accompanying this book, you can watch the video of that reenactment. *State v. Roth*, 75 Wash. App. 808, 881 P.2d 268 (Wash. App. Div. 1 1994).

Another illustration of this proposition is a case involving the murder of an 11-month-old child who suffered a fractured skull. The defendant's story was that the baby accidentally fell down a flight of stairs. The prosecution used a computer animation video of a football-like object (representing the baby) going down the stairs to show the improbability of this happening without otherwise injuring the child whose only injury was the skull fracture. This video animation is also on the DVD that comes with this book. In both this and the *Randy Roth* case, the defendants were convicted. On the other hand, the impeachment of a key detective by a computer photo enhancement during cross-examination was a powerful piece of evidence in a trial ending in the acquittal of actor Robert Blake for murder.

As will be discussed in the next section, courtroom demonstrations are another way to show the jury (or your adversary in settlement) the improbability of the other side's story. But for now, the following is a cumulative list to this point of times when you should create visuals.

✔ CHECKLIST

When You Should Use Visuals

- **Storytelling**—When you want to tell a story well
- **Complexities**—When the case is complex
- **Story is Implausible**—When you want to show the other side's story is implausible

---

D. Courtroom Demonstrations

Courtroom demonstrations can be effective in bringing a story to life. For example, in the *ATM Murder* case, the prosecutor could have Ms. O'Toole step down from the witness chair, stand in front of the jury, and demonstrate, with you acting as her husband, how he struggled with the defendant over the wallet and how the defendant stabbed him.

However, courtroom demonstrations can prove fatal to a case theory. Most courtroom demonstrations fail because they were not rehearsed during pretrial preparation. Not only should the participants practice the demonstration but the attorney should also carefully plan how and where it will be conducted in the courtroom. If you are thinking about conducting a demonstration with a witness called by your opposing party, the demonstration will not have been rehearsed. It is a gamble. It very well may backfire or be met with resistance.

✔ **CHECKLIST**

When You Should Not Use Trial Or Settlement Visuals

- **Overuse**—When the trial or settlement conference becomes overloaded with hardware and software to the point of interfering with communication
- **Unprepared**—When the attorney and/or witness is unprepared to work with the technology or other visual
- **Gamble**—When you are gambling that the visual will work, e.g., an unrehearsed demonstration

---

E. Argument Visuals

Argument visuals can serve several purposes including:

- Explaining the law,
- Reviewing the facts,
- Defining terms,
- Showing relationships between the participants,
- Applying law to the facts, and
- Arguing the case.

Argument visuals can be used during jury argument or pretrial in settlement negotiations or arbitration for instance.

For example, you as the prosecutor in the *ATM Murder* case, could use an elements chart like the one below to explain to the jury or your adversary that the conduct of the person who took Robert O'Toole's wallet fulfilled all the elements of robbery.

To review the facts for the jury or during settlement discussions you could employ the timeline chart described earlier in the chapter. Also in reviewing the facts, you could show photographs and the diagram of the scene.

Then, in your discussion of the credibility of the witnesses, you could display a chart that shows on one side the list of witnesses in the case and on the other side the criteria for judging witness credibility, which are con-

---

ROBBERY

A person commits robbery when they:

- **Take personal property of another;**

- **uses or threatens to use immediate force, violence, or fear of injury to that person; and**

- **such force or fear is used to obtain or retain possession of the property or to prevent or overcome resistance to the taking.**

---

tained in the court's instruction to the jury. Then, you could talk about each witness in terms of the criteria: "Was the pathologist credible? Let's look at the criteria for determining the credibility of a witness as stated in the court's instructions. One criterion is whether the witness has an interest in the outcome of the case. Does the doctor have such an interest?"

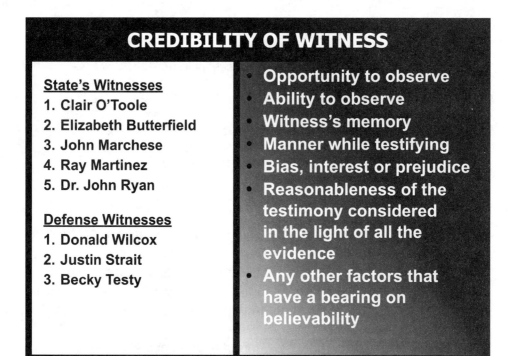

CREDIBILITY OF WITNESS

State's Witnesses
1. Clair O'Toole
2. Elizabeth Butterfield
3. John Marchese
4. Ray Martinez
5. Dr. John Ryan

Defense Witnesses
1. Donald Wilcox
2. Justin Strait
3. Becky Testy

- **Opportunity to observe**
- **Ability to observe**
- **Witness's memory**
- **Manner while testifying**
- **Bias, interest or prejudice**
- **Reasonableness of the testimony considered in the light of all the evidence**
- **Any other factors that have a bearing on believability**

You would argue that the single issue in the case is whether the defendant is the man who robbed and stabbed Robert O'Toole to death. To emphasize your argument you could avail yourself of the following target argument visual. Starting with the outside circle, you argue that Wilcox had five $20 bills, the amount of money and in the same number of bills as Robert had just taken out of the ATM. Pointing to the second circle, you would say that not only did he have the amount of money in the same denominations as the robber but also he was arrested within two blocks of where the robbery and stabbing took place. Your argument would continue as you point to the inner consecutive circles: Wilcox meets the initial description given by Ms. O'Toole; the ATM photograph looks like the defendant. All of this corroborates Ms. O'Toole's identification of Wilcox. All the evidence points to the defendant as the murderer.

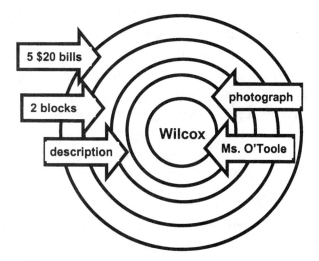

IV. ETHICAL CONSIDERATIONS

The ethical considerations in preparing visuals echo those discussed in Chapter 2 regarding developing a case theory. As mentioned there, the core concern is that ABA Rule of Professional Conduct 3.4 not be violated. That Rule states: "A lawyer shall not: . . . (b) falsify evidence, counsel or assist a witness to testify falsely, or offer an inducement to a witness that is prohibited by law."

In the case theory chapter, we used the illustration of coaching Ms. O'Toole to falsely testify about her identification of Wilcox as the murderer. Here, the concern is that the exhibit literally not give a false picture of the facts. For example, in the *ATM Murder* case, this could be done by taking a picture not from where she looked out of her car window but from a place where she would get a better view. The photographs of the scene should not mislead the jury to believe that Ms. Wilcox had a better vantage point to see what happened at the ATM than she really did. If a misleading visual is offered, it will likely be objected to and should be excluded. Therefore, careful preparation and prudent use of your visual evidence should be a paramount consideration.

The following are standards of performance for pretrial creation of trial visuals:

Visuals

❑ Appreciate the value of trial visuals in persuasion because visuals:
  ✓ Correspond with the way jurors learn,
  ✓ Are vehicles for highlighting and emphasizing testimony, and
  ✓ Can be created to deliver the advocate's message.
❑ Select the media (high-, medium-, low-, or no-tech) that will deliver the information in the most meaningful way.
❑ Take advantage of the display options that software permits, e.g., slide-show or enlargement of a single slide into a poster.

Planning Visuals

❑ Utilize the case theory as a guide in deciding what visuals to create:
  ✓ Visuals to communicate the legal theory and
  ✓ To tell a persuasive factual story.
❑ Visit the scene of the event.
❑ Research the evidentiary predicate.
❑ Decide who will prepare the visual in-house or hire someone.

Taking Advantage of Visuals

❑ Prepare visuals that will aid in storytelling, e.g., opening statement.
❑ Make complex information comprehensible, e.g., summary chart.
❑ Expose the implausibility of the other side's story.
❑ Bring the story alive (a courtroom demonstration).
❑ Avoid overusing visuals and working with a visual.

Ethical Considerations

In designing a trial visual, make sure that it is neither false nor misleading.

✓ PRETRIAL LITIGATION LIBRARY

The following references are resources for further research into the topics discussed in this chapter:

❑ New York Law School's Visual Persuasion Project website at *www.nyls.edu* created by Professor Richard Sherwin.

❑ Litigation Technology: Becoming a High-Tech Trial Lawyer, Mike Rogers, Aspen Publishers (2006)

❑ The Lawyer's Guide to Creating Persuasive Computer Presentations, Ann E. Brenden and John D. Goodhue, ABA Law Practice Management Section, Second Edition (2005)

SOFTWARE FOR VISUALS

- PowerPoint—*www.microsoft.com.* PowerPoint from Microsoft, available with Windows enables the user to create a slide show presentation to show or to be printed out.
- Sanction by Verdict Systems—*www.verdictsystems.com;* and
- Trial Director by inData Corp—*www.indatacorp.com.* Both software programs can generate, among other things, slides that can be easily retrieved and shown.
- Timemap—*www.casesoft.com/timemap/index.shtml.* This software can be used to create timelines.
- Broderbund—*www.broderbund.com.* With Broderbund software you can diagram scenes.

11 *Pretrial Motion Advocacy*

11 *Pretrial Motion Advocacy*

"Speech is power: speech is to persuade, to convert, to compel. It is to bring another out of his bad sense into your good sense."

Ralph Waldo Emerson (1803–1882)

"'Wait a minute,' interrupted the judge. 'There's going to be enough spitting back and forth without you starting so soon.' He glared at Cheeseman awaiting his response." (Cheeseman brings a pretrial Rule 11 motion)

Jonathan Harr, *A Civil Action* (1995)

I. PRETRIAL MOTION PRACTICE

This chapter examines how to develop motion theories for both making and responding to a pretrial motion. We also discuss how to set a motion, plan an evidentiary hearing, write a compelling motion or response and persuasively advocate to the judge. Here we refer to the motion's judge although that person may be the trial judge as well.

Motions are requests for a court order; they can take many forms. As your case progresses, you will file many types of pretrial and trial motions—pretrial *in limine* motions to exclude evidence or to use a particular exhibit, motions during trial, and post-trial motions. They can include an oral request for a five-minute continuance, an emergency motion for bail or a temporary restraining order, a 30-page motion for summary judgment, or a motion to suppress evidence accompanied by a full evidentiary hearing that resembles a mini-trial. In this chapter, we focus on written pretrial motions, although the ideas and procedures presented in this chapter apply to any of these motions.

II.   PLANNING THE MOTION

A.   Setting Objectives:
Ends–Means Thinking

The process of setting the objectives for your motion begins with the needs of your case. It is a process grounded in ends-means analysis. You begin by perceiving the needs of your case from its inception, during settlement negotiations, litigation, and to its conclusion. Once you have identified the needs, then look for motions to fulfill those needs. In essence, the motions that you develop are designed to satisfy the needs of your case. From our experience, these needs will roughly fall into one or more of what we call "control categories":

- Control of *information:*
    - ◇ keeping your adversary's information out of evidence, e.g., a motion to preclude use of subsequent repairs,
    - ◇ obtaining information for your case theory, e.g., a motion to compel discovery for a failure to answer,
    - ◇ getting your information into evidence, e.g., a motion to let an expert show the jury the videotape that formed the basis of the expert's opinion, and
    - ◇ giving information, e.g., presenting the court with a favorable image of your client or your client's cause through a motion for bail.
- Control of the *final outcome*—dispositive motions to resolve the case, e.g., a motion to dismiss, summary judgment, directed verdict, judgment as a matter of law; a motion to control information may also resolve the case, e.g., a suppression motion may deny the prosecution the information it needs to support its factual theory.
- Control of the *procedure*—motion for change of venue, motion regarding rules for trial, a motion to exclude mentioning of certain matters in voir dire or opening statement, or a motion for a particular procedure for jury selection.
- Control of the *participants*—motion to compel a party to appear at deposition, motion for a material witness warrant to stop a witness from leaving the jurisdiction, motion for order restraining one party from personally contacting the other.

B. Developing a Motion Theory

An effective method for formulating a motion argument is by developing a strategic theory analogous to the case theory. Like its case theory counterpart, this motion theory (MT) is a plan developed out of an ends-means analysis directed at achieving overall objectives. The ends of the case theory are to achieve the client's overall objectives in the case. The ends of the MT are to achieve the control objectives just described. Specifically, the MT is comprised of a motion legal theory (MLT) and a motion factual theory (MFT). These are directly analogous to the legal theory and factual theory that make up the case theory. In fact, just as the legal and factual theories interact so each suggests and limits the other, the MLT and MFT are likewise interrelated.

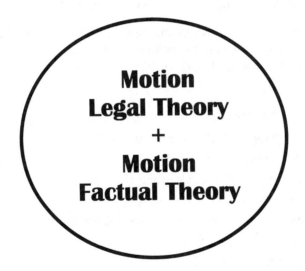

C. Motion Legal Theory

The motion legal theory (MLT) of the moving party parallels the plaintiff's legal theory in the case theory. But, unlike the case theory and its single underlying legal theory, a motion will often be based on several MLTs: a motion to suppress evidence may be brought on the legal basis that no probable cause exists to support the search warrant, there is an overly broad description of the thing to be seized, and the information is insufficient to establish the credibility of an informant. Asserting various motion factual theories (MFTs) will not present a problem if the respective legal theories present consistent stories.

Identifying your MLT

How do you identify the motion legal theory for your case? You begin with your motion objective to control either the information, the final outcome, the procedure, or the participants. With the objective in mind, you work backwards (ends-means thinking) to look for authority for a MLT that can aid you in achieving your objective. This authority may be on your list of typical motions. The following are lists of typical civil and criminal motions that may provide you with the type of motion and legal authority that you may wish to use.

CHECKLIST

Potential Topics for Civil Pretrial Motions

This list of civil motions provides examples of potential motion topics; we believe that such a list can be helpful when brainstorming for possible motions and motion legal theories (MLTs).

Dismiss
- Lack of subject matter—Fed. R. Civ. P. 12(b)(1)
- Lack of personal jurisdiction—Rule 12(b)(2)
- Improper venue—Rule 12(b)(3)
- Improper service of process—Rule 12(b)(5)
- Failure to state a claim—Rule 12(b)(6)
- Failure to join an indispensable party—Rule 12(b)(7)
- Judgment on the pleadings—Rule 12(c)
- Voluntary dismissal—Rule 41(a)
- Involuntary dismissal for failure to prosecute, comply with the rules or a court order

Default judgment—Rule 55(a)
Set aside default judgment—Rule 55(c)
Summary judgment—Rule 56
Pleadings
- Sanction for frivolous pleading—Rule 11
- Strike for redundant, immaterial, impertinent, or scandalous matter—Rule 12(f)
- Add counterclaim—Rule 13(f)
- Amend pleadings—Rule 15
- Add, drop, or substitute a party—Rule 21

- Interplead—Rule 22
- Intervene—Rule 24

Discovery

- Protective order—Rule 26(c)
- Mental or physical examination—Rule 35
- Compel discovery—Rule 37
- Limiting or terminating a deposition

Remedy

- Preliminary injunction—Rule 65(a)
- Temporary restraining order—Rule 65(b)

Trial

- Disqualify the assigned judge
- Alternative dispute resolution
- Venue change
- Jury trial—Rule 39(b)
- Separate trials or bifurcation—Rule 42
- *In limine* matters (e.g., admissibility of expert's opinion)
- Directed verdict

CHECKLIST

Potential Topics for Criminal Pretrial Motions

Like the civil motions list, this list provides examples of potential motion topics—a list can be helpful when brainstorming for possible motions and motion legal theories (MLTs).

Diversion
Venue change
Bail/own recognizance
Competency hearing
Dismissal—speedy trial violation—prearrest delay
Continuance
Appointment of expert
Discovery violation—destruction/loss of evidence
Free transcript
Informant identity

continues ▶

Dismiss—double jeopardy

For a line-up

Reduce felony to misdemeanor

Review preliminary hearing/indictment for lack of probable cause or procedural defects

Severance of counts and/or defendants

Suppression of evidence (search & seizure)

- detention ("stop")
- frisk
- search warrant (place, thing, time, hearsay)
- arrest (with/without warrant)
- search incident to arrest
- search of automobiles
- emergency search
- administrative search
- inventory/booking search plain view
- consent
- taint

Suppress statement of defendant

- *Miranda* violation
- taint
- involuntary statement

Challenge of judge

- cause
- preemptory

Suppress identification suggestive

- unduly suggestive procedure
- failure to provide counsel at post-indictment line-up

In limine evidence matters (e.g., use of prior uncharged acts, use of prior conviction for impeachment, admissibility of novel scientific test)

Identifying the Standard Motion Legal Theory— An Illustration

Now let's apply the method for identifying a motion legal theory. Recall the *Alby* automobile case from the pleading chapter.

The *Alby* Case

Story

On June 15, 20XX Alby and Clark Brady were driving on Interstate Highway 5 in the State of Major. Brady crashed into the rear of Alby's red sports car. The week before the crash, Alby made an appointment to have his gas pedal adjusted. At the scene, Alby told the police that his car abruptly slowed down. Both Alby and Brady suffered personal injuries and property damage. Brady was given a breathalyzer test at the scene and registered a .25 blood-alcohol level. The state highway police issued a citation to Brady for violation of State of Major motor vehicle code section 14.0, which provides "it is unlawful to operate a motor vehicle while intoxicated. . . . Presumption of intoxication is .08."

As plaintiff's counsel your case objective is to obtain a judgment that the defendant is liable. You review the list of standard civil motions and conclude that you will bring a motion for summary judgment on the issue of liability. Specifically, you will seek summary judgment on your claim of negligence per se, i.e., driving while intoxicated in violation of a state statute. Your MLT tracks the local procedural rule for summary judgment—"That there is no genuine issue on any material fact and that the moving party is entitled to judgment as a matter of law." This local rule is in accord with Fed. R. Civ. P. 56(c). Your motion factual theory is based on an affidavit by the police officer stating that the defendant had a .25 breathalyzer. Under the statute in this jurisdiction, evidence of a .08 breathalyzer establishes an irrebuttable presumption of intoxication in criminal cases, and you plan to ask the court in your motion to take judicial notice of the driving-while-intoxicated statute. Coupled with the .25 breathalyzer, you believe your chances for winning the motion are excellent.

Creating a Non-Standard Motion

You may, however, have to look beyond your motion list and create a non-standard motion from a synthesis of existing authority and analogy. This creative approach to motions is again analogous to our pleading examples in Chapter 7, where we developed cutting-edge claims, parties, and relief. In this regard, imagine you want a psychiatrist to interview your criminal client under sodium amytol. The problem is your client is in jail, and the jail has no facility for such an interview. Your objective falls under the "control of information" category. Specifically, you need to obtain the information your client might give under the drug-induced interview; but no existing motion of which you are aware is available to achieve this end. So you begin to create.

But, remember, even your created motion must be based on a legal theory that the court can rely on and consider. In fact, virtually all presentations to the court have legal and factual theories. You know that your client has a Sixth Amendment right to counsel and a Fifth Amendment right to put on a defense. You know that in various cases courts have found experts to be a necessary part of the attorney-client relationship and that statutes implicitly recognize the importance of experts by providing funds for indigents to obtain experts whom the court finds appropriate. Mixing all these fragments together with your need still in mind, you might create "A Motion for Temporary Release (to Ensure Defendant's Fifth and Sixth Amendment Rights to a Fair Trial)." This would provide the objective and would be your motion to remove your client to some hospital for the interview on the grounds that it is the only way to obtain information that must necessarily be obtained if you are to function as an effective Sixth Amendment counsel and your client is to realize his or her rights under the due process clause of the Fifth Amendment to bring forth a defense.

Putting a Standard Motion to a Creative Use

At other times, your case objective may instead lead you to put an existing motion to creative use. Imagine a criminal case in which your client is a co-defendant. Early in the case, you have determined that a plea bargain is the most likely outcome and that you have a case objective falling again under the "control of information" category to establish for the prosecutor (court, probation officer, investigating police officer) that your client's culpability is less than that of the co-defendants. With this need in mind, information emphasizing your client's peripheral role and relatively lower culpability in the matter could be brought out in such standard motions as a motion for release on personal recognizance or bail reduction or motion to dismiss a complaint at a preliminary hearing for lack of cause.

D. Motion Factual Theory

Like the factual theory underlying the case theory, the "story" that makes up the MFT supports the motion. This factual information in a criminal motion will usually be presented to the court through testimony at a motion's evidentiary hearing, a declaration, or an offer of proof. In a civil motion, the MFT usually is presented in declarations, deposition transcripts, affidavits, and other exhibits submitted to the court along with the motion. Similar to the factual theory prong of a case theory, the MFT must be both factually sufficient and persuasive or, to look at it another way, be able to withstand attacks upon factual sufficiency and persuasiveness by your opponent.

Factually Sufficient

In the context of an MFT, we are using factual sufficiency as a rough analogy to how that term is used when discussing the case theory. Unlike the situation with the case theory, lack of factual sufficiency in your MFT will not subject you to a formal motion to dismiss. Rather, the court will likely just find your motion lacks merit and deny it and any request for an evidentiary hearing. This is not a desirable result. You will have wasted your client's money, potentially injured your overall credibility in the case, and lost even the opportunity for achieving possible sub-objectives (put witnesses on the stand and test their credibility, find out further information). Therefore, generally you should present sufficient facts to avoid a denial of your motion. However, certain motions do not require a factual record. See III A at page 386.

Persuasiveness

Even if the court finds your MFT to be factually sufficient, you must still persuade the court to rule in your favor. Just as the factual case theory, the MFT must fulfill the concerns of quantity and quality discussed in the context of case theory (see pages 23-30). You must persuade the court that your argument has merit.

Logic and Human Values

The "story" underlying the MFT must make logical sense. Accordingly, it must comport with human experience, that is, it must make common sense. Also, when developing an MFT, the story should tie into the underlying legal rationale (gleaned directly from cases, common sense, implications in the doctrine, treatises) that supports the MLT. The judge deciding a motion will be mindful of making a legal decision, although factual findings may be determinative of the issue. To the extent you can focus the judge on values that transcend the individual case by linking your story to underlying policy rationales in the law that is embodied in the MLT, the court is likely to take your position far more seriously.

E. Responding to a Party's Motion Theory

So much for a moving party's MLT, but what about that of a responding party? The formation of a responding party's MLT exactly parallels the development of the defense legal theory discussed in Chapter 2.

- **Attacking the moving party's MLT**—A responding party can attack the moving party's MLT for legality ("This motion claims the client was denied the right to an attorney in the grand jury room, but there is no such right") and procedural insufficiency ("This motion was not filed within required time limits;" "This is not the proper court to hear this motion").

- **Attacking the moving party's MFT**—Or a responding party can attack the proponent's MFT for persuasive sufficiency ("There is simply not much evidence that the officer did anything but treat the defendant with respect when he questioned him, let alone coercively took the statement") and for something akin to factual sufficiency ("It is simply hard for me to believe that the 70-minute delay in letting counsel see the client in the jail can constitute a total denial of effective counsel in this case").

- **Affirmative defense to the motion**—Moreover, a respondent can raise what is, in effect, an affirmative defense—for example, in opposing a motion to compel discovery, a party might argue, "The moving party is not entitled to what would otherwise be discoverable information in this case since my client can rely on the patient-psychiatrist privilege (which in this situation is an affirmative defense to the motion for production) to resist this motion." Analogously, in the case of a defense suppression motion, once it is established that there was no warrant and the burden of justifying the search shifts to the government, the government, if it is not to lose the motion, must in effect establish the affirmative defense that every factor that constitutes probable cause is met.

On the other hand, you may agree that the motion has merit and that you will not oppose it. To cancel the hearing on the motion, inform opposing counsel of your position. An agreed order can be prepared by opposing counsel, signed by you and then submitted to the motion's judge.

F. Putting the Process Together—The Motion Theory—An Illustration

Let's apply all of these processes by developing a motion theory. We'll use the hypothetical *Portage Bay News* robbery case you first encountered in the Pleadings Chapter 7. The defendant was stopped by the police based on a general description by the victim, and subsequently was identified by the victim.

The *Portage Bay News* Case

Story

Portage Bay News is a popular newspaper and magazine shop. It is open 24 hours a day. At about 11:30 p.m. on January 15th of this year, Cory Kostich, the clerk, noticed a man, who had been browsing at the magazine rack, approach the counter. No one else was in the store. The man, who wore a red vest and had his baseball hat pulled down, laid the magazine he was carrying on the counter, put his hand into his coat pocket, and demanded cash from the register. The clerk handed over the money, and the man fled on foot. At 1:30 a.m. on the 16th a police officer arrested Jeff Lukens because he matched the general description given by Mr. Kostich and wore a red vest and baseball hat. The officer drove the suspect Lukens to the store where Kostich identified Lukens as the robber. A partial print on the magazine matched the fingerprint of the twenty-three year old defendant, Jeff Lukens, who has a lengthy juvenile criminal history for shoplifts and a robbery.

Legal Theory

This time imagine you represent the defendant Jeff Lukens, and, because of some shadowy memory from law school criminal procedure, your intuitive sense is that there is something wrong with the way the identification was conducted, and recognizing that this event was a crucial evidentiary juncture in the case, you sense that some motion may be indicated. But what will be your MLT?

Start searching for possible MLTs and look back and forth between the facts and your list of typical motions at pages 377-78. The "Motion to Suppress an Identification" on your list comports with the idea that something might be wrong with the identification procedure. Focused research, made possible by this first level of analysis, will result in refinement. Your legal research has revealed that identifications can be suppressed on a number of grounds ("taint" from an illegal seizure, a witness is otherwise incompetent, the identification procedure was unduly suggestive, no attorney was present at a post-indictment line-up). Which ground applies to this motion? When you look back to your facts the "unduly suggestive identification procedure" ground tentatively seems to be the most appropriate source for an MLT.

Your research uncovers the leading case in the state of Major, *State v. Maenhout. Maenhout* holds that the burden is on the defendant to establish that a show-up procedure was suggestive and if that is proven, then the judge must decide whether that suggestiveness caused a substantial likelihood of irreparable misidentification. The court's decision is to be guided by several factors—now referred to as the "*Maenhout* factors"—including: the witness's opportunity to view the suspect at the time of the crime, the accuracy of the initial description of the suspect, the degree of certainty expressed by the witness at the time of the initial identification, and the span of time between the crime and the identification. If the court concludes that there is a "substantial likelihood of irreparable misidentification," then the in-court identification will be suppressed.

You know that without the victim's in-court identification, the prosecution will not have sufficient evidence to go to the jury on the element of identification. Accordingly, your objective is to keep this vital information out of evidence. A suppression motion can achieve this objective. The evidentiary hearing on the motion can also provide you with a general assessment of the credibility of the victim and information for impeachment. In this example, your tentative MLT would be that the in-court identification should be suppressed because it was the result of a suggestive identification procedure, violative of due process. The elements of this MLT would be that you can establish that (1) the government used identification procedures (2) that were so suggestive (3) as to lead to a reasonable likelihood of irreparable misidentification.

Factual Theory

Factual Sufficiency

In your proposed motion, you probably will be able to amass sufficient facts as to each element of the legal theory so as to credibly raise this motion: (1) The government used identification procedures (the police conducted a show-up of the suspect on the street), (2) the procedures were suggestive (the defendant was by himself, handcuffed, in front of a police car, flanked by police, and wearing a red vest), and (3) the procedures were likely to lead to irreparable misidentification (the victim did not get a long look at the robber, the robber's face was partially covered by a baseball hat, the victim gave only a general description). So much for factual sufficiency.

Persuasiveness

Now, how are you going to make all this persuasive within applicable burdens of proof? The court is not going to be eager to throw out the prosecution's case, which would be the result of granting the motion. Your story, therefore, should try to present its component information in such a way that, comporting with common sense, the information is tied to the underlying policy rationale that justifies such an MLT in the first place. In the present case, the underlying rationale involves our concern that suggestive identification procedures could result in the conviction of innocent people—a human value that will persuade the judge. With this in mind, your story might be that that your client is innocent and was misidentified and that the procedures of the show-up were so suggestive that the victim was misled into identifying your client as the robber, which could result in the conviction of your innocent client. For a further discussion how to write and argue the motion persuasively see pages 393-96 and 399-409.

G. Motion Theme

After you have settled upon both the motion legal and factual theories, you should formulate a motion theme. Some attorneys refer to it as the "hook" because in a jury trial context, the theme catches the juror's attention and pulls them back to the proponent's case theory. The theme is used to persuade. It is a short statement, phrase, or even a single word that encapsulates an analytic framework—a legal theory that will compel the result you want to achieve with your motion. This theme is the core of your motion. You will use it in both your written motion and your oral argument. While a trial theme directed at a jury is normally factually based (e.g., "this is a case about greed"), a motion theme aimed at the judge should be based on the legal theory and its application to the case. If possible, you will want to work in the public policies that drive the rationale. For example, in the robbery case, the theme could be: "Your Honor, the in-court identification should be suppressed because the show-up was so suggestive that it was inevitable that the victim, who didn't get a good view of the robber, would misidentify Mr. Lukens as the robber." This theme incorporates the two values that are persuasive to the motion's judge: fairness in the show-up identification procedure and justice—not convicting an innocent, misidentified person. These values in turn are linked to the rationale underpinning the *Maenhout* decision. Put simply, the theme summarizes your motion theory, and if the judge agrees with your theme, the judge will be compelled to rule favorably on your motion.

H. Relationship Between the Motion Theory and Case Theory

The sole purpose of a particular motion may be to help your case theory by obtaining information for your factual theory (your story), or by keeping out information helpful to your opponent's theory. Or the issues underlying a motion may directly parallel issues in the case. For example, suppose you brought a motion to keep a crucial document out of evidence on the ground that its method of preparation was too unreliable to permit the document to qualify as a business record. If successful, this would support an attack on the persuasive (and perhaps even factual) sufficiency of the opposing party's case.

III. MAKING THE FACTUAL RECORD

A. The Burden and the Type of Record

Civil motions ordinarily are presented on paper with the facts set out by declarations, affidavits, deposition transcript excerpts and other documents. Some civil motions do not require a factual record. For instance, a motion for dismissal for failure to state a claim under Fed. R. Civ. P. 12(b)(6) can be made on the pleadings, and no factual record need be made. However, if a factual record is required, the next question is who has the burden to establish the factual record. In the *Portage Bay News* robbery case, the *Maenhout* decision places the burden on the defense to establish a suggestive procedure in order to support its motion to suppress the in-court identification.

Fundamentally, two types of factual records are made to support a motion. First, both civil and criminal motions may be supported by documents. Second, a criminal motion may call for an evidentiary hearing where witnesses are called and exhibits admitted.

B. Documentary Factual Record

Typically the factual record is composed of documents attached to the motion. For example, in the *Alby* automobile accident case, the plaintiff moved for summary judgment on the grounds that no genuine issue of material fact existed on whether the defendant was negligent per se when a breathalyzer over .08 establishes an irrebuttable presumption of intoxication. That motion could be supported by a police officer affidavit stating that the defendant had a .25 breathalyzer and that the breathalyzer was in proper working order.

The documents need to meet evidentiary requirements. Fed. R. Civ. P. 56(e), dealing with summary judgments, provides that "(s)upporting and opposing affidavits shall be made on personal knowledge, shall set forth such facts as would be admissible in evidence, and shall show affirmatively that the affiant is competent to testify to the matters stated therein." If the document is self-authenticating (e.g., a public record), nothing is required to establish its authentication. However, if an evidentiary foundation must be laid to prove the authentication, an affidavit needs to be prepared. For instance, to use a handwritten letter as an exhibit for the motion, an affidavit by the author of the letter stating that she authored it or an affidavit by a person who could swear that it is the author's signature would suffice to prove the letter's authenticity. Besides authentication, the document must satisfy other evidentiary requirements. For instance, a witness's account in the document should be from first-hand knowledge and should not recount inadmissible hearsay.

Documents that may be attached to the motion include:

- **Affidavit or Declaration**—An affidavit is a witness statement sworn to under oath. The affidavit is a statement in lieu of witness testimony in court. The factual recitations should be drafted with evidentiary rules in mind. A declaration is a witness's statement declaring that the information contained in it are true under penalty of perjury. Generally an affidavit and declaration can be used interchangeably unless rules or statutes provide otherwise.

- **Discovery Responses**—The responses to discovery requests by the opposing party, e.g., the answers to interrogatories, may be attached to the motion.

- **Depositions**—Copies of relevant pages from a deposition may be submitted with the motion. Highlight the segments of the deposition that you want the judge to read.

- **Exhibits**—Other documents, including photographs, public records, and witness statements among others, may be attached to the motion and given an exhibit letter or number (e.g., Exhibit A). Usually, these documents are copies. To authenticate this type of documentation as well as the portions of depositions and unsigned discovery responses, an affidavit or declaration of the attorney may be used to prove that they are true and correct copies and are authentic.

C. Evidentiary Hearing Factual Record

Motions call for evidentiary hearings, particularly when it is necessary to have the judge evaluate the credibility of witnesses. Criminal cases, which do not have extensive pretrial documentation, such as depositions and responses to requests for discovery, call for an evidentiary hearing to establish details of an event (a search or the taking of a confession). Civil motions for preliminary injunctions can often result in an evidentiary hearing. An evidentiary hearing could be conducted in the *Portage Bay News* robbery case to lay the factual record for the suppression of identification motion.

Evidentiary hearings are like a mini-trial. Thus, they involve many basic trial skills that are not dealt with extensively in this chapter. We do, however, provide some guidance. Parallels to presenting evidence at a hearing can be drawn to preparation of witnesses for trial, Chapter 6 at pages 152-56 and examination of witnesses at a preservation deposition, Chapter 9 at pages 306-10.

IV. A HEARING ON THE MOTION

There are several procedural concerns to consider when you want to get your motion heard. Will you note the motion with the court clerk or have it set in open court by the judge? Is there a minimum number of days' notice that you must give opposing counsel prior to a hearing on the motion? Can this time be shortened by the judge? Under what circumstances and criteria will the court shorten the time? Must all pretrial motions be set for one hearing? If such a single setting is not mandatory, what are the advantages and disadvantages for your position of having the individual motions heard at separate times?

To properly get your motion heard you need to know the procedural requirements for filing, calendaring, and presenting motions. From reading local court rules and discussing procedural concerns with other attorneys and court clerks, you can learn the procedures for proof of service, orders shortening time, declarations and exhibits, and subpoenaing witnesses to an evidentiary hearing.

Just because counsel wishes a hearing does not mean that counsel will get one. The court may decide the matter on the written motion and response. If a hearing is set, it may involve the presentment of evidence, as discussed above. Whether or not evidence is presented, the motion's judge will hear argument of counsel. Moving counsel argues first, followed by responding counsel, and then the moving attorney will be given a chance to offer a rebuttal. If the court has a time limit, the moving attorney should at the outset of argument ask to reserve time for rebuttal.

A. Filing and Service

Ordinarily, the motion is filed with the court clerk. Some court rules have authorized electronic filing. Fed. R. Civ. P. 5(e) provides that a court can permit "papers to be filed, signed, or verified by electronic means. . . " The federal system, for instance, is designed to accept only Portable Document Format (PDF) electronic files.

Fed. R. Civ. P. 5 governs service of a motion. Many state rules are patterned after this rule. All parties must be served with the motion. In some instances, defendant parties, such as government officials, require special service, so you should consult the court rules. If the other party is represented, service is upon counsel. The service may be done by first-class U.S. mail or delivery to the attorney's office of record.

B. Conference with Opposing Counsel

Before a motion will be heard, the applicable court rule may require that the moving attorney confer with opposing counsel. The intent of the rule is to alleviate busy court dockets by encouraging counsel to resolve matters when possible. The rule will usually require that the motion be accompanied by a statement by counsel that either a conference took place or that an attempt was made to conference along with a description of what attempt was made.

C. Single Hearing or Separately

Generally, whether to calendar all your motions for a single hearing or separately involves a variety of concerns. If all motions are brought at once, the court may have difficulty focusing on individual motions. If a large number of motions are brought together, the court may become impatient or bored and deal with each on a rather summary level or just provide some rulings for one party, some to the other so the process will feel fair. To combat this, you can try to submit less important motions on the papers (only in written form) and limit your argument and presentation to a few, significant motions (requesting a hearing on these important motions). Fed. R. Civ. P. 16(b)(2 and (15) govern scheduling and planning for motions. The court might set schedules for motions. Also, the local rules of the district and the practice of the judge, according to judge memoranda, will govern motion procedure.

On the other hand, if you bring the motions separately (assuming that you can), the court may be annoyed that you are dealing with the motions in piecemeal fashion or may not give you much time because yours is just one motion in the middle of an entire day's motion calendar (i.e., the court will not have set aside a separate block of time for just hearing your motions). Generally, it's a good idea to first check with court personnel to determine the judge's preference. Remember, however, that if you have a choice, the tactical decision is yours to make. Of course, the court's preference in the matter will be a factor that will weigh heavily in that choice.

D. Notice of Motion

The moving attorney who wants a hearing before the judge assigned to the case or the motion's judge will need to schedule a hearing date and time with the court and give notice to the other parties. The attorney will normally serve the Notice of Motion (see page 416 for an example) along with the motion. Fed. R. Civ. P. 6(d) provides that the notice must be served not later than five days before the hearing.

The court may have a judge assigned to hear motions or the trial judge may have a day of the week or a time of day set aside to hear motions. Under any of these situations, the moving attorney contacts the court's clerk and sets the day and time of the motion before preparing the Notice of Motion. In some federal courts, the court, rather than counsel, notifies the parties.

V.   WRITING THE COMPELLING MOTION OR RESPONSE

A.   The Essential Baker's Dozen Elements

Although the precise form required for a motion will vary with the particular motion and jurisdiction, and while you must always check local court rules regarding proper paper size, typeface, spacing, indexes, and so on, the elements that make up a motion are fairly standard. A sample civil motion and other documents are included at the end of this chapter (pages 416-24) to illustrate these elements. Essentially when filing a motion there will be the Notice of Motion, the Motion, a Memorandum of Law, a Proposed Order, and Proof of Service. The elements of a response to a motion correspond to these elements, except of course the responding attorney need not prepare a notice for the motion or a motion

1.   Heading and Caption

The name of the court to which you are addressing the motion appears as the heading at the top of the first page of the motion. The caption is placed just below this heading and is made up of several parts. On the left side of the page, the names of the parties are listed just as they are in the complaint. On the right side, the case number, which will be assigned by the court clerk when the complaint is filed, appears. Directly under the case number, the name of the document being filed appears (e.g., Motion for Protective Order; Declaration of B.Y. Davis in Support of Defendant Proust's Motion for a Protective Order). See page 417. Note, however, that in some jurisdictions, in addition to this information or as an alternative, the attorney lists on the first page of the motion all the documents that are being presented to the court.

2.   Notice of Motion

The notice, which is a separate document, establishes the date, time, and courtroom for the hearing on the motion and also states the nature of the motion. See pages 416-17.

3. Motion and Memorandum of Law

The motion itself describes the nature of the request. It also includes a statement of the record on which the motion will be based and may include a summary statement of the grounds for the motion. Fed. R. Civ. P. 7(b) provides that the motion must "state with particularity the ground therefor" and the relief requested.

The statements, argument, and conclusion (numbers 5-10 below) are components of the document supporting the motion, and they usually are set out in this order. Depending upon the applicable procedural rules, the components may be part of the motion document itself or may be a separate document.

While these components are somewhat uniform, the order of the components is not. Many lawyers organize documents in the sequence suggested above. However, as the sample civil motion illustrates, there are other possibilities. Thus, in the sample motion below the Statement of the Case and the Statement of Facts are contained as subheadings within the Memorandum of Law (page 420). The exhibits follow the motion, but precede the Memorandum. This structure is certainly acceptable. Unless there is a particular court rule that governs, your actual construction of the motion should be guided by local rule and custom and the effectiveness of the presentation.

4. Signature

Ordinarily, the attorney making the motion and all other pleadings must sign the document. Under Fed. R. Civ. P. 11(a), the attorney's signature assures the court that the attorney has made a reasonable investigation and inquiry of law and fact and that the motion is for a proper purpose. If the motion is filed for improper purposes (e.g., delay), Fed. R. Civ. P. 11 (c) provides for the imposition of sanctions upon the offending attorney.

5. Relief Requested

This statement of the relief requested, usually at the outset of the memorandum of law tells the court what the moving party is seeking from the court and the rule or statute that authorizes it. See "Memorandum of Law in Support of Defendant Proust's Motion for Protective Order" at page 420.

6. Statement of Case

A statement sets out the procedural history. This statement is generally rather summary, but it may be a crucial section if the issue is grounded in the procedural history of the case (e.g., a double jeopardy motion). See "Memorandum of Law in Support of Defendant Proust's Motion for Protective Order" at page 420.

7. Statement of Facts

The Statement of Facts is usually contained in the memorandum of law or in the motion itself. In constructing this statement, you may use only facts supported in the existing case record (to which you should specifically refer) or in the attachments filed with the motion, which you cite to. See "Memorandum or Law in Support of Defendant Proust's Motion for Protective Order" at page 421.

8. Statement of the Issues

This section of the legal memorandum states the issues that the court is to decide. See "Memorandum of Law in Support of Defendant Proust's Motion for Protective Order" at page 421.

9. Argument

The citation of applicable legal authorities and your arguments based on the law supported by your statement of the factual record. See "Memorandum of Law in Support of Defendant Proust's Motion for Protective Order" at page 422.

10. Conclusion

A brief summary of the remedy you are seeking from the court and the persuasive rationale for that request. See "Memorandum of Law in Support of Defendant Proust's Motion for Protective Order" at page 423.

11. Attachments

Attachments are the documents upon which you are making your factual claims. According to court rule and practice, these attachments are usually attached to the motion or bound separately and labeled. Attachments may include: affidavits, declarations, documents, records, offers of proof, excerpts from transcripts, and so on. Note that if the transcript or any other document is already part of the case record, technically you do not have to include it in your motion. Nonetheless, you may still want to include it for the court's convenience, for emphasis, or for some other tactical consideration, and you may want to highlight the portions of the case record that are significant to your arguments. See, e.g., page 422. However, keep in mind that some courts will not permit you, as the attorney, to assert facts in an affidavit or declaration since it would be likely to put you in the unethical position of being a witness in a case where you are the attorney. Rather, some courts view an attorney declaration as more properly a vehicle for recounting the procedural posture of the case and the exhibits that are being attached to the motion ("I am submitting in support of this motion Exhibit A, the declaration of Dr. Frances, the treating psychologist").

12. Proposed Order

Most jurisdictions require that you prepare and include a copy of the written order, if any, you are seeking from the court. Also, a self-addressed stamped return envelope may be required. Even if a draft order is not required, you may wish to include an order to expedite matters if the court rules in your favor. See page 419.

13. Proof of Service

Proof of service generally appears on an approved court form. It will establish the proof of service of a copy of your motion papers—by personal service or by mail—on all persons entitled to such service (generally, opposing counsel). See page 424.

The Response

The response to the motion will be composed of many but not all of the same components. Typical components are the memorandum of law in opposition to the motion (with correct caption, request for relief, statement of the case, statement of the facts, statement of the issues, argument, and conclusion, together with attachments), proposed order, and proof of service. The local court rules must be consulted to determine the time within which a response must be served and filed.

B. Telling a Persuasive Story—The Statement of Facts

Either in your motion or in the memorandum of law supporting the motion is a section for the statement of the facts. A responding memorandum of law in opposition to the motion will also have a section for the statement of facts. In this you should include a statement of the overall facts in the case. A statement of facts should not be argumentative and therefore should not state conclusions. It is nevertheless a piece of advocacy and should be organized in such a way as to be persuasive in support of your position on the motion. The following are the ingredients of a factually sufficient and persuasive statement of facts.

Factually Sufficient

First and foremost, the story that you write in the statement of facts should be sufficient to support your legal theory. In drafting this section, you can be guided by the elements of your motion legal theory. In the *Portage Bay News* robbery case, you would refer to *State v. Maenhout*, the controlling case. Your would tell the story of your client Jeff Lukens being arrested, taken to the store, and shown to the victim in an unduly suggestive manner. You would also cover the judicially relevant *Maenhout* factors that the judge should consider if the judge were to find that the show-up identification procedures were impermissibly suggestive, that is, the witness's opportunity to view the suspect at the time of the crime, the accuracy of the initial description of the suspect, the degree of certainty expressed by the witness at the time of the initial identification, and the span of time between the crime and the identification.

Persuasive Storytelling

The Two Critical Characteristics

The two most important characteristics of persuasive storytelling, as we have stated previously, are that it recounts the story about human values that the audience, here the motion's judge, cares about and shares and that it is a human story. The values that you communicate in the rendition of the story should be linked to the rationale for your legal theory. For example, remember that our legal theory in the robbery case is that suggestive identification procedures can lead to misidentification and the conviction of an innocent person. Obviously no decent judge wants an innocent person to be convicted. The human story in the robbery case is the story of Jeff Lukens being arrested just because he matched the general description of the robber and wore a red vest and baseball hat. The more you can bring the defendant to life in telling that story the better.

Storytelling Techniques

Judges, like everyone else, can be engaged by a story well told; they can also be bored by a dull recitation of facts. Capture the judge's attention at the outset of the factual statement. One way to do this is to find the critical and interesting factual situation and begin with that. Think about techniques used in movies—that are used to tell a story and engage an audience. You can flash forward or flash back. After that, use a chronological account because it will be easy to follow. Stick to facts essential to deciding the legal issue. This will also please the judge pressed by a heavy docket. Busy judges appreciate brevity. Then, again, emphasize the critical characteristics. Tell a story that is value-based. Tell a human story. As an illustration of some of these techniques you might read the factual argument on the Portage Bay News case at page 401.

C. Framing the Issues—The Statement of Issues

The goal is to frame the issue so that if the court agrees with how you view it, a ruling in your favor will follow. The statement of the issue should not just identify the legal issue. For example in the *Portage Bay News* case, a traditional statement of the issue might be:

> Whether the pretrial identification procedure was so suggestive that it created a substantial likelihood of irreparable misidentification?

While this is a succinct and accurate statement, it tells the court little about the case at hand. However, in the *Portage Bay News* case, the defense view is that the circumstances under which the victim viewed the robber were such that a risk of misidentification existed and then the police show-up was so suggestive that it caused the misidentification of the innocent defendant as the robber. To convey this in formulating the issue, you can include what you consider the pivotal facts into the issue statement. Because the *Maenhout* decision dictates a two-step analysis, the statement of issues might parallel the analysis and contain two issues, such as:

> Issue 1: Was the police identification procedure of showing the defendant to the victim when the defendant was handcuffed, in front of a police car, flanked by two police officers, and dressed in a vest similar to the one worn by the robber to the victim unduly suggestive?
>
> Issue 2: Did this show-up identification procedure create a substantial likelihood of irreparable misidentification when the robbery

victim had seen the robber for only a brief time and when the robber's face was partially covered by a baseball hat?

Framing the issues in this way is intended to persuade the court to answer "Yes" and to rule in your favor if the court adopts the logic.

D. Arguing the Law—The Argument Section

Aristotelian Appeals

Aristotle, who lived from 384–322 BC, promulgated the concept of three appeals that may be used to convince an audience. These three appeals have stood the test of time. In drafting both your factual and legal statements, you should concentrate on using all three appeals because they are what sway an audience.

ARISTOTELIAN ARGUMENT

The *Portage Bay News* Case

- Logos—The first appeal is logic. Logical arguments stress patterns of thought, rational thinking, and a sense of logic. A motion's judges will rule on a motion by applying the law to the facts—a logical process. Therefore, arguments appealing to logic and the law are the centerpiece of a motion's argument. In the robbery case, you can structure your argument in the logical pattern prescribed by the Maenhout decision.

- Ethos—The second appeal is an ethical appeal. When making this argument, you appeal to the audience's highest moral sense. The argument speaks in terms of truth, duty, honor, justice, generosity, mercy, and the like. In your factual statement and legal arguments in the Portage Bay News case, you can repeatedly return to the unfairness of the identification procedure and how it led to the unjust identification and potential conviction of your client and robbery charge.

- Pathos—Pathos, the emotional appeal, is the third type of argument. Of course, you cannot improperly appeal to the passion and prejudice of your audience whether judge or jury. While inexperienced lawyers often think that logical arguments are all that are important in arguing a motion (after all, rational appellate decisions are the core of law school education), they soon learn that that is not the case. Judges are human too. Justice William O. Douglas (1898-1980) once observed: "At

---

> the constitutional level where we work, 90 percent of any decision is emotional. The rational part of us supplies the reasons for supporting our predilections." When your facts are emotional and shed light on the case, they provide a strong appeal to the court. The emotional appeal in the robbery case is the risk of incarceration of your innocent client.

Syllogistic Argument

The syllogistic structure of argument is well accepted. The classic syllogism is:

1. All men are mortal.
2. Aristotle is a man.
3. Therefore, Aristotle is mortal.

The syllogism begins with the all-encompassing premise. The second statement puts the fact within the proposition. This leads to the logical conclusion. Customarily, arguments in support of motions begin with the controlling law. Then, that law is applied to the facts of the case, leading to the logical conclusion. In the *Portage Bay News* case, the argument might be stated in this way.

> ## SYLLOGISTIC ARGUMENT
> ### The *Portage Bay News* Case
>
> 1. If the *Maenhout* factors indicate that there was a substantial likelihood of irreparable misidentification, the in-court identification should be suppressed.
> 2. When the *Maenhout* factors are applied to the *Portage Bay News* case, they indicate that there was a substantial likelihood of irreparable misidentification of Jeff Lukens.
> 3. Therefore, the in-court identification of Jeff Lukens should be suppressed.

E.   Interweaving the Theme

As with the old adage of "Vote early, vote often," state your theme early and often. The judge will appreciate the early statement particularly if your motion theme tells the court not only the basis of your motion but also what you are seeking from the court. Your goal is to provide the court with a legal analysis that will lead to a favorable result. At the same time, ideally you want to communicate the value that is the basis of the rationale for the legal analysis and for your factual theory. Remember the theme in the robbery case was tied to the values of fairness in how identification procedures are conducted and justice in not convicting an innocent person:

> "Your Honor, any in-court identification should be suppressed because the show-up procedure was so suggestive that it was inevitable that the victim, who didn't get a good view of the robber, would misidentify Mr. Lukens as the robber."

The Memorandum of Law in support of your motion could begin with this theme statement used to express the Relief Requested from the court:

> "Defendant Jeff Lukens moves for suppression of any in-court identification because the show-up identification procedure used here was so unduly suggestive that it created a substantial likelihood of irreparable misidentification."

The Statement of Issues (above), and the Argument and Conclusion sections of the brief provide other opportunities to repeat the theme.

F.   Writing Style, Structure, and Gaffs

Writing is a demanding endeavor, requiring an understanding of grammar, punctuation, sentence structure, and much more than can be comprehensively discussed in this chapter. Nevertheless, certain writing requirements are so vital for a well-written memorandum of law, that we provide a checklist here:

✔ **CHECKLIST**

Writing Requirements

- **Accuracy**—Nothing can mar a motion or response to a motion more than a misstatement of law, fact, or anything else for that matter. If you cannot be relied upon for accuracy, the judge will most likely view you with distrust.
- **Clarity of Expression**—Use the simple declarative sentence. It will lend clarity to your written work. Use everyday English. Avoid legalisms ("Comes now," "wherefore," "the aforementioned") that will distract the

reader. The active voice is better than passive (He wrote the motion. Not: The motion was written by him).

- **Avoid Hyperbole**—Cull out exaggerations. Most unnecessary adjectives and adverbs should be promptly edited out, e.g., "very," "the worst," "the most egregious."
- **Proofread**—Too often the written work provided to judges suffers from typographical and other clerical errors. After the document is in a final form, spell and grammar check it. Then, set the document aside and come back to it later with fresh eyes and proofread again. Usually, you will be surprised to discover an obvious error in the text that you thought was ready to publish. Pay particular attention to titles, headers, and other important words since these are most often the words in which an error occurs.
- **Proper Citations**—The Bluebook provides the proper way to cite and should be adhered to. Certain states have citation form rules, e.g.., Texas, that must be complied with.
- **Avoid Personal Attacks**—Judges do not look favorably upon acrimony between counsel. If you are the victim of such an attack, rise above it because the court will not appreciate a retaliatory personal response.
- **Cite Contrary Authority**—See Ethical Considerations at pages 410-11.
- **Meet Deadlines**—Motions practice, like most other aspects of pretrial and trial work, is fraught with deadlines that must be met. Failure to meet a deadline for submission of a motion or response may result in striking the motion, sanctions being imposed, possibly even civil liability (e.g., for failure to pursue a motion), and damage to the lawyer's reputation. To avoid the all-too-common problem of tardiness, adopt the practice of setting your own deadline for completion of your work that is far enough in advance of the court or other exterior imposed deadline with enough time to complete the work if something unexpected happens (e.g., your computer system malfunctions).

VI. PERSUASIVELY ARGUING THE MOTION OR RESPONSE

A. The Beginning—Get the Judge's Attention

The Rule of Primacy holds that what is heard first will register well with the listener. Therefore, the first minute or so of the oral argument on the motion should be carefully designed to communicate your theme and capture the judge's attention. Because opening remarks are some of the most important words in oral advocacy, it is good practice to write them out, edit them, and then rehearse them until you can deliver them naturally and with confidence. By preparing well, you will also lessen your nervousness.

Normally, a busy judge will appreciate it if you get to the essence of your motion or response and tell the court what you are seeking and why it is the right thing for the court to do right at the start.

After the judge or clerk has called the case ("The next case on the calendar is a motion to suppress in *State v. Lukens*. Are the parties ready?") The court may ask counsel to identify themselves and who they represent. If the court does not ask, do so when you begin the argument unless the judge knows you. For instance, the opening remarks in the robbery could mirror the theme expressed in the written motion:

THE BEGINNING

The *Portage Bay News* Case

"Your Honor, my name is Monique Thompson, and I represent Jeff Lukens who has been charged with robbery. [If the court has a time limit, add—"May I reserve five minutes for rebuttal?"] The motion before you requests that you suppress any in-court identification of my client. The police one-person show-up in this case was so suggestive that it was inevitable that the victim, who didn't get a good view of the robber at the time of the crime, would misidentify Mr. Lukens as the robber."

B. The Middle—Use Compelling Legal and Factual Arguments

Organization

The organization of the body of the argument should usually begin with the strongest argument point. This will put your best foot forward on the merits of your motion or response. Do not devote much time to weaker arguments, and better yet, avoid them altogether. The best practice is to get to the heart of it—those persuasive arguments that in your judgment will cause the judge to rule in your favor.

Factual Argument

In the body of the argument, a factual argument may be made. But, lengthy recitations of facts distract from the persuasiveness of the argument. The court has had an opportunity to read the motion and supporting or responding memorandum laying out the facts. Rather, the factual argument may be crafted to be brief, emphasize only essential facts, and communicate the values that will appeal to the bench.

For instance, in the robbery case the values are the unfairness of the show-up and the need to serve justice by ensuring that an innocent person is not convicted. The argument might go something like this:

FACTUAL ARGUMENT

The *Portage Bay News* Case

"My client, Mr. Lukens, is accused of robbery. His real crime is wearing a red down vest. Anyone among the tens of thousands of men in this city who are my client's size would be facing trial today if they too had been wearing a red vest while walking in the area where my client was stopped.

Let's go back to the evening of January 16th and see how this identification happened. The victim, upset from being robbed, is taken to see if he can identify a man whom he must believe the police strongly suspect is the robber—otherwise, why are they going to all the trouble to drive him over? What does he see outside the store? A full line-up? No. A single man. My client. Handcuffed. Standing in front of a police car, flanked by officers Garrity and Roan. They might as well have put a neon sign over him—'This is the man. This is the man.'

The victim could give only a general description of his assailant. He said the robber had a baseball hat pulled down over his face. What did he see besides the finger of the police department pointing at my client? All he saw was a red vest, a common, innocuous piece of clothing. This red vest confirmed in his mind everything the conduct of this show-up identification procedure screamed to him. 'That's the man,' he shouts. What a surprise. This identification procedure was not just reasonably likely to lead to irreparable misidentification. It was all but certain to lead to a misidentification."

Legal Argument

A useful oral argument structure is the syllogistic pattern discussed earlier. State the law, and then apply it to the facts of the case. For example, in the robbery case defense counsel might begin by discussing the controlling law—the four *Maenhout* factors (the witness's opportunity to view the suspect at the time of the crime, the accuracy of the initial description of the suspect, the degree of certainty expressed by the witness at the time of the initial identification, and the span of time between the crime and the identification) and then one by one apply the factors to the facts of the robbery case. Counsel would then state that the factors lead to the conclusion that an irreparable risk of misidentification exists and therefore any in-court identification should be suppressed.

Focus the judge's attention on any controlling statute, court rule, or appellate decision (e.g., *Maenhout*). Avoid string citing appellate decisions to the motion's judge because the judge is listening for legal principles, rationales, and key facts that will help decide the motion, not for box scores. When opposing counsel relies on a particular case, you should explain how it is distinguished from the case at hand (assuming that it can be).

C.   The End—Present a Strong Conclusion

Like the opening of the argument, the conclusion should be carefully planned so that the argument ends on a high note. It is a good place to reiterate your theme and to ask the court for the relief that you are seeking. It's a good practice to write it out and rehearse. Unless you are experienced and an extremely skilled advocate, this chance to leave a last and lasting impression (the Rule of Recency) should not be left to the inspiration of the moment. When you have said what you have to say, sit down—this will be much appreciated by the judge. If you go on, it is likely that you'll muddle a perfectly good argument.

D.   Know the Judge

To the extent possible, the advocate should try to learn about the judge's personality, temperament, approach to decision making, particular preferences for how various aspects of the case should be conducted (e.g., marking exhibits), and such. Suppose the robbery suppression motion is set before a judge who has a particular concern about misidentification in criminal cases and has expressed it in other cases. Wouldn't that be useful information for both the moving and responding lawyers? It is possible to scout the motion's judge by speaking to other lawyers or reading the judge's past rulings or opinions or at least by going to the judge's court to observe the judge preside in other cases.

E.   Fielding Questions—A Dialogue with the Bench

A half dozen principles guide how to field questions from the motions judge:

✔ **CHECKLIST**

Fielding Questions from the Judge

1. **Watch, Stop, and Listen**—Presenting a motion or response to a judge is like carrying on a conversation. Is the judge engaged, following your argument, displeased, leaning in your direction? The only way to know is to closely watch the judge. If the judge seems to favor the argument, press on. If the judge seems skeptical, you may need to clarify or tack to another direction. If the judge begins to speak, stop speaking, not another word until the judge has completed the question. Not only is it common courtesy but also the person on the other end of the conversation deserves the deference given one who can rule either for or against you. Listen carefully to the question so you get the gist of it.

2. **Answer the Question**—You may have planned an orderly presentation that would answer the judge's question later in your outline. However, it is ill-advised to tell the judge that you'll be getting to that later. Obviously, this is an important question for the court; best to get right to it. Putting off answering the judge's question may result in losing an opportunity to keep the judge engaged.

3. **Prepare for the Questions**—The best way to effectively answer questions from the bench is to prepare for them. And, the way to prepare is to brainstorm to determine all the questions that might be asked. This brainstorming begins with all the attacks that opposing counsel has made upon your arguments. Focus on any weaknesses in your arguments. Then, plan the responses to the questions.

4. **Composure**—When questioned, maintain your composure. The preparation process described here is the best medicine for quelling nervousness when you are questioned.

5. **Candor**—Nothing is more important to an advocate than your credibility. Only by maintaining that integrity can the judge come to rely on the lawyer presenting the motion or response. A misleading statement made in oral argument can destroy the lawyer's credibility. Therefore, candor with the court is critical. If a question is posed and you do not know the answer, say so. You could also offer to do further research if necessary.

6. **Engage in the Dialogue**—Finally, welcome questions from the judge. The judge is not an antagonist; the judge may just have some questions about the motion or response. This is a chance to engage in a conversation with the judge and answer any concerns that the court may have. Be sensitive to the court's concerns.

F.   Be Prepared on the Facts and Law

A vital aspect of the successful oral argument of a motion is a firm grasp of both the facts and law. This builds the advocate's confidence and persuades the judge to rely on the lawyer because the lawyer has a firm command of both the law and facts. To achieve this competence requires dedication and hard work preparing for the motion.

G.   Courtesy and Respect

An important characteristic of an effective advocate is professional behavior. Professionalism means that the lawyer treats everyone in the court system with respect and courtesy. Naturally, lawyers are deferential, courteous, and respectful to the judge (when addressing the bench, the first words uttered are "Your Honor"). Courteous behavior should be displayed towards the lower bench (bailiff, clerk, court reporter) as well because it is the right thing to do and because each member of the lower bench is a direct pipeline for information about you to the judge. Moreover, your showing of respect and courtesy to court staff will be returned.

Professional behavior will not only make you a welcome visitor to the courtroom but will also enhance your reputation. Courthouses are small communities, even in large judicial systems, and before a lawyer steps into the courtroom the lawyer's reputation has already arrived. A good reputation acts like a shield, and when missiles begin to fly as often happens in pretrial and trial situations, that reputation can protect you. For example, if opposing counsel challenges your integrity, your good reputation can shield you from unjust attack.

This principle of courtesy and respect holds true for how counsel should behave toward opposing counsel. No matter how much you detest opposing counsel, never let it show unless you are confident that a tactical attack on opposing counsel is absolutely necessary and will be of benefit to you in both the short and long term. Judges become upset in the extreme when one attorney attacks another. They believe, as G. K. Chesterton, the notable journalist and writer, put it, "People generally quarrel because they cannot argue." A personal attack is sure to bring at minimum a verbal admonition to address remarks to the court not to counsel. Focus energy on undercutting opposing counsel's arguments and not on personal affronts.

H.   Courtroom Positioning

The advocate's goal in positioning him or herself in the courtroom is to find the most advantageous place to communicate with the judge. Courtroom custom, however, may dictate where you stand. If you have never been to the judge's courtroom, you need to learn where counsel usually stands when arguing to the judge. Get this information from other attorneys familiar with the judge's preferences, from court personnel or, best of all, by going and watching the judge hear a motion or two. Once you know the court's custom, try to figure out how to use it to your advantage.

Some state and local courts and all federal courts require that counsel stand at a podium. The problem is that a podium is not only a barrier between you and the judge but also it infects advocates with bad habits (leaning on it, hugging it). Avoid the podium if possible. If it is required that you stand at a podium, you may be able to stand away from it if you keep one hand on it at all times. Some courts have developed the custom of having counsel argue from counsel table. This too presents communication problems; the lawyer is some distance from the judge and often fails to speak loudly enough. If permitted, come forward to a position where you can easily converse with the judge. Many courts have a lower bench where court personnel sit and in front of them is a divider. Step up to that divider, place your notes on top of the bar and argue from there. It is an ideal location, close to the judge. Once there, stay in that position throughout the argument even when opposing counsel is speaking. After all, it's your courtroom.

I.   Visuals

A dramatic change has taken place over the last couple of decades for attorneys in terms of what they can do visually, not just in trial but also during a pretrial motion. Visuals can be displayed during both the evidentiary hearing—the way visuals are utilized in trial—and they can be used during the argument to the judge. This advancement and the importance of using visuals to communicate with the judge and jury is covered in more depth in Chapter 10, where we discuss the creation of visuals for pretrial and trial.

This change in both the quality and quantity of visuals is the product of two significant developments: (1) the technology for displaying visuals in the courtroom and (2) the software available to create those visuals.

The Technology

Twenty years ago the lawyer was mostly limited to the flip chart, white board, or overhead projector. Today, a document camera enables the advocate to provide the court with images projected onto a screen or television monitor in multiple ways, including, most commonly, enlargement of any document (photograph, map, chart, timeline), x-rays or other transparencies, and objects (the handgun enlarged so that the serial numbers can be read by the judge or jury). How the visuals may be used during a pretrial motion is limited only by the imagination of the lawyer and the receptivity of the judge to visuals. For example, if a summary judgment argument involved a specific provision in an employment contract, the lawyer could place the contract page on the document camera so that it is projected on the screen and then the lawyer can zoom in on the pertinent provision.

The Software

Various software programs are available to aid the lawyer in creating visuals for both pretrial and trial. PowerPoint, Sanction, and Corel can be used to create a seemingly infinite number of visual aids. For example, in the robbery case, these can be used to insert a photograph of the Portage Bay News store onto a map with an arrow from the picture to where the building is located on the map.

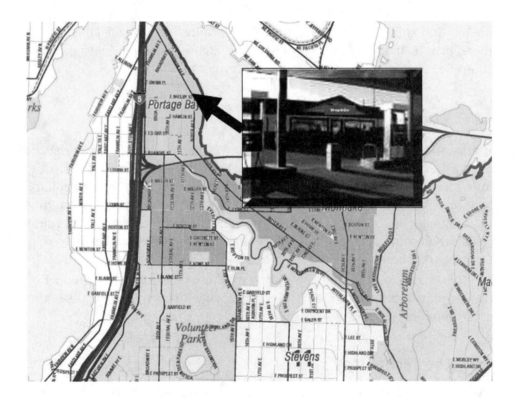

PowerPoint can be used to create slideshows of words, pictures, charts, graphics, and so on that can be projected onto a large screen. The slideshow can be animated, so that words fly in. Audio can be added such as a recording of a 911 phone call or the sounds along a roadway (when that is relevant to your argument). The PowerPoint visual can be printed on letter-size paper and then enlarged by a chart maker or handed to the judge for closer inspection. For example, the Portage Bay News store enlarged map can be affixed to poster board and taken to court and placed on an easel. Or, at a pretrial motion hearing a PowerPoint slide could be enlarged, and displayed on an easel to visually communicate the defense's arguments to the judge. For example, the factors for identification as set out in the Maenhout case could be displayed in the robbery case.

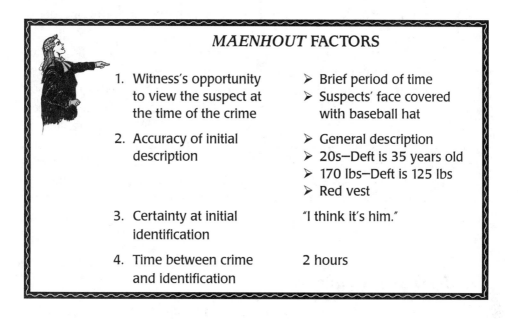

MAENHOUT FACTORS	
1. Witness's opportunity to view the suspect at the time of the crime	➤ Brief period of time ➤ Suspects' face covered with baseball hat
2. Accuracy of initial description	➤ General description ➤ 20s–Deft is 35 years old ➤ 170 lbs–Deft is 125 lbs ➤ Red vest
3. Certainty at initial identification	"I think it's him."
4. Time between crime and identification	2 hours

Casesoft, *www.casesoft.com,* is an example of a company that provides software that enables lawyers to create visuals in a fraction of the time it used to take and relatively inexpensively. For example, Casesoft has a program called Timemap that will generate a timeline. All the lawyer needs to do is input relevant dates and information to create the timeline. Broderbund, *www.broderbund.com,* is another useful software program for lawyers. With this program and a modicum of skill, diagrams of buildings, rooms, and even landscaping can be created.

While a lawyer or law office staff may design the visual, a lawyer may instead employ an organization that is in the business of designing courtroom visuals. No matter whom the lawyer hires, the ultimate responsibility for deciding what visuals will be effective rests with the trial lawyer. A major factor is whether the motion's judge is receptive to the use of visuals during the motion argument, assuming of course that the visual otherwise would advance the presentation. This can only be determined by scouting the judge as we discussed earlier.

J.   Appearance and Delivery

Body Language

Appearance is important, and the appearance that the advocate should project to the judge is that of a professional who is engaged in a dialogue with that judge. Look the judge in the eye, maintain a dignified posture, and avoid distracting habits. Sounds simple, but too often this is not achieved. The lawyer hugs the podium. Taps away with pen in hand. Or, most commonly, reads from prepared notes. Often the distracting behavior is the product of nervousness.

The cure for most of these behaviors is to be a minimalist. If the lawyer doesn't have a pen in hand, a transcript within reach, or change in the pocket to juggle, then the lawyer has no choice but to focus on the judge. But, what about reading? Again, less is better. If the lawyer has detailed notes, invariably the lawyer's eyes will be drawn to the notes like a magnet and he or she will begin to read. Some advocates take no notes, but that's for the greats and the inept. Most people need some notes to rely upon. A proven technique is notes in large print mostly in outline form on the inside of a manila folder. This will free the advocate to deliver the presentation without reading. The notes ideally contain an outline, key-phrase quotes, and essential citations.

Speaking Techniques

All good speech techniques—clear voice, modulation, pausing, and so on—apply to arguing a motion. Also, verbal hiccups should be avoided. They are space holders—the "Okay," "You know," "Aaah," "Hmm," and so forth—repeated over and over to the distraction of the judge. Speak at a comfortable pace for the judge and court reporter. Finally, use speech devices including analogies, rhetorical questions, similes, and so on to keep the court's interest on your argument.

K.   On Time

You walk into court five minutes late. The judge called the calendar, noted that you were not present, and struck your motion. Your client is there and is not happy. Always plan on the worst—a traffic jam, your car breaks down. Arrive at least 15 minutes early. Besides being on time, this extra time gives you the opportunity to evaluate the lay of the courtroom, the judge, and opposing counsel.

VII. THE ADVERSE RULING

You just lost the motion. The next question is: Do you live with it or can you get the court to reconsider or get the ruling overturned by a higher court?

A. Reconsideration

If the court ruled against you, prefacing that ruling with "on the record before me . . . ," the possibility of later providing a different or fuller record is open. If the court stated when making its ruling that "At this time, I am not inclined . . . ," the possibility is left open. The judge's position could change with the court's experiences over time as you develop a better record or provide additional authority. In these instances, move for reconsideration or at least make a statement, "Your Honor, as we progress in the case, we'd like the opportunity to revisit this issue." The local court rules must be consulted to determine if and when a motion for reconsideration will be considered appropriate.

B. Appellate Review

Appealable?

The first question is: Can you appeal the judge's ruling? While applicable court rules and case law in your jurisdiction will answer this question, normally only final orders are appealable. Otherwise, appellate courts would be besieged with appeals from incomplete trial records and bit-by-bit appeals. Final orders are those that terminate or substantially abate the action. In the civil context, for example, rulings granting either a motion to dismiss or a summary judgment and leaving no further action on the merits would be final orders. In a criminal case, a pretrial order dismissing the charges on grounds that the statute on which the allegations were based is unconstitutional would be final. A ruling granting a suppression motion to exclude the prosecution's key evidence (e.g., the defendant's confession) and leaving no evidence for further prosecution would so abate the action that the ruling could under some rules be appealed. Some exceptions to this finality rule exist, including interlocutory review by appeal (e.g., 28 U.S.C. §1292 authorizes discretionary and as-a-matter-of-right interlocutory appeals from particular types of orders) or by extraordinary writ (e.g., prohibition and mandamus).

Sensible?

Although the ruling is appealable, the next question is: Is it sensible to appeal the ruling? Obviously, the critical consideration is whether you will succeed in getting the appellate court to reverse the motion's judge. This in turn involves the consideration of several factors, including the standard of review on appeal (e.g., does the appellate court have to find an abuse of discretion to reverse the motion's judge), the nature of the issue involved (e.g., if it involved a finding of fact dependent on the court determining the credibility of witnesses, it is unlikely that the appellate court will substitute its judgment for that of the motion's judge who heard the testimony and saw the witness), whether the motion judge's ruling is consistent with appellate case law, and so on.

Perhaps you assess your chances on appeal as pretty good. Yet, you know that it is going to be time-consuming and expensive. The most sensible thing to do at this juncture may be to settle the case.

The decision not to appeal may turn on the desire not to make appellate case law that would run against your client's interest. For example, the motion's judge has granted a defendant's motion for summary judgment based on a statutory construction that resulted in the plaintiff having no cause of action. Your client, the plaintiff, is pursuing other defendants in other county courts of the same state based upon the same legal theory and would rather have the other trial courts decide the motions than have the appellate court decide the matter and create controlling precedent for the trial courts (e.g., the standard of review running against the plaintiff makes it less likely that the plaintiff will get the motion's judge reversed).

One additional point: Sometimes when you believe you are right, you must appeal a judge's pretrial ruling. Just knowing that you're willing to put in this work often makes a judge take your position in subsequent motions seriously. This will be especially true if you receive anything but a summary denial from the court of appeals—(e.g., a stay while the issue is being considered, an order to the opposing party to file a response).

VIII. ETHICAL CONSIDERATIONS

A. Opposing Legal Authority

Is it ever ethical to omit legal authority that is opposite to your arguments? If so, is it tactically wise to do so in your case? If you choose to meet the adverse authority and question its reasoning, attack your opponent's interpretation, or distinguish the facts or law, will you do so in the main body of your motion or in a footnote?

This issue has both an ethical and a practical aspect. Ethically, you must cite all controlling authority in your jurisdiction on an issue even if your opponent does not. ABA Model Rule of Professional Conduct 3.3 (a) (3). Practically, you risk losing the respect of the court in this and future cases if you leave out an important case adverse to your position. If you do, the court will either question your thoroughness and competence or your integrity. Neither option is desirable. Think what your opponent will do if you leave out this authority when you file the motion and opposing counsel then files a response to your motion ("It's interesting that in this 15-page brief, just loaded with cases favoring the plaintiff, the only case plaintiff omits is one that is dispositive in defendant's favor"). Rather, citing the case will give you an opportunity to weaken its impact ("Although *Gordon v. Hayes* may superficially seem somewhat troublesome, it offers no problem for plaintiff's position in this motion because . . .").

B. Not Frivolous

Lawyers are prohibited from asserting or controverting an issue in a case "unless there is a basis in law and fact for doing so that is not frivolous, which includes a good faith argument for an extension, modification or reversal of existing law." ABA Model Rule of Professional Conduct 3.1 and Fed. R. Civ. P. 11. Consequently, a totally frivolous summary judgment motion brought only to familiarize the judge with your side of the case or as a trial balloon to see how your evidence will be perceived is ethically suspect. The ethical standards are relaxed for defense counsel in criminal cases who can defend so as to "require that every element of the case be established."

C. Not for an Improper Purpose

Motions must be pursued only for proper purposes and not to cause delay. ABA Model Rule of Professional Conduct 3.2 requires counsel "make reasonable efforts to expedite litigation consistent with the interests of the client." The commentary to this Rule states, "Dilatory practices bring the administration of justice into disrepute." Fed. R. Civ. P. 11(b) states that when an attorney presents a motion to the court, the attorney is certifying to the court that "(1) it is not being presented for any improper purpose, such as to harass or to cause unnecessary delay or needless increase in the cost of litigation. . .", and sanctions can be imposed for violations.

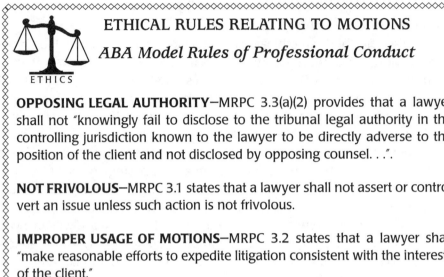

OPPOSING LEGAL AUTHORITY—MRPC 3.3(a)(2) provides that a lawyer shall not "knowingly fail to disclose to the tribunal legal authority in the controlling jurisdiction known to the lawyer to be directly adverse to the position of the client and not disclosed by opposing counsel. . .".

NOT FRIVOLOUS—MRPC 3.1 states that a lawyer shall not assert or controvert an issue unless such action is not frivolous.

IMPROPER USAGE OF MOTIONS—MRPC 3.2 states that a lawyer shall "make reasonable efforts to expedite litigation consistent with the interests of the client."

✓ THE PRETRIAL MOTION ADVOCACY CHECKLIST

Motion Theory and Theme

❑ Appreciate the objective of the motion (control the information, control the outcome, control the procedure, or control the participants).

❑ Have a Motion Legal Theory (MLT) to achieve the objective of the motion.

❑ As the responding party, have a motion legal theory that:
  - ✓ Attacks the moving party's MLT,
  - ✓ Attacks the moving party's MFT, or
  - ✓ Provides an affirmative defense to the motion.

❑ Have a Motion Factual Theory (MFT) that is:
  - ✓ both sufficient in that it supports the MLT and
  - ✓ persuasive because it makes sense, is logical, reveals values that the judge will hold (linking the values to the rationale behind the MLT), and is a human story.

❑ Have a Motion Theme, a short statement that encapsulates the Motion Theory—particularly the MLT and expresses the values that will appeal to the motion's judge.

Making a Factual Record

❑ Determine whether the motion requires a factual record or not, and if so who has the burden of making the record.

❑ In making a *documentary factual record* (affidavit, discovery response, deposition excerpts, exhibits), ensure that it is a sufficient factual record supporting the motion and that the documents are authenticated and otherwise satisfy the evidentiary rules.

❑ When presenting evidence at an *evidentiary hearing* create a factual record, utilizing the skills and techniques covered on pages 387-90.

Getting a Hearing on the Motion

❑ Properly serve the motion on opposing counsel.

❑ Confer with opposing counsel regarding the motion and prepare a certificate of the conference if required by the jurisdiction.

❑ Think about the strategies of requesting a single or separate hearings.

❑ Obtain a hearing time and date and serve a notice of the motion.

The Written Motion or Response

❑ Make sure the motion has all the essential supporting components:
   - ✓ Notice of motion,
   - ✓ Memorandum of law with the appropriate subsections (statement of the case, request for relief, statement of facts, statement of issues, argument and conclusion),
   - ✓ Attachments,
   - ✓ Proposed order, and
   - ✓ Proof of service.

❑ Make sure the response to the motion has the essential elements—the memorandum of law, attachment, proposed order, proof of service.

❑ Write a persuasive story in the statement of facts:
   - ✓ Tell a story about human values that will appeal to the motion's judge and demonstrates a human story.
   - ✓ Use storytelling devices, such as beginning in a way that will capture the judge's attention.

❑ Frame the issues favorably to the client and accurately reflect the facts and law while attempting to obtain the agreement of the judge.

❑ In the argument section of the legal memorandum:
   - ✓ employ the three Aristotelian arguments—logical, ethical, and emotional, and

✓ follow the syllogistic structure of argument (state the law, apply it to the facts, and state the conclusion).

❑ Throughout the motion and memorandum, repeat the motion theme and rephrase it so that it remains fresh.

❑ Take advantage of effective writing styles and structures:

✓ Accuracy,

✓ Clarity of expression,

✓ Avoiding hyperbole,

✓ Avoiding personal attacks,

✓ Proper citing of legal authority,

✓ Citing and dealing with contrary controlling legal authority,

✓ Carefully proofread for errors and misspellings, and

✓ Timely submitted.

Oral Argument on the Motion or Response

❑ Begin by:

✓ Preparing for this part of the argument by writing it out and practicing it,

✓ Introducing yourself and who you represent,

✓ Asking to reserve time for rebuttal if you are the moving party,

✓ Capturing the judge's attention,

✓ Getting to the essence of your motion or response,

✓ Stating your theme.

❑ The middle—making the arguments:

✓ Organize the arguments so you lead with your strongest argument,

✓ Make a factual argument that tells a human story and one about human values that underpin the rationale behind the advocate's MLT, and

✓ Present the legal argument in the syllogistic structure, rely on controlling statutory, case law, or other authority and avoid string citing.

❑ Conclude with your theme and a request for what you want (request to grant or deny the motion). As with your beginning, write this part out and practice it over and over until you can deliver it smoothly and naturally. Finally, when you have said what you have to say, sit down.

❑ Know the judge by scouting.

❑ Field the judges questions well by adhering to these techniques:

✓ Preparing for the questions by brainstorming to determine what the tough questions will be and planning answers to them,

✓ Watching to see how the argument is being received and adjusting if needed,

✓ Stopping if the judge speaks and not interrupting,

✓ Listening carefully to the judge's question,

✓ Pausing before answering and organizing your thoughts,

✓ Answering the question and not saying it will be answered later,

✓ Preparing for the questions,

✓ Maintaining composure—the best remedy for nervousness is hard work in preparation and practicing,

✓ Being candid with the court—saying that you don't know is alright, and

✓ Engaging in a dialogue with the motion's judge—welcome the exchange.

❑ Be thoroughly prepared on the facts and law.

❑ Utilize visuals to enhance the argument.

❑ Show courtesy and respect to everyone in the court system—judge, lower bench, and opposing counsel (never engage in personal attacks on opposing counsel).

❑ Find the right courtroom position—behind a podium only if required, stand up at the bar if permitted, and most of all, find the position that enhances your communication with the motion's judge.

❑ Dress and groom professionally.

❑ Use appropriate body language:

✓ No distracting habits (tapping the pen),

✓ Avoid reading and maintain good eye contact by having a minimal amount of paper at hand—use the folder technique (page 408), and

✓ Make appropriate hand gestures.

❑ Apply good speech techniques:

✓ Clear voice,

✓ Modulated voice,

✓ Pause, particularly between arguments,

✓ Watch out for place holders and hiccups—"You know," "Um," and such repeated over and over, and

✓ Take advantage of speech devices to keep your presentation interesting (analogies, rhetorical questions, similes, and the like).

❑ Handle problems posed by problematic, adverse, and/or hostile witnesses.

Reacting to an Adverse Ruling on the Motion

❑ Determine whether there is authority authorizing an appeal of the ruling.

❑ Exercise common sense in deciding whether to appeal:
- ✓ Determine if the appellate court is likely to reverse,
- ✓ Decide whether it is worth the time and expense, and
- ✓ Decide if there are other unfavorable consequences of an appeal.

Ethical Considerations

❑ Offer adverse controlling legal authority and distinguish it if appropriate.

❑ Do not make a frivolous motion.

❑ Use the motion only for an appropriate purpose.

SAMPLE CIVIL MOTION
SAMPLE NOTICE FOR CIVIL MOTION

SUPERIOR COURT OF MAJOR,
JAMNER COUNTY

GLENNA WASHINGTON,	)	
	)	Case No.: No. 7-43-20XX
Plaintiff,	)	
	)	
vs.	)	NOTICE AND MOTION FOR
	)	CIVIL MOTION CALENDAR
	)	(Clerk's Action Required)
MARC PROUST,	)	
	)	
Defendant	)	

TO: THE CLERK OF THE COURT; and to all parties named below:

PLEASE TAKE NOTICE that a motion for protective order in the matter of *Washington v. Proust* will be heard on the date below and the Clerk place this issue on the Civil Motion Calendar.

DATE OF HEARING: <u>Wednesday</u>   <u>March 15, 20XX</u>
                              (Day of Week)   (Calendar Date)

TIME OF HEARING: <u>9:30 a.m.</u>

PLACE OF HEARING: <u>Before Hon. S. Frankel, Courtroom W965</u>
                              Superior Court of Jamner County
                              101643 John Street,
                              Ruston, Major

NATURE OF MOTION: <u>MOTION FOR PROTECTIVE ORDER</u>

DATED: <u>February 27, 20XX</u>   _____
                              Typed Name: B.Y. Davis
                              Attorney for Defendant Proust
                              16 Stratton Road
                              Ruston, Major 96120
                              Tel.: (206) 421-0280
                              Bar No.: 8367

<u>OTHER PARTIES REQUIRING NOTICE:</u>
Fill In & Check Box If Backside Is Used [ ]

Name: <u>F. C. Townsend</u>   Name: _____
Address: <u>1600 Nat'l Bank Bldg.</u>   Address: <u>Jamner, Major 96120</u>
Phone: <u>(206) 825-6245</u>   Phone: _____
Attorney for: Plaintiff   Attorney for: _____

SAMPLE EXHIBIT

<u>Exhibit B</u>

SUPERIOR COURT OF MAJOR
JAMNER COUNTY

GLENNA WASHINGTON,	)	
	)	No. 7-43-20XX
Plaintiff,	)	
v.	)	PLAINTIFF WASHINGTON'S FIRST
	)	SET OF INTERROGATORIES
MARC PROUST,	)	AND REQUEST FOR DOCUMENTS
	)	TO DEFENDANT PROUST
Defendant.	)	
_____	)	

TO: Defendant Marc Proust and his attorney, B. Y. Davis.

continues ▶

In accordance with Rules 26, 33, and 34 of the Civil Rules for Superior Court, please answer the following interrogatories and requests for production under oath separately, fully, in the space provided, adding pages if additional pages are necessary, within twenty (20) days of the date of service upon you.

If any part of the following interrogatories or requests cannot be answered in full, please answer to the extent possible, specifying the reasons for your inability to answer fully and stating whatever information or knowledge you have concerning the unanswered portion.

These interrogatories and requests for production are continuing in nature, and you are requested to provide any information which alters or augments the answers given through supplemental answers. Supplemental answers should be provided within a reasonable time following discovery of the additional information and prior to trial.

MATTERS OF GENERAL APPLICATION AND DEFINITIONS

A.   The answer to each interrogatory or request for production shall include such knowledge of the defendant as is within the defendant's custody, possession, or control. Such knowledge includes documents in the defendant's custody, possession, or control, or those documents under common control, the control of predecessors in interest, consultants, accountants, attorneys, or other agents. When facts set forth in answers or portions of answers are supplied upon information and belief rather than upon actual knowledge, the defendant should specifically describe or identify the source or sources of such information and belief. Should the defendant be unable to answer any interrogatory or portion of an interrogatory by either actual knowledge or upon information and belief, the defendant should describe all efforts to obtain such information.

B.   In response to each interrogatory or request for production, if the defendant does not answer the interrogatory or request for production in whole or in part because the defendant is unable to do so, defendant should identify each person the defendant believes has information regarding the subject of such interrogatory.

C.   If the defendant contends that the answer to any interrogatory or request for production is privileged in whole or in part, or otherwise objects to any part of any interrogatory or request for production, or maintains that an identified document would be excludable from production to the defendants in discovery regardless of its relevance, defendant should state the reasons for each objection or grounds for exclusion and identify each person having knowledge of the factual basis, if any, on which the privilege or other ground is asserted.

D.   For the purpose of these interrogatories and requests for production, the term "document" shall mean any book, pamphlet, periodical, letter, report, memorandum, notation, message, telegram, cable, record, study, working paper, chart, index, tape, correspondence, records of purchase or sale, contracts, agreements, leases, invoices, electronic transcriptions or taping of telephone or personal conversations or conferences, or any and all other written, typed, punched, taped, filmed, or graphic matter, or thing, however produced or reproduced.

E.   For the purpose of these interrogatories and for production:

1. The terms "identify" or "identification" when used in reference to an individual person shall mean to state the person's full name, present address, telephone number, and, if known, a present position and business affiliation.

<u>INTERROGATORY 10(E):</u>

Please attach copies or releases for all medical bills, statements, narrative medical reports, hospital records, medical test results, receipts for prescriptions, written documents, notes and other materials concerning your health, injuries or illnesses during the past ten years which have been suffered by you prior to the incident which is the subject matter of this lawsuit.

<u>ANSWER</u>: Objection. Privileged.

DATE: January 1, 20XX.

By: _____

Attorney for Plaintiff Washington
F. C. Townsend
Townsend & Seebreeze
1600 Nat'l Bank Building
Jamner, Major 96120
Telephone No. (206) 825-6245
Bar No.: 1341

Plaintiff Washington' First Page - 3
Interrogatories

Townsend & Seebreeze
Attorneys far Plaintiff

SAMPLE PROPOSED ORDER

SUPERIOR COURT OF MAJOR,
JAMNER COUNTY

GLENNA WASHINGTON,	)	
	)	
Plaintiff,	)	No. 7-43-20XX
v.	)	
	)	PROTECTIVE ORDER
MARC PROUST,	)	
	)	
Defendant.	)	
	)	

Defendant Marc Proust applied for a Protective Order in the matter of Washington v. Proust. This Court considered the motion, affidavit of Dr. Johnson and Declaration of B.Y. Davis, the Memorandum of Law submitted by plaintiff and defendant and the arguments of counsel. It is ordered:

Plaintiff Washington is prohibited from discovering the psychological treatment records of the defendant Marc Proust.

continues ▶

Additional Provision. Nothing in this Order shall preclude any party from applying to the court for additional or different protective provisions in respect to specific documents if the need should arise during this litigation.

DATED: March 16, 20XX.

_____
Judge

Presented by:

_____
B.Y. Davis
Attorney for Defendant Marc Proust
16 Stratton Road
Ruston, Major 96120
Tel.: (206) 241-0280
Bar No.: 8267

Approved as to Form,
Notice of Presentation Waived:

_____

F.C. Townsend Attorney for Plaintiff
1600 Nat'l Bank Bldg.
Ruston, Major 96120
Tel.: (206) 825-6245
Bar No.: 1341
Protective Order Page - 1   B.Y. Davis _____

SAMPLE MEMORANDUM OF LAW

SUPERIOR COURT OF MAJOR,
JAMNER COUNTY

GLENNA WASHINGTON,	)	
	)	No. 7-43-20XX
Plaintiff,	)	
	)	
v.	)	MEMORANDUM OF LAW IN SUPPORT
	)	OF DEFENDANT PROUST'S MOTION
MARC PROUST,	)	FOR PROTECTIVE ORDER
	)	
Defendant.	)	
	)	

STATEMENT OF THE CASE

A complaint alleging negligent operation of a vehicle and resulting personal injury and property damage was filed in the Major Superior Court on November 1, 20XX-1 by Plaintiff,

Glenna Washington. Plaintiff's request for a jury trial accompanied her complaint. On December 7, 20XX-1, Defendant Marc Proust filed an answer and a counterclaim, also alleging negligence. The parties are currently in the process of discovery. No trial date has yet been set.

STATEMENT OF THE FACTS

This memorandum is in support of defendant Marc Proust's motion for a Protective Order to protect the medical records of Proust's psychological treatment from discovery by plaintiff Glenna Washington in the action of *Washington v. Proust*.

Washington v. Proust arises from a rear-end collision which occurred on September 12, 20XX-1. Washington is claiming personal injury and property damages totaling $25,000, and special damages of $5,600. Proust denies any liability and is counterclaiming for $1,500 property damage.

Plaintiff Washington sent defendant Proust interrogatories and a request for production of documents. Interrogatory no. 10(E) requested production of the following items:

> All medical bills, statements, narrative medical reports, hospital records, medical test results, receipts for prescriptions, written documents, notes and other materials concerning the defendant's injuries and/or damages as a result of the incident which is the subject matter of this lawsuit.

A copy of the request is attached as Exhibit B. Defendant Proust has fully complied with this overly broad request, with the exception of notes and evaluations made in the course of Proust's psychological treatment under Dr. Johnson. It should be noted that Proust, totally unrelated to this case, is currently undergoing psychological treatment with Dr. Joaquin Johnson, a licensed psychologist. Proust has been under Dr. Johnson's care for the past three years for treatment of arachnophobia, the unreasonable fear of spiders. (Exhibit C.)

Proust seeks to prevent disclosure of these documents on the following grounds: 1) the notes and evaluations are not relevant to the subject matter of the action pursuant to Court Rule 26(b)(1); 2) the notes and evaluations are privileged matter pursuant to Civil Rule 26(b)(1). Alternatively, Proust seeks to prevent disclosure of the notes and to limit the disclosure of the evaluations to an *in camera* examination pursuant to Civil Rules 26(c)(2) and 26(c)(4).

STATEMENT OF THE ISSUES

THE NOTES AND EVALUATIONS ARISING OUT OF PSYCHOLOGICAL THERAPY ARE PRIVILEGED AND IRRELEVANT TO THE PENDING ACTION.

Civil Rule 26(b)(1) provides:

> Parties may obtain discovery regarding any matter not privileged, which is relevant to the subject matter involved in the pending action. . .

A party may not discover privileged matter or matter irrelevant to the action. To ensure that such matters are not disclosed, a party may bring a motion for a Protective Order pursuant to Civil Rule 26(c), which provides:

continues ▶

> Upon motion by a party or by the person from who discovery is sought, and for good cause shown, the court in which the action is pending . . . may make any order which justice requires to protect a party or person from annoyance, embarrassment, oppression, or undue burden or expense, including one or more of the following: 1) that the discovery not be had; 2) that the discovery may be had only on specified terms and conditions, including a designation of the time or place . . . 4) that certain matters not be inquired into, or that the scope of the discovery be limited to certain matters.

Thus, the court may order that discovery of certain matters be prohibited, or limited in scope, or both.

THE NOTES AND EVALUATIONS ARE NOT RELEVANT TO THE ACTION

The threshold test for discovery is relevance to the pending action. Civil Rule 26(b)(1) requires that the matter sought to be discovered be relevant to the subject matter of the pending action. Proust's mental condition is not an issue in the action, nor does his mental condition bear on a claimed issue or defense. The documents arising out of psychological therapy simply are not relevant to this action.

THE PSYCHOLOGICAL/PATIENT PRIVILEGE

Once the psychologist/patient privilege attaches, pretrial discovery as to the privileged matter is prohibited. *Clark v. Dist. Ct.*, 668 Maj.2d 3 (1983). Dr. Johnson is a licensed psychologist in the State of Major. His relationship with Proust is a psychologist/patient relationship. Moreover, notes and evaluations arising out of such therapy are protected by this privilege.

Effective diagnosis and treatment require protecting the patient from the embarrassment and humiliation caused by the psychologist's disclosure of information revealed during therapy. *Bond v. Dist. Ct.,* 682 Maj.2d 33, 38 (1984). The affidavit of Dr. Johnson, Exhibit C, discussing the nature of Proust's therapy states:

> Because his initial childhood trauma and subsequent manifestations are so very personal, successful treatment necessarily depends on Proust's sense of security and confidentiality in his communication with me.

Dr. Johnson emphasizes that Proust's therapy would be severely impaired by disclosure of the notes and evaluations of treatment. Further, current and future treatment would be impaired by a loss of confidentiality.

The privilege may be waived by the patient. *Clark* at 8. The patient has waived the privilege when he has "injected his mental condition into the case as a basis of a claim or an affirmative defense." *Clark* at 10. Proust has not waived the psychologist/patient privilege and the notes and evaluations arising out of that relationship are privileged and not discoverable.

ALTERNATIVELY, THE COURT MAY EXAMINE THE EVALUATIONS <u>IN CAMERA</u>

If the court finds that the evaluations are not protected by the psychologist/patient privilege or that the evaluations are relevant to the action, we request an <u>in</u> camera examination of the evaluations by the court.

Civil Rule 26(c) provides:

> Upon motion by a party . . . and for good cause shown, the court in which the action is pending . . . may take any action which justice requires to protect a party from annoyance, embarrassment, oppression, including . . . (2) that the discovery may be had only on specified terms and conditions, including a designation of the time and place . . . (4) that certain matters not be inquired into, or that the scope of the discovery be limited to certain matters. . . .

There is sufficient cause to limit the disclosure of the documents. Dr. Johnson's affidavit emphasizes the personal and potentially embarrassing nature of the therapy. Dr. Johnson also warns that disclosure of the documents is likely to severely impair the current psychologist/patient relationship as well as future treatment. By limiting disclosure to an *in camera* examination of the documents, the dangers arising from complete disclosure are mitigated.

The notes taken during therapy may be misleading because they express the thoughts and observations of Dr. Johnson during treatment. While we request that the evaluations should also be protected, the notes are far less dispositive and are potentially more destructive to Proust's therapy than the evaluations. The evaluations provide a more accurate estimate of Proust's mental condition.

Thus, we request that the court examine the evaluations <u>in</u> camera, since a wrongful disclosure of the evaluations would cause unwarranted damage to Proust's therapy that could not be cured on appeal.

CONCLUSION

Court Rule 26 prohibits discovery of privileged matters that are irrelevant to the action. Likewise, the Rule limits discovery when a party is likely to be unduly oppressed or embarrassed. Thus, the Rule enables all relevant matter to be discovered while ensuring that parties will not be discouraged from necessary litigation by the fear that every aspect of their lives will be scrutinized. Since the records of psychological treatment are unrelated to this action, the motion for a Protective Order should be granted.

DATED: February 19, 20XX.

B.Y. Davis, P.S.

_____

B.Y. Davis
Attorney for Defendant Proust
61 Stratton Road
Ruston, Major 96120
Telephone No. (206) 421-0280
Bar No.: 8267

SAMPLE DECLARATION OF SERVICE

SUPERIOR COURT OF MAJOR,
JAMNER COUNTY

GLENNA WASHINGTON,	)	
	)	
Plaintiff,	)	NO. 7-43-20XX
	)	
v.	)	DECLARATION OF SERVICE (MAIL)
	)	
MARC PROUST,	)	
	)	
Defendant.	)	
	)	

I, STEVEN GROSS, declare the following:

1.   At the time of service I was at least eighteen years of age and not a party to this cause.

2.   I served on: F.C. Townsend, Attorney for Plaintiff the following documents: Motion for Protective Order, Memorandum of Points and Authorities, and Declarations.

3.   Manner of Service: United States Mail

4.   Date of Mailing: 2-19-20XX

Address to which document(s) were mailed:

1600 National Bank Building
Ruston, Major 96120

I declare under penalty of perjury that this information is true and correct.

Date: 2-19-20XX   Place: Ruston, Major

12 *Negotiating the Best Disposition*

I. Negotiation

II. Planning Negotiation

    A. Setting Objectives

    B. Developing a Negotiation Theory

    C. Facts

    D. Law

    E. Client's Needs and Wishes

    F. Incentives

III. The Bargaining Range

    A. A Persuasive Range of Solutions

    B. Determining the Range

    C. The Optimum Solution

    D. The Least Desirable Solution

    E. Solutions Within the Range

IV. Successful Negotiation

    A. The Right Mind Frame

    B. Negotiation Styles—Competitive vs. Cooperative

    C. Applying the Negotiation Theory

V. Negotiation Techniques

    A. Administrative Matters

    B. A Favorable Setting and Time

    C. Bargaining

    D. Pressure

    E. Exchanging Information

    F. Settlement Conference

    G. Bringing Negotiation to Closure

<h1>12 Negotiating the Best Disposition</h1>

"Uh, no. It's an agreement reached by mutual consent. Now, here's the way it works. You concede the necessity of goin' to school, we'll keep right on readin' the same every night, just as we always have. Is that a bargain?"

Atticus Finch In Harper Lee's *To Kill a Mockingbird* (1963)

"The Son'a wish to negotiate a cease-fire. It may have to do with the fact that we only have three minutes of air left."

Lieutenant Commander Worf—*Star Trek: Insurrection* (1998)

I. NEGOTIATION

Because over 90 percent of both civil and criminal cases are disposed of without trial, the strategies, skills, and techniques of successful negotiation are essential tools of an attorney. In a criminal case the negotiation may be for a deferred prosecution, a guilty plea agreement, a dismissal, or any resolution other than by trial. In a civil action the parties are usually attempting to resolve their dispute by agreeing to terms that favor both parties, rather than the winner-take-all result of trial. In this chapter, you will learn how to plan for and conduct negotiation for the best disposition. While the discussion primarily focuses on negotiation in the context of civil litigation, most of the principles are applicable to criminal cases as well.

The approach covered here is designed to achieve the best disposition. "Best" does not mean that you get your optimum result, such as a plaintiff's counsel getting a settlement at the top of the plaintiff's bargaining range. Rather, it means you arrive at a durable and lasting solution that you believe is just under the facts and law of the case and one that is acceptable to your client. This chapter shows you how to arrive at the best disposition by developing a negotiation theory that will guide your negotiation planning and execution and by adopting the philosophies, characteristics, and techniques of a good negotiator.

II. PLANNING NEGOTIATION

A. Setting Objectives

Seldom do you have only one objective. Often, clients have multiple objectives that may appear to be conflicting. This makes the concept of The Objective or The One Solution for the negotiation something of a myth.

Seldom will your adversary accept your optimum or only solution. Negotiation frequently involves making concessions to the other side. However, it also is an opportunity to creatively explore those areas where the underlying needs and interests of your respective clients are in conflict and where they are aligned.

Where the underlying interests of your clients are directly opposed, it is likely that your negotiation will consist of hierarchical negotiation preferences. You will usually find yourself considering a range of solutions or a spectrum of potential dispositions running from the most favorable result you can obtain to the least appealing.

B. Developing a Negotiation Theory

This section covers how key information can be organized into a negotiation theory and how an analysis of that information will guide you in crafting the negotiation hierarchy.

In formulating a negotiation strategy you consider how you will persuade your adversary to accept your client's proposed solutions and you consider what aspects of your adversary's proposed solutions are acceptable to your client. One method of approaching this task is to plan your negotiation in the context of information organized into a coherent theory that supports your proposals and distinguishes the weak points.

Just as in all other aspects of your pretrial and trial work, an underlying theory provides the organizational framework for planning and conducting negotiation. We refer to this theory as the "negotiation theory." Negotiation theory serves much the same function in negotiation as your case theory does in litigation. When you negotiate, your theory provides the context for your negotiation. Negotiation theory is relevant regardless of differing negotiation philosophies because it provides the basic context for organizing the four key elements discussed below into cohesive and persuasive discussions to support your positions.

The four key elements that compose the negotiation theory are:

- the facts of the case,
- the pertinent law,
- your client's needs and wishes, and
- the economic and non-economic incentives of your client and the opposing party.

Your hierarchical order of solutions will most likely be based on your analysis of these key elements. Put simply, the more the information supports your client's position, the stronger your position, and the higher you might set your objectives.

The process of formulating this range of negotiation solutions, moreover, is identical to that of developing case theories and back-up theories. We saw that as information is discovered and evaluated, weaknesses may appear in your primary case theory making that theory less persuasive (e.g., doubtful credibility of witnesses, inconsistency in evidence to support your case theory, inadmissibility of evidence). Likewise, negotiation solutions may encounter weaknesses. An optimum solution may be less persuasive if a similar case was settled for less than you as plaintiff's counsel are demanding in your negotiation, or if your client needs an immediate settlement and is willing to "take anything they offer" if it is paid within two weeks.

Throughout the next four sections, the four key elements of the negotiation theory are thoroughly examined.

NEGOTIATION THEORY

Facts
+
Law
+
Client's Needs
& Wishes
+
Incentives

C. Facts

To be successful in negotiation, you will need to obtain and be thoroughly familiar with the same factual information that you would use if you were trying the case (e.g., witness availability, credibility of witnesses, witness stories, potential evidentiary problems and rulings, availability of documents). This preparation is important in formulating negotiation proposals and in your discussion of those proposals. You will not be persuasive if you are not prepared.

Only by knowing the factual strengths and weaknesses of the case can you persuasively discuss your proposed disposition with opposing counsel. To illustrate, suppose that you are retained in the *Amber Ski Resort* case. This case will be used throughout the remainder of this chapter to illustrate negotiation principles, strategies, and techniques in the civil context.

The *Amber Ski Resort* Case

Story

You represent the plaintiff, 17-year-old Lisa Nevin, an injured skier. Lisa and her partner Susan went away for a skiing weekend. When Susan went back to the lodge, Lisa went for one last run. Lisa fell from a runaway cable car when a cable connecting the car in which she was riding broke. Lisa suffered multiple fractures to her right leg and arm. The prognosis is that she will not regain the mobility of two fingers on her right hand. She also reports loss of sleep, nightmares, and a fear of moving vehicles, which has been diagnosed as Post-Traumatic Stress Disorder (PTSD). Although she is afraid of being enclosed in a moving vehicle or gondola she remains an avid skier and has used skiing as a means to regain strength and confidence. At this juncture, you know of no other witness to the incident besides your client. You have filed a lawsuit alleging negligence and claiming the Amber Ski Lodge Corporation failed to maintain the cables on the ski cable cars. The damages allegations and other costs are:

- Total—Plead $2 million
- Special damages (medical expenses), $300,000,
- Non-Market Services $500,000 (caring for her mother),
- Loss of earnings, $300,000 (lost wages),
- Pain and suffering claim $900,000,
- Attorney fees are a 33.3 percent contingent fee of the net recovery,
- The estimate of trial costs (expert witness fees, court costs, demonstrative evidence exhibits) is approximately $30,000.

> Amber responded, denying liability and pleading Lisa's contributory fault. Amber has an insurance liability policy allowing recovery of $400,000 for each occurrence.

How you evaluate the strength of Lisa's case will effect how high you place the top settlement solution. The stronger the facts of your case, the higher the solution. Lisa will be a key witness. You believe she will be a credible witness. Her story is sympathetic and she presents an excellent appearance. In other words, you would have a strong and credible factual theory. As her attorney, you might place great weight on these credibility indicia because she is the plaintiff. You believe the facts that she reports enhance the strength of your case, making it more likely and consistent with an optimistically high result.

D. Law

When referring to "law" in this context, we are not referring solely to substantive doctrine. Rather, we are referring both to the outcomes of relevant prior cases and the types of rulings on liability and damage issues made by the respective trial courts. The law, thus, is a barometer to determine strengths and weaknesses in negotiation strategies. By examining legal precedent you can determine how favorable the precedent is to your negotiation position. The more it supports your position, the stronger your negotiation proposal could be. Acquiring information as to jury verdicts and settlements in similar litigated cases (multiple services exist for obtaining settlement and verdict information) may help you evaluate and compare the outcome. For example, in representing Lisa, your legal research led you to *Fletcher v. Ryan*, which involved a boating accident, and information about a settlement in a situation similar to Lisa's case.

THE LAW AS A BAROMETER

The *Amber Ski Resort* Case

Fletcher v. Ryan—In *Fletcher v. Ryan*, the trial judge instructed the jury that they should consider and weigh the eyewitness testimony in determining the percentage of negligence. The jury found plaintiff 40 percent at fault and defendant 60 percent. The appellate court stated, "We

continues ▶

> find that in determining comparative negligence of the parties, a defendant's negligence in the course of defendant's commercial recreational business creates a rebuttable presumption of total liability on the part of defendant in any resulting recreational accident. This presumption can be rebutted only by direct, not circumstantial, evidence."
>
> **Similar Cases**—Your research also uncovered a similar ski case in which a negotiated settlement was reached. The settlement was for $600,000. Also, in discussion with other lawyers, you were told that pleading requests for damages in recreational sport cases generally range from one to four million dollars while jury verdicts range from $500,000 to two million dollars.

The law affects the content of Lisa's optimum solution in three ways, as:

1. Legal precedent supporting Lisa's position,
2. A guideline as to what to propose, and
3. A limitation.

Supporting Legal Precedent

If *legal precedent* supports Lisa's negligence claim, then she has a viable claim that creates a risk of a verdict in her favor. This means that should Amber chose to fight her claim, it is likely that they will have to pay something at the end of the fight. This likelihood creates a different risk profile for Amber than a frivolous claim where a court fight would most likely end in a defense verdict.

Based on the viability of her claim, it is realistic for you to request and anticipate a higher optimum negotiation settlement. The stronger Lisa's legal case, the more likely it is that her case would survive motions to dismiss, for summary judgment, and for directed verdict. The likelihood of a verdict in some amount in her favor presents greater risk for Amber to refuse to negotiate and settle.

As Lisa's attorney, you might optimistically, but rationally, interpret *Fletcher v. Ryan* in a manner that supports 100 percent fault by the defendant, Amber. By relying on the *Fletcher* case you could suggest that the 60-40 percent solution is limited to the particular facts in *Fletcher*. Because there is no direct eyewitness to rebut a presumption of total negligence on the part of Amber in Lisa's case, a jury reasonably could find Amber 100 percent at fault. This also strengthens the potential value of Lisa's case.

Finally, the case law also provides some guidance as to what range of potential verdicts or settlements might be an appropriate optimum solution.

Guideline for Optimum Solution

Legal precedent provides a potential *guideline* as to how to actually determine the type and amount of Lisa's optimum disposition. You might be guided by what other litigants have pled, obtained in settlement, or obtained by jury verdict.

You might look to that precedent to define a range of potential solutions. For instance, how do you know what Lisa's optimum solution should be? Should Lisa request ten million dollars? Or perhaps only two million? Legal precedent as a guideline might strongly support an optimum result of one million dollars. You could reasonably base your optimistic determination on any of three precedents: the pleading range (one to four million dollars), the negotiated settlement of the other ski case ($600,000), and the range of jury verdicts ($500,000 to two million).

Because you are being optimistic, you might decide to look at the higher end requested in pleadings and in jury verdicts and use those precedents as a guideline. But if you request four million dollars based on pleading requests instead of two million based on jury verdicts, you should also be aware that because pleadings are notoriously inaccurate (attorneys may lack precise knowledge at the pleading stage to realistically predict the amount in controversy, and may view the initial pleading as a "first price" offer), your proposal may be suspect and vulnerable to attack by your opponent.

Limitation on Optimum Disposition

You must also consider whether substantive law or procedural rules place any *limitation* on your optimum solution. In particular, this may occur when there are multiple parties involved in the dispute that is being negotiated. As an example, consider what is also known as the "sliding scale agreement," which has been prohibited by law in some jurisdictions. This agreement occurs where there are multiple parties in a tort case who may be responsible for the injury, and some, but not all the parties agree to settle. Under terms of such an agreement, a plaintiff is prohibited from either agreeing to dismiss or not actively pursuing litigation against a settling defendant who, in exchange for the settlement, guarantees judgment whether the plaintiff wins or loses, *see* description of Mary Carter agreements, on pages 461-62.

E. Client's Needs and Wishes

Generally, by the time you negotiate you will know your client's needs and wishes. In negotiation, however, both your client's needs and wishes and those of your adversary's client are of importance and should be reflected in the negotiation. After all, it is the clients who must ultimately accept a negotiated settlement. If you know about the other side's needs, you may be able to propose solutions that will meet both clients' needs.

These solutions may include remedies and terms that would not otherwise be available in the context of a jury verdict. In fact, one of the most attractive elements of settlement over trial is that the parties control the exact nature of the outcome and can craft a resolution that optimizes the needs of both sides.

What are your client's wishes in the *Amber Ski Resort* case? Lisa told you:

YOUR CLIENT'S WISHES

The *Amber Ski Resort* Case

Story

"I want six million dollars. It would be nice to have a lot of money, and I heard that another skier who was injured got six million dollars. I want the Amber Ski Lodge to apologize for its failure to repair the defective cable that caused the accident. I also need to pay for my college education and help pay for my mother's assisted living situation. Since the accident, I can no longer take care of my mother."

Lisa's six million dollar wish might be based on whim or on a calculation of what she needs to care for her mother or on a sense of equity from her perceptions as to what others have received.

Sometimes your client will be pessimistic and will have an unrealistically low expectation. Of course, you could strategically present your client's wish even if it is in truth a whim without regard to realistic factors. Nevertheless, you certainly do not want to disregard the story about another skier's six million dollar settlement. You want to find out more about that other case.

It is possible that in your jurisdiction you will not be able to recover Lisa's college expenses and the cost of her mother's care through the lawsuit. However, you certainly should consider the amount of money Lisa needs to help pay for her mother's care.

You may also want to include an apology by the defendant as part of the negotiation content so the settlement reflects Lisa's stated desires. In doing so, it is important to clearly understand how important this issue is to Lisa, and whether Amber has any countervailing interest in maintaining confidentiality of any settlement. You probably will need to evaluate additional information and again discuss the matter with Lisa.

F.   Incentives

Incentives refer to the wide range of circumstances that may affect your and your adversary's motivations to resolve the dispute. For ease of analysis, we classify incentive information into two categories, economic and non-economic, although to some extent information classified as non-economic ultimately might also have economic consequences.

To obtain incentive information, you should think about everything that could possibly affect the dispute and its outcome. This process is identical to brainstorming a case theory. You may need to consult many diverse sources—your client, other attorneys, court personnel, family or friends of your client and of your adversary's client, trade periodicals, and so on. You might also have to include formal investigation and/or discovery to identify pressures that might be affecting either your client or your adversary.

Non-Economic

Types of Incentives

CHECKLIST

Non-Economic Incentives

Non-economic incentives include such things as:

- The emotional stability of the clients—Can your client or your opponent's client endure a trial?
- The impact on your client's relationship with the adversary—Does your client want to maintain a continuing working relationship with her adversary?
- Either client's need for a public trial—Is the party litigating the case to establish a principle?
- The impact of favorable or adverse publicity on your client or opponent—Does the defendant want to avoid bad publicity?
- The jury appeal of the case—Will the presentation of plaintiff's case be likely to favorably impress the fact finder because of the sympathetic injured young woman? If so, that factor might provide a strong incentive for a defendant to settle close to plaintiff's demand because a jury award might result in much higher damages than the amount for which the case can be settled.

Non-economic information can also help you to decide such issues as whether to negotiate and for what amount. Imagine that your client Lisa, the injured skier, has told you she cannot endure the emotional trauma of a trial. Yet, you need her testimony at trial to convince the jury. Negotiation may be your only alternative. This type of information will not only help you decide to negotiate but will also affect the ultimate limits of what you might be willing to accept to reach a resolution short of trial.

Your Adversary's Needs

The more your negotiation solutions reflect your adversary's interests and needs, the more likely your adversary may find the solution acceptable. In order to propose solutions that meet your adversary's needs, you clearly want to be familiar with what they are. Although you could evaluate your adversary's needs when you evaluate your own client's needs, we have analyzed them separately. This ensures that they are properly and extensively considered.

Think about what will make your proposed solution acceptable to Amber Ski Resort. Examining your solutions, ask:

- Do these suggested solutions reflect any of Amber's needs or interests?
- Is there a way to express or present Lisa's solutions in a manner that achieves Lisa's objectives and also takes into account Amber's needs?

One of Amber Ski Resort's primary needs may be to preserve the anonymity of any settlement so there will be no adverse publicity. You might be tempted to consider as part of your proposals a suggestion that the settlement be confidential. Many attorneys consider it the norm for a large settlement to be kept confidential. However, in some jurisdictions, state law prohibits settlement that will be confidential when the subject of the lawsuit involves issues of health and safety of the public. Some attorneys consider it morally offensive to enter into secret settlements. Those attorneys inform their clients at the start of the case that they will not enter into a confidentiality agreement and they ask their clients to acknowledge a waiver on this issue in their employment retainer agreement.

Similarly, a solution that takes into consideration Amber's cash-flow problems, such as gradual payments instead of a large lump sum, might be more acceptable to Amber and therefore more likely to succeed.

Do not forget to consider the possibility that your adversary and their representatives may be composed of multiple individuals. Each of those individual decision makers may have different perspectives on the underlying needs and priorities of your adversary. As an example, Amber's insurance carrier may have legal obligations to settle the case for an amount under the policy limits, which might make the Amber team very willing to consider an offer under $400,000 but quick to reject an offer in excess of $400,000.

In evaluating how to best approach addressing those needs it is important to consider to whom you will be communicating and how that communication may be transmitted and evaluated by the team of decision makers that represent your adversary.

Economic

Some negotiation theorists use mathematical formulas for determining the effect of economic incentives on a particular negotiation. By assigning values to each piece of information, these theorists believe they can calculate the influence that an incentive may have on decisions to negotiate, negotiation proposals, and negotiation performance strategies.

While we might choose to avoid such sophisticated mathematical models, economic information can help you evaluate the financial impacts on your client should the client accept a proposed solution by your adversary. You should consider whether your client will be better or worse off if the dispute is settled. Is there benefit to your adversary's client from the proposed negotiated settlement?

Economic factors related to the litigation can include litigation expenses (discovery costs, court costs, witness fees, evidence preparation, legal fees, collection of the judgment, and so on) as well as the tax aspects of judgments. Economic concerns generally stem from the financial position of the parties and their monetary concerns.

Other economic factors may be based on your best estimate of the financial outcome of the case (e.g., the likelihood of a favorable outcome and the amount of verdicts for similar cases, customs in the industry and in the geographical area, and the attitudes of court personnel, the judge, and jury). This type of information can be acquired by consulting specialized legal periodicals and by talking with other attorneys, court personnel, and your client.

III. THE BARGAINING RANGE

A. A Persuasive Range of Solutions

In order to be persuasive, the range of solutions should be based on information that rationally supports each proposed solution. In our approach, the proposed solutions are based on our consideration of the four elements that make up the negotiation theory—facts, law, client's wishes and needs, and incentives.

Your solutions should also be creative, presenting alternative ways to resolve the dispute. Creative and innovative solutions that present your adversary with alternatives that meet client needs are persuasive and present a greater likelihood of being considered acceptable. For example, if Amber Ski Resort has a cash-flow problem and could not afford to pay an immediate lump sum, you could offer a creative economic incentive. A possible solution that meets Amber's needs might be a delay in paying a lump sum. Does that meet Lisa's needs? It might, if Amber paid sufficient interest. Or perhaps you could suggest that Amber pay all or part of Lisa's mother's care now as part of the settlement, and Lisa would agree to a delay in receiving the remaining amount of the settlement. In addition to money, consider other services that Amber might provide Lisa. Would life-time membership or lift tickets be attractive to Lisa? Can the restaurant that services the ski resort provide meals to Lisa's mother or to Lisa? Does Amber have the ability to fund or assist with Lisa's college education?

B. Determining the Range

Although various ways exist for developing a bargaining range for negotiation, we suggest that you begin by determining the optimum solution you believe you can credibly request. You do this by optimistically interpreting the four elements in your negotiation theory (facts, law, client's wishes and needs, and incentives). While you are thinking optimistically, however, you may well note flaws in your analysis. Those flaws will begin to suggest that you should also consider less optimistic solutions. You will begin to develop a range of solutions from these flaws or weaknesses until you hit the bottom.

"Hitting the bottom" generally means, "I'd rather risk everything and go to trial." This bottom line is the lowest possible point that you and your client will accept instead of trying the case. This does not mean that there are no risks even if you win at trial. You have risks caused by delay while the case is on appeal and costs of appeal, as well as the risk that the case may be reversed by the appellate court.

Next, take the information you have about your adversary and apply the same analysis. Try to determine what the result would be if the four factors were evaluated most optimistically in favor of your opponent, based on the underlying interests of your adversary. This will represent your best estimate as to the top of their bargaining range. Note the flaws in the analysis, and try to determine the lowest possible point that your adversary will accept instead of trying the case.

If you overlay these two ranges, you may gain an understanding of the actual range of resolution, that is, where your lowest and their highest overlap. This actual range will be the most likely range of ultimate resolution.

Of course, neither side is likely to begin the negotiations within that range of resolution. Both sides will most likely be trying to jockey the other side into their range. To reach the optimum disposition and reach the range of resolution we will use our negotiation theory to build a negotiation plan to move our adversary into this zone and to effect the optimum disposition that will favor both sides.

C.   The Optimum Solution

You have now analyzed each of your negotiation theory's elements in the *Amber Ski Resort* case. You can now tentatively set the optimum solution you think you should seek. It may be higher than any of the precedents that guided you because it represents your optimistic view of what you think you can obtain for Lisa. Or you may decide, upon reflection, that only one position, your client's optimum solution, would be acceptable as a negotiated settlement.

However, be aware that almost never will your adversary accept your first and only suggestion or settlement demand, even if it is reasonable and persuasive. In fact, a failure to recognize that your adversary has a need to feel that the process has been a collaborative negotiation can lead to impasse, no matter how reasonable your initial offer. The practice of making one "fair and final" offer without any back and forth negotiation is known in some circles as "Boulwarism" and is generally considered to be synonymous with a failure to negotiate in good faith. Boulwarism is named after Lemuel Boulware, who served as the personnel director of General Electric many years ago. Boulware attempted to shorten a difficult collaborative bargaining process by simply presenting GE's best and final offer at the start of the negotiation. Rather than being perceived as enlightened and cooperative, he and GE were perceived as stonewalling and obstructive. Accordingly, it is important to plan your first offer as establishing the bargaining range, while still planning for room for movement into the range of resolution.

In our illustration, there is clearly more than one proposed solution, because as we considered the four elements optimistically, we also noted flaws in our analysis. However, let's suppose that we believe that the appropriate optimum solution for your client Lisa would be two million dollars—the highest jury verdict.

⚖ Settlement Value

However, two million dollars is not the real settlement value to your client, Lisa. First, two million dollars assumes that your client has a 100 percent chance of winning two million dollars at trial with no possibility of appeal and without expending any resources to achieve that result.

Obviously, to determine the appropriate settlement value we need to modify that two million dollar optimum solution to account for these other risks and expenses.

Probability of Liability

First, the top result should be decreased by a percentage equivalent to your chance of losing. This will be your best estimate, and it may be to a degree influenced by research into what percent of the time juries return verdicts that the defendants were liable in cases similar to yours. Optimistically, you determine that there is an 80 percent chance of proving liability. So, the two million is reduced to $1,600,000 to reflect the defendant's likelihood of winning.

Comparative Fault

Based upon your optimistic reading of *Fletcher v. Ryan*, you have concluded that the jury will find the defendant 100 percent at fault. Therefore, you do not decrease the settlement value because of the case law. However, if your research indicated that some percentage of comparative fault would be a likely outcome, you would want to factor that likelihood into your analysis as well.

Costs of Trial

You conclude that settlement would eliminate trial expenses of $30,000, which include among other things: expert witness fees, court costs, costs of demonstrative exhibits (e.g., the animated video you plan to create to show what happened when the cable broke sending Lisa out the door, appeal, and so on). We might subtract those costs out of our optimum value. Now, the settlement value is $1,570,000.

This factor may be complicated by the law of the jurisdiction concerning trial costs and fees. Many jurisdictions provide that costs may be recovered by the prevailing party. In this circumstance you would want to evaluate the likelihood that you would be considered the prevailing party for purposes of reimbursement of trial costs (an offer of judgment or settlement under some court rules and statutes can shift the point at which we become the prevailing party). You would also want to consider the effect of inflation resulting from the delay before recovery of costs can be achieved.

D.   The Least Desirable Solution

Having formulated the top of the range for Lisa, you can now consider the least, but still acceptable, solution for your client. The least acceptable solution is the worst possible result that your client should agree to accept as settlement of the dispute. This bottom position defines the boundary where you will tentatively abandon negotiation. The least, but still acceptable, result is the BATNA, the "Best Alternative to a Negotiated Agreement," a principle discussed by Fisher, Ury and Patton in *Getting to Yes,* 2nd Ed., Penguin Book (1991). Fisher and Ury suggest the least but still acceptable result can be determined by comparing the negotiated settlement with other alternatives, including no settlement. If the bottom is worse than any other alternative, then it is not an acceptable position.

When determining the bottom position, you want to know how far down you should set your lowest objective. The weaker Lisa's case in terms of the elements in the negotiation theory, the less you may be able to attain if you pursue other alternatives. Your adversary may be aware of these weaknesses and be willing to settle for your bottom position only. Therefore, you need a plan to determine your least but still acceptable result. You may find that when you actually negotiate, this bottom position may be raised or lowered if different information is revealed or opposing counsel provides you with a different perspective.

The weakness in your client's case is determined by considering the most pessimistic view of the facts, the law, and the incentives, which, conversely, is also the most optimistic view of your adversary's position.

Settlement Value

Probability of Liability

In calculating your optimum settlement value, you were optimistic and used an 80 percent probability of liability. A worst case scenario would be a belief that you have only a 60 percent chance of proving liability. Reducing your $500,000 (the bottom of the jury verdict range) by 40 percent means that the value is really $300,000.

Comparative Negligence

Next, consider *Fletcher v. Ryan.* Your most pessimistic interpretation of the leading case, *Fletcher v. Ryan*, is that potentially Lisa might be 40 percent at fault. You base your view that Lisa could be found comparatively negligent on the possibility that a court could interpret the phrase "direct evidence" in the *Ryan* case as encompassing more than just eyewitness testimony (e.g., direct physical evidence). You base your view of the percentage of comparative fault on jury trial verdicts in three cases, all similar to Lisa's, that found plaintiffs 20 to 40 percent at fault. Reducing the $300,000 by 40 percent leaves $180,000.

Costs of Trial

The $180,000 still needs to be reduced by $30,000 trial costs to arrive at the worst trial result of $150,000. This is theoretically the worst that you think your client would receive if the case went to trial.

The Client's Recovery

When the contingent attorney's fee of 33 percent ($50,000) is subtracted the client would receive $100,000.

SETTLEMENT VALUES SUMMARY
The *Amber Ski Resort* Case

Optimum		Worst Scenario	
Optimum Award	$2,000, 000	Worst Award	$500,000
80% Probability of liability	$1,600,000	60% Probability of liability	$300,000
0% reduction for for comparative negligence	0	40% reduction for comparative negligence	$180,000
Settlement Value after trial costs reduction of $30,000	**$1,570,000**	**Settlement Value** after trial cost reduction of $30,000	**$150,000**

Client's Needs and Wishes

Now consider whether Lisa would accept this as the bottom. Your client will determine the bargaining range—the top to the bottom. The settlement value is between the optimum of $1,570,000 and $150,000. Would she accept $150,000? Would you recommend it to her?

Reconsider—Alternatives and Consequences

Before you arrive at the bottom figure, consider again the incentives on both sides, the alternatives, and the consequences.

Incentives

Lisa has a strong incentive to settle. She insists she needs the settlement money immediately to help pay for college and her mother's assisted living situation.

Reviewing Amber's position, you believe that Amber Ski Resort, although wanting to settle, might not be very anxious to settle except for a minimal amount—Lisa's bottom position. You base your belief on its financial position. At the present time Amber will be unable to pay a lump sum damage award above $400,000 (its insurance coverage for liability) because of its cash-flow problems you learned about from discovery. You also do not believe Amber has much fear of having to make a public apology as the result of trial because that is not a remedy that a judge would order (although a trial may well result in unfavorable publicity).

Considering the Alternatives

You should discuss the optimum settlement value ($1,570,000) and worse settlement value ($150,000) with Lisa. Before setting the bottom of the range, explore the consequences of walking away from the negotiation. In some instances, either Lisa or Amber Ski Resort might want to accept a negotiated settlement that does not achieve anything either client wants because going to trial is less preferable.

On the other hand, Lisa can go to trial. You have considered how likely it is that Lisa will prevail at trial from a 60 percent to an 80 percent chance. You believe a judgment may be as low as $500,000 (the bottom of the range of jury verdicts). You estimate three years if no appeal, and, if a successful appeal grants Amber a new trial, perhaps as long as seven years. Evaluating all the factors, weighing the risks, assessing Lisa's needs, you believe the bottom you would recommend to Lisa would be a settlement of approximately $500,000, consisting of an initial lump sum payment of $400,000 (the limits of the insurance policy) to be paid immediately and $100,000 paid by Amber in periodic installment payments—structured to meet Amber's needs. For any amount less than $500,000, you will advise Lisa to walk away from negotiation.

PLAINTIFF'S BARGAINING RANGE

The *Amber Ski Resort* Case

OPTIMUM	BOTTOM
$1,570,000	**$500,000**

E.   Solutions Within the Range

Now consider the solutions between your optimum and bottom solutions. The range is a matter of judgment because you must decide how much each flaw or weakness adversely affects your optimum solution. For example, in representing Lisa you could conclude that the legal precedent of a jury verdict is important. This in turn many lead you and Lisa to conclude that your bargaining range is from $500,000 to $1,570,000 and that a disposition within that range is reasonable and should be seriously considered by Lisa. Remember, this range is the result of your analysis of the factors discussed.

When you bargain within the range, you will discuss issues over which you disagree. Then, one side will concede a weakness and with that concession move down the hierarchy to another less desirable solution. Dollar values can be assigned to each weakness in the case. During negotiation, you could concede a weakness and reduce the demand (plaintiff) or increase the offer (defendant) a percentage. It is good practice to plan in advance the concessions that you are willing to make. It is during this bargaining process that you will make your arguments guided by your negotiation theory of facts, law, incentives, and client's needs and wishes.

IV. SUCCESSFUL NEGOTIATION

A.   The Right Frame of Mind

Your frame of mind is critical in being able to plan, analyze, and strategize prior to and during negotiation. Two mental processes that are interrelated and necessary for negotiators are ends-means thinking and creativity.

Ends-Means Thinking

Ends-means thinking is an integral part of negotiation. During your negotiation, everything you do should be directed toward achieving the end result you want to accomplish. Consciously adopting ends-means thinking puts you in a frame of mind to analyze, strategize, and restrategize based on goals. For instance, when you negotiate you need to instantaneously analyze, react, and respond to proposals and tactics. By adopting a frame of mind where you constantly think about the end result, you are accustoming yourself to automatically thinking and responding in this manner.

Examining the basic strategy for a game of checkers illustrates the ends-means frame of mind that you will need for negotiation (each move is made to take you closer to the winning position). However, a word of caution. Although planning game strategies and negotiation strategies are similar, they are not identical. Nor are we suggesting that you should negotiate sole-ly to win. Negotiation has more sophisticated objectives than just winning. Negotiation strategies also consider your adversary's and other interests and needs.

But, let's continue with the game metaphor—playing checkers—because it is useful in understanding end-means thinking and developing negotiation strategies. The strategy for a game of checkers is straightforward. You want to win. In order to win, your checkers are not moved randomly. Rather, you move your checkers according to a plan, a game strategy. Your strategy is based on the rules of the game and your knowledge or prediction of how your opponent might be expected to play the game. In planning your game strategy, you will develop strategies by analyzing each move you can make and predicting the responses that your opponent could or would in all likeli-hood make, and their effect on your ultimate goal. You will plan alternative strategies. As you play, you will ask yourself questions. If I move my checker to this position, what is the likely result for that checker? The rest of my checkers? The result for the move after that? What will be the likely response by my opponent? If my opponent responds in this manner, what are my alternatives? Each move is calculated to bring you closer to home, as is each plan and each fresh strategy. Planning your game strategy has required you to adopt a frame of mind that is directed toward achieving an objective, which here, in a checker game, is to win.

Using ends-means thinking for planning how you will negotiate is much like formulating a checker game strategy. Negotiation strategy requires plan-ning the content of your negotiation and how you will achieve your client's objectives—the best disposition. Just as you need the ends-means frame of mind in checkers, you will be planning negotiation by concentrating on your goal—achieving your client's objectives. You will plan your moves, which may be offers, counter-offers, or concessions. You will analyze and assess your opponent's responses. As you plan and negotiate, you will analyze and restrategize with your objectives as your guide.

Creative Thinking

As a negotiator, you must think creatively about information to use, tech-niques to employ, and solutions to propose. As a negotiator, you can use dif-ferent types of information that often would be inadmissible if presented in trial. In negotiation, you can rely on any information that is helpful as long as you are ethical and do not violate the law. You can be creative in plan-ning novel solutions—such as periodic payments or requiring an apology. For instance, if you know that your adversary's client is fearful of adverse publicity, you can use that information to persuade your adversary to settle by including in your proposal an accommodation that the settlement will be confidential. If a defendant is adamant about not acknowledging fault, you can create a proposal that permits defendant to disclaim liability. You can even negotiate a solution contrary to substantive law. For example, you might represent the defendant in a jurisdiction where the law provides that in a rear-end collision the following driver is presumptively negligent. Nevertheless, you could ignore that principle of law in a negotiated resolution (e.g., both parties to the settlement agree the following driver was not negligent).

The techniques you use as a negotiator can be wide-ranging and not constrained by procedural rules, except for professional ethics and criminal sanctions. You can threaten to walk out, picket, strike, or advertise your client's position in a newspaper.

The more creative and receptive you are to novel ideas, the greater might be the potential for resolving the dispute. However, alienating the opposing party may shut down the negotiations and make settlement that much harder to accomplish.

Reasonable and Rational

The negotiation ranges and your arguments in support of your position must be rationally related to the facts and the law that provide a solution. For example, Lisa's argument that she needs "sufficient money to pay for her college education" is not a persuasive argument to the opposing party for supporting the proposed settlement range. However, if it had a rational link to Amber's conduct and subsequent liability then it could be persuasive to Amber. For instance, if Lisa, because of her injuries needs to pursue a particular career at a specific university because of her disabilities, then the argument about money to finance such a rehabilitation plan would have a rational basis.

B.   Negotiation Styles—Competitive vs. Cooperative

While each negotiator has a unique style reflecting his or her personality, certain generalizations can be made about negotiation styles. These generalizations can help you understand and develop your own style and assist you in understanding and reacting to the styles of other attorney negotiators.

Gerald Williams, researcher in the area of attorney negotiation and author of *Legal Negotiation and Settlement* (West Publishing, 1983), in studying behavioral characteristics of attorney negotiators, typecast negotiators based on behavior patterns ranging from the cooperative to the competitive type. According to Professor Williams, the characteristics of these two types are as follows:

NEGOTIATOR CHARACTERISTICS

Cooperative Negotiator

The **cooperative** negotiator is:

- fair,
- objective,
- reasonable,
- logical,
- willing to move from established positions,
- friendly,
- trustworthy,
- ethical,
- interested in a fair settlement,
- wants to meet the client's needs,
- likes to avoid litigation, and
- tries to establish or maintain a good personal relationship with the opponent.

The cooperative negotiator makes realistic opening positions, supports positions with facts, and is forthright.

Competitive Negotiator

The **competitive** negotiator is:

- dominating,
- competitive,
- forceful,
- tough,
- arrogant, and
- uncooperative.

Generally, the competitive negotiator makes high opening demands, uses threats, is willing to stretch facts in favor of a client's position, sticks to positions, is parsimonious with information about the dispute, and appears to take a gamesmanship approach to negotiation.

Generally, negotiators who share similar behavior characteristics use similar negotiation tactics. Of course, a negotiator may exhibit all, some, or none of the characteristics of a particular type of negotiator. A competitive negotiator may be soft spoken, courteous, and friendly and never use threats. But it is more than likely that at least some of the behavior characteristics will be evident and the attorney will use some negotiation tactics that are characteristic of a behavior type. Researchers have even identified different styles of reasoning and different ways of resolving problems based on gender differences.

To illustrate negotiation styles, imagine now that you have been retained by Amber Ski Resort's insurance company as counsel in the ski accident case.

NEGOTIATION STYLE

The *Amber Ski Resort* Case

Lisa's attorney is J. M. Galvin, known affectionately as JMG. Mr. Galvin sent you a demand letter for $2 million, documented by $100,000 in medical bills, an economic loss report claiming $300,000 in lost income, the appellate decision of *Fletcher v. Ryan,* and jury verdict information from similar cases. Mr. Galvin then telephoned you to see "if we can work out a settlement." You are scheduled to meet with Mr. Galvin.

You have heard from many attorneys that JMG, Lisa's attorney, is generally obnoxious, argumentative, and bluffs as to his real position. Nevertheless, you plan to begin negotiation with the following opening remarks:

"Good to see you, JMG. I'd like to discuss my client's interest in this case. As you can imagine, Amber has no desire to litigate this matter. Am I correct in interpreting from Ms. Nevin's remarks in her deposition that she would like an immediate settlement for financial reasons? As I see this negotiation, we have a mutual interest—arriving at a fair settlement. Correct? Now tell me what Ms. Nevin's financial needs are."

Can you predict how JMG might respond?

If you are able to predict how your adversary might behave, you can tentatively plan which tactics will be most effective to counter your adversary's behavior. If your adversary then uses tactics in the actual negotiation that you thought he or she would use, you will be able to anticipate the pattern of offers and counter-offers and respond effectively. You can also assess how close to a final solution of the dispute you might be by comparing what you thought your adversary might demand and what he or she actually requested and considering points the adversary might be willing to concede.

Looking at the Negotiator Characteristics Chart on page 447, you can see from the list of attributes that both cooperative and competitive negotiations can be successful. They also can be unsuccessful. Generally, ineffective cooperative negotiators exhibit socially desirable traits: honesty, trustworthiness, courtesy, but lack the attitudes that effective cooperative negotiators have. They are not perceptive, convincing, analytical, realistic, creative, disciplined, self-controlled, or versatile. Ineffective competitive negotiators are all aggression and bluff, not backed up by careful preparation and analysis.

From your research into JMG's prior negotiations and resulting reports of his hostile and competitive negotiation style, you anticipate that JMG will refuse to discuss his client's mutual interests and needs, will initially stay firm on the demand of two million dollars, then will be likely to present a counter-offer that is outrageously high and announce the offer as final, and probably will not readily exchange confidential information. You also believe JMG is likely to insult your client, try to obtain evidentiary information or information as to your client's weaknesses, and use threats as pressure tactics. With your understanding of this likely behavior, you can decide not to be intimidated, to not disclose much information, to maintain your poise, and to calmly present your initial position. While you recognize the importance of this opening discussion, you are not expecting the case to resolve at this initial meeting.

C.   Applying the Negotiation Theory

Just as your negotiation theory guides you in planning negotiation and arriving at a bargaining range, the theory can guide you in successfully negotiating with opposing counsel. In conducting negotiation, your goal is to persuade the opposing party to agree to your best disposition within your bargaining range. To show how to conduct negotiation with the negotiation theory as a guide, continue to assume that you represent Amber.

NEGOTIATION THEORY AS A NEGOTIATION GUIDE

Client's Needs and Wishes

The *Amber Ski Resort* Case

You have ascertained your client's needs and wishes, one of the four elements of your negotiation theory. Amber is most anxious to settle and has approved a tentative range of up to $600,000 ($200,000 in excess of the

continues ▶

> policy limits), if the settlement can be confidential and paid in installments. Amber's insurance company and Amber, however, would like to settle for much less than the policy limit of $400,000. You believe there is a good chance to prove that Lisa was 40 percent at fault. You have located an eyewitness (thereby satisfying any interpretation of the *Ryan* case) who will testify, "Just before the cable broke I saw Lisa standing up in the cable car and leaning over the side." Your company engineer will testify that such a position would place extra strain on the cable, and that for that reason each gondola has a small sign that says "For the Safety of All—Remain Seated at All Times".

As Amber's attorney you wish to persuade Lisa's attorney, to settle the dispute for $100,000—well within the insurance policy limits. You wish to avoid adverse publicity for Amber Ski Resort and to reduce the emotional strain of a trial for Mr. Amber, Amber Corporation's CEO. A secondary and complementary objective is to obtain as much evidentiary information from plaintiff's attorney as possible in case the dispute does not settle and you are forced to go to trial. In particular, as Amber's attorney, you want to know how plaintiff intends to refute the claim that Lisa bears comparative fault for the cable failure.

The $100,000 optimum solution represents your most optimistic evaluation of Amber's case. The $100,000 was derived by calculating 20 percent of Lisa's medical expenses, loss of earnings, and pain and suffering. You optimistically believe that Lisa was 40 percent negligent. You base your evaluation on four specific pieces of information:

1. An eyewitness who will testify that Lisa was leaning out of the cable car shortly before the accident occurred,

2. Lisa's expert witness failed to affirmatively state in his deposition that the cable was defective or in need of repair,

3. Legal precedent, a jury verdict award, supports 40 percent contributory negligence (in a similar case, *Fletcher*, involving a boating accident, the jury found plaintiff 40 percent at fault), and

4. The physician that you retained to conduct a defense medical exam for the purpose of creating admissible credible evidence, Dr. Nancy, stated in her report after examining Lisa that she does not believe Lisa was seriously hurt. She believes that Lisa might even be malingering and is prepared to testify to those opinions on a more probable than not basis.

PRESENTING THE OPTIMUM PROPOSAL

The *Amber Ski Resort* Case

These four specific pieces of information can be used as a basis to argue Amber's $100,000 optimum proposal:

"Well, JMG, I think you know the strong and weak points of your case as well as I do. Liability is not clear-cut. In fact, Lisa's case is similar to that boating accident case in Kitsap County where the jury found plaintiff 40 percent at fault. It is evident that Lisa was at fault. Eyewitness and expert witness testimony support that position. But even supposing that liability is found against Amber, damages are not strong. As you know from defense medical report, Lisa's injuries do not appear serious. Dr. Nancy even states she believes your client is malingering.

V.   NEGOTIATION TECHNIQUES

You can employ a variety of techniques to persuade your adversary to accept your proposed solution. For instance, there are many techniques for commencing negotiation discussions—making a first offer, inviting a first offer from your adversary, making a high or low offer, communicating in writing or verbally, and tying the offer to other issues.

There are ways of attempting to put pressure on your adversary by communicating a lack of negotiating flexibility. These techniques include statements such as "This is our first and last offer," "This offer is available for the next 30 minutes," or conversely by expressly stating "Our opening offer is . . ." or "This offer is negotiable."

Techniques that can help persuade may range from things that superficially appear to be inconsequential, such as administrative matters (seating arrangements for the negotiation meeting), to those that appear to be near the crux of the negotiation (pressure to obtain critical information such as disclosure of witnesses).

For your use and convenience, we have roughly classified techniques into seven areas:

1. Administrative matters,

2. Favorable setting and time,

3. Bargaining,

4. Pressure,

5. Exchanging information,

6. Settlement conference, and

7. Closing the negotiation.

These areas present frequent negotiation tactics that you might encounter in any negotiation session. This grouping is not exhaustive but rather presents some common techniques you can consider and anticipate when planning your negotiation strategy.

A. Administrative Matters

You may find yourself negotiating administrative matters before you negotiate the substantive issues in the dispute, or you may find when you actually negotiate that many of these nuts-and-bolts issues do not present any particular problems. Nevertheless, you still need to have a tentative plan to deal with an administrative issue if it should arise. Otherwise, you might react haphazardly if it suddenly arises in negotiation and adversely affects your client's objectives.

One important point that you will want to clarify before the meeting is authority to settle. You will want to be assured that your client's representative has discussed settlement potentials and has the authority to "seal the deal." You will want to discuss what authority your client will initially provide to you as you enter the negotiation. You will also want assurances from your adversary that they are coming to the negotiation with authority to resolve the matter.

An administrative matter that often is itself the subject of negotiation is the agenda. Typically, the agenda can influence the outcome of the negotiation. When setting the agenda, some of the following can be decided: the nature of the issues, the order in which they will be discussed, a time frame for the meeting.

In designing the agenda, it is a good idea to start with matters upon which the parties can agree. Generally, having these matters first will set a tone of cooperation and move negotiation forward. Some issues are more easily resolved than others or may be disposed of more favorably for one of the clients, consequently, you and your adversary may differ as to which issues or sequence of issues to discuss. For example, assuming that before negotiating you have a strategic plan as to the issues you want to negotiate and their sequence. You will want an agenda that arranges the issues you want resolved in the order that you wish them addressed. Propose an agenda that is most favorable to achieving your result. Anticipate the effect that alternative agendas may have on obtaining your client's objectives. Ask yourself how a different agenda could affect the ultimate result.

B.   A Favorable Setting and Time

Negotiation can be conducted over the phone, on the Internet, in writing, or in person. The most effective negotiations takes place in person, where you can fully assess the other attorney and where you can be your most persuasive. The nature of the negotiation setting and timing present tactical opportunities to influence negotiation. Typically, you could be concerned with such matters as:

- **Where**—Negotiation could take place in your office, your adversary's office, the courtroom, or on other neutral turf. If it is conducted in your office, you are in familiar surroundings with supporting evidence (e.g., documentation), your support and legal staffs, your computers, and other useful resources close by. Unfortunately, it is difficult to walk out of your own office if the negotiation falters. Additionally, your adversary may feel less at ease in your office and less willing to compromise on key points.

- **Arrangement of the Setting**—You can arrange the seating in a way that will make you most comfortable and encourage communication.

- **People Present**—You need to decide who you want present—clients, third parties, judge (if it is a settlement conference proposed and conducted by a judge), and/or others. In some instances, it is not advisable to have the client there because the client might get upset at opposing counsel, agree to a bad settlement proposal, disagree with your techniques, and so on. Instead, you may want your client available by phone or in another office at your firm. In other instances having your client present can provide additional insight, and you may want your client involved because the client can provide information and answer questions that would facilitate the negotiation. In formal negotiations, opposing counsel may make a condition of the negotiation that your client, or a person with authority to bind your client, be physically present.

- **When**—You need to consider setting the time of day for the negotiation to avoid interruptions. You should identify how long you will negotiate and plan your schedule accordingly. It is important that you be sensitive to the pressures that other looming deadlines and meetings might have on your ability to negotiate.

C.   Bargaining

In every negotiation, each party must find out what the other party wants. Each side might have a general understanding because of prior contact—a demand letter, a pleading, a telephone discussion, and so on. However, even if both sides have an understanding of the issues to be negotiated, each will need to discuss its objectives with particularity. How and when you and your adversary communicate your respective proposals presents important tactical choices in bargaining.

Choices in Bargaining Tactics

Begin in a Cooperative or Competitive Way

Should you begin negotiation in a cooperative manner with a discussion of mutual interests? For example, you as Amber's counsel might say, "I think we both have an interest in saving the time and money involved in trial and in avoiding the risks of trial." Or, you could start with an optimum solution: "Amber is willing to settle for $100,000." Either way, it's advisable to begin in a congenial manner and build some rapport before beginning negotiation.

Take a Position First

Should you make the first demand? Or, should you refrain from making a demand and wait until opposing counsel makes the first demand. If you make the first demand, you establish the bargaining range and set expectations. However, you also may be shooting in the dark as to what your adversary would be willing to accept.

Whether you or opposing counsel takes a position first, it is best to start with a demand that is better than your expected outcome This will leave latitude for later compromise. Some negotiators feel that you should begin above the range of reasonableness and allow your adversary to draw you down into your bargaining range. Others suggest that a better approach is to show the other side that you are willing to engage in negotiation by stating an initial position that is on the high side of realistic and supported by a discussion of how you arrived at the figure.

Make Concessions Where Reasonable to Do So

If opposing counsel rejects your solution, offering reasonable arguments, an effective bargaining technique is to be prepared to make concessions. For example, "I can see your point. I'd be willing to come up a little bit from $100,000."

Generally, you will try to adhere to the solutions you prepared when planning your bargaining range. But there are circumstances which may occur that will compel you to alter or abandon your plan. For instance, during the negotiation you might learn from your adversary critical information you did not have or that you relied on incorrect information to formulate your range of solutions. Either of these circumstances might make your negotiation proposals incomplete, illogical, unreasonable, or inconsistent.

If this occurs it is important that you regroup and integrate this information into your negotiation strategy. It is also critical that you be clear on the authority that your client has extended to you and whether that authority is still valid in light of this new information.

Tie Your Solution to Other Issues

Another technique is to tie your demand to other concessions. For instance, you might say, "I'm willing to offer you $150,000 if you agree to a confidentiality agreement."

Applying the Bargaining Tactics

Now, let's apply some of these tactics to your bargaining in the *Amber Ski Resort* case. You have learned from your supervisor that the custom among insurance defense attorneys in your jurisdiction is to make a low offer, then move slowly to a point of reasonableness. You have a few choices. Suppose we examine two tactics. You can begin with a low offer. "We are willing to settle this case for $100,000." But, is a low counter-offer strategically appropriate in Amber's situation? Because the offer is rational and can be explained by the facts and law of the case, it might seem to be a good bargaining tactic.

Let's analyze the benefits if you, as Amber's attorney, begin the negotiation by discussing mutual interests, rather than by making the offer. You can then do a similar analysis yourself imagining that you had started instead with the offer. A benefit to beginning negotiation with a discussion of the interests and needs of the client is that positions might not harden and it might be more likely that an agreement will be reached. Beginning the negotiation might allow you to control the negotiation—discussion may be likely to center around Amber's interests and needs. Lisa Nevin's attorney may have great respect for you if the offer or discussion of interests appears reasonable and will allow you to lead the negotiation discussion.

One risk if you proceed with an interest discussion is that you might be informing Lisa's attorney of your view of the case. Of course, if you would have done so anyway, this may not be a negative. If Amber's interests appear irrational, however, the esteem in the eyes of Lisa's attorney may quickly vanish and you as Amber's attorney will appear weak and ineffectual. Or Lisa's attorney, by learning about Amber's interests, might be able to use that discussion to obtain concessions from you.

D. Pressure

Pressure can be an effective tool. It can be particularly useful when negotiation has bogged down for reasons such as opposing counsel refuses to seriously consider your proposed solutions, discussions have concentrated on tangential issues, opposing counsel is being obnoxious or irrational, or you and opposing counsel are too far apart in terms of an acceptable solution.

Your adversary will also be choosing and using pressure tactics to persuade you, focus discussion, end discussions, and so forth. You will need a plan for how you will respond if your adversary threatens to walk out, litigate, or even call the press.

Carrot or Stick

Pressure tactics include the carrot-or-stick techniques intended to influence action. The carrot is an incentive, and the stick a deterrent. For instance, incentive pressure tactics can be used to persuade your adversary to take your client's solutions seriously. As an example, you might suggest something like, "JMG, if you agree to a structured payout over 5 years, we can offer Lisa an extra $5,000 total compensation."

Or you might use a deterrent pressure tactic if negotiation becomes unproductive and you want to rejuvenate discussion. You might pressure the opposing party using time pressure by stating, "I have only one hour to discuss this matter; I'm due in court at 3:00 P.M." You might also use refusal to continue to negotiate as a pressure. However, be careful of statements such as, "We're going to trial if we can't agree on this minor point," unless you are prepared to back them up. Generally, you would use such a tactic when the point is minor to the other side but important to you.

Ultimatum

Outside your personal credibility with your adversary, the ability to walk away, perhaps until another day, is your greatest power in negotiation. It surely may be preferable to abandon negotiation when further discussion is resulting only in your making concessions and compromises that you don't want to make. Pressure tactics can help you conclude negotiations. You may want a graceful exit so negotiation may resume at a future date ("I'll think about our discussions . . .") or you can suggest a cooling off period ("Let's get together in two weeks and discuss the matter of damages"). Or, you might want to abruptly close the door because you believe signaling to your adversary that you have reached the end of your flexibility may precipitate your adversary into making a better offer in the future.

We caution against the indiscriminate use of take-it-or-leave-it offers, unless they are truly your final offer, after which you expect to go to trial. While there is a school of thought that suggests that such brinkmanship may pressure your adversary into making a better offer, it is more often the case that such statements undermine your credibility with your opponent as someone who means what they say. Obviously, if every offer you make is accompanied with a "take it or leave it," it won't take long for your opponent to figure out that your use of that tactic is simply theater. What is worse, your opponent will not know when you really are at a take-it-or-leave-it position, and an offer that might be within their bargaining range could be rejected because your opponent does not trust you to stop negotiating.

E.   Exchanging Information

When you negotiate, you will be making tactical choices about the information that you give and the information you want to receive. These choices will include considering the kind of information you will reveal or seek, how much information you will reveal or seek, and when you will reveal or seek it.

Persuasion—Settlement Presentations

During negotiation, you will be concerned with persuading your adversary to accept your client's solution. As we've discussed, to persuade you will discuss your negotiation theory—client needs and interests and factual, legal, and incentive information that supports your client's position or refutes your adversary's position. You will need to consider tactically how much of your negotiation theory to reveal. Some of the legal, factual, and incentive information may be known by your adversary. Other information may be privileged communication under the attorney-client or work product privilege. Equally important, you will not want to reveal trial strategies and nondiscoverable information (e.g., assessment of a witness's credibility).

It is a good practice to prepare for settlement as if you were going to trial. To persuade the opposing party, you will need to prepare and then prove your positions. Presentations may include a settlement booklet or brochure that includes a narrative of the case or cover letter, bills, calculations, witness statements, expert reports, and so forth. There are legal services that specialize in the preparation of settlement brochures. Settlement presentations may also include a PowerPoint presentation with a print-out for your adversary. In the Amber Ski Resort case, counsel for Lisa Nevins could support settlement proposals with evidence—documents (e.g., medical bills, pay checks, bills, a copy of *Fletcher v. Ryan*, pages showing verdicts and settlements in similar cases), and a DVD or video of a day in the life of Lisa. The proposal and supporting evidence could be provided in a settlement brochure, in a notebook, or on a DVD.

Discovery—Gathering Information

One of your negotiation objectives is to obtain information from opposing counsel. To accomplish this, you may reveal information and your analysis so that opposing counsel will trade information. Another approach is to ask questions (e.g., "Why do you believe your client has such a strong affirmative defense?"). A little pressure may result in the disclosure of information.

F.   Settlement Conference

Negotiation frequently takes place without any judicial involvement. An agreement can be struck without a lawsuit ever being filed—an ideal situation. After filing, negotiation may still involve no judicial intervention. The court may not even require a settlement conference. Then again, judges in your jurisdiction may routinely hold settlement conferences. Fed. R. Civ. P. 16(a) requires pretrial conferences and in conducting the pretrial conference, settlement may be an issue the court will examine. The conference may be designed to, at a minimum, monitor whether the parties are heading toward settlement with the judge taking no active role in settlement. Or the judge may actively encourage settlement.

You need to determine whether your jurisdiction holds pretrial conferences that include settlement talks. It is also helpful to understand how your assigned judge may approach settlement discussions. If the judge will explore settlement, you should come prepared to advocate your position to the judge. The elements of your negotiation theory are the key points for you to present. Argue the strength of your *factual* evidence on liability and damages. Explain to the judge your *legal* strengths, such as jury verdicts supporting the settlement amount your client will accept. Inform the court why it makes sense for the parties to settle—the *incentives*. Be prepared to meet opposing counsel's arguments and the judge's questions about your positions. And be ready to consider the judge's recommendations, if any.

G.   Bringing Negotiation to Closure

The last part of a negotiation concerns thinking about the conclusion. Too often, negotiation ends inconclusively or at an impasse because negotiators are tired or disillusioned or even because they are elated. Therefore, let's consider planning based on three potential conclusions to the negotiation:

1. You are close to a settlement, but have not pinned down terms,
2. The terms of the settlement are in sight, and
3. Settlement has been generally agreed on.

Remember, however, as in all of our discussion of negotiation, the following present some ideas for you to consider; they do not present all the variables that are likely to occur. The underlying principle was succinctly put into A, B, C terms by playwright David Mamet in his play *Glengarry Glen Ross:* "Always Be Closing." Don't let the agreement get away from you!

Split the Difference

SPLIT THE DIFFERENCE

The *Amber Ski Resort* Case

JMG proposes, "I suggest we split the difference between our proposals. We aren't that far apart." Or JMG might propose, "If you increase those special damages by $10,000, we have a deal."

Such suggestions are typical. You must now reconsider your plan and how you can deal with these proposals tactically. You might suggest, "JMG, let's go back to our last proposals. First, let's examine my last proposal; it is based on the following facts. . .".

You may want to go back to your previous proposal because it was based on specific factors that made your proposal reasonable. JMG's latest suggestions, "splitting the difference" or "adding $10,000" to your proposal, essentially are not reasonable proposals but rather reflect JMG's last-ditch effort to increase what appears to be your last and final offer. But if you can return to your proposal, you might be able to persuade JMG that your proposal is rational, fair, and acceptable. Or you might convince JMG to drop his current compromise or propose a better deal: "OK, let's go with a 40-60 split between our proposal or a $5,000 increase and we have a deal." Or when you are putting together your proposal, consider the points at which you would find it acceptable and within your negotiation solution to "split the difference."

Of course, you might not be able to convince JMG to change to split the difference or settle for the "$10,000 increase." A number of different factors may influence JMG to hang tight—a belief that you will not walk away from the deal now, skepticism concerning your reasons for rejecting his proposals, or JMG's client instructions. In any case, you might have to take JMG's offer or formula if there is to be a settlement.

Cooling Off

Or consider the second potential situation: Anticipating the possibility that no settlement will be reached, you might suggest a cooling-off period.

COOLING OFF

The *Amber Ski Resort* Case

You: "Let's meet again in two weeks. In the meantime, we can talk things over again with our clients. You might want to consider Lisa's need for financial support and my client can consider Amber's cash flow. Perhaps we can think about mutually beneficial proposals and meet again."

JMG might then agree or suggest that a neutral third party act as a facilitator or that the clients be present in follow-up negotiations or that the parties should abandon negotiation altogether.

VI. SETTLEMENT

Finally, a settlement has been reached.

Following the negotiation, generally there are many things left to do—draft the settlement agreement, then sign, file, or distribute it. Agreeing on who will draft the agreement can be an important part of whether the settlement will be finalized or even implemented. Being well aware of this, you might plan to keep progress notes of the discussion, thus making it more likely that you will be the drafter.

You will want to consider all the items that need to be completed in order to implement the settlement and plan how these will be accomplished before the negotiation discussions terminate. Who will sign the agreement? Should the signatures be witnessed? Is there a timetable for signature? Does the agreement need to be filed? Who will file it? What will be the format? Is there specific language that must be included or not included? The answers to these questions are provided by the law and practice of your jurisdiction. However, this section generally describes, among other things: the types of settlement agreements (e.g., structured settlement or lump sum settlement), the types of documents that are used to settle an action, and how to terminate the action with a court order or stipulated dismissal.

A.   Settlement Agreement

The Contract

The agreed-upon terms of the settlement should be reduced to writing. This document is a contract between the parties, and is drafted like any contract. A sample settlement agreement is at page 475.

Types of Settlement Agreements

A variety of settlement agreements are available, and knowing what is possible can aid you in finding a creative solution to propose during negotiation. The following are some of the settlement arrangements that are possible.

Structured Settlement

Rather than providing the plaintiff with a lump sum, the settlement agreement provides for a series of payments over time (usually, an annuity-type of arrangement). Reasons for this approach include, among others: the party cannot make the lump sum payment and because personal injury payments are generally not income if payments are spread out, the recipient may receive them tax-free (as opposed to incurring tax liability for earning off of a lump sum). The structured settlement may include a lump sum payment up front to cover expenses followed by periodic payments. However, a lump sum representing the present value of a reduced structured settlement may be attractive and may avoid a concern with mismanagement of a settlement paid out over time. Be creative.

High-Low Settlement

This form of agreement is designed to avoid the extreme risks of trial. Plaintiff and defendant agree that the case will go to trial but that the plaintiff will not receive more than a set high figure nor less than a low figure. For example, if you are seeking four million in trial on behalf of Lisa in the *Amber Ski Resort* case, a high-low agreement could be entered (e.g., not more than $1,000,000 and not less than $400,000). Lisa Nevin can't lose more than $400,000 and Amber Corp. cannot lose more than $1,000,000. This agreement is not disclosed to the jury.

Mary Carter Agreement

This sort of agreement is used in some states when the case involves multiple defendants. Some states have held Mary Carter agreements to be void because in essence the agreement tends to promote litigation. Under this type of agreement, the plaintiff secretly agrees with a defendant that while the defendant remains in the suit, that defendant's extent of liability is set— the defendant gives the plaintiff an interest-free loan and the defendant's liability will be decreased by the increased liability of other defendants—the defendant's loan is repaid out of the plaintiff's recovery at trial above a set amount. This is often considered a "piecemeal" settlement process that may affect the rights, such as contribution, of one or more multiple defendants. Concerns arise when the court informs the jury of settlement between the plaintiff and one defendant.

B.   Other Settlement Documents

Dismissal

Once a settlement is reached, a filed action will need to be terminated with a dismissal. Fed. R. Civ. P. 41(a)(1) authorizes the dismissal of an action by the plaintiff or by stipulation without a court order. The plaintiff may dismiss by filing a notice of dismissal before the opposing party serves an answer or motion for summary judgment. An action can be dismissed without an order if all the parties sign the stipulation of dismissal. The dismissal must state that it is "with prejudice" in order to end the matter. A sample of a stipulated dismissal is found on page 476.

A Release

Although a release of claims statement can be placed in a separate document, it just as well can be in the settlement agreement itself. The release states in essence that the party permanently releases from any claims both the opposing party and any others against whom the claim could be made (e.g., heirs, employees).

Covenant Not to Sue

Like the release, the covenant not to sue can be included in the settlement agreement. However, it is not a release. Instead, it is an agreement not to sue in the future based on an existing claim. It can be used in partial settlements (e.g., settle some claims against some defendants).

VII. ETHICAL CONSIDERATIONS

As a negotiator you are selling a product—the best deal you can obtain for your client. To accomplish that goal, you will try to be as convincing as possible. You might exaggerate, belittle, selectively present information, or use incentives or threats to achieve your goal. The question nonetheless is: What are the ethical boundaries in negotiating conduct? Just as with other pretrial skills, whether conduct is unethical is usually clear only when the most egregious ethical violations occur—dishonesty, fraud, deceit, misrepresentation.

A.   False Representations

ABA Model Rule of Professional Conduct 4.1 provides: "In the course of representing a client a lawyer shall not knowingly: (a) make a false statement of material fact or law to a third person. . .". The Comment to this Rule states: "A lawyer is required to be truthful when dealing with others on a client's behalf, but generally has no affirmative duty to inform an opposing party of relevant facts. A misrepresentation can occur if the lawyer incorporates or affirms a statement of another person that the lawyer knows is false. Misrepresentations can also occur by partially true but misleading statements or omissions that are the equivalent of affirmative false statements. . .".

MISLEADING STATEMENTS

The *Amber Ski Resort* Case

You represent Amber Ski Resort. Suppose that you know that the eyewitness who claims to have seen Lisa lean out of the cable car just before the cable broke may not be available for a deposition or trial. Is it ethical for you to state the following during negotiation with Lisa's attorney: "We have an eyewitness to the accident who can testify that just prior to Lisa's falling out of the cable car, Lisa was standing up and leaning out the side." Is this ethically all right because you do have a witness who *can*—it's just that the witness *won't* be around to testify? Still, don't you know and in fact intend that this statement will be taken to describe a witness who will appear for trial? On the other hand, it is Lisa's attorney's responsibility to ask, "Will the witness be available at trial?" In the same vein, when, if ever, must a party volunteer weaknesses in its position during negotiation?

Arguably, your statement is not an affirmative falsehood and is not explicitly prohibited by the language of Rule 4.1. As the Comment to the Rule states, you have no obligation to inform Lisa's lawyer that the witness is unavailable for trial. Then again, the statement would seem to be in the words of the Comment a partially true statement that is the "equivalent of an affirmative false statement." Assuming that an argument exists that the statement is not an affirmative falsehood prohibited by the Rule, the best ethical check and balance will be your desire to maintain a reputation for using ethical practices in the jurisdiction in which you practice. You will thus want to maintain behavior that is fair and not misleading. Therefore, even though your failure to disclose the unavailability of an eyewitness if not directly asked is not a falsehood and might not be prohibited by professional rules of conduct or actionable under criminal or civil law, issues of fairness and concern for your reputation should define the ethical boundaries of your negotiation tactics.

B.   The Client's Decision

The ultimate decision maker when it comes to settlement of a civil case or whether to enter a guilty plea in a criminal case is the client. ABA Model Rule of Professional Conduct 1.2 (a) states:

> Subject to paragraphs (c) and (d), a lawyer shall abide by a client's decisions concerning the objectives of representation and, as required by Rule 1.4, shall consult with the client as to the means by which they are to be pursued. A lawyer may take such action on behalf of the client as is impliedly authorized to carry out the representation. A lawyer shall abide by a client's decision whether to settle a matter. In a criminal case, the lawyer shall abide by the client's decision, after consultation with the lawyer, as to a plea to be entered, whether to waive jury trial and whether the client will testify.

The Comment to the Rule recognizes that the client may in advance grant authority to his or her attorney "to take specific action on the client's behalf without further consultation." So, a lawyer and client may settle upon a bargaining range and the lawyer need not discuss the matter further as long as the lawyer stays within the range. The client at any time can rescind the lawyer's authority to negotiate.

C.   Communication with the Client

As negotiation progresses, the lawyer has an obligation to keep the client informed. ABA Model Rule of Professional Conduct 1.4(a) (3) states that the "lawyer must keep the client reasonably informed about the status of the matter. . .". The Comments to Rule 1.4 also provide useful guidance regarding communication during negotiation:

> . . . (2) . . . For example, a lawyer who receives from opposing counsel an offer of settlement in a civil controversy or a proffered plea bargain in a criminal case must promptly inform the client

of its substance unless the client has previously indicated that the proposal will be acceptable or unacceptable or has authorized the lawyer to accept or to reject the offer. .

(5) The client should have sufficient information to participate intelligently in decisions concerning the objectives of the representation and the means by which they are to be pursued, to the extent the client is willing and able to do so. Adequacy of communication depends in part on the kind of advice or assistance that is involved. For example, when there is time to explain a proposal made in a negotiation, the lawyer should review all important provisions with the client before proceeding to an agreement.

ETHICAL RULES RELATING TO NEGOTIATION—SUMMARY

ABA Model Rules of Professional Conduct

TRUTHFULNESS—MRPC 4.1 provides: "In the course of representing a client a lawyer shall not knowingly: (a) make a false statement of material fact or law to a third person. . .".

THE CLIENT'S DECISION—It is ultimately the client's decision regarding settlement of a civil case and entry of a plea in a criminal case. MRPC 1.2(a)

KEEPING THE CLIENT INFORMED—MRPC 1.4(a)(3) states that the "lawyer must keep the client reasonably informed about the status of the matter. . ." . If counsel received a settlement offer (civil) or proposed plea agreement (criminal), counsel must promptly inform the client unless the client has pre-approved the offer as acceptable on unacceptable.

VIII. NEGOTIATION IN THE CRIMINAL JUSTICE SYSTEM: PARALLELS TO AND CONTRASTS WITH CIVIL CASE NEGOTIATION

You have already been provided with a great deal of information about negotiation in a civil litigation context. An appreciation of negotiation in the criminal context, commonly referred to as plea bargaining or plea negotiation, requires that you use the material you have already assimilated to understand the similarities and differences between negotiations in the civil and criminal arenas.

A.   Parallels

Negotiation of a criminal case is analogous to negotiation in the civil arena in at least four major respects.

1.   Whether to Negotiate

In both the civil and criminal justice systems, you must initially decide whether to negotiate at all. A prosecutor may have a variety of reasons for not negotiating although some of the following reasons may seem inappropriate to many, including some prosecutors. A prosecutor's office may have a policy not to offer plea bargains in certain types of serious cases. A particular case may have sparked such strong community feelings a trial seems unavoidable. Or a particular prosecutor may feel that the evidence in the prosecution's case is so open and shut that he or she might as well go to trial and get a guilty verdict if the defendant will not plead guilty to the crimes as charged.

A defendant, on the other hand, may have nothing to lose by going to trial (e.g., with any conviction—and a guilty plea is a conviction—the defendant will be deported or will have a probation revoked and a sentence imposed in another case that is longer than the potential sentence on the current charge). Or the defendant may have everything to lose by not going to trial (e.g., it is imperative to the defendant to clear his or her name). In contrast, the defendant may have nothing to gain by going to trial. For example, the defendant may have no real defense and the trial judge, who will also pronounce sentence, will be annoyed by the waste of court time and the lack of contrition especially if the court believes that the defendant presented a false story.

2.   Preparation for Negotiation

In both arenas you must prepare for negotiation. Preparation will involve reviewing relevant statutes and case law regarding available penalties and sentencing alternatives (e.g., diversion), learning the defendant's and victim's backgrounds, talking to other attorneys (about your adversary, about the sentencing policies of the institution of which your adversary is a member, and about the sentencing judge), thoroughly knowing the facts of the crime, and so on.

3.   Plan a Hierarchy of Solutions

In both civil and criminal arenas, you must develop a plan for the proposed dispositions of your negotiation. In the criminal arena, planning for negotiation can also begin by your positing a wish list of optimum solutions that will likely range from dismissal of all charges for the defendant to pleading guilty to all charges and seeking the court's mercy in sentencing.

The Hierarchy

Like its civil counterpart, this criminal negotiation plan can then be constructed by developing a bargaining range with a hierarchy of solutions, moving down along your wish list, that reflects an assessment of the potential risks and costs involved if the case goes to trial, as viewed in the total context of the strengths and weaknesses of the respective case theories. The prosecutor may face risks such as the escape from justice of a guilty person. A defendant may risk a longer sentence, the death penalty, the stigma of being convicted of a serious charge, increased legal expenses, the loss of a professional opportunity (e.g., when a felony conviction bars one from a profession and the defendant has been offered a misdemeanor plea), deportation, the pressure of trial, the anticipation of trial publicity and the attendant embarrassment for one's family, or loss of a job (e.g., when a conviction will result in incarceration, but work furlough has been offered as part of a plea bargain).

Types of Dispositions

As an illustration of three forms that your disposition solutions might take, imagine you represent Jeff Lukens, who has been charged with robbery in the first degree for robbing Portage Bay News, a convenience store. A robbery in the first degree conviction carries a sentence of five to twenty years in prison, to be set by the sentencing judge. You could bargain in one or a combination of the following three ways (your client must approve the disposition):

- **Charge Bargain**—You could charge bargain: "My client will plead to a charge of the lesser included offense of second-degree robbery (one to five years). Charge bargaining may include striking of enhancements (e.g., extra penalties for using a weapon, prior convictions).
- **Sentence Bargain**—You could sentence bargain: "My client will plead to the robbery in the first degree if you agree to recommend a suspended sentence and probation to the judge. . .".
- **Creative Alternative**—Or you could seek a creative alternative, which will generally manifest itself as a condition of probation—restitution, treatment program, halfway house, community service, or civil compromise. Again, these forms, of course, are not mutually exclusive. Restitution or a treatment program may be part of a bargain for a suspended sentence. Reduction to second-degree robbery may affect the

sentence as well as the charge. In fact, that may have been the whole point of the deal.

Negotiation Style

These positions can be developed, moreover, with either a cooperative or competitive bargaining style underlying their formation.

NEGOTIATION STYLE

The *Portage Bay News* Case

Defense Attorney: I want my client on probation with a short jail term.

Prosecutor: No way. I want your client off the streets. He's going to prison.

Defense Attorney: Why do you want my client in jail?

Prosecutor: Because I'm sick of all the trouble he causes in this town. In prison, he'll cause no trouble. Besides, the punishment will fit the crime.

Defense Attorney: What if we put him on probation and transfer the probation to another county? That way I'll get my probation and you'll get my client out of town.

Prosecutor: Sorry, we can't pass him on to another town. Let's discuss the length of incarceration in my recommendation to the court for prison time for your client.

Power of the Parties

As in civil negotiations, the relative power of the parties, that is, the ability to influence other parties to do as you wish, plays a role. For either side in the criminal process, trial is a risk, an uncertainty. There are so many contingencies at trial: the judge, the jury panel, how witnesses perform, whether the jury begins deliberation on a Friday or the day before a holiday, and the defense needs only one vote to hang the jury. Because of the uncertainty of trial, cases taken to trial are generally characterized by the attorney with the cautious label "triable," and rarely the confident label "clear winner."

The Prosecutor

Within this context of risk, the prosecutor can affect the risk through the interplay of three sources of power:

1. The merits of the prosecution's position,
2. The prosecutor's skill, and
3. The available time and money resources.

The stronger the case theory, the better the prosecutor is as an attorney, and the more time and money available to spend on the case, the more the risk shifts to the other side. The prosecutor can "insure" the defendant against risk ("plead to robbery in the second degree, which carries a one to five-year penalty and you are insured that your client will not face the twenty-year penalty for robbery in the first degree.). With the risk so great at the extremes—one to five years versus twenty years—and the risk of trying even a strong case so difficult to calculate, this "insurance policy" is likely to be tempting.

The Defense

The defense has two basic sources of power. The first is precisely analogous to the prosecution's ability to affect risk that is discussed above: the merits of the defense case, the skill of defense counsel, and the available time and financial resources of the defendant. The second does not come from anything unique to a particular defense or defendant. It derives from the reality of the criminal justice system in which neither prosecutors nor courts have sufficient resources for the task of trying all the cases that have been charged. As an institution, the prosecutor's office thus is often faced with the administrative need to negotiate the majority of its cases. This need of the prosecutor puts some power in the hands of the defense.

4. Peripheral Benefits

In both arenas, counsel may gain peripheral benefits from the process. These benefits may include obtaining information about your opponent and your opponent's case. Rules of Evidence, however, generally bar the use at trial of statements that were made during the negotiation process.

B. Contrasts

The four ways in which criminal negotiation differs from civil bargaining are subtle, being principally attributable to four aspects of the criminal process itself.

1. Moral Values

When you negotiate in the criminal justice system, you are operating in a system where the law is based exclusively on moral values. Unlike the civil system where the allocation of economic resources between parties as compensation for harm is the central focus, dollars are not at issue in the criminal system. Rather, the criminal system is structured around an inquiry into the culpability of the individual allegedly causing harm. Does the defendant deserve punishment and, if so, how much? As a result, you will have few options, or, at best, a narrow range of options, available for bargaining in all but relatively minor criminal cases. Why? Because in criminal law, intuitive community moral judgments, codified by the legislature, establish categories bearing a criminal stigma of various magnitudes (robber, rapist, petty thief) and penalties roughly reflecting the relative culpability that the community attaches to each of those categories. In this realm, a rapist is not the same as a petty thief. They are of different categories, which cannot be mixed. They deserve different treatment according to some external community moral sense. Thus, while you might bargain a million-dollar civil case down to $500,000, you won't bargain a rape case for a plea to petty theft where there is credible evidence that the defendant raped the victim and then stole her wedding ring.

2. Protection of the Innocent

You are negotiating in a system that is procedurally oriented toward protecting the innocent from governmental power. The central theoretical inquiry in the process is whether the government can prove guilt beyond a reasonable doubt. How does this affect bargaining? This systematic focus on assuming innocence on the part of the defendant and requiring proof of guilt by the prosecution structurally places you at a point that is the mutually exclusive opposite of your adversary ("My client is innocent," "Your client is guilty," "You can't prove that beyond a reasonable doubt," "Yes, I can"). You and your adversary will thus theoretically begin your bargaining at positions that are as far apart as possible.

3. Institutional Players

Those participating in negotiation in the criminal justice system are generally institutional players.

The Prosecutor

Except in relatively minor cases (where satisfaction of the victim or compassion for the defendant may come into play), the nature of the prosecutor's office itself may be far more significant in bargaining than the perspective of the individual prosecutor who is handling a case. Although there are prosecutor's offices where each attorney has complete authority to make his or her deals, there are a variety of institutional possibilities that will affect negotiations with the prosecution.

The prosecutor's office may have a set of disposition standards for reduction of charges or standard plea agreements (e.g., first-time theft in the second degree normally will result in a prosecutor's recommendation of probation and one month in the county jail). Such standardization may be motivated by a desire to conserve resources, a concern for equal treatment in the bargaining system, and a desire that the plea agreement reflect institutional policy and not individual discretion. Standardization can also be mandated by statutes that leave little discretion for the prosecutor once charges are filed or require extensive proof before deviation from statutory standards is permissible. Bargaining in this type of office will generally be limited to take-it-or-leave-it positions mixed with some discussion over the application of the guidelines. Prosecutor's offices do not depend on fees generated by billable hours. Thus, the cost of the trial process to the client or law office, which weighs so heavily in the calculus when negotiating in civil cases, will generally have no bearing in the criminal area.

Even in an office without written standards, tacit institutional policies of the office will determine what the defense can offer in a negotiation that will be of value to the prosecution. When the prosecutor's office has an overwhelming caseload, the defense can offer to remove a case from the prosecution's caseload in return for a disposition favorable to the defense. If the office focuses its plea bargain determinations on the nature of the crime itself, then the defense can offer a perspective, say, that the case at hand was not "really a burglary but the result of a lack of judgment"—the defendant was hungry, a little drunk, saw the food through the kitchen window, and he should be allowed to plead guilty to criminal trespass.

The Defense

The prosecution, of course, is not the only institutional player in the system. Judges and most defense attorneys, who are public defenders, work within bureaucratic institutions. The institutional framework of public defender offices will also affect negotiation. In many of these offices, direction from institutional leadership, coupled with time and money resource constraints in the office, and the reality of the legal positions of many of the office's clients, may result in an institutional policy strongly favoring plea bargaining. In such circumstances, the public defenders and the prosecutors with whom they deal daily will often develop an informal set of routine deals for various types of cases and defendants. In any event, both the public defender and the prosecutor will be well aware of the institutional constraints that bear on taking a case to trial.

4. Constitutional Rights

Negotiation in the criminal justice system is constitutionally circumscribed. This has a number of specific ramifications. The defendant who pleads guilty must knowingly and freely waive the constitutional rights the defendant is foregoing (e.g., cross-examination, trial) and must understand the nature and consequences of that to which he or she is pleading. The prosecutor is bound by promises made in a plea bargain. The prosecution must provide the defendant, prior to the plea, with all exculpatory evidence in the government's possession that is material to adjudication or sentencing.

✓ CIVIL NEGOTIATION CHECKLIST

The following are standards of performance for negotiating for the best civil disposition:

Negotiation Theory

- ❑ Have a negotiation theory that will guide both the planning for negotiation and the negotiation presentations.
- ❑ Use the comprehensive negotiation theory composed of these four elements:
  - ✓ Facts: The factual strengths and weakness of the case are considered in planning negotiation and in presenting the negotiation solution.
  - ✓ Law: The strengths and weaknesses of the case are considered in conjunction with the law and are employed in planning and presentation. The law includes not just substantive law but also legal precedent relevant to damages, e.g., jury verdicts in similar cases.
  - ✓ Economic and other incentives influencing each party to settle.
  - ✓ The client's needs and wishes: The negotiation comports with the client's needs and wishes.

Bargaining Range

- ❑ Plan the range of solutions so it is persuasive and supported by the elements of the negotiation theory—facts, law, incentives, and client's wishes wants and needs.

❑ The tentative optimum solution rationally considers the elements in the most optimistic way.

❑ The least desirable solution for negotiation is the most pessimistic view of the facts, law, and incentives.

❑ Settlement values—considering trial contingencies (e.g., probability of proving liability, trial costs)—were calculated for both the optimum and bottom solutions.

❑ A bargaining range is arrived at with the client (and committed to in writing) after discussion of settlement values, trial risks, and so on.

❑ Plan solutions within the range and potential concessions that might be made.

Successful Negotiation

❑ Adopt the right frame of mind for negotiation:

✓ Use ends-means thinking to drive negotiation—always moving toward the ultimate solution with negotiation maneuvers.

✓ Think creatively to find solutions that are persuasive to the other side.

Negotiation Style

❑ Understand the differences between the cooperative and competitive negotiator.

❑ Recognize the traits of the cooperative or competitive negotiator in the opposing attorney (understanding that the attorney may display some of each) and use them to your advantage.

❑ Adopt the traits of effective negotiators.

Negotiation Theory and Presenting the Position

❑ Use the negotiation theory elements to present the negotiation position (e.g., arguing the strength of the facts of the case to support a good settlement solution).

Negotiation Techniques

❑ Negotiate administrative matters to your advantage (e.g., the agenda that favors your result).

❑ Work to have a favorable setting and time for negotiation:

✓ The place where negotiation takes place works to your advantage,

✓ The right people are present, and

✓ The time set for negotiation is favorable.

❑ Make choices in bargaining tactics that are helpful:

✓ Begin negotiation in an effective way to promote negotiation (e.g., cooperative).

✓ Decide whether taking the first position is the most effective approach.

✓ Make concessions.

✓ Tie solutions to other issues.

✓ Understand and use pressure tactics when called for including the carrot and the stick or the ultimatum.

❑ Exchange information appropriately—give information to persuade and gather information to discover more about the other side's case strengths and weaknesses.

❑ Always be seeking to conclude the negotiation, which can include the use of such tactics as splitting the difference and suggesting a cooling-off period.

Settlement

❑ Know what types of settlement agreements are possible (e.g. structured settlement, high-low agreement).

❑ After reaching a settlement, ideally you should draft the settlement agreement.

❑ Prepare other settlement documents, such as releases.

Ethical Considerations

❑ Do not make false or misleading statements during negotiation.

❑ Keep the client informed about the status of negotiation.

❑ Make sure that the client makes the ultimate decision about settlement.

SAMPLE SETTLEMENT AGREEMENT

GENERAL RELEASE AND SETTLEMENT OF CLAIM

For the sole consideration of ◇ to me in hand paid, the receipt of which is acknowledged, I, _____, Releasor, being over 21 years of age, do hereby for myself, my spouse, heirs, executors, administrators, successors, assigns and next of kin, release, and forever discharge, ◇, and all of ◇his/her past, present, and future officers, agents, employees, representatives and assigns and any other persons, firms, or corporations (hereinafter "Releasees") from any and all claims, demands, rights, actions, causes of action, or damages of any type whatsoever, known or unknown, (and consequences thereof, including any injuries or damages which may develop at some time in the future, and all unforeseen developments arising from known injuries or damages) and any and all damages and/or financial loss arising out of or resulting an alleged incident on the   day of   , 19◇ wherein RELEASOR alleges ◇he was injured by the operation of ◇ of a motor vehicle in ◇Pierce County, Washington.

Releasor does hereby for ◇himself, ◇his spouse, ◇his heirs, executors, administrators, successors, assigns and next of kin, covenant and agree to indemnify and save Releasees harmless from all claims, demands, costs, loss of services, expenses, and compensation arising out of or resulting from the incident on the ____ day of _____, 19◇, in ◇ County, Washington, in which Releasor alleges that ◇he was damaged, specifically including but not limited to attorney liens, subrogation claims of an insurance carrier making payments to or on behalf of the Releasor, medical liens, liens for nonpayment of mortgage payments, liens for payment of county, state or federal taxes, including federal income taxes and state/county property taxes, any and all claims or liens by doctors, hospitals, treatment centers and health care facilities, all other medical bills for services, liens under RCW 60.44 and RCW 74.09, liens or claims of the United States of America, and liens or subrogation claims of the State of Washington and its departments, including but not limited to the Department of Labor and Industries and the Department of Social and Health Services. This hold harmless specifically includes all liens or claims by any and all of Releasor's attorneys, health care providers, Medicare, Medicaid and all other such federal and state programs.

It is expressly understood and agreed that the payment of the foregoing amount is not an admission of liability or negligence by the Releasee.

I understand and agree that I may have this reviewed by legal counsel and, by not having this reviewed, I waive my right to do so.

WITNESS: _____, 20XX.

_____
Signature
Printed Name: _____

CERTIFICATE OF WITNESS

We certify that this release was signed in our presence by the above person who acknowledged that s/he understood it fully.

Witness_____   Witness _____

Address_____   Address _____

STIPULATION OF DISMISSAL

UNITED STATES DISTRICT COURT MIDDLE DISTRICT OF MAJOR

LISA NEVIN,	)	
	)	
Plaintiff,	)	
	)	Civil Action, File Number 4817
v.	)	
	)	STIPULATION OF DISMISSAL
	)	
AMBER SKI RESORT, INC.,	)	
DARREN AMBER AND	)	
STEPHANIE AMBER,	)	
Defendant	)	
_____	)	

In accordance with Fed. R. Civ. P. 41, the parties in the above-entitled action agree to dismiss the action with prejudice.

DATE _____March 15_____ , 20XX
(month and day)   (year)

Michelle Hollifield, Attorney for Plaintiff,
6122 Clark Ave.
Ruston, Major 96120
Tel.: (206) 241-0518
Bar No.: 2792

J.M. Galvin, Attorney for Defendants
42 Magnolia Lane
Ruston, Major 96120
Tel.: (206) 241-0107
Bar No.: 7910

13 *Alternative Dispute Resolution*

Associate Professor Alan Kirtley of the University of Washington School of Law was the lead author for this chapter. The authors wish to express their gratitude to Professor Kirtley for his valuable and major contributions to this chapter.

13 *Alternative Dispute Resolution*

"To give a satisfactory decision as to the truth, it is necessary to be rather an arbitrator than a party to the dispute."

Aristotle (384–322 BC)

"The mere formulation of a problem is far more often essential than its solution, which may be merely a matter of mathematical or experimental skill."

Albert Einstein (1879–1955)

I. CONSIDER ALTERNATIVE DISPUTE RESOLUTION

The title of this chapter refers to dispute resolution processes used as an alternative to litigation and trial. Under the banner of alternative dispute resolution, referred to as ADR, a myriad of processes have been created to resolve conflicts. The purpose of this chapter is to introduce you to the various ADR processes. We emphasize arbitration and mediation because they are the most frequently used ADR processes, and the "original stock" from which numerous hybrids have been developed, including final offer arbitration, early neutral evaluation, nonbinding arbitration, mini-trial, summary jury trials, and med/arb (mediation-arbitration).

A word of caution is in order. This chapter will not tell you how to arbitrate or mediate a case or conduct any of the hybrid process. There are excellent resources that can provide a how-to approach for arbitration and mediation, such as John Cooley and Steven Lubet's, *Arbitration Advocacy*, 2nd ed. (NITA, 2003); Dwight Golann's *Mediating Legal Dispute*, Aspen Law & Business (1996); and Jay Folberg, Dwight Golann, Lisa Kloppenberg and Thomas Stipanowich, *Resolving Disputes: Theory, Practice, and Law*, Aspen Publishers (2005).

So why include this chapter if it does not provide a how-to approach to ADR? The focus of this book is pretrial advocacy in the litigation context: the traditional process of resolving disputes in our legal system. Today's attorneys and clients, however, also have various ADR forums available for resolving their disputes. Moreover, the courts increasingly require that parties engage in an ADR process before a trial is granted.

We include this chapter because we believe clients are entitled to be informed of their ADR options before deciding to pursue litigation and a trial. Attorneys cannot counsel their clients effectively if they are not familiar with the attributes of the various ADR processes. Our overview of ADR is intended as a starting point to help you assist clients in choosing the dispute resolution process that best fits their case. The information will also help you consider the discussion questions that follow regarding arbitration and mediation. The attorney and client dialogue regarding the choice of dispute resolution process is a critical aspect of pretrial practice. We have touched on decision making of this type already regarding the choice of whether to go to trial or negotiate a settlement.

For these reasons, we believe that a text on pretrial practice would be incomplete without at least some introduction to ADR. Placing the ADR chapter at the end of the text should not be taken as an indicator of the importance of these processes. Rather, we believe that before you can appreciate the value of the ADR options, you must first have a thorough understanding of what these options are an alternative to—pretrial litigation and trial. Finally, our prediction is that the use of ADR will continue to increase over the course of your career. We hope that this limited exposure to ADR will encourage you to learn more about ADR and to always explore ADR options with your clients.

As a starting point, the chart below illustrates some of the core characteristics of litigation and negotiation, which you have already studied, and those of arbitration and mediation.

II. ATTRIBUTES OF ARBITRATION AND MEDIATION

You should be aware that characteristics of an ADR process may vary depending on the type of dispute and the jurisdiction. Examining the ways the alternative processes differ from each other, and from trial, provides guidance in selecting the process that will best serve your client's needs. In the chart that follows, we have not attempted to list or discuss every attribute of the four major processes; instead, we have included some of their most distinctive features.

Characteristics of ADR Processes and Litigation

Characteristic	Negotiation	Mediation	Arbitration	Litigation
Voluntary/Involuntary	Voluntary	Voluntary, unless mandated by a court	Voluntary, unless mandated by a court	Involuntary (at least for the defendant)
Involvement of Third-Party Neutral	None	Yes, a mediator	Yes, one or a panel of arbitrators	Yes, a trial judge, jury
Role of Third-Party Neutral	No neutral	Guides process and facilitates negotiation discussions	Decision maker	Decision maker
Type of Proceeding	None, free flowing private discussion	Informal, mediator facilitates discussion	Informal hearing; relaxed procedural and evidence rules	Formal trial; rules of procedure and evidence enforced
Discovery	Not applicable	Not applicable; evidence not presented	More limited than in litigation	Full scope under established rules
Time from Start to Finish	Very fast if parties are cooperative	Short time to schedule mediation (within weeks); 4- to 8-hour mediation session	Short time to hearing if discovery limited; one day to several weeks hearing	One to 3 years before trial; 1 day to weeks of trial
Expense	Cost free to the parties unless they involve attorneys	Moderate costs for mediator's fee and attorney time	Significant cost for arbitrator's fee and attorney time	Substantial cost for attorney's time; no fee for judge
Outcome	Negotiated Settlement	Enforceable mediation agreement	Enforceable Award	Enforceable judgment
Appeal Rights	No appeal	No appeal	Very limited (expect in mandatory arbitration: trial de novo)	Full scope on the merits

Arbitration and mediation are the most well-accepted and frequently used methods for settling both public and private disputes outside the courtroom. For those reasons, in this chapter we will focus on arbitration and mediation, and compare those processes with dispute resolution via negotiation or litigation. Even though arbitration and mediation are dissimilar in their approach, their goals are to settle differences between two or more parties in a way that supplements the trial process and maintains the structure of our society.

III. ARBITRATION

A. The Arbitration Process

Arbitration is a process in which disputing parties present their case to a neutral third person or persons who are empowered to render a decision. Of the various ADR processes, arbitration most closely mirrors court adjudication of cases. Both arbitration and trials are adversarial processes, conducted under sets of procedural rules, presided over by an impartial decision maker, and finalized with a binding decision. Arbitration, however, is unique in many respects as described below.

Most commonly, arbitration begins with a provision in a contract. The parties agree, in advance, to arbitrate their disputes, rather than go to court, and to abide by the arbitrator's decision, called an award. Parties may also agree to arbitrate after a dispute arises. In either case, arbitration is an attractive alternative to litigation because the process tends to be faster and less expensive.

Contracting parties have freedom to design an arbitration process that best meets their particular circumstances. They can designate the disputes subject to arbitration, the process for selecting the arbitrator(s); the number of arbitrators (one or a panel of three); the rules of procedure, discovery, and evidence; and the types of damages the arbitrator may award. For example, if the contract involves perishable goods, the parties could pick their arbitrator in advance, agree to no discovery and an expedited hearing with relaxed rules of evidence, no punitive damages and a short deadline for the arbitrator to render the award.

For most parties a generic set of arbitration rules is sufficient and saves the time needed to negotiate and draft a custom made process. Common practice is for the arbitration clause to incorporate the rules of an established provider of arbitration services, such as the American Arbitration Association's proposed clause in its publication "Drafting Dispute Resolution Clauses—A Practical Guide:"

> Any controversy or claim arising out of or relating to this contract,
> or the breach thereof, shall be settled by arbitration administered by
> the American Arbitration Association in accordance with its Commer-
> cial Arbitration Rules, and judgment on the award rendered by the
> arbitrator(s) may be entered in any court having jurisdiction thereof.

The private arbitration process is supported by statute in most states. The majority of states and Congress have enacted arbitration laws based on the Uniform Arbitration Act created by the National Conference of Commissioners on Uniform State Law. Very recently, the Revised Uniform Arbitration Act was issued. These statutes authorize courts to compel reluctant parties to arbitrate, to stay pending litigation when the dispute is subject to an arbitration agreement, to issue a judgment based on an arbitration award, and to set aside an award but on very narrow grounds.

B. Voluntary or Mandatory

Voluntary

In most instances arbitration is voluntary. Private parties make a decision to resolve their dispute in arbitration either before or after the conflict arises. The business community in particular has a long history, beginning with merchants in the Middle Ages, of submitting disputes to an arbitrator. Arbitration agreements are included in business-to-business contracts as a matter of course.

Over the last 25 years, corporations have begun inserting clauses in their form contracts with customers and employees requiring that all disputes be arbitrated. These contracts have been criticized for their lack of voluntariness and often one-sided terms, resulting from the parties' unequal bargaining power. The clauses have led to claims of unconscionability and a flood of litigation. At stake is the right to trial by jury.

The United States Supreme Court has issued a line of cases steadfastly espousing its support for the arbitration process and enforcing arbitration agreements, including those between businesses and their customers and employees. Among the Court's rulings are those that uphold clauses that require arbitration of statutory civil rights claims.

Since moving beyond business-to-business disputes, arbitration has been under tremendous pressure to allow for more discovery, to follow the rules of evidence, to include written findings of fact and conclusions of law in support of awards, and to broaden appeal rights. As arbitration becomes more like litigation, it is less of an alternative to trial. The lesson for lawyers is that arbitration practice is likely to continue to grow and become more complex.

Mandatory

Not all arbitration is private and voluntary. Some judicial systems have implemented mandatory arbitration programs for certain types of cases or for all civil disputes. For example, a court system may require parties to arbitrate their case if the only relief requested is monetary damages and the amount in controversy is $50,000 or less.

Mandatory arbitrations are conducted under rules promulgated by the local court. The arbitrator's award is binding. Court programs permit an appeal to a trial de novo so as not to run afoul of the Seventh Amendment right to trial by jury. Often the appeal right comes with disincentives. For example, if the party challenging the award does not fare better at trial (by x% or $xx), it must pay the other side's attorneys fees and costs for the *trial de novo.*

C.   The Arbitrator

The arbitrator's role is like that of a judge in a bench trial. Although arbitrators function like a judge, they need not be lawyers and in fact many are not. Businesses in dispute often prefer an arbitrator who is a member of their "guild" and a decision based on accepted practices within their industry. Arbitrators are free to decide cases based on their sense of justice, unless the arbitration agreement requires them to follow the law.

The traditional model of arbitration has become less viable with arbitration's expansion beyond business-to-business disputes. Under current practice, arbitrators are called upon to determine arbitrability, that is, whether the particular dispute is covered by the contract's arbitration clause, make rulings on procedural and discovery questions, issue subpoenas, preside over courtroom-like adversarial proceedings, rule on questions of evidence, and issue written, reasoned decisions consistent with the law. In this new arbitration environment, legal training becomes more necessary and attorney-arbitrators more likely.

Generally, a single arbitrator is chosen by the parties. Some arbitration contracts provide for a panel of three arbitrators: each party selects an arbitrator and those two designate the third neutral arbitrator. Arbitrators are usually selected from a list furnished by firms providing arbitration services. Parties seek arbitrators who are honest, impartial, judicial in their demeanor, and, especially, knowledgeable in the law related to the subject matter of the dispute.

The law treats arbitrators as quasi-judicial officers. Arbitrators are immune from civil liability while carrying out their role. Arbitrators are also given testimonial immunity preventing them from being called as witnesses to explain or defend their award or official actions.

D. Arbitration Proceedings

Arbitration proceedings in traditional business-to-business arbitration were characterized by speed, procedural simplicity, relaxed legal rules, and limited appealability. Parties, often unrepresented, informally presented evidence and arguments in the normal trial format: openings, direct and cross-examination of witnesses, presentation of exhibits, and closing arguments. It was not unusual for the arbitrator to announce the award at the end of the hearing. If written, awards were short and straightforward. For example, "I decide for Able Corp. and award it $39,000." Businesses valued arbitration's efficiency, informality, and finality more than legal exactness. It was "cheap" litigation.

While the traditional arbitration model is still used, arbitration has taken on many of the characteristics of litigation and trials. These changes have been brought on by the new classes of claims and the increased involvement of lawyers. Current arbitration practice has become more rule-bound. Here is a sample of rules from the American Arbitration Association's (AAA) "Commercial Arbitration Rules and Mediation Procedures:"

SAMPLE ARBITRATION RULES

The American Arbitration Association

RULES

R-21. Exchange of Information

(a) At the request of any party or at the discretion of the arbitrator, consistent with the expedited nature of arbitration, the arbitrator may direct

i) the production of documents and other information, and

ii) the identification of any witnesses to be called.

* * * * *

R-30. Conduct of Proceedings

(a) The claimant shall present evidence to support its claim. The respondent shall then present evidence to support its defense. Witnesses for each party shall also submit to questions from the arbitrator and the adverse party. The arbitrator has the discretion to vary this procedure, provided that the parties are treated with equality and that each party has the right to be heard and is given a fair opportunity to present its case.

* * * * *

R-31. Evidence

(a) The parties may offer such evidence as is relevant and material to the dispute and shall produce such evidence as the arbitrator may deem necessary

continues ▶

to an understanding and determination of the dispute. Conformity to legal rules of evidence shall not be necessary. All evidence shall be taken in the presence of all of the arbitrators and all of the parties, except where any of the parties is absent, in default or has waived the right to be present.

(b) The arbitrator shall determine the admissibility, relevance, and materiality of the evidence offered and may exclude evidence deemed by the arbitrator to be cumulative or irrelevant.

(c) The arbitrator shall take into account applicable principles of legal privilege, such as those involving the confidentiality of communications between a lawyer and client.

* * * * *

Arbitration agreements and provider rules may now allow for one or more of the following: provisional relief to preserve the status quo (injunction and attachment), full discovery, motion practice including summary judgment, strict adherence to the rule of evidence, a transcript of the hearing, a written reasoned decision based on the law, and, even, a substantive appeal right to the courts. With such characteristics, arbitration proceedings are no longer a "cheap" alternative to litigation.

It is the lawyer's responsibility to design an arbitration process that fits the client's needs and budget. For example, in a contract between small businesses, the lawyer should draft an agreement that calls for a simple, informal arbitration process. Whereas, a plaintiff's attorney should insist on an arbitration process with extensive discovery rights, if the client's claim involves her employer's pattern and practice of racial discrimination.

E. Appeal

Arbitration awards may be appealed to the courts, but the grounds for an appeal are extremely limited (except in court mandated arbitration where a trial de novo is a matter of right). Arbitration appeal rights are statutorily based. The grounds for appeal found in the Uniform Arbitration Act, adopted by many states, the new Revised Uniform Arbitration Act, and Federal Arbitration Act are very similar. For example, on an arbitration party's motion, the court is to vacate an award if it determines that:

- the award was procured by corruption, fraud, or other undue means or

- the arbitrator was partial, corrupt, engaged in prejudicial misconduct, exceeded his or her powers, refused to grant a reasonable request for postponement, or failed to afford the parties due process rights.

Beyond these statutory grounds, the courts have been reluctant to interfere with arbitration awards. Arbitration appeals are unlikely to have a complete record of the proceedings. Without a transcript and/or a reasoned decision, judges are unwilling to speculate as to the basis of the arbitrator's decision. The courts also recognize that appeals severely undercut the benefits of arbitration's finality. However, in a few instances, the courts have vacated arbitration awards, when the award is in "manifest disregard of the law" or violates explicit public policy. These grounds remain vaguely defined and not uniformly applied by the courts.

A recent development is arbitration agreements providing for full rights of appeal to the courts. These clauses are intended to give judges the power to vacate an arbitration award on the same bases as a judgment following trial. These clauses have received a mixed reaction in the courts. Some courts have accepted jurisdiction believing they are obliged to honor contract rights. Courts taking the opposite view have been unwilling to allow private parties to contract for jurisdiction in the public courts.

On balance, appeal rights remain very limited in arbitration.

IV. MEDIATION

A. The Mediation Process

Mediation is a process in which a third-party neutral, the mediator, facilitates communication and negotiation between parties to assist them in reaching a voluntary settlement of their dispute. The mediator, unlike an arbitrator, does not make a decision in favor of one party or the other. Instead, the mediator assists parties in negotiating a resolution that is acceptable to both sides.

The mediation process offers a number of benefits. As compared to arbitration and trials, mediation is generally faster, less costly, less formal, and more likely to preserve the parties' personal or business relationship. In mediation, the parties retain control of the outcome of their dispute, rather than turning it over to a third-party decision maker. Mediation is private and the parties can select a mediator with the background and skills that fit their dispute. Parties can develop creative solutions to their disputes without being restricted to legal remedies. Compliance rates are higher with mediation agreements than court judgments. Presumably, parties are more willing to follow through on their voluntary promises than a resolution imposed upon them by a court.

Mediation, however, is not the right process for all disputes. A mediated settlement does not establish a legal precedent. If the goal is to make changes in the law, court is the proper process choice. The lack of due process protections in mediation has raised concerns about powerful parties taking advantage of parties with fewer resources. Mediation is not the right process if you have serious doubts about the other party's willingness to mediate in good faith. For example, beware of the opposing party who might mediate only to conduct cheap, informal discovery; who may provide information and make statements that cannot be relied on; or who is unlikely to follow through on any agreement that is reached. The cost of mediation is a final concern. A trial judge's services are free, whereas a mediator's fee represents additional costs. If mediation does not settle the case, parties have the double expense of two processes: mediation and a trial. (Although it is not uncommon for a case that fails to settle at the actual mediation to subsequently resolve based upon the ground work done in the mediation process.) When these listed concerns are not present, mediation has a lot to offer.

Mediation is an expeditious and efficient process for resolving disputes. A mediation becomes a settlement event that assembles all the necessary players around one table to engage in a concerted effort to reach resolution. Mediations generally are scheduled for two hours to a full day, which is a fraction of the length of most arbitrations and trials. Since time translates to money, the cost of mediating a dispute is much less than arbitrating and substantially less than litigation and trial.

Mediation is an informal and private process usually conducted in an office building conference room. How mediators conduct the mediation process varies. Some mediators ask the parties to submit pre-mediation memoranda outlining the factual background of the dispute, their legal position, and any negotiations that have already occurred. The mediator may or may not require the parties to exchange memoranda. If an exchange is required, mediators generally allow parties to submit a second confidential memorandum for the mediator only.

Typically, a mediation session begins with the mediator explaining the process and the participants signing an agreement to mediate that should include a confidentiality provision. Next the parties in turn make opening statements presenting their views of the dispute and possible settlement terms. Negotiations then begin and continue until the parties either reach an agreement or an impasse.

Some mediations are conducted entirely in joint session with all the participants present. Increasingly, however, negotiations in mediation take place as a series of caucus sessions in which each party meets privately with the mediator. In caucus style mediation, the mediator becomes the conduit through which all information and settlement proposals are passed between the parties.

Caucus sessions with the mediator generally have an added layer of confidentiality. Most mediators will not share information learned in a caucus with the other side without the disclosing party's consent. Other mediators will share what they learn in caucus when they believe it will help resolve the case. Because mediator practice varies, it is important for lawyers to learn, in advance, how the mediator in their case will treat caucus information.

Advocacy in mediation is similar to what works best when simply negotiating with the opposing party. Lawyers must convey both an openness to settlement and a willingness to go to trial if necessary—not easy to do effectively. Attorneys can set the proper tone in their opening statements in mediation. The following illustration shows how counsel might do that in a sexual harassment case.

OPENING STATEMENT FOR MEDIATION
The *Sexual Harassment* Case

Defense Attorney: Ms. Butler, we are very pleased that you and your attorney agreed to mediate with us. My client, Mr. Vinson of the Ajax Company, and I are here today to negotiate in good faith and we sincerely hope that an amicable settlement can be reached. Mr. Vinson would like to say something initially.

Mr. Vinson: Ms. Butler, on behalf of Ajax I want you to know how much I regret the negative experiences you had while working for us. Our company does not tolerate sexual harassment and we have a strong policy to prevent it. I'm here to learn if there is some way Ajax can improve its procedures.

Defense Attorney: As Mr. Vinson indicates, we are here today to reach a settlement. At the same time, if Ajax does have to go to court we are very confident of our legal position. Ms. Butler complained to co-workers about her supervisor's behavior at work, but she never filed a written complaint of sexual harassment to a manager as required by Ajax's policy. And Ms. Butler quit her job without giving Ajax the opportunity to investigate and address her concerns. Under the law, Ajax is not liable for what management does not know about. If Ajax is forced to go to trial we believe we have a very strong case. Nonetheless, Ajax wants to avoid the expense, delays, and uncertainties of going to court, as I'm sure you do, Ms. Butler.

Mediation is time for both sides to lay down their legal swords and attempt to reach a fair resolution. Ajax is here to do exactly that.

B. Participation

Participation in mediation is generally voluntary. When parties are unable to resolve their dispute, they agree to bring in a mediator. In some business agreements and divorce decrees, the parties agree in advance to mediate their disputes before resorting to the courts.

Because of mediation's success in resolving disputes, many federal and state trial and appellate courts have implemented mandatory mediation programs. While participation in these programs is mandatory, reaching agreement is not. Nonetheless, many courts insist that the parties participate in "good faith," and will assess costs and sanctions for violations. Since the meaning of mediating in "good faith" varies among judges, it is important for lawyers to learn the expectations of their jurisdiction.

C.   Confidentiality

A major benefit of mediation is that it provides a safe negotiating environment. Parties can openly and candidly discuss their case without fear that their words will be repeated in court if the case does not settle. The confidentiality of mediation communications is protected by privilege statutes in nearly every jurisdiction. Several states have recently adopted the new Uniform Mediation Act, a creation of the National Conference of Commissioners on Uniform State Law and the ABA's Dispute Resolution Section.

A privilege provides more protection for mediation communications than Evidence Rule 408, which applies generally to negotiations. A mediation privilege bars both discovery of mediation communication and their admission into evidence. In contrast, Evidence Rule 408 only restricts admissibility and its "for another purpose" exception significantly limits its usefulness as a means of protecting mediation discussions.

Although almost all jurisdictions have a mediation privilege, their statutes vary widely in content, scope, and operation. Because of these differences, lawyers must become familiar with the privilege statute that will apply in their case (before the mediation begins). Some of the questions lawyers need to answer are:

- What has to happen to trigger the privilege?
- What types of disputes are covered?
- When does the privilege begin and end?
- Who is covered by the privilege?
- What types of information are covered or excluded?
- Does the privilege apply in a civil case? criminal case? arbitration? legislative hearing?
- Who can enforce the privilege?
- How is the privilege waived?

The mediation privilege is not absolute. For example, the privilege does not bar the use of mediation information as a basis for future discovery efforts. Imagine that your opposing party, George, reveals in mediation that the day after the automobile accident he told his friend Carol: "I was at least 25 miles over the speed limit when I hit them." The mediation privilege will bar discovery and evidence of the words spoken by George in the mediation. However, you may use what you learned in mediation by deposing Carol to obtain the same information. As a result, counsel and client need to exercise caution in mediation to avoid giving away discovery tips.

The mediation privilege does not apply to evidence that existed before the mediation. For example, a client's damning letter to the other party sent before the mediation does not become privileged by slapping the letter down on the mediation table. Otherwise mediation would become a "black hole" for depositing all unhelpful evidence.

Finally, the mediation privilege only applies to subsequent legal proceedings. If sensitive personal or commercial information is likely to come up in a mediation, attorneys should insist on a confidentiality agreement in order to prevent disclosures, for example, to the media or their client's business competitor.

SAMPLE AGREEMENT TO MEDIATE

AGREEMENT TO MEDIATE

THIS IS AN AGREEMENT between the undersigned parties ("parties") and Jamal Shakelford ("mediator") to mediate under the following terms and conditions:

1. The parties consent to the appointment of Jamal Shakelford to act as their mediator in this matter. The mediator will use his best efforts to assist the parties in reaching a mutually acceptable settlement of their dispute. The mediator however does not warrant or represent that settlement will result from the mediation process or that settlement is in the best interest of any or all of the parties.

2. The mediator will serve exclusively as a neutral and impartial third-party facilitator. The mediator is not a judge or arbitrator, and thus will not be making a decision, ruling, or award.

3. Mediation is a voluntary process for settlement negotiations. The mediator does not have the power or authority to force a settlement upon a party or the parties. A party may withdraw from the mediation at any point. The mediator reserves the right to terminate the mediation at his discretion.

4. The mediator will not provide legal advice nor will he represent or advocate for any party. The parties are strongly encouraged to consult with their individual attorneys regarding their legal rights and responsibilities before the mediation, at any time during the mediation session, and before signing any final binding settlement agreement.

5. All those signing this Agreement understand and agree that all mediation communications will be confidential, unless agreed otherwise. Mediation communications are also privileged, which means they may not be disclosed in any later legal proceeding

continues ▶

under [a state mediation privilege statute based on the Uniform Mediation Act]; except the following will not be confidential or privileged and may be disclosed:

- Any written agreement (e.g., this Agreement to Mediate and any settlement agreement),
- Threats to inflict bodily injury or commit crimes of violence,
- Plans to commit a crime or conceal ongoing criminal activity,
- Claims of professional misconduct or malpractice based upon conduct during the mediation, and
- Admissions of abuse or neglect of a child, adult, or disabled person.

All those signing this Agreement understand that under limited circumstances a judge may allow mediation communications to be introduced in a criminal felony proceeding or a proceeding challenging the mediation settlement agreement. Finally, documents and evidence that existed before the mediation do not become privileged by reason of their use in the mediation.

6. The mediator may hold private meetings or caucuses with one or more of the parties. Information disclosed during a caucus will not be revealed by the mediator unless authorized to do so by the party making the disclosure.

7. The parties agree not to subpoena or otherwise require the mediator to testify or produce records, reports, notes, or other documents received, reviewed, or prepared by or for the mediator during the mediation proceeding. The parties agree to pay all the mediator's expenses (including but not limited to the mediator's hourly rate, the mediator's attorneys fees, and costs) related to his resisting and/or quashing a subpoena issued by a party.

8. The parties agree to be jointly and severally responsible for paying the mediator's fees, which will be charged at the rate of $XXX.00 per hour.

9. If this Agreement to Mediate is signed at separate locations and/or at differing times, the counterparts will be treated as a single original constituting the agreement of all signing parties.

Dated: _____, 20XX

_____   _____
Party   Party

_____
James Jones
Mediator
Address: XXX
Tel.: XXX

In exchange for the mediator agreeing to conduct this mediation for their clients, the undersigned attorneys agree to abide by paragraphs 5 and 7 of this Agreement to Mediate.

_____   _____
Attorney   Attorney

D. Choosing a Mediator

Mediation is an emerging profession that is not yet regulated in most jurisdictions. Mediators are not required to have any particular qualifications or even mediation training. Mandatory mediation programs connected with the courts are an exception. Those programs normally require panel members to have a law or other advanced degree (e.g., MBA or MSW) and mediation training. Most private firms and nonprofit organizations offering mediation services require their mediators to be trained.

Selecting the right mediator for your case is important. The first step is to learn the mediator's background and qualifications. Questioning a potential mediator directly is appropriate. Talking to several attorneys who used the mediator recently is often the best means of assessing mediator competence and appropriateness for a particular dispute.

Mediators have different styles of practice. You will need a mediator whose style fits your client and your case. Mediator styles have been categorized as narrow versus broad in terms of problem definition, and facilitative versus evaluative in the way the mediator interacts with the parties. Mediators are then classified as falling within one of four quadrants as illustrated in the chart below: narrow/evaluative, broad/evaluative, narrow/facilitative or broad/facilitative.

Mediator Techniques

Leonard L. Riskin, "Understanding Mediators' Orientations, Strategies, and Techniques: A Grid for the Perplexed," 1 HARV. NEG. J. 7 (1996).

	Role of Mediator *Evaluative*	
Problem Definition Narrow	**Urges/pushes parties** to accept narrow (position-based) settlement **Proposes** narrow (position-based) agreement **Predicts** court or other outcomes **Assesses** strengths and weaknesses of each side's case	**Urges/pushes parties** to accept broad (interest-based) settlement **Develops and proposes** broad (interest-based) agreement **Predicts** impact (on interests) of not settling **Educates self** about parties' interests

Problem Definition Broad

continues ▶

Helps parties evaluate proposals	**Helps parties** evaluate proposals
Helps parties develop & exchange narrow (position-based) proposals	**Helps parties** develop and exchange broad (interest-based) proposals
Asks about consequences of not settling	**Helps parties** develop options that respond to interests
Asks about likely court or other outcomes	**Helps parties** understand interests
Asks about strengths and weaknesses of each side's case	

Facilitative

Narrow style mediators tend to focus only on the legal aspects of the case and the likely litigated result. Mediators with a broader style will add business interests and personal relationships to the problem definition and its resolution.

A facilitative mediator is more likely to give parties latitude in finding their own solution to the conflict. Facilitative mediators tend to favor mediating in joint session. Evaluative mediators are more likely to direct the parties' discussions and give their opinion on the merits of a parties' case, and some will predict the results of the trial. Evaluative mediators prefer to use the caucus style for their mediation.

Interestingly, studies have shown that while individual mediators may identify their style as narrow/evaluative or broad/facilitative, when mediating they are not wedded to a particular style. Instead, a mediator's style will vary with the nature of the case and the stage of the mediation proceeding. During the early stages of the mediation or if the case involves parties who have a continuing relationship, mediators are more likely to fall into the broad/facilitative style. Mediators will move toward a more narrow/evaluative style later in the mediation or if the case is mostly about the legal issues.

You and your client may want a broad/facilitative mediator if the parties hope to preserve their business or personal relationship, for example, employer and employee, business partners, or a divorcing couple sharing child rearing responsibilities. The broad/facilitative mediator will focus not only on the immediate dispute but will help the parties improve their communication and problem solving skills for their future interactions by keeping them in joint session.

If, instead, the only thing connecting the parties in your case, for example, is a personal injury suit, a narrow/evaluative mediator may be the better choice. Such a mediator will focus on the strengths and weaknesses of the parties' legal positions and stress the costs and risks of the impending trial. To lessen the effects of adversarial behavior and provide privacy for evaluating each party's case, this mediator will use caucuses extensively. You will want your evaluative mediator to have legal expertise and familiarity with trial results in cases similar to yours. Finally, in caucus style mediation, the mediator, and not you, will be presenting your arguments and proposals to the other side. Therefore, it is critical to select a mediator the opposing party will respect, trust, and listen to.

A caucus in the latter stages of the mediation of the sexual harassment case might look something like this:

MEDIATION CAUCUS

The *Sexual Harassment* Case

Mediator: [entering the plaintiff's caucus room] Hello there, anything new come to mind while I was meeting with the company?

Attorney: Not really. We have been reviewing their last proposal.

Mediator: Ok, well the company has asked me to convey some points. Please remember I'm just the messenger.

The folks in the other room are expressing some frustration. They say they heard from you that improving working conditions for the women at the company was most important and that compensation was secondary.

From their point of view they believe they have made important commitments to improve the working environment. In their last proposal, they agreed to beef up their sexual harassment policy, in the ways you wanted, and to require sexual harassment training for all their managers. Also, the company president has agreed to write you a positive letter of reference, something which you had not even asked for.

Given these commitments, the company is very disappointed to hear that you would not accept their $15,000 offer. They believe $15,000 is more than fair under the circumstances, particularly since you have said that money is a secondary concern. So, what I'm hearing from them is that they have been giving, giving, giving, and you guys have not.

continues ▶

However, they have said that, in the spirit of compromise, they are willing to increase their offer of $20,000.

Client: When I said money was secondary, I didn't mean it was unimportant. What happened to me at the company was wrong, and it has hurt me deeply. One reason I don't have a job yet is because they took away my confidence. $20, 000 doesn't seem fair for what I've been though.

Attorney: I agree. $20,000 is not in the ball park.

Mediator: Ok, I understand. But, right now the company thinks its legal position is strong. For you to get them to offer more, they will have to be convinced otherwise. You need to give me your best factual and legal arguments for why they should pay more. And, I'll need a new number to take over to them.

Attorney: [The attorney then sets out for the mediator the strengths of the plaintiff's case and the weaknesses of the company's. The attorney also shows the mediator a list of jury verdicts in similar cases.]

So, based on the law and what juries have done in the past, our case is worth a lot more than $20,000.

Tell the company we appreciate their willingness to improve their sexual harassment policies and that we will come down from $115,000 to $95,000.

Mediator: Ok. I'll go talk to them. Am I authorized to disclose the points you made to support your $95,000 demand?

Attorney: Yes. And, take this copy of the jury results to show them.

E.   Law, Evidence, and Procedures

Law

Parties in mediation bargain in the "shadow of the law." Mediation settlement proposals are measured against the parties' estimates of the likely litigated result under the governing law. However, mediation parties are often willing to accept less than they might receive in court because a mediation settlement is "a bird in hand" without the risks and costs of going to trial.

A great advantage of mediation is that the parties are not limited to legal precedent and remedies in formulating a resolution. In contrast to arbitration awards and court judgments, which must be based in law and generally involve only the payment of money, the parties in mediation are free to disregard the law and base their settlement on what seems fair and reasonable under their particular circumstances. Mediation settlements can take into account the parties' personal values and business interests. Mediation allows parties to be creative in reaching agreements that satisfy their values and broader interests. For example, in a sexual harassment case, the terms of settlement, in addition to compensation, can include improvements to the company's sexual harassment policy, sexual harassment awareness training for all managers, a transfer of the harasser to a distant work site, and a promise by the former employee not to disparage the company or reveal the financial terms of the settlement.

The law comes into play if the mediation parties agree to settle. Mediation settlement agreements fall under traditional contract law principles. Therefore, it is important for lawyers to make sure their settlement agreement meets the legal requirements of contract formation and the statute of frauds. Best practice is not to leave the mediation session without a written settlement agreement signed by all the parties and their attorneys. An alternative, if there are time constraints or the settlement is very complex, is a written *memorandum of understanding* containing the essential terms, again, signed by all the parties and their attorneys. As a note of caution, some jurisdictions will not enforce oral mediation settlements. In other jurisdictions, the mediation privilege statute is likely to severely restrict the availability of evidence to prove the existence of such oral agreements.

✔ **CHECKLIST**

Key Elements of a Mediation Memorandum

Items to include in a mediation memorandum of understanding are:

- Key points of the terms of agreement: who, what, when, where, how, and how much
- Criteria for determining if performance has occurred
- Terms of any release of claims
- Confidentiality of the settlement terms if important
- Designation of the attorney who will draft the formal Settlement Agreement
- A deadline for the draft
- A process for resolving drafting disagreements or disputes over implementation e.g., negotiation, return to mediation, or authorizing the mediator (now acting as an arbitrator) to make a ruling
- Signatures of all parties to the settlement and their attorneys

Evidence and Procedural Rules

Evidentiary and procedural rules designed to control the flow of information at trial do not apply in the mediation process. These rules are essential for orderly court proceedings, but lack flexibility and do not permit direct communications between the parties. In contrast, mediation participants have the freedom to custom-make their process to fit their particular dispute. Within the mediation framework, parties may decide what, when, and how they will talk about the issues. Mediation parties and their counsel have the opportunity to speak and negotiate directly with each other (under mediator enforced ground rules to keep the discussions civil, businesslike, and on task). On the other hand, some parties may instead decide that caucus style mediation would work better for their case.

V. CHOOSING, PLANNING, AND PREPARING FOR AN ADR PROCESS

Choosing an ADR Process

When helping clients choose a process to resolve their dispute, the attorney's job is to "Fit the Forum to the Fuss." F. Sander and S. Goldberg, "Fitting the Forum to the Fuss: A User-Friendly Guide to Selecting an ADR Process," 10 NEG. J. 49 (1994). In other words, the choice of process should be driven by factors that will satisfy the client's objectives, which may include: minimize cost, speed, privacy, maintain or improve relationship, vindication, neutral opinion, precedent, or potential type and amount of recovery.

Making the choice of process, as with all pretrial planning, requires familiarity with the factual and legal aspects of the dispute, your client's interests and objectives, as well as the other parties', and the attributes of each of the available processes.

Use of a chart like the one at page 481 of this chapter may help clients and their attorneys decide which process is most suitable for their case.

Choosing whether to pursue resolution of a case through ADR or litigation requires a discussion between lawyer and client. In the earlier sexual harassment case such a discussion might proceed like this:

THE "ADR CHOICE" DISCUSSION WITH THE CLIENT

The *Sexual Harassment* Case

Lawyer: From our earlier discussions, I understand Ms. Butler that your goals for the case are changing the working environment for women at the company and being fairly compensated for what you had to go through. You want to see the company strengthen its sexual harassment policy and train managers to deal with sexual harassment complaints proactively. Do I have it straight?

Client: That's right. I really want the Ajax company to clean up its act! I still have friends that work there. But finances are important too since I haven't been able to find a new job yet.

Lawyer: Well, there are a number of processes we could use to achieve your goals. Let me describe them. [Then the lawyer and client have an extended discussion regarding the characteristics and pros and cons of the various ADR processes, perhaps using a chart like the on page 481.]

* * * * *

Client: OK, given what you have said, how about this: We negotiate with the company's lawyer first and, if that doesn't work, suggest mediation to them. That will keep my costs down and maybe we can settle quickly. Also, I may be able to avoid having to relive the experience in a public courtroom. Let's put court on the back burner for right now.

What do you think?

Lawyer: Sounds sensible to me. That's your best shot at getting the company to change its policy and provide training to the managers. A judge would never order that.

Let's go forward and see what happens. I'll call the company's lawyer tomorrow and set up a meeting. If they are unreasonable, we can always revisit the litigation option later.

Planning and Preparing for the ADR Process

Planning and preparing for an ADR process will be similar to readiness for either a trial or settlement discussions. Preparing for arbitration is very much like getting ready for a trial. You will marshal and then present your evidence in an adversarial hearing to the arbitrator who will make a binding decision. Rules governing arbitration mirror court procedures but with significant differences in the areas of discovery (less), rules of evidence (relaxed), and rights of appeal (virtually none). There is no single set of arbitration rules. Arbitrations are conducted under rules established by the provider of arbitration services, such as, the American Arbitration Association or Judicial Arbitration and Mediation Services. Attorneys must become thoroughly familiar with the particular arbitration procedures that will apply in their case.

Planning and preparing for a mediation has all the same elements as getting ready for direct settlement negotiations with the opposing party, which we covered in Chapter 12. For a mediation, you must also decide what style of mediation fits your case and identify appropriate mediators. Once the mediator is selected, you need to get your client ready for mediation, initially by explaining how the mediation process works. Clients need to be forewarned that mediation can be an intense and stressful experience. It is helpful to establish a role the client feels comfortable playing during the mediation. For example, will the attorney do all the talking when the other side is present, or will the client present the business aspects of the case? Most important is for the client and attorney to remain in sync as to their negotiation strategy and ultimate objectives. This will require consultation throughout the mediation as new facts, arguments, and settlement proposals are presented.

Attorneys need to remember that mediation is not an adjudicative process. The objective is to persuade the other party, not the mediator. Aggressive, adversarial behavior is generally counterproductive. A more successful stance is a balanced one illustrated in the earlier example of an attorney's opening statement in mediation.

VI. HYBRID ADR PROCESSES

Our focus has been on arbitration and mediation, as we said, because they are the most widely used ADR processes. The flexibility of ADR has allowed for the creation of hybrid processes drawing from arbitration and mediation. An introduction to a few of the hybrids follows.

In what is known as "final offer," "baseball," or "high-low arbitration," the arbitrator may only decide between the parties' last offers to each other. This hybrid, used in major league baseball, motivates the parties to make reasonable final offers as a means of persuading the arbitrator to rule in their favor. The arbitrator's decision is binding.

A number of hybrid processes are designed to place an estimated value on a case. Parties using *early neutral evaluation* make presentations to a neutral lawyer who gives estimates of a party's chances of winning particular issues or the entire case. In *nonbinding arbitration* the arbitrator's award is not final. Instead, the amount of the award is used as a basis for further negotiations. With a *summary jury trial,* an elected judge presides over an abbreviated trial using jurors selected from the court's pool. The jurors are presented key testimony and exhibits and hear the lawyer's arguments. The jury's verdict becomes an estimate of what a "real" jury will do with the case. Summary jury trials are only used in high stakes trials that are expected to be very long. Summary jury trials have been criticized for "tricking" jurors by not informing them that their service and verdict are for advisory purposes only.

Mini-trials are used in large business disputes and may incorporate elements of negotiation, early neutral evaluation, and mediation. First, a mini-trial is not a trial. Instead, the lawyers present truncated versions of their cases to a panel consisting of each party's CEO and a third-party neutral who oversees the process. After the presentations the CEOs meet to negotiate a resolution. The neutral's role can vary. The CEOs may ask the neutral to provide an evaluation of the case, serve as their mediator, and/or issue a nonbinding decision.

Med-arb starts with mediation, but if the parties are unable to reach settlement, the case is decided by arbitration. The attraction of med-arb is the availability of a final decision "in the wings" if mediation does not work. The process is highly efficient when the same neutral serves both roles—the parties only have to tell their stories once. However, knowing that an arbitration phase is looming, parties may be less candid with their mediator, who may later be a decision-making arbitrator. Parties in the arbitration phase may have concerns whether the arbitrator's decision is based on confidential mediation communications. If the arbitrator relies only on information gained during mediation, the parties do not have the opportunity to present additional evidence or to cross examine witnesses.

These hybrid processes are examples of ADR's wonderful flexibility. As a lawyer you will have numerous process choices to meet your clients' needs.

VII. ETHICAL CONSIDERATIONS

Alternative dispute resolution processes raise familiar ethical issues. When arbitrating a case, the ethical requirements of trial practice are relevant. Ethical standards governing negotiation apply to an attorney representing a client in mediation.

An ethical issue unique to ADR relates to client counseling. The question is whether an attorney is ethically obligated to discuss ADR options with a client before beginning a lawsuit. Fear of lost fees is not an appropriate reason for attorneys to skip the ADR discussion with their client. Whether ethically required or not, the best practice for attorneys is to outline the available ADR options for the client before initiating litigation and during the litigation process. For the client to make an informed choice, attorneys must review the pros and cons of litigation as compared to the various ADR processes, including considerations of costs, time, privacy, emotional stress, and the effect on the parties' future relationship.

✓ ADR CHECKLIST

Preparation to Meet with the Client to Assist in Selecting an ADR Process

❑ Thoroughly understand the characteristics and pros and cons of arbitration, mediation, and the various hybrid ADR process.

❑ Know what ADR resources are available in your area.

❑ Know whether your state has adopted either the Uniform Arbitration Act or the newer Revised Uniform Arbitration Act.

❑ Know whether your state has a mediation privilege statute and, if so, what confidentiality protection it provides.

❑ Determine the estimated costs for each of the ADR alternatives available to your client.

❑ Know whether the court will require ADR if suit is filed.

Gather This Information in Order to Assist Your Client in the Selection Process

❑ The client's goals in resolving the dispute:
  ✓ A money judgment
  ✓ Injunctive relief
  ✓ Creating a precedent
  ✓ Non-legal relief
  ✓ Maintaining an ongoing relationship
  ✓ Concern for privacy

❑ The barriers to settlement
  ✓ Poor communication
  ✓ Need to vent emotions
  ✓ Broken relationship
  ✓ Differing view of the facts
  ✓ Differing view of the law
  ✓ An important principle involved

❏ The "likely litigated result" estimate will help the client weigh the ADR alternatives against going to trial

Conducting the Meeting

❏ Have a meeting agenda designed to learn your client's goals and to determine what the barriers are.

❏ Decide how will you explain the characteristics and pros and cons of the various processes:

    ✓ Send your client written materials on ADR before the meeting

    ✓ Use a visual aid (chart or diagram) to explain the ADR processes

❏ Select topics you will cover when describing the ADR process and comparing the process to litigation:

    ✓ Presence of a third-party neutral

    ✓ Neutral's role: decision maker or facilitator of negotiations

    ✓ Available Relief: legal only or parties determine

    ✓ Outcome: settlement contract, enforceable award, or legal judgment

    ✓ Nature of the proceeding: formal or informal

    ✓ Opportunity to deal with emotional issues: none or in a controlled setting

    ✓ Degree of privacy: public hearing or private process

    ✓ Time to resolution: protracted process to relatively quick

    ✓ Estimated cost: very costly to relatively inexpensive

    ✓ Stance of Parties: adversarial or problem solving

Assisting the Client to Make the Choice of Process

❏ Summarize what the client has said to make sure you know what is most important to the client in a dispute resolution process

❏ List factors for you and your client to discuss

❏ Decide whether you will offer a recommendation or do so only if asked

❏ Decide whether you will review the decision with the client to make sure you fully understand the client's wishes.

14 Introducing the Cases and Assignments

14 *Introducing the Cases and Assignments*

"I hear and I forget. I see and I remember. I do and I understand."

Confucius

"What one has not experienced one will never understand in print."

Isadora Duncan

"We learn by example and by direct experience because there are real limits to the adequacy of verbal instruction."

Malcolm Gladwell,
Blink. The Power of Thinking Without Thinking (2005)

"With every experience, you alone are painting your own canvas, thought by thought, choice by choice."

Oprah Winfrey (1954–)

I.   EXPERIENTIAL LEARNING

You will learn how to effectively engage in pretrial activities by experiencing them as set forth in text, assignments, and the case files that include the documents and mock law you will need to perform the assignments. The chapters in the book correspond to the skills you will need in order to do pretrial work. Each of the chapters in this book has a corresponding set of checklists and performance exercises, called assignments, which will give you experience in the chapter's activity. The checklists are at the end of the chapters, but assignments for all of the chapters are in this chapter, starting at page 517. For example, the chapter on depositions has corresponding performance assignments in which you will take and defend depositions.

507

In addition to the assignments, this chapter provides a factual summary of both a civil and criminal case that arises out of a series of incidents. You are about to be introduced to factual situations that lead to pretrial activities for criminal litigation, civil litigation, or both. Your professor will assign you to the case or cases, *State v. Hard, Summers v. Hard* and you will learn by performing the assignments—developing a case theory and theme, interviewing, pleading, engaging in discovery, negotiating, creating persuasive visuals, researching and arguing a motion, and so on

II. FACTUAL SUMMARY

The following factual summary gives you an overview of what happened in *Summers v. Hard* and *State v. Hard*. It is a composite of highlights of what some of the witnesses claim occurred. For specifics and greater detail, refer to the documents in the Case Files, which are contained in the CD that accompanies this book. Also, during case development and discovery exercises you will uncover many additional facts that are neither described in this summary nor contained in the Case Files.

During the evening of August 20th of last year, Bruno Summers and his fiancée, Deborah Miller, were in the Garage, a tavern in the city of Ruston, state of Major. The Garage has both a bowling alley and pool hall on different sides of the building. Bruno and Deborah were seated in the bar area adjacent to the pool hall. The Garage tavern is owned by M. C. Davola and his wife. Edward Taylor Hard also was in the tavern that day. Ed Hard, allegedly intoxicated and boisterous, approached the Summers-Miller table and began making advances toward Deborah Miller, his former girlfriend. Bruno Summers and Deborah Miller rose to pay the bill and leave. Ed Hard grabbed

Bruno Summers around the neck and a struggle ensued. Bruno Summers knocked Hard to the floor, splitting Hard's lip and chipping a tooth. Bartender Tom Donaldson ordered both men to leave the tavern. Tavern patrons overheard the exchange between Summers and Hard and saw what happened.

At the time of the August 20th incident, Bruno Summers was 30 years old and the owner of University Fitness Center. He also was a member of a neo-Nazi organization. Ed Hard was 29 years of age, and he worked as a house painter.

On August 22, Ed Hard went to the American Gun Shop located in Neva, Major, and he purchased a .22-caliber revolver. On August 27, after the statutory five-day waiting period had passed, Hard paid for and received the gun and bought some ammunition. On the same day—the 27th—Bruno Summers married Deborah Miller. This was Bruno Summers's second marriage. His first marriage lasted six years, and he was awarded custody of his two children by that marriage, Ronnie, age 8 and Amanda, age 12.

On September 3 of last year, at approximately 8:00 P.M., Ed Hard and two friends, John Gooding and Rebecca Karr, were in the Garage Tavern seated at the bar. They had several drinks before arriving at the tavern. Bartender Donaldson served them rounds of drinks. They were talking loudly.

Bruno Summers, his new wife Deborah Summers, and their friend Peter Dean entered the pool hall side of the Garage Tavern at approximately 9:00 P.M. They had spent the previous couple of hours on the bowling side of the Garage Tavern, where they bowled and drank. The three walked to the entrance of the bar area and saw Hard sitting at the bar. Hard was overheard making a comment about the presence of the Summers in the tavern. Deborah wanted to leave, but Bruno said that instead they would sit in a booth near the front of the tavern, some distance away from Hard.

Roughly five minutes after the Summers and Peter Dean entered the pool hall side of the Garage, Bruno got up from the booth and went to the restroom near the front door of the tavern. Hard confronted Bruno Summers as he left the restroom. An exchange took place. Hard produced a gun and shot Bruno Summers. Deborah ran to her husband who lay shot on the tavern floor. The bartender called 911. Hard immediately left the Garage.

Peter Dean called Hans Summers, Bruno Summers's father, who along with his wife Gretchen were at Bruno and Deborah's house taking care of their two grandchildren, Ronnie and Amanda. The grandparents loaded the two children into the car and drove to the Garage and parked on the street in front of pool hall side of the tavern. Hans Summer went to the front door of the tavern where he was stopped by a Ruston Police Officer who told him that he would have to wait while the EMTs took care of his son. Hans Summers could see his son's bleeding body from the doorway. His daughter-in-law was standing near Bruno's body, and she was crying and screaming. Hans Summers looked down to find that his grandson had left the car and was standing at his side. When Ronnie saw his father, he also began screaming and crying. Bruno's parents and children followed the ambulance to Mercy Hospital where Bruno was treated.

Ruston police officers were dispatched to Hard's residence where they entered without a warrant, arrested Hard, and seized a revolver that later a firearm's expert was able to match with the slug recovered from Bruno's body. The officers took Hard to the precinct where detective Russell Tharp took a statement from him. In that statement, Hard among other things said that he had feared for his life and shot Summers by accident. Also, a breathalyzer test was administered, and Hard's blood-alcohol level was .16.

Both Deborah and the eight-year-old Ronnie Summers suffered emotional disturbances from witnessing what happened to Bruno Summers. They both saw a psychologist, who after administering a battery of tests, opined that they suffer from post-traumatic stress disorder.

Bruno Summers at first seemed to be recovering from the gunshot wound. However, he contracted pneumonia and died on September 7. As you first enter the criminal case, Ed Hard, who had originally been charged with first degree assault, may now be charged with homicide. As you enter the civil case, you will have just been retained and will engage in plaintiff and/or defense case theory development.

III. THE CD

The Case Files

On the CD that accompanies this book, you will find Case Files for *Summers v. Hard* and *State v. Hard*, the civil and criminal cases respectively.

The Case Files include diagrams, documents, expert reports, jury instructions, pleadings, research memoranda, statutes, and witness statements. The research memoranda are a special feature. The memoranda are composed of fictional appellate decisions in a fictional jurisdiction, the State of Major. The memos provide all the research you need to deal with the legal issues in the problems. Of course, your instructor may prefer that you instead research and use appropriate real cases from your jurisdiction. You can print out portions of the Case Files from the CD to use during an exercise. For instance, you can print out exhibits, such as a diagram and photographs, to use during the deposition. A Table of Contents of the CD is on the CD and also on page 600.

IV. THE DVD

A DVD is also a companion to this book. It is designed to further enrich your experience of studying pretrial advocacy. On the DVD, you will find:

- *DVD of the scene*—The prosecutor's investigator will walk you through the Garage tavern where the central events of the civil and criminal cases take place;
- *DVD depositions*—By watching excerpts of DVD depositions you can learn firsthand how to take and defend a deposition;
- *Computer slide show*—Using computer software, such as PowerPoint, litigators create dramatic pretrial presentations, e.g. for settlement, and trial presentations, e.g. for opening statement. The DVD offers examples of what the software can produce, and
- *Computer animation*—The DVD contains examples of computer animation, the type of demonstrative evidence that can be created pretrial.

V. RULES OF THE "GAME"

A. Jurisdiction

These two fictitious cases take place in the jurisdiction of the State of Major. The specific setting encompasses the adjoining counties of Jamner and Neva.

The city of Ruston is within the County of Jamner. Neva City is the main city in Neva County.

The jurisdiction of the State of Major was chosen for a number of reasons. Its laws reflect, although they are probably not identical with, current law on the various issues raised in the cases. The memorandum opinions in the jurisdiction of Major are short and to the point, replacing what would be hundreds of pages in other jurisdictions with a small fraction of that volume. The opinions, nevertheless, require careful reading and interpretation; they provide a foundation for a series of assignments whose purpose is to teach you how to think about a body of law in an active adversary context, rather than to teach you substantive criminal and civil procedure and doctrine. Do not do *any* outside research unless your instructor tells you to.

B. The Procedural and Professional Responsibility Rules

The State of Major Court Rules and Rules of Criminal and Civil Procedure are in most instances identical to the Federal Rules of Civil Procedure and the Federal Rules of Criminal Procedure. The Major Evidence Code is identical to the Federal Rules of Evidence. The standards of professional responsibility in the State of Major are based on ABA Model Rules of Professional Conduct. These rules are intended to provide a legal structure against which you can analyze the particular ethical situations in the assignments. Of course, your instructor may instead ask you to deal with the ethical situations under the current rules in your jurisdiction.

C. Dates

The fictitious incidents take place in the following years:

> 20XX Last year—the year that the shooting took place.
> 20XX + Years after last year (20XX + 1 is this year).
> 20XX—Years prior to the incident (20XX-2 is three years ago).

To give the cases a feeling of reality, the dates in the Case Files should be converted into actual dates, so that "20XX + 4" is changed to four years after last year's date.

D. Civil Case

Whenever you deal with the civil case of *Summers v. Hard*, you should assume that the criminal case has been disposed of in such a manner that the main character, Ed Hard, cannot legitimately resist answering in the civil case by claiming that he will incriminate himself.

E.   Your Responsibilities

As a class member or as an attorney assigned to conduct a particular performance, your own good sense and the directions of your instructor will make your responsibilities clear. Your responsibilities when role-playing a witness, however, are a different matter. The quality of your effort in preparation, and in the subsequent performance of your role, can make or break the class. Effort put into your role-playing can make an interview come alive by challenging the planning and performance skills of the student who is playing the attorney. Lack of effort and enthusiasm can result in an unrealistic, fragmented, boring shambles.

As a witness, you have two responsibilities:

1. *Preparation.* You should prepare for your witness performance by reviewing the Assignment and readings, the confidential witness information from the Actors' Guide, the pretrial Case File documents listed for the Assignment for which you are playing the role of a witness, special documents provided by your instructor, and any specific witness instructions for the Assignment. Be certain to bring to class all your witness information.

2. *Innovation.* Although we have tried to make the materials as complete as possible, there may be circumstances in which the factual materials furnished to you are insufficient. Therefore, you will have to be somewhat innovative at times. If you are asked questions on matters not covered by the facts you have been furnished, you may add any facts that are consistent with the supplied facts. You may also add details that provide color and reality to your character. You should not add a fact, however, that would be so important that it would determine the outcome of the lawsuit. If in doubt, ask your instructor.

Depending on the actual selection and sequence and performance of the Assignment in your class, you may encounter gaps in information or may fail to make the acquaintance of some of the witnesses who figure in the principal cases. It has been our experience that such potential gaps in information should not seriously impair your case preparation. If the gaps do present any difficulties, however, consult your instructor.

F.   The "Game"

We have just discussed the rules of the game for the performance assignments because it is a game. No clients will go to prison for life. No one will lose a home or business or be denied access to his or her children. So feel free to play, because, ironically, the more you play, the better you will do when you enter the real world of pretrial. Work hard at your play. Your clients are awaiting you in the next few years, and they are completely and totally dependent on you and on your having learned your lessons well.

We hope you enjoy using this book and the accompanying materials and living with the characters as much as we enjoyed creating them. If any character or situation reminds you of someone you know, so much the better for the game to seem real. It is not our intention, however, to represent any real person or situation; this a work of fiction.

ASSIGNMENTS TABLE OF CONTENTS

VI. PRETRIAL ADVOCACY: ASSIGNMENTS

Chapter 1: Entering The Advocate's World

ASSIGNMENT 1: The Role of an Attorney in the Adversary System

You are about to be totally immersed in the world of a practicing attorney. To maximize this experience, these materials will place you in a variety of roles (plaintiff, defense, government, and private counsel) and legal arenas (civil and criminal litigation and alternative dispute resolution). But always you will be an advocate.

This environment, however, is more than an amalgam of skills and tactical decisions. It is a human, flesh-and-blood world in which a clear understanding of your role as an attorney is a vital predicate to your effectiveness. But what is your role?

PREPARATION

READ: (1) Pretrial Case Files Entry 64; (2) Chapters 1 and 13.

ASSIGNMENT FOR CLASS

DISCUSSION: Be prepared to discuss the following questions:

1. What is the theory behind our adversary system?
2. What is your role as an attorney in this system?
3. Do you have ethical or other obligations to anyone or anything other than your client?

Chapter 2. Formulating the Case Theory— Assignments

Criminal Case Assignments

ASSIGNMENT 2: Prosecutor: Initial Development of a Case Theory (Homicide)

You are employed in the criminal division of the prosecutor's office for Jamner County, State of Major. The local police sent over their reports of a shooting at the Garage Tavern for your review and filing decision. A man named Edward Taylor Hard is being held in custody for shooting Bruno Summers at the Garage Tavern on September 3, 20XX. Summers survived the shooting and was in intensive care. You charged Hard with assault in the first degree.

It is now September 8, 20XX, and you just received a telephone message from Detective Tharp, the case detective. The Edward Hard case has changed: Bruno Summers, who everyone thought was going to recover from his gunshot wound, took a sudden unexpected turn for the worse over the weekend and died last night at 7:00 P.M. in Mercy Hospital.

You must now consider filing a new complaint. A man is dead as the result of Hard's conduct and the charge of assault no longer reflects this reality. Yet you must think carefully whether the charge should be first-degree, premeditated murder, felony-murder, second-degree murder, voluntary manslaughter, or involuntary manslaughter. The wrong charging theory at the inception could affect the ultimate success of the prosecution.

PREPARATION

READ: (1) Pretrial Case Files Entries 4-6, 10,14, 15, 17, 19, 26, 29, 30, 32, 33, 61, 65, 71; (2) Chapters 1 and 2.

ASSIGNMENTS FOR CLASS

DISCUSSION: Be prepared to discuss the following questions:

1. After reviewing the applicable statutes and jury instructions, what criminal charges could be filed based upon the available evidence?
2. If you charge first-degree premeditated murder, do you foresee any problem in establishing premeditation?
3. The defense may have a self-defense claim, do you have an ethical or other obligation to have Detective Tharp investigate it?

PERFORMANCE

In class, meet with your supervising attorneys in order to brainstorm your theory of the case and to determine further tasks and investigation to be done.

ASSIGNMENT 3: Defense Attorney: Initial Development of a Case Theory (Charge of Premeditated First Degree Murder)

You are employed at a small private firm specializing in criminal defense. It is September 8, and the prosecutor has just telephoned you. Bruno Summers died last evening in Mercy Hospital. Your client is no longer facing the original charge of assault in the first degree for shooting Summers in the Garage Tavern; instead the prosecutor has informed you that Edward Hard will be charged with first-degree murder, based on premeditation. You must, therefore, begin again to develop a tentative legal and factual theory for the defense.

The Jamner County Prosecutor's office has a policy of providing police reports to defense counsel shortly after counsel's entrance into the case without a formal discovery request or motion and you have received that report.

PREPARATION

READ: (1) Pretrial Case Files Entries 1, 4, 5, 14, 17, 61, 65; (2) Chapters 1 and 2.

ASSIGNMENT FOR CLASS

DISCUSSION: Be prepared to discuss the following questions:

1. After reviewing the applicable statutes and jury instructions, what are the possible complete or partial defenses to the charge of first-degree premeditated murder?
2. At this point, what is your most likely legal theory of defense? Why?
3. At this early juncture in the case and before the defendant discusses what happened at the time of the shooting, would you lay out the legal requirements of self defense and tell him that it is his best defense (assuming that you believe it is)? Does this present any ethical problem?

PERFORMANCE

In class, meet with the senior partners in order to think about and develop theories of the case and to develop a list of further tasks and investigation to be done.

Civil Case Assignments

ASSIGNMENT 4: Plaintiffs' Attorney: Theorizing About *Summers v. Hard*

You received a telephone call from a law school classmate who told you she referred Deborah Summers to you for consultation. You recall reading about a shooting and death involving Deborah Summers's husband, Bruno. After interviewing Deborah Summers, you also met with Gretchen and Hans Summers, Bruno Summers's surviving parents. Deborah, Gretchen, and Hans Summers have asked you to investigate possibilities for obtaining monetary recovery for themselves and Bruno's minor children, Ronnie and Amanda. You obtained signed retainer agreements and consent forms to act on behalf of the Summers family.

You have subpoenaed and received the criminal file, *State v. Hard*, from the prosecutor's office. As you know, the prosecutor has dismissed the criminal case against Ed Hard and will not be filing it again. Your law clerk completed a preliminary legal memorandum that you requested. You are now ready to theorize about legal and factual theories for *Summers v. Hard*. Theorizing at this stage of a case is a creative process since you have many potential defendants—Ed Hard, M.C. Davola, the Garage Tavern owner and his employees, Mary Apple and Tom Donaldson, Dr. Brett Day, and others.

PREPARATION

READ: (1) Pretrial Case Files Entries 1-33, 62, 63, 66, 85; (2) Chapters 2 and 7.

ASSIGNMENTS FOR CLASS

DISCUSSION: Be prepared to discuss the following questions:

1. Who are the potential plaintiffs and defendants in the case?
2. After reviewing the applicable statutes, jury instructions, and legal memoranda, what are the possible claims (legal theories) that could be made against the potential defendants?
3. What, if any, ethical and/or other responsibilities do you have that could preclude you from filing a claim?

PERFORMANCE

In class, meet with the senior partners and present the case of the death of Bruno Summers at the law firm's weekly session for discussing cases.

ASSIGNMENT 5: Attorney for Defendant Hard: Theorizing About *Summers v. Hard*

Ed Hard received a complaint naming M.C. Davola, Tom Donaldson, Mary Apple, and Ed Hard as defendants in the *Summers v. Hard* lawsuit. You are an associate in a law firm retained by Ed Hard because of the possibility of a judgment in excess of his insurance coverage. (Ed Hard has a homeowner's insurance policy with SAPO Insurance Company.)

You have agreed to represent Ed Hard in the civil lawsuit brought by Deborah Summers and family. You have explained fully in writing to Ed Hard that he may be entitled to be represented by the SAPO Insurance Company, but that there may be a conflict between SAPO and Hard because of the possibility of a judgment in excess of the insurance policy. The SAPO Insurance Company has indicated to you that it is still evaluating the Hard case. You and Ed Hard have decided that, as Ed's private attorney, you should proceed with Ed's defense while awaiting SAPO's decision.

You have interviewed Ed Hard, researched the law, and your investigator has prepared a report for you. You obtained the *State v. Hard* file from the prosecutor's office.

You plan to discuss the *Summers v. Hard* lawsuit with your partners. The meeting with your partners will be a planning, theorizing, and brainstorming session.

PREPARATION

READ: (1) Pretrial Case Files Entries 1-37, 43, 62, 63, 66, 85; (2) Chapters 2 and 7; (3) Notes of your interview with Ed Hard. Furthermore, in theorizing about Ed Hard's defense to *Summers v. Hard*, refer to the civil complaint (Case Files Entry 37) solely for critique purposes.

ASSIGNMENT FOR CLASS

DISCUSSION: Be prepared to discuss the following questions:

1. Reviewing plaintiffs' complaint and the documents you possess, what are the defenses that defendant Hard could theoretically assert?
2. Refer to your list of possible defenses:
    a. List the facts that support each defense.
    b. List the witnesses and documents that support each defense.
3. The state of Major has a wrongful death and survival statute.
    a. Are both of these statutes applicable in this case? Explain.

b. Did plaintiffs properly (factually, legally) allege claims based on the state of Major wrongful death and survival statutes? Explain.

4. Is contributory negligence a possible affirmative defense for Hard? Why or why not?

a. Factually is this defense supportable?

b. Will defendant Davola and/or plaintiffs attack this defense? Why?

PERFORMANCE

1. Outside of class, assume you are an associate in a law office representing Ed Hard in the civil lawsuit, *Summers v. Hard*. You are to present Hard's case at the law firm's weekly meeting for discussing cases. Prepare a memorandum discussing your theories of Hard's case. Give your memorandum to your senior partners.

2. In class, meet with the senior partners.

ASSIGNMENT 6: Attorney for Defendant Davola: Theorizing About *Summers v. Hard*

M.C. Davola received a complaint naming M.C. Davola, Tom Donaldson, Mary Apple, and Ed Hard as defendants in a lawsuit, *Summers v. Hard*. You are an associate in a law firm on retainer to the EKKO Insurance Company, which is representing Davola, Donaldson, and Apple pursuant to Davola's EKKO insurance policy. Davola also retained a private attorney because of the possibility of a judgment in excess of his insurance coverage. The necessary disclosures in writing were made to Davola concerning possible conflicts of interest.

You interviewed Davola, Donaldson, and Apple, researched the law, and your investigator D. Dapple prepared a report for you. You obtained the *State v. Hard* file from the prosecutor's office.

You plan to discuss the *Summers v. Hard* lawsuit with your partners. The meeting with your partners will be a planning, theorizing, and brainstorming session.

PREPARATION

READ: (1) Pretrial Case Files Entries 1-37, 42, 49, 62, 63, 66, 85; (2) Chapters 2 and 7. Furthermore, in theorizing about Davola's defense to *Summers v. Hard*, refer to the civil complaint (Case Files Entry 37) solely for critique purposes.

ASSIGNMENTS FOR CLASS

DISCUSSION: Be prepared to discuss the following questions:

1. Reviewing plaintiffs' complaint and the documents you possess, what are the defenses that Davola, Apple, and Donaldson could assert?
2. What available evidence supports each defense?
3. Could the same attorney ethically represent all the defendants if the clients did not enter a waiver of conflicts?

PERFORMANCE

In class, meet with the senior partners and discuss *Summers v. Hard*.

ASSIGNMENT 7: Attorneys for Defendants Hard and Davola: Meeting and Theorizing About *Summers v. Hard*

Defendants Hard and Davola received a complaint naming M.C. Davola, Tom Donaldson, Mary Apple, and Ed Hard as defendants in the *Summers v. Hard* lawsuit. Ed Hard has a homeowner's insurance policy with SAPO Insurance Company. He retained a private attorney to represent him because of the possibility of a judgment in excess of his insurance coverage.

The SAPO Insurance Company has indicated that it is still evaluating the Hard case. Ed Hard's private attorney has decided to proceed with Ed's defense while awaiting SAPO's decision.

Davola is represented by the EKKO Insurance Company. Both Hard's and Davola's attorneys have interviewed their clients, researched the law, and obtained the *State v. Hard* file from the prosecutor's office.

Ed Hard's attorney has telephoned Davola's attorney to discuss coordinating the defendants' defenses to the *Summers v. Hard* lawsuit. Before this meeting, both Davola's attorney and Ed Hard's attorney individually discussed the lawsuit with their partners.

Now it is time to think about coordinating the defense case.

PREPARATION

READ: (1) Pretrial Case Files Entries 1-37, 42, 43, 62-64, 66, 85; (2) Chapters 2 and 7; (3) Notes of interviews with respective clients.

ASSIGNMENT FOR CLASS

DISCUSSION: Be prepared to discuss the following questions:

1. Will you discuss your case theories and/or discovery plans with the other defense attorneys? Explain.

2. When planning and theorizing about the Summers v. Hard case defendants should consider what coordinating action, if any, to take in order to dismiss or diminish the effectiveness of plaintiffs' claims. Analyze plaintiffs' claims in terms of coordinating defense actions.

    a. What facts seem most problematic for plaintiffs with their claims?

    b. What claims seem factually inadequate in plaintiffs' claims? Why?

    c. Do any of the claims seem to be legally inadequate? Why?

    d. Explain defendants' tentative ideas of how and why defendants plan to deal with plaintiffs' claims (e.g., motions, defenses, discovery).

PERFORMANCE

In class, Davola's and Hard's attorneys meet, discuss, and plan strategies for defending the *Summers v. Hard* lawsuit.

Chapter 3. Developing and Managing the Case— Assignments

Criminal Case Assignments

ASSIGNMENT 8: Prosecutor and Defense Attorney: Case Fact Development Overview

You have developed tentative legal and factual theories regarding the current charge of first-degree murder against Edward Taylor Hard. Those theories, when placed in the context of your case strategy, will serve as guides for your investigation to find additional evidence supporting your case theory. Conversely, the results of your investigation may lead you to alter your current case theory. You have many methods available to you to obtain information. At this point, you should think broadly about their use.

For this problem defense counsel may assume that the *only* information you have received from the pretrial Case Files at this point is the police reports.

PREPARATION

READ: (1) Pretrial Case Files Entries 4, 5, 7, 10, 14, 15, 17, 19, 26, 29, 30, 61, 65, 74; (2) Chapters 2 and 3.

ASSIGNMENT FOR CLASS

DISCUSSION: Be prepared to discuss the following questions:

1. What specific information will you seek during the fact investigation? Why, in terms of your case theory, do you want it?
2. What is the likely source of the information that you are seeking?
3. What precautions will you take to ensure that your investigator does not commit an ethical violation during the investigation?

PERFORMANCE

In class, discuss your case development plan from the perspective of the prosecutor and defense attorney.

Civil Case Assignments

ASSIGNMENT 9: Plaintiffs' and Defendants' Attorneys: Case Fact Development Overview

You have developed tentative legal and factual theories regarding *Summers v. Hard*. Those theories, when placed in the context of your tentative representational strategies, will serve as guides for your factual investigation. Conversely, the results of your factual investigation may lead you to alter your current case theory. You have many methods available to you to obtain information. At this point, you should think broadly about their use.

PREPARATION

READ: (1) Pretrial Case Files Entries 1-33, 61, 63, 65, 85; (2) Chapters 2 and 3.

ASSIGNMENT FOR CLASS

DISCUSSION: Be prepared to discuss the following questions:

1. What specific information will you seek during the fact investigation? Why, in terms of your case theory, do you want it?
2. What is the likely source of the information that you are seeking?
3. What precautions will you take to ensure that your investigator does not commit an ethical violation during the investigation?

PERFORMANCE

In class, discuss your case development plan from the perspective of both plaintiff(s) and defendant(s).

ASSIGNMENT 10: Plaintiffs' and Defendants' Attorneys: Utilizing Case Analysis and Management Software

You have concluded that the *Summers v. Hard* case is complex enough that your pretrial organization, management, and analysis of the case may be alleviated by utilizing computer software. Your law office does not own any case management software, and you would like to explore what is available and whether it would be helpful both on this case and on future cases. You have learned that companies offer potential customers an opportunity to test their software for trial periods. You decide to explore the potential use of software to assist you in the case.

For the purpose of this assignment, visit and test one or more of the websites mentioned in Chapter 3 on page 75 (Concordance from Dataflight Software, Inc. *www.dataflight.com.* Casemap from Casesoft *www.casesoft.com,* Summation from CT Summation *www.summation.com* or Visionary from Visionary Legal Technologies—*www.visionarylegaltechnologies.com*) or a web site selected by your instructor.

PREPARATION

READ: (1) All Pretrial Case Files Entries; (2) Chapters 2 and 3, and (3) Internet exploration of websites offering software for case management and analysis.

ASSIGNMENT FOR CLASS

DISCUSSION: Be prepared to discuss the following questions:

1. What does the software that you tested offer in terms of case organization, management, and analysis?
2. Describe the trial run that you took utilizing the website.
3. Are there any concerns that you have about your firm purchasing the software (e.g., expense, time devoted to entering the case data, other)?

PERFORMANCE

In class, discuss your experience with the software, the feasibility of purchasing the software, and what it can do for your case and future cases handled by your office.

Chapter 4. Forging the Attorney-Client Relationship—Assignments

Criminal Case Assignments

ASSIGNMENT 11: Defense Attorney: Interviewing Ed Hard Regarding a First-Degree Murder (The Formation of an Attorney-Client Relationship)

It is mid-morning, September 8. Things have been moving fast since your initial interview with Edward Taylor Hard a few days ago in the county jail where you met him and then represented him at the bail hearing. At that time Hard was charged with assault in the first degree, as the result of his alleged shooting of Bruno Summers in a tavern. As a result of that appearance on Hard's behalf, you have received the police report on the assault case. Since your first brief contact with Hard, Summers has died, and Hard now faces a charge of premeditated, first-degree murder. You are now on your way to county jail for an extensive interview with Hard in light of these new charges.

PREPARATION

READ: (1) Pretrial Case Files Entries 3-7, 10, 14, 15, 17, 19, 61, 64, 65 (2) Chapters 4, 6, and 7.

ASSIGNMENTS FOR CLASS

DISCUSSION: Be prepared to discuss the following questions:

1. What are your overall and specific objectives for this interview?
2. What will be the factual focus of this interview? Why?
3. Hard's statements to detective Tharp claims accident, self-defense, or both. What will you do if you ask Hard about the ambiguity and he responds: "I'm innocent. Which version is most likely to get me off?"

PERFORMANCE

In class, interview your client Edward Taylor Hard. Either (1) assume he is indigent and imagine you are a public defender or (2) assume he has money and you are retained private counsel. Your instructor will tell you which option to choose.

ASSIGNMENT 12: Defense Attorney: Interviewing Ed Hard for a Bail Reduction Motion (Charge of First-Degree Murder)

Your client has been sitting in jail on a $30,000 bail that he can't make. That bail was set when Bruno Summers was still alive and Hard was facing charges of assault in the first degree. Your client is now facing a first-degree murder charge. As your research has indicated, unlike many jurisdictions, bail is available in the State of Major even in capital cases. You still want to try to reduce bail (or at least limit the amount it may be raised in light of the new charges), and thus you will need to obtain information for a bail reduction motion.

PREPARATION

READ: (1) Pretrial Case Files Entry 68; (2) Chapter 4.

ASSIGNMENTS FOR CLASS

DISCUSSION: Be prepared to discuss the following questions:

1. What is the importance of obtaining bail for Hard?
2. What are the legal standards for bail?

3. What information should you seek from Hard in preparing for a bail motion? Why?

4. What will you do if Hard says, "Just get me out on bail and I'll be in South America in 24 hours"?

PERFORMANCE

In class, be prepared to meet with Hard and obtain the necessary information for your bail reduction motion.

Civil Case Assignments

ASSIGNMENT 13: Plaintiffs' Attorney: Interview of Deborah Summers

You are an associate attorney in a law firm. Deborah Summers was referred to you by your law school classmate Casper Corey Williams, an assistant prosecutor. The receptionist has scheduled an appointment for you to meet with Ms. Summers. When making the appointment, Ms. Summers stated: "I need help in obtaining money owed to my late husband, Bruno Summers, from his employer."

You have heard and read about Bruno Summers being shot and killed by Edward Taylor Hard. You are also aware that the prosecutor has decided not to prosecute Ed Hard for the shooting. The criminal case, *State v. Hard*, has been dismissed.

PREPARATION

READ: (1) Pretrial Case Files Entries 1, 2, 62; (2) Chapters 4, 6, and 7.

ASSIGNMENT FOR CLASS

DISCUSSION: Be prepared to discuss the following questions:

1. Will the statement made by Deborah Summers, "I need help in obtaining money owed to my late husband, Bruno, from his employer," have an effect on this interview? Explain.

2. Bruno Summers allegedly died after he was shot by a third person in a tavern. Does that incident have any effect on this interview? Explain.

3. What are your ethical responsibilities in setting an attorney's fee with Deborah?

PERFORMANCE

In class, interview Deborah Summers.

ASSIGNMENT 14: Plaintiffs' Attorney: Interview of Ronnie Summers

A few weeks have passed since Bruno Summers's death. Deborah, Gretchen, and Hans Summers have retained you as their attorney. You are considering whether to file a wrongful death lawsuit. As plaintiffs' attorney, you have wanted to interview Ronnie (age 8), because Ronnie is one of Bruno Summers's minor children and he saw his father bleeding after he had been shot. You refrained from interviewing Ronnie because of the emotional trauma Ronnie may have experienced upon his father's death.

Ronnie has been living with his grandparents, Gretchen and Hans Summers, since September 4 of last year. Gretchen Summers, although not happy with your request to interview Ronnie, has reluctantly agreed.

Gretchen Summers and Ronnie will be at your office at 4:00 P.M.

PREPARATION

READ: (1) Pretrial Case Files Entries 1-33, 62, 63, 66, 85; (2) Chapters 2-4. Note, however, that this problem can be assigned at any time, whether before or after a lawsuit has been filed. If assigned after the lawsuit is filed, your reading should include Case Files Entries 1-37, 40-41, 62, 63, 66, 85, and Chapters 2-6.

ASSIGNMENTS FOR CLASS

DISCUSSION: Be prepared to discuss the following questions:

1. What are your objectives for the interview with Ronnie?
2. Explain the legal theory that you will use to structure the interview with Ronnie.
3. How can the civil jury instructions help you in structuring the content of the interview? Explain.
4. Will you interview Ronnie the same way you would an adult witness? If not, explain the differences in your approach to the child witness.

PERFORMANCE

In class, conduct the interview of Ronnie Summers.

ASSIGNMENT 15: Attorney for Defendant Hard: Client Interview

Ed Hard has told your receptionist he would like to talk to a lawyer about a civil lawsuit brought against him for shooting and killing someone at the Garage Tavern. You are quite familiar with the shooting incident referred to by Hard from reading newspaper articles, and your friend represented Hard in the criminal case. Ed Hard has left the complaint for *Summers v. Hard* and his SAPO insurance policy with your receptionist. An appointment has been scheduled with Ed Hard for later in the week at 9:00 A.M.

PREPARATION

READ: (1) Pretrial Case Files Entries 1, 2, 34, 35, 43, 62-64, 82, 85; (2) Chapters 4, 6, and 7.

ASSIGNMENT FOR CLASS

DISCUSSION: Be prepared to discuss the following questions:

1. What relevance, if any, does Hard's SAPO insurance have on *Summers v. Hard*?
2. What questions will you ask Hard after reviewing the complaint in *Summers v. Hard*?
3. Suppose Hard begins the interview saying: "Tell me what the defenses are to this lawsuit, then I'll talk." What will you say?

PERFORMANCE

In class, interview Edward Hard.

ASSIGNMENT 16: Attorney for Defendant Davola: Client Interview

M.C. Davola has told your receptionist he would like to talk to a lawyer about a lawsuit brought against him as the owner of the Garage Tavern. He has left the *Summers v. Hard* complaint with your receptionist. He also muttered something about "slashed seats in his tavern."

Mr. Davola has been scheduled for an appointment later in the week at 9:00 A.M.

PREPARATION

READ: (1) Pretrial Case Files Entries 1, 2, 34, 35, 62-64, 85; (2) Chapters 4, 6, and 7.

ASSIGNMENT FOR CLASS

DISCUSSION: Be prepared to discuss the following questions:

1. Do you have any tentative theories about Davola's defense? Explain.
2. Suppose Mr. Davola is a very angry about the lawsuit. How will that attitude affect the interview? Explain.
3. Suppose Mr. Davola insists that you "counter-sue" the plaintiffs. How will you respond?

PERFORMANCE

In class, interview M. C. Davola.

ASSIGNMENT 17: Attorney for Defendant Davola: Interview of Mary Apple

You have interviewed M.C. Davola and read the criminal file that you obtained from the prosecutor's office. You are interviewing clients and witnesses before drafting a response to the plaintiffs' complaint in *Summers v. Hard*. You have arranged to interview Mary Apple, who has been named as a defendant in the lawsuit filed by the Summers family.

You have heard that a patron in the tavern, Bert Kain, claims he overheard Mary Apple say: "Oh God, I shouldn't have served them." Be sure you obtain the facts about the circumstances surrounding this statement directly from Ms. Apple.

PREPARATION

READ: (1) Pretrial Case Files Entries 1-35, 42, 62-64, 85; (2) Chapter 4 and 6 (3) Notes of interview with M.C. Davola.

ASSIGNMENTS FOR CLASS

DISCUSSION: Be prepared to discuss the following questions:

1. What are your objectives for the interview with Mary Apple?

2. Suppose Mary Apple gives inconsistent responses to your questions. What will you do? Why?

3. Will you confront Ms. Apple with the statement that Bert Kain, an eyewitness, claims he heard Apple say: "Oh, my God, I shouldn't have served them?" Explain.

4. Suppose Mary Apple becomes hostile during the interview. What will you do?

PERFORMANCE

In class, along with your investigator, interview Mary Apple.

Chapter 5. Counseling the Client—Assignments

Criminal Case Assignments

ASSIGNMENT 18: Prosecutor: Counseling a Witness Whether to Talk to Your Adversary (Peter Dean)

Peter Dean has telephoned you at your office to tell you that Ed Hard's investigator is at his home and wishes to interview him. Peter Dean wants your advice regarding what to do. You are aware that the guiding rule in such cases is that a witness has the right to talk with any attorney (or agent of the attorney) and no other attorney (or agent) can interfere with this right. On the other hand, a witness has no obligation to talk with anyone, except when testifying in court proceedings.

PREPARATION

READ: (1) Pretrial Case Files Entry 64; (2) Chapter 5.

ASSIGNMENTS FOR CLASS

DISCUSSION: Be prepared to discuss the following questions:

1. Do you want to know what Dean wants to do?
2. What do you want to do in this situation? Why?
3. What about telling Dean the substance of the guiding ethical rule?
   a. Will you emphasize any portion of the rule? Which portion?
   b. Does such emphasis comport with what you perceive to be your ethical responsibilities?
4. What if you ask Dean what he wants to do and, he says:
   a. "Whatever you think is best"?
   b. "I'll talk, but only if you're here"?
   c. "Let me put the investigator on the telephone, so you can discuss it and see what he wants"?

PERFORMANCE

In class, discuss this matter with Peter Dean on the telephone.

ASSIGNMENT 19: Prosecutor: Counseling a Key Witness Who Is Threatening to Leave Town (Deborah Summers)

Deborah Summers has just telephoned you on her cell phone and told you that she is leaving town and will not testify in the *Hard* case. "This case is tearing me apart. I feel so guilty, so responsible. I think I'm going crazy. You understand; I just have to leave. I just have to."

Too bad—the day was going well. Well, this is not the first time Deborah has balked at testifying. Earlier in the month she was in your office crying, but somehow you convinced her that it was her duty to testify.

PREPARATION

READ: (1) Pretrial Case Files Entries 64, 75; (2) Chapters 4 and 5.

ASSIGNMENTS FOR CLASS

DISCUSSION: Be prepared to discuss the following questions:

1. What realistically will be the effect on your case if Deborah does not testify?
   a. How would it affect your case theory?
   b. How would it affect your case strategy?
2. What will you do?

3. What are your ethical obligations to Deborah and to the people of the state of Major?

PERFORMANCE

In class, discuss the matter with Deborah on the phone.

ASSIGNMENT 20: Defense Attorney: Counseling the Defendant Concerning a Drinking Problem and Testifying at a Suppression Motion

It is now a few months since criminal charges were filed. Your client Ed Hard is out on bail. You are preparing for a motion to suppress the gun Hard used to shoot Summers, the statement Hard made to Yale, and the statement Hard gave to Tharp. Your arguments range from attacking the lack of an arrest warrant and the lack of a valid consent to enter Hard's home, to Hard's failure to waive his *Mintz* rights when questioned by Detective Tharp. As you are discussing these motions with Hard he says, "I want to testify at the hearing. Those cops are liars. They kicked in my door and that Tharp never gave me any warnings. I know I signed something after I talked to the cops, but I didn't read the fine print on the form because I was so upset."

As pretrial preparation has proceeded; you have noticed that Hard has appeared intoxicated the last two times you met. According to his friend, John Gooding, Hard has been drinking a great deal since the shooting of Bruno Summers. You are concerned that he will become even more difficult to work with, make a bad appearance before a court and jury, will be less effective in his testimony, and will reinforce the view that he was drunk on the night of the shooting. Although you know it will be difficult to discuss Ed's "drinking problem" with Ed, you have decided to meet with him because you can no longer ignore it.

PREPARATION

READ: (1) Pretrial Case Files Entries 5, 19, 28, 64, 69; and (2) Chapters 4, 5, and 7.

ASSIGNMENTS FOR CLASS

DISCUSSION: Be prepared to discuss the following questions:

1. What does the defense gain if Hard testifies at the suppression hearing? What are the disadvantages to the defense if he testifies?

2. Do you have any responsibilities for counseling your client about the drinking?

3. What are your ethical obligations if Hard insists on testifying at the hearing?

PERFORMANCE

In class, meet with your client and advise him regarding testifying at the suppression hearing. Assume that you have decided to dissuade him from testifying. Also, during the meeting, try to deal with this drinking problem. (Note: This is likely to be a very difficult and uncomfortable confrontation with your client. Nevertheless, you must carry through to some resolution.)

Civil Case Assignments

ASSIGNMENT 21: Plaintiffs' Attorney: Counseling Client to See a Psychologist (Deborah Summers)

You have completed informal discovery in *Summers v. Hard.* You interviewed witnesses, filed a complaint, and received defendants' responses.

One of the claims you assert on behalf of Deborah Summers is that she has suffered emotional distress. It would be helpful to obtain a psychologist's evaluation of Deborah's emotional condition.

Since your initial meeting with Deborah in September 20XX, you have suggested that she obtain professional help, but your suggestion was not acted on. You have made an appointment for December 1, 20XX, for Deborah Summers to come to your office to discuss this matter.

PREPARATION

READ: (1) Pretrial Case Files Entries 1-39, 50, 51, 57, 62-64, 66, 67, 85; (2) Chapter 4 and 5.

ASSIGNMENTS FOR CLASS

DISCUSSION: Be prepared to discuss the following questions:

1. Discuss what you will do before meeting with Deborah.
2. Suppose that Deborah is hostile and does not want to go to a psychologist. How will you obtain her cooperation?

3. Suppose that after repeated attempts during the interview to obtain Deborah's cooperation, she still refuses to go to a psychologist. What will you do?

PERFORMANCE

In class, meet with Deborah Summers about going to a psychologist.

ASSIGNMENT 22: Plaintiffs' Attorney: Counseling Client Concerning Remarriage (Deborah Summers)

Approximately five months have passed since Bruno Summers died. Deborah Summers has consulted you concerning her desire to marry her boyfriend, Gary Korn. Deborah told you:

> "I may have a better chance in the future to obtain custody of the Summers children and make something of my life if I get married and have some money. But I don't want to mess up the *Summers v. Hard* lawsuit. What should I do?"

After Bruno died, Gretchen and Hans invited Deborah and the children to move in with them. Every time you have talked with Deborah, she has been vague about her plans for the future. The last time you talked to Gretchen she expressed concern that Deborah was still living with them. Gretchen said, "Surely, Deborah should think of going to work, moving out on her own, or at least going to her own parents."

Then Gretchen and Hans consulted a lawyer about obtaining custody of Amanda and Ronnie. Deborah immediately moved out of the Summers's house and moved in with her parents. The children remained with Gretchen and Hans.

With Deborah's permission, you have discussed the issue of her remarriage with the attorney representing Deborah in the child custody dispute. Her child custody attorney assured you that the child custody matter was settled. (Deborah voluntarily agreed that Hans and Gretchen retain custody of the children.) Your instructor will inform you whether to consider the child custody dispute and its effect on *Summers v. Hard*.

You have scheduled an appointment with Deborah on February 1, 20XX + 1 to discuss the issue of her remarriage.

PREPARATION

READ: (1) Pretrial Case Files Entries 1-39, 57, 59, 62-64, 66, 67, 84, 85; (2) Chapters 4, 5, and 7.

ASSIGNMENTS FOR CLASS

DISCUSSION: Be prepared to discuss the following questions:

1. Do you have a position as to whether Deborah's remarriage will hurt the *Summers v. Hard* lawsuit?
    a. What is your position based on?
    b. Will you communicate your position to Deborah? Why or why not?
2. If it is your opinion that the remarriage will damage the lawsuit, do you have an ethical obligation to advise her of the ramifications or is this just too personal a matter?
3. Suppose Deborah states: "I've got to get out of my parent's house, get some money to get on my feet." What will you say?

PERFORMANCE

In class, be prepared to discuss your objectives. Meet with Deborah Summers concerning the issue of her remarriage.

ASSIGNMENT 23: Plaintiffs' Attorney: Counseling Client Concerning Granddaughter's School Truancy (Gretchen Summers)

Three months have passed since Bruno's death. A complaint on behalf of the Summers family, Deborah, Gretchen, Hans, Ronnie, and Amanda, was filed on November 1, and defendants responded seven days later. Gretchen Summers has taken over the care of Amanda, age 12, and Ronnie, age 8, the children of Bruno from his prior marriage. The children are currently receiving social security, supplemented by welfare.

Gretchen has been plagued by personal and financial problems and by coping with two children. Since you are her attorney, Gretchen has unburdened herself to you, telling you of some of her distress and inability to cope. She claims that she has no one else to talk to whom she respects. She telephones you at least three times a week. In fact, you have just spoken with her concerning her most recent upset—Amanda's school truancy. You have made an appointment with Gretchen to discuss Amanda's truancy.

PREPARATION

READ: (1) Pretrial Case Files Entries 1-37, 64; (2) Chapters 4, 5, and 7.

ASSIGNMENTS FOR CLASS

DISCUSSION: Be prepared to discuss the following questions:

1. Should you have agreed to see Gretchen Summers? Why or why not?

2. Should you counsel her on this matter? If so, what should be the extent of your counseling?

PERFORMANCE

In class, meet with Gretchen Summers.

ASSIGNMENT 24: Attorney for Defendant Hard: Counseling Client Concerning His Objections to Deposition of Adverse Witness (Deborah Summers)

You were just planning to notice the deposition of Deborah Summers when Ed Hard calls you sounding very upset. Suddenly he says: "Look, I love her and I've caused her enough pain. You're just not going to bother her or make her look like a liar. I won't let you!" Ed Hard insists that you refrain from deposing Deborah Summers.

You have made an appointment to talk with Ed Hard at your office tomorrow September 20, 20XX, (only 13 days after the shooting at the Garage Tavern) so you can discuss this matter with him.

PREPARATION

READ: (1) Pretrial Case Files Entries 1-37, 43, 62-64, 66, 81, 85; (2) Chapters 4, 5, and 7.

ASSIGNMENTS FOR CLASS

DISCUSSION: Be prepared to discuss the following questions:

1. As Ed Hard's personal attorney, what will you say to him?

2. What would you say to Ed Hard if you were defending him under his SAPO insurance policy?

3. Isn't it Ed Hard's case? Although he is paying you to represent him can't he proceed as he desires as long as he appreciates the consequences of his decision? Explain.

PERFORMANCE

In class, meet with Ed Hard.

ASSIGNMENT 25: Attorney for Defendant Davola: Counseling Client About the Litigation

Plaintiffs filed a complaint naming Ed Hard, Mary Apple, Tom Donaldson, and M.C. Davola as defendants. Defendants responded. Discovery has been conducted by both plaintiffs and defendants. A year has passed and M.C. Davola contacts you as his attorney and requests to speak with you concerning a problem he is having. He does not say anything else and sounds too upset to question further over the telephone.

You have scheduled an appointment to see M.C. Davola.

PREPARATION

READ: (1) Pretrial Case Files Entries 1-37, 43, 62-64, 66, 81, 85; (2) Chapters 4, 5, and 7.

ASSIGNMENTS FOR CLASS

DISCUSSION: Be prepared to discuss the following questions:

1. Can you prepare for your meeting with Mr. Davola? Explain.
2. Suppose one year has passed since filing an answer in the Summers case. Mr. Davola walks into your office and begins berating you for the delay in litigating his case. Discuss how you will respond.
3. Suppose that Mr. Davola blames the Summers case for his fall-off in business at the Garage. He wants to sue the Summers family for libel, slander, and loss of business. This is not the first time he has mentioned wanting to "counter-sue." He did so also early in the pretrial process, but changed his mind. What will you say? Why?

PERFORMANCE

In class, meet with your client M.C. Davola.

ASSIGNMENT 26: Plaintiff's and Defendants' Attorneys: Counseling Clients to Accept Settlement

During the meeting with opposing counsel, plaintiffs' counsel made a demand within the range agreed to by the plaintiffs. Defense counsel countered that they were not yet authorized to settle and what they were about to propose did not constitute an offer (because it was the clients' decision to actually make an offer). However, if it would settle the case, the defense counsel would go to the clients and recommend that the defendants accept the following (which is lower than the first number mentioned by plaintiff's counsel):

> *Hard:* payment of $80,000 (the limit of his SAPO insurance policy is $100,000). The $80,000 to be distributed as follows: $10,000 to Deborah Summers; $70,000 to be divided equally between two trusts to be established for Ronnie and Amanda.

> *Davola:* payment by EKKO insurance company of $450,000 (the limit of the policy is $600,000). This amount will be paid to the estate of Bruno Summers.

It is now time to discuss the settlement with your client(s) to see if the client(s) will agree to settlement. You have an appointment to meet with your client(s) on February 1, 20XX + 2.

PREPARATION

READ: (1) Pretrial Case Files Entries 1-60, 62-64, 66, 82, 84, 85; (2) Chapter 4 and 5; (3) Fed. R. Civ. P. 68.

ASSIGNMENTS FOR CLASS

DISCUSSION: Be prepared to discuss the following questions from the perspective of your client's (or clients') interests:

1. Generally, what could you do prior to presenting an offer of settlement to your client(s) to ensure that a valid offer of settlement is acceptable?
2. What will be your role during the meeting with your client(s)?
   a. Will you try to convince your client(s) to accept the offer? Explain.
   b. Will you be neutral? Explain.

3. Suppose plaintiffs offered to settle for an amount within the insurance policy limits.

    a. Should Hard settle?

    b. Should Davola settle?

PERFORMANCE

For this particular problem, your instructor may advise you to negotiate a settlement and to use your own settlement figures instead of those in this problem.

In class, attorneys for plaintiffs Gretchen, Hans, Ronnie, Amanda and Deborah Summers and defendants Davola and Hard, meet individually with your respective client(s) to discuss the settle.

Chapter 6. Witness Interviewing—Assignments

Criminal Case Assignments

ASSIGNMENT 27: Prosecutor: Interview of Dr. L. H. Jackson (Medical Examiner)

You have filed a first-degree murder charge in *State v. Hard*. You still have some questions, however, about Summers's death. After all, one minute Summers was supposed to be fine; the next, he was dead. You have an appointment with the medical examiner who did the autopsy and wrote the pathologist's report, Dr. L. H. Jackson.

PREPARATION

READ: (1) Pretrial Case Files Entries 4, 7, 8, 18, 22, 61, 65; (2) Chapter 6; (3) Fed. R. Evid. 701-705.

ASSIGNMENTS FOR CLASS

DISCUSSION: Be prepared to discuss the following questions:

1. How will you prepare for this interview?

2. Is the medical examiner an expert on "proximate causation" ?

PERFORMANCE

In class, meet with the medical examiner. In particular, you should discuss and assess with the medical examiner the question of Bruno's death from pneumonia and the legal element for murder of "proximate cause."

ASSIGNMENT 28: Prosecutor: Interview of Peter Dean

You should prepare for an interview with Peter Dean in the *State v. Hard* murder case. Mr. Dean was a close friend of the deceased, Bruno Summers. He was with Summers at the Garage on September 3, and at his parents' home on August 22 when Hard allegedly telephoned and threatened Bruno.

PREPARATION

READ: (1) Pretrial Case Files Entries 4, 14, 15, 26, 29, 30, 64; (2) Chapter 6; (3) Fed. R. Evid. 803(2), 901.

ASSIGNMENTS FOR CLASS

DISCUSSION: Be prepared to discuss the following questions:

1. What information can Peter Dean provide in the context of your case theory?
2. Are there potential problems with the fact that Peter Dean was Bruno's friend? Explain.
3. Assume you decide to bring photographs of the Garage Tavern with you. How specifically will you use the photographs?
4. What if Dean asks: "What do you want me to say?" How will you respond?

PERFORMANCE

In class, you and your investigator interview Peter Dean. Bring the diagram and/or photographs of the Garage Tavern (Case Files Entries 28, 31, 32) with you to the interview.

ASSIGNMENT 29: Prosecutor: Interview of Jack Waters

You are about to interview Jack Waters as part of your pretrial investigation for the *State v. Hard* murder case. Waters, who has a significant criminal history, is currently in jail on charges of receiving stolen property.

Waters came to your attention through a somewhat circuitous route. Waters contacted police officers a few days ago while in jail, claiming he had valuable information in the Hard case. The police brought him to you, where Waters asked for full immunity in return for his information. You refused. After further negotiations, however, you agreed to ask for leniency from the sentencing judge in Waters's current case (after Waters pleads guilty) in return for Waters's information and testimony in Hard's case.

Waters claims that he was at the Garage on September 3, 20XX and that, just before the shooting, he heard Hard tell Summers, "You asked for it and now you're going to get it." To which Summers allegedly responded, "Don't do it. I'm not armed."

PREPARATION

READ: (1) Pretrial Case Files Entries 4,10, 14-16, 64; (2) Chapter 6; (3) Fed. R. Evid. 801(d)(2), 803(2)(3).

ASSIGNMENTS FOR CLASS

DISCUSSION: Be prepared to discuss the following questions:

1. First, think about Waters's evidence:
   a. How exactly does it help your case?
   b. How do you expect the defense to discuss Waters's and his testimony in closing argument?
2. Now focus on the deal you have given Waters in exchange for his testimony.
   a. Is it ethical making such a deal in exchange for his testimony?
   b. Could the defense promise benefits, e.g., money to its non-expert witnesses?
   c. Regardless of when the deal is fulfilled, are you obligated to inform the defense of its existence under *Branty v. State* and *State v. Augle* (See Case Files Entry 75)

PERFORMANCE

In class, you and your investigator interview Jack Waters.

ASSIGNMENT 30: Prosecutor: Interview of Detective Tharp (Investigating Officer for the Case)

Detective Tharp is sitting in the waiting room outside of your office. Detective Tharp directed the investigation in the *State v. Hard* murder case, and thus will sit by you at the counsel table during trial as your investigating officer. At this point, you are interested that Detective Tharp:

1. directed the taking of photographs at the scene of the shooting on September 3,
2. took measurements at the scene and made a rough sketch,
3. supervised the preparation of a detailed diagram of the scene,
4. authored the initial suspect information report and the follow-up report,
5. took the statement of Deborah Summers the day after the shooting,
6. took the statement of Tom Donaldson on the night of the shooting, and
7. took Ed Hard's statement.

In approaching this interview, keep in mind that Hard's grounds for suppression will likely be:

1. that he was too intoxicated to either voluntarily give a statement or to knowingly waive his constitutional rights, and/or
2. that his *Mintz* (identical to *Miranda*) rights were not respected.

PREPARATION

READ: (1) Pretrial Case Files Entries 4, 5, 14, 15, 17, 26, 29, 30; (2) Chapter 6; (3) Fed. R. Evid. 401, 801(d)(1).

ASSIGNMENTS FOR CLASS

DISCUSSION: Be prepared to discuss the following questions:

1. Initially, think about this meeting (you have already had a number of brief conversations with Detective Tharp), but this is the first extensive interview you will have):
   a. What institutionally is the appropriate relationship between you as the prosecutor and the police?
   b. What do you see as the nature of Detective Tharp's and your respective roles in the meeting and in the case?

2. What are the requirements for the use and admissibility of the photographs and the diagram?
3. Why would the defense want to suppress Hard's statement?
4. Why do you oppose the suppression?

PERFORMANCE

In class, meet with Detective Tharp, your investigating officer on the Hard case. Unless your instructor directs you otherwise, interview Tharp regarding the seven areas noted.

ASSIGNMENT 31: Defense Attorney: Interview of John Gooding

You plan to seek discovery from the prosecution as part of your case development for the *State v. Hard* murder case. At the same time, you must continue your own investigation. You and your investigator are therefore about to interview John Gooding.

Mr. Gooding is a friend of the defendant who was with Hard (1) at the Garage on August 20 and (2) at the Garage again on September 3. Further, according to your client, Mr. Gooding is also willing to speak about Hard's good, nonviolent character and Summers's violent character.

PREPARATION

READ: (1) Pretrial Case Files Entries 4, 5, 14, 15, 17, 26, 29, 30, 64; (2) Chapter 6; (3) Fed. R. Evid. 404, 405, 608.

ASSIGNMENTS FOR CLASS

DISCUSSION: Be prepared to discuss the following questions:

1. What information can Mr. Gooding provide to support your case theory? What specific information do you want from him?
2. What will you want to know about Gooding's proposed character testimony? Why?
   a. What are the evidentiary requirements for the admission of that testimony?
   b. How will this evidentiary perspective affect your interview?
3. Suppose you ask Mr. Gooding about the August 20 incident and he states, "It's very important in this case that I saw Bruno threaten Ed, isn't it?" How will you respond?

PERFORMANCE

In class, you and your investigator interview John Gooding. Take notes. Be sure to assess Mr. Gooding as a character witness for Hard and against Summers.

ASSIGNMENT 32: Defense Attorney: Interview of Cindy Rigg

As part of your investigation in the *State v. Hard* murder case, it is now time to plan your interview with Cindy Rigg. Ms. Rigg is an eyewitness to the August 20 fight between Hard and Summers at the Garage Tavern. She does not seem to be friends with either Summers or Hard.

PREPARATION

READ: (1) Pretrial Case Files Entries 4, 14, 17, 26, 29, 30, 64; (2) Chapter 6.

ASSIGNMENTS FOR CLASS

DISCUSSION: Be prepared to discuss the following questions:

1. What will you ask Cindy Rigg about? Why?
2. Suppose you just show up and tell her that you want to discuss the shooting at the Garage Tavern with her, and she states, "I don't really want to get involved."
3. Suppose Ms. Rigg says she will only speak to you alone without your investigator. How will you respond? What are your concerns?

PERFORMANCE

In class, be prepared to discuss your objectives and strategies for your interview and any ethical concerns you may have. Then, you and your investigator do the interview.

ASSIGNMENT 33: Defense Attorney: Interview of Marty Saunders (Witness for a Suppression Motion)

Within a few hours after the shooting of Bruno Summers at the Garage, police, led by Officer Yale went to Hard's home. According to the police, Hard agreed to let the police into his home, where the gun was found and seized.

In planning a suppression motion (a motion to keep the gun out of evidence), you have been developing a twofold legal attack.

First, you are prepared to argue that the police needed an arrest warrant to enter Hard's home prior to seizing the gun.

Second, you will take the position that there existed neither exigency nor valid consent as could obviate the need for an arrest warrant because, among other grounds, Hard's consent was a mere submission to authority.

A discussion with your client this morning has added a totally new dimension to this search issue. According to Hard, the police report is "A bunch of nonsense! Consent nothing! They just kicked my door in, and I had a guest there who was a witness—Marty Saunders."

Hard's story is legally significant because such an action by the police would also undermine any government attempt to use consent as a theory that could circumvent the need for an arrest warrant.

You have made plans to meet with Marty Saunders.

PREPARATION

READ: (1) Pretrial Case Files Entries 19, 20, 28, 76, 77; (2) Chapters 6, 8; (3) Notes from all the interviews you have seen and done in class.

ASSIGNMENTS FOR CLASS

DISCUSSION: Be prepared to discuss the following questions:

1. When you first meet with Saunders, will you tell him what Hard has told you? Why? Why not?
2. What information will you seek from Saunders? Why?
3. If you call Saunders to testify at the suppression hearing, won't you be calling the police liars?
   a. What problems may this cause you with the judge?
   b. How will you deal with such problems?
   c. Who is the court more likely to believe, Hard's friend or the police?
4. Assume the prosecution has the burden of persuasion by a preponderance of the evidence to establish consent. Can you use this burden to avoid calling the police liars? How?

PERFORMANCE

In class, you and your investigator interview Marty Saunders.

ASSIGNMENT 34: Defense Attorney: Interview of James Raven (Polygrapher)

Your client has consistently maintained his innocence to the first-degree murder charge in *State v. Hard*. You are now considering giving Hard a polygraph. As such, you have set up a meeting with polygrapher James Raven. You have obtained Mr. Raven's resume prior to the interview.

PREPARATION

READ: (1) Pretrial Case Files Entries 5, 15, 17, 24, 75, 86; (2) Chapters 6; (3) Fed. R. Evid. 701-705.

ASSIGNMENTS FOR CLASS

DISCUSSION: Be prepared to discuss the following questions:

1. Assume the results of the polygraph are inadmissible in court. List all the reasons you might still want to give a client a polygraph. Are any of these reasons persuasive in this case?
2. As to the polygraph itself:
    a. What generally do you want to know?
    b. What do you want to know about the procedure and technique?
    c. Do you want to know what it can show about Hard? The risks of inaccuracy? The variables that affect accuracy?
    d. What is the significance of the *Dilbert* case for this interview?
3. If a prosecution witness took a polygraph and failed, could you argue that the prosecutor has a duty to disclose the information?

PERFORMANCE

In class, interview James Raven. Be prepared to discuss with your supervisor whether Hard should take a polygraph.

Civil Case Assignments

ASSIGNMENT 35: Plaintiffs' Attorney: Interview of Bert Kain

You have interviewed Deborah Summers, reviewed the criminal file that you obtained from the prosecutor's office, and researched the law. Deborah,

Gretchen, and Hans Summers have retained you as their attorney concerning the death of Bruno Summers. You plan to informally investigate the incidents at the Garage Tavern and Ed Hard's role in the shooting in order to assess whether to file a lawsuit.

Peter Nye, your investigator, has located three potential eyewitnesses to the August 20 incident and the September 3 shooting—Bert Kain, Tom Donaldson, and Peter Dean. Bert Kain has agreed to be interviewed by you and Peter Nye at your office at 9:00 A.M.

PREPARATION

READ: (1) Pretrial Case Files Entries 1-33, 62-64, 66, 85; (2) Chapter 6.

ASSIGNMENTS FOR CLASS

DISCUSSION: Be prepared to discuss the following questions:

1. What are your objectives for the interview with Bert Kain? Why?
2. Should the law affect your interview?
3. What factual information will you seek from Bert Kain to support your theory of the case?

PERFORMANCE

In class, conduct the interview of Bert Kain.

ASSIGNMENT 36: Plaintiffs' Attorney: Interview of Dr. Brett Day

You have interviewed Deborah Summers, reviewed the criminal file that you obtained from the prosecutors office, researched the law, and obtained Bruno Summers's hospital records. Deborah, Gretchen, and Hans Summers have retained you as their attorney concerning the death of Bruno Summers. You plan to informally investigate the incidents at the Garage Tavern and Ed Hard's role in the shooting in order to assess whether to file a lawsuit.

According to Peter Nye, your investigator, Dr. Brett Day was the surgeon who operated on Bruno Summers the night of the shooting and attended Bruno until he died. Dr. Day has agreed to see you at his office at 5:30 P.M.

PREPARATION

READ: (1) Pretrial Case Files Entries 1, 2, 4, 5, 7, 8, 11, 21, 22, 33, 38, 39, 62-64, 66, 67, 85; (2) Chapter 6; (3) Fed. R. Civ. P. 26(b)(4), 35.

ASSIGNMENTS FOR CLASS

DISCUSSION: Be prepared to discuss the following questions:

1. In the criminal matter against Edward Hard, the prosecutor would have interviewed the medical examiner and explored the issue of proximate cause of death. When you interview Dr. Day you will also most likely be interested in the issue of proximate cause. Compare how you would explore the issue in both the criminal and civil context.

2. Dr. Day is a potential expert witness, as opposed to a lay witness. How will that affect preparation for the interview?

3. Potentially, Dr. Day could be friendly, neutral, or hostile toward your case. Can you explain what would cause him to adopt one of these attitudes? How will you approach Dr. Day if he is hostile?

PERFORMANCE

In class, conduct the interview of Dr. Day.

ASSIGNMENT 37: Plaintiffs' Attorney: Interview of Karen Sway

Deborah, Gretchen, and Hans Summers have retained you as their attorney concerning the death of Bruno Summers. It is a few months since the shooting and death of Bruno Summers, and Deborah still appears to be upset about Bruno Summers's death. You would like to explore Deborah's emotional condition more fully.

You have just received a telephone call from Deborah Summers. She has told you that she has retained an attorney to represent her in a child custody matter. It seems that Bruno Summers's parents have filed for legal custody of Ronnie and Amanda, Bruno's children by his prior marriage. Deborah may contest the petition filed by Gretchen and Hans Summers. Deborah's child custody attorney has interviewed Karen Sway, who is a close friend of Deborah.

A few months ago, you spoke with Karen Sway by telephone to confirm her willingness to be a potential witness in a wrongful death case. Karen

Sway has agreed to be interviewed by you and Peter Nye, your investigator. She will be at your office at 9:00 A.M.

PREPARATION

READ: (1) Pretrial Case Files Entries 1-33, 38, 39, 62, 64, 66, 67, 79, 85; (2) Chapter 6.

ASSIGNMENTS FOR CLASS

DISCUSSION: Be prepared to discuss the following questions:

1. Explain how Civil Instruction 4 can provide guidance in planning the content of this witness interview.
2. Will the child custody matter and Karen Sway's role in that case influence your interview of Karen Sway? Explain.
3. Suppose Karen Sway is reluctant to talk to you. What will you do?
    a. Is that helpful for Deborah's emotional distress claim?
    b. Harmful? Explain.

PERFORMANCE

In class, conduct the interview of Karen Sway.

ASSIGNMENT 38: Attorney for Defendant Hard: Interview of Rebecca Karr

You have interviewed Ed Hard, reviewed Ed Hard's homeowner's insurance policy with SAPO Insurance Company, read the criminal file that you obtained from the prosecutors office, and researched the law. Ed Hard's rich cousin has paid your fee. You have agreed to represent Ed Hard in the *Summers v. Hard* lawsuit.

Ed Hard went to the Garage Tavern on August 20 and September 3 with John Gooding and Rebecca Karr. During the past few weeks, Ed has asked you, as his attorney, to speak with Rebecca. On three occasions, you had appointments with Rebecca, but each time she did not call or appear for her appointment. You have not told Ed that Rebecca has not been a cooperative witness.

You have scheduled one last appointment to speak with Rebecca concerning the Bruno Summers-Edward Hard incidents.

Rebecca has agreed to be interviewed by you and your investigator. She will be at your law office at 2:00 P.M.

PREPARATION

READ: (1) Pretrial Case Files Entries 1-35, 62-64, 66, 85; (2) Chapter 6.

ASSIGNMENTS FOR CLASS

DISCUSSION: Be prepared to discuss the following questions:

1. You have heard a rumor that Rebecca attended a neo-Nazi survivalist meeting. Will you ask her about her experience? Why?
2. Are there any circumstances under which you should preserve the interview with Ms. Karr? Explain.
   a. How can you preserve the interview? Discuss.
   b. If you preserve the interview and Rebecca Karr is no longer available as a witness, will you have to give defendant Davola and plaintiffs access to your witness interview? Explain.
3. Should you confront Ms. Karr about the three appointments she failed to keep? Why?

PERFORMANCE

In class, conduct the interview with Rebecca Karr.

_____

ASSIGNMENT 39: EKKO Attorney for Defendant Davola: Interview of Roberta Montbank

You have received and reviewed the Summers complaint. Before responding to the Summers's complaint, you plan to informally investigate the incidents alleged.

The EKKO insurance investigator located another patron, Roberta Montbank, who claims to have been at the Garage Tavern on September 3. (It seems that the police had inadvertently written down Robin Luntlebunk as being a patron at the Garage Tavern instead of Roberta Montbank. Therefore, the police never located her for the criminal case, *State v. Hard*.) As Davola's insurance company attorney, you have arranged to interview Ms. Montbank at the Stillwater Retirement Home on October.

PREPARATION

READ: (1) Pretrial Case Files Entries 1-35, 42, 62-64, 66, 85; (2) Chapter 6; (3) Fed. R. Evid. 601, 612.

ASSIGNMENTS FOR CLASS

DISCUSSION: Be prepared to discuss the following questions:

1. Roberta Montbank was not interviewed, nor did she give a statement to the police after the shooting. She was discovered by the investigator for the EKKO Insurance Company. How do these facts affect your interview?

2. Ms. Montbank is 78 years of age. She appears to be slightly hard of hearing. Will this factor have any influence on the interview? Explain.

3. Would a diagram of the Garage Tavern be helpful to you in conducting the interview of Roberta Montbank? Why or why not?

4. Suppose Ms. Montbank provides helpful information for Ed Hard's defense. What will you do after the interview?

PERFORMANCE

In class, along with the EKKO investigator, interview Roberta Montbank.

Chapter 7. Strategic Pleading—Assignments

Criminal Case Assignments

ASSIGNMENT 40: Prosecutor: Drafting a Criminal Pleading

You have already filed a charging pleading (a criminal complaint) accusing Ed Hard of first-degree premeditated murder in *State v. Hard*. Your pleading embodied your legal theory and formed a part of your representational strategy. That pleading also began the formal criminal judicial process and constituted the charge to which Hard pleaded "not guilty." Your supervisor has now asked you to draft three additional complaints—one charging Hard with unpremeditated, intentional second-degree murder, one charging second-degree extreme recklessness murder, and one charging voluntary manslaughter. "We need these on hand in the event of a possible plea bargain," your supervisor said. "The deal would be that we'd file the new charge we agreed on (if any) with defense counsel, and the defendant would plead to the new charge. Then we'd dismiss the first-degree murder charge."

PREPARATION

READ: (1) Pretrial Case Files Entries 3, 4, 61, 65; (2) Chapter 7.

ASSIGNMENTS FOR CLASS

DISCUSSION: Be prepared to discuss the following questions:

1. Generally, what should you put in a complaint?
2. Imagine your investigation indicated that Hard was trying to rob Summers when he shot him. Any problem with filing a new felony murder complaint at trial? The month before?
3. Is this different than asking for a "lesser included" instruction of second-degree unpremeditated murder at the close of a trial where Hard has been charged with first-degree premeditated murder?
4. Does it matter if you include the exact date of the crime? Is "on or about" a certain date good enough? Explain.

PERFORMANCE

Outside of class, draft a separate complaint charging Hard with second-degree unpremeditated intentional murder.

Civil Case Assignments

ASSIGNMENT 41: Plaintiffs' Attorney: Planning and Drafting Pleadings

You have interviewed the Summers family (Deborah, Gretchen, Hans, and the children, Amanda and Ronnie), reviewed the criminal file you obtained from the prosecutor's office, obtained medical records, bills, and other documents, researched the law, theorized about the case, and interviewed some witnesses.

The Summers family has requested that you represent them. They requested that you contact the potential defendants in the case to see if the defendants will settle. You have done so but were not successful in settling the case. The Summers family has requested that you pursue litigation; that means you should draft a complaint.

PREPARATION

READ: (1) Pretrial Case Files Entries 1-33, 38, 39, 62-64, 66, 82, 85; (2) Chapter 7; (3) Fed. R. Civ. P. 7-21.

ASSIGNMENTS FOR CLASS

DISCUSSION: Be prepared to discuss the following questions:

1. Whom will you join as defendants?
   a. Explain the legal basis (substantive law, procedural rules, evidentiary concerns).
   b. Explain the factual basis.
2. What claims for relief will you state? Against whom?
3. Suppose that after filing your complaint in the Summers case, you find out that a critical fact in the complaint is incorrect. What will you do? Why?

PERFORMANCE

Outside of class, draft a summons, an affidavit of service, and a complaint seeking redress for Bruno Summers's death. Your instructor will discuss the format to follow in preparing your complaint and will assign your opposing counsel. Serve your complaint on opposing counsel who will draft an answer to the complaint.

ASSIGNMENT 42: Defendants' Attorneys: Planning and Drafting Responsive Pleadings

You have reviewed the summons and complaint in *Summers v. Hard*, interviewed your respective clients (Ed Hard, M.C. Davola, Mary Apple, and Tom Donaldson), reviewed the criminal file you obtained from the prosecutor's office, obtained some of the relevant documents (medical records of Bruno Summers), researched the law, informally interviewed some witnesses, and theorized about defenses to the lawsuit.

Informal discovery has concluded. Of course there are additional witnesses and documents to examine, but you have enough information to respond to the *Summers v. Hard* complaint.

A major problem that is still unsettled is whether the SAPO Insurance Company lawyer or Ed Hard's own lawyer will be representing Ed Hard. Ed Hard's insurance company has agreed that it will draft the appropriate responsive pleadings invoking its reservation of rights clause in the insurance contract in order to protect the issue of "duty to defend." M.C. Davola and his employees, Mary Apple and Tom Donaldson, are represented by both EKKO Insurance Company and a private lawyer.

PREPARATION

READ: (1) Pretrial Case Files Entries 1-37, 42, 43, 62-64, 66, 82, 85; (2) Chapter 7.

ASSIGNMENTS FOR CLASS

DISCUSSION: Be prepared to discuss the following questions:

1. Explain the steps you have taken to prepare to draft an answer.
2. Will you assert any cross-claims?
   a. List the cross-claims you will assert, if any.
   b. Explain the legal theory you are relying on for each cross-claim.
   c. Explain the factual theory you are relying on for each cross-claim.
3. How does Federal Rule of Civil Procedure 11 influence your decision to admit or deny allegations in plaintiff's complaint?

PERFORMANCE

Outside of class, draft an answer and affidavit of service to the complaint that a student served on you. Hand in your answer and affidavit of service to your senior partner.

Chapter 8. Creating a Coordinated Discovery Plan—Assignments

Criminal Case Assignments

ASSIGNMENT 43: Defense Attorney: Seeking Discovery from the Government

Ed Hard finally obtained bail. A wealthy relative provided the cash premium and even threw a nice little party to celebrate Ed's release. You know, however, that unless you can obtain ultimate vindication for Ed or something less than total victory if that is all that is reasonably possible there is little cause for celebration. So back to work. Fact-finding in the context of your tentative case theory is now your dominant concern. You want to learn more about the prosecution's case, including its strengths and weaknesses, and to discover evidence that you may want to use should you choose to present a case. While organizing your approach to witness interviews, you are simultaneously planning a formal discovery motion in order to obtain all the information that is in the possession of the government.

For this problem, assume that the only documents that you have received from the Case Files at this point are the police reports.

PREPARATION

READ: (1) Pretrial Case Files Entries 4, 75; (2) Chapters 8.

ASSIGNMENTS FOR CLASS

DISCUSSION: Be prepared to discuss the following questions:

1. The prosecution has obtained a great deal of information. You must carefully plan a discovery request in order to gain access to this information.
   a. What information will you seek in light of your theory of the case? Why?
   b. Why is it reasonable to think that the prosecution may have this information?
   c. Do you want this information before you do any witness interviews? Why?
      1) If so, are there practical problems with delaying the interviews? Explain.
      2) How will you resolve this dilemma?
      3) Does your answer depend upon the length of the delay? The particular witness? Anything else?
2. What is the nature of the prosecution's duties under *Branty v. State* and *State v. Augle* (See Case File Entry 75)?
3. What is the relationship between the nature of your discovery request at the trial level and the application of Branty/Augle principles on appeal?

PERFORMANCE

In class, be prepared to meet with your supervisor to discuss discovery planning for the defense of Ed Hard, including the specific information that you would seek in a discovery motion.

Civil Case Assignments

ASSIGNMENT 44: Plaintiffs' and Defendants' Attorneys: Discovery Planning

Summers v. Hard progressed through theorizing, informal interviewing, pleading, and response. Plaintiffs and defendants even had extensive discussions concerning arbitrating or mediating the case. But, alas, no agreement was reached. Settlement also was rejected because the facts are not entirely evident. Therefore, it appears that the parties will proceed with the pretrial process.

The next stage of the pretrial process involves formal discovery. It is important to plan what discovery devices will be used, to whom they will be directed, and what items, things, and facts need to be discovered. Discovery planning is particularly important because many courts, in order to control the discovery process, require that each party submit a discovery plan.

PREPARATION

READ: (1) Pretrial Case Files Entries 1-37, 62, 63, 66, 81, 85; (2) Chapters 8 and 9; (3) Fed. R. Civ. P. 26-37.

ASSIGNMENTS FOR CLASS

DISCUSSION: Be prepared to discuss the following questions:

1. Explain how discovery will help you achieve your case strategies.
2. What are the advantages and disadvantages of each discovery device?
3.. How will you decide what information you need? What will you consult?
4. Will you use the discovery devices in any particular sequence? Explain.

5. How will a scheduling conference be conducted according to the Federal Rules of Civil Procedure 26(f)?

PERFORMANCE

In class:

1. Be prepared to discuss the discovery plans for the plaintiffs and defendants Hard and Davola.
2. Meet with your opposing counsel to work out an agreeable discovery plan to present to the judge in a scheduling conference conducted (unless directed otherwise by your instructor) in conformance with the Federal Rules of Civil Procedure.

ASSIGNMENT 45: Plaintiffs' and Defendants' Attorneys: Initial Disclosure and Written Discovery Requests

Summers v. Hard has progressed through theorizing, informal interviewing, pleading, and response. The parties are proceeding with the litigation process and discovery.

You have drafted a discovery plan for *Summers v. Hard* that sets forth the discovery you need to complete. It is time to commence written discovery. Plaintiffs' and defendants' attorneys have prepared a list of written discovery requests that should be drafted. Since discovery appears to be extensive, you will have to be careful in selecting which written discovery to pursue.

PREPARATION

READ: (1) Pretrial Case Files Entries 1-37, 62, 63, 66, 81, 85; (2) Chapters 8 and 9; (3) Fed. R. Civ. P. 26-37 and 45.

ASSIGNMENTS FOR CLASS

DISCUSSION: Be prepared to discuss the following questions:

1. Explain what was produced during the initial disclosure process according to State of Major Civil Rule of Procedure 26(a).
2. Explain how discovery will help you achieve your representational strategies.
3. What are the advantages and disadvantages of each discovery device?

4. How will you decide what information you need? What will you consult?

5. Will you use the discovery devices in any particular sequence? Explain.

PERFORMANCE

Outside of class, draft discovery requests as follows: 12 interrogatories; 3 requests for production and 2 requests for admissions (subparts to interrogatories and requests for production do not count separately). You may chose to represent any party in the *Summers v. Hard* case. Give your senior partner a copy of your discovery requests.

Chapter 9. Taking and Defending Depositions— Assignments

Civil Case Assignments

ASSIGNMENT 46: Plaintiffs' Attorney: Preparing a Client for a Deposition (Deborah Summers)

Summers v. Hard has progressed through theorizing, informal interviewing, pleading, and response. Attorneys for plaintiffs and defendants are proceeding with formal discovery.

As Deborah's attorney, you received a notice from defendants pursuant to Federal Rule of Civil Procedure 30(b)(1) to take the oral deposition of your client Deborah Summers on October 30, 20XX + 1. It will be necessary for you to prepare Deborah for her deposition.

PREPARATION

READ: (1) Pretrial Case Files Entries 1-39, 51, 57, 62-64, 66, 67, 81, 85; (2) Chapter 9; (3) Fed. R. Civ. P. 26, 29-32, 37.

ASSIGNMENTS FOR CLASS

DISCUSSION: Be prepared to discuss the following questions:

1. What factual information will you prepare your client Deborah Summers to cover during her deposition?
2. How will you explain the deposition process to Deborah?
3. Suppose that Deborah tells you that she is planning to withhold information about her personal life from opposing counsel at the deposition.
   a. What are your ethical obligations (to your client, your adversary, yourself)?
   b. Explain what you will do.

PERFORMANCE

In class, prepare your client, Deborah Summers, for her deposition.

ASSIGNMENT 47: Attorney for Defendant Davola: Preparing a Client for a Deposition (M.C. Davola)

Plaintiffs and defendants are proceeding with the pretrial process and formal discovery.

As M. C. Davola's attorney, you received a notice from plaintiffs pursuant to Federal Rule of Civil Procedure 30(b)(1) to take the oral deposition of one of your clients, M.C. Davola, on October 25, 20XX + 1.

PREPARATION

READ: (1) Pretrial Case Files Entries 1-37, 42, 62-64, 66, 81, 85; (2) Chapter 9; (3) Fed. R. Civ. P. 26, 29-32, 37.

ASSIGNMENTS FOR CLASS

DISCUSSION: Be prepared to discuss the following questions:

1. Discuss how you will explain the deposition process to Mr. Davola.
2. Will you have Davola bring anything to the meeting with you in which you prepare him for the deposition (e.g., office manual)?
3. Will you prepare Davola for using a diagram of the Garage Tavern at the deposition? Why?

PERFORMANCE

In class, prepare your client, M.C. Davola, for his deposition.

ASSIGNMENT 48: Attorney for Defendant Davola: Preparing an Expert Witness for a Deposition (Dr. Thomas Monday, Economist)

Plaintiffs' and defendants' attorneys have agreed that all experts who will testify at trial can be deposed without a court order. Defendant Davola hired an expert witness to present the valuation of Bruno Summers's life and refute the opinion of plaintiffs' economist, Dr. Bruce Hann. The deposition of defendant's economist has been scheduled to be taken at the law office of plaintiffs' attorney at 9:00 A.M. on November 13, 20XX + 1.

PREPARATION

READ: (1) Pretrial Case Files Entries 1-37, 40, 41, 53, 56, 62-64, 66, 81, 85; (2) Chapter 9; (3) Fed. R. Civ. P. 26, 29-32, 37.

ASSIGNMENTS FOR CLASS

DISCUSSION: Be prepared to discuss the following questions:

1. Is there anything you should do before meeting with Dr. Monday?
2. List the specific differences between preparing an expert witness for deposition and preparing a lay witness client.
3. What will you advise Monday to do when you make objections to Plaintiff's questions?
   a. Can you anticipate what objections you may assert? Explain.
   b. Should you tell your economist to refuse to answer questions you've objected to?
4. Suppose Dr. Monday has a habit of dressing in blue jeans and blue work shirts when he is not officially working at his employment. Should you tell him how to dress for the deposition? Why or why not?

PERFORMANCE

In class, prepare your economist, Dr. Thomas Monday, for his deposition.

ASSIGNMENT 49: Plaintiffs' Attorney: Preparing an Expert Witness for a Deposition (Dr. Brett Day, Treating Physician)

Plaintiffs' and defendants' attorneys have agreed that all experts who will testify at trial can be deposed without a court order. Dr. Brett Day was the surgeon who operated on Bruno Summers the night of the shooting and attended and treated Bruno until he died. You have previously interviewed Dr. Day briefly at the outset of the case and decided not to pursue a medical malpractice case. Currently, you intend to call the doctor to testify at trial, among other things, about Bruno Summers's treatment, statements, and his pain and suffering before he died.

Defendant's attorney has scheduled Dr. Day for a deposition on November 10, 20XX + 1 at 9:00 A.M.

PREPARATION

READ: (1) Pretrial Case Files Entries 1-39, 61-63, 66; (2) Chapter 9; (3) Fed. R. Civ. P. 26, 29-32, 37.

ASSIGNMENTS FOR CLASS

DISCUSSION: Be prepared to discuss the following questions:

1. Is there anything you should do before meeting with Dr. Day?
2. What particular areas of concern do you have about Dr. Day's deposition testimony?
3. Specifically, what are your objectives in preparing Dr. Day for the deposition?
4. What guidance do you plan to give Dr. Day about how to conduct himself during the deposition?
5. What will you do if Dr. Day demands expert witness fees not only for the deposition but also for trial and this session that you are conducting with him in preparation for the deposition?

PERFORMANCE

In class, prepare the treating physician, Dr. Brett Day, for his deposition.

ASSIGNMENT 50: Plaintiffs' Attorney: Taking the Deposition of an Adverse Party (Tom Donaldson)

Plaintiffs' attorney sent a notice to take the deposition of Tom Donaldson.

Plaintiffs' attorney served written interrogatories on Tom Donaldson. In response to an interrogatory requesting information about Ed Hard's appearance, demeanor, or drinking the night of September 3, Donaldson refused to answer the interrogatories, claiming that to answer would incriminate him. Plaintiffs' attorney has decided to depose Donaldson instead of compelling answers to the interrogatories.

Defendant Davola's attorney, representing Donaldson, has prepared Donaldson for this deposition. The deposition is scheduled for November 6, 20XX + 1 at 9:00 A.M. at the law office of plaintiffs' attorney. Attorneys for defendants Hard and Davola will be attending the deposition. They may examine the deponent if time permits.

PREPARATION

READ: (1) Pretrial Case Files Entries 1-37, 42, 62-64, 66, 81, 85; (2) Chapter 9; (3) Fed. R. Civ. P. 26, 29-32, 37.

ASSIGNMENTS FOR CLASS

DISCUSSION: Be prepared to discuss the following questions:

1. What topics and events will you cover during the deposition?
2. Suppose that Mr. Donaldson changes some critical facts that are material to the issues.
   a. List all the things plaintiffs' counsel can do.
   b. What will you do? Explain why.
3. Suppose that you ask Mr. Donaldson: "Tell me about Ed Hard's appearance on the night of September 3, 20XX + 1." Donaldson states: "I refuse to answer on the grounds it may incriminate me."
   a. What is the basis for Donaldson's refusal?
   b. What options do you have if Donaldson continues to refuse to answer questions on the topic of Ed Hard's drinking, demeanor, or appearance?
   c. What will you do? Why?

PERFORMANCE

In class:

1. Plaintiffs' attorney: Conduct the deposition of Tom Donaldson.
2. Attorneys for defendants Davola and Hard: Attend the deposition, and, if desired, examine Tom Donaldson.

––––––––––––––––––––––––––

ASSIGNMENT 51: Attorney for Defendant Hard: Taking the Deposition of an Adverse Party (Deborah Summers)

Summers v. Hard has progressed through theorizing, informal interviewing, pleading, and response. Attorneys for plaintiffs and defendants are in the midst of the litigation process and formal discovery.

Defendant Ed Hard's attorney sent a notice to take the deposition of Deborah Summers. The deposition is scheduled for October 30, 20XX+ at 9:00 A.M. at the law office of Hard's attorney. Attorneys for plaintiffs and Davola will be attending the deposition. They may examine the deponent if time permits.

PREPARATION

READ: (1) Pretrial Case Files Entries 1-37, 38, 39, 62-64, 66, 81, 84, 85; (2) Chapter 9; (3) Fed. R. Civ. P. 26, 29-32, 37.

ASSIGNMENTS FOR CLASS

DISCUSSION: Be prepared to discuss the following questions:

1. What are your objectives in deposing Deborah Summers?
2. What topics will you examine? Explain.
3. Suppose that you ask Deborah Summers if she has a boyfriend. Deborah's Attorney answers: "She refuses to answer."
   a. Why are you interested in this information?
   b. Have you posed an objectionable question? Explain.
   c. List all the ways that you could obtain the information if plaintiffs' counsel continues to instruct Deborah to refuse to answer the question?

PERFORMANCE

In class:

1. Attorney for defendant Hard: Conduct the deposition of Deborah Summers.
2. Attorneys for plaintiffs and defendant Davola: Attend the deposition and, if desired, examine Deborah Summers.

ASSIGNMENT 52: Attorney for Defendant Hard: Taking the Deposition of an Adverse Party (Gretchen Summers)

Gretchen Summers, Bruno's mother, can be a key witness for plaintiffs as to damages and Bruno's reputation for violence. She has taken care of Bruno's children and presently has custody of Amanda and Ronnie. She also might be knowledgeable about Bruno's neo-Nazi activities.

You sent a notice to take the deposition of Gretchen Summers. The deposition is scheduled for November 2, 20XX + 1 at 9:00 A.M. at your law office. Attorneys for plaintiffs and defendant Davola will be attending the deposition. They may examine if time permits.

PREPARATION

READ: (1) Pretrial Case Files Entries 1-37, 62-64, 66, 81, 85; (2) Chapter 9; (3) Fed. R. Civ. P. 26, 29-32, 37.

ASSIGNMENTS FOR CLASS

DISCUSSION: Be prepared to discuss the following questions:

1. Considering plaintiffs' complaint (Case Files Entry 37), can you use the deposition to develop evidence for a summary judgment motion?

2. Suppose that you ask Gretchen Summers: "Your son, Bruno, was a member of a neo-Nazi survivalist group. What do you know about his participation in that group?" Gretchen Summers responds: "None of your business."
   a. What, if anything, can you as Hard's attorney do or say?
   b. Do you anticipate that plaintiffs' counsel will say or do anything? Explain.

3. Suppose that you ask Gretchen Summers: "Would you like to settle the *Summers v. Hard* lawsuit?" Plaintiffs' counsel objects and instructs Mrs. Summers to not answer the question.
   a. Is plaintiffs' counsel correct to object? Upon what grounds?
   b. What, if anything, should you as Hard's counsel say or do? Why?

PERFORMANCE

In class:

1. Attorney for defendant Hard: Conduct the deposition of Gretchen Summers.

2. Attorneys for plaintiffs and defendant Davola: Attend the deposition and, if desired, examine Gretchen Summers.

ASSIGNMENT 53: Attorney for Defendant Hard: Taking the Deposition of a Neutral Witness (Roberta Montbank)

You sent a notice to take the deposition of Ms. Roberta Montbank. The deposition is scheduled for November 7, 20XX + 1 at 9:00 A.M. at the law office of defendant Hard's attorney. Attorneys for plaintiffs and defendant Davola will be attending the deposition. They may examine the deponent if time permits.

The deposition may be critical to establish Ed Hard's defenses. A little history of this witness is important.

Ms. Montbank, 78 years of age, was a patron at the Garage Tavern on the night Bruno Summers was shot. The police incorrectly listed Robin Lundebunk as a witness instead of Roberta Montbank, so no statement was taken from her until November 3 (after the criminal case was dismissed). The police claim they could not locate Ms. Montbank because they were given the name Robin Luntlebunk instead of Roberta Montbank.

Plaintiffs sent written interrogatories to defendant Davola on May 15, 20XX + 1. Attorney for defendant Hard learned from those interrogatories that the EKKO Insurance Company interviewed and received a signed statement under oath from Ms. Roberta Montbank on October 26. Ms. Montbank declined to give either plaintiffs' attorney or Ed Hard's attorney a copy of her statement. Plaintiffs' written request for the document has been the subject of an unsuccessful plaintiffs' motion to compel Davola to produce the Montbank statement. The court tentatively ruled the statement work product. This ruling is for purposes of this Assignment only. See the motion, Assignment 73.

PREPARATION

READ: (1) Pretrial Case Files Entries 1-37, 48, 60, 62-64, 66, 81, 85; (2) Chapter 9; (3) Fed. R. Civ. P. 26, 29-32, 37.

ASSIGNMENTS FOR CLASS

DISCUSSION: Be prepared to discuss the following questions:

1. What are the topics you will cover during your examination? Explain.

    a. Will you follow a particular sequence?

    b. Why?

2. Is it ethical and wise for either plaintiffs' attorney or any of defendants' attorneys to contact Roberta Montbank prior to her deposition? Explain.

3. Do you think plaintiffs' counsel should examine Ms. Montbank? Why or why not?

    a. If you were plaintiffs' counsel, what topics would you select? Why?

    b. Can plaintiffs' attorney ask leading questions? Why or why not?

    c. Can defense counsel ask leading questions? Why or why not?

PERFORMANCE

In class:

1. Attorney for defendant Hard: Conduct the deposition of Roberta Montbank.

2. Attorneys for plaintiffs and defendant Davola: Attend the deposition, and if desired, examine Ms. Roberta Montbank.

ASSIGNMENT 54: Attorney for Defendant Davola: Taking the Deposition of a Neutral Witness (Bert Kain)

Bert Kain was a patron at the Garage Tavern on both August 20 and September 3, 20XX. You have heard that he spoke to plaintiffs' attorney, but he has not answered your telephone calls.

You sent a notice to take the deposition of Bert Kain. The deposition is scheduled for November 8, 20XX + 1 at 9:00 A.M. at your law office. Attorneys for plaintiffs and defendant Hard will be attending the deposition. They may examine the deponent if time permits.

PREPARATION

READ: (1) Pretrial Case Files Entries 1-37, 62-64, 66, 81, 85; (2) Chapter 9; (3) Fed. R. Civ. P. 26, 29-32, 37.

ASSIGNMENTS FOR CLASS

DISCUSSION: Be prepared to discuss the following questions:

1. What are your objectives in deposing Bert Kain?

2. Suppose that Bert Kain begins the depositions stating, "I have to miss a day's work because of this deposition. Who is going to pay me for my loss of pay and for the travel and my lunch?
   a. How should defendants' counsel respond?
   b. How should plaintiffs' counsel respond?

3. Suppose that at the deposition Bert Kain states, "I can't remember if I heard Mary Apple on August 20 or September 3 say 'I shouldn't have served them.'"
   a. Should you question Kain further on this topic? Explain.
   b. Should you try to refresh Kain's memory? Why? Why not?

4. Suppose that at the deposition one of the defendants' attorneys asks Bert Kain: "I understand you met with plaintiffs' attorney before *Summers v. Hard* was filed. Tell me what you told their attorney."
   a. Is it ethical for defendants' counsel to ask such a question? Explain.
   b. If plaintiffs want to object, is there any appropriate objection that plaintiffs' attorney could make? Explain.

PERFORMANCE

Your instructor may select which attorneys will examine the deponent and the topics to be covered in the deposition

---

In class:

1. Attorney for defendant Davola: Conduct the deposition of Bert Kain.
2. Attorneys for plaintiffs and defendant Hard: Attend the deposition, and, if desired, examine Bert Kain.

ASSIGNMENT 55: Attorney for Defendant Davola: Taking the Deposition of Neutral Witness (Betty Frank, Nurse)

Nurse Frank watched over Bruno Summers in the intensive care unit when he was admitted to Mercy shortly after the shooting at the Garage Tavern. In a previous visit to the hospital, your investigator reviewed portions of Summers's hospital records in order to evaluate the alleged cause of death and saw a hospital record in which a statement was recorded that was attributed by Nurse Frank to Summers: "I should have left when I saw him."

You have subpoenaed Nurse Frank to take her deposition. The deposition is schedule for November 9, 20XX + 1 at 9:00 A.M. in your law office. Attorneys for the plaintiffs and other defendants will be attending the deposition. They may examine the deponent if time permits.

PREPARATION

READ: (1) Pretrial Case Files Entries 4, 7; (2) Chapter 9; (3) Fed. R. Evid. 803(2)(6), 804(6)(2)(3), 901; (4) Notes from all the interviews you have seen and done in class.

ASSIGNMENTS FOR CLASS

DISCUSSION: Be prepared to discuss the following questions:

1. What specific bearing does Nurse Frank's information have on your case theory?
   a. Would you want to use the statement at trial?
   b. Explain.
2. Now think about its admissibility:
   a. What evidentiary problems do you face?
   b. How will you deal with the problems?
3. Imagine that you subpoenaed the hospital records for Bruno Summers and the hospital resisted, claiming physician-patient privilege.
   a. What will you respond?
   b. What bearing, if any, is the fact that a medical records clerk had previously permitted your investigator to review the records?

PERFORMANCE

In class:

1. Attorneys for defendant Davola: Conduct the deposition of Nurse Frank.
2. Attorneys for plaintiffs and defendant Hard: Attend the deposition, and, if desired, examine Nurse Frank.

ASSIGNMENT 56: Defendant Davola's Attorney: Taking the Deposition of an Adverse Expert Witness (Dr. David Bowman, Plaintiffs' Behavioral Psychologist)

The parties have proceeded with the litigation process and formal discovery. Plaintiffs' and defendants' attorneys have voluntarily provided each other with copies of the reports submitted by their expert witnesses. Defendant Davola's attorney has learned through answers to interrogatories that Plaintiff's behavioral psychiatrist, Dr. David Bowman, will testify that a reasonable person familiar with the tavern/pub environment could have predicted a shooting between Ed Hard and Bruno Summers at the Garage Tavern. Defendant Davola's counsel sent a subpoena to take the deposition for Dr. Bowman.

The deposition is scheduled for November 20, 20XX + 1 at 9:00 A.M. at Dr. Bowman's office. Attorneys for Plaintiffs will be attending the deposition. They may examine the deponent if time permits.

Preparation to take a deposition and preparation of the deponent for a deposition are important. Attorney for Defendant Davola, in order to prepare to take an adverse expert witness's deposition it is usually advisable to consult with an expert to educate yourself about the specialty. You have retained Dr. Hollis Lufkin, a clinical psychiatrist, who believes "that there is no reliable methodology in the psychological discipline that would permit an opinion like Bowman's." Dr. Lufkin is available to consult with defendant's attorney.

PREPARATION

READ: (1) Pretrial Case Files Entries 1-37, 50, 54, 62-64, 66, 67, 81, 85, 86; (2) Chapter 9; (3) Fed. R. Civ. P. 26, 29-32, 37.

ASSIGNMENTS FOR CLASS

DISCUSSION: Be prepared to discuss the following questions:

1. How will you prepare for taking the deposition of Dr. Bowman?
2. What are your objectives in deposing Dr. Bowman?
3. Dr. Bowman's opinion that a reasonable person could have predicted a shooting between Ed Hard and Bruno Summers at the Unicom Tavern is not helpful to your case theory.
   a. What questions will you ask Dr. Bowman to keep his opinion from being admissible in evidence? [How will you use *Dilbert*?]
   b. What questions will you ask Dr. Bowman to weaken the impact of his opinion if the court rules that Bowman's opinion is admissible?

PERFORMANCE

In class:

1. Defendant Davola's attorney: Depose Plaintiff's behavioral psychiatrist, Dr. Bowman.

2. Plaintiffs' attorney: Attend the deposition and, if desired, examine the expert at the deposition.

ASSIGNMENT 57: Defendants' Attorneys: Taking the Deposition of an Adverse Expert Witness (Dr. Bruce Hann, Plaintiffs' Economist)

Plaintiffs' and defendants' attorneys have provided each other with copies of the reports submitted by their expert witnesses. Defendants' attorneys scheduled a deposition of plaintiffs' economist, Dr. Bruce Hann, for November 3, 20XX + 1 at 9:00 A.M. at the law office of defendant Davola's attorney. Attorneys for both defendants and for plaintiffs will be attending the deposition.

Preparation to take a deposition and preparation of the deponent for a deposition are important. In order to prepare to take an adverse expert witness's deposition it is usually advisable to consult with an expert to educate yourself about the specialty. Defendants have retained Dr. Thomas Monday, an economist who believes: "The economic loss for the wrongful death of Bruno Summers is substantially less than the amount calculated by plaintiffs' economist, Dr. Bruce Hann." Dr. Monday is available to consult with defendants' attorneys.

PREPARATION

READ: (1) Pretrial Case Files Entries 1-41, 53, 56, 62-64, 66, 81, 85; (2) Chapter 9; (3) Fed. R. Civ. P. 26, 29-32, 37.

ASSIGNMENTS FOR CLASS

DISCUSSION: Be prepared to discuss the following questions:

1. You should usually begin an expert witness deposition by inquiring into the expert's background and education to determine whether the expert is qualified to testify at trial, whether additional or different experts are needed to compete favorably with opposing counsels' expert, and generally to educate yourself as to the persuasiveness of the expert's opinion. What specific background and education areas will you question Dr. Hann about as to his qualifications?

2. What substantive topics will you question Dr. Hann about?
   a. Will the deposition topics be arranged in any particular sequence?
   b. Why?

3. Dr. Hann will in all likelihood state his opinion that the death of Bruno Summers has resulted in a significant economic loss to plaintiffs.

   a. What questions, if any, would you ask Dr. Hann about his opinion?

   b. What questions, if any, can you ask him that would weaken his opinion?

   c. Do you want to weaken his opinion at the deposition? Explain.

PERFORMANCE

In class:

1. Attorneys for defendants Davola and Hard: Prepare to take the deposition of Dr. Hann.

2. Plaintiffs' attorney: Attend the deposition and, if desired, examine the expert at the deposition.

ASSIGNMENT 58: Attorney for Defendant Hard: Taking the Deposition of an Adverse Expert Witness (Dr. Brett Day, Plaintiffs' Medical Expert)

Plaintiffs' and defendants' attorneys have agreed that all experts who will testify at trial can be deposed without a court order. In addition, the plaintiffs' attorney has voluntarily provided defendants with copies of the hospital records of Bruno Summers. Defendant Hard's attorney sent a subpoena to take the deposition of one of plaintiffs' medical experts, Dr. Brett Day. The deposition is scheduled for November 10, 20XX + 1 at 9:00 A.M. at the law office of defendant Hard's attorney. Attorneys for plaintiffs and defendant Davola will be attending the deposition. They may examine the deponent if time permits.

PREPARATION

READ: (1) Pretrial Case Files Entries 1-39, 51, 57, 62-64, 66, 67, 81, 85; (2) Chapter 9; (3) Fed. R. Civ. P. 26, 29-32, 37.

1. What substantive topics will you question the doctor on?
   a. Will the deposition topics be arranged in a particular sequence?
   b. Why?

2. Dr. Day heard Bruno Summers state: "I should have left when I saw him."

   a. Would questioning Dr. Day about this statement help or hurt your theory of the case? Explain.

b. Would it help or hurt Davola's theory of his case? Explain.

c. Would it help or hurt plaintiffs' theory of their case? Explain.

d. Suppose you want the statement admitted into evidence at trial. What questions could you ask Dr. Day to help you admit the statement in evidence at trial?

3. Do you think plaintiffs' attorney should examine Dr. Day at this deposition? Explain.

PERFORMANCE

In class:

1. Attorney for defendant Hard: Depose Dr. Brett Day.

2. Attorneys for plaintiffs and defendant Davola: Attend the deposition and, if desired, examine Dr. Day at the deposition.

ASSIGNMENT 59: Defendants' Attorneys: Taking the Deposition of an Adverse Expert Witness (Hao Tredwell, Firearms Expert)

Defendants' attorneys scheduled a deposition of firearms expert, Hao Tredwell, for November 9, 20XX + 1 at 9:00 A.M. at the law office of defendant Davola's attorney. Tredwell is an employee of the Major State Patrol Crime Laboratory, whom the plaintiffs have indicated that they will call as an expert witness at trial. Attorneys for both defendants and for plaintiffs will be attending the deposition.

In preparation for taking the deposition of Tredwell, you have reviewed his Crime Laboratory Report (Case File Entry 15), Tredwell's Curriculum Vitae, and available literature on firearm's comparison, trigger pull, and gunshot residue and the determination of proximity of the firearm's barrel to the impacted target.

PREPARATION

READ: (1) Pretrial Case Files 1-33, 61, 63; (2) Chapter 9.

ASSIGNMENTS FOR CLASS

DISCUSSION: Be prepared to discuss the following questions:

1. How are Tredwell's findings in the Crime Laboratory Report detrimental to your clients' case theory? Helpful to your case theory?

2. About what substantive topics will you question Tredwell during the deposition?

3. Will you serve Tredwell with a subpoena duces tecum for the deposition, and, if so, what do you want Tredwell to bring to the deposition?

PERFORMANCE

In class:

1. As the attorney for defendants Davola and Hard: Take the deposition of Tredwell.

2. Plaintiffs' attorney: Attend the deposition and, if desired, examine the expert at the deposition.

ASSIGNMENT 60: Defendants' Attorneys: Taking the Deposition of an Adverse Expert Witness (Dr. Pat Gage, Psychiatrist)

Dr. Pat Gage has been scheduled to be deposed by defendants' attorneys at 9:00 A.M. on November 15, 20XX + 1 at the office of counsel for defendant Davola. Attorneys for both defendants and for plaintiffs will be attending the deposition.

As defendants' attorney, you have already received Dr. Pat Gage's pertinent files and report stating in essence that Deborah Summers suffers from post-traumatic stress disorder (PTSD) as a result of the shooting of Bruno Summers on September 3, 20XX. Also, in preparation for the deposition you have examined Dr. Gage's curriculum vitae. (The fact that Ronnie Summers is not included in this report is really not that much of a surprise. In your conversations over the past weeks, Plaintiff's counsel has given you a sense that they will not be pursuing a claim that Ronnie suffered from PTSD as a result of the shooting—likely, their expert witness could not back up the claim; anyway, you always thought that there were legal problems with the claim as well as problems from the fact that the grandparents had knowingly taken the child to the scene of the shooting.)

PREPARATION

READ: (1) Pretrial Case Files Entries 1-41, 44, 45, 52, 86; (2) Chapter 9.

ASSIGNMENTS FOR CLASS

DISCUSSION: Be prepared to discuss the following questions:

1. What does Gage's opinion add to Deborah Summers' existing emotional distress damage claim (after all, plaintiffs' counsel can already establish that she is depressed and cries a lot)?
2. What preparation will you conduct to ready yourself to depose Dr. Gage?
3. What areas of potential vulnerability to impeachment and/or to revealing weakness in her opinion will you cover during your examination of Dr. Gage?

PERFORMANCE

In class:

1. As the attorney for defendants Davola and Hard: Take the deposition of Dr. Gage.
2. Plaintiffs' attorney: Attend the deposition and, if desired, examine the expert at the deposition.

ASSIGNMENT 61: Plaintiffs' Attorneys: Taking the Deposition of an Adverse Expert Witness (Dr. Ennis Martinez, Psychologist)

As plaintiffs' counsel, you have scheduled Dr. Ennis Martinez to be deposed in your office at 9:00 A.M. on December 11, 20XX + 1. Attorneys for both defendants and for plaintiffs will be attending the deposition.

You have already reviewed Dr. Martinez's expert witness report stating in essence that Deborah Summers did not suffer from post-traumatic stress disorder as a result of the shooting of Bruno Summers on September 3, 20XX. Also, in preparation for the deposition you have examined Dr. Martinez's curriculum vitae. Further, you have conferred with your expert, Dr. Gage, and (if you did Assignment 60) attended the defendants' deposition of your expert on November 15, 20XX + 1.

PREPARATION

READ: (1) Pretrial Case Files Entries 1-41; 44, 45, 55, 86; (2) Chapter 9.

ASSIGNMENTS FOR CLASS

DISCUSSION: Be prepared to discuss the following questions:

1. What are your objectives in deposing Dr. Martinez?

2. Suppose that you issued a subpoena duces tecum for Dr. Martinez to bring the doctor's file on the case to the deposition. Dr. Martinez brought only the expert report and refuses to bring the case file to the deposition. What, if anything, will you do?

3. What areas of potential vulnerability to impeachment and/or weaknesses in his opinion will you cover during your examination of Dr. Martinez?

4. Does Dr. Martinez possess any information that can *help* bolster your case theory?

PERFORMANCE

In class:

1. As the attorney for plaintiffs Ronnie and Deborah Summers: Take the deposition of Dr. Martinez.

2. Defendants' attorney: Attend the deposition and, if desired, examine the expert at the deposition.

ASSIGNMENT 62: Plaintiffs' Attorneys: Taking the Deposition of an Adverse Expert Witness (Dr. Dale Thompson, Hotel Management)

As plaintiffs' counsel, you have scheduled Dr. Dale Thompson to be deposed in your office at 9:00 A.M. on November 22, 20XX + 1. Attorneys for defendants and for plaintiffs will be attending the deposition.

You have already reviewed Dr. Thompson's expert witness report to the effect that the management of the Garage Tavern on September 3, 20XX was consistent with tavern practice and standards in the tavern/restaurant industry. This defense expert contradicts the expert, Ben Kaplan, whom you have employed and who concluded that the operation of the Garage Tavern on September 3 was not in accord with standards for the industry. You have conferred with your expert and read your expert's file and report in preparation for taking Dr. Thompson's deposition.

PREPARATION

READ: (1) Pretrial Case Files Entries 1-44, 46 ,47, 58; (2) Chapter 9.

ASSIGNMENTS FOR CLASS

DISCUSSION: Be prepared to discuss the following questions:

1. What are your objectives in deposing Dr. Thompson?
2. List the ways in which your expert differs from Dr. Thompson.
3. About what, if any, documents will you question this defense expert?
   a. What documents support your clients' position?
   b. What documents undermine your clients' position?

PERFORMANCE

In class:

1. As the attorney for plaintiffs: Take the deposition of Dr. Thompson.
2. Defendants' attorney: Attend the deposition and, if desired, examine the expert at the deposition.

Chapter 10. Creating Visuals—Assignments

Criminal Case Assignments

ASSIGNMENT 63: Prosecutor and Defense Attorney: Planning and Visiting the Scene

You should prepare to go to the scene of the shooting. You have seen photographs and diagrams of the Garage Tavern, but actually going there provides an entirely different feeling and perspective.

PREPARATION

READ: (1) Pretrial Case Files Entries 4, 14, 15, 17, 26, 29, 30; (2) Chapter 10. View the video of the Garage Tavern on the DVD that is a companion to this text or, alternatively, your instructor may direct you to visit a tavern that will be designated as your Garage Tavern for the performance exercise.

ASSIGNMENTS FOR CLASS

DISCUSSION: Be prepared to discuss the following questions:

1. What specifically will you be looking for during your scene visit? Explain.
2. How did the reality compare with your mental image of the tavern?
3. Do you want the jury to visit the scene? Explain.

PERFORMANCE

In class, be prepared to visit and discuss the Garage Tavern scene.

ASSIGNMENT 64: Prosecutor and Defense Attorney Prepare Exhibits and Other Visuals

You are preparing for trial, and you want to bring the case to life visually for the jury. You plan to do that with your exhibits, which include real, documentary, and demonstrative evidence. It is time for you to organize and prepare your exhibits and most of all to use your imagination to create demonstrative evidence and other visuals for the *State v. Hard* case.

PREPARATION

READ: (1) Pretrial Case Files Entries 26-32; (2) Chapter 10.

ASSIGNMENTS FOR CLASS

DISCUSSION: Be prepared to discuss the following questions:

1. What visuals would you create for settlement? What additional visuals for the phases of trial from jury selection through closing argument? Explain why you think they would enhance your presentation.
2. What are the evidentiary foundations for those visuals that you can introduce into evidence?
3. What, if any, courtroom demonstration would you consider conducting?
4. What ethical concerns do you have about the visuals you are considering? About the visuals opposing counsel may offer?

PERFORMANCE

In class, be prepared to display and discuss a visual you have created for the *State v. Hard* case. The visual you create may be either demonstrative evidence (e.g., a scene diagram) or an illustrative one (e.g., an argument visual). Your instructor will designate whether you are a prosecutor or defense counsel.

Civil Case Assignments

ASSIGNMENT 65: Plaintiffs' and Defendants' Attorneys: Planning and Visiting the Scene

You should prepare to go to the scene of the shooting. You have seen photographs and diagrams of the Garage Tavern, but actually going there provides an entirely different feeling and perspective.

PREPARATION

READ: (1) Pretrial Case Files Entries 1-33, 62, 63, 66, 85; (2) Chapter 10. (2) View the video of the Garage Tavern on the DVD that is a companion to this text or, alternatively, your instructor may direct you to visit a tavern that will be designated as your Garage Tavern for the performance exercise.

ASSIGNMENTS FOR CLASS

DISCUSSION: Be prepared to discuss the following questions:

1. What specifically will you be looking for during your scene visit? Explain.
2. How did the reality compare with your mental image of the tavern?
3. Do you want the jury to visit the scene? Explain.

PERFORMANCE

In class, be prepared to visit and discuss the Garage Tavern scene.

ASSIGNMENT 66: Plaintiffs' and Defendants' Attorneys Prepare Exhibits and Other Visuals

You are preparing for trial, and you want to bring the case to life visually for the jury. You plan to do that with your exhibits, which include real, documentary, and demonstrative evidence. It is time for you to organize and prepare your exhibits and most of all to use your imagination to create demonstrative evidence and other visuals for the *Summers v. Hard* case.

PREPARATION

READ: (1) Pretrial Case Files Entries 26-32; (2) Chapter 10.

ASSIGNMENTS FOR CLASS

DISCUSSION: Be prepared to discuss the following questions:

1. What visuals would you create for the phases of settlement and for trial from jury selection through closing argument? Explain why you think they would enhance your presentation.
2. What are the evidentiary foundations for those visuals that you can introduce into evidence?
3. What, if any, courtroom demonstration would you consider conducting?
4. What ethical concerns do you have about the visuals you are considering? About the visuals opposing counsel may offer?

PERFORMANCE

In class, be prepared to display and discuss a visual you have created for the *Summers v. Hard* case. The visual you create may be either demonstrative evidence (e.g., a scene diagram) or an illustrative one (e.g., an argument visual). Your instructor will designate whether you are a plaintiff's or defendant's counsel.

Chapter 11. Pretrial Motion Advocacy— Assignments

Criminal Case Assignments

ASSIGNMENT 67: Defense Attorney: Planning Constitution-Based Pretrial Motions

You have already raised several common law and statute-based pretrial motions (e.g., discovery and bail motions). Later, you will bring motions before the trial judge, that is, *in limine,* in order to resolve a variety of evidentiary issues. Now is the time to begin to plan constitution-based pretrial motions. Such motions can exclude evidence vital to the prosecution's case, resolve procedural matters in your favor (e.g., change of venue), or incidentally provide you with additional discovery for your case at trial through evidentiary hearings associated with the motions. Motions can also be part of a case strategy, because by putting constant pressure on the prosecution they may lead to a fairer disposition of the case.

PREPARATION

READ: (1) Pretrial Case Files Entries 1, 2, 4, 5, 15, 19, 32; (2) Chapter 11.

ASSIGNMENTS FOR CLASS

DISCUSSION: Be prepared to discuss the following questions:

1. Which motions (that are constitution-based) could you raise in this case?
2. Without doing any research, see how many of the following questions you can answer:
   a. What is the legal basis of each motion?
   b. Does this legal basis require a factual showing (e.g., the lack of an arrest warrant becomes an issue only when an arrest takes place in a home, as opposed to in public)?
   c. If the legal basis requires a factual showing, how will you make this showing (e.g., witnesses at an evidentiary hearing, declarations)?
   d. What will be the prosecutor's response to each such motion?
   e. What will be the legal basis of each such response?
   f. Which of these motions will result in the suppression of prosecution evidence if successful?
3. Suppose you believe that your legal basis for these motions is questionable and you are certain to lose. However, just the volume of paper will put pressure on the already overworked prosecution, who then may be likely to give your client a good deal to avoid having to answer your paper onslaught. Is this ethical?

PERFORMANCE

In class, be prepared to discuss and justify your selection.

ASSIGNMENT 68: Prosecutor: Planning Responses to Constitution-Based Pretrial Motions (Suppression Motions)

In pretrial and trial work you must plan for every eventuality, good or bad. There are potential defense pretrial motions that, if successful, will exclude evidence in your case. It is important that you now assess the consequences of this possibility.

Do an item-by-item analysis of the effect on the presentation of your case theory to the jury if the defense is successful in its motion to suppress each such item (e.g., the gun).

PREPARATION

READ: (1) Pretrial Case Files Entries 4-6, 15, 19, 32; (2) Chapter 11.

ASSIGNMENTS FOR CLASS

DISCUSSION: Be prepared to discuss the following questions:

1. What evidence in your case provides a potential subject for defense motions to suppress? Why?
2. What is the legal basis for each attempt to suppress evidence?
3. Look individually at each piece of evidence that you analyzed and imagine that it has been suppressed. Now taking these pieces of evidence one at a time, analyze how you would then alter or restructure your case in order to achieve your objectives in light of the loss of the particular piece of evidence.

PERFORMANCE

In class, be prepared to discuss your analysis under Discussion Question 3 above.

ASSIGNMENT 69: Defense Attorney and Prosecutor: Constitution-Based Pretrial Motion (Suppression of Ed Hard's Gun)

Defense counsel will move to suppress the gun seized at Ed Hard's house. In order to successfully bring the suppression motion, defense counsel must develop the legal basis for the motion. The first step in this endeavor is to develop the chain of relevant events that led to the seizure of the evidence. If the defense can break the chain by finding illegal or unsupportable government (police) conduct at any link, the evidence can be suppressed. The prosecution will respond to the defense suppression motion.

Unless your instructor tells you otherwise, your analysis of this problem should be based solely on Officer Yale's version of the search as described in his report and statement to the prosecutor. (Case Files Entries 20, 21).

PREPARATION

READ: (1) Pretrial Case Files Entries 4, 19, 20, 28, 76, 77; (2) Chapter 11.

ASSIGNMENTS FOR CLASS

DISCUSSION: Be prepared to discuss the following questions:

1. Again, the first step in evolving a defense theory to suppress the gun is to articulate the chain of events that led to its seizure. This chain begins when the police come to Hard's home to arrest him without a warrant, the police tell Hard that they could get a warrant to search his house, etc., etc.

    Hint: It's easiest to develop this chain by starting with what you want to suppress, in this example it is the gun, and then trace backwards through the events that led to the seizure.

    a. List the chain of relevant events that led to the seizure of the gun.

    b. Is there any government conduct at any link in the chain in seizing the gun that you believe may be illegal or unsupportable? Explain.

2. Let's start with a theory for suppression based on the lack of an arrest warrant.

    a. Suppose that the judge agrees that the police should have had an arrest warrant.

        1) What bearing does that have on the prosecution's right to introduce the gun at trial? Why?

        2) What legal authority would the judge rely on in deciding the police should have had an arrest warrant?

    b. Now suppose, as is likely, that the necessity of an arrest warrant is in dispute. How will the defense respond if the prosecutor states, "No warrant was needed. This was an emergency—police were in `hot pursuit' of an armed and dangerous man"?

3. The prosecution will attempt to justify the seizure of the weapon, once the police were inside the house, under the "plain-view" doctrine.

a. Does *Tex v. Warden*, (See Case Files Entry 75) help the prosecution?

b. Does the defense have a reply?

c. Would *Tex v. Warden* help the prosecution if it were presented at the evidentiary hearing that the gun had been found in a back room, rather than the living room as stated in the report? Why or why not? Does your answer "depend"? If so, upon what?

PERFORMANCE

1. Outside of class, draft either the defense motion and memorandum of law supporting the motion or the prosecution's response to the motion. Your instructor will indicate who will represent the parties.

2. In class, be prepared to argue your motion or response to the motion.

ASSIGNMENT 70: Defense Attorney: Constitution-Based Pretrial Motion (Evidentiary Hearing. Suppression of Statements to Officer Yale)

You now wish to plan to suppress defendant's false exculpatory statement to Officer Yale ("I was home watching TV.") that Hard allegedly made when the police came to his home. The court has reserved ruling on your motion to suppress the gun. Unless your instructor tells you otherwise, your analysis of this problem should be based solely on Officer Yale's version of the search as described in his report and statement to the prosecutor. (Pretrial Case Files Entries 19, 20.)

PREPARATION

READ: (1) Pretrial Case Files Entries 19, 20, 28, 73, 76, 77; (2) Chapter 11.

ASSIGNMENTS FOR CLASS

DISCUSSION: Be prepared to discuss the following questions:

1. If you fail to suppress this statement, how specifically will you deal with it in:

   a. Defendant's testimony?

   b. Closing argument?

2. Focusing on suppression:

   a. What legal theories exist for suppressing the statement?

   b. What is the basis for each theory?

   c. What are the problems with each theory? How will you deal with these problems?

   d. What are the strengths of each theory?

   e. What other specific factual information would you want to know? Why?

3. Now, let's think in *Mintz* terms. Suppose that you raise the lack of *Mintz* warnings preceding Hard's statement and the court states, "I think *State v. Rhodes*, (Case Files Entry 72) is dispositive against you."

   a. What does the judge mean? Explain.

   b. How will you respond to the judge's statement?

   c. Does *State v. Rhodes* provide guidance regarding how you must characterize the initial encounter at the door in order to raise the Mintz issue? Explain.

4. What will you respond if the prosecutor takes the position that because the general inquiry that produced this response was directed at locating the gun under the interest of public safety, no *Mintz* warnings were required under *State v. Quirk*, 257 Maj. App. 3d 406.

PERFORMANCE

In class:

1. Imagine that Officer Yale is testifying at the evidentiary hearing regarding the defense motion to suppress the false exculpatory statements (made at the door). Unless your instructor tells you otherwise, you will not actually put on the testimony of the witness.

   Prosecutor: Determine the points you would want to bring out in Yale's testimony in order to support your legal position, if applicable. Be certain to consider how you would want Yale to characterize the relevant events, particularly those that are problematic for you.

2. **Defense attorney:** Determine the points you would want to bring out in Yale's testimony at the evidentiary hearing in support of the defense motion to suppress the false exculpatory statements (made at the door).

3. **Prosecutor and defense attorney:** Be prepared to argue your respective positions to the trial judge concerning the suppression of the false exculpatory statement.

ASSIGNMENT 71: Defense Attorney and Prosecutor: Constitution-Based Pretrial Motion (Suppression of the Statement Given to Detective Tharp)

The defense will move to suppress Hard's statements to Detective Tharp, and the prosecution will resist the motion. Be careful not to confuse: (1) an involuntary statement, which violates due process; and (2) a violation of defendant's rights under *Mintz* (failure to give proper warnings, ineffective "waiver").

You recall that, according to the police report, Ed Hard was interviewed by Detective Tharp at 11:00 P.M. at the police station. In that interview, Hard allegedly told Tharp that at approximately 9:00 P.M. Hard and two friends, John Gooding and Rebecca Karr, went to the Garage Tavern for a drink. Hard was sitting at the bar, got up, and went to the restroom. As he approached the restroom, Bruno Summers came out of the restroom and confronted him. Hard stated that he was surprised to see Summers and had been unaware of the fact Summers had been in the tavern prior to the confrontation. Hard said he had not looked around the tavern but had been drinking and conversing with his friends. Hard stated that Summers threatened and shoved him and then reached into his pocket. Hard stated that, in response, in order to protect himself he pulled a .22 caliber revolver from his coat pocket, cocked it, and pointed it at the wall. But the gun accidentally discharged, hitting Bruno Summers.

Tharp confronted Hard with the fact that (1) Hard had to have been aware of Summers in the tavern before meeting him coming out of the restroom, and (2) it would have been impossible to misjudge the aim at such a short distance. The following conversation then occurred:

Hard: I think I'd better get an attorney. Don't you think I'd better get an attorney?

Tharp: If you want an attorney, I can't ask you any further questions.

Hard: Do you think an attorney could help me?

Tharp: That's up to you to decide. Do you want an attorney?

Hard: I want to tell what happened. That guy is a Nazi. Yes, I knew he was there. He deserved what he got. I couldn't continue to be afraid.

Tharp: Do you want an attorney?

Hard: Yes, I probably better get one.

At the hearing Hard's written statement will be offered by the prosecution. The defense will call no witnesses.

PREPARATION

READ: (1) Pretrial Case Files Entries 4, 5, 15, 73, 76, 77; (2) Chapter 11.

ASSIGNMENTS FOR CLASS

DISCUSSION: Be prepared to discuss the following questions:

1. Consider a Fifth Amendment due process analysis:
   a. What is the difference between an involuntary statement, which violates due process, and a statement obtained in contravention of *Mintz*?
   b. What bearing does this distinction have in this case?
   c. What bearing does it have on the nature of the testimony that you would want to present at an evidentiary hearing?
2. Now, for the *Mintz* analysis. (Note that *Mintz* embodies a concept that Fifth Amendment rights are protected by the Sixth Amendment assistance of counsel.)
   a. What legal significance will you argue that the dialogue concerning "needing an attorney" has? Why?
   b. How will the defense characterize this discussion?
   c. How can the prosecution argue that this was not a request for an attorney?
   d. What would be your reply as defense attorney?

PERFORMANCE

1. Outside of class, draft either the defense motion and memorandum of law supporting the motion or the prosecution's response to the motion. Your instructor will indicate who will represent the parties.
2. In class, prosecutor and defense attorney, be prepared to argue your respective positions to the trial judge concerning the suppression of the statement.

Civil Case Assignments

ASSIGNMENT 72: Defendants' and Plaintiffs' Attorneys: Defendants' Motion for Summary Judgment and Plaintiffs' Response (Mental Distress)

Plaintiffs' complaint in *Summers v. Hard* was filed on November 1, 20XX. Plaintiffs and defendants sent written interrogatories, requests for documents, requests for admission, and completed depositions. It is now December 20, 20XX + 1. Discovery in *Summers v. Hard* is completed and a trial date has been set.

Defendants' attorneys believe the sixth claim for relief for intentional and negligent emotional distress asserted by plaintiffs Deborah, Amanda, Ronnie, Gretchen, and Hans Summers is particularly vulnerable for summary judgment. Attorneys for defendants Hard and Davola plan to file a motion for summary judgment.

PREPARATION

READ: (1) Pretrial Case Files Entries 1-39, 51, 57, 59, 62-64, 66, 67, 85; (2) Chapter 11; (3) Fed. R. Civ. Proc. 5-7; 11-12; 56.

ASSIGNMENTS FOR CLASS

DISCUSSION: Be prepared to discuss the following questions:

1. What are defendants' objectives in filing this motion for summary judgment?
   a. List the advantages of being the moving party.
   b. List the disadvantages of being the moving party.
2. What arguments should defendants present in support of their motion for summary judgment?
   a. Legal arguments?
   b. Factual arguments?
3. What response will the Summers's attorney make to oppose summary judgment?
   a. Legal arguments?
   b. Factual arguments?
4.. In order to present your factual position in making or responding to summary judgment:

a. What, if any, documents will you file? Why?

b. Whose affidavits, if any, will you file?

c. What facts will you include in the affidavits? Why?

d. Are there evidentiary problems that you may encounter in filing the affidavits? Explain.

e. Are there ethical problems that you may encounter if you include an affidavit as the attorney? Explain.

PERFORMANCE

1. Outside of class:
   a. Defendants' attorneys: Prepare a written motion for summary judgment.
   b. Plaintiffs' attorney: Prepare a response to the motion.
2. In class, plaintiffs and defendants argue or discuss the motion.

ASSIGNMENT 73: Plaintiffs' Attorney and Defendant Davola's EKKO Attorney: Plaintiffs' Motion to Compel Production of Documents and Defendant Davola's Response

Before filing a complaint for wrongful death, plaintiffs obtained the prosecutors file in *State v. Hard*, which contained the police witness statements from Deborah Summers, Tom Donaldson, and Officers Yale and West. The police also incorrectly listed Robin Luntlebunk instead of Roberta Montbank as a witness, so no statement was taken from her until November 3, 20XX (after the criminal case was dismissed). The police claim that they could not locate Ms. Montbank because they were given the name Robin Luntlebunk instead of Roberta Montbank. Plaintiffs' complaint, *Summers v. Hard*, was filed on November 1, 20XX. Defendants responded to the complaint on November 8, 20XX.

Plaintiffs sent written interrogatories to defendant Davola on May 15, 20XX + 1. In response to plaintiffs' written interrogatories, plaintiffs learned that the EKKO Insurance Company interviewed and received a signed statement under oath from Roberta Montbank on October 26, 20XX. Ms. Montbank, 78 years of age, was a patron at the Garage Tavern on the night Bruno Summers was shot.

Plaintiffs contacted Ms. Montbank on June 1, 20XX + 1. They asked her for the statement she gave to EKKO. Ms. Montbank declined to give it to plaintiffs' attorney. Ms. Montbank explained that she was still a patron at the Garage Tavern and did not want to anger Mr. Davola.

Plaintiffs sent defendant Davola a written request for documents on July 15, 20XX + 1, requesting the witness statement of Roberta Montbank. Defendant Davola refused to produce the statement. Defendant Davola responded:

> PLAINTIFFS' REQUEST TO PRODUCE DOCUMENTS DIRECTED TO DEFENDANT DAVOLA: REQUEST NO. 4. Witness statement of Roberta Montbank, taken by EKKO Insurance Company on behalf of defendant Davola shortly before *Summers v. Hard* was commenced on November 1, 20XX.
>
> *Answer:* Work Product.

After receiving defendant Davola's response, plaintiffs' attorney met with defendant Davola's attorney on August 12, 20XX + 1, but they were unable to resolve the matter. The plaintiffs' attorney plans to file a motion to compel Davola to produce the Montbank statement. Defendant Davola's attorney will resist plaintiffs' motion. Davola is represented by a private attorney and the EKKO Insurance Company. For the purpose of this Assignment, the EKKO Insurance Company is handling the entire motion.

PREPARATION

READ: (1) Pretrial Case Files Entries 1-37, 48, 50, 54, 60, 62-64, 66, 81, 85; (2) Chapter 11; (3) Fed. R. Civ. P. 11-12; 26-37.

ASSIGNMENTS FOR CLASS

DISCUSSION: Be prepared to discuss the following questions:

1. What arguments can plaintiffs present to refute Davola's assertion that Montbank's statement is work product?
   a. Legal arguments?
   b. Factual arguments?
2. Even if the court rules that the Montbank statement is Davola's work product, plaintiffs' attorney may still be able to obtain the statement since work product is a qualified privilege. The plaintiffs will have to show (factually) that plaintiffs have substantial need of the materials to prepare their case and that they are unable without undue hardship to obtain the substantial equivalent of the materials by other means. In order to make a factual presentation:
   a. What documents, if any, will you file? Why?
   b. If you file affidavits, whose affidavits will you file?
   c. What facts will you include in the affidavits?

3. What are your objectives in refusing to provide plaintiffs' attorney with the statement you have from Roberta Montbank in terms of
   a. Your case theory?
   b. Other reasons?

PERFORMANCE

1. Outside of class:
   a. Plaintiffs' attorney: Prepare a written motion or a written outline of a motion to compel production of documents on Request No. 4. If you believe you should not proceed with a motion compelling discovery, draft a memorandum to your senior partner explaining your reasons for not proceeding.
   b. Attorney for defendant Davola: Prepare a written response or a written outline of a response to plaintiffs' motion to compel production of documents on Request No. 4.
2. In class: argue or discuss your written motion, memorandum, or response.

Chapter 12. Negotiating the Best Disposition— Assignments

Criminal Case Assignments

ASSIGNMENT 74: Defense Attorney and Prosecutor: Negotiation (Plea Bargaining)

The judge has denied all defense motions. The prosecutor and defense attorney bumped into each other at the courthouse, and the prosecutor suggested that they might explore a plea agreement. While both attorneys believe they have a very triable case, as a matter of thoroughness they must give some consideration to the possibility of plea bargain.

Counsel agree to meet and discuss a possible plea agreement

PREPARATION

READ: (1) Pretrial Case Files Entries 3-6, 8, 10, 14, 15, 17, 26, 61, 64, 65; (2) Chapter 12.

ASSIGNMENTS FOR CLASS

DISCUSSION: Be prepared to discuss the following questions:

1. Generally, what would motivate you to seek a deal in any case?
2. Why would you plea bargain the *State v. Hard* case? What are your incentives to negotiate?
3. What is the best deal you can reasonably imagine would be offered or agreed upon by the prosecution in *State v. Hard*? By the defense?

PERFORMANCE

In class, you will be designated either to be a prosecutor or defense attorney and you will engage in plea negotiations with opposing counsel.

Civil Case Assignments

ASSIGNMENT 75: Attorneys for Defendant Hard and SAPO Insurance Company: Negotiation Concerning Duty to Defend

Plaintiffs Deborah, Hans, Gretchen, Ronnie, and Amanda Summers filed a complaint on November 1, 20XX, naming Ed Hard, Mary Apple, Tom Donaldson, and M.C. Davola, as defendants. Plaintiffs allege that defendants are responsible for the wrongful death of Bruno Summers. Ed Hard contacted an attorney to represent him in this case, *Summers v. Hard*.

Ed Hard has a homeowner's insurance policy with the SAPO Insurance Company. Ed Hard's attorney contacted the SAPO Insurance Company and requested that SAPO defend Ed Hard in *Summers v. Hard*, a civil lawsuit. SAPO's position is that it does not have a duty to defend Ed Hard because the shooting by Ed Hard was a premeditated, willful act and therefore not covered by the insurance contract. Ed Hard asserts the shooting was not an intentional or willful act and that the insurance company has a duty to defend him.

A meeting between Hard's attorney and the attorney representing SAPO Insurance Company is scheduled. The purpose of the meeting is to try to reach a settlement of this issue. Planning and preparing for the negotiation are critical.

Unless your instructor informs you otherwise, this negotiation occurs before an answer is filed in *Summers v. Hard*.

PREPARATION

READ: (1) Pretrial Case Files Entries 1-35, 43, 62-64, 66, 82, 85 (2) Chapter 12; (3) 28 U.S.C. §2072.

ASSIGNMENTS FOR CLASS

DISCUSSION: Be prepared to discuss the following questions:

1. Will you present legal arguments? If so, what are they?
2. What response do you expect from your opponent? Explain.
3. What facts will you present to support your position?
   a. Which facts are the weakest for your position?
   b. How will you deal with the weakest facts?
4. Suppose Ed Hard's attorney suggests that if agreement is not reached, Ed Hard will litigate the tort of bad-faith breach of contract and seek punitive damages. Is it ethical for Ed Hard's attorney to threaten litigation of the tort of bad-faith breach of contract? Explain.

PERFORMANCE

In class, the attorneys for Ed Hard and the SAPO Insurance Company meet and negotiate on the issue of duty to defend under the SAPO Insurance contract.

ASSIGNMENT 76: Plaintiffs' and Defendants' Attorneys: Negotiation Between Plaintiffs and Defendants

Bruno Summers was shot by Ed Hard at the Garage Tavern on September 3, 20XX and died on September 7, 20XX. A criminal case for first-degree murder, *State v. Hard*, was brought and subsequently dismissed on October 1, 20XX. The Summers family filed a wrongful death and emotional distress case against Ed Hard, Mary Apple, Tom Donaldson, and M.C. Davola on November 1, 20XX. Defendants responded on November 8, 20XX. Discovery has been completed in *Summers v. Hard*. The trial has been scheduled to begin on April 1, 20XX +2. Plaintiffs' attorney has requested a meeting to discuss settlement.

Attorneys for both sides have met with their respective clients prior to this meeting. This settlement discussion is scheduled for January 20, 20XX +2 at 9:00 A.M. in the law offices of plaintiffs' attorney.

PREPARATION

READ: (1) Pretrial Case Files Entries 1-60, 62-64, 66, 67, 81-85; (2) Chapter 12; (3) Fed. R. Civ. P. 16, 68.

ASSIGNMENTS FOR CLASS

DISCUSSION: Be prepared to discuss the following questions:

1. Generally, what preparation will you do prior to this meeting? Why?
2. In your opinion, should this case be settled prior to trial? Why or why not?
3. How would you detail your method and its specific application in this case for calculation of damages?
4. Suppose defendant Hard's attorney, in discussing the *Summers v. Hard* case, tells the plaintiffs' attorney that if the case goes to trial, he is going to "get even" with "that flake" Deborah Summers. He is going to show her prior emotional problems, her juvenile record, and that even before "Bruno's body was cold in the ground" she had a new boyfriend.
   a. Are such threats ethical?
   b. Can defendant Hard's attorney ethically make such a threat if he knows Ed Hard does not want him to cross-examine Deborah?
   c. What response would you have if you were plaintiffs' attorney? Why?

PERFORMANCE

In class, attorneys for defendants and plaintiffs conduct settlement discussions in accordance with their clients' instructions.

Chapter 13. Alternative Dispute Resolution

ASSIGNMENT 77: Plaintiff's and Defendants' Attorneys: Arbitration and Mediation

Plaintiffs and defendants have been pursuing litigation to resolve the wrongful death and emotional distress claims brought by plaintiffs in *Summers v. Hard*. Formal discovery has been completed by the parties. The discovery process has been time consuming and expensive. However, as new attorneys, your experience with litigation was limited. Now that you have experienced pretrial preparation, you can imagine how time consuming and costly litigation in the *Summers v. Hard* case will be.

The plaintiffs' attorney has decided to investigate the possibility of mediation. Plaintiffs' attorney telephoned the defendants' attorneys and suggested a meeting to discuss mediation as an alternative.

PREPARATION

READ: (1) Pretrial Case Files Entries 1-37, 62-64, 66, 85; (2) Chapter 13.

ASSIGNMENTS FOR CLASS

DISCUSSION: Be prepared to discuss the following questions:

1. Generally, what are the advantages and disadvantages of using mediation in the *Summers v. Hard* case?
2. Can mediation work in a litigation situation such as the *Summers v. Hard* case? Explain.
3. In *Summers v. Hard* would mediation benefit:
   a. Plaintiffs? Why?
   b. Defendants? Why?
4. Generally, why select arbitration instead of trial?
5. What are the advantages and disadvantages of selecting arbitration for the *Summers v. Hard* case?

PERFORMANCE

1. In class, plaintiffs' and defendants' attorneys meet and discuss mediation and arbitration and their specific use in *Summers v. Hard*.
2. In class, your instructor may ask you to mediate this case.

VII. TABLE OF CONTENTS FOR CASE FILES ON CD

The following documents listed in this Table of Contents can be located on the CD in this book's back cover pocket:

CRIMINAL CASE FILE ENTRIES: *STATE V. HARD*

E-19.   Officer M. Yale

E-20.   Officer Yale Interview Transcript

Curriculum Vitae

E-21.   Dr. Brett Day, Attending Doctor

E-22.   Dr. L.R. Jackson, Medical Examiner

E-23.   Dr. T.A. Loopman, Pharmacologist

E-24.   James Raven, Polygrapher

E-25.   H. Tredwell, Firearms Examiner

Diagrams

E-26.   Scale Diagram, Garage Tavern

E-27.   Scale Diagram, Gull Gas Station

E-28.   Diagram (not to scale) Edward Hard's House

Photographs

E-29.   Garage Tavern Photos

Garage Tavern (Garage Exterior Photo A)

Garage Tavern (Garage Exterior Photo B)

Garage Tavern (Garage Exterior Photo C)

Garage Tavern (Garage Interior Photo D)

Garage Tavern (Garage Interior Photo E)

Garage Tavern (Garage Interior Photo F)

Garage Tavern (Garage Interior Photo G)

Garage Tavern (Garage Interior Photo H)

Garage Tavern (Garage Interior Photo I)

Garage Tavern (Garage Interior Photo J)

Garage Tavern (Garage Interior Photo K)

Garage Tavern (Garage Interior Photo L)

Garage Tavern (Garage Interior Photo M)

Garage Tavern (Garage Interior Photo N)

Garage Tavern (Garage Interior Photo O)

Garage Tavern (Garage Interior Photo P)

Garage Tavern (Garage Interior Photo Q)

E-30.   Photos After Shooting of Bruno Summers

Photos After Shooting of Bruno Summers, 09.03.20XX (Photo A)

Photos After Shooting of Bruno Summers, 09.03.20XX (Photo B)

E-31.   Photos of Bruno, Deborah, and the Summers Children

Photos of Bruno, Deborah, and the Summers Children (Photo A)

Photos of Bruno, Deborah, and the Summers Children (Photo B)

Photos of Bruno, Deborah, and the Summers Children (Photo C)

Photos of Bruno, Deborah, and the Summers Children (Photo D)

Photos of Bruno, Deborah, and the Summers Children (Photo E)

Photos of Bruno, Deborah, and the Summers Children (Photo F)

Photos of Bruno, Deborah, and the Summers Children (Photo G)

Photos of Bruno, Deborah, and the Summers Children (Photo H)

Photos of Bruno, Deborah, and the Summers Children (Photo I)

Photos of Bruno, Deborah, and the Summers Children (Photo J)

E-32.   Photos of Gun and Bullets

Gun (Photo A)

Bullets (Photo B)

E-33.   Knife (Photo)

CIVIL CASE FILE ENTRIES: *SUMMERS V. HARD* (INCLUDES CRIMINAL PRETRIAL CASE FILE, ENTRIES 1-33)

Pleadings

E-34.   Summons

E-35.   Complaint (for critique only)

E-36.   Ed Hard Answer (for critique only)

E-37.   Davola, Donaldson, and Apple Answer (for critique only)

Deborah Summers' Medical Records

E-38.   Jamner County Health Department

E-39.   Neva County Medical Services

Economic Reports and Photographs

E-40.   Dr. Bruce Hann Report and Photos

Dr. Bruce Hann Report

University Fitness Photos (Photo A)

University Fitness Photos (Photo B)

University Fitness Photos (Photo C)

E-41.   Dr. Thomas Monday

Insurance Company Policies

E-42.   EKKO Insurance Policy

E-43.   SAPO Insurance Policy

Psychologists Reports and Files—Emotional Distress

E-44.   Report and Files of Dr. Pat Gage, Doctor for Deborah Summers

E-45.   Report of Dr. Ennis Martinez

Tavern Management Reports

E-46.   Dr. Dale Thompson, Operations Practices Report

GENERAL RESEARCH CASE FILE

THE GARAGE TAVERN

A visit to the Garage tavern is on the DVD that is a companion to this book.

Index